Motul de San José

Maya Studies

UNIVERSITY PRESS OF FLORIDA

Florida A&M University, Tallahassee
Florida Atlantic University, Boca Raton
Florida Gulf Coast University, Ft. Myers
Florida International University, Miami
Florida State University, Tallahassee
New College of Florida, Sarasota
University of Central Florida, Orlando
University of Florida, Gainesville
University of North Florida, Jacksonville
University of South Florida, Tampa
University of West Florida, Pensacola

Motul de
San José

Politics, History, and Economy
in a Classic Maya Polity

Edited by Antonia E. Foias
and Kitty F. Emery

University Press of Florida

Gainesville · Tallahassee · Tampa · Boca Raton

Pensacola · Orlando · Miami · Jacksonville · Ft. Myers · Sarasota

First cloth printing, 2012
First paperback printing, 2015

Library of Congress Cataloging-in-Publication Data

Motul de San José : politics, history, and economy in a Maya polity / edited by Antonia
E. Foias and Kitty F. Emery.
    p. cm.—(Maya studies)
Includes bibliographical references and index.
ISBN 978-0-8130-4190-2 (cloth: alk. paper)
ISBN 978-0-8130-6146-7 (pbk.)
    1. Mayas—Guatemala—Peten (Dept.)—Antiquities.   2. Excavations (Archaeology)—
Guatemala—Peten (Dept.)   3. Peten (Guatemala : Dept.)—Antiquities.   I. Foias,
Antonia E.   II. Emery, Kitty F.   III. Series: Maya studies.
    F1435.1.P47M65 2012
    972.81 2—dc23   2012009832

The University Press of Florida is the scholarly publishing agency for the State University
System of Florida, comprising Florida A&M University, Florida Atlantic University,
Florida Gulf Coast University, Florida International University, Florida State University,
New College of Florida, University of Central Florida, University of Florida, University
of North Florida, University of South Florida, and University of West Florida.

University Press of Florida
15 Northwest 15th Street
Gainesville, FL 32611-2079
http://www.upf.com

Contents

Figures

Tables

Acknowledgments

We would like to thank all the organizations and institutions that supported the Motul de San José Archaeological Project (NSF SBR-9905456, FAMSI, Wenner-Gren, Heinz Foundation, Sigma Xi, Fulbright, Williams College, Tulane University, SUNY-Potsdam, the University of Florida, University of California-Riverside, Yale University, Boston University). We are immensely grateful to the Williams College's Dean of Faculty Dr. William Wagner, who provided subsidy funding for this volume; to the former director of the Williams Center for Environmental Studies, Dr. Kai Lee, who funded the project in its early years; and to the Anthropology-Sociology administrative assistant, Donna Chenail, who assisted tirelessly with many versions of the book's bibliography and many other tasks. We thank former UPF editor Kara Schwartz, as well as Dr. James Garber, and an anonymous reviewer for their valuable comments. We express our gratitude to the Departamento de Monumentos Prehispánicos y Coloniales of the Institute of Anthropology and History of Guatemala (IDAEH) for their permission to conduct research at Motul de San José, and especially to Dr. Juan Antonio Valdés, Dr. Hector Escobedo, Lic. Erick Ponciano, Lic. Salvador Lopez, Lic. Paulino Morales, Licda. Yvonne Putzeys and Gustavo Amarra. We also recognize the support of the Municipio of San José, Petén, Guatemala, and its mayor, Don Julian Tesucún y Tesucún, to whom we send our deepest thanks. Finally, this book would not have been possible without the assistance of all the members of the Motul de San José Archaeological Project, including Matthew Moriarty, José Sanchez, Jeanette E. Castellanos, Christina Halperin, Oswaldo Chinchilla, Elly Spensley Moriarty, Erin Thornton, Fredy Ramirez, Aaron Deter-Wolf, Andrew Wyatt, Melanie Kingsley, Suzanna Yorgey, Daniel Glick, Francine Guffey, George Higginbotham, Jessica Charland, Rebecca Goldfine, Benito Burgos, Eliza Suntecun, Anna Lapin, Caroline Ryan, Cathy Warren, Tirso Morales, Gerson Martinez Salguero, Anita Sanchez, Maria Alvarado, Yukiko Tonoike, Megan Foster, Patricia Rivera, Rigden Glaab, Jessica Deckard, Camilo Luin, Erin McCracken, Monica Alvarez, Jeffrey Buechler, Chris Jensen, Kris Johnson, Julia Drapkin, Eric Kerns, Freeden Oeur, William Hahn, Benjamin Haldeman, Yovany Hernández Véliz, Nancy Monterroso, Jonathan Cartagena, Scott Brian,

Crorey Lawton, Ingrid Seyb, Jorge Gúzman, Bevin Stevens, Adriaan Denkers and our numerous field-workers from San José and Nuevo San José. We dedicate this volume to two of our first field assistants and local experts, Salvador Zac and Jorge Zac.

1

Politics and Economics

Theoretical Perspectives of the Motul de San José Project

ANTONIA E. FOIAS AND KITTY F. EMERY

A major debate in Maya archaeology has centered on the nature of its political organization during the Classic period (AD 250–950): was the Maya state centralized or decentralized (Chase and Chase 1996; Demarest 1996; Fox et al. 1996; Houston 1993; J. Marcus 1993; Sharer 1993; Stuart 1993)? However, more recent treatises have underscored the dynamic nature of Classic Maya political institutions (Demarest 1996; J. Marcus 1998; Iannone 2002; Sharer and Golden 2004). The "dynamic model" proposed by J. Marcus (1998) affirms that all ancient civilizations have cycled between periods with highly centralized, territorially extensive states and periods of fragmentation with small-scale decentralized (or weakly centralized) polities (J. Marcus 1998). But Iannone (2002) signals that the dynamic model leaves the question of causality in Maya political dynamics unanswered. To approach this question, we must shift from simple and generalized concepts such as "centralization" and "decentralization" to the actual political practices and mechanisms used by active political actors and/or factions to gain more power and to pursue their agendas within their individual polities (Brumfiel and Fox 1994; Ehrenreich, Crumley, and Levy 1995; Blanton 1998; Carmack 1981; Claessen 1984; Earle 1997, 2001; Feinman 1998; Urban and Schortman 2004; A. Smith 2003; see also Foias 2003, 2007).

One mechanism deployed by ancient elites to advance their political power was control over economic matters. The relationship between political and economic power is crucial to our reconstruction of the nature of Maya states and of the trajectory of this pre-Hispanic Mesoamerican civilization. The Motul de San José Archaeological Project, a long-term interdisciplinary research program, was formulated to provide a better understanding of the intersection between economics and politics from the perspective of one Classic Maya center within the larger context of the southern Maya lowlands. The first phase of research explored the site of Motul de San José and its periphery between 1998 and 2005. Designed to set the groundwork to address the issues of political relationships and economic controls, the first phase involved settlement surveys, a focused sampling of the central and peripheral settlement, strategic excavations of small to large residential units, and the analyses of artifact collections. This volume presents the results of this first phase of research.

Motul de San José in Maya Archaeology

Although Central Petén has attracted a great deal of archaeological attention over the last century (e.g., W. Coe 1965a, 1965b, 1990; Coggins 1975; Culbert 1991, 1993; Sabloff 2003; Fedick and Ford 1990; Ford 1986; Harrison 1999; Jones 1991; Jones and Satterthwaite 1982; Laporte and Fialko 1995; Maler 1908–10; Morley 1938; D. Rice 1986; P. Rice 1986; P. Rice and D. Rice 2009; Tozzer 1911), the nature of political and economic relationships between the major and minor centers in the region remains less clear. Within this core zone of the southern Maya lowlands, long-term ecological studies have correlated environmental shifts with the growth of Maya civilization, while glyphic studies have identified certain political ties between the regional capitals. Among these Central Petén centers is the site of Motul de San José (Figure 1.1).

Motul de San José was an important political center according to hieroglyphic sources. J. Marcus (1976) was the first to identify its Emblem Glyph[1] containing the Ik' symbol (similar to our letter T) as its main element (often called the Ik' Emblem Glyph). Recent decipherments have confirmed this identification (Mathews 1985, 1991; Reents-Budet, Bishop, and MacLeod 1994; Schele and Mathews 1998, 187, 203), although Houston and Stuart (personal communication, 1998) have suggested that the Ik' polity may have encompassed multiple capitals (at the same or at different times), one of which was Motul de San José. During the Late Classic period (AD 600–850), Ik' rulers or nobles were mentioned either as allies or enemies in the monuments of near and far Maya cities, such as Dos Pilas, Seibal, and Yaxchilán (Houston 1993; Stuart and Houston 1994; Schele and Mathews 1991, 1998). The most important of these references appears on Seibal Stela 10 (dated to AD 849), which records rituals witnessed by the rulers of Tikal or Dos Pilas/Aguateca (which share the same Emblem Glyph), Calakmul, and Motul de San José (Schele and Mathews 1998, 187;

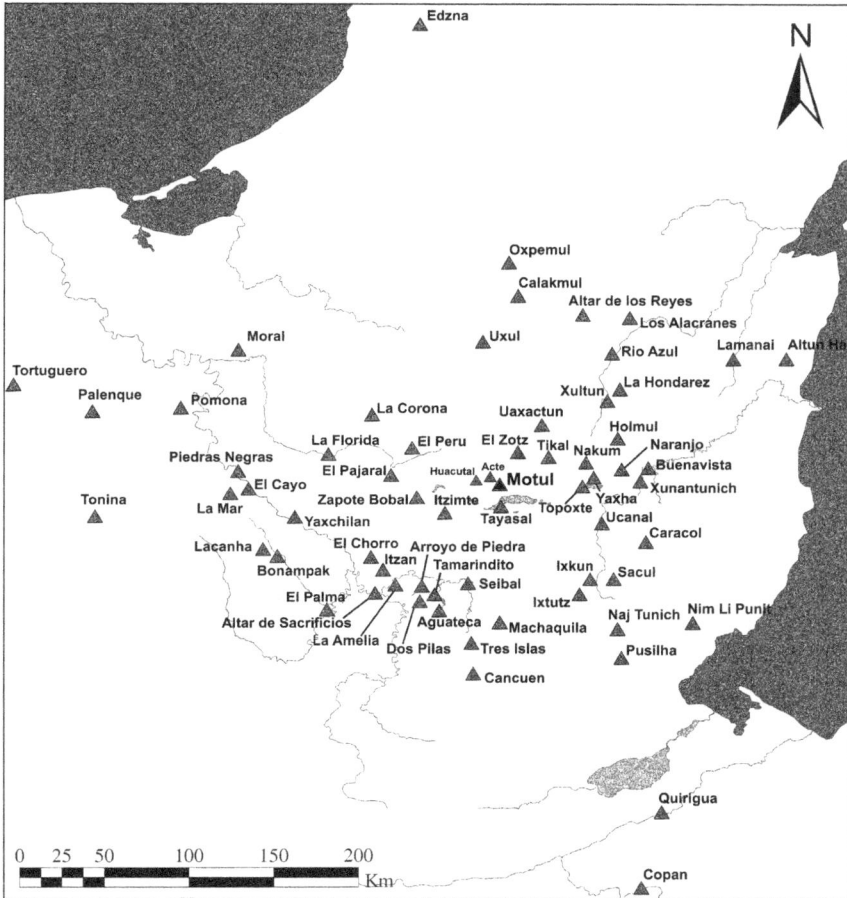

Figure 1.1. Location of Motul de San José in the southern Maya Lowlands (drawing by A. Tokovinine, courtesy of A. Tokovinine).

see Tokovinine and Zender, this volume). J. Marcus interprets this text as naming the capitals of four regional states at the end of the Late Classic (1993, 152). In contrast, Schele and Mathews (1998) view this monument as recording period-ending rituals undertaken by the Seibal king Wat'ul Chatel (possibly from the site of Ucanal in Central Petén) and witnessed by the rulers of the other sites, including Motul de San José. The participation of the Motul or Ik' dynast (called Kan Ek') together with Tikal/Dos Pilas/ Aguateca and Calakmul suggests that it was one of the major actors on the Classic Maya political arena at the end of the Classic period (Schele and Mathews 1998, 185).

Motul de San José was also a center of production of polychrome vessels painted with texts that name the rulers of the Ik' site, hence called the Ik' Polychrome Style (see Reents-Budet et al., this volume; Halperin and Foias, this volume). Previous chemical sourcing of some of these elaborate polychrome vases has shown that they were made in the Motul de San José area, although there was enough chemical variation to suggest the existence of multiple workshops in the region (Reents-Budet 1994). There are now a significant number of such vessels in the so-called Ik' corpus (see Reents-Budet et al., this volume). Although many of these are in private collections, and their provenience is therefore unknown (Kerr 1989–97; Reents-Budet 1994), some are from archaeological contexts, especially from the Petexbatún region (Foias 1996) and now from Motul de San José. The wide distribution of these glyphic vessels, which were given as gifts to cement alliances between the royal elites and nobility of different polities, attests to the extensive political network established by Motul de San José. The close ties with the Petexbatún region, known to be allied with Calakmul during the Late Classic (Martin and Grube 1995, 2000), hint that at some point in its history, Motul was also part of the Calakmul sphere, and therefore in opposition to Tikal, its close neighbor to the north. Building on these earlier studies, our archaeological investigations at Motul offer us a window into its political and economic role in the larger Maya civilization, together with the latest epigraphic decipherments described by Tokovinine and Zender here, as well as the art historical and chemical analyses of the Ik' polychrome pottery presented in this volume by Reents-Budet and colleagues.

A third reason for the importance of Motul de San José in Maya archaeology is that long-term ecological, archaeological and ethnohistorical projects in the Central Petén Lakes region over the last twenty years have provided us with a rich regional context (D. Rice 1986; P. Rice 1986; Deevey et al. 1979; G. Jones 1989, 1998; D. Rice and P. Rice 1980, 1984, 1990; P. Rice and D. Rice 2009). Detailed research by the Rices, Jones, Deevey, Brenner, and their colleagues have built on early work by George Cowgill (1963), William Bullard (1970, 1973), and Arlen Chase (1983). These investigations have reconstructed the long history of occupation of the lacustrine basins from the Middle Preclassic to the Late Postclassic (P. Rice 1986, 1996, 2004; Sánchez Polo et al. 1995; Cecil and Neff 2006; Pugh 2003, 2005; Rice, Demarest, and Rice 2004; P. Rice and D. Rice 2009), and its impact on the tropical environment of the Central Petén Lakes (Deevey 1978, 1984; Deevey et al. 1979; Deevey, Brenner, and Binford 1983; Anselmetti et al.

2007; Brenner et al. 2002; Hodell, Brenner, and Curtis 2000; Mueller et al. 2009). The Maya-Colonial Political Geography Project has extended these studies to the Colonial period and expanded both the surveys and excavations to the areas surrounding the largest Lake Petén Itzá (Sanchez Polo et al. 1995; Rice, Rice, and Jones 1993; Rice, Rice, and Pugh 1997; Rice, Sánchez Polo, and Rice 2007; P. Rice and D. Rice 2009). The focus of these projects has been on the Postclassic and Colonial periods. Their extensive surveys of the Central Petén Lakes basin provide a rich base on which the Motul de San José Archaeological Project builds a site-focused intensive analysis of Classic Maya politics and economics.

Models of Maya Economies and Politics

Changing Paradigms

Reconstructions of Maya economies have changed in the last century as interpretations of Classic society have been refined (McAnany 1989, 1993b; Wells 2006; Smith and Schreiber 2005, 2006). According to the earliest theocratic model, this ancient society consisted of two classes: the peaceful priests who concerned themselves with calendrics and astronomy in vacant ceremonial centers, and the peasants or farmers who lived dispersed around the "empty" centers (Thompson 1942, 1966; Becker 1979; Bullard 1960, 1964; Morley and Brainerd 1956). The dispersed peasant population shifted through the countryside following the requirements of extensive slash-and-burn agriculture. As a result of population dispersion and the self-sufficiency imposed by this simple agricultural system, craft specialization and local exchange were underdeveloped. Only long-distance trade, described in ethnohistorical sources from the time of the Spanish Conquest as an important part of the ancient economy (Thompson 1966), was sustained by, and for, the religious elite.

During the 1960s, a second model of Classic Maya society developed in association with a burgeoning interest in the role of environmental factors in sociopolitical change (McAnany 1993b). Influenced by regional highland Mexican projects that emphasized the correlation between regional settlement and environment, a "highland ecological model" was applied to Classic Maya society (Sanders and Price 1968). In the absence of comparable settlement research in eastern Mesoamerica, the environment of the Maya lowlands was described as homogeneous and resource-poor, and as such, it did not require large, centralized economic and political institutions to integrate distinct ecological zones as seen in Central Mexico (Sanders and Price 1968; Sanders 1962, 1963). According to this model, the homogeneity of resources across the Maya lowlands necessitated no local or intraregional exchange and, therefore, craft production and exchange were small scale. Within this model, Maya civilization was characterized by a weak central government because it did not fulfill an integrating economic-environmental role.

Both of these early models have been effectively refuted by several decades of settlement and environmental research in the Maya lowlands (Culbert and Rice 1990; Culbert 1988b; Tourtellot 1988; Turner and Harrison 1983; Fedick 1996; Golden and Borgstede 2004) and by recent hieroglyphic decipherments (Culbert 1988a; Schele and Miller 1986; Schele and Freidel 1990; Houston 1993; Culbert 1991; Houston and Inomata 2009). These studies revealed that eastern Mesoamerica was more densely populated both within the city centers and throughout the countryside (Culbert 1988b; Culbert and Rice 1990; Iannone and Connell 2003; Scarborough, Valdez Jr., and Dunning 2003), and that sociopolitical structures and historical trajectories were much more variable and complex (Hammond 1981, 1991; D. Chase 1986; A. Chase 1992; Martin and Grube 1995, 2000). Furthermore, the epigraphic revolution shed light on the nature of Maya rulership as "divine warrior kings" who drew their political power from royal descent, success in warfare, and shamanistic priestly rituals (Schele and Miller 1986; Schele and Freidel 1990; Demarest 1992; Ciudad Ruiz 2001; Zender 2004b).

Simultaneously, the integration of ecological research into archaeological projects has illuminated the true heterogeneity and diversity of tropical lowland environments and resources. Numerous studies have revealed the mosaic nature of the lowlands and the presence of localized resources in restricted areas, for example, the Colha high-quality chert and volcanic stone in the Maya Mountains (E. Graham 1987; McAnany 1993b; Potter 1993; Potter and King 1995; Shafer and Hester 1983; Scarborough, Valdez Jr., and Dunning 2003; Scarborough and Valdez Jr. 2009). The humid tropical lowlands are also rich in environmental resources critical both for subsistence and for the production of prestige or wealth items such as jaguar pelts, precious bird feathers, honey, hardwoods, spices, cacao, and cotton (Sharer 1994). Furthermore, variability in monthly and yearly rainfall across the Maya lowlands would lead to distinct times for harvesting the most important crops, such as corn, beans, squash, etc. (see similar discussion in Scarborough, Valdez, and Dunning 2003). Such harvest irregularities would have been balanced through trade of agricultural surplus between regions, subregions, or communities, as they were in the Mixtec region (Lind 2000). The complexity of Maya agriculture has also been explored, leaving behind the image of a simple, extensive swidden system (Atran 1993; Dunning et al. 1999; Fedick 1996; Ford 2008; Johnston 2003; Nations and Nigh 1980; Scarborough and Valdez Jr. 2009; Whitmore and Turner 1992).

More importantly, studies of highly diverse environments such as those found in Central Mexico, Peru, and Hawaii have shown that the presence of marked vertical environmental strata discourages regional exchange and encourages political control over all ecological zones in the hands of one polity (McAnany 1989; Earle 1987). In contrast, the lack of marked vertical environmental zones and the presence of mosaic resource diversity as found in the Maya lowlands may well have led "to the development of community specialization and of a regional exchange system to obtain these localized goods" (McAnany 1989, 362). In support of this new perspective, lithic and ceramic studies have found significant local craft production and exchange in Belize (Shafer and Hester 1983, 1986; McAnany 1989; Lewis 2003), in Central Petén (Fry 1979, 1980; Becker 2003a; Moholy-Nagy 1997), in the southeastern periphery (Beaudry 1984; Aoyama 2001; Schortman, Urban, and Ausec 2001; Urban, Wells, and Ausec 1997; Andrews and Bill 2005), in the Palenque area (Rands and Bishop 1980; Bishop 1994), in the western periphery (Bishop and Rands 1982; Rands, Bishop, and Sabloff 1982), and in the Petexbatún region (Foias 1996, 2002, 2004; Foias and Bishop 1997, 2007; Inomata 2001b; Inomata and Stiver 1998; Inomata et al. 2002; Aoyama 2007; Emery and Aoyama 2007).

Recent Models and Debates

In response to these two early paradigms, a diversity of new synthetic revisionist economic and sociopolitical models has been proposed (Adams and Smith 1981; Ball and Taschek 1991; Demarest 1992; J. W. Fox 1987, 1989; Freidel 1981; Houston 1993; J. Marcus 1976; Sanders and Webster 1988). However, a review of these models shows the emergence of two polemics. On the one hand, a "centralist camp" (e.g., Chase and Chase 1996) describes a system of centralized Maya states with elite control over production and exchange. On the other hand, the "decentralist camp" (e.g., Demarest 1992) envisions Classic Maya states as weakly integrated polities with little elite control over production and exchange beyond the tribute system and/or the social valuables sphere. Thus, it becomes clear that most Maya archaeologists correlate political centralization (or strong centralization) with elite control over the economic infrastructure, and decentralization (or weak centralization) with a lack of elite involvement in economic matters of production and exchange. The degree or even presence of elite economic control is seen as a key mechanism in the centralization of political power (cf. Brumfiel 1994), but needs further archaeological testing to assess its importance.

A brief summary of the decentralist and centralist models illuminates that they are two extremes at each end of a continuum,[2] and that Classic Maya polities probably varied along this range as most recent scholarship has underscored (J. Marcus 1993, 1998; Haviland 1997; Chase, Chase, and Haviland 1990; Demarest 1996; Iannone 2002; Foias 2007).

The decentralist camp has engendered the application of multiple cross-cultural political models, such as the peer polity (Renfrew 1982; Renfrew and Cherry 1986; Freidel 1986; Sabloff 1986), segmentary state (Southall 1988; J. W. Fox 1987; Fox et al. 1996), "theater state" (Geertz 1980; Demarest 1992), "galactic polity" (Tambiah 1976, 1977; Demarest 1992; Houston 1993), regal-ritual centers (R. Fox 1977; Ball and Taschek 1991; Ball 1993), city-state model (Grube 2000), and heterarchical models (Crumley 1979; Ehrenreich, Crumley, and Levy 1995; Potter and King 1995). Although they vary in detail, all these constructs pertain to a weakly centralized state model. The main features of such a state are: (1) the polity consists of a capital and its hinterland, with weakly controlled secondary and tertiary centers where there is clear replication of both structures and functions found in the primary center; (2) the power of the ruler is predicated on his personal charisma and his success in prestige-enhancing warfare, ritual, and marriage alliances; (3) a general lack of economic control by the political institution underscores its ritual foundation and legitimation (Demarest 1992; Iannone 2002).

In contrast, the centralized state model (Chase and Chase 1996; J. Marcus 1993; R. Adams 1986; Haviland 1992, 1997; Chase, Chase, and Haviland 1990) proposes that the largest Maya cities, Tikal, Calakmul, and Caracol (and possibly others), were characterized by rulers who were able to amass and centralize considerable political power. Such political panache is reflected in their ability to construct massive public works, not only monumental pyramids, but also economic infrastructure, such as the extensive causeways and standardized terrace systems at Caracol (Chase and Chase 1996; Chase, Chase, and Haviland 1990) and the defensive earthworks and possibly drainage systems in adjacent bajos at Tikal (Haviland 1997; Culbert 1988b; Chase, Chase, and Haviland 1990; Fialko, personal communication, 2000). Centralized political control is also reflected in the large-scale population relocation that took place at Tikal at the beginning of the Late Classic (ca. AD 550; see Haviland 1997, 443; Chase, Chase, and Haviland 1990, 500). Centralized states are, therefore, seen to be able to control economic systems, such as intensive agriculture, or production and exchange. Tight political control and integration of the middle and lower levels of the political hierarchy are visible in the archaeological record in limited functional and structural replication at secondary and tertiary centers, as in the case of the causeway termini at Caracol (Chase and Chase 1996) which show distinct architecture and functions from the capital city (see also Iannone 2002). The centralized state model also supposes a much more complex social system, one based on differentiated socioeconomic classes and not exclusively on kinship, with an extensive middle class as evidenced at Caracol (Chase and Chase 1996), although the existence of lineages or other kin-based social groups like houses (Fox et al. 1996; McAnany 1995; Hageman 2004; Gillespie 2000; Ringle and Bey 2001; Hutson, Magnoni, and Stanton 2004) would not be antithetical to a centralized state (Haviland 1997, 444).

Most recent discussions (J. Marcus 1998; Demarest 1996; Iannone 2002; Sharer and Golden 2004; A. Smith 2003) highlight the dynamic nature of Maya states, as different rulers and their polities may have successfully centralized their political base, expanded, flourished, and then contracted to more weakly centralized units. Although such multiple trajectories of expansion and contraction specific to each polity are encompassed by the "galactic polity" model borrowed from Southeast Asia (Tambiah 1976, 1977) and applied to the Maya case by Demarest (1992) and Houston (1993), we need to understand why some Maya rulers could centralize power while others didn't. We need to inquire: what allowed them to strengthen their power, and what then led to their disintegration? To answer these questions, we need to examine the internal dynamics of each Maya state.

One of the reasons for this variability in political structure may be variation in state involvement in economic matters. In some polities—for example, Caracol (Chase and Chase 1996) and Sayil (Smyth, Dore, and Dunning 1995)—the rulers may have had more direct control over the economic infrastructure, which gave them an added power base for more extensive political control. Therefore, we need to understand the degree of elite control over economy in each Maya polity to attempt to explain variations in political structures across the Maya lowlands during the Late Classic period (AD 600–830). The concept of ritual economy proposed recently by Wells (2006; see also Wells and Davis-Salazar 2007; Wells and

McAnany 2008; McAnany 2010) ties the knot between politics, economics, and rituals. Ritual economy, as "the materialization of values and beliefs through acquisition and consumption [of goods] for managing meaning and shaping interpretation . . . is central to the study of . . . [Maya] political authority" (McAnany 2010, 159). In his review of the role of performance in premodern polities, Inomata (2006, 805) echoes the critical role of political ritual: "subject populations' perception and experience of authorities and national unity were highly uneven, accentuated in the specific temporal and spatial contexts of state-sponsored events such as ceremonies and construction projects . . . [in] the tangible images of the ruler's body, state buildings, and collective acts." Finally, to quote one final scholar, ritual is critical in premodern societies because *"in the absence of writing, it was ritual that defined people's power relations"* (Kertzer 1988, 104; italics added). The relationship between economy and politics (through ritual) is the primary focus of the Motul de San José Archaeological Project (see Foias et al., this volume; Emery, this volume; Emery and Foias, this volume; Moriarty, this volume).

Current Maya Political Debates and the Motul de San José Research

As one of the main questions concerning Classic Maya political structure is the degree of political centralization, it behooves us to begin with a definition of this term. There are many definitions of centralization, but let us propose a preliminary etic[3] one. Most anthropologists would agree that a centralized state is characterized by a professional cadre of administrators (or a protobureaucracy), organized on several tiers with distinct powers and responsibilities, with the top tier (located in the main capital of the state) as the one controlling all political decisions (see Foias 2007, forthcoming; Roscoe 1993; Doyle 1986; Eisenstadt 1993). Roscoe (1993) more specifically considers the degree of political centralization tied to fewer and fewer individuals making the political decisions.

When the centralist camp argues that the Classic Maya ruling elite controlled the economic structure, they are discussing the power base of the political institutions rather than its centralization (which refers specifically to how many individuals make political decisions; cf. Roscoe 1993). Following a Marxist perspective, they argue that the strongest source of power is economic through the control of basic resources needed for survival. However, there are other sources of political power, such as military, social,[4] and religious (see Earle 1997). Military sources of power are predicated on the strength and size of the army, and through the threat of coercion or force. Such military power can be enforced through the presence of a standing army of some strength and skill. Social bases of power are predicated on kinship relations, interpersonal alliance systems, patron–client networks, social status or prestige, and so on (see Blanton 1998). The ideological or religious source of power is founded on the belief that the political leaders are semidivine or divine, as among the ancient Egyptians and Classic Mayas. As many anthropologists have remarked, coercive or military power is much harder and more costly to maintain than ideological power: the threat of supernatural punishment is much more enforceable than the threat of physical coercion (Doyle 1986; Earle 1997; Sinopoli 1994).

More importantly, when the centralists posit that the Classic Maya rulership was centralized, they are implying that it was autocratic, with the ruler wielding absolute power (Foias 2007, 169). But, autocratic rulers could also exist in decentralized political systems. Their absolute power may extend only over the capital city, whereas each of the subsidiary centers has its own elite leaders who may or may not follow the orders of the ruler (Claessen 1984). Nevertheless, both centralists and decentralists would agree that in order for a centralized system to work, a professional administrative staff or protobureaucracy is needed to monitor and extend that control beyond the confines of the capital (Eisenstadt 1993; Kiser and Cai 2003; Foias 2007, forthcoming). Most ancient states could not create such a centralized protobureaucracy that drew its power exclusively from the ruler (Foias 2003, 2007). Rather, ancient rulers most often had to rely on the elite class to administer the political affairs of the state. The problem is that the nobles were not dependent on the ruler for their power, but rather had their own power base (social, economic, religious, etc.) due to their social rank as members of the aristocratic class. Thus, it is likely that the instances in which ancient states were truly centralized were extremely rare, and that the typical ancient state was weakly centralized (Foias 2007; see also Graham, this volume).

Turning back to the Maya case, one source of evidence on the existence of a political administrative hierarchy is the Classic period hieroglyphic texts. Therein, we find subsidiary administrative titles, but they do not appear frequently: *sahal*, *ah k'uhun*, and *yajaw k'ak* (Sharer and Golden 2004; Inomata 2001a; Houston and Stuart 2001; Houston 1993; Grube quoted in Coe and Kerr 1998; Jackson and Stuart 2001). The title *sahal* refers to a subsidiary noble governing a secondary center, whereas *ah k'uhun* has been interpreted variously as "keeper of the sacred books," "royal scribe," "keeper of tribute" (or of sacred/special objects), or "venerator" of specific rulers (Jackson and Stuart 2001). However, the latest decipherments of the *ah k'uhun* title see it as a high-ranking priestly position (Zender 2004b). *Yajaw k'ak* can be translated as "the fire's lord" and was also a priestly title below the rank of *ah k'uhun* (ibid.). This does not deny the possibility that these priestly positions also fulfilled administrative roles (ibid.). Hierarchical ordering using the modifier *ba* or "first" were sometimes made among these titles, such as *ba-sahal*, or "first governor" or *ba-ajaw*, or "first lord" (Sharer and Golden 2004); however, Zender (2004b) suggests that *ba-ajaw* was a lower priestly post. Another possible administrative title found recently is *lakam*, which appears on a few polychrome vases rather than on public monuments (Lacadena 2008). Even so, these administrative titles were uncommon, mostly appearing in the western lowlands (Houston and Stuart 2001). Furthermore, an intense personal association between these titles and an individual ruler specified by the glyphs argues for a strong personal relationship between the ruler and his administrators, rather than an impersonal, bureaucratic connection.

The administrative structure of Classic Maya states, then, consisted of the nobles who had their own power base because of their social rank, and therefore were not completely dependent on the ruler for their power and privilege. Based on this evidence alone, it seems more likely that the Classic Maya states were generally not strongly centralized. This does not deny the possibility that at some point in time, some states (such as Tikal, Calakmul, and/or Caracol) did accomplish the feat of political centralization, called the "Augustan threshold" of centralization by Michael Doyle (1986).

At this point, we also need to consider the long-term pattern of political organization in the Maya lowlands. In other words, when considering Maya state organization over the millennia from its inception until the Spanish Conquest, can we determine which was the most common form of the Maya state: the strongly centralized, territorially extensive "superstate" or the small-scale, weakly centralized polity? Let's consider a similar case from the Near East. The long-term political pattern in Sumerian history (from circa 4000 BC until 1800 BC) is of small city-states that are then conquered and unified into an empire for relatively shorter periods of time, which then disintegrate again and again into the original city-states. Why was no Sumerian empire forged as a long-term stable political entity? Westenholz (1993) responds by pointing to the dominant Sumerian political ideology that the legitimate political unit was the city-state, each one tied to its particular location and its associated tutelary gods (see also discussion in Steinkeller 1993, 116–29). A similar ideology existed among the Classic Maya as first suggested by Rosemary Joyce (1986), and now supported by epigraphic studies (Houston and Stuart 2001; Grube 2000, 552–53). This ideology focused on the capital at the center of each Maya polity and its associated royal dynasty:

> The reading of the Emblem Glyph title shows the rulers' claim to a form of "divine kingship." These were not competing claims to a singular authority since each [king] drew his power from, and was specific to, a given seat or locality [the capital], better seen as a central source rather than a bounded and demarcated territory. (Grube 2000, 552)

The divine Maya rulers (*k'ujul ajaw*) drew part of their power from their descent through a long line of illustrious ancestors back to deities tied to a specific locality in the capital city (e.g., the Palenque Triad). Territorial conquest, therefore, was not possible as a long-term policy because the conquerors were never seen as legitimate since their ancestors were not tied to the vanquished city (Grube 2000, 552).

In spite of this overarching ideology that both the Sumerian city-states and the Maya polities shared (although different in detail), some rulers and some states were able to surpass it. Sargon of Akkad managed it and united for the first time all Sumerian city-states into the Akkadian Empire in 2371 BC (Liverani 1993). Martin and Grube (2000; see also Grube 2000) have argued that the rulers of Tikal and Calakmul also were able to manage this feat. They ground this assertion in the archaeological evidence that these sites are much larger in size and scale of monumental public construction than most other Classic Maya capital centers. They argue that such large-scale constructions "would have required centralized planning and the control of substantial manpower," which could be achieved only through the formation of hegemonies or hegemonic superstates (Grube 2000, 550; Martin and Grube 1995, 2000). Such hegemonic control is marked through the hieroglyphic expressions of *y-ajaw*, "the lord of" or "his vassal," and the verbal phrase *u kabhiy*, "it was done under his tutelage [of the overlord]" (Martin and Grube 1995, 2000). These expressions involve Tikal's or Calakmul's rulers over several generations, suggesting a long-term system of hegemonies centered upon these two major cities. However, it is important to remark that these hegemonies are not envisioned as strongly centralized states. Grube describes them in the following manner:

Conquests made by the dominant states were not consolidated by military occupation or centrally administered. Local lords were usually restored to their offices and allowed to rule their states without further hindrance. (2000, 550)

Nevertheless, these vassal states had to pay tribute to the dominant ones who also held sway in their external affairs (following the definition of a hegemony [Doyle 1986]). Grube's description of Tikal's and Calakmul's hegemonies indicate that these were not highly centralized bureaucratic polities, even though clearly there was central and powerful political authority in the hands of their divine rulers (also see Ciudad Ruiz 2001, 209, 234). Although the presence of hegemonies has been accepted by many Maya scholars, their actual organization or the nature of the connections between the vassal states and their overlords have not been investigated (see also Ciudad Ruiz [2001, 209–10] for Postclassic Maya examples of hegemonic control). Motul de San José participated in these regional politics, and Tokovinine and Zender (this volume) discuss Tikal's hegemonic control over Motul during part of the Late Classic period.

Grube and Martin do not address how or why Tikal or Calakmul were successful in forming these hegemonies where most other Maya states were not. It is likely that one reason some Maya states were able to pass the "Augustan threshold of centralization" was because the state managed to gain control over a larger portion of the economic system, such as, possibly, the water system as suggested by Scarborough and Lucero (Scarborough 1996, 2003; Lucero 2002, 2006). Both Tikal and Calakmul had massive water reservoirs within their cores (Lucero 2002), and at least at Tikal, more and more evidence is discovered that suggests that some water-management works may have been initiated, built, and maintained by the state (Fialko, personal communication, 2001; Scarborough 1996, 2003). Control over a larger portion of the economic system (whether water-management systems, agricultural lands, craft production, or exchange) would have created for these states a greater surplus that could be translated into more military personnel, or a larger administrative cadre, that could serve to enforce the ruler's power. Our investigations at Motul de San José (a minor center on the periphery of, but within the hegemony of, Tikal and Calakmul at different times) are perfectly positioned to examine the internal dynamics of smaller states, especially ones that were tied to a dominant "superstate." Many scholars have also asserted that intermediate centers, like Motul de San José, and their elites had a critical role in causing the dynamics of ancient polities (e.g., J. Marcus 1983; Elson and Covey 2006). Research targeting heterogeneous commoners and hinterlands has also revealed that political power not only emanates from the top, but is also negotiated between social groups, leading to the dynamic nature of political trajectories (Elson and Covey 2006; Schwartz and Falconer 1994a, 1994b; Canuto and Yaeger 2000; Lohse and Valdez 2004; Scarborough, Valdez Jr., and Dunning 2003; Iannone and Connell 2003; Scarborough and Valdez Jr. 2009). Thus, the relationships between top elites, secondary elites, and nonelites (the negotiations, resistance, contestations, or impositions between them) are critical pieces of the political dynamics of Classic Maya states.

Current Maya Economic Debates and the Motul de San José Research

The role of economic factors in sociocultural evolution remains an important concern in anthropological and archaeological studies of cultural change. Control over basic economic resources, such as land, technology, and the means of production, has been considered the basis for gaining and increasing political power from the earliest complex societies until the present time (e.g., Blanton et al. 1996; Brumfiel and Earle 1987; Earle 1997; Fried 1967; Harris 1968; Johnson and Earle 1987; Morgan 1964; Marx 1949; Service 1962, 1975; White 1959). In every ancient civilization, whether in Mesopotamia, Egypt, China, Valley of Mexico, or Andean Peru, the ruling elites had some degree of control over economic systems (R. McC. Adams 1965, 1966, 1981; Brumfiel 1980; Chang 1986; D'Altroy and Earle 1985; Earle 1987, 1997; Isbell 1978; Kemp 1989; Murra 1980; Sanders and Price 1968; Sanders, Parsons, and Santley 1979; Yoffee 1988; Feinman and Nicholas 2004; Smith and Schreiber 2005, 2006; P. Rice 2009b). The question of elite involvement in economic institutions is important in understanding not only diachronic processes of cultural evolution, but also the nature of political systems in ancient societies.

The most recent syntheses of Classic Maya economy reconstruct it as a pluralistic precapitalist system consisting of two spheres: the "prestige economy" and the "general economy" (McAnany 1993a; Ball and Taschek 1992; Feldman 1985; Foias 2002, 2004). The *prestige economy* refers specifically and restrictively to "the production, acquisition, and disposition of articles used for purposes of status affirmation or in elite-initiated transactions through which bonds are formed and maintained between the elites of differing polities and among the [elite] members of individual polities" (Ball and Taschek 1992, 17). In contrast to the prestige economy, the *general economy* is defined as the economic activities pertaining to the production, exchange, and consumption of subsistence goods such as common foodstuffs, utilitarian pottery (including lower-grade polychromes), and stone and bone tools (Ball and Taschek 1992; McAnany 1989, 1993a). Alternatively, Prudence Rice discusses the prestige economy as the *political economy* (distinct from the *domestic economy*): "the management of types and sources of wealth and power in a sociopolitical system through decisions made and implemented at levels above that of the domestic group" (2009b, 70). Each of these two spheres (prestige-political versus general-domestic economies) may have had different and partially or completely separate systems of production and distribution.

Within the *prestige economy*, elite patronage of the artisans is assumed to have been the normal pattern of manufacture of elaborate polychromes, ritual pottery, stone eccentrics, and jade or shell jewelry; this reconstruction is based on few cases, though. The existence of elite pottery "workshops" or "palace schools" has been inferred from the epigraphic and iconographic studies of Reents-Budet and MacLeod, who have shown that scribal signatures include the elite title of *ajaw* and even possibly the word for apprentice (MacLeod and Reents-Budet 1994; Reents-Budet 1994; Reents 1985). Ball has discovered a possible "palace school" at Buenavista in Belize, where Holmul-style polychromes were crafted (Ball 1993; Taschek and Ball 1992; Reents-Budet et al. 2000). Inomata has also found a scribe's palace in the epicenter of Aguateca, where shell jewelry was made and painting (of vessels and other artifacts) took place (1995, 2001b). These elite scribes or artisans devoted the majority or all of their time to these multiple crafting activities. Elite control over the production of such prestige items is suggested by these limited examples. Excavations in the Acropolis of Motul de San José have uncovered another example of a "palace school" of polychrome production related to the Ik' Polychrome Style (Halperin and Foias 2010, this volume; Reents-Budet et al., this volume).

The exchange of these prestige or sumptuary goods was most likely through gifting between royal dynasties and nobility as they are found in restricted elite contexts, although studies of this aspect are also rare (Tourtellot and Sabloff 1972; P. Rice 1987a, 1987b, 2009b; Ball 1993; Reents-Budet 1994; Bishop 1994; see also Reents-Budet et al., this volume). However, the lack of elite control over the distribution of elaborate Codex-style polychromes at the site of Nakbe is reflected in the broad distribution of these fancy pots in almost all Late Classic households (Hansen, Bishop, and Fahsen 1991), but Nakbe appears to have a special status as the production center of Codex-style polychrome.

Studies of figurines at Motul de San José have also highlighted the complexities of the prestige economy and its junction with the general economy (Halperin 2004a, 2004b, 2007, 2009, this volume; Halperin et al. 2009). These small media are found commonly in household contexts and depict a broad array of images from simple women holding a child or a food plate to elaborately attired rulers (Halperin, this volume). In addition, the common use of figurine molds at Motul de San José makes them into "a type of [early] mass media" (Halperin 2009, 385). Furthermore, recent scholarship within and beyond the Maya area has provided a more nuanced perspective on prestige economies, locating them socially and historically (Bayman 1999, 2002; Hruby and Flad 2007; Mills 2004).

The *general economy* appears to follow different patterns from the prestige sphere. Within the general economy, utilitarian pottery (unslipped, monochrome, and simple polychromes), stone or bone tools, and other craft items were generally produced by possibly part-time, nonelite specialists in independent, generally small-scale family "workshops" dispersed beyond the major centers (P. Rice 1985, 1987a; Fry 1980; Rands and Bishop 1980; Beaudry 1984; Ball 1993; Reents-Budet, Bishop, and MacLeod 1994; Potter 1993; Bishop, Rands, and Holley 1982; Culbert and Schwalbe 1987; Potter and King 1995). Because of this dispersed organization of production, Maya cities are seen as the consumers of these utilitarian products rather than as production hubs (Ball 1993). Ball (1993), McAnany (1993b), and Scarborough, Valdez Jr., and Dunning (2003) have contended that small communities outside the major centers may have specialized in the manufacture of particular items. Chert workshops at Colha, Belize, were dense accumulations of manufacturing debris that would suggest more intensive or larger-scale production (Hester and Shafer 1984; Hester, Eaton, and Shafer 1980; Shafer and Hester 1983, 1986, 1991). Similar remains of chert production have also been discovered recently by Crorey Lawton and project members at La Estrella, Nuevo San José, in the periphery of Motul de San José (Lawton 2007a, 2007b; Moriarty, this volume). Arnold (1985), P. Rice (1981), and Ford (1991, 1992, 2004) have argued that there is a positive correlation between Classic Maya craft specialization and poor soil fertility, suggesting that where food production was insufficient, basic foods were acquired intraregionally in exchange for utilitarian craft goods. This stresses the importance of exchange on the regional and interregional levels, and the interrelatedness of small specialized communities (Scarborough, Valdez Jr., and Dunning 2003; Scarborough and Valdez Jr. 2009). In contrast, McAnany (2010) hypothesizes that craft production gave Maya commoners pride and increased prestige, and had less to do with lower soil fertility in their communities.

Variability within Maya general economies is also reflected at the sites of Sayil and Caracol. Studies at Sayil in the Puuc region of the northern Maya lowlands have uncovered a large-scale utilitarian ceramic production zone within the Southwest Elite Group in the site core (Smyth, Dore, and Dunning 1995, 331), showing that some utilitarian production was more concentrated in elite centers. Numerous production activities have also been discovered at Caracol, leading its excavators to nominate this city as a production hub (Chase and Chase 1996). Site-wide spatial analysis of manufacturing activities at Quiriguá revealed that both obsidian and pottery production took place in the site core and periphery, sometimes in association with elaborate or elite architectural groups (Ashmore 1988, 2007). Obsidian and chert production has also been identified in elite households at El Pilar (Ford 2004). Thus, both elite control and the scale of production are variable aspects that have to be explored in detail in every Maya polity.

The exchange of subsistence goods may have varied from simple barter to a complex market system, possibly associated with fairs or embedded in the social organization (Rands and Bishop 1980; Fry 1979, 1980, 1981; Freidel 1981; P. Rice 1987a; West 2002; Halperin 2007; Halperin et al. 2009). According to the decentralist camp, the elite had little control over the distribution of these subsistence goods and utilitarian wares (Fry 1980, 1981; P. Rice 1987a; Rands and Bishop 1980; McAnany 1993a). But, elites could easily control exchange if it took place in a central location either through redistribution or market exchange. Carol Smith (1976) has emphasized that control over distribution is the foundation for elite power in agrarian societies (see also West 2002). Markets have been difficult to detect archaeologically (Hirth 1998; Minc 2005), although the large central plazas in Maya centers are often seen as functioning in such a role (Freidel 1981; Hirth 1998; West 2002). Unfortunately, no features or artifact accumulations have been found in these central plazas, so this hypothesis remains under debate. Nevertheless, a possible market has been discovered at Sayil within one of the core architectural complexes, the Mirador Complex, because of linear stone features suggestive of market stalls and a high density of utilitarian ceramic wares suggestive of marketing or storage (Tourtellot, Sabloff, and Carmean 1992; Smyth, Dore, and Dunning 1995). Even more recently, Chunchucmil has also been described as the location of a market using new innovative soil chemistry studies (Dahlin et al. 2007). Recent soil studies at Motul and the secondary center of La Trinidad have provided intriguing data suggestive that this port on the north shore of Lake Petén Itzá and one of the central plazas at Motul may have held markets (Bair and Terry, this volume; Dahlin et al. 2009).

Studies of distribution have also been applied to understand the nature and scale of exchange. The most successful have been based on chemical or petrological sourcing analyses of pottery (Fry 1979, 1980, 1981; Rands and Bishop 1980; Bishop 1994; Culbert and Schwalbe 1987; see also Hirth 1998). These studies have shown lively exchange organized in multiple ways, from localized barter or supply zone exchange, to possible markets, central place redistribution, and kinship-based exchange (Fry 1979, 1980; Rands and Bishop 1980; Bishop 1994; P. Rice 1987a, 1987b; West 2002; Dahlin et al. 2007).

The lack of animal or wheeled transportation in Mesoamerica clearly limited the scale of possible exchange in pre-Hispanic times (Hassig 1985, 1992; Drennan 1984a, 1984b). Inland regions like the central lowlands would have relied on human transportation of exchange goods. It is important to note, though, that the Central Petén Lakes system (where the ancient Maya constructed canals connecting the major lakes from east to west [D. Rice 1996]), together with several river systems, which in the past may have had a higher water flow (Fialko, personal communication, 1999–2000)—the San Pedro Martir River toward the western lowlands, the Holmul River toward the eastern lowlands, and the Pasion-Chixoy-Usumacinta rivers in the southern and southwestern lowlands—would have allowed partial movement of goods by water routes. Boat transportation is much more efficient than human porters, and may have led to a larger scale of exchange in the Maya lowlands than usually envisioned.

Finally, to explore the intersection between politics and economics, we need to consider the relationship between environment and human society. Landscape archaeology and historical ecology perspectives emphasize the links between the cultural, ecological, and historical contexts of ancient societies. They argue for the importance of the specifics of site-based environmental patterning and the history of its development as a result of synergistic relationships between people and their natural and human-modified surroundings (Balee 2006; Balee and Erickson 2006; Crumley 2003; Graham 1998, 1999). The Motul de San José environment was an ideologically loaded, modified landscape created by the process of impacts and responses of humans with the plants, animals, geology, and other resources of the region. We are interested in the extent to which the Motul de San José "landscape" was manipulated for both economic and political reasons through construction, land-use, and control of natural resources (Brady and Ashmore 1999; Dwyer 1996; Hirsch 1995; Ingold 1993; McAnany 1998). Bair and Terry (this volume) and Webb and Schwarcz (this volume) apply soil geomorphology and soil chemical studies to reconstruct the soil qualities and resources, as well as agricultural systems at Motul de San José and its periphery. Emery (this volume) and Thornton (this volume) use zooarchaeological approaches to examine human–animal interactions and their changes over time at Motul. Wyatt et al. (this volume) present the ongoing analysis of macro- and microbotanical remains at Motul to understand the plant resources available and/or used by the ancient Maya.

Introduction to Motul de San José and the Motul de San José Archaeological Project

Motul de San José, situated approximately 3.5 kilometers north of Lake Petén Itzá in the Central Petén Lakes region (Figure 1.1), was first visited by Maler in 1895 (Maler 1908–10). Because the ruins had been recently cleared for milpa cultivation, he was able to judge the considerable size of the site extending from east to west (Maler 1908–10, 132). He recorded two stelae, one of which he photographed and described in detail (134–35). Twenty years later, Sylvanus G. Morley also visited the site and reported on the same two stelae (1938, 415–21). In the 1950s, Ian Graham recorded and photographed five monuments at the site and made a preliminary accurate map. Arlen Chase also included Motul de San José in his survey of the Lake Petén Itzá zone, although the focus was on the Peninsula Tayasal (1983).

The first extensive archaeological fieldwork began during the summer of 1998 by the Williams College Motul de San José Archaeological Project under the direction of Foias and Emery (Foias 1998, 1999, 2001; Foias and Castellanos 2000; Moriarty 2002; Moriarty et al. 2004). Intensive survey of the site and its periphery between 1998 and 2000 has produced the first extensive and accurate map (Foias 2003; Moriarty 2004d).

The core of the site covers an area of approximately 1.4 square kilometers, with a total of 230 structures (Figure 1.2). This is at the moment a national park protected by the Guatemalan National Institute of Anthropology and History (Instituto Nacional de Antropologia e Historia; see Figure 1.3a).

However, contiguous settlement pertaining to Motul de San José continues beyond the park limits, and based on the survey data, probably encompassed a larger area of 4.2 square kilometers (Moriarty 2004d, 30). Nevertheless, Motul remains a small regional center in Central Petén, dwarfed by Tikal, Holmul, Naranjo, and Yaxhá, to mention a few.

The monumental architecture of the site core is organized into five groups (named Groups A to E) arranged from west to east (Figure 1.2). Each of these major groups consists of several courtyards with substantial residential multiroom range structures, and one or more temple-pyramids ranging in height from 4 to 20 meters (see Foias 2003). Group C is the largest and includes the Main Plaza (Plaza I) and the Acropolis (which probably functioned as the royal palace and court of the Late Classic rulers). The Main Plaza is defined by twin pyramids[5] in the east (reaching 18 meters in height), the highest pyramid in the south (reaching 20 meters in height), Group D in the north, and the Acropolis in the north and west. Six stelae are found in the Main Plaza: Stelae 3, 4, and 5 are situated on small platforms aligned in front of the twin pyramids; Stela 6 was discovered in 1998, along the north façade of the southern pyramid (Foias 2000a, 2000b); finally, Stelae 1 (first recorded by Maler) and 7 (possibly an independent stela fragment or a very eroded altar) are located along the northwestern corner of the Main Plaza. The final Motul monument, Stela 2 (photographed by Maler), is found in Group B, on the west side of its major south pyramid. Group B is connected to Group E by a north–south avenue that ends at the north pyramid of Group E. This north–south avenue or *sacbe* is lined on both the east and west sides by medium-size plaza groups.

Beyond this monumental core, settlement is more dispersed, with residential plaza groups extending on high ground north (North Zone) and east (East Zone), whereas to the south and west, low-lying areas (small, seasonally flooded bajos) are not conducive to human occupation but may have been used for agricultural purposes by the ancient inhabitants (see also Foias 2003; Moriarty 2004d).

Archaeologists have used settlement pattern analysis to understand site organization and human activities, but have relied heavily on architectural variability as an indication of sociopolitical or functional distinctions (Tourtellot 1988; Carmean 1991; Webster and Gonlin 1988; Hendon 1991; Fash et al. 1992; Freidel and Sabloff 1984; Smyth and Dore 1992, 1994). However, architectural features are not the best indicators of the functions of different buildings (Smyth, Dore, and Dunning 1995; Inomata 1995). Associated artifacts (in primary floor deposits or adjacent refuse deposits) and

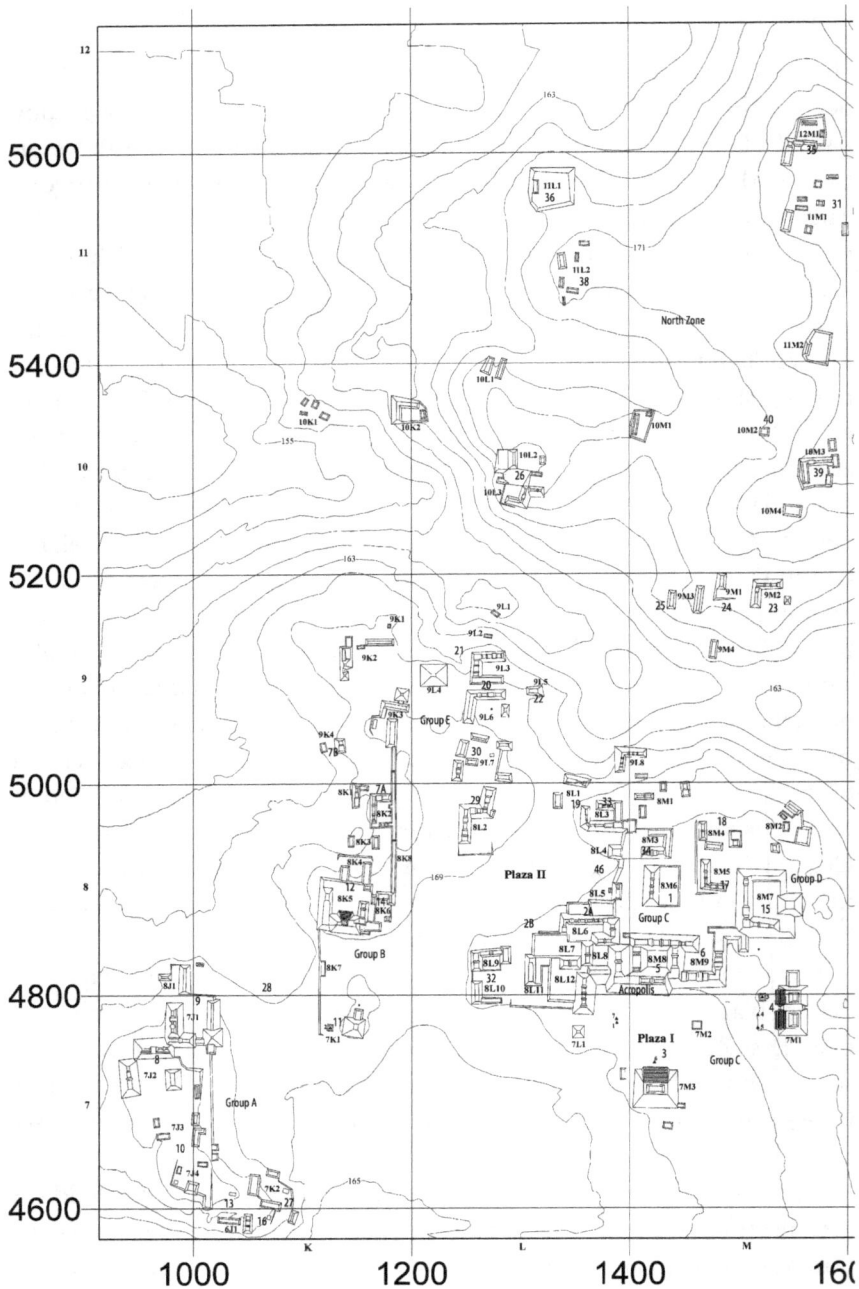

Figure 1.2. Map of Motul de San José showing group names (mapped by A. Foias and project members; drawing by M. Moriarty). Groups and structures are named sequentially in each quadrant, and carry the quadrant name. Numbers below group names refer to the excavation operations. Stelae 1–7 are marked with small triangles. Major groups and site zones are also marked.

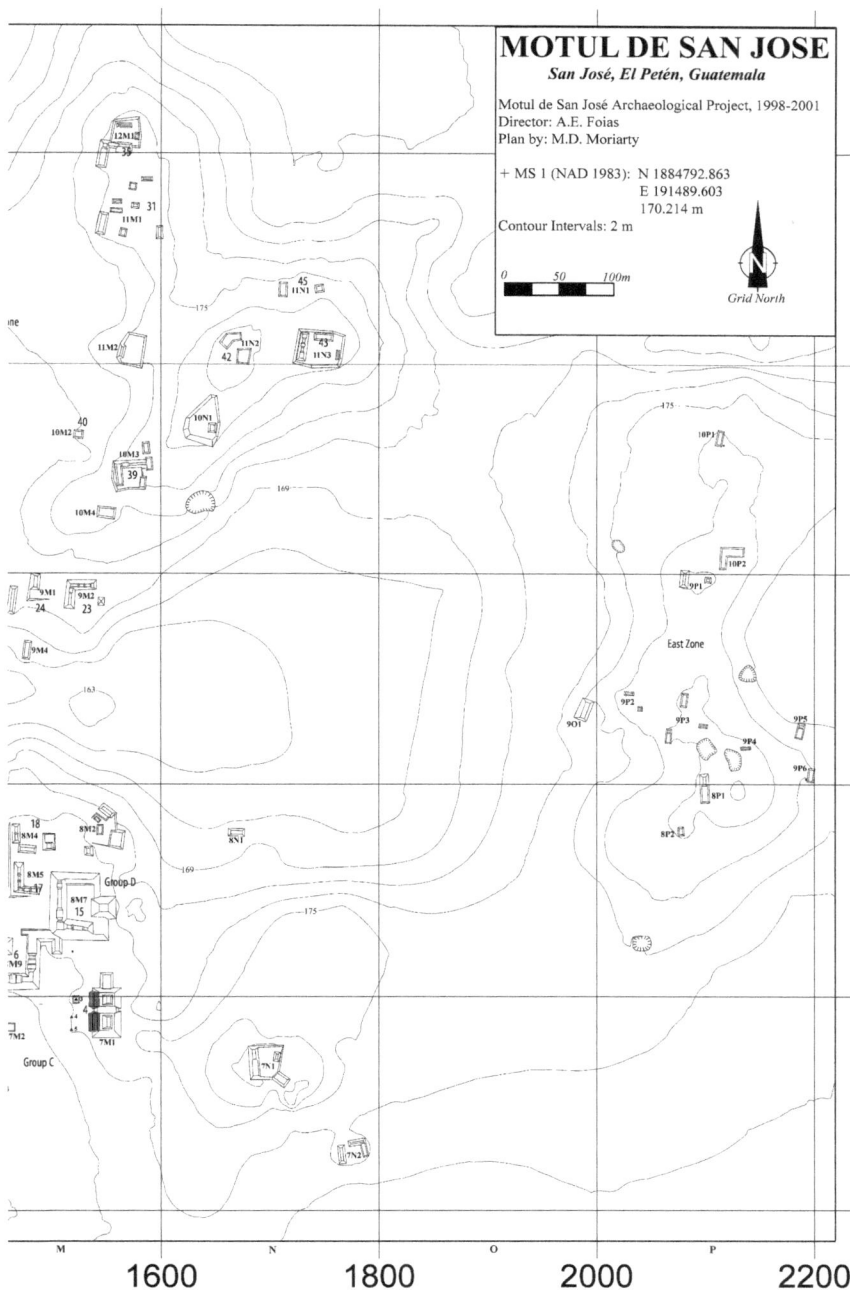

MOTUL DE SAN JOSE
San José, El Petén, Guatemala

Motul de San José Archaeological Project, 1998-2001
Director: A.E. Foias
Plan by: M.D. Moriarty

+ MS 1 (NAD 1983): N 1884792.863
E 191489.603
170.214 m

Contour Intervals: 2 m

0   50   100m

Grid North

East Zone

Group D

Group C

1600   1800   2000   2200

geochemical-geomorphological studies of floor stucco provide additional indications of the activities that took place within and around architectural features (Inomata 1995, 1997; Smyth, Dore, and Dunning 1995; Hendon 1991; Fash et al. 1992; Ford 1991, 1992; Schiffer 1976, 1987; Spensley, this volume; Bair and Terry, this volume). Hence, an extensive testing program has investigated over 60 percent of the plaza groups of the site. This has involved at least two small test pits in each patio group, and dozens of shovel tests targeting zones likely to contain refuse deposits on the perimeter of each residential group (Deter-Wolf and Charland 1998; Halperin et al. 2001; Ramirez, Sanchez, and Alvarado 2000). Moreover, five elite structures were intensively explored using clearing excavations: two of these are in Group D, one in Group C, two in Group B, and the final one in the North Zone of the site (see Foias et al., this volume; Bair and Terry, this volume).

The test-pitting program has revealed a long history of human occupation at Motul de San José and its periphery from the Middle Preclassic (600–300 BC) until the Early Postclassic (AD 950/1000–1200), although its apogee was clearly during the Late Classic (AD 600/650–830; see Foias 2003). The periphery of Motul was occupied even earlier, possibly as early as 800–700 BC (Castellanos 2007), and experienced a first boom during the Late Preclassic period (300 BC–AD 300) and a second one during the Late Classic (Moriarty, this volume).

The test-pitting program also delineated the range of economic activities that took place in the different plaza groups through a comparison of the materials deposited in residential middens. We were able to identify one or multiple refuse deposits in almost all patio groups. For example, a 1-by-1-meter unit discovered the richest midden at the site, along the northwest edge of the Acropolis in Group C (Emery and Higginbotham 1998; Guffey, Tonoike, and Castellanos 2000). The high density of polychromes, the presence of various wasters, a miniature pot with specular hematite, a figurine mold, and ash lenses have all suggested that this massive deposit was at least in part the debris from a ceramic "workshop" or "palace school" in the vicinity of the Acropolis (Halperin and Foias, this volume). Because pottery production loci have been so difficult to identify in the Maya lowlands, this midden holds special importance for understanding not only ceramic manufacture, but also the nature of elite control over such production (Halperin and Foias, this volume). The Motul de San José excavations have underscored the variety of production activities carried out in the residential groups at Motul (including the royal and subroyal elites in the major groups), from weaving (Halperin 2008), lithic production (Brian

2005), bone tool manufacture (Emery, this volume), figurine production (Halperin, this volume), to, finally, polychrome pottery crafting (Halperin and Foias, this volume). In other words, the Motul elites were producers or artists, alongside the middle and lower ranks of Classic Maya society.

Beyond the core of Motul de San José, peripheral settlement was documented through three transects oriented south, east, and northeast in 2000 and 2001 (Figure 1.3a). The transects extended between 1.5 and 3.5 kilometers, beyond the protected archaeological park, and measured between 250 and 400 meters in width (Moriarty, Rivera, and Ramirez 2000; Moriarty et al. 2001; Moriarty and Wyatt 2001; Moriarty 2004d). These formal and additional informal surveys have discovered the presence of minor centers (secondary and tertiary) situated approximately 2 to 3 kilometers away from Motul to the southwest (Buenavista-Nuevo San José), southeast (La Trinidad de Nosotros), east (Chäkokot, Figure 1.3b), and northwest (Kante't'u'ul; see Moriarty 2004d; Moriarty and Wyatt 2001; Figure 1.4). Although further excavation and reconnaissance are needed and planned for future seasons, the presence of such a ring of secondary and/or tertiary centers at a relatively standard distance (comparable to that found at La Milpa [Tourtellot et al. 2000, 2002], Belize Valley [Iannone 2004; Driver and Garber 2004], and Nohmul [Hammond 1985]) suggests a more formal politico-administrative structure for the Motul polity than previously considered.

Several of these subsidiary centers were the focus of later field seasons: Akte during 2002 (Yorgey and Moriarty, this volume) and La Trinidad de Nosotros and Buenavista-Nuevo San José in 2003 and 2005 (Moriarty, this volume; Spensley, this volume; Lawton 2007a, 2007b; Castellanos 2007). These secondary centers are also strategically positioned close to important resources. Buenavista is situated on a low rise and has visibility of the Main Plaza of Motul and a large portion of Lake Petén Itzá (Castellanos 2007). La Trinidad de Nosotros is the easiest disembarking point along the north shore of Lake Petén Itzá, and probably functioned as the port facility of Motul de San José (Moriarty, this volume). Furthermore, Buenavista, La Trinidad de Nosotros, and the newly discovered La Estrella, Nuevo San José (Chak Maman Tok') were extraction and production sites for chert tools (Lawton 2007a, 2007b). To complicate matters even more, La Trinidad has a ball court, whereas Motul does not (Moriarty, this volume). Akte had seven stelae, like Motul, in spite of its diminutive size (Yorgey and Moriarty, this volume). These multiple aspects of Motul's regional settlement weave a pattern of rich complexity in political, ritual, and economic threads. The

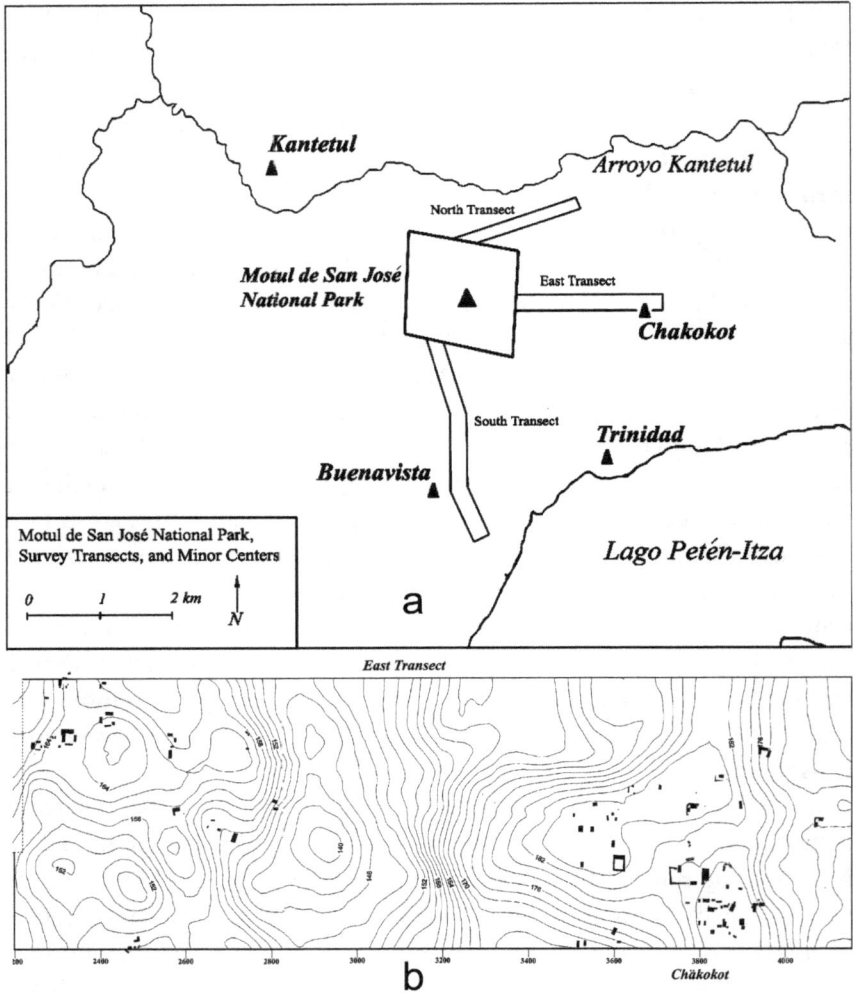

Figure 1.3. Survey transects in the periphery of Motul de San José: a. general view (drawing by M. Moriarty); b. East Transect (mapped and drawing by M. Moriarty, courtesy of M. Moriarty).

multiauthored contributions to the present volume detail many of these threads of the ancient Maya polity centered on Motul de San José.

To provide the historical context for these archaeological explorations, we include two chapters devoted to the epigraphic records of Motul de San José rulers who presented their exploits on both stone monuments and polychrome pottery. Although there are some disagreements between Tokovinine and Zender's reconstruction of Motul's dynastic history in Chapter

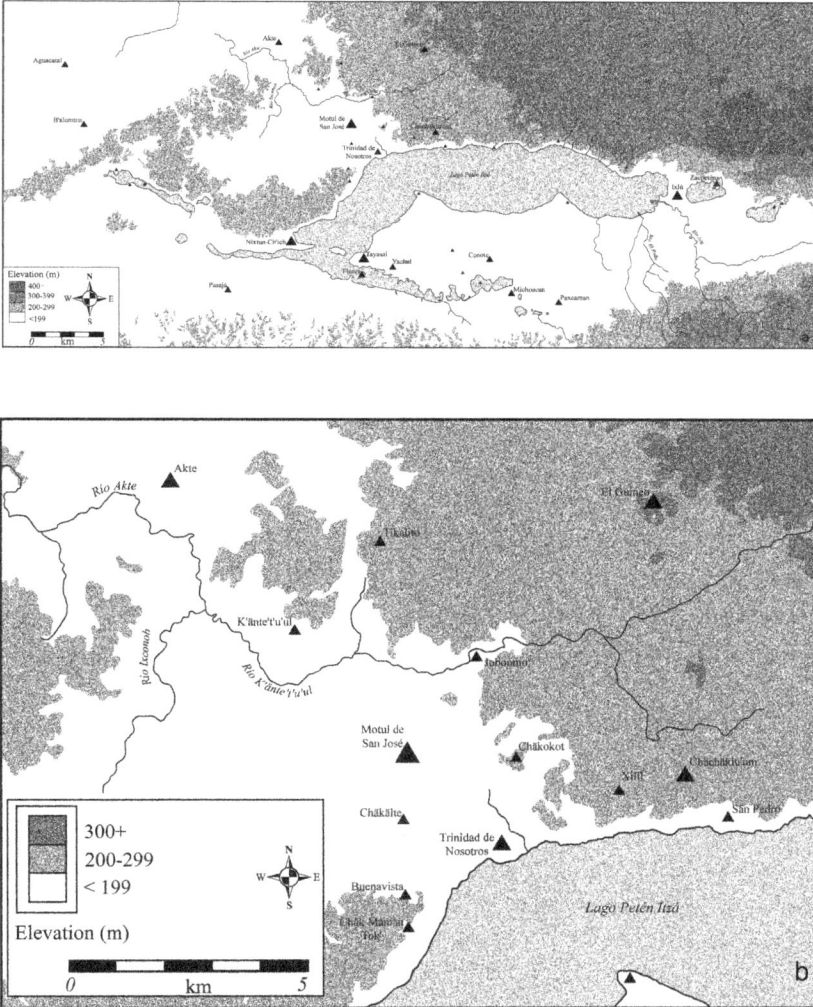

Figure 1.4. a. Central Petén Lakes zone: a. general map showing Lake Petén Itzá (drawing by E. Spensley, courtesy of E. Spensley); b. close-up of the periphery of Motul de San José (drawing by E. Spensley, courtesy of E. Spensley).

2 and that presented by Reents-Budet et al. in Chapter 3, these should not overshadow the major concordances. Both teams of epigraphers agree that Motul dynasts were most active during the eighth century, and this agrees with the archaeological evidence from the site where all surface monumental architecture was built during the Tepeu 2 ceramic phase (generally dated between AD 680/700 and 830/850; see Foias et al., this volume). Both teams

agree that the two most powerful rulers were Yajawte' K'inich (Fat Cacique) and the subsequent ruler K'inich Lamaw Ek' (Lord Termination Star), who ruled during the middle to late eighth century AD. These two rulers have left behind most hieroglyphic texts on polychrome vessels and were also probably the sponsors of most monumental architecture at Motul de San José. The authors of both chapters also agree that several rulers (such as White Bird/Sak Muwaan and Taj Yal/Tayal Chan K'inich) preceded these two great rulers, but Tokovinine and Zender place them in slightly different order from Reents-Budet et al. These discordances are due to the fact that we don't have Long Count dates for the Motul rulers, who prefer to use Calendar Round dates on their polychrome vases. Thus, epigraphers have to rely on vessels that record Motul rulers and have certain contexts, such as tombs of rulers with known death dates that were excavated archaeologically (rather than looted). Needless to say, these are rare. Both groups of epigraphers also agree that after K'inich Lamaw Ek', the zenith of Motul is past, and only a few rulers after him still sponsor the painting of Ik'-style polychrome vessels. Reents-Budet et al. place Tayel Chan K'inich as one of these late dynasts, whereas Tokovinine and Zender put him in the first half of the eighth century because of his frequent mention on vases in Petexbatún tombs from that earlier time. Tokovinine and Zender include several other dynasts in their chapter (K'inich . . . in the late seventh century AD; Yeh Te' K'inich I in the first decade of the eighth century; Sihyaj K'awiil preceding Yajawte' K'inich; Yeh Te' K'inich II in the last decades of the eighth century), but Reents-Budet et al. remain much more conservative and do not because of either the very little information about these or the eroded state of the polychrome vessels that record them.

Conclusion

As recent scholarship (J. Marcus 1998; Iannone 2002; Turchin 2003) has stressed, early civilizations across the world are characterized by continuous cycles of expansion and collapse. The role of political leaders in these multiple political trajectories is central, be it to integrate and maintain their states or to cause dissent, resistance, and finally disintegration. Political power has numerous bases in different societies, from an emphasis on social networks, military might, economic control, and ideological means to a combination of these (Blanton 1998; Claessen 1984; Clark 1997; Earle 1997; Eisenstadt 1993; Foucault 1991; Iannone 2002). However, the manner in which these different "ingredients" are combined with environmental exploitation may determine the stability and longevity of that particular state. Nevertheless, all political power has an economic aspect that has to be considered in order to address issues of sociocultural evolution, stability, and collapse. The role of economic factors in the transformations of ancient Maya states cannot be established without a better understanding of economic organization and the degree of elite control over economic matters. This volume sheds light on the organization of Classic Maya economy and its intersection with political power at the Central Petén site of Motul de San José in northern Guatemala. It thus aims to address the causality of Classic Maya political dynamics. This will allow a more nuanced perspective of the role of the Maya ruling elites in the Classic economy and of the differences in political structure across the whole Maya lowlands.

2

Lords of Windy Water

The Royal Court of Motul de San José in Classic Maya Inscriptions

ALEXANDRE TOKOVININE AND MARC ZENDER

The archaeological site of Motul de San José is famous for a corpus of splendid polychrome vases detailing the social and political lives of its rulers (Reents-Budet, Bishop, and MacLeod 1994, 172–79). Yet despite several pioneering studies on the "king list" presented by these largely unprovenanced ceramics (Agoos 2007; Reents-Budet et al. 2007; Velásquez García 2009), the monuments of Motul de San José remain unpublished and understudied, and there is no integrated overview of the history of this prominent Classic Maya polity, its place in a larger political landscape, and the activities of its royal court. This chapter will attempt at long last to fill this gap. The first section will discuss the ancient name of Motul de San José, followed by a consideration of its rulers, its interactions with other polities, and its internal affairs as represented on both monuments and painted vases.

There are major difficulties in dealing with the written sources on Motul de San José's history. Not only are there very few monuments with inscriptions (four stelae and several fragments of uncertain origin), but their current state of preservation is remarkably poor. Similarly, most of the vases attributed to Motul de San José's rulers by dedicatory inscriptions have no provenance and provide only Calendar Round dates. Sadly, none of the royal names on these vases is attested on the legible sections of the fragments of Motul de San José monuments. Nonetheless, as we shall see, it is possible to propose a tentative sequence of local rulers and examine how their reigns fit into the history of the region.

The Ancient Name of Motul de San José

The association between an Emblem Glyph with the **IK'** logogram and the site of Motul de San José was first suggested by J. Marcus (1973, 912; 1976, 17–19). This observation was subsequently confirmed by Stuart and Houston (1994, 27–28), who noted a passage in the text on Stela 2 of Motul de San José (Figure 2.1a) that referred to a dance (apparently depicted on the same monument) as having "happened at Ik'a'" (*uhtiiy ik'a'*).[1] Stuart and Houston also noticed that "men of Ik'a'" (*aj-ik'a'*) were mentioned on the monuments at nearby sites and that some carvers who signed Motul de San José monuments (MTL St 2 and 4) also identified themselves as "men of Ik'a'" or "young Ik'a' lords" (Figure 2.1b, c).[2] Given these associations, Stuart and Houston (ibid.) concluded that the ancient name of Motul de San José was Ik'a' (spelled **IK'-a**).

Lest there be any doubt, we can now say that the text of Motul de San José Stela 1 (Figure 2.2, Table 2.1) offers still further support for Stuart and Houston's identification of the Ik'a' toponym with Motul de San José. The narrative details the accession of a "holy **IK'** lord" (*k'uhul ik'[a'] ajaw*) and then describes a later period ending event "before the waters of Ik'a'" (*tahn ha' ik'a'*) in glyph blocks C8–D8. This extended version of the place-name is of a type of location statement well known from other contexts, and there can be no doubt that Ik'a' includes the spot on which Stela 1 stood because its dedication was part of the period-ending ritual (Table 2.1).

Although the place-name for Motul de San José is always spelled as **IK'-a**, the toponym in the title of its rulers is consistently spelled as **IK'**. Stuart and Houston (1994) have suggested that **IK'** and **IK'-a** were two distinct place-names, perhaps designating entities of different spatial scale (e.g., the city and the kingdom). However, **IK'** alone is never used as a place-name, and some examples of the Emblem Glyph do contain the full spelling **IK'-a**. One of them is the inscription on Altar 3 at Altar de los Reyes (Figure 2.1d; see site location in Figure 1.1), which clearly spells **K'UH IK'-a AJAW-wa** for *k'uh[ul] ik'a' ajaw* (Grube 2008, 180–82, fig. 8.6). Another example of a complete rendering comes from an unprovenanced codex-style vase, now in the Princeton University Art Museum (MVD:K1546; Figure 2.1e), where the spelling is also **IK'-a AJAW-wa**.

There are several comparable cases of place-names ending in -*a'* that are dropped when the toponym is incorporated into a title before the word "lord" (*ajaw*), such as **3-WITS-AJAW** for *uhx witsa' ajaw*, **wa-ka-AJAW**

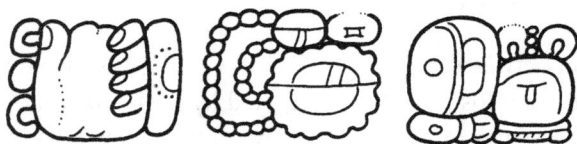

a

b

c

d

e

Figure 2.1. Ik'a' as the ancient name of Motul de San José: a. reference to Ik'a' on MTL St 2 (all drawings by A. Tokovinine unless stated otherwise); b. carver's signature on MTL St 2; c. carver's signature on MTL St 4; d. *ik'a' ajaw* as **IK'-a AJAW-wa** on ALR Alt 3; e. *ik'a' ajaw* as **IK'-a AJAW**-wa on MVD:K1546.

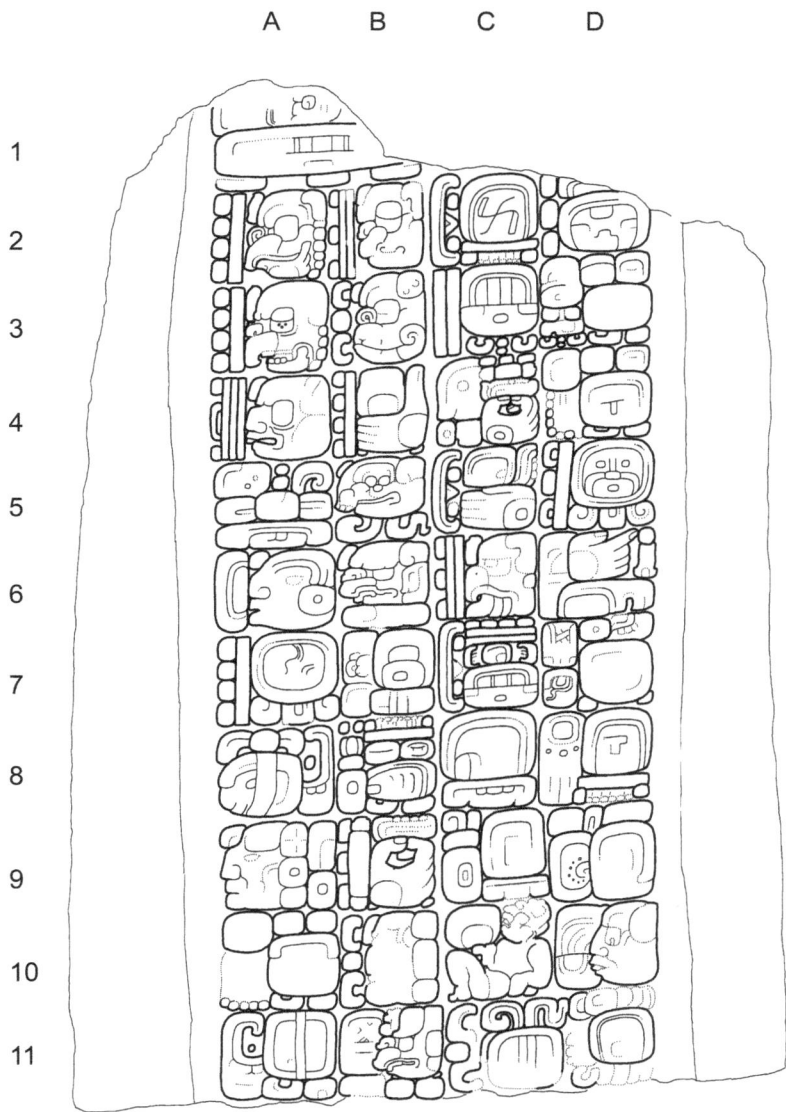

Figure 2.2. Inscription on MTL St 1.

Table 2.1. Transcriptions of hieroglyphic inscriptions on Motul de San José Stela 1 and Itzan Stela 17

Transcription	Transliteration	Translation
MOTUL DE SAN JOSÉ STELA 1 (FIGURE 2.2)		
(A1-B1) ISIG (A2) 9-PIK (B2) 13-WINIK-HAAB (A3) 9-HAAB (B3) 1-WINIK (A4) 17-K'IN (B4) 9-CH'AM-? (A5) TI'-HUUN-na (B5) TIL-K'AHK' (A6) T24-? (B6) ?KAN-? (A7) 9-KABAN (B7) CHUM IK'-[AT]-ta (A8) jo-JOY-ja (B8) ti a-AJAW-wa-²le (A9) ye-TE' (B9) K'INICH-ni-chi (A10) K'UH ?IK' AJAW-wa (B10) ya-AJAW (A11) ja-sa-wa (B11) CHAN K'AWIIL-la (C1) [missing] (D1) [missing] (C2) u-TS'AK-a (D2) 3-?-WINIK (C3) 10-HAAB-ya (D3) CHUM-?-ya AJAW-wa (C4) ye-TE' K'INICH-ni-chi (D4) K'UH IK' AJAW-wa (C5) u-K'AL-TUUN-ni (D5) 6-AJAW (C6) 13-MUWAAN-ni (D6) i-TSUTS-yi (C7) u-14-WINIK-HAAB (D7) CHAN KAB ?-NAL (C8) TAHN-na (D8) HA'-IK'-a (C9) SAK-?-? (D9) KAL-ma-?TE' (C10) UNEN-K'AWIIL (D10) i-JGU (C11) 1-K'AHK' (D11) ?-?	. . . baluun pik uhxlajuun winikhaab baluun haab juun winik huk-lajuun k'in . . . ti' huun til-k'ahk' . . . [ta] bal-uun kaban chum ik'at joyaj ti ajawlel ye[h] te' k'inich k'uh[ul] ik'[a'] ajaw y-ajaw jasaw chan k'awiil . . . uts'aka[j] hux[-hew] [waklajuun] winik[jiiy] lajuun haabiiy chum[lajii] y [ti] ajaw[lel] ye[h] te' k'inich k'uh[ul] ik'[a'] ajaw u-k'al-tuun [ta] wak ajaw uhxlajuun[te'] muwaan i-tsutsuyi u-chanlajuun winikhaab chan kab . . . nal tahn ha' Ik'a' sak . . . kaloomte' unen k'awiil . . . juun k'ahk' . . .	". . . nine baktuns, thirteen katuns, nine years, one month, seventeen days; G1 at the edge of the headband; on 9 Kaban, seating of Wo, Yeh Te' K'inich, holy Ik'a' lord, vassal of Jasaw Chan K'awiil makes a debut in lordship . . . three days, sixteen months, ten years since Yeh Te' K'inich, holy Ik'a' lord sat in lordship, [it is] his stone-binding of 6 Ajaw, 13 of Muwan. His fourteenth katun ends, sky (?), earth (?) . . . before the waters of Ik'a,' Sak . . . kaloomte,' Unen K'awiil, JGU, Juun K'ahk' . . ."
FIRST CAMPAIGN AGAINST MOTUL DE SAN JOSÉ ON STELA 17 AT ITZAN (FIGURE 2.10A)		
(H3) u-jo-ch'o-wa (G4) K'AHK' IK'-a (H4) u-CHAN-na IK' chi-?ji (G5) ?XOOK-ki (H5) LAKAM-TUUN-ni AJAW (G6) yi-ta-ji (H6) u-CHAN-na ?-BAHLAM-ma	u-joch'ow k'ahk' ik'a' u-chan ik' chij xook lakam tuun ajaw yitaaj u-chan ?-bahlam	the guardian of Ik' Chij Xook, Lord of Laka-mtuun, drilled fire [in] Ik'a'; the guardian of ?-Bahlam accompanied him
SECOND CAMPAIGN AGAINST MOTUL DE SAN JOSÉ ON STELA 17 AT ITZAN (FIGURE 2.10B)		
ju-bu-yi (G11) a-IK'-a (H11) u-?-BAAK-ki (G12) u-CHAN-na ?-BAHLAM-ma (H12) AJ-20-BAAK T556.686-TE' AJAW	jubuyi a[j]-ik'a' u-... baak u-chan ?-bahlam aj-winik baak . . . te' ajaw	the man of Ik'a' fell. He is . . . captive of the guardian of ?-Bahlam, he of twenty captives, lord of . . . Te'

for *waka' ajaw*, and, perhaps, **K'IN-ni-AJAW** for *k'ina' ajaw* (see Zender 2002). The exception are Emblem Glyphs where *-a'* is spelled with "main signs," as in **pi-pi-a AJAW** for *pipa' ajaw* and **YAX-a AJAW** for *yaxa' ajaw* (Tokovinine 2008, 78–79). The rationale for such underspellings seems to be partly graphic (underspellings being restricted to cases where *-a'* is not spelled with a "main sign") and partly phonetic (syncopation or segment reduction of the sequence *-a' ajaw*). For these reasons, it is quite plausible that the toponym in the Emblem Glyph was also Ik'a'; there is no evidence of the contrary.

One interesting question is whether Ik'a' may also have been the ancient name of Lake Petén Itzá, or even of the surrounding area. On the basis of present evidence, there is still no indication that the name stood for anything but the area associated with the site of Motul de San José, the dwelling place of the king, his nobles, and his artists. But it is by no means impossible that Ik'a' could have referred to both the lake and the ancient city. The toponym literally means "Windy Water" and seems to be an appropriate name for Lake Petén. Further, it is worth considering that Motul de San José may have taken its ancient name from the nearby lake. Yaxa' provides a perfect example of a toponym that designated the lake and its nearby settlement in the past and continues to do so in the present (Stuart 1985). In fact, many Classic Maya place-names associated with ancient sites seem to be based on landscape features in their vicinity (Tokovinine 2008, 83–86).

Lords of Ik'a'

Early Classic Silence

Discussions of Ik'a' rulers often begin with the inscription on Bejucal Stela 2 (Schele and Grube 1994, 88; Velasquez 2009, 48–50) celebrating the period ending of 8.17.17.0.0 in AD 393. This is followed by a reference to the accession (whether before or after the period ending is still unclear) of an individual whose name is usually read as Mam Yax Ik' Ajaw Chak ? Ahk, identified as the "vassal" of *kaloomte'* Sihyaj K'ahk', an apical figure in charge of most of the Petén at that time (Estrada Belli et al. 2009, 245, fig. 9d). Yet any assumption that Yax Ik' Ajaw is just an early variant of the late Classic Ik'a' Emblem Glyph runs afoul of the observed conventions of Maya nominal syntax: the supposed emblem is in the wrong part of the protagonist's name phrase. An emblem should rather appear at the end of a phrase than at the beginning. As Houston (2008) points out, the name itself is suspiciously identical to the names of one or more Early Classic Pa' Chan lords of El Zotz. Moreover, it is not even clear that the superfix in the phrase Yax Ik' Ajaw should be identified as **AJAW**. It more strongly resembles an undeciphered sign that appears as a superfix of the **IK'** logogram in a title on several Early Classic vases (Boot 2005, 12, fig. 8). This title is also attested in the names of some Late Classic Ik'a' lords (see below), but it is not restricted to Ik'a' lords, and it is not their Emblem Glyph. Therefore, it is very unlikely that the inscription on Bejucal Stela 2 mentions an Early Classic member of the Ik'a' royal dynasty.

The Early Classic roots of Ik'a' lords perhaps lie much closer to their Late Classic seat at Motul de San José. The eroded inscription on Tayasal Stela 3 (Chase 1983, 376, 1207), an Early Classic monument judging by its style, contains the **IK'** logogram in the name of the protagonist. The sign immediately preceding it looks very similar to **K'INICH**, a frequent part of Ik'a' royal names as we shall see below. The sign after **IK'** is largely gone, although the surviving portion does not exclude the possibility that it could have been **AJAW**—the second half of the Emblem Glyph title. The Ik'a' place-name is also attested on an early Late Classic vessel in the Santa Barbara museum in Flores (Gronemeyer 2010). The context of this example seems to be an extended toponymic phrase or a list of four distinct place-names. The vessel was allegedly found in the Lake Petén area. Therefore, we would suggest, albeit very tentatively, that the royal family of Motul de San José might have already resided in the Lake Petén region during the Early Classic period.

-K'inich

The first clear sign of Motul de San José rulers comes in the form of Stela 4 at the site. This monument is badly damaged, yet it is possible to discern at least two dates: a period ending of 9.12.10.0.0 in AD 682 mentioned in a determinative future form[3] and the Tzolkin position 4 Ajaw, perhaps the dedication date of the stela itself (Figure 2.3a, e; Table 2.2). If we assume that the monument was carved shortly before AD 682 and that its dedication also corresponded to a Long Count station of some kind, the likeliest date would be 9.12.8.0.0 or AD 680.

There is enough left of the stela to say that it once represented a standing lord with a k'awiil scepter in his hand accompanied by a dwarf (Houston 1992, fig. 3), one of the most common themes of Late Classic Maya monuments. The eroded text on the back of the stela (Figure 2.3d, pE5) mentions a "k'awiil-taking" (*ch'amaw k'awiil*), a ceremony often linked to the

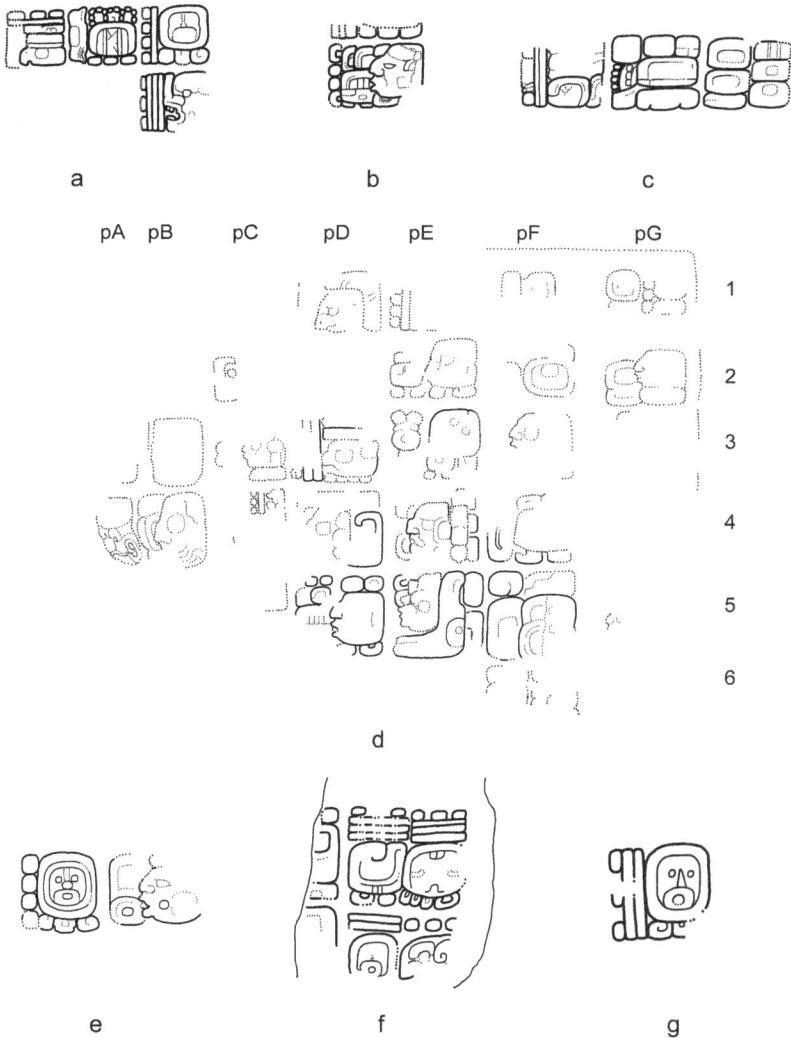

Figure 2.3. Inscriptions on monument fragments at Motul de San José: a–c. MTL St 4 (front); d–e. MTL St 4 (back); f. an MTL stela fragment with the Calendar Round 10 Ajaw 3 Xul; g. Tzolkin day of 13 Ajaw on the MTL stela fragment.

assumption of authority. All sections of the text with the name of the protagonist, however, are heavily damaged. The most preserved example (Figure 2.3d, pE4) suggests that the final portion of his name was "K'inich." He also carries the title "two katun lord" or *cha' winikhaab ajaw* (Figure 2.3b,

Table 2.2. Known events in the history of Ik'a' lords

Long count	Calendar round	Date	Event	Source
			Accession of -K'inich	
[9.12.08.0.0]	4 Ahau [8 Tzec]	680		MTLᵃ ST 4
[9.12.10.0.0]	9 Ahau 18 Zodz	682	Future period ending (*utoom*)	MTL ST 4
			Accession of White Bird	
9.13.9.1.17	4 Kaban 0 Uo	701	Accession of Yeh Te' K'inich I	MTL ST 1
9.14.0.0.0	6 Ahau 13 Muan	711	Period ending of Yeh Te' K'inich I	MTL ST 1
			Accession of Tayel Chan K'inich	
[9.15.3.6.6]	1 Cimi 4 Pax	734	Tayel Chan K'inich receives tribute from three *lakam* officials	K4996
			Accession of Sihyaj K'awiil	
			Sihyaj K'awiil drinks	K1453
			Accession of Yajawte' K'inich	
[9.15.6.8.9]	6 Muluc 12 Kayab	738	Yajawte' K'inich dances	K1452
9.15.10.0.0	3 Ahau 3 Mol	741	A captive "Ik'a' lord" mentioned at Machaquila	MQL ST 11
[9.15.12.7.15]	7 Men 13 Muan	743	Yajawte' K'inich dances	K1439
9.15.13.15.19	11 Cauac 2 Tzec	745	Ik'a' lord ?Chuliw Hix is captured by K'awiil Chan K'inich of Dos Pilas	DPL HS 3
9.15.16.0.0	5 Ahau 13 Xul	747	Local lord dedicates a stela	Acte St 1
9.15.18.0.0	10 ?Ahau 3 Xul	749	MTL Stela fragment	MTL frag
9.16.0.0.0	2 Ahau 13 Tzec	751	Sun God's Seed, the holy Yokeel lord, erects a stela at Huacutal	HUA St 1
9.16.1.2.0	12 Ahau 8 Yaxkin	752	Bird Jaguar dances with his wife Lady Wak Jalam Chan Ajaw of MTL	YAX Ln 5
[9.16.3.0.0]	3 Ahau 18 Zodz	754	Dedication of a vase for Yajawte' K'inich that ends up at ALS	K3120
[9.16.3.13.14]	4 Ix 12 Cumku	755	Dedication of a vase for Yajawte' K'inich	K791
9.16.3.16.19	4 Cauac 12 Zip	755	Bird Jaguar's wife Lady Wak Tuun of MTL conjures a serpent	YAX Ln 15
9.16.4.1.1	7 Imix 14 Tzec	755	Bird Jaguar's wife Lady Wak Jalam Chan Ajaw attends him in war (dance?)	YAX Ln 41

Long Count	Calendar Round	Year	Event	Source
[9.16.5.11.17]	11 Caban 5 Pax	756	A vase with a scene of the Namaan (La Florida) royal court is painted for K'inich Lamaw Ek' (as *buah tsàm*)	K5418
[9.16.6.5.12] [9.16.14.7.12]	12 [Eb] 15 Chèn; 7 [Eb] 15 Chèn	757; 765	K'inich Lamaw Ek' as *buah tsàm* attends to Yajawte' K'inich	K1463
[9.16.8.9.14]	8 Ix 7 Mac	759	Yajawte' K'inich receives gifts	K8889
[9.16.9.12.5]	3 ?Chicchan 13 Muan	760	Yajawte' K'inich dances	K533
9.17.15.6.17	3 Ix 7 Mol	763	Bird Jaguar's wife Lady Wak Tuun of MTL conjures a *kàwiil*	YAX Ln 38
Accession of K'inich Lamaw Ek'				
9.16.16.11.5	7 Chicchan 18 Ceh	767	Lakamtuun lord of El Palma attacks Motul de San José	ITN St 17
9.16.17.4.18	6 Edznab 6 Xul	768	Itzan ruler defeats somebody from Motul de San José	ITN St 17
[9.16.17.6.2]	4 [Ik] 10 Yaxkin	768	Yajawte' K'inich and K'inich Lamaw Ek' attend a ceremony	K3054
		769	Itsamnaaj Bahlam accedes shortly before this year in Yaxchilan	
9.17.0.0.0	13 Ahau 18 Cumku	771	Itsa' lord Juun Tsak Took' dedicates a stela at Itzimte	ITS St 7
9.17.0.0.0	13 Ahau 18 Cumku	771	Another Juun Tsak Took' called "Lakamtuun lord" dedicates a stela at El Palma	El Palma St 5
[9.17.0.0.0]	13 Ahau [18 Cumku]		MTL Stela fragment	MTL frag
[9.17.8.0.7]	1 Manik 5 Kayab	778	Presentation of tribute for K'inich Lamaw Ek'	K1728
[9.17.8.9.15]	7 Men 8 Mol	779	A vase is dedicated for K'inich Lamaw Ek'	K1728
Accession of Yeh Te' K'inich II				
[9.17.10.8.17]	7 Caban 0 Yaxkin	781	Yeh Te' K'inich II in a *joyaj* ceremony	LC.cb2.441
[9.17.12.17.14]; [9.18.6.2.19]	7 [Ix] 7 Muan; 7 [Cauac] 7 Muan	783; 796	Yeh Te' K'inich II dances with a lesser Ik'a' lord	K1399
[9.17.18.1.13]; [9.18.10.4.13]	[13] Ben 1 Pax; [12] Ben 1 Pax	788; 800	A captured "man of Ik'a'" is mentioned at Yaxchilan	YAX St 21
Accession of Chan Ek'				
10.1.0.0.0	5 Ahau 3 Kayab	849	Ik'a' lord Chan Ek' witnesses a period ending ceremony in Seibal	SBL St 10
10.2.0.0.0	3 Ahau 3 Ceh	869	Ik'a' lord dedicates a stela in Tayasal or Flores	FLS St 1

a MTL is Motul de San José

2.3d, pD5). This title indicates that the Motul de San José lord in question was between twenty and forty years of age.

White Bird

Two unprovenanced painted vases—one in the Dallas Museum of Art, the other at Dumbarton Oaks—provide us with references to a ruler who we believe may have succeeded ". . . K'inich" and reigned between AD 682 and 701. The scene on the Dallas vase (MVD:K2803) shows a ball game and tags one of the players as "young man, White Bird, holy Ik'a' lord" (*chak ch'ok keleem sak ? k'uh[ul] ik'[a'] ajaw*) (Figure 2.4a).[4] The same White Bird, this time provided with the additional titles "holy Ik'a' lord, first *kaloomte', baahkab" (k'uh[ul] ik'[a'] ajaw yax kaloomte' baah kab*), is mentioned as a father of the owner of the Dumbarton Oaks vase (MVD:K2784; Figure 2.4b), K'ebij ti Chan. The two vases differ from the later corpus of Ik'-style pottery and look like they could well have been painted in the late seventh century. White Bird's titles perhaps correspond to earlier and later stages in his life and political career, although we would caution that the vases cannot be securely dated.[5]

a

b

Figure 2.4. References to White Bird: a. MVD:K2803; b. Dumbarton Oaks vase PC.B.564.

Yeh Te' K'inich I

The previously discussed inscription on Stela 1 at Motul de San José (Figure 2.2, Table 2.1) reports the accession of a new ruler in AD 701 and the period-ending rituals overseen by him in 9.14.0.0.0 (AD 711; see Schele and Grube 1994, 145). As we have mentioned, the text on this monument is highly significant as the only surviving reference to the accession of a holy Ik'a' lord tied to a later ceremony at Ik'a'. The ruler's name is provided twice in the spelling **ye-TE'-K'INICH-ni-chi** (in glyph blocks A9–B10 and C4) probably to be transliterated as *ye[h] te' k'inich*. Unfortunately, there are presently no known references to Yeh Te' K'inich I in any other texts or scenes. Nevertheless, as we shall see below, he does have a late eighth-century namesake. It is also noteworthy that Yeh Te' K'inich I accedes to the throne as the vassal of Tikal's famous ruler Jasaw Chan K'awiil I (as will be discussed further below).

Tayal Chan K'inich/Tayel Chan K'inich

The next Motul de San José ruler (if not, in fact, more than one) is known from a number of polychrome vases, some of which were excavated in tombs at Dos Pilas, Tamarindito, and maybe even El Peru (Eppich 2007, 8, figs. 7, 8, 10).[6] Others, unfortunately, have no firm provenience. There are no monuments at Motul de San José that could be attributed to his reign.

There is uncertainty in deciding whether we are dealing with one or two similarly named lords. The name of the owner of the plate found in the tomb of Dos Pilas Ruler 2 (Houston 1993, 110; Martin and Grube 2008, 59) is spelled **ta-?YAL-CHAN-na K'INICH** and includes the titles of "holy Ik'a' lord" and "sixteen *yook k'in*" (Figure 2.5a). All other examples of the name are instead spelled **ta-ye-(le) CHAN-na K'INICH-(ni)** (Figure 2.5b-d). One of them also features the title "nine *yook k'in*" (Miller and Martin 2004, plate 7).[7] At first glance, the number might seem to provide a designation in sequence of separate kings with similar names. However, most examples lack the *-tal* suffix of ordinal numbers that we would expect to find in glyphs recording true sequences. Further, nine *yook k'in* and sixteen *yook k'in* are deities associated with period endings. Consequently, the titles may merely indicate the king's special affinity to these gods and not his place in the dynastic sequence. Moreover, in the caption on an Ik'-style vase from Tamarindito (Valdés 1997, fig. 11), Tayel Chan K'inich is designated "seventh *yook k'in*" with the *-tal* suffix (Figure 2.5b). This example perhaps does

a

b

c

d

Figure 2.5. References to Tayel Chan K'inich: a. vase from Ruler 2's burial, Dos Pilas; b. Tamarindito vase; c. K2573; d. vase from Burial 20, Dos Pilas.

represent the king's place in the dynastic sequence, albeit of a presently unclear type (see the discussion of Sihyaj K'awiil below).

One clear Calendar Round associated with Tayel Chan K'inich is found on an unprovenanced vase (MVD:4996) and can be reconstructed as AD 734 or 786 (Figure 2.11a; Table 2.1).[8] However, the vessels from tombs at

Dos Pilas provide excellent *terminus ante quem* controls. The Ik'a' ruler responsible for the plate in Ruler 2's tomb (Figure 2.5a) should have acceded before Ruler 2's death in AD 726. As Stephen Houston (personal communication, 2009) pointed out to us, an Ik'a' vase with Tayel Chan K'inich's name (Figure 2.5d) was found in the tomb of the Lady of Cancuen (Burial 20). It means that this vase had to be at Dos Pilas before AD 742, the date of the Lady's death as recorded on Hieroglyphic Bench 1 (Houston 1993, 108, 115, figs. 4–9). Therefore, Tayal Chan K'inich was in power by AD 726 and Tayel Chan K'inich was king in AD 734. As we believe that this is most likely the same person, the plate provides the earliest *terminus ante quem* date for his reign. This seems corroborated by the text on one of the unprovenanced vases published by Miller and Martin (2004, plate 7) that suggests that Tayel Chan K'inich reached a rather advanced age of four katuns (sixty to eighty years).[9]

The presence of Tayel Chan K'inich's vases in tombs dated to the second half of the eighth century at Tamarindito (Valdés 1997, fig. 11) and El Peru (Eppich 2007, 8, figs. 7, 8, 10) led some scholars to place his reign in the late eighth century (Reents-Budet at al., this volume) or to suggest that he had a late eighth-century namesake (Velásquez García 2010, 66–68). The first hypothesis is refuted by the presence of Tayel Chan K'inich's vases in the tombs of Dos Pilas individuals who were interred no later than AD 726 and 742. The second hypothesis seems unlikely because, as we shall see below, there are better candidates for Motul de San José rulers in the last quarter of the eighth century. The style of the images and inscriptions on the Tamarindito and El Peru vessels is similar to early eighth-century and not late eighth-century Ik'a' pottery. As for their apparently late placement in tombs, it only attests to the long social life of certain objects as prized gifts and heirlooms at the courts of Classic Maya rulers.

The caption to the figure of Tayel Chan K'inich on the vase from Burial 20 at Dos Pilas (Figure 2.5d) may contain clues about his origins. As Stephen Houston (personal communication, 2009) suggests, the initial part of the text is eroded but the remaining section can be read as *ti chan tayel chan k'inich k'uh[ul] ik'a' ajaw*. The phrase *ti chan* may be a reference to the nature of the event as a public performance (Tokovinine 2003). However, if it is part of the king's name, then it is suspiciously similar to the name of White Bird's son K'ebij ti Chan, discussed previously (see Figure 2.4b). K'ebij ti Chan could well have been the pre-accession name of Tayel Chan K'inich. If Tayel Chan K'inich was White Bird's son, it may explain his advanced age at the time of his accession.

Sihyaj K'awiil

A scene on the unprovenanced vase (MVD:K1453; Miller and Martin 2004, 43) shows a corpulent ruler tagged "Sihyaj K'awiil, *ch'ajoom* of three years, eighth *yook k'in*, holy Ik'a' lord" (Figure 2.6a). There is no date and no other mention of this king, although his "eighth *yook k'in*" title may suggest that he acceded after Tayel Chan K'inich. Therefore, his reign could be between AD 734 and 738, probably hardly any longer than his title of "*ch'ajoom* of three years" would suggest.

Yajawte' K'inich

Tayel Chan K'inich and Sihyaj K'awiil were likely succeeded by Yajawte' K'inich (previously known as the "Fat Cacique"). His name is consistently

a

b

c

d

Figure 2.6. Sihyaj K'awiil and Yajawte' K'inich: a. reference to Sihyaj K'awiil on MVD:K2803; b–d. name and titles of Yajawte' K'inich on MVD:K1452, MVD:K533, and MVD:K1896.

spelled as **ya-AJAW-TE' K'INICH**, and he carries a number of additional titles that will be discussed in more detail in a later section of this chapter (Figure 2.6b–d). For the time being, it will be sufficient to note that his name and titles on K1452 are *yajawte' k'inich k'uhul ik'a' ajaw baah kab kaloomte' uhxlajuun k'uh chak el*, or "Yajawte' K'inich, holy Ik'a' lord, *baahkab, kaloomte'*, Thirteen Gods, Great/Red Burning" (Figure 2.6b). The name phrase on K533 is another common combination: *yajawte' k'inich uchan ik' bul k'uhul ik'a' ajaw chan te' chan uhxlajuun k'uh baah kab*, or "Yajawte' K'inich, the guardian of Ik' Bul, holy Ik'a' lord, Chan Te' Chan, Thirteen Gods, *baahkab*" (Figure 2.6c). Finally, the inscription on K1004 offers a version that begins with "Kaats Kab Naah lord." The initial position of this title makes it somewhat unlikely that it refers to a real location ruled by Yajawte' K'inich: it could perhaps be the name of a deity that the king impersonated.

Sadly, we have no date for the accession of Yajawte' K'inich and there is no mention of him on surviving Motul de San José monuments. However, as many as eight Calendar Round dates on vases with his name and titles cluster around the mid-eighth century and the only way to accommodate them all in relation to earlier and later kings is to assume that his reign began as early as AD 738 and ended as late as AD 768. One of the stela fragments at Motul de San José (Figure 2.3f) seems to have the Calendar Round of 10 Ajaw 3 Xul that may correspond to the Long Count of 9.15.18.0.0 (AD 749) or roughly the middle of Yajawte' K'inich's tenure. Although no monument can be securely attributed to Yajawte' K'inich, his high visibility in pottery texts and scenes suggests that he was one of the most successful sovereigns of Motul de San José.

K'inich Lamaw Ek'

K'inich Lamaw Ek' (spelled **K'INICH-LAM-EK'**)[10] formally known as "Lord Completion Star," appears to have risen through the ranks of Ik'a' princes during the reign of his predecessor. An inscription on one unprovenanced vase (MVD:K5418) with a scene dated to AD 756 mentions K'inich Lamaw Ek' as the vessel's owner, but gives only his *baah ts'am* ("head throne") title (Figure 2.7a). Another scene on a vase of unknown provenance (MVD:K1463) has a Calendar Round that could be interpreted as AD 757 or 765 and again shows K'inich Lamaw Ek' as *baah ts'am* before the eyes of "holy Ik'a' lord" Yajawte' K'inich during a *joyaj* ceremony. A third inscription on yet another unprovenanced vessel (MBD:K3054), this time with a badly preserved Calendar Round that can be tentatively reconstructed as AD 768, identifies both, K'inich Lamaw Ek' and Yajawte' K'inich, as "holy Ik'a' lords." This is the last time we hear of the latter. It seems as if there may have been a gradual transition of power or perhaps even a period of co-rulership with Yajawte' K'inich as a high king because K'inich Lamaw Ek' takes the *kaloomte'* title only after Yajawte's death. The last Calendar Round associated with K'inich Lamaw Ek' is in the dedicatory text on an unprovenanced vase in the Boston Museum of Fine Arts (MVD:K1728). The associated date suggests that he was in power as late as AD 779 (Figure 2.7b).

The same inscription states that the father of K'inich Lamaw Ek' was a certain "three katun lord" named Took' Yaas K'inich. It is this latter individual who carries the title mentioned earlier, consisting of **K'UH** and **IK'** with a rare superfix that looks like some kind of vegetation. The same title appears after the Emblem Glyph in the name phrase of Yajawte' K'inich on K1463. The titles of a ruler on two unprovenanced monuments published by Mayer (1989, plate 101; 1991, plate 118) suggest that the combination of **IK'** and that unusual superfix can be substituted by a head of the young Wind God. As such, the title of Took' Yaas K'inich title is identical to the title carried by Tayal Chan K'inich in the inscription on the plate from Dos Pilas (see Figure 2.5a). This suggests that Took' Yaas K'inich might have been of royal blood, though there is presently no evidence that he was ever a king.

A fragment of a Calendar Round from Motul de San José may correspond to the period ending of 9.17.0.0.0 in AD 771 (Figure 2.3g). For reasons to be discussed below, Stela 2 is likely to have been commissioned by K'inich Lamaw Ek'.

Yeh Te' K'inich II

The next Motul de San José ruler appears to be the namesake of the early eighth-century king discussed previously. The earliest reference to Yeh Te' K'inich II (spelled **ye-TE'-K'INICH**) as a ruler in his own right boasting a *kaloomte'* title comes from a *joyaj* ceremony scene on an unprovenanced vase (LC.cb2.441), photographs of which are available in the archive at Dumbarton Oaks (Figure 2.7c–e). The Calendar Round date associated with the scene can be reconstructed as AD 781. We know very little of his reign except for dancing scenes on two unprovenanced vases (MVD:K534, K1399) with illegible dates that show him with individuals who are also called "Ik'a' lords." One of the dates could be very tentatively reconstructed as AD 783 or 796, but the poor preservation makes such reconstruction highly tenuous.

a

b

c

d e

Figure 2.7. K'inich Lamaw Ek' and Yeh Te' K'inich II: a–b. the name and titles of K'inich Lamaw Ek' on MVD:K5418 and MVD:K1728; c–e. Yeh Te' K'inich II and his courtiers in the inscription on the vase LC.cb2.441.

Chan Ek'

The next known mention of holy Ik'a' lords comes from the inscription on Seibal Stela 10 that celebrates the period ending of 10.1.0.0.0 in AD 849 (Graham 1996 36). Chan Ek', or perhaps Kan Ek' (the hieroglyphic spelling is the ambiguous **4-e-k'e**), is granted a full Emblem Glyph title, and appears to have taken part in a joint ceremony at Seibal involving the holy lords of Mutal and Kanuul, who all allegedly witnessed the rituals undertaken by the ajaw of Seibal. There is no way to verify if Chan Ek' resided at Motul de San José. There are no ninth-century monuments at the site. The inscription on a possibly Tayasal stela now in Flores (Figure 2.8a) states that it was dedicated by a "holy Ik'a' lord" who also carries the title of *uhxlajuun k'uh* frequently claimed by Yajawte' K'inich. The likely dedication date of 10.2.0.0.0 (AD 869) suggests that it could have been commissioned by Chan Ek' or his successor, given that what remains of his name looks rather different.

Other Ik'a' lords

As we have mentioned above, Yeh Te' K'inich II appears in the company of two Ik'a' lords. The main protagonist of the scene on K534 is a certain ?Yopaat Bahlam, carrying the emblem "holy Ik'a' lord" (Figure 2.8b). The

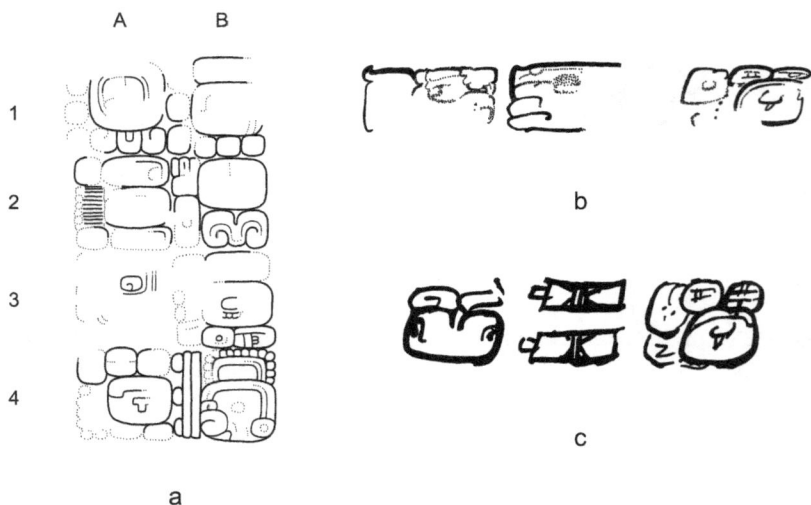

Figure 2.8. Last Ik'a' lords: a. inscription on Tayasal/Flores Stela 1; b. reference to ?Yopaat Bahlam (MVD:K534); c. reference to ?Tsij . . . (MVD:K1399).

second "holy Ik'a' lord" on K1399 is an individual named in part Tsij- (Figure 2.8c). Interestingly enough, the third dancer in both scenes is a "worshipper" (*aj-k'uhuun*) named ?Juun Tuun Chak. Consequently, the scenes should be roughly contemporaneous. However, we do not know if these Ik'a' lords were kings-to-be, rulers of secondary sites, or independent members of a dynasty that split apart.

There were at least two Ik'a' lords captured in war. The inscription on Dos Pilas Stairway 3 reports the capture of the Ik'a' lord ?Chuliw Hix in AD 745. The ruler of Machaquila claims the title of "the guardian of the Ik'a' lord" in the text on Machaquila Stela 11 dedicated in AD 741, suggesting another capture. However, the absence of a *k'uhul* prefix in these foreign citations suggests that ?Chuliw Hix likely never acceded to kingship and that he and the captive mentioned at Machaquila were probably junior members of the royal family of Ik'a' who never had the opportunity to become "holy lords."

Motul de San José in the Late Classic Political History

The dynasty of Motul de San José made a rather late entrance into the political landscape of the southern lowlands. If Tayel Chan K'inich was seventh in the line of Ik'a' rulers, it means that there are no more than three kings before -K'inich on MTL Stela 4 and White Bird, all presently unknown to us historically. It is also hardly accidental that -K'inich and White Bird presided over Ik'a's rise to prominence. By AD 679, Tikal's defeats in wars against Calakmul and Dos Pilas (Martin and Grube 2008, 42–43, 57) most likely created a situation in which lesser dynasties in the Lake Petén region could strive for greater power in the last quarter of the seventh century. A fragment from the front of Motul de San José Stela 4 (Figure 2.3c) may imply that -K'inich captured lords of Lakamtuun and Namaan sometime before AD 680. On the Dallas vase (MVD:K2803), mentioned earlier, White Bird is shown playing ball alongside several other lords, but the vase's owner is identified as a "(holy) lord of Hix Wits." As David Stuart (2003) has shown, this polity is associated with the archaeological sites of El Pajaral, Zapote Bobal, and La Joyanca. These sites are all located between the site of La Florida, the location of the Namaan court as suggested independently by several scholars (for more details see Lopes n.d., 167; Zender 2002) and Motul de San José itself (Miller and Martin 2004, 91; Schele and Miller 1986, 255; Tokovinine 2002, 5). Therefore, we can deduce that that the relationship of -K'inich with Namaan and Lakamtuun lords was antagonistic and that White Bird was either an ally or vassal of the Hix Wits rulers.

Intriguingly, the previously mentioned Dumbarton Oaks vase designated for White Bird's son shows the accession of a Namaan lord[11] and was possibly made at La Florida itself (see also discussion of this vessel's chemical signature in Reents-Budet et al., this volume). This suggests either that La Florida had become an ally or dependent of Motul de San José or that diplomatic relations between the two polities had subsequently improved.

As the confrontation between Tikal and Calakmul-Dos Pilas continued to unfold, it affected the regional political landscape in which the Ik'a' polity had begun to play a significant role. The Calakmul king was defeated in AD 695 (Martin and Grube 2008, 44–45) and Tikal began to reassert its influence in the Lake Petén Itzá region. According to the text on Motul de San José Stela 1, A7–B11 (Figure 2.2, Table 2.1), the next Ik'a' ruler, Yeh Te' K'inich I, acceded in AD 701 as a "vassal" (*y-ajaw*) of the victorious Tikal ruler, Jasaw Chan K'awiil I (Martin and Grube 1994; Schele and Grube 1994, 145).

However, Tikal lords did not always have the upper hand against their Dos Pilas rivals and suffered a defeat in AD 705 (Martin and Grube 2008, 58). The competing dynasties probably reached a kind of status quo following this engagement, which may have meant that the Ik'a' lords had to keep their options open. The next Motul de San José ruler, Tayel Chan K'inich, was apparently a successful practitioner of the art of geopolitical survival. Although never identified as a vassal, one unprovenanced vase (MVD:K2573) shows him alongside a Mutal princess, perhaps his wife. We do not know which of the two Mutal dynasties she was from, Dos Pilas or Tikal.[12] Another vessel (MVD:K4996) shows him in the company of a woman with a different name, here almost certainly a wife. In addition to a common queenly title, she is also identified as an "*i' ajaw*"—a title otherwise only known from the Mutal lords of Tikal (Figure 2.9a).[13] The dedicatory text on the same vase (Figure 2.9b), however, states that it belongs to a princess who appears to be from the Xultun royal family (on Xultun rulers' titles, see Houston 1986, 8–9). Of course, Xultun is rather far from Motul de San José, but then there is yet another vase (MVD:K2295) signed by a scribe from Ik'a' (Figure 2.9c), but owned by an individual with the titles of Rio Azul rulers (Tokovinine 2008, 94–96). In our opinion, this network of associations can be taken to suggest that Tayel Chan K'inich was on good terms with the lords of Tikal and that his political alliances in the northeast went as far as Xultun and Rio Azul. Similarly, the presence of Tayel Chan K'inich's vessels in the tombs of Itsamnaaj K'awiil and the Lady of Cancuen in Dos Pilas suggests that there was at least some exchange of gifts during

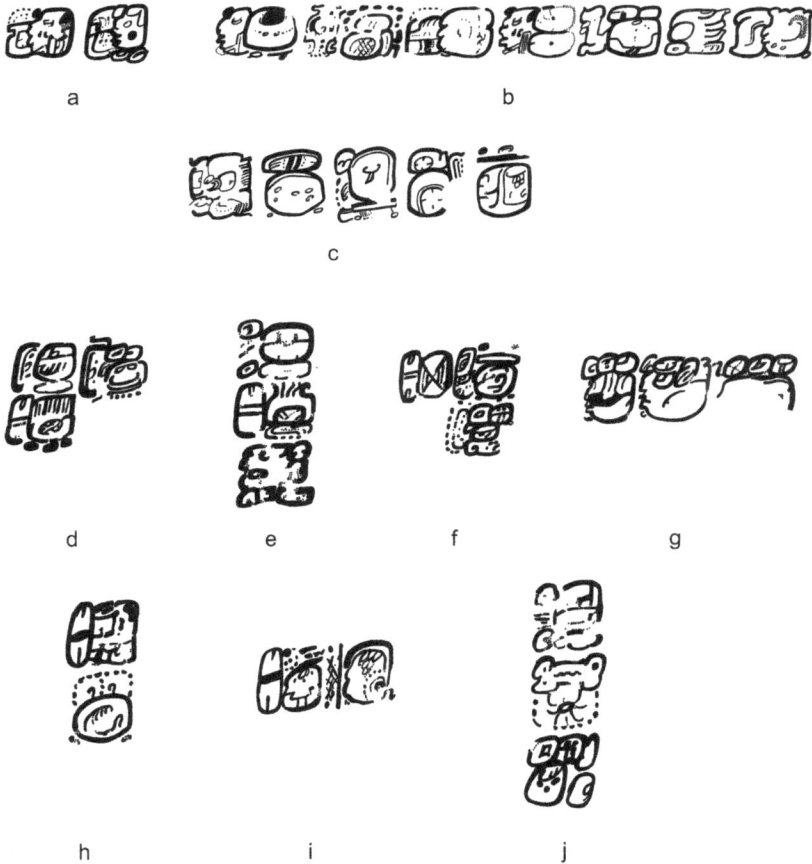

Figure 2.9. Late Classic external connections of Ik'a' rulers: a. titles of Tayel Chan K'inich's wife on MVD:K4996; b. the name of the owner of the vase MVD:K4996; c. scribal signature on MVD:K2295; d–e. visiting lord in the scene on MVD:1439 and another occurrence of the same name on a vase from Tayasal; f–g. visiting lords in the scene on MVD:1439; h–j. dance participants in the scene on MVD:K533.

this period, and that diplomatic relations may have remained cordial during the reigns of Dos Pilas Rulers 2 and 3.

Motul de San José rulers must have conducted at least some military campaigns during this otherwise calm period. One of Tayel Chan K'inich's subordinates on the Tamarindito vase carries the title of "the guardian of ?Ch'aaj Tuun" (Figure 2.11f). The later Ik'a' lord Yajawte' K'inich is called "the guardian of Ik' Bul" (Figure 2.6c, d), in reference to a captive he must have taken before AD 738. Unfortunately, we do not know where Ik' Bul or ?Ch'aaj Tuun were from. Their names do not resemble those of the major royal dynasties in the area, nor are they provided with Emblem Glyphs or other identifications. Most likely, they were rulers of lesser polities and/or subordinates of more powerful lords.

This period of successful diplomacy and little warfare came to an end sometime between AD 734 and 741. It looks as if Sihyaj K'awiil and particularly Yajawte' K'inich presided over a major change in Motul de San José's foreign relations. However, they were part of a larger trend: a new generation of rulers came to power at Tikal, Dos Pilas, Motul de San José, and Yaxchilán and they did not seem to be satisfied with the existing state of affairs. The next period in the history of Ik'a' is characterized by an alliance (or similar association involving bride transfer) with the Pa' Chan lords of Yaxchilán and by several military engagements with Dos Pilas and Lakamtuun, the latter likely to be identified with the site of El Palma on the Lacantun River (Bernal Romero 2006).[14] We do not know precisely when the Ik'a' princesses, Lady Wak Jalam Chan Ajaw and Lady Wak Tuun, were sent to Yaxchilán as the brides of Bird Jaguar IV. But since Classic Maya royal marriages were usually overseen by children's parents and Bird Jaguar IV's father died in AD 742, this may suggest that the alliance (if such it was) began somewhat earlier.

We can expand the list of Motul de San José allies and/or affiliates thanks to a dance scene on the unprovenanced vase (MVD:K1439). Dated to AD 743, the vase shows Yajawte' K'inich accompanied by three visiting rulers. One of them is a "holy Hix Wits lord" (Figure 2.9f), so it looks like this royal family continued in its alliance or association with Motul de San José. The name of another participant (Figure 2.9d) greatly resembles that of the seated ruler on the vase T7B/6–22 from Tayasal (Figure 2.9e; see also Chase 1985, fig. 3), possibly, another ally or a vassal from that site. Sadly, the name phrase of a third individual (Figure 2.9g) is unrecognizable, and his Emblem Glyph is obliterated.

It also appears that Tikal may have largely withdrawn from the geopolitical process in the Lake Petén Itzá area, possibly because many of its resources were directed to wars against the Kanuul lords of Calakmul, Sa'aal lords of Naranjo, and Waka' lords of El Peru (Martin and Grube 2008, 49–50). A vessel with a scene of the court of the Dos Pilas ruler K'awiil Chan K'inich (MNAE 11418 /K2697; see also Martin and Grube 2008, 62) discovered in association with the Structure 5C-49 at Tikal implies that Tikal rulers received gifts from their Dos Pilas counterparts. It looks as if the two

Mutal dynasties reached a rapprochement allowing them to pursue a more aggressive policy in the distinct spheres of influence.

The first sign of trouble for Motul de San José rulers comes in the inscription on Machaquila Stela 11 erected in AD 741, the same year that K'awiil Chan K'inich of Dos Pilas acceded to kingship. The local lord at Machaquila claims the title of "the guardian of Ik'a' lord." Apparently, then, there must have been a somewhat earlier confrontation in which a ruler or a member of the royal family of Motul de San José was captured (Grube and Schele 1996, 99). It is tempting to speculate that this capture may have been linked to the abrupt end of Sihyaj K'awiil's political career and the accession of Yajawte' K'inich. We do not know if Dos Pilas was involved in this capture, but there would be no clear reason why Machaquila lords would have attacked Motul de San José in the first place: the two polities did not even share a border and were separated from each other by lands under the sway of Dos Pilas and its vassals. Therefore, this military victory was probably part of a larger campaign and the most likely power behind such a campaign would be Dos Pilas.

This period certainly seems to be the turning point in the previously cordial relations between the two polities. In AD 743, according to the inscription on Dos Pilas HS 3, K'awiil Chan K'inich of Dos Pilas attacked El Chorro and captured a local lord (Martin and Grube 2008, 62–63). Less than a year later, Bird Jaguar IV of Yaxchilán, still not a king, captured and sacrificed a Lakamtuun lord.[15] Several months later, according to Dos Pilas HS 3, K'awiil Chan K'inich defeated lords of Yaxchilán and Motul de San José and captured a certain Ik'a' lord named ?Chuliw Hix, as already mentioned. The timing of these defeats (within three days of each other) strongly suggests that Yaxchilán and Motul de San José acted in concert and that the attacks against El Chorro and El Palma were part of a larger campaign that ended in the defeat of Pa' Chan and Ik'a' lords by K'awiil Chan K'inich.

Although Yajawte' K'inich was not captured, it looks like the defeat evidently had cost him and his court some political capital, at least as measured against the increasing visibility of lesser royal families in the vicinity of Motul de San José within a few years of AD 744. For instance, a stela was erected by a local lord at the site of Akte in AD 747 (Mayer 2000b; see also Yorgey and Moriarty, this volume). Although his name and titles are unfortunately illegible, they nonetheless seem to include an unfamiliar Emblem Glyph. Four years later, in 751, a "holy Yokeel lord" at Huacutal (or Aguacatal) named Sun God's Seed celebrated the period ending of 9.16.0.0.0 and erected a stela (Mayer 2000a).

Evidence of the diplomatic efforts of Ik'a' lords comes to us in the form of the famous "Altar Vase" (MVD:K3120) discovered in a royal tomb in Mound A-III of Altar de Sacrificios in 1962 (R. Adams 1963). Although long assumed to be of direct relevance to local dynastic history (R. Adams 1977), the vase was clearly commissioned by Yajawte' K'inich of Motul de San José in AD 754 and was most likely a gift of this king to local rulers.[16] Another vessel (MVD:5418) is labeled as the property of K'inich Lamaw Ek' during his early days as *baah ts'am* at the court of Yajawte' K'inich (Figure 2.7a). Painted by one of his favorite artists, Tubal Ajaw, it shows the accession of the Namaan ruler Chan Yopaat in AD 756, which we have taken as a sign of some rapprochement between the two royal families. It also implies that relations with the court of Hix Wits lords located between Namaan and Ik'a' were cordial enough to allow the flow of gifts and messengers. In AD 760, a "holy Hix Wits lord" (Figure 2.9j) accompanied Yajawte' K'inich in a dancing ceremony depicted on still another unprovenanced vessel (MVD:K533). Finally, the Motul de San José wives of Bird Jaguar IV began to play a prominent role at his court after his accession in AD 752 and several Yaxchilán monuments celebrate their participation in various ceremonies between AD 753 and 763.[17]

The political landscape in the Lake Petén Itzá region during the 760s was affected by the collapse of the Dos Pilas hegemony (Martin and Grube 2008, 63–64). One of the key geopolitical actors was gone and new centers of power were emerging. According to the inscription on Itzan Stela 17 (Grube and Schele 1996, 131), the Lakamtuun lord of El Palma and the contemporary lord of Itzan campaigned successfully against Motul de San José in AD 767 and 768 (Figure 2.10, Table 2.1). They "drilled fire in Ik'a'" (*ujoch'ow k'ahk' ik'a'*) and "a man of Ik'a' fell" (*jubuyi aj-ik'a'*). There are also signs of some strain in the relations with Yaxchilán during the last years of Bird Jaguar IV's reign. It is at this time that the Ik'a' queens disappear from Yaxchilán monuments and new prominence is given to Bird Jaguar IV's third, local wife of *sajal* descent. Her son was groomed as the future heir to the throne and her brother evidently played an important role at the court. We do not know the circumstances that led to these changes, but Ik'a' supporters in Pa' Chan might no longer have been in the king's favor. The new Yaxchilán ruler, Itsamnaaj Bahlam IV, who acceded around AD 769 was likely not an Ik'a' sympathizer, although there are no signs of open confrontation during K'inich Lamaw Ek's tenure.

K'inich Lamaw Ek' acceded to kingship shortly after the setback at the hands of Itzan and El Palma, and he may well have been in need of new allies.

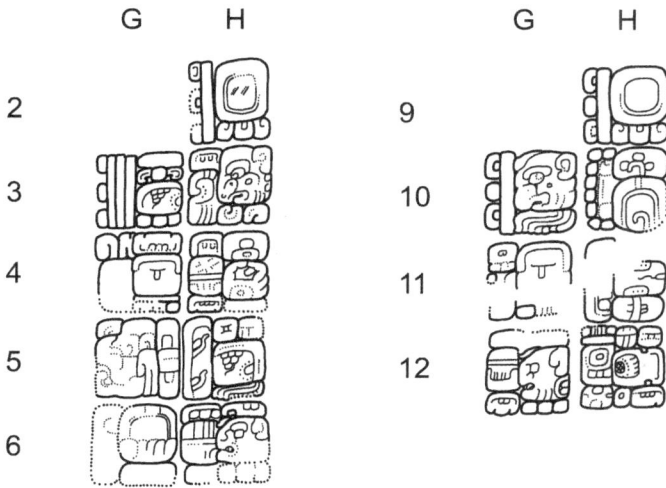

Figure 2.10. References to campaigns against Motul de San José on Itzan St 17.

Stela 2 of Motul de San José may portray him (that part of the caption is missing) dancing with Juun Tsak Took', the contemporary Itsa' lord of nearby Itzimte.[18] Juun Tsak Took' celebrated the period ending 9.17.0.0.0 in AD 771 with his own stela at Itzimte (Mejía and García Campillo 2004), so the Motul de San José monument should be roughly contemporaneous. Another stela fragment at Motul de San José features the Tzolkin position of 13 Ajaw, likely corresponding to the same period ending in AD 771 (Figure 2.3g). The alliance with the rulers of Itzimte, placed strategically to the southwest of Lake Petén, was possibly meant to prevent further aggression from Itzan and El Palma. If so, this strategy would seem to have worked, because the only other known event from the 770s is a collection of tribute payments in AD 778 depicted on an unprovenanced vase in the Boston Museum of Fine Arts (MVD:K1728; Reents-Budet, Bishop, and MacLeod 1994, 174–75).

A fragment of a carved-incised late Tepeu 2 vessel found in the midden behind the Structure L4-43 at Dos Pilas (Foias 1996, 555, fig. 6.51) offers some evidence of further contacts between the site and Motul de San José. The surviving section of the scene shows a seated ruler with a partial caption that identifies him as " . . . K'inich, holy Ik'a' lord."[19] Velásquez García (2010, 69–70) correctly points out that this gift from Motul rulers must postdate the collapse of the Dos Pilas hegemony. Yeh Te' K'inich II would then be the likeliest candidate for the ruler depicted on this vase.

The main geopolitical problem for Ik'a' rulers in the last decade of the eighth century were the relentless military campaigns undertaken by Itsamnaaj Bahlam IV of Yaxchilán (Safronov 2005). The Hieroglyphic Stairway 5 at Yaxchilán details his victories against Namaan, Hix Wits, Lakamtuun, and possibly Itsa' (ibid., 54–55, fig. 4.4) between AD 796 and 800. Although fragmentary and preserving only a single Calendar Round, Yaxchilán Stela 21 (Tate 1992, fig. 151; Mathews 1997, fig. 7-5) can be dated somewhere between AD 788 and 800. On this monument, Itsamnaaj Bahlam IV takes the titles "guardian of Tajal Mo', guardian of Baluun Ajawlel, guardian of the man of Namaan, guardian of the man of Ik'a'." These titles may refer to the conquests of AD 796–800 or to some unknown earlier campaigns, but there can be little doubt that Yaxchilán rulers targeted Motul de San José and its key allies.

Although there are no references to Ik'a' lords in the inscriptions around Lake Petén for the next half a century, they receive mention in a list of dynasties on Altar 3 at Altar de Los Reyes in Campeche that can be tentatively dated to the period ending of 9.18.10.0.0 in AD 800 (Grube 2008, 180–82, fig. 8.6; for site location see Figure 1.1). The same list includes Mutal and Kanuul lords as well as rulers of Palenque and Edzna (see below). Apparently, Ik'a' lords still had the reputation of one of the most prominent Classic Maya dynasties.

The last outside mention of holy Ik'a' lords comes from Seibal Stela 10. There is no indication that Ik'a' lords were subjugated by Seibal. They just seem to be one of four prominent dynasties apparently still functioning around AD 849. This in itself was quite an achievement during the political chaos of the Classic Maya collapse. It is possible that Ik'a' lords were not entirely unaffected, however, as Flores Stela 1 of AD 869 suggests that their court may have relocated to Tayasal or Flores.

The Court of Ik'a' Rukers: A View from Vase Paintings

At least fifteen painted vases provide us with a unique series of snapshots of the life of the Ik'a' royal court through time. The earliest of these scenes shows Tayel Chan K'inich receiving tribute (*patan*) from three officials holding the title of *lakam* that, as Lacadena (2008) has recently suggested, may correspond to ward governors (Figure 2.11a). One of these *lakams* is named ?Ahkul Ichiim (Figure 2.11b), and the other is named ?Yaxuun Bahlam (Figure 2.11c). The vase from Tamarindito depicts Tayel Chan K'inich "with pulque" (*ti chih*) attended by two *ajk'uhuuns*: ?Ajwo'ol Bahlam

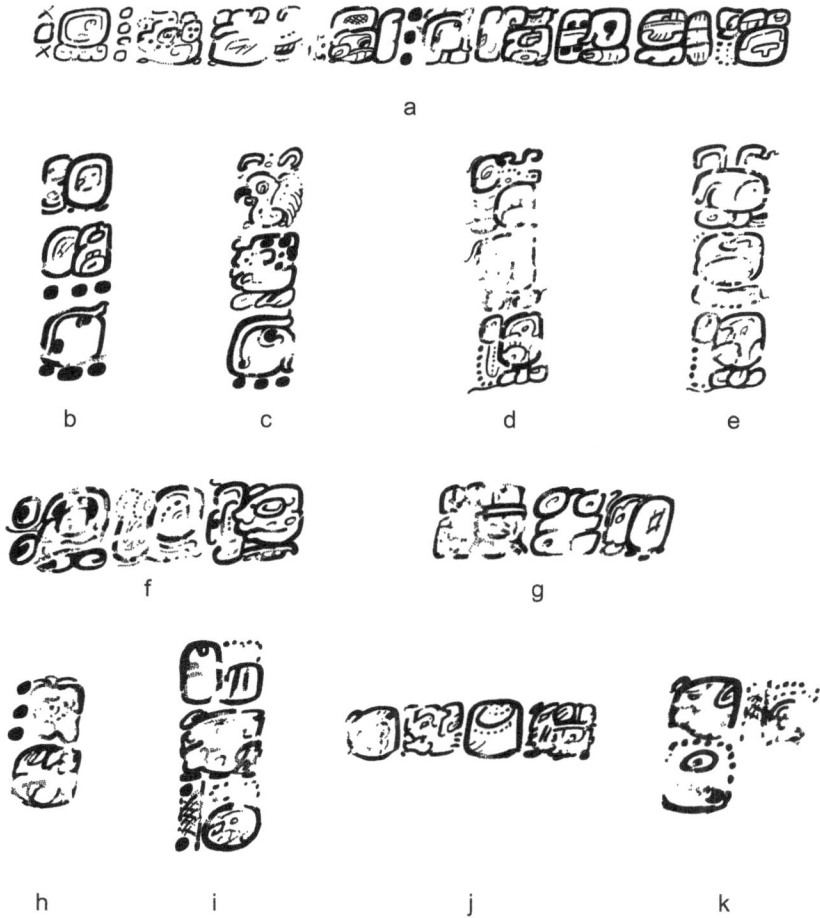

Figure 2.11. The court of Ik'a' in the inscriptions on painted vases: a. tribute presentation on the MVD:K4996; b. *lakam* ?Ahkul Ichiim on MVD:K4996; c. *lakam* ?Yaxuun Bahlam on MVD:K4996; d–f. names of courtiers on the Tamarindito vase; g–i. titles of courtiers in the scene on MVD:K1463; j. Lady Tsam in the scene on MVD:K3054; k. Lady *ajk'uhuun* in the scene on MVD:K3054.

(Figure 2.11d) and K'ahk' Yopaat K'inich (Figure 2.11e), as well as a certain Yax Hixil who carries the title "guardian of ?Ch'aaj Tuun" (Figure 2.11f). The vase found in the burial of the Lady of Cancuen at Dos Pilas mentions two courtiers. One caption is too eroded, but the other can be read. It identifies the king's attendant as an *ajk'uhuun* named Janaab (**ja-na-bi AJ-K'UH-?na**). The only depiction of the court of his potential successor,

Sihyaj K'awiil (MVD:K1453), shows a drinking scene featuring two atten-
dants with illegible names, a hunchback, and a dwarf. Three musicians are
playing trumpets in the background while the king seems to be examining
his fingernails in a mirror.

In the first known dancing ceremony during the reign of Yajawte' K'inich
(depicted on K1452), two *ajk'uhuun* officials appear before the seated ruler.
Unfortunately, their names are too eroded to be read. Another dancing
ritual in AD 743 seems to involve three invited rulers including lords of
Hix Wits and, possibly, Tayasal (Figure 2.9d–g), as already mentioned. A
further dance in AD 760 features a new Hix Wits lord (Figure 2.9j) and two
more individuals, Chak ?Kan ?Took' (Figure 2.9h) and Chak Ohl Ahk (Figure 2.9i). The latter seems to be an important member of Yajawte' K'inich's
court because he accompanies the king along with two more officials of
illegible names in still another dance depicted on K1896. Unfortunately, his
precise status and office remain unknown.

As we move into the later part of Yajawte' K'inich's reign, the future king
K'inich Lamaw Ek' begins to appear in several scenes carrying the subordinate title *baah ts'am* (Figure 2.11g). The first of these is the *joyaj* event of
AD 757 or 765 (MVD:K1463). The same ceremony (hardly an accession
in this case) featured an *ajk'uhuun* (or, perhaps, a variant title of the form
ajk'uh) named Chak Tok Bahlam (Figure 2.11i) alongside a certain Uhx
?Paax Bahlam of unknown status (Figure 2.11h). A very similar ceremony
took place in AD 768 (MVD:K3054), though here K'inich Lamaw Ek' is
now given the title "holy Ik'a' lord." The scene also includes the wife of Yajawte' K'inich', whose name might suggest that she was from Tsam (Figure
2.11j), a location known from the inscriptions of Caracol. She is attended
by a female *ajk'uhuun*, although it is also possible that this is a second wife
of the king, of *ajk'uhuun* descent (Figure 2.11k). This crucial scene therefore
represents not only the first public acknowledgment of K'inich Lamaw Ek'
as the next Motul de San José ruler, but it also reveals the importance of
female members of the court in key political and ritual events.

The scene on the Boston Museum of Fine Arts vessel (MVD:K1728;
Reents-Budet, Bishop, and MacLeod 1994, 174–75, figs. 5.10, 5.11) provides
important insights into the court of K'inich Lamaw Ek', but nonetheless remains difficult to interpret. It shows several individuals presenting bundles
and mantles called *yubte'* to a seated ruler. An associated text spoken by
the ruler seems to refer to *yubte'* and other objects as the "payment" (*to-
jool*) of a *sajal* named . . . Muut. Given that the dedicatory text on the vase
names K'inich Lamaw Ek' as its owner, the likeliest interpretation of the

scene would be that it represents him receiving a payment from his *sajal*. The captions identify the nearest seated figure as Chij Lam, unfortunately of unknown rank and affiliation.[20] One of the two standing characters is a "young man of mantles" (*aj-yubte' ch'ok*); the other is an *ajk'uhuun* named Way Baah Haats. A final member of the court of K'inich Lamaw Ek' appears on an unprovenanced vase in the Dumbarton Oaks photo archive (LC. cb2.415), but the name is too eroded to be read.

Very little is known about the Ik'a' court during the reign of Yeh Te' K'inich II. One vase (LC.cb2.441; Figure 2.7d, e) identifies two of his subordinates, but their names are largely illegible. One of them carries the same undeciphered title as the carver of one of the Motul de San José monuments (Figure 2.7d). Two dancing scenes on unprovenanced vases (MVD:K1399, K534) show the king in the company of one ?Juun Tuun Chak, an important individual who may have carried the slightly enigmatic *ajk'uh* title, perhaps a reduced variant of the better-known *ajk'uhuun* (see Zender 2004b, 164–95).

The most interesting aspect of the scenes involving Yeh Te' K'inich II is the presence of other "holy Ik'a' lords," ?Yopaat Bahlam (Figure 2.8b) and Tsij . . . (Figure 2.8c). We do not know if they were the king's designated heirs or high-ranking relatives in charge of secondary sites. The latter seems more likely. It suggests a shift in the way the Ik'a' court operated, perhaps the first sign of a political strain caused by the overproliferation of nobility sometimes highlighted as one of the factors in the Classic Maya collapse (Fash 1991, 175–76; Houston and Stuart 2001, 73–76).

A few patterns emerge from these glimpses spread over a period of nearly a century. Even if we assume that the scenes only show a few most elevated members of each king's close circle, the court was apparently rather small. Tayel Chan K'inich seems to have relied on three district governors (*lakams*), and his own administration consisted of several *ajk'uhuuns* and a few other officials. These numbers appear to remain more or less constant during the reigns of his successors. There is no sign of expansion or contraction. The scene on K1728 reveals the presence of *sajal* officials at the court during the tenure of K'inich Lamaw Ek'. *Sajals* were the backbone of the Yaxchilán administration, so one may speculate whether it was an alliance with Pa' Chan lords that led to the adoption of some of their practices in the Petén. At present, no court officials are known to have retained their positions through more than one reign. It looks like every new king appointed his own men.

With the exception of a jovial scene of drinking in the company of musicians, dwarves, and hunchbacks in Sihyaj K'awiil's palace, and possibly two earlier receptions at the court of his predecessor depicted on the Tamarin-dito vase and K2573, the rest of the scenes show three kinds of activities: presentation of tribute, dancing, and *joyaj*. The *joyaj* ceremony involves putting on royal regalia in front of a mirror surrounded by a few atten-dants. Despite the use of the verb *joyaj* (most common in the *joyaj ti ajawil* "appeared in lordship" construction of royal accession), the dates and as-sociated iconography indicate that these are unlikely to have been royal accessions. Such events seem to have taken place "behind closed doors" in the royal court, and we are invited to see them with the eyes of lesser court members who might have actually witnessed the ceremonies. The likely audience seems to be internal except for some dancing ceremonies involv-ing rulers of multiple polities. It is unlikely that lords would have traveled to such events without their retinues. Consequently, the scene on K1439 implies a particularly large gathering of visiting nobility.

The scribes of the Motul de San José court also deserve mention in this section, although this subject has been extensively discussed elsewhere (e.g., Reents-Budet, Bishop, and MacLeod 1994, 172–79; Reents-Budet et al., this volume). Some of them, like the scribe responsible for painting vases K791 and K1728, apparently enjoyed long and productive careers spanning the tenures of more than one ruler. For the most part they were probably local artists, with the significant exception of Tub[al] Ajaw, who signed several vessels featuring scenes with Yajawte' K'inich and K'inich Lamaw Ek'. The name of this scribe suggests some relation to the royal line of Tubal, an unknown location mentioned in the inscriptions of both Tikal (Figure 2.12c) and Naranjo (Figure 2.12b) and situated within about a day's trip of these two sites (Martin and Grube 2008, 76–77; Zender 2005, 14). The main problem here is different spellings. Although we only have two examples, the scribe at Motul de San José spelled his name as **tu-ba AJAW** in both of them (Figure 2.12a). The place-name at Tikal (Figure 2.12c) is somewhat equivocal, because although the elements beneath **tu-ba** appear identical to the -**la** syllable beneath the **K'AWIIL** (immediately above the sign in question), they might also be seen as a common "flourish" on the **ba** sign, without phonetic value. In any case, we can probably assume an underspelled final -**la** in the designation of the Motul de San José painter. Underspellings of this place-name have clear precedent in the inscriptions of Naranjo, where they occur in the name of a queen from Tubal on Nara-njo Stela 13:G6 (Figure 2.12d) and possibly also on Stela 19:L1, although the latter text is eroded. Other examples of the same name contain the full **tu-ba-la** spelling (Figure 2.12e). For these reasons, we suggest that the Motul

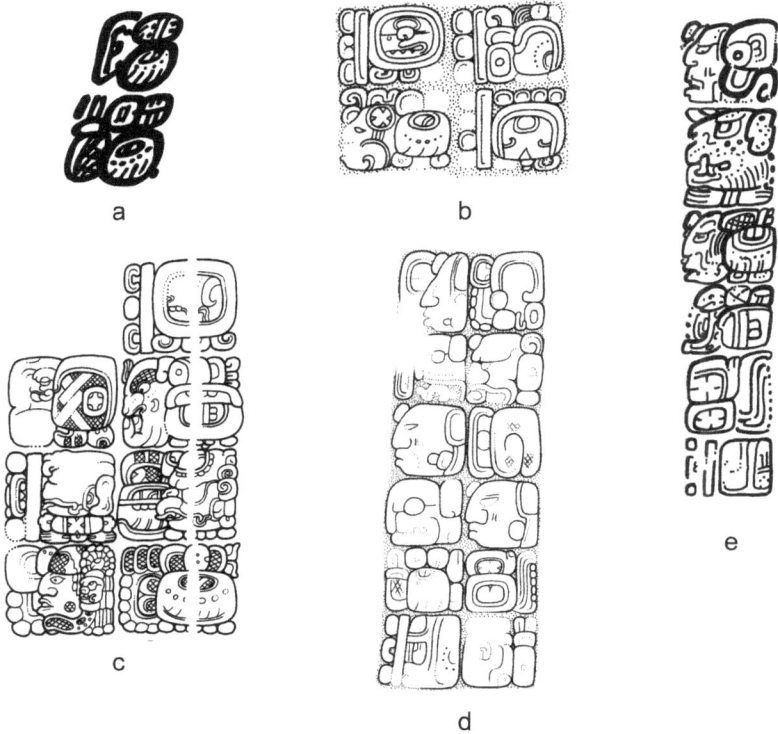

Figure 2.12. References to Tubal at Motul de San José and other sites: a. signature by Tuba[l] Ajaw on K3054; b. burning of Tubal mentioned on Naranjo Stela 22 (drawing by Ian Graham); c. Yik'in Chan K'awiil's arrival at Tuba[l] in the inscription on Lintel 2 in Temple 4, Tikal (drawing by M. Zender); d. Lady of Tubal in the text on Naranjo Stela 13 (drawing by I. Graham); e. Lady of Tubal on the unprovenanced vase K7750.

de San José scribe could have come from Tubal.[21] This connection to Tubal is interesting, because Tubal lords apparently belonged to the western part of a regional group of *huk tsuk* or "Seven Divisions" where Naranjo usually dominated (Beliaev 2000). This would be the only known link between Motul de San José and polities in this region.

Ik'a' Rulers in the Ideational Landscape of Classic Maya Dynasties

Generations of scholars have discussed the inscription on Seibal Stela 10 that includes the Ik'a' lord Chan Ek' among a list of four dynasts arranged in a kind of quadripartite order resembling the idealized organization of Chichen Itza in the Books of Chilam Balam (Barthel 1968; J. Marcus 1973, 1976; Wagner 2006). Similar lists also appear on Copan Stela A (Barthel 1968) and Ixtutz Stela 4 (Zender 2001), among other monuments. A priori, earlier models proposing that such lists truly refer to the paramount states of idealized geopolitical landscapes must be rejected given the pronounced historicity of all such texts, where individually named rulers are merely cited as having cooperated in the performance of joint ritual events. Further, there is little historical evidence to support any notion that Motul de San José was the seat of one of the four most powerful dynasties of AD 849. In Martin and Grube's words (2008, 227), "by now these kingdoms were mere shadows of their former selves and the lofty titles probably mask little more than pretenders to fragmented realms." Nevertheless, and all apart from the geopolitical reality at any given time, some of these group rituals and the texts commemorating them may have reflected the geopolitical ambitions of their participants. Is such an emic appraisal of the Seibal Stela 10 text warranted in the light of what is known about Motul de San José's political history and monumental rhetoric?

The earliest sign that Motul de San José rulers wielded at least some regional political clout comes in White Bird's titles in the inscription on the Dumbarton Oaks vase (Figure 2.4b). He is called "first *kaloomte*'" (*yax kaloomte'*). Although the title remains poorly understood, its most frequent context is in claims to authority over other kings. Tikal and Calakmul lords used it most consistently. As we have previously mentioned, White Bird was probably one of the first powerful Ik'a' lords. The best analogy here is to the titles of Itsamnaaj Bahlam III of Yaxchilán. This highly successful Pa' Chan lord laid the foundations of Yaxchilán's rise to geopolitical prominence (Martin and Grube 2008, 123–26), and was perhaps significantly referred to as "first *kaloomte*'" by his successor, Bird Jaguar IV, in the inscription on Yaxchilán Stela 12, G2–H2 (Tate 1992, fig. 137).

Whereas Tikal's vassal Yeh Te' K'inich I dropped the *kaloomte*' title for rather obvious reasons, his successors would claim it again. In the reign of Yajawte' K'inich, almost every known example of the king's name features the *kaloomte*' title. This insistence on regional prominence seems even to have been acknowledged by some of Yajawte' K'inich's allies. On Yaxchilán Lintel 38 (C4), for example, Lady Wak Tuun of Ik'a' was called an "eastern *kaloomte*'." Some of Yajawte' K'inich's titles also hint at a link to the east. His full name frequently includes the place-name Chan Te' Chan (Figure 2.6c, d).

This mythical toponym appears in the quadripartite list on Copan Stela A, where it is associated with the east (J. Marcus 1973, fig. 3).

Yajawte' K'inich's other common title—*uhxlajuun k'uh* or "Thirteen Gods" (Figure 2.6b–d)—possibly refers to another important geopolitical concept that was evoked in the previously mentioned list on Altar 3 at the site of Altar de Los Reyes in Campeche (Grube 2008, fig. 8.6). The top of the altar features a caption that states *k'uh[ul] kab uhxlajuun [tsuk]* or "(they are) divine land(s), (they are) thirteen divisions." Although the final hieroglyphic block is eroded, the size of the signs is different from the nearby **ka-KAB** or **ka-ba** spelling (also somewhat eroded), and the reading of this block could well be **tsu-ku**. The sides of the altar carry an inscription that likely begins with a statement like "it is their [x] thrones" and then continues by naming thirteen Emblem Glyphs, although part of the text is missing. The list of preserved Emblem Glyphs includes "holy Mutal lord," "holy ?Chachtahn person," "holy Baakal lord," "holy Kanuul lord," "holy Ik'a' lord," "holy [T1008.552]," and "holy [T579] lord."[22]

It appears that the list on Altar 3 references the same concept as the title "Thirteen Divisions" (*uhxlajuun tsuk*) that appears in the names of the rulers of Tikal, Xultun, Rio Azul, and La Honradez but is also used to designate groups of lords from these sites (Beliaev 2000; Tokovinine 2008, 250–60). We believe that "Thirteen Gods" is a variation of the title "Thirteen Divisions." In addition to the names of Motul de San José rulers, it also appears on the inscribed earflares from Tomb A-1/1 at Altun Ha. The owner of the object is said to be the mother of a lord who carries the titles *baahtuun* ("head stone") and *uhxlajuun k'uh* ("Thirteen Gods"). As mentioned above, the Altun Ha Emblem Glyph may be included in the Altar de Los Reyes list.

As suggested by Houston, Stuart, and Taube (2006, 89–97, fig. 2.30), the arrangement of thirteen dynasties on a circular altar resembles Postclassic Maya representations of an ideal spatial-temporal organization of the political landscape also attested in Early Colonial sources. A list of thirteen holy lords looks like a katun wheel, a key space-time concept for Postclassic Maya evidenced in precontact objects like the Mayapán turtle sculptures encircled with thirteen Ajaw signs (Taube 1988a, fig. 2a). What is potentially significant for the present discussion of Ik'a' lords is that, as noted long ago by Ralph L. Roys (1954), similar concepts were attested by the Spaniards in the Lake Petén Itzá region. According to Avendaño y Loyola's seventeenth-century account of the Itza shortly before the conquest, the people were divided into thirteen parts associated with their own deities, priests, and katun seatings:

> These ages are thirteen in number; each has its separate idol and its priest with a separate prophecy of its events. These thirteen ages are divided into thirteen parts which divide this kingdom of Yucathan and each age with its idol, priest and prophecy rules in one of these thirteen parts of the land according as they have divided it. (Means 1917, 141)

Therefore, we may be able to tentatively link Motul de San José rulers' concepts of an ideal geopolitical order, and their place in it, to Early Colonial accounts from the same area. The main caveat here comes from the scribal signature on the unprovenanced vase K2295 mentioned above (Figure 2.9c). The artist calls himself a "man of Ik'a'" (aj-ik'a') and "Western Seven Divisions" (ochk'in huk tsuk). Seven Divisions is another regional group located to the east of Thirteen Divisions and this inscription unequivocally claims that at least some residents of Motul de San José associated themselves with it.

There are, of course, different ways to address this apparent contradiction. There may have never been a single classification of Maya polities and their inhabitants, so that these titles reflect multiple and inevitably contradictory visions of a geopolitical landscape. Moreover, the terms "Thirteen Divisions," "Thirteen Gods," and "Seven Divisions" are never used as toponyms and always designate individuals and groups of people, the implication being that members of various regional groups may have lived in Motul de San José. In fact, if the scribe Tub[al] Ajaw was indeed from Tubal he would also have been a "Western Seven Divisions" person at the court of Ik'a'. Interestingly, some lesser members of the court (Figure 2.1c, 2.7d) identified themselves with an altogether different regional group. In other words, people who lived at Motul de San José and served its rulers did not necessarily share a single vision of the geopolitical landscape and did not necessarily ascribe themselves to the same regional group.

Concluding Remarks

A careful review of the carved monuments and painted vessels from Motul de San José, a settlement known as Ik'a' to the ancient Maya themselves, has made possible the recovery of some two centuries of the history of the local royal dynasty. We have identified at least eight rulers ("holy Ik'a' lords") who reigned through some of the most interesting and turbulent centuries of the Late Classic to Terminal Classic transition.

The history of the Ik'a' royal dynasty is a remarkable story of opportunism and survival amidst a very challenging and fluid geopolitical environment. It offers us a unique glimpse into the world of middle-range Classic Maya polities, which oscillated between client states, independent political centers, and regional hegemonies relying more on diplomacy than on outright warfare to achieve their political ambitions. It is also illustrative of how such polities were integrated into larger geopolitical networks in terms of specific bilateral ties to neighboring royal courts and also in terms of membership in larger geopolitical groups based on certain concepts of spatiotemporal order. Despite the unimaginable damage done to archaeological contexts by looting, the geographical distribution of such Ik'a' vases whose provenance can be recovered nonetheless reveals the incredible scale of Motul de San José's ancient geopolitical network. That Ik'a' lords consistently allied themselves to Hix Wits and Namaan suggests that these polities shared some lasting common interests, such as the confrontation of more powerful neighbors or perhaps the control of trade routes along the Rio San Pedro to the Lake Petén Itzá.

The record of the Motul de San José court is also unique in providing multiple snapshots of its inner workings. We are witness to receptions and feasts, to tribute presentations and courtly diplomacy, and to performances ranging from the intensely private to the ostentatiously public. Even though the court was rather small, every new ruler relied on his own trusted subordinates. In addition to visitors from other royal courts, scenes on Ik'a' vessels reveal the presence of *ajk'uhuun* administrators, *lakam* district governors, and *sajal* officials, the latter being a potentially late innovation. The titles of some courtiers suggest participation in warfare. Other members of the royal court included heirs apparent, most clearly in the case of K'inich Lamaw Ek', who is visible in the unclear role of *baah ts'am* for more than a decade prior to his own accession. Toward the end of the Classic Period, a form of co-rulership may perhaps have been introduced under Yeh Te' K'inich II, with lesser Ik'a' lords possibly left in charge of secondary sites.

Acknowledgments

In our study of the Motul de San José monuments, we relied on Ian Graham's photographs in the archive of the Corpus of Maya Hieroglyphic Inscriptions in the Peabody Museum of Archaeology and Ethnography,

Harvard University. We wish to thank Barbara Fash, the corpus director, for her invaluable help in accessing this material. Our study of vessels attributed to Motul de San José was greatly facilitated by access to Justin Kerr's Maya Vase Database (including high-resolution images of some vases) and to photographic archives at the Dumbarton Oaks Research Library and Collections. Miriam Doutriaux, exhibition associate of the Pre-Columbian Collection at Dumbarton Oaks, helped us with the study of this archive. The authors would also like to thank Dmitry Beliaev for many excellent comments on the manuscript and the illustrations. We greatly appreciate informal discussions with colleagues and friends touching upon questions investigated herein, particularly Antonia Foias, Erik Velásquez García, Stanley Guenter, Stephen Houston, Simon Martin, Joel Skidmore, and David Stuart.

3

Identity and Interaction

Ceramic Styles and Social History of the Ik' Polity, Guatemala

DORIE REENTS-BUDET, STANLEY GUENTER, RONALD L. BISHOP,
AND M. JAMES BLACKMAN

A hallmark of Classic Maya civilization (AD 250–850) is its elaborately decorated pottery, primarily made for and used by the ruling elite (Coe 1973, 1978; Merwin and Vaillant 1932; Reents-Budet, Bishop, and MacLeod 1994, 72–105). Prior to ending their lives in tombs and burials, many vessels functioned as high-status food service ware and as gifts for guests attending elite-sponsored feasts (Reents-Budet 1998, 2000b). The elite feast functioned as a key sociopolitical mechanism for the Maya as it did elsewhere in Mesoamerica and among many world cultures (Brumfiel 1987; Burgoa [1674] 1989; Dietler 1996; Earle 1977; Junker 1999; Monaghan 1990; J. Pohl 1999; Vogt 1969, 1993). As food service wares, the tall cylinder vases were used for serving and drinking cacao (*kakaw*) beverages, and the flat-bottomed dishes typically contained maize gruel or atole (*ul*; see Reents-Budet, Bishop, and MacLeod 1994, 127–28; Stuart 1987). Their elaborate, painted decoration includes pictorial and hieroglyphic imagery, which often is of a historical nature (e.g., see Coe 1973, 1978; Reents 1985; Reents-Budet 19872000a). As gifts, these painted wares became portable proclamations of the prestige and power of the feasting host (Brumfiel 1987; Reents-Budet 1998). Recognition of this important facet of the pictorial pottery underlies recent inquiries into the sociopolitical nature of its production and use (e.g., see Ball 1993; Reents-Budet, Bishop, and MacLeod 1994; Reents-Budet et al. 2000; Reents-Budet et al. 2004; Halperin and Foias 2010).

The Ik' Ceramic Corpus of the Late Classic Period

This chapter discusses a short-lived polychrome pottery expression of the eighth century AD known variously as the X-ray Style (Coe 1973, 1978;

Figure 3.1. MS1121/K1439, a Motul Group 1 vessel portraying the eighth-century Ik' ruler Yajawte' K'inich. Note the rendering of physical likeness of each performer, especially the rotund governor and his characteristically delicate facial features (photograph ©Justin Kerr).

also see Paul 1976) and the Pink Glyph Style (Kerr and Kerr 1981; e.g., Figures 3.1, 3.2). More recently, the corpus has been labeled the Ik' Emblem Glyph Style, so named because many vessels include the Ik' Emblem Glyph in their hieroglyphic texts (Figure 3.1; Reents-Budet, Bishop, and MacLeod 1994, 164–79; also see Velásquez García 2007). It is assumed that many of these vessels were used during feasting events sponsored by the Ik' polity elite, based on aesthetic characteristics, painted narrative contents, and archaeological data.

J. Marcus (1973, 1976) and Coe (1978) equate the archaeological site of Motul de San José with the Classic period Ik' site, and Coe identified it as the location of the X-ray Style pottery workshops (1978, 130). Support for Marcus's and Coe's attribution comes from epigraphic research by Martin and Grube (2000) and Houston (1993), among others. Archaeological research at Motul de San José by Foias and colleagues (Foias 1998, 2001; Foias et al. 1999; Moriarty, Castellanos and Foias 2004; Foias and Emery, this volume; Halperin and Foias, this volume) has provided additional substantiation of the Marcus and Coe attribution.

Our investigation of the Ik' Emblem Glyph Style pottery combines epigraphic, stylistic and chemical compositional data to confirm the style's geographic attribution (Reents-Budet, Bishop, and MacLeod 1994, 172–79; Reents-Budet and Bishop 1989; Reents-Budet et al. 2007). This chapter

Figure 3.2. K5418, an Ik'-style vase. Note the pink glyphs and finely drawn human figures (photograph ©Justin Kerr).

focuses on the chemically analyzed Ik'-style pottery associated with a few eighth-century Ik' rulers rather than the site/polity's entire corpus due to page limitations and the preponderance of chemically sampled pottery from the eighth century, the chemical data being crucial to our research strategy. When critical to our arguments, however, nonsampled vessels may be discussed.

Membership in the Ik'-style corpus is determined by a combination of stylistic features (see the definition of style in Akerman 1962; Lemmonier 1986; Reents-Budet 1994). These include: (1) cylinder vases or tall dishes with parallel or slightly out-flaring walls, (2) a cream or orange background color, (3) pink and rose-hued hieroglyphs, (4) black rim and basal bands defining the pictorial space, (5) a black scalloped or streaky black decorative motif on the vessels' rim interiors, (6) pictorial scenes filling the vases' circumference and lacking a vertical visual break such as an architectural element, (7) scenes recounting certain historical events among the Ik' polity elite, (8) a large number of nobles portrayed and named in the accompanying hieroglyphic texts, (9) male performers wearing elaborate costumes and masks rendered in x-ray fashion (the performers' faces are rendered behind the masks), (10) female participants, often wearing long black huipils (dresses), and (11) costume feathers painted with a dense black slip or a once-green slip (now faded to gray), the feathers often filling a significant percentage of the pictorial space and overlapping the hieroglyphic rim texts.

A salient stylistic feature is portraiture of historical individuals manifested as the hieroglyphic recording of personal names and titles and the

Table 3.1. Dates on the Ik' Pottery Corpus (Julian calendar dates)[a]

Mayan calendar	Julian calendar	Vessel number
7(?) Oc (?) 13(?) Xul (?) 9.15.18.0.10(?)	25 May AD 749[b]	MS1121/K1439
		[MS1403/K533, MS1419/K1399, K1452, MS1418/K1463]
3 Ajaw 18 Z'otz' 9.16.3.0.0	19 April AD 754	The Altar de Sacrificios Vase
4 Ix 12 K'umku 9.16.3.13.14	18 Jan. AD 755	MS1769/K791
11 Caban 5 Pax 9.16.5.11.17	1 Dec. AD 756	K5418
1 Manik' 5 K'ayab' 9.17.8.0.7	16 Dec. AD 778	MS1373/K1728
7 Men 8 Mol 9.17.8.9.15	22 June AD 779	MS1373/K1728
? ? Uo/Zip???		K534

[a] Many Ik'-style vessels bear texts with Calendar Round dates for the portrayed event. Unfortunately, all have suffered erosion and some have been repainted in modern times. Thus, the correct reading of the original date on the majority of vessels remains problematic at best and impossible to reconstruct at worst. Vessels that bear unreadable or uncertain dates include K2795, MS1403/K533, K534, MS1419/K1399, K1452, MS1418/K1463, and K3054. For example, the latter vase may record the date 4 ? 10 Yaxkin 9.16.4.2.17 (if 4 Caban) [24 June AD 755] or 9.16.17.6.2 (if 4 Ik) [10 June AD 765] or 9.17.10.9.7 (if 4 Manik) [7 June AD 781].[c]
[b] AD 743, according to Tokovinine and Zender (this volume).
[c] AD 757 or 765, according to Tokovinine and Zender (this volume).

rendering of physical likeness (Steiner 1987), a rare feature in Mesoamerican art (Figure 3.1). Epigraphically, the Ik'-style is characterized by texts recording historical events rather than the more common vessel-dedicatory text known as the Primary Standard Sequence (PSS; see Coe 1973). The historically focused narratives typically are composed of a Calendar Round date, a verbal phrase, and the name of the vase's patron/owner and sometimes that of the painter (Table 3.1). The nominal phrase often ends with the Ik' Emblem Glyph, and short glyphic texts within the pictorial field name the depicted individuals.

The historical episodes recount a limited set of elite rites concerning eighth-century politics in the Lake Petén Itzá area. The events include rites during which participants donned royal regalia, vision quest rituals, tribute presentation, the sacrifice of war captives, and performances during which participants performed as supernatural beings and made personal blood offerings (see also Tokovinine and Zender, this volume). A narrative parallel may be drawn with the famous wall murals at Bonampak, Mexico (Miller 1986), which recount a similar constellation of events.

The Ik'-style corpus includes more than forty-five whole vessels, most lacking archaeological provenience. The loss of provenience has dramatically lessened the eighth-century history that could have been gleaned from them. However, the corpus remains useful to the pursuit of sociopolitical insights when analyzed from a collaborative, multidisciplinary approach, with art history, epigraphy, archaeology, and paste compositional analysis contributing to our inquiry.

The Maya Ceramics Project

Classic Maya pictorial pottery can elucidate facets of culture history beyond the information proffered by its pictorial and hieroglyphic imagery. Specifically, when a pottery style can be connected to a specific location of manufacture, it can shed light on the nature of ceramic production and use. Toward this end, the Maya Ceramics Project[1] uses Instrumental Neutron Activation Analysis (INAA) to chemically characterize the ceramic pastes of potsherds and whole vessels. The pastes' constituent elements reflect the use of different clay resources within a fairly small geographic area (Bishop, Rands, and Holley 1982) and thereby function as a "chemical fingerprint" of the idiosyncratic mixture of local clays and tempers formulated by ancient potters. Matches between unprovenanced and archaeologically excavated samples may indicate the location of the workshop(s) where they were made[2] so that ceramic objects, archaeological pottery types, or a painting style may be attributed to a geographic region, a clay procurement zone, or even an archaeological site. Pottery that shares a specific constellation of stylistic features and a distinct compositional profile should represent the output of a group of potters working closely together, possibly in one community or even within one production unit (Arnold, Neff, and Bishop 1991; Arnold et al. 1999). Our research has confirmed the Motul de San José area as the locale of manufacture of Ik'-style pottery, the corpus generally falling into two chemically determined groups.

Compositional Analysis of Ik'-Style Feasting Pottery

Attribution of Ik'-style pottery to the greater Petén Lakes region has been difficult up to now because the target region is one of extensive geological similarity, its clays having formed from Cretaceous and Tertiary limestones. Gradually, with a detailed analysis of large quantities of pottery from Motul de San José and nearby La Trinidad de Nosotros, as well as other sites around Lake Petén Itzá, we now are able to discern subregional compositional differences with an acceptable degree of confidence. Moreover, the analyses finally have led to determining the specifics of the chemical differences between Motul-area-produced pottery and that made in the vicinity of nearby Tikal (Reents-Budet et al. 2008). Some of the compositional differences are quite small, which frustrated all previous efforts at discrimination. For example, we have determined that pottery produced in the Motul area is likely to contain slightly lower concentrations of barium but higher rare earths values than pottery produced at Tikal. This minor, but highly discriminating, variance reflects the lake sediment geochemistry of the Motul de San José vicinity that contrasts with that of Tikal, in spite of the fact that all the clays derived from a relatively common geological source. Furthermore, under the constraints of limited INAA sampling and the chemical variation inherent to different potting practices, there is little reason to expect distinct, nonoverlapping groups in such a geochemically similar environment.

The modeling of the chemical variation in Ik'-style pottery was carried out relative to the compositional data for the Ik' regional and Tikal ceramics using an approach that differs from those that we have employed in the past (e.g., Bishop and Neff 1988). Compositional groups were formed through the use of Fuzzy K-means clustering accompanied by outlier removal.[3] The procedure is based on the concept of fuzzy set theory (Bezdek 1981, 1993) as implemented by Minasny and McBratney (2002; also see De Gruijter and McBratney 1988). The groups thus formed are similar to those created for ceramic types, which are conceptually polythetic, with group members sharing sufficient numbers of attributes so that they can be considered similar. The groups' divisions variously will be "softer" or "harder," with some specimens having ambiguous placement because their attributes fall into more than one group. Confirmatory evidence includes the extent to which the chemically derived patterns were found to correlate with archaeological and stylistic information, the combined data giving rise to a "best fit" among the diverse data sets (Bishop, Rands, and Holley 1982; Bishop 2008).

The specific implementation of fuzzy analysis for the Ik'-Tikal regions pottery involved multiple random starts and iterative trials to determine sample relationships based on Mahalanobis distances, after the removal of outliers. The use of Mahalanobis distances to assess similarity adds the information about the pattern of elemental covariance to the data matrix. In this manner, clustering is not only concerned with absolute differences in composition, but also with the "shape" of elemental profiles. The statistical program was stepped through five to twenty-five groups that were weighted according to sample distance from the multivariate groups' centroids. The permitted degree of "fuzziness," or group overlap, was set experimentally. The thirteen-group partition of the data set was seen as the "best fit" because it showed a relatively sharp change of slope in the graph of the "fuzzy performance index" relative to the number of classes formed and the number of outliers identified. Logically, the creation of additional groups might accommodate more of the samples regarded as outliers. In the present application, however, most of the outliers were consistently identified as such, regardless of the number of groups. Of the 911 samples in the Motul-and-Ik' data set, seventy-eight were excluded from the analysis as outliers, including a few Ik'-style vessels atypically tempered with crushed carbonate.

The majority of the Ik'-style vessels was found to occur in two partitions (Motul Groups 1 and 2) and clustered with Motul de San José–excavated pottery, indicating their close chemical similarity (Table 3.2, which lists only the Ik'-style whole vessels). A few stylistically related specimens exhibited fuzzy membership with another group dominated by pottery from the Tikal area (Tikal Group 1; see Table 3.2). All three groups were statistically refined at the 95 percent confidence interval. They then served as the basis for searching the entire Maya Ceramics Project database, which exceeds thirty thousand analyses, for any additional samples that lay within the confidence interval. In this manner, we observed that several of the Ik'-style vessels excavated from sites in the Petexbatún region were classifiable, based on chemical composition, as members of the two major Motul-produced groups. The refined groups constitute our Motul Group 1, Motul Group 2, and Tikal Group 1. The centers of these three are presented in Table 3.3, and their separation is shown graphically in Figure 3.3 relative to the "hard" partitions of a linear discriminant analysis. Variable weights comprising the canonical discriminant functions are listed in Table 3.4.

The corpus of whole vessels associated with eighth-century, Ik'-style ceramic production initially was compiled based on stylistic assessments and epigraphic data, and then refined through the paste chemical compositional analysis described above. The corpus of whole vessels matches our chemically refined Motul Groups 1 and 2, which include materials archaeologically excavated from Motul de San José and surrounding sites. Slight chemical variations among the two groups result from differences in clay and temper resources and/or paste preparation, which likely reflect specific choices of clay resources and/or idiosyncratic mixtures of clays and tempers on the part of the potters.

The relationship between the whole vessels and the Motul compositional Groups 1 and 2 is depicted graphically in Figure 3.3, using a minimum

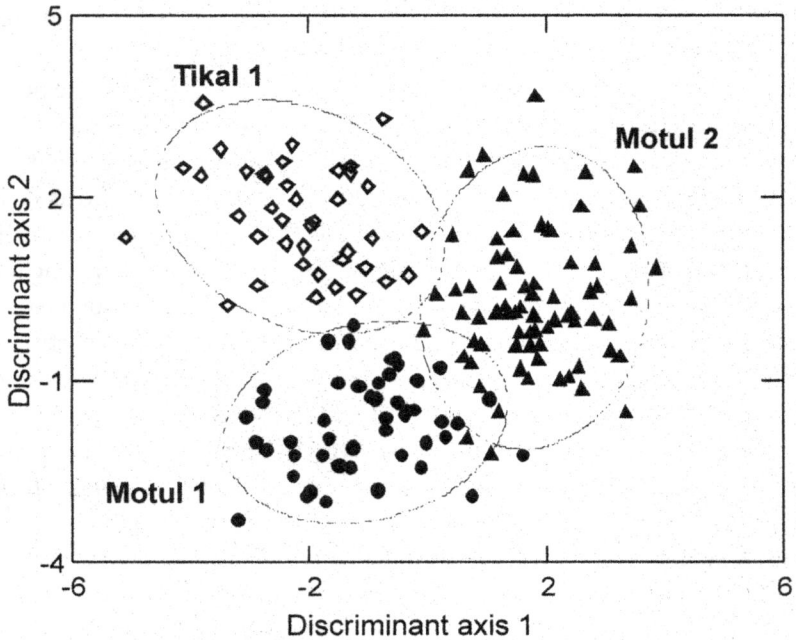

Figure 3.3. Discriminant analysis plot of main fuzzy-derived and statistically refined groups containing vessels painted in the Ik' style.

spanning tree. This type of graph visually links the vessels as they are distributed on a bivariate plot from a linear (nonfuzzy) principal components analysis based on the correlation matrix of Motul Group 2 samples (see Table 3.5 for the elemental contributions to the extracted components). It is important to note that the compositional groups have been refined in a multivariate space whereas Figure 3.3 shows only the first two dimensions.

Motul Group 1 contains the larger number of whole vessels (thirty-two of forty-four) and also displays a broader stylistic spread than those in Motul Group 2. Group 1 also represents the work of at least six artists, discerned by distinctive painting characteristics and artist signatures. Group 1 includes two of the vessels featuring the mid-eighth-century ruler Yajawte' K'inich and painted by the Tuubal Ajaw artist (MS1121/K1439 and DPCS25 from the Petexbatún region; perhaps also the eroded vase MS0313, see Figures 3.1 and 3.4). Yajawte' K'inich's other vessels are members of Group 2 (MS1403/K533 and MS1418/K1463). Group 1 also contains the vase MS0031, which resembles vessels painted by the Tuubal Ajaw artist but lacks his figural and

Table 3.2. Chemically defined groups of eighth-century Ik' painted pottery

Motul Group 1	Motul Group 2	Tikal Group 1
MS0031[a]	MS0179	MS0064
MS0047	MS0903	MS0273
MS0057	MS1373/K1728	MS0070
MS0074/K5445	MS1403/K533	MS0156
MS0313	MS1418/K1463	MS1098
MS0334/K5370[a]	MS1419/K1399	MS1156
MS0445/K2784[a,b]	MS1442/K4606	MS1784
MS0522	MS1769/K791	MS1867
MS0636	MS1770/K793	DPD033/K5695
MS0902	MS1771/K792	
MS1054	MS1783	
MS1121/K1439	MS1795/K4825	
MS1123/K688[a]		
MS1134		
MS1160		
MS1166		
MS1436		
MS1437		
MS1562		
MS1648		
MS1699[a]		
MS1805[a]		
MS1814/K4120		
MS2019		
MSA007[a]		
MSG470[a]		
DPAP24		
DPD009		
DPD013		
DPCS25		
LPO325[a,b]		
LP0327		

[a] Group outlier.
[b] Carbonate tempered.

hieroglyphic expertise; we suggest this other painter was copying works by the Tuubal Ajaw based on their similar pictorial style.[4] Interestingly, MS0031 (Boston Museum of Fine Arts 2003.777) exhibits lower rare earths than those of the Tuubal Ajaw's vessels, suggesting different Motul-area clay resources or a different paste recipe used for this vase. Whether the chemical differences among MS1121/K1439, DPCS25, and MS0031 indicate the products of two workshops or a minor change in paste recipe within

Table 3.3. Fuzzy cluster mean values (in ppm, unless otherwise specified)

	Motul 1 (n = 51)	Motul 2 (n = 77)	Tikal 1 (n = 40)
K%	1.35	2.02	1.08
Sc	10.9	9.9	12.3
Cr	39.5	34.5	51.7
Fe%	2.97	2.58	3.14
Rb	80.6	99.3	67.1
Sb	1.37	1.66	1.56
Cs	5.21	5.38	5.14
Ba	796	894	997
La	30.2	25.1	18.0
Sm	5.36	4.31	2.65
Eu	1.00	0.79	0.48
Yb	3.23	2.72	1.81
Lu	0.45	0.40	0.26
Hf	7.62	6.37	6.95
Th	14.5	13.0	14.5

Table 3.4. Linear discriminant functions

	DF 1	DF 2
K	1.107	0.176
Sc	−0.235	0.437
Cr	0.024	0.125
Fe	0.231	−0.189
Rb	−0.305	−0.330
Sb	0.083	0.737
Cs	0.272	−0.156
Ba	−0.205	0.286
La	0.858	1.099
Sm	−0.797	0.080
Eu	0.031	−1.408
Yb	−0.170	−1.054
Lu	0.566	0.606
Hf	−0.109	−0.072
Th	−0.500	−0.448

Table 3.5. Principal components from Motul Group 2

	PCA 1	PCA 2	PCA 3	PCA 4	PCA 5
K	−0.19	0.45	0.39	0.24	−0.61
Sc	0.15	−0.82	0.39	0.05	−0.14
Cr	−0.05	−0.84	0.14	0.21	−0.01
Fe	0.40	−0.69	0.37	0.20	0.07
Rb	0.05	0.52	0.27	0.59	−0.26
Sb	−0.04	−0.05	0.67	−0.29	−0.33
Cs	−0.30	0.36	0.53	0.09	0.52
Ba	−0.24	0.25	0.58	0.10	0.52
La	0.88	0.16	0.08	−0.08	0.05
Sm	0.90	0.15	0.02	−0.25	−0.04
Eu	0.90	0.12	0.09	−0.29	−0.03
Yb	0.89	0.12	0.13	−0.13	0.06
Lu	0.83	0.11	0.15	−0.13	0.03
Hf	0.64	−0.03	−0.27	0.57	0.11
Th	0.56	0.00	−0.07	0.69	0.05
Percent variance	33.1	17.3	11.5	10.4	7.6

the same workshop is unknown. Group 1 is also distinguished by the lack of any vessels whose imagery or chemical composition pertains to the next Ik' ruler K'inich Lamaw Ek'.

Group 2, the smaller of the two Motul groups (twelve of forty-five whole vessels tested; see Table 3.2), is strongly associated with the next ruler K'inich Lamaw Ek'. Its constituent vessels are more restricted in their stylistic characteristics than are those of Group 1, and represent the work of at least five artists. The largest number of vases was painted by Mo . . . n Buluch Laj, whose masterworks date from circa AD 755 (MS0179, MS1373/K1728, MS1769/K791, MS1770/K793, and MS1771/K792; Figures 3.5 and 3.7). Interestingly, a sixth vase painted in the Mo . . . n Buluch Laj style (MS0074/K5445) is an exception, being a chemically defined member of Group 1 (Figure 3.6).

Group 2 also contains four vessels featuring the previous ruler Yajawte' K'inich (MS1403/K533, MS1419/K1399, MS1418/K1463, MS1442/K4606), although the last two render him in the company of K'inich Lamaw Ek'. MS1419/K1399 features an auto-sacrifice performance by Yeh Te' K'inich, a name that simply may be an underspelling of Yajawte' K'inich (see alternative interpretation in Tokovinine and Zender, this volume). On this vase, Yeh Te' K'inich is accompanied by two lords, one whose name may be Juun??? Tuun Chak. The latter nobleman is also pictured in the same kind

Figure 3.4. DPCS25, a vase excavated at Cueva de Sangre, Petexbatún region, Guatemala, but made at Motul de San José (Motul Group 1).

of event on K534, a vase painted by yet another Ik' artist and featuring Yeh Te' K'inich (no chemical data are available for K534).

Two Group 2 vases were painted by the Tuubal Ajaw for Yajawte' K'inich (MS1418/K1463 and MS1403/K533). On the former, Yajawte' K'inich and K'inich Lamaw Ek' participate together in a joyaj rite. In the text, Yajawte' K'inich is noted as the divine Ik' lord whereas K'inich Lamaw Ek' is named only as a noble person (see also Tokovinine and Zender, this volume). Yet on another vessel painted by the Tuubal Ajaw (K3054) both men participate

Figure 3.5. MS1373/K1728, a Motul Group 2 vessel (photograph by D. Reents-Budet).

in a similar ritual (dating to either AD 755 or 768) and simultaneously carry the divine lordship title. Subsequently, on what may be the last vase painted by the Tuubal Ajaw (K5418, dated to AD 756), the artist's patron no longer is Yajawte' K'inich but instead K'inich Lamaw Ek', the subsequent divine Ik' lord. Hereafter, the Tuubal Ajaw artist disappears from the ceramic record, and Mo . . . n Buluch Laj takes center artistic stage for K'inich Lamaw Ek'.

Paste chemistry and painting style shed some light on this complicated artistic and aristocratic historical scenario. The presence of Yajawte' K'inich–associated vessels in Group 2 (primarily associated with K'inich Lamaw Ek') and one K'inich Lamaw Ek'–associated example in Group 1 (primarily associated with Yajawte' K'inich) indicate the close chemical compositions among the vessels produced for these two

Figure 3.6. MS0074/K5445, a Motul Group 1 vessel (photograph by D. Reents-Budet).

mid-eighth-century rulers of Motul de San José. The chemical similarity may indicate an equally close relationship between their two artists, who perhaps were sharing clay resources, paste recipes, and even workshop locale(s) (see Halperin and Foias, this volume, for evidence for such a workshop at Motul de San José).

Nevertheless, the presence of some variety in stylistic and paste compositional patterns of Ik'-style pottery suggest that multiple workshops produced feasting vessels for the eighth-century Ik' nobility. The chemical data intimate the workshops' location at Motul de San José and its immediate vicinity. Patronage likely came primarily from the royal court, which may have had palaces (and craft workshops) throughout the area, a situation

Figure 3.7. MS0179, a Motul Group 2 vessel (photograph by D. Reents-Budet).

found elsewhere during Late Classic times (Ball and Taschek 2001; Demarest 1997). Yet the entire corpus' stylistic and chemical variability also implies production at the behest of secondary members of the nobility residing at Motul de San José as well as in nearby subsidiary sites. This hypothesis would explain the presence of so many Ik'-style vessels whose texts name otherwise unknown lords. Yet the relatively close chemical compositions and stylistic features indicate production within a restricted geographic area by ceramicists sharing an artistic tradition, clay resources, and/or paste recipes, as well as patron-consumer audience.

Ik'-Style Pottery and Political History

The eighth-century Ik'-style ceramic corpus embodies a century of remarkable artistic and sociopolitical exploits among the Ik' polity's elite. Such activity likely was in response to the volatile social and political landscapes that characterized the Petén lowlands at this time (Culbert 1988a, 1991; Webster 1993). As we discuss in this section, the epigraphic record on these vessels suggests that the Ik' polity played relatively prominent but shifting roles as a moderately powerful secondary center located at the nexus of the Tikal, Petexbatún, and northwestern Petén spheres of influence. The large number of Ik'-style feasting vessels featuring the political endeavors of its patrons prompts the hypothesis that the Ik' elite utilized the feast as an important tool of negotiation and advancement (see also Halperin and Foias 2010).

To discuss this complicated corpus of painted pottery and its sociopolitical implications, we partition the corpus by ruler and focus on artistic style and ceramic paste compositional chemistry. We conservatively interpret the historical dynastic contents of the vessels' texts and images that we suggest record five rulers of the eighth century.[5] In chronological order, these are Taj Yal Chan K'inich, Sak Muwaan, Yajaw Te' K'inich, K'inich Lamaw Ek', and Tayel Chan K'inich.[6] Unfortunately, no accession or certain death dates are known for any of them. Thus, the length and period of their reigns can only be determined roughly, and we place some of the rulers at different points in time from Tokovinine and Zender (this volume) based on our interpretations of the chronology of the vessels. Their manuscript was not available when we wrote this chapter, and thus we cannot comment specifically on the epigraphic discrepancies.

Vessels of Taj Yal Chan K'inich (early eighth century)

Taj Yal Chan K'inich is named on a square plate (DPD033/K5695) excavated from the tomb of Itzamnaaj K'awil, an early eighth-century ruler of Dos Pilas who died in AD 726 (Demarest et al. 1991; Martin and Grube 2000, 58–59).[7] The plate's chemical composition indicates it was not made at Motul de San José but instead at Tikal (Tikal Group 1). Corroborating the chemical data is its painting style, which diverges from that of the Ik'-style corpus and recalls patterns observed in Tikal painted pottery.

On the plate, Taj Yal Chan K'inich is named a kaloomte', a title that usually implies political independence and domination over other lords

(Stuart, Grube, and Schele 1989). Interestingly, the contemporary Tikal ruler Jasaw Chan K'awil is noted as having overseen the accession of a ruler of Motul de San José in AD 702 (Schele and Grube 1994, 145), and other epigraphic evidence indicates the Ik' polity's subservience to Tikal during the early decades of the eighth century (see also Tokovinine and Zender, this volume). At the time this plate was placed in Itzamnaaj K'awil's tomb (AD 726), Dos Pilas and Tikal seemingly were at political odds although an apparent détente was less than ten years away. This Ik'-named, Tikal-made square plate and its final Dos Pilas resting place may preserve a trace of "backroom politics" among these three polities, indicating some degree of nonadversarial relations between them (or at least between Motul and Dos Pilas). Perhaps the plate was made at the behest of Tikal nobility for the Ik' ruler Taj Yal Chan K'inich. Then, either he regifted the plate or through other means it found its way into the hands of Itzamnaaj K'awil of Dos Pilas, and finally ended its journey in his sumptuous tomb.

As already mentioned, Tikal's hegemony over the Ik' polity dates to the early eighth century (Martin and Grube 1995; 2000, 48–50). At this same time, high level, nonadversarial contact between the Ik' and Petexbatún polities is indicated by the presence of Ik'-produced ceramics (both Ik'-style and other polychrome types) at sites in the Petexbatún region, in spite of the fact that Tikal and Dos Pilas were politically at odds with each other. These vessels and their archaeological contexts pertain to the eighth century AD. These include the ritual venue Cueva de Sangre (the Cave of Blood; DPCS13, DPCS25, DPCS28, DPCS80; Figure 3.4; also see Brady 1996) and palace and other midden contexts at Aguateca, Arroyo de Piedra, Dos Pilas, and Tamarindito (DPA162, DPAP24, DPD014, DPT009; see Foias 1996; Valdes 1997; Inomata 1995). The ceramic evidence indicates elite contact, perhaps even a sociopolitical alliance, between the Ik' and Petexbatún polities, which may have become stronger during the mid-eighth century based on ceramic and archaeological indicators.

Vessels of Sak Muwaan (early to mid-eighth century)

Mention of the next Ik' ruler Sak Muwaan is found only on two pottery vessels (MS1526/K2803 and MS0445/K2784).[8] On MS1526/K2803 he plays the ball game with noblemen from other sites. The owner/patron of this vase is "Spangle Head," a lord of the Hiix Witz polity (El Pajaral-Zapote Bobal; Stuart 2003). "Spangle Head" may be the same Hiix Witz lord mentioned on Yaxchilán's Hieroglyphic Staircase 3, Step V, dated at AD 732. This provides a general time frame for his rule, and, by extension, that of Sak Muwaan (see Tokovinine and Zender, this volume, for an earlier placement of this ruler, called White Bird). The vase's painting style and paste chemistry indicate a non-Ik' origin, and its paste composition suggests production in the western region of the Petén lowlands toward the location of Hiix Witz.

Sak Muwaan is also mentioned on MS0445/K2784 as the father of the vase's owner/patron, K'ej Ti Chan. Given his royal father, K'ej Ti Chan must have been a member of the Ik' royal line, likely a prince. However, there is no evidence that he ever acceded as king and may well have been a younger son who never was in line for the throne. The vase's painting style is unlike most polychrome pottery made at Motul de San José. However, it shares elements of pictorial format and figural features with MS1373/K1728 (Figure 3.5), a vase made as many as forty years later for the fourth ruler in our royal sequence, K'inich Lamaw Ek'. MS0445/K2784 could be an earlier, idiosyncratic creation by an accomplished Ik' artist; yet it is curious that no other works by this painter seem to have survived. Its chemical composition is similarly enigmatic, being characterized by calcium carbonate temper in contrast to the more typical volcanic ash tradition of Motul de San José polychrome ceramics. Excluding the carbonate temper, however, the vase's composition is proportionally similar to that of Motul ceramics. Therefore, we tentatively suggest MS0445/K2784 was made in the Motul de San José area during the early eighth century as a member of Motul Group 1 although its composition remains outside the chief chemical patterns of Late Classic Motul ceramic production.

Vessels of Yajawte' K'inich (mid-eighth century)

The largest number (eighteen plus) of Ik'-style pictorial vessels pertains to the reign of the next ruler Yajawte' K'inich. Four of those painted by the ruler's master artist Tuubal Ajaw (or closely aligned artists), which name and/or portray Yajawte' K'inich, are compositionally aligned with Motul Group 2 (MS1403/K533, MS1418/K1463, MS1419/K1399, MS1769/K791); in contrast, three reside in Motul Group 1 (MS0031/Museum of Fine Arts Boston 2003.777, MS1121/K1439, DPCS25).

The group is characterized by a wide range in painting quality from high technical and artistic ability (e.g., MS1121/K1439, MS1403/K533, MS1418/K1463, MS1419/K1399; Figure 3.1) to clumsy figural portrayals (e.g., MS1442/K4606) and maladroit use of pictorial space (e.g., MS0031).

Epigraphic aptitude is equally varied, from expert calligraphy to inelegant texts (e.g., compare MS1121/K1439 and K2795 with MS1442/K4606). At least four artists are represented in the group, including the aristocratic painter, the Tuubal Ajaw, who signed three of the eight vases (MS1418/ K1463, K3054, K5418) in his known corpus (also including MS1121/K1439, K2795, K1452, DPCS25, and K8889).[9] Vase K5418 may carry the latest date associated with this artist and his primary royal patron Yajawte' K'inich (11 Caban 5 Pax 9.16.5.11.17 [Dec. 1, 756]; Figure 3.2).

The scenes portray a restricted number of events relating to rites of rulership and portray from two to as many as ten participants, frequently identified in intra-scene, short nominal texts composed of personal names and/or elite titles. Depicted events include tribute presentation or reception scenes (K8889 and perhaps MS0313 [a highly eroded vase]) and joyaj rites (MS1418/K1463, MS1160, LC-cb2-441, and perhaps K2763 and MS0031). Whereas the verb *joyaj* has been interpreted as indicating accession, this is only the case when the text explicitly states *joyaj ti ajawlel*, "was wrapped/ dressed in rulership." None of the Ik' vessels includes the latter part of the phrase, and it appears that the depicted events simply refer to the king getting dressed for ritual performance. This interpretation is supported by MS1418/K1463, the Ik' corpus vessel with the most explicit joyaj text, which shows an attendant sitting next to the ruler and holding a mirror at the ready.

Many vessels depict ritual dances, some even bearing texts that make this explicit (Grube 1992; Looper 2009). The performers may wear fantastical costumes with full head masks, their faces rendered inside the masks in X-ray fashion (MS1121/K1439, MS1403/K533, MS1442/K4606, K1896, K2795, and perhaps the eroded vase DPCS25). The X-ray depiction is typical of the work of the Tuubal Ajaw painter; yet this feature was copied by at least two other artists who may have been producing for Yajawte' K'inich (MS0031) and other Ik' nobility (MS1442/K4606).[10] Some scenes render the performers holding feathered batons or large banners (MS1134, MS1437/ K3464, K534) or playing percussion instruments as they dance (MS1419/ K1399, MS1442/K4606, MS1436, a vase at the Mint Museum [89.64.4], and one at the Museo de Vidrio, Antigua, Guatemala). Many performance scenes include rites of personal blood offerings (MS1121/K1439, MS1419/ K1399, K1452, and DPCS25 [tentative identification]) or the scaffold sacrifice of war prisoners (K2795), a rite frequently connected to accession (Taube 1988b).

Vessels of K'inich Lamaw Ek' (third quarter of the eighth century)

The next Ik' ruler, K'inich Lamaw Ek', is associated with six vessels based on painting style and hieroglyphic texts (MS0074/K5445, MS0179, MS1373/K1728, MS1769/K791, MS1770/K793, and MS1771/K792; see also Tokovinine and Zender, this volume). All were painted by an accomplished artist named Mo . . . n Buluch Laj (or Mo . . . n B'uluch Laj) who signed the exceptional vase MS1769/K791 (Reents-Budet, Bishop, and MacLeod 1994, 174–77; Reents-Budet, Guenter, and Bishop 2001, 10). The famous Altar de Sacrificios vase (R. Adams 1971, fig. 92) also may be one of his creations. His vessels apparently were produced during a relatively short period of time (ca. AD 754–779) and were made at Motul de San José based on hieroglyphic inference and substantiated by paste chemistry. Five of the six vessels' compositional profiles closely resemble each other and are members of Motul Group 2 (see Table 3.2). Such close chemical similarity implies they were made from the same mixture of clays and tempers, suggesting the products of one or a very few closely related workshops. MS0074/K5445 (Figure 3.6), on the other hand, belongs to Motul Group 1, although its style connects it to painter Mo . . . n Buluch Laj and the artistically similar Group 2 vessels associated with K'inich Lamaw Ek'.

The imagery painted by Mo . . . n Buluch Laj recounts a restricted set of elite-sponsored events with ritual performance being most prominent. Dancers are not rendered in X-ray-style masks as seen on the previous ruler's vessels (e.g., MS0179; Figure 3.7). Instead they either are portrayed in their fantastical animal spirit–companion forms or are named as such in the accompanying nominal phrases (MS1770/K793, MS1771/K792; see also Looper 2009). The corpus also includes records of tribute payment events (MS1373/K1728; Figure 3.5) and an enigmatic elite rite of drinking and smoking tobacco (MS0074/K5445; Figure 3.6). Mo . . . n Buluch Laj's vessels are distinguished from other Ik'-style pottery by the use of the PSS rim text and the lack of pink-hued glyphs. However, as is typical of the broader Ik' corpus, they begin with Calendar Round dates. Clearly chronology was central to the role and function of these eighth-century feasting wares.

K'inich Lamaw Ek' is the patron of vase MS1373/K1728 (Figure 3.5). Its PSS text opens with the Calendar Round date 7 Men 8 Mol (9.17.8.9.15; 22 June AD 779), and concludes with the name of his father, Took' Yaas K'inich, a lord of Ik' but not a *k'uhul ajaw* (a divine lord/paramount ruler). A secondary text located within the scene describes the activity as the presentation of tribute at his court, half a year earlier on 1 Manik' 5 K'ayab' (9.17.8.0.7; 16 December AD 778).

MS1769 (K791; Princeton Museum of Art) is an exceptionally fine example of Late Classic ceramic painting. The vase has been repainted in modern times, which obscures the finesse of the original artistry as well as lends uncertainty to any transcription of the hieroglyphic text, especially in the nominal sections. Yet the repainting seems to follow the original work, and thus we may, at the least, assess the extraordinary control by Mo . . . n Buluch Laj of the challenging slip paint medium. This exceptional artist created an exuberant pictorial field that visually vibrates with spirit beings accompanied by exquisitely rendered nominal phrases. The PSS text begins with the date 4 Ix 12 K'umku (9.16.3.13.14; 18 January AD 755) and names the patron/owner Yajawte' K'inich. This may be a reference to the previous ruler Yajawte' K'inich, a possibility strengthened by the recorded date of AD 755, a time when both he and K'inich Lamaw Ek' were co-participating in rulership events. The seemingly different Emblem Glyph ending his name phrase, however, is the result of modern repainting of the vase. A prerestoration photograph shows the original left portion of what likely was the Ik' Emblem Glyph.[11]

Vessels of Tayel Chan K'inich (late eighth century)

Tayel Chan K'inich, the final ruler in our Ik' sequence, is known from texts painted on three vases, including K2573, K4996, and Vessel 4 of Burial 21 from El Perú-Waká, dated to post-760 based on archaeological context (Eppich 2007, fig. 10; see alternative placement of this ruler earlier in the eighth century in Tokovinine and Zender, this volume). Only the El Perú-Waká vessel may have been made at Motul de San José (Eppich 2007, 9–10), an assessment based on its stylistic similarities to other Ik' pottery including MS0313, an eroded vase in Motul Group 1. The El Perú vessel portrays a vassal lord, identified by a *baah ajaw* title, kneeling in front of Tayel Chan K'inich. Keith Eppich interprets Burial 21 as that of an El Perú-Waká nobleman who may be the *baah ajaw* portrayed on the vase (2007, 9–10). Unfortunately, the text on this eroded vessel is too weathered to confirm his identification. An alternative interpretation is that the scene renders an Ik' *baah ajaw* because there are no known instances of sub-lords of one kingdom offering tribute or kneeling in obeisance to the lord of a foreign kingdom, unless as captives.

A fourth vessel, from Tamarindito, also has been attributed to Tayel Chan K'inich (Figure 3.8; Vessel 5 from the royal Burial 6; Foias 1996, fig. C.22;

chemical sample DPT009; see also Tokovinine and Zender, this volume). However, the main nominal text is too eroded for certain identification of the protagonist, the only clear glyph being *k'inich*. We suggest instead that the vase features the Dos Pilas ruler K'awil Chan K'inich (reigned ca. AD 741–761) receiving tribute and hosting a feast because its pictorial style and chemical composition recall those of Petexbatún-produced ceramics such as MS0651/K1599 (Figure 3.9).

K2573 pictures Tayel Chan K'inich sitting on a throne, which typically would identify him as the dominant person in the scene and the likely patron of the vase. However, the greatest amount of visual weight is given to a finely dressed woman kneeling in front of the throne. She gestures dynamically toward Tayel Chan K'inich and is named as a noblewoman of Tikal/Dos Pilas. The vase's painting style excludes it from membership in the artistic tradition of Late Classic Motul de San José ceramics; its style instead

Figure 3.8. DPT009, excavated at Tamarindito, Petexbatún region, Guatemala, and likely made in the same area (photograph by A. Foias, courtesy of the Vanderbilt University Press).

Figure 3.9. MS0651/K1599, a vase made in the Petexbatún region, Guatemala, based on ceramic style and paste composition (photograph ©Justin Kerr). Compare with DPT009 (Figure 3.8).

recalls vessels associated with Tikal-produced pottery (Reents-Budet et al. 2008). K4996, too, is not a style member of Motul de San José pottery but rather is associated with those of the Tikal region. On this vase, tribute is being offered "in the presence of Tayel Chan K'inich," who is pictured sitting on the bench/throne accompanied by a royal woman.

As the Late Classic period was coming to a close, the ceramic record indicates that Tayel Chan K'inich engaged elites in the Tikal and Río San Pedro regions. The fewer number of pictorial vessels featuring Tayel Chan K'inich and the fact that only one of our small corpus was produced at Motul de San José may point to a lessening of power for the Ik' polity during the final decades of the eighth century. Alternatively, the smaller corpus may indicate a short time span for his reign at the beginning of the Late Classic collapse of Petén Maya civilization and the general downturn in production of painted feasting vessels (Rice, Demarest, and Rice 2004).

Post–Tayel Chan K'inich Vessels (ca. 800 and beyond)

The Ik' polity continued to play a role in lowland social politics after the reign of Tayel Chan K'inich, indicated by the continued production of pictorial pottery at Motul de San José. Cylindrically shaped drinking vessels now take on a barrel shape with slightly out-curved walls and occasional nubbin supports, a form associated with Late to Terminal Classic times (ca. AD 800–875; see Culbert 1993, fig. 981c; Gifford 1976, fig. 166e; R. Smith 1955, figs. 2p [MSG470], 3j, 44f). The vessels' painting style and pictorial narratives maintain the local tradition, including renderings of tribute presentation and ritual performances (MS0903, MS1054, MS1648, MS1814/K4120, MS2019, LP0327, MSA007, MSG470). The rim text on MS1814/K4120 ends with the name Yete' K'inich, the divine lord of Ik'. It is possible that, rather than being an alternative name for the earlier ruler Yajawte' K'inich, this is a later ruler after Tayel Chan K'inich (see also discussion in Tokovinine and Zender, this volume, of late ruler Yeh Te' K'inich II).

The aggregate chemical composition of these late vessels pertains to Motul Group 1, although they reside along the outer end of its statistical axis (see Figure 3.3). Such compositional variability may be due to minor changes in resource procurement zones and/or paste recipes, both of which are typical of pottery production behavior over time. These late vessels suggest the continued employment of feasting rites by Ik' nobility as an important sociopolitical mechanism. Additional validation is provided by barrel-shaped, Ik'-produced feasting vessels found at Uaxactún (MSG470), El Chal (LP0327), and Altun Ha (MSA007). Soon hereafter, however, the pottery record falls silent concerning Ik'-style elite ceramics.

Conclusions

The eighth-century, Ik'-style corpus of feasting pottery is composed of more than forty-five vessels sharing stylistic and paste chemical features, which together identify them as the output of interrelated workshops producing for an associated consumer audience. The shared features distinguish them from the broader corpus of Late Classic lowland Maya painted pottery. Yet when viewed internally, they exhibit stylistic, artistic qualitative, and chemical diversity. This type of variance intimates a nonmonolithic, local production system involving a broader segment of the Ik' population beyond that of the paramount ruler and the immediate palace retinue. The variability also suggests production by potters exploiting a variety of local clay resources and/or following idiosyncratic paste recipes. Some variation may be due to potting modifications over time, the corpus representing approximately one hundred years of production (AD 710–810). This time span provides sufficient opportunity for adjustments in resource procurement zones, paste formulation, elite patronage preferences, and artistic discrimination.

Eighth-century, Ik'-style pottery is equally notable for its pictorial scenes featuring numerous nobles—both men and women—who are named in accompanying nominal phrases. Clearly, it was important to render these many members of the Ik' elite, an artistic situation not encountered to this degree in the ceramic record from most other Late Classic polities. Further, the glyphic texts indicate the unusual situation of more than one person simultaneously carrying the title of paramount ruler (*k'uhul ajaw*). Considered together, the artistic style, paste chemistry, and narrative contents of the pottery corpus suggest that the Ik' polity was composed of a royal lineage and a number of aristocratic families that were especially active during the late seventh and eighth centuries.[12] The presence of multiple noble families wielding considerable local power may be reflected in the architectural features at Motul de San José. Foias and colleagues have identified five elite administrative-residential compounds in the center of the site that may pertain to different lineages (Foias 1998, 2003; Moriarty 2004d; Foias et al., this volume; Emery and Foias, this volume). The eighth-century ceramic record echoes this architectural complexity and intimates that their respective feasting pottery needs were considerable.

Furthermore, the presence of at least two Emblem Glyphs in the Ik' ceramic corpus and the monumental inscriptions at Motul de San José suggests the development of alliances among local and independent corporate entities as a sociopolitical survival tactic that gave rise to the relatively powerful Late Classic Ik' polity. Based on the ceramic evidence, we argue that the Ik' polity was composed of a confederation of noble families amongst whom paramount authority could shift. This state of affairs would explain the presence of two *k'uhul ajaws* (Yajawte' K'inich and K'inich Lamaw Ek') co-participating in regal events as paramount rulers (see MS1418/K1463 and K3054).

The two vessels depicting Yajawte' K'inich and K'inich Lamaw Ek' together as *k'uhul ajaws* could alternatively indicate retrospective production, that is, vases made after the depicted events transpired and at the behest of the later royal patron rather than the simultaneous presence of two *k'uhul ajaws*. This alternative interpretation would accommodate the portrayal of K'inich Lamaw Ek' on MS1814/K4120 as a high-status lord and his also being rendered, by the same artist whose works are otherwise associated with the previous ruler Yajawte' K'inich, on another vase (K5418; Figure 3.2) where he is designated the *k'uhul ajaw*. K5418 is the last known vase painted by the Tuubal Ajaw, after which Mo . . . n Buluch Naj becomes the preeminent painter of high-quality vessels featuring K'inich Lamaw Ek'. This artistic situation could be evidence for Yajawte' K'inich sanctioning K'inich Lamaw Ek', via feasting pottery, as his chosen successor. It is possible, too, that the Tuubal Ajaw may have worked for two successive rulers, a patron–artist relationship noted elsewhere in the corpus of high-status painted pottery.[13]

Among the five rulers of the Ik' polity during the eighth century, Yajawte' K'inich and K'inich Lamaw Ek' were the most famous. Interestingly, they patronized a different noble artist, the Tuubal Ajaw and Mo . . . n Buluch Laj, respectively. Their ceramic creations are differentiated by painting style and paste chemistry. Yet their aggregate paste recipe is similar enough to indicate a likewise close production environment (in paste recipe and/or resource procurement zones). The intimation of production proximity is strengthened by the presence of a vase featuring Yajawte' K'inich and painted by the Tuubal Ajaw (MS1814/K4120) in the chemically defined group of K'inich Lamaw Ek'/Mo . . . n Buluch Laj vessels. These circumstances suggest continuity of elite ceramic production despite dynastic changes and the presence of a second regal artist. K'inich Lamaw Ek's expression, in the form of feasting pottery, of his independence from the shadow of Yajawte' K'inich may be signaled by his later, exclusive patronage of the artist Mo . . . n Buluch Naj. This artist developed an innovative adaptation of the narrative configuration favored by his immediate artistic predecessor, the Tuubal Ajaw. He further distinguished himself by reviving a pictorial format found on the Ik'-produced vase MS0445/K2784 which was made during the reign of Sak Muwaan some thirty years or more earlier (compare with MS1373/K1728). In summary, the importance of tradition and independence to these two regal patrons was manifested by their respective distinctive pottery styles that accentuated their sociopolitical legitimacy as divine rulers while simultaneously expressing patrician autonomy.

The Ik' polity is notable for its location on a boundary between two powerful Late Classic adversarial constituencies—those of Tikal and the Petexbatún. As Bruce Byland and John Pohl (1994) discuss for the Postclassic Mixtec, boundary sites in Oaxaca were the preferred location for elite feasting rites and the accompanying market fiestas for the general populace. The Ik' polity occupied a similar locale—a vulnerable yet potent geographic and sociopolitical position wherein the polity variously could suffer or profit from the politics of its neighbors. Feasting rituals, as evidenced in Ik'-style polychrome vases, provided a forum for creating alliances and garnering the power needed to compete in the contentious and unstable environment of the day (see also Bair and Terry, this volume, for the possible existence of a market at Motul).

The proliferation of feasting vessels during the mid-eighth century in the Ik' polity, and specifically at Motul de San José, suggests a lively sociopolitical environment in which Ik' nobility actively sought to augment power via internal relationships and external alliances among the myriad Late Classic polities competing for dominance (see also Halperin and Foias 2010). The production of so many Ik'-style feasting vessels painted by different artists, of variable aptitude, and the paste compositional variation among these products combine to intimate equally broad patronage/artist/workshop networks among the polity's aristocracy. And the presence of eighth-century, Ik'-style pottery in the ceramic records of other sites throughout the Petén lowlands provides material evidence of extra-polity efforts and specific indications of the geopolitical relationships. The ceramic evidence points to focal areas being the Petexbatún polity; the Río San Pedro Martir drainage and adjacent Usumacinta River area; El Chal to the southeast; and Altun Ha, Belize, to the east.

4

Architecture, Volumetrics, and Social Stratification at Motul de San José during the Late and Terminal Classic

ANTONIA E. FOIAS, CHRISTINA T. HALPERIN, ELLEN SPENSLEY
MORIARTY, AND JEANETTE CASTELLANOS

Social stratification has been considered one of the central features of complex societies (A. Chase and D. Chase 1992, 1996; Elson and Covey 2006; G. Marcus 1983, 1992; Garraty 2000; Smith and Schreiber 2005, 2006). It is predicated on significant differences in wealth, status, and power between members of a society, but details of the nature of the socioeconomic strata and the actual differences in power, wealth, and status among these strata in ancient civilizations merit further investigation.

Social classes have been defined in a myriad of ways by scholars. Classical Marxist theory separates classes based on ownership of the means of production. However, Marx also spoke of the existence of class consciousness, or the awareness of individuals in each class that they pertain to it. Whether such class consciousness developed among pre-Hispanic Mesoamerican societies is questionable as significant vertical kinship ties crosscut economic-based distinctions (see also A. Chase and D. Chase 1992, 11). The Classical Marxist definition of class relies on demonstrating ownership of the means of production, which in the case of agrarian societies in premodern times was land, the principal resource for production. Landownership has been hard to pinpoint archaeologically, although most Maya scholars agree that the dominant land practice was small-scale ownership by families, lineages, houses ("maison"), or communities,[1] rather than centralized under elite estates (these would have also existed but as separate entities from commoner landholdings; see also discussion in D. Chase and A. Chase 1992, 309).

The concept of social status, inherited status, or *estate* is another aspect of Maya social stratification systems. Among Mesoamerican scholars, the term *estate* often refers to birthrights and obligations separating a noble "class" or "inherited status" from a commoner "class" or "inherited status" (Hicks 1999, 409–10), and likely corresponds to some degree with lordly titles (e.g., *k'ujul ajaw, ajaw*; see Martin and Grube 2000; Stuart 1993). These *estates* or inherited social statuses are ethnohistorically defined by rights and responsibilities. Nevertheless, the exercise of these hereditary privileges would have varied in practice as not all members of the elite estate possessed the same quantity of resources or engaged in the same politicking strategies.

Political scientists have been inclined to define class based on differences in political power (G. Marcus 1983, 1992), and such an approach has been pursued by some archaeologists (e.g., Hicks 1999). Hicks defines "class" as "persons in a society who stand in a similar relationship to the apparatus of control and who possess similar amounts of power over allocation of wealth and privilege" (1999, 410). But determining political power archaeologically in the absence of clear political insignia, apparel, and/or administrative tools may be difficult (A. Chase and D. Chase 1992, 3; Kowalewski, Feinman, and Finsten 1992; cf. Emerson 1997). If political power is closely connected to material wealth (as Hicks seems to imply), material indices of wealth could provide one measure of political power. A. Chase and D. Chase (1996, 2001) follow this political definition of class, recognizing three classes with a middle one of bureaucrats. Elson and Covey (2006, 8) and Brumfiel (2006, 166) also pursue this definition by considering intermediate elites as the lower level officials or provincial authorities.

Another approach to social stratification expands on these political-based (or politico-economic-based) systems by tying in craft specialization with a middle class. Although he defines the Aztec class system based on differences in political power, Hicks (1999) describes the middle class as consisting of six major groups that have mostly clear specializations: "(1) lesser political officials, (2) stewards in charge of labor and goods, (3) artisans in the luxury trades, (4) merchants [of fancier items or resources] . . . (5) ritual and ideological specialists, (6) enforcers and military professionals" (413). Adams (1970), Becker (1973), Sharer (1994), and Schortman and Urban (2004) also outline the importance of craft specialization in creating a middle-status group (possibly class) in the Maya region. However, we also know that crafting was associated with the upper class, whose members could be sculptors, wood-carvers, shell and lapidary jewelry artisans, painters, or scribes (Reents-Budet 1994, 1998; Inomata 2001b). Hence, crafting appears to crosscut other economic and estate inequalities.

Rather than focusing on issues of classification, Garraty (2000, 324) presents a more practice-oriented concept of "eliteness" founded on the same three dimensions: political power, estate,[2] and wealth. Elites demonstrate their social positions through practices such as "overt consumption and display, especially during feast occasions" (ibid., 323). They differentiate themselves from other groups through "*practices* used to establish and socially reproduce the unequal 'distributive systems' of wealth, power, and estate" (ibid.). We endeavor to approach social stratification at Motul de San José from a perspective similar to Garraty's.

The nature of social stratification in Classic Maya society has been under scrutiny for a long time. One current debate is whether Maya society was divided into two or three major social strata.[3] This is intimately tied to political and economic questions about the Classic Maya states (discussed by Foias and Emery, this volume). The "centralist camp" among Maya political scholars proposes that a three-class system existed during Classic times, with a commoner-farmer stratum at the bottom; a middle "class" of bureaucrats, crafts artisans, and merchants; and a top elite "class" (see A. Chase 1992; A. Chase and D. Chase 1992, 1996; Haviland and Moholy-Nagy 1992). The "decentralist camp" proposes a less stratified society with two major strata (commoner and elite; see, e.g., J. Marcus 1992, 1995), although several subdivisions within these two classes probably existed. The three-class system is based on interpretations of Classic Maya economies as vibrant, with strong craft specialization (A. Chase and D. Chase 1992, 9; Sharer 1994). In contrast, the two-class system assumes a view of Maya economies that are relatively small scale and self-sufficient. Other scholars have preferred to use the concept of heterarchy as an alternative to social hierarchy (Ehrenreich, Crumley, and Levy 1995; Scarborough, Valdez Jr., and Dunning 2003). But, as Smith and Schreiber (2005, 205) reflect, heterarchy (or horizontal complexity) is part of all complex systems, and hence both hierarchy and heterarchy should be considered. The crux of the debate is whether the social, political, and economic systems are perfectly articulated, where differentials in political power aligned perfectly with differentials in economic wealth, inherited position of status, and craft specialization. We would argue that such a proposition is highly unlikely for the Classic Maya, as described below.

Moving beyond such simple debates (Smith and Schreiber 2005) and general models of Maya social stratification, it would be important to understand what it meant to be a commoner and how he or she lived, in comparison to what it meant to be a middle-rank or an elite individual in Classic Maya society (see comments in Smith and Schreiber 2005, 205). Abrams (1994) has approached such questions by considering distinctions between labor investment in the residences of royal elite, secondary elite, and commoners at Copán. Abrams estimates that the royal palaces in the Main Group at Copán required several tens of thousands of person-days of labor (thirty thousand person-days for Str. 22), whereas subroyal palaces such as in Group 8N-11 required between three thousand and ten thousand person-days (in Webster et al. 1998), and rural commoner structures only necessitated between sixteen and 150 person-days (Gonlin 1993). Such major differences argue for significant social stratification. Architectural volume, elaborateness, and/or labor investment have been used by many archaeologists as a measure of socioeconomic status (e.g., M. Smith 1987; Tourtellot, Sabloff, and Carmean 1992; Palka 1997). We have also used architectural volume to model social stratification at Motul de San José. However, because extensive architectural excavations have been limited,[4] structural volume can only serve as one index of the socioeconomic pyramid.

Although elaborate or major architecture marks differential control over labor (authoritative resources for power [Giddens 1984, 373] and, inferentially, wealth and symbolic), artifactual distributions record the activities and practices that took place within patio groups that served to identify its residents as pertaining to particular social groups (Garraty 2000; M. Smith 1987). Hence, another aspect of our investigation at Motul de San José has focused on patterns of production and consumption in both foods and artifactual goods, and of access to exotic or labor-intensive artifacts. For example, productive activities were suggested by differential distributions of ground stone, spindle whorls, chert and bone tool debris, and figurine and pottery wasters, highlighting that different social strata were involved in distinct activities at different scales and/or intensity. The consumption of exotics (A. Chase and D. Chase 1992, 4) and/or hypertrophic (or labor-intensive; Clark and Parry 1990) artifacts provides a final reflection on differences in power, status, wealth, and practice among the social strata of Motul de San José.

Architectural Volumetrics

Architectural patterns detected from surface surveys provide one of the most common criteria for classifying and ranking Maya social groups.

Typologies of architectural groups, or clusters of mounds, that attempt to measure rank or wealth differentials throughout a region often consider group and mound size because they provide relative indicators for labor investment required in their construction and presumably also served as inscribed symbols of wealth and power (Abrams 1989, 1994; Ashmore 2007, 58–66; Hendon 1992b; Palka 1997; Tourtellot 1988). For example, the typology established by the Harvard University expedition in the Copán Valley, Honduras, considers mound height, number of mounds, number of patios, and building materials to create a four-tiered architectural group ranking system (Willey and Leventhal 1979).

The heuristic typology used here also considers architectural group size, but in the form of architectural group volume. It, thus, combines surface area (which partially reflects the size and the number of patios and mounds in each group), with architecture heights. Architectural volumes were calculated from data retrieved from the 1998–2001 field season total station survey of the Motul de San José site core and northern and eastern peripheries using the 3-D Analyst tools within a Geographic Information Systems (GIS) software program (ArcGIS). Calculations followed methods employed by the Yalahau Regional Human Ecology Project (Sorensen, Glover, and Fedick 2003). Substructures or formal platforms were included in the calculations if detected by the surveyors. Fine-tuned calculations of labor investment by individual architectural features (e.g., stucco flooring versus fill) into person-days of labor (see Abrams 1994; Arnold and Ford 1980) were not attempted.

Volumetrics were calculated for sixty-nine groups, which were divided into three categories, Rank 1–3 (defined below). Our discussion here, however, excludes groups identified as exclusively civic-ceremonial in nature (e.g., groups 7M1, 7M2, 7M3, 7L1, 7K1, 8K3, 9L4) bringing our total to sixty-two residential groups (Table 4.1, Figure 4.1). Rank 1 architectural groups were the largest and possessed volumes greater than 6,797 cubic meters. These groups are associated with the major architectural groups at the site (named using letters,[5] Groups A through E, see description in Foias and Emery, this volume). They are clustered within the epicenter of the site adjacent to the temple-pyramid complexes, public plazas, and stela monuments.

A natural break occurs between the lower end of Rank 1 and the upper end of Rank 2 architectural groups, which ranged between 4,443 and 1,100 cubic meters. These groups may have been associated with middle-status inhabitants and are located both in the epicenter and peripheral zones of

Architectural Group Volumetrics

Rank 1   Rank 2   Rank 3

[Chart: Volume (m) on y-axis from 0 to 70000; x-axis from 0 to 70. A single high point near 65000 at left, remaining points descending rapidly below 10000.]

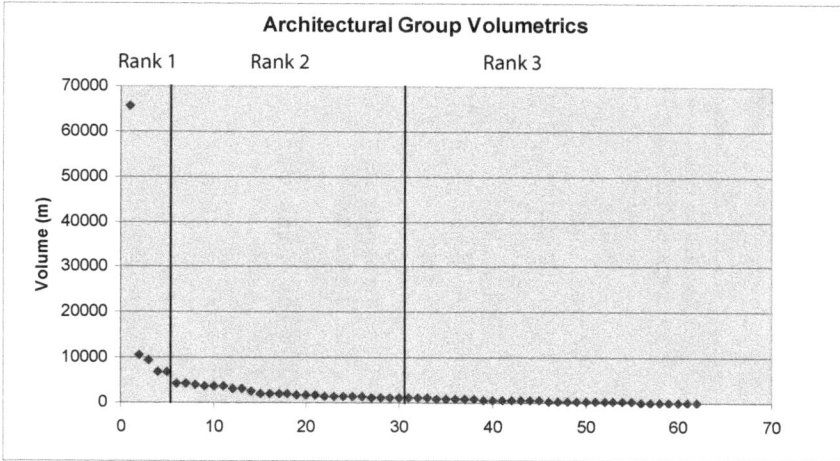

Figure 4.1. Definition of three ranks of groups based on architectural group volumetrics.

Motul. However, the common use of stone roof vaults among this rank suggests that they are not necessarily nonelite (but see discussion in Tourtellot, Sabloff, and Carmean 1992).

The smallest architectural groups, Rank 3, possessed volumes of less than 1,100 cubic meters and probably represent the lower echelons of the social structure. These groups are scattered throughout the site. Whereas the break between Rank 2 and 3 is somewhat arbitrary as no natural break occurs, some attempt was made to exclude groups with vaulted architecture, as identified by surface evidence, from Rank 3 (although see the review of excavation data below for possible exceptions).

This volumetric ranking system provides only general and preliminary status parameters as much variability in architectural form and consumption patterns occurs within and between groups as discussed below. It also ignores internal variation of structure size and type within each group as well as the groups' distance to the civic-ceremonial center. Furthermore, it does not account for variations in time-depth in which labor investments may have occurred gradually over time as a result of multiple refurbishings of a structure rather than its construction in a single episode. This inconsistency is counterbalanced, to some degree, in that these larger kin groups may have possessed better access to land, and, thus, resources, in what McAnany (1995, 96–99) calls the "principal of first occupancy."

The use of architecture volume to detect possible differences in socioeconomic status is useful because it provides an easy means to compare

Table 4.1. List of Motul de San José groups, their architectural volume, rank, excavation operation, and group type

Subarea	Group	Op	Details	Volume (m)	Volume rank	Inferred context[a]	Settlement type[b]
Site core	8L	2,5,6		65,740.698	1	Residential	NA[c]
Site core	8K5&6	12, 14	Entire group	10,600.56	1	Residential	6
Site core	8M7	15	Entire group	9,566.168	1	Residential	5
Site core	7J1	9		7,018.391	1	Residential	6
Site core	7J2	8	Includes "patio"	6,796.535	1	Residential	6
North periphery	10L2&3	26	Entire group	4,443.337	2	Residential	2
Site core	7J4	10	Includes "patio"	4,437.032	2	Residential	
Site core	9L7	30		3,998.421	2	Residential	2
North periphery	11L1	36	Entire group	3,851.028	2	Residential	3
Site core	8L2	29		3,824.69	2	Residential	2
Site core	8L4	32		3,752.842	2	Residential	2
North periphery	11N3	43	Entire group	3,205.984	2	Residential	2or5
Site core	8M6	1		3,065.945	2	Residential	2
Site core	8L3	33	Entire group	2,440.044	2	Residential	2
North periphery	10M3	39	Entire group	2,065.575	2	Residential	2or5
North periphery	12M1	35	Entire group	2,054.919	2	Residential	2or5
Site core	9K2	NA		1,900.275	2	Residential	2
Site core	8L5	46		1,878.999	2	Residential	NA
Site core	9K3	NA		1,715.45	2	Residential	2
Site core	9L3	20		1,640.475	2	Residential	2
Site core	9L6	20		1,613.005	2	Residential	5
Site core	8M2	NA	Entire group	1,545.624	2	Residential	1
North periphery	10K2	NA	Entire group	1,480.843	2	Residential	2or5
Site core	8L1	19	Entire group	1,464.623	2	Residential	2

Location	Code	No.	Description	Area	Level	Type	No.
Site core	8J1	9		1,349.235	2	Residential	2
Site core	8K2	7	West of causeway	1,325.696	2	Residential	
North periphery	10M1	NA	Entire group	1,265.08	2	Residential	3
Site core	7K2	16, 27	Structures, patio not included	1,168.331	2	Residential	2or5
Site core	8K1	NA	West of causeway	1,137.304	2	Residential	2
North periphery	10N1	NA	Entire group	1,090.867	3	Residential	
North periphery	11N2	42	Entire group	1,067.871	3	Residential	1
North periphery	11M2	NA	Entire group	1,062.265	3	Residential	1
Site core	9L1&2	NA	Entire group	1,026.687	3	Residential	1
East periphery	10P2	NA	Three str. group	984.165	3	Residential	2
Site core	7N2	NA	Estimate only	923.208	3	Residential	2
Site core	8M4	18	Entire group	851.106	2	Residential	2
Site core	6J1	13		847.482	3	Residential	2
North periphery	11L2	38		730.567	3	Residential	1
North periphery	9M3	23	Entire group	697.761	3	Residential	5
Site core	8K4	NA	Both east and west structures; north of Op.12	662.626	3	Residential	2
Site core	8M5	17	Entire group	605.75	3	Residential	2
Site core	9K4	7	Both east and west structures	574.518	3	Residential	
North periphery	11M1	31	Entire group	560.974	3	Residential	1
North periphery	9M1	NA	Entire group	491.743	3	Residential	1
East periphery	9O1	NA		456.875	3	Residential	1
North periphery	9M2	24,25	Entire group	424.403	3	Residential	2
North periphery	10L1	NA	Entire group	392.006	3	Residential	2
Site core	7J3	10	Entire group	389.275	3	Residential	
North periphery	9M4	NA	Entire group	239.287	3	Residential	1
East periphery	8P1	NA		222.614	3	Residential	1
East periphery	9P3	NA	Four str. group next to quarries	219.471	3	Residential	1

(continued)

Table 4.1. (Continued)

Subarea	Group	Op	Details	Volume (m)	Volume rank	Inferred context[a]	Settlement type[b]
North periphery	11N1	45	Entire group	211.679	3	Residential	1
East periphery	9P1	NA	Isolated structure	192.966	3	Residential	2or5
East periphery	9P5	NA	Isolated structure	192.609	3	Residential	1
East periphery	10P1	NA	Isolated structure	184.777	3	Residential	1
North periphery	10K1	NA	Entire group	137.692	3	Residential	1
North periphery	10M4	39	Entire group	118.983	3	Residential	1
North periphery	10M2	40	Entire group	67.013	3	Residential	1
East periphery	8P2	NA		58.632	3	Residential	1
East periphery	9P2	NA	Isolated structure	51.392	3	Residential	2or5
East periphery	9P6	NA		51.392	3	Residential	1
East periphery	9P4	NA	Two str. group	25.181	3	Residential	1
Site core	7M3	3	Southern Pyramid & associated small strs.	9,962.778	1	Public	NA
Site core	7M1	4	Twin Temples & associated stela platform	9,162.256	1	Public	NA
Site core	9L4	21	Pyramid at end of causeway	3,291.429	2	Public	NA
Site core	8K3	causeway	Sacbe only; does not include auxiliary str.	1,627.88	2	Public	NA
Site core	7K1	11	Group B; pyramid, extension, stela platform	1,574.108	2	Public	NA
Site core	7L1	NA	Pyramid (south of Acropolis; NW of largest pyramid)	1,001.436	3	Public	NA
Site core	8K7	NA	Structure north of Group B's pyramid	102.982	3	Public	NA

[a] Some residential groups likely held multiple functions.

[b] Settlement types proposed by Moriarty (2004) are based partly on shape and layout of architectural groups (see Figure 4.2 for illustrations of these types).

[c] Not applicable (either because no excavation took place in that group, or because it was not classified by Moriarty).

groups in *relative* terms using a single variable. It also avoids the wholesale borrowing of architectural typologies based on the presence or absence of features that may not adequately fit with the Motul data. For example, Tourtellot, Sabloff, and Carmean (1992, tables 6.1, 6.2) compared architecture types between the major centers of Sayil and Seibal to find that stone buildings with or without vaulted roofs are significantly more abundant at the former site (51.9 percent of mapped buildings) than the latter (8.8 percent of excavated structures). They suggested that particular architectural features, such as vaulted buildings, do not signify an "ever-present" connection with elites, but must be contextualized within the *range* of architectural elements present within each site (ibid., 88). In addition, the focus on architectural volume avoids the problem associated with counting structures from surface surveys as these counts do not always correlate with those identified after excavations (Hendon 1992b).

The investigation of architectural volume complements the Motul de San José settlement classification by Moriarty (2004d, 28–30, fig. 4), which considers the number of structures as well as the shape and layout of a group's architectural features detected from surface survey (Figure 4.2). This classification omits civic-ceremonial buildings and is restricted to groups presumed to have been, in whole or in part, residences. The focus on shape and layout draws on previous research by Becker (1999, 2003b), who designates different "plaza plans" at the site of Tikal. These plaza plans conform to an "architectural grammar" that is thought to have been the basis of differences in group function or social organization (e.g., corporate groups, occupation, ethnicities, moieties) and have been understood by the Maya builders and users of the groups (see also Ashmore 2007, 55–58, 137–47; Hageman and Lohse 2003).

Although it is unclear, based on present data, what type of social organization the plaza plans may manifest at Tikal, Becker (2004) argues that they were heterarchical because they occur in various sizes and degrees of elaboration. Similarly, the Motul de San José settlement classification crosscuts volumetric rankings. For example, settlement classification Type V, which contains a ritual structure on the eastern side of the group (as in Becker's Plaza Plan 2), is represented in volumetric Ranks 1, 2, and 3, and Type II, which comprise formal groups of two to seven structures arranged around a square or rectangular patio, is represented in both volumetric Ranks 2 and 3. Both the Motul de San José settlement and volumetric typologies provide heuristic categories about hierarchy (and possibly heterarchy), but do not form a priori assumptions. We will use the volumetric ranking as

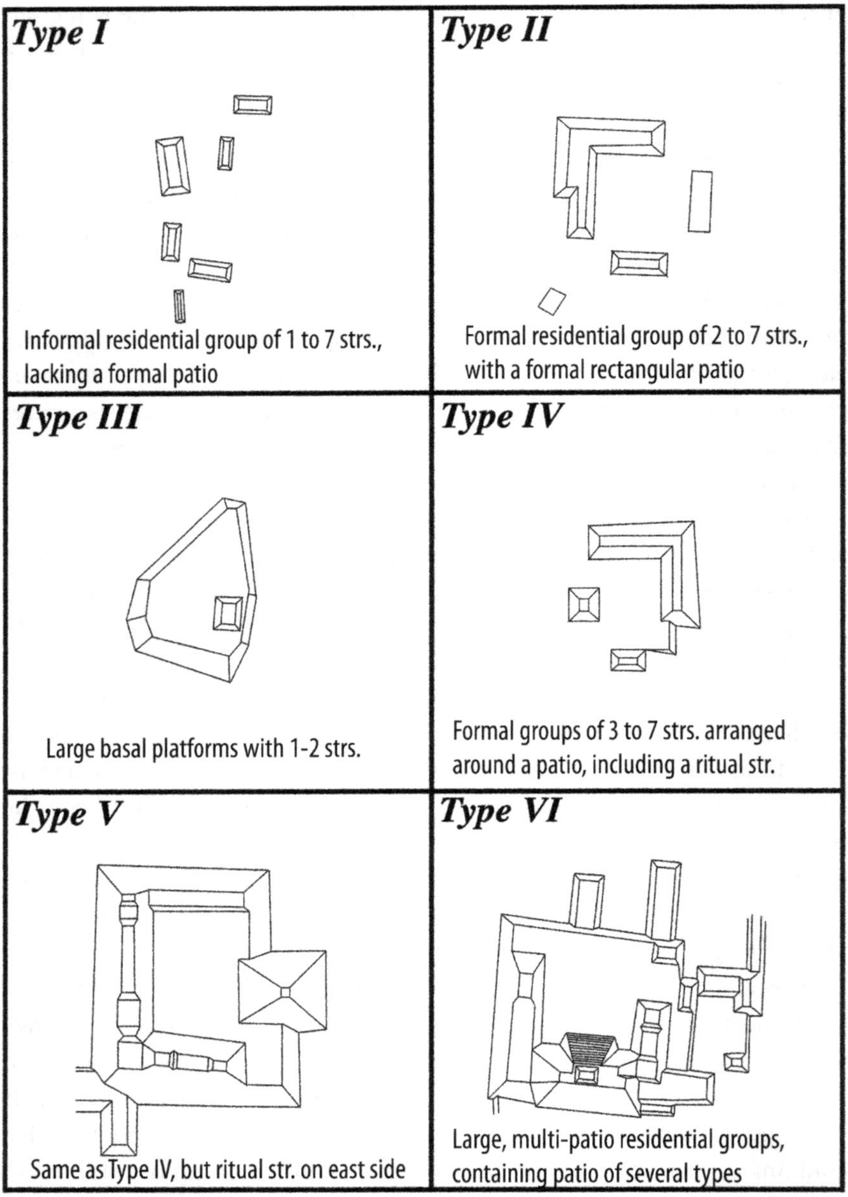

Type I	Type II
Informal residential group of 1 to 7 strs., lacking a formal patio	Formal residential group of 2 to 7 strs., with a formal rectangular patio
Type III	Type IV
Large basal platforms with 1-2 strs.	Formal groups of 3 to 7 strs. arranged around a patio, including a ritual str.
Type V	Type VI
Same as Type IV, but ritual str. on east side	Large, multi-patio residential groups, containing patio of several types

Figure 4.2. Definition of group types in the Motul de San José zone based on architectural features and number of structures (modified from Moriarty 2004d, 28–30, fig. 4).

a heuristic device in which the results of further excavations and artifact analyses can be considered. It is to these directions that we now turn.

Excavations, Architecture, and Stratification

The Motul de San José Archaeological Project conducted mostly small-scale excavations and a few extensive horizontal operations from 1998 to 2005 (Figure 1.2). These aimed to establish the chronological and material parameters of the site through time. Specific plaza groups were targeted both randomly and intuitively. For example, looted groups were selected because they required stabilization or salvage. In this section, we summarize the extensive excavations carried out in the epicenter and near periphery (North Zone) to underscore the complexity of architecture and the differences in labor investment between and within volumetric ranks during the Late and Terminal Classic periods.

Operations 2 and 15 explored Rank 1 groups that represent the most complex constructions at the site, and so pertained to elites, and more specifically, upper or royal elites (Figure 1.2). Operation 2 targeted the northern building (Str. 8L-9) in the northwest corner (Court #4) of the Acropolis in Group C (Figure 4.3, Figure 6.1). Because the Acropolis is the single largest architectural complex at Motul and is directly associated with the Main Plaza (or Plaza I) that hosts six of the seven[6] stelae found at the site, we suggest that it served as the royal court and residence of its paramount rulers at the heyday of the site during the Late Classic.

In Operation 2, the exposed stone vaulted Str. 8L-9 (measuring 20 meters in length by 4 meters in width, with an average height of 1.5–2 meters) is comprised of three principal rooms (separated by internal dividing walls), each opening south to the plaza of Court #4 (Castellanos 2000). This is a typical plan of lowland "palaces" (or elite, residential range structures) of the Late Classic. Complete excavation of the east and central rooms showed each to be dominated by a massive bench (2 meters by 5.84 meters and 0.66 meters high), and it is likely that the third room to the west is as well (ibid.; Figure 4.4). The two rooms had broad doorways, 2.20 and 2.10 meters wide. Walls of this three-room palace were constructed mostly of irregular slab stones with thick stucco veneer.[7] This construction style is characteristic of Motul during the Late Classic, as it is also visible in the south pyramid and the twin eastern temple-pyramids in the Main Plaza, the three single major constructions at the site. Because the pottery associated with this structure pertains to a more restricted period between AD 680/700 and

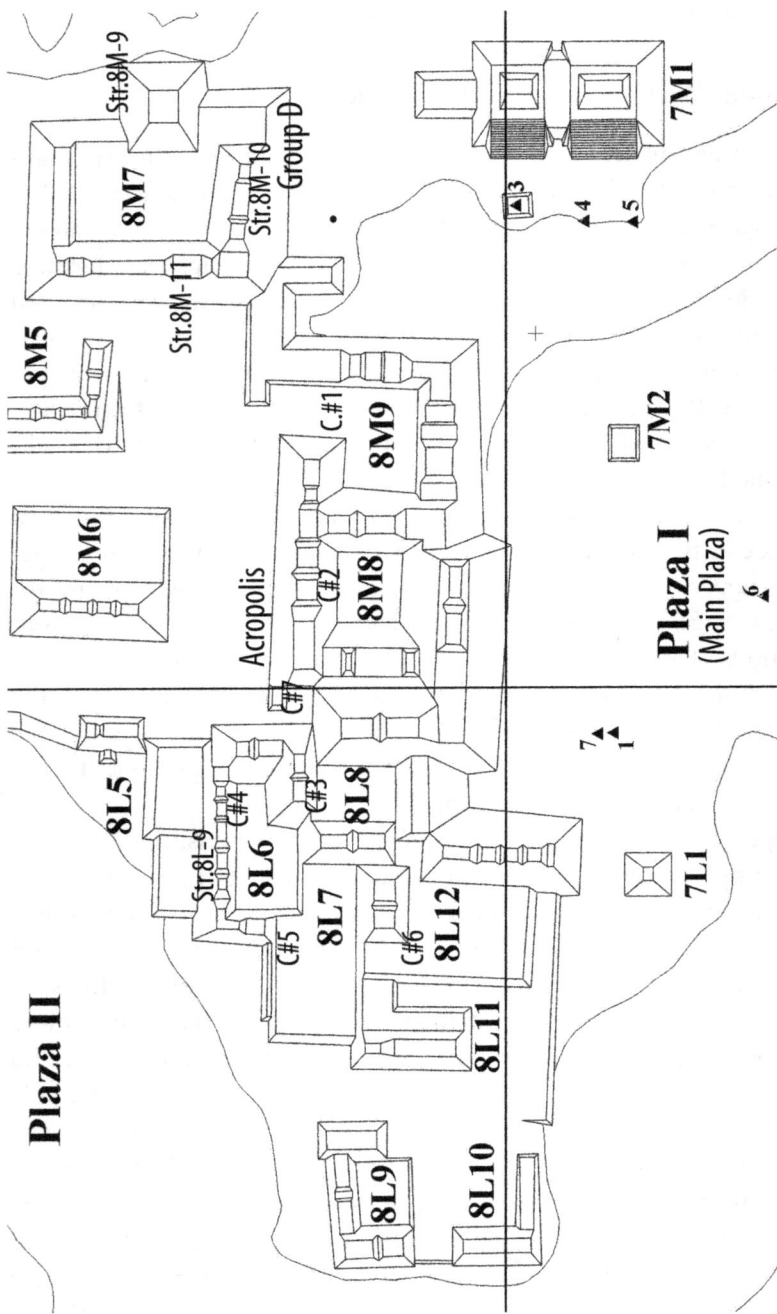

Figure 4.3. Close-up of Groups C and D, showing Strs. 8L-9 in the Acropolis (Operation MSJ2A), and Strs. 8M-9, 10, 11 in Group D (Operation MSJ15).

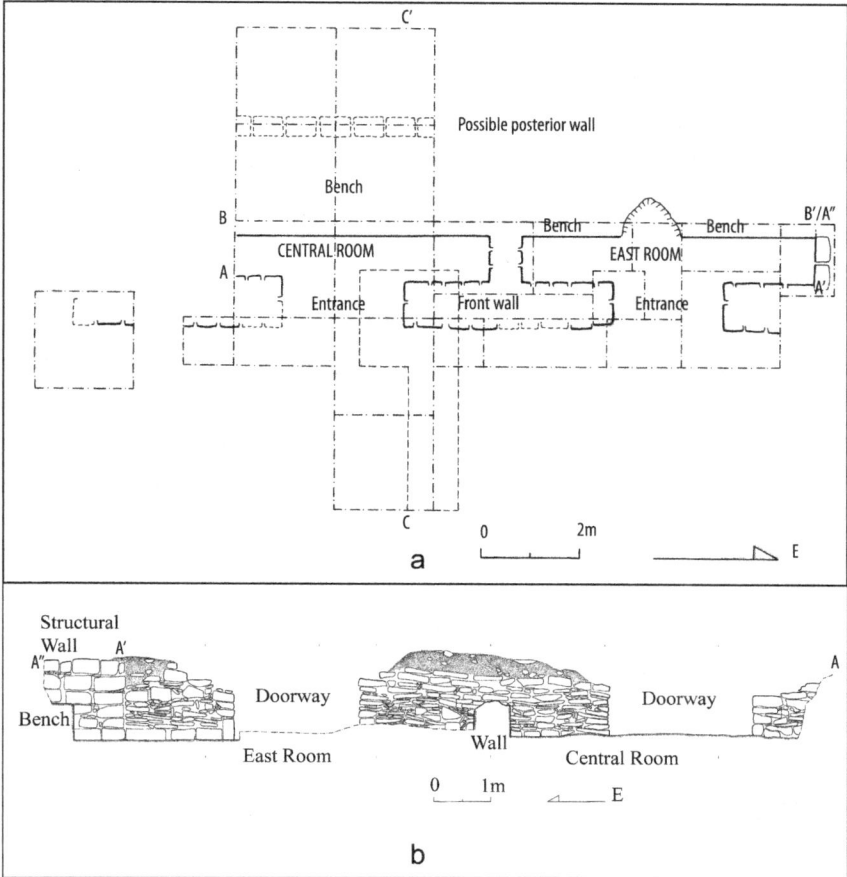

Figure 4.4. a. Plan of excavations in Str. 8L-9 (Operation MSJ2A, all drawings by Luis Luin, unless otherwise specified); b. east–west profile of interior of the south and east walls in Str. 8L-9, along profile line A-A'. Profiles along lines B-B' and C-C' available at http://motul-archaeology.williams.edu.

830 (Tepeu 2), we are able to more accurately date the major construction projects at Motul to this specific time period.

A hint about the possible identity of the residents of this palace was retrieved from both the massive secondary midden discovered behind it and from two ceramic artifacts found within it. The latter artifacts are fine polychrome sherds, typical of the Ik' Polychrome style (Halperin and Foias, this volume, Figure 6.5c). Most important, both have post-break use wear and shapes similar to sherd polishers used in a pottery workshop identified at K'axob, Belize (Lopez Varela, McAnany, and Berry 2001; Lopez Varela, van Gijn, and Jacobs 2002; McAnany 2004b). The deep midden found behind this palace also had the highest density of pottery and numerous other indices of pottery production (see Halperin and Foias, this volume). Thus, we hypothesize that this edifice was the residence of a royal scribe(s) or painter(s) of elaborate polychrome vessels, like the Ik' style.

Operation 15 exposed two buildings in Group D, which is a smaller major group in the epicenter, situated along the eastern edge of the Acropolis and the northeastern limit of the Main Plaza (Figure 1.2, Figure 4.3). The discovery of a looted royal tomb in the eastern pyramid of this group identifies the rank of this compound as royal elite, although in architectural volume, it is dwarfed by Groups C and B. The location of the tomb in the small eastern pyramid, its architecture consisting of a chamber partly dug into bedrock, and the thick layers of chert (mixed with some obsidian) covering the flat slab roof are typical of royal tombs in the Tikal area and in the Petexbatún region—where the Dos Pilas dynasty is known to have been a branch of the Tikal royal lineage (Houston 1993; Martin and Grube 2000; Figure 4.5). Furthermore, even though looted, there were numerous artifacts found within the chamber that are indicative of a royal interment: jade (ten complete or fragmented beads, twenty mosaic pieces); shell, including spondylus and mother of pearl (seventy-seven whole or fragmented beads; 145 pieces of mosaic; eleven fragmented or complete medium-size spondylus shells; at least one fragment is carved and painted with red); pyrite (ninety-eight mosaic pieces); stingray spine (one complete); two small broken polychrome vessels (Foias, Foster, and Spensley 2000, figs. 4.9–4.11). Only a few remains of the human skeleton were recovered, but these were all painted red (possibly with cinnabar). Such ritual is typical of ancestor worship where the tombs of important ancestors are revisited and the bones are painted (and sometimes removed) as part of veneration rites (McAnany 1995). Thus, it seems likely that this was an important royal ancestor, if not the founder of the Motul de San José royal dynasty, as the fragmented pots recovered pertain to the Late Classic.

Whereas Operation 2 gives us insight into the royal court of the Late Classic period, Operation 15 offers us a window into the royal elite of the Terminal Classic period (AD 830–950) when these structures were last occupied.[8]

The architecture of Str. 8M-11 (the western building in Group D) appears more conducive to public rather than private affairs, and therefore, it is possible that this represents a special purpose structure, at least in its final form. This edifice does not have the typical architectural plan of a

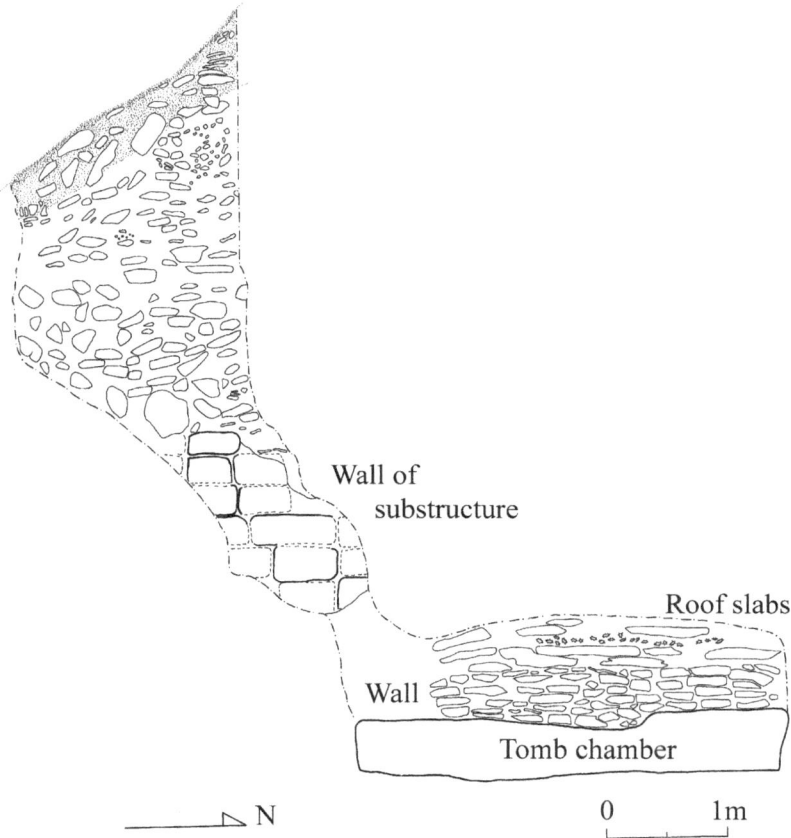

Figure 4.5. Profile of looting trench (sub-Operation MSJ15F) in the eastern pyramid of Group D, showing the royal tomb chamber at the base.

Late Classic "palace" (Figures 4.6, 4.8), but resembles Terminal Classic and Postclassic residences of the Central Petén Lakes region (Pugh 2004; D. Rice 1986, 1988) and possibly the open halls of the Late Postclassic Yucatán (Pugh 2003, figs. 5, 6). We explored two rooms (designated north and south). It is possible that a third room, the mirror image of the south room, was attached at the north end (Figure 4.8). The northern room (the largest) consisted of two long and narrow, parallel (or tandem) galleries with the back gallery slightly higher (Figures 4.6–4.9). The reconstructed north to south length of these galleries was approximately 12.20 meters, whereas the interior width of the back gallery was a very narrow 1.2 meters. The back gallery had stuccoed masonry walls that rose 0.5 meters above the interior stucco floor, but lacked a stone roof and benches. The masonry construction of the back gallery is distinct from the slab style seen in Operation 2 and in the large temple-pyramids of the Main Plaza: here, walls consist of rectangular, dressed blocks made of relatively soft limestone, with thin stucco veneer. The southern room of Str. 8M-11 has a more typical Late Classic palace plan: it is rectangular in shape, with thick masonry walls, and an L-shaped bench that covers almost completely the interior of the room (Figure 4.6). This is the only stone vaulted space in the western structure, and may have been a later addition because its masonry style of thin horizontal slab stones covered with thick stucco veneer (sometimes as thick as 10 centimeters) conforms to the style seen in Operation 2. Two entrances made its interior quite public: the main door faced toward the south (2.1 meters wide), and the western door (2 meters wide) faced west (Figure 4.6). Numerous artifacts were found directly in front of the south doorway, mixed with wall fall or directly on the exterior terrace floor. As none of these were complete, we suspect that they are from nearby refuse deposits and were brought here in a rite of termination for the building or for the whole group during the Terminal Classic, after this room was burnt.

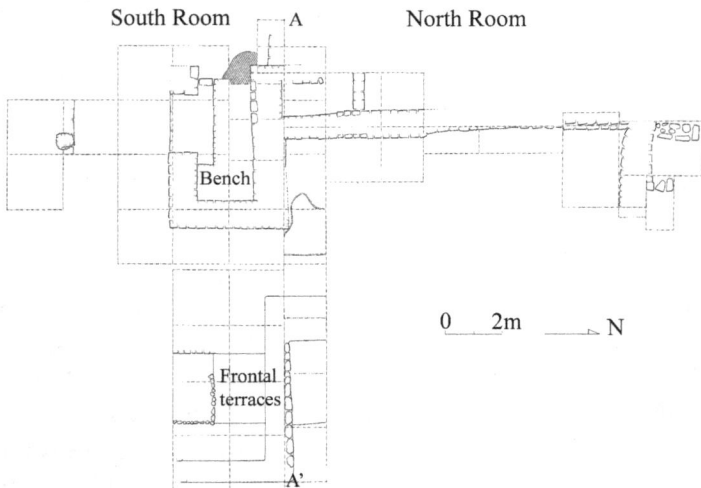

Figure 4.6. Plan of excavations in Str. 8M-11. Profile along line A-A' is shown in the next illustration. Hatched area is the original looting.

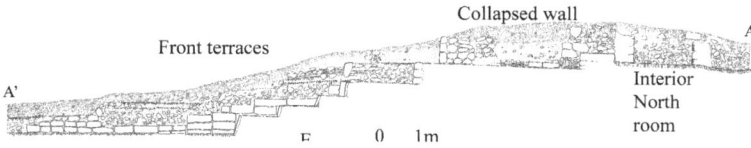

Figure 4.7. Profile of Str. 8M-11 along east–west line A-A'.

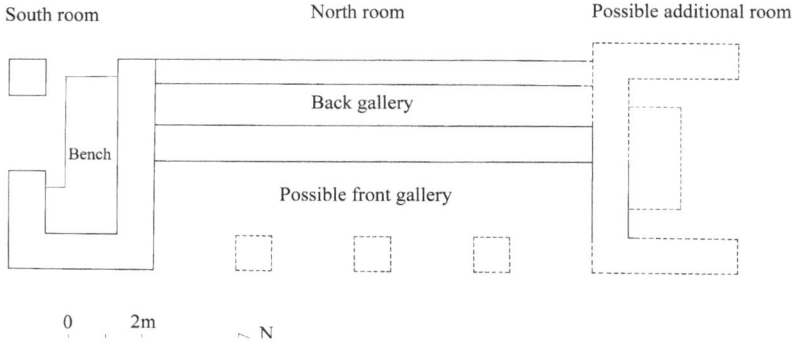

Figure 4.8. Artist's reconstruction of Str. 8M-11 in its final version. Dashed lines are reconstructed features.

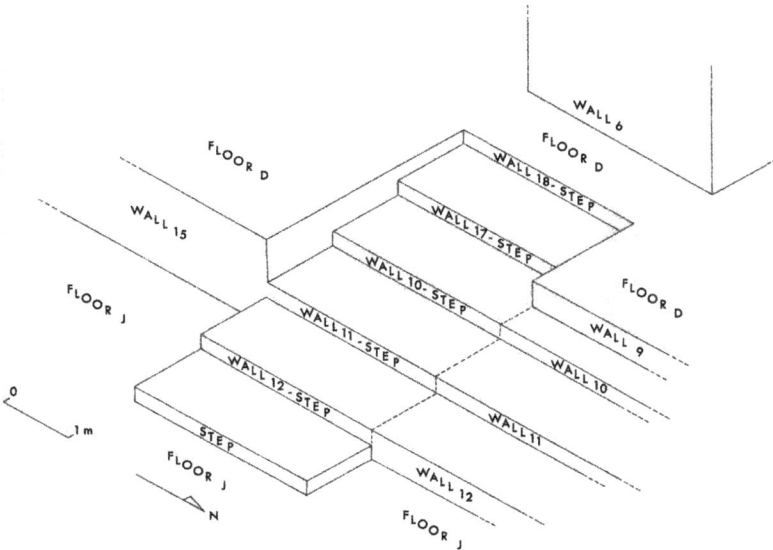

Figure 4.9. Artist's reconstruction of the front terraces and stairway of Str. 8M-11 in its earlier version.

Excavation of the southern structure in Group D (Str. 8M-10) has yielded evidence of two rooms (both with masonry vaults), although only the main room was completely exposed (Alvarez, Castillo, and Foias 2001; Figure 4.10). About two-thirds of the interior space was covered by three benches: the main bench against the back wall that had high armrests, and two lateral and smaller benches on the east and west that extended from the front wall to the back wall. The doorway providing access to the main room is very wide, measuring 2.4 meters. The second side room of this building opened toward the east, rather than the north as the main room. Hence, this building seems to have had a similar plan to the western building: a main room that opened toward the courtyard had attached one (or possibly two) side rooms that

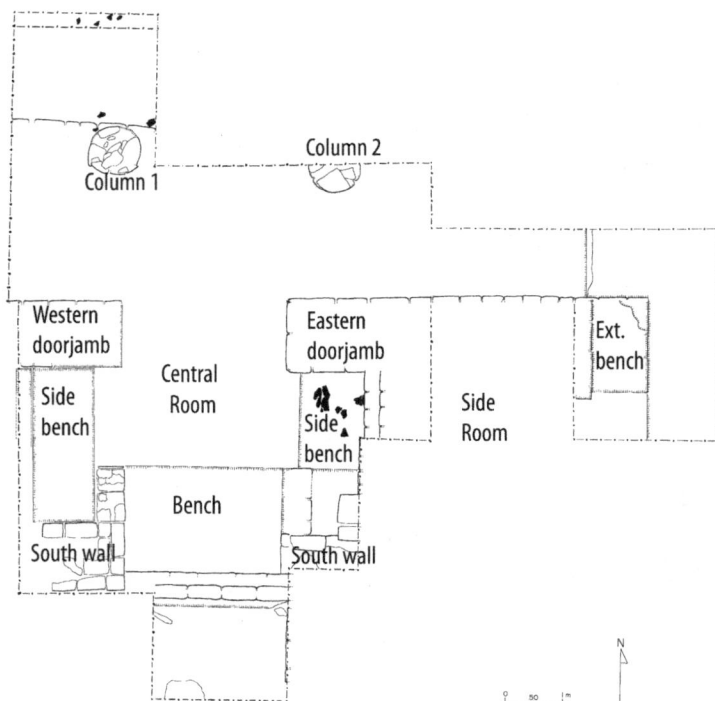

Figure 4.10. Plan of excavations in the southern Str. 8M-10, showing central room with three benches, smaller side room with exterior bench, and two round columns in frontal patio.

opened away from the patio. The eastern room of the south palace had an exterior bench (1.4 meters long by 0.80 meters wide by 0.4 meters high) built against the south wall of the room, immediately to the north of the doorjamb.

Operation 15 is the largest undertaking at Motul up to date, and has revealed the most complex and longest stratigraphy, beginning in the Middle Preclassic (600–300 BC). Group D was also extensively occupied in the Terminal Classic (with activities possibly continuing into the Postclassic). The two explored structures appear to have had multiple functions, including domestic ones (as domestic refuse was associated with both), but this operation had the greatest variety in its artifacts, pointing to numerous economic activities carried out by its residents (see below). Foias (in Alvarez, Castillo, and Foias 2001) has hypothesized that the two structures may have been occupied by priests (and their families?) who were responsible for the cult of the venerated royal ancestor buried in the eastern pyramid. Alternatively, these structures were occupied by the descendants of this royal ancestor, who could have also been responsible for the cult of their progenitor.

Three additional extensive operations targeted groups that pertain to Ranks 2 and 3: Operations 29, 31, and 42. Operation 29 explored two structures in Group 8L2 at the south end of the north-south avenue connecting Group E with Groups B and C (Figure 1.2; Ramirez, Sanchez, and Alvarado 2000). One of the two structures explored in Operation 29 revealed a stone vault, generally taken as a marker of elite status. Thus, we could initially categorize Rank 2 groups as secondary elites (but see discussion below). This operation produced a few examples of Terminal Classic diagnostic types, such as Fine Orange, suggesting that occupation in this part of the site continued into this later period. The southern structure (Str. 8L-28) is a typical Late Classic "palace" construction (Figure 4.11). It appears to have been a one-room building with a wide door (measuring between 2.5 meters and 2.95 meters) that opened toward the east. Its interior had a large half-meter-high bench that possessed arm supports and that likely ran the length of its back wall. The masonry roof was vaulted and the walls were preserved up to a significant height between 1.38 and 1.60 meters. Wall construction consisted of rectangular stones, many dressed (or well cut), with relatively thin stucco veneer. In front of this edifice, there was a small platform that may have been a bench, about 0.54 meters high, shaped probably as a cross (Figure 4.11).

The central structure (Str. 8L-27) was heavily remodeled and its overall plan is distinct from the southern building (Figure 4.12). We exposed two rooms, the main one facing south toward the south patio and the second

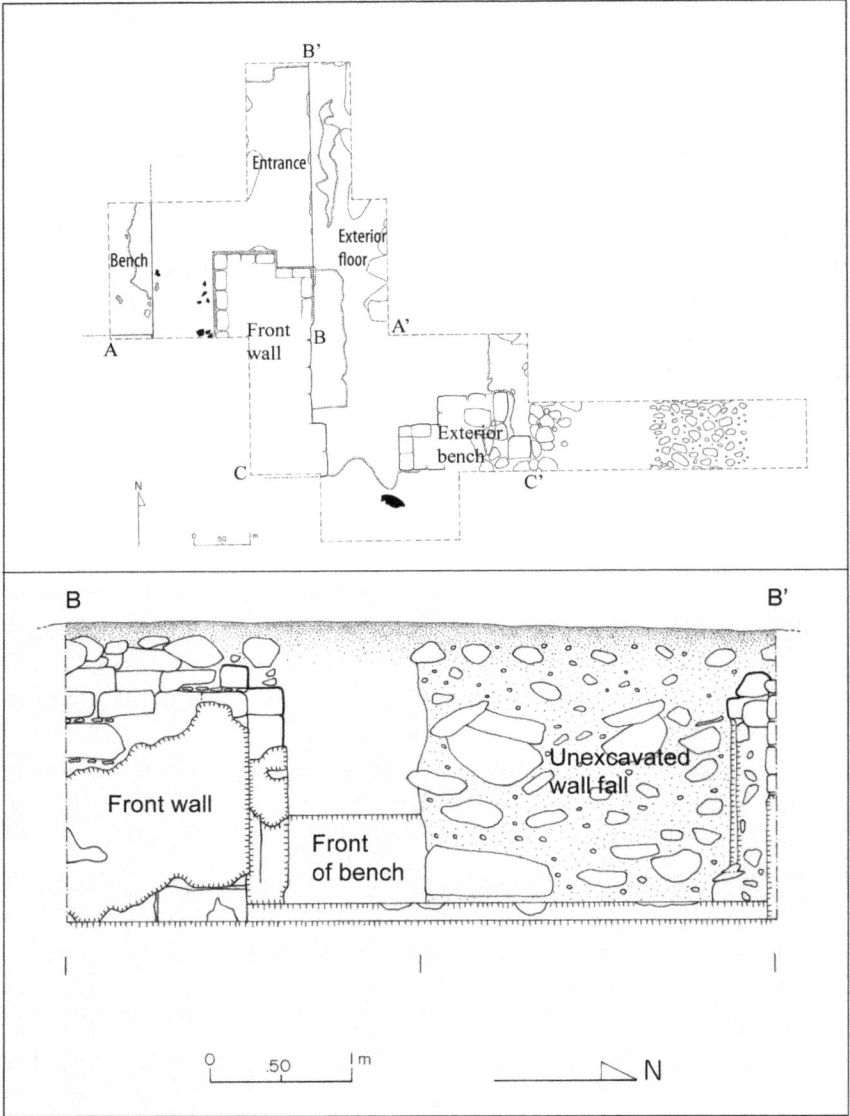

Figure 4.11a. Plan of excavations in southern Str. 8L-28 (MSJ29F), showing front wall with inset corners in the doorjambs and exterior corner, interior bench with armrest, and exterior bench; b. north–south profile (between B and B') of unit 29F-10 showing the front wall, inset doorjambs, and interior bench. Profiles along lines A-A' and C-C' available at http://motul-archaeology.williams.edu.

facing west (away from the patio). Both rooms lacked interior benches, had low stone walls (0.40–0.50 meters high), but were positioned on a 0.65-meter-high platform above the south plaza floor. The dividing wall between the main and the western rooms consisting of upright slab stones was a late addition that created two separate spaces out of one original room. Most fascinating is that even though the preserved walls appear to be quite low, several layers of large, thin slab stones were exposed embedded in the interior floor at sharp angles (about 70 degrees), suggesting that these were part of a rough stone vault (Halperin and Deckard 2001, 64). Only one door provided access into each room. The western door (1.34 meters wide at its narrowest point) of the side room contained one inset step between the interior and the exterior floor of the terrace. The south door (2.10 meters wide) of the main room had three inset steps that allowed access from the plaza into the high interior. The lack of benches in both rooms argues for a nondomestic function for this building, but artifacts found within and around the structure are suggestive of domestic occupation (maybe of the adjacent southern palace). The presence of inset steps in the doorways is also aberrant, and not seen in the other structures excavated at Motul. This architectural feature may be more characteristic of the Terminal Classic and even more so of the Postclassic, and suggests that these modifications to the central building of this group were done very late in its occupation, probably in the Terminal Classic.

Significantly, the architectural style in these two buildings was unique at Motul: both structural corners and doorjamb corners had double corners (see Figures 4.11, 4.12). This transformed the shape of each whole building into giant *I* or *T* letters. The doors can also be called "double-threshold" as seen in Puuc buildings at Uxmal. Because these notched corners were on the exterior rather than interior parts of the structures, they likely comprised some type of indexical communication or nonverbal social signifiers marking intracommunity distinction (Blanton 1994, 8–10).

In contrast to Rank 2, Rank 3 groups (Operations 31 and 42) are smaller constructions that generally lack stone vaults. However, as the excavations in Operation 31 revealed, the architecture can still be elaborate. It is difficult to conclude, then, that Rank 3 represents nonelite with such hypertrophic architecture. Hence, we may be seeing another third level of "eliteness" or "middle-rank" in the Rank 3 groups at Motul. Unfortunately, this would suggest that only "elites" lived at Motul de San José, an unlikely proposition.

Operation 31 is located approximately 1 kilometer north of Motul's Main Plaza, on another natural plateau (called the North Zone). The operation

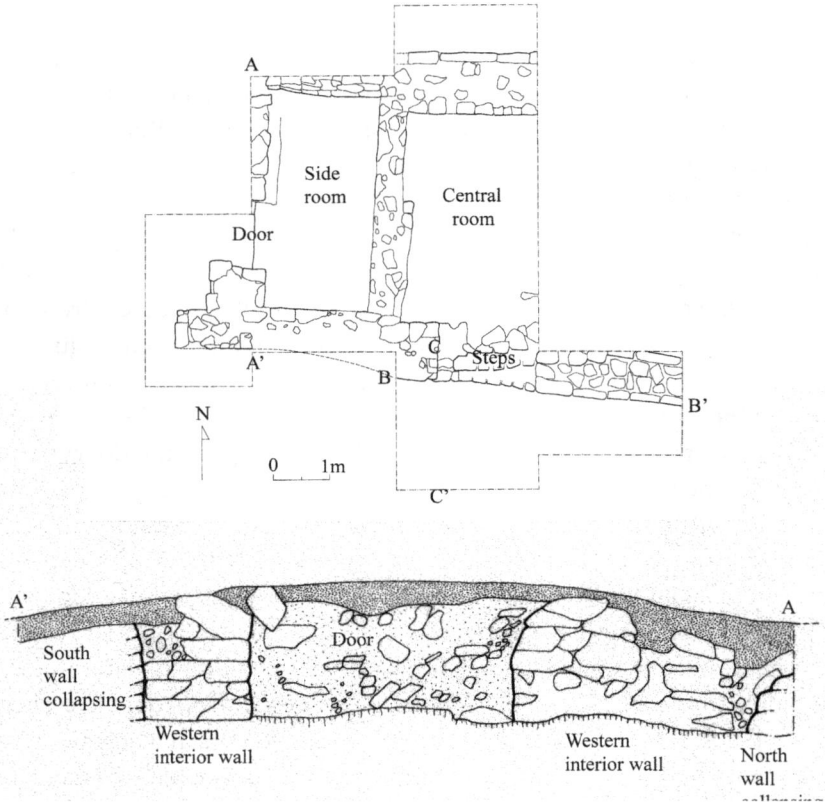

Figure 4.12a. Plan of excavations in the central Str. 8L-27 (MSJ29G), showing larger central room and smaller side room, with inset corners on the doorjamb in the side room; b. north–south profile (between A and A') of units 29G-7, 8 showing door and west wall of side room; profiles along lines B-B' and C-C' available at http://motul-archaeology.williams.edu.

explored a dispersed plazuela group of mounds (Group 11M1) that is situated directly to the south of a larger group (Group 12M1) of Rank 2 (see Figure 1.2). Placed in Rank 3, the structures of Group 11M1 are significantly smaller than those located within the site core, and the goal of the excavation was to compare such lower-status residences from the site's near periphery with those from the core. We only partially uncovered one structure

(Str. 11M-9) that had been severely damaged by looting. Str. 11M-9 is the largest of eight mounds in this highly dispersed plaza group. Its exterior dimensions were 18.8 meters in length by 4.2 meters in width. The structure had two (and possibly three) small rooms, with large interior benches and vaulted stone roof (Figure 4.13; Moriarty 2000). The interior benches were placed against the back wall of each room, had high arm supports, and rose 0.55 meters above the interior stucco floors. Wall construction consisted of large, rectangular, dressed blocks with thick stucco veneer. The lowest row of stones projected approximately 3 centimeters beyond the rest of the wall (a basal molding), an architectural feature not encountered in the other excavations at Motul. The entrance into the main central room that faced east, and had a width of approximately 2.2 meters. Although this seems wide in comparison to modern doors, the fact that the same size is repeated again and again in almost all the structures excavated at Motul suggests that this was characteristic of residential architecture and does not suggest that they were public or nondomestic buildings (although multifunctionality of structures is quite likely). Despite the elaborate masonry architecture of Str. 11M-9, the other structures in the group were significantly smaller and less architecturally complex. Test units placed on Str. 11M-5, for example, exposed a small cobblestone platform less than 50 centimeters in height (Halperin et al. 2001, 20). The remaining structures quite likely also comprised stone platforms that supported walls and roofs of perishable materials. Nonetheless, the masonry architecture of Str. 11M-9 suggests that even though the whole group possesses a small construction volume, this household was inhabited by individuals of a middle status who could command enough labor for masonry and stucco construction. The relatively high density of polychromes (see below) reinforces the higher status of the residents of this building. It is possible that the whole group was of commoner status, but had gained more wealth than other commoners, and could therefore display it through the construction of a larger and finer residence, possibly for the lineage or house head.

Operation 42 comprises test-pitting and small-scale architectural excavations of Group 11N2, another Rank 3 compound, located also in the North Zone of Motul (Figure 4.14a). This group sits at the upper end of the Rank 3 volumetric rating system, with 1,068 cubic meters and comprises two structures, 11N-6 and 11N-7, the former oddly shaped in comparison to other right-angled (L-shaped) buildings. These structures are located on a natural rise in the bedrock rather than on a formal masonry platform. Architectural excavations during 2005 targeted only the southern

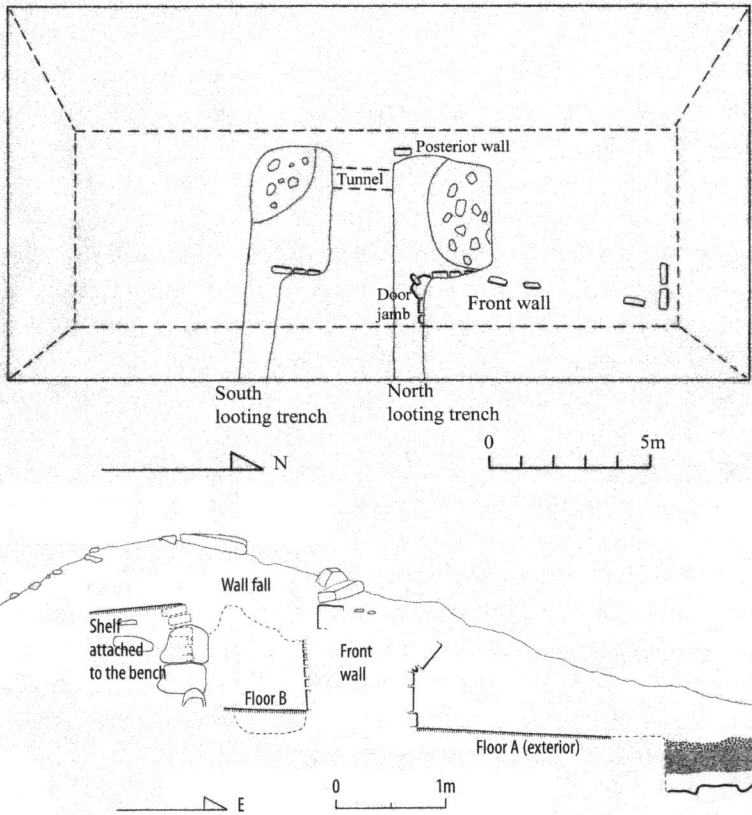

Figure 4.13. a. Plan of looting damage in Str. 11M-9 (Operation MSJ31A); b. profile of Str. 11M-9 showing front wall with outset base row (possible molding), and interior bench with shelf or high armrest.

half of Str. 11N-7 (Halperin and Martinez Salguero 2007a, 2007b). Ceramics recovered from both test-pitting and architectural excavations revealed a long occupation history from the Middle Preclassic to the Early Postclassic, with the majority dating to the Late Classic period. Dense middens were found behind both structures of this minor group. In addition, three Late Classic period burials were excavated from the interior of Str. 11N-7 (Figure 4.14b). Although the limited nature of the architectural excavations did not allow for the complete recovery of two of the burials (as they bisected the units), they demonstrate, not surprisingly, qualitative differences from the elaborate tomb in Operation 15 (Group D). Furthermore, grave goods were also relatively meager with a single Tepeu 2 phase polychrome bowl to accompany the adult individual in Burial #6, a few broken shell fragments and eroded polychrome vessel fragments accompanied a single adult individual in Burial #7, and a single polychrome dish was found with the adult individual from Burial #8. Eastern structures in the Maya area tend to be the revered places for ancestor burials (McAnany 1995, 53–54). Thus, despite the relative simplicity of their grave accompaniments and architecture, these individuals were likely more esteemed than others occupying this group. In comparison with the largest structure from the previously discussed group, Group 11M1, the architecture of the eastern Str. 11N-7 is less elaborate: it consists of a rectangular masonry platform that served as the foundation for a perishable structure (Figure 4.14b). The platform comprised at least three construction phases with the latest, Phase A, dating to the Late Classic period. During this time, the platform measured approximately 8.5 meters wide, 11.0 meters long, and between 0.5 and 1.0 meter in height (depending on the slope of the ground). It contained at least three and likely five masonry steps located on its western side toward the group plaza. The steps were lined with dressed stone blocks, and the platform itself was constructed out of small slab stones. Although excavations of Str. 11N-6, an irregularly shaped building to the northwest, were not undertaken, it possessed approximately the same height as Str. 11N-7 and likely also comprised a masonry platform foundation.

Motul de San José Elites and Production Activities

A key issue in discussions of Classic Maya political structure has been the degree of elite control over economic institutions. One approach to understanding economic involvement is to assess productive activities undertaken (or sponsored) by the elites in their residential compounds. Both the horizontal excavations (described above) and the midden prospecting program from the 1998–2001 field seasons have provided evidence for production that took place within elite to nonelite plaza groups at Motul de San José. Because abandonment processes and postdepositional transformational processes were probably distinct within the site (Schiffer 1985), we have relied heavily on midden assemblages associated with particular plaza groups (rather than floor assemblages) to reconstruct the activities and consumption patterns of each residential group.[9]

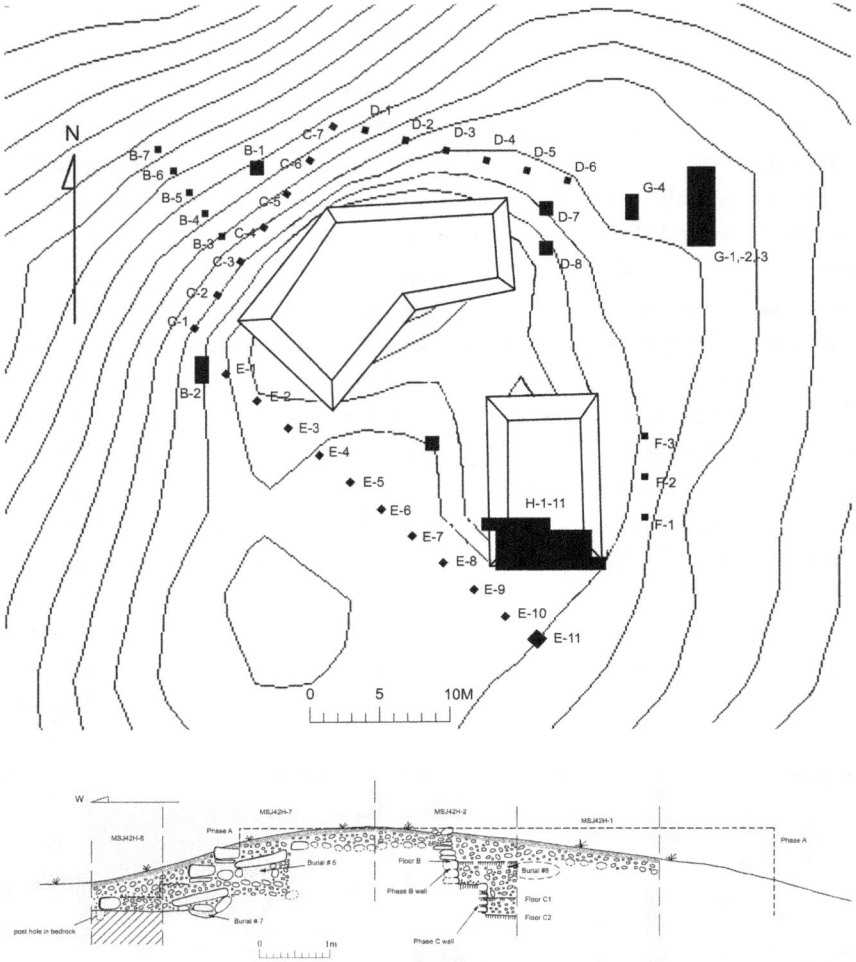

Figure 4.14a. Plan of Group 11N2 showing the location of excavation units and shovel tests of Operation MSJ42; b. east–west profile of Str. 11N-7 (sub-Operation 42H), showing three phases of construction and associated burials.

Food Production and Ground Stone Distribution

Food production is one of the most basic economic activities carried out in every household. The activity areas related to food production generally include a kitchen or cooking area with its hearth, and a food preparation area with a mano and metate, the most important food preparation tools of pre-Hispanic Mesoamerica (e.g., Sheets 2000, 2002). Contemporary Central American households generally have one metate and one accompanying mano (Sheets 2000, 225). In a small to medium-size center like Motul de San José, we would expect most residential plaza groups to be producing their own food and, therefore, to own at least one set of metate and mano. Surprisingly, metates and manos were rare at Motul, although one operation (MSJ15A) had most of them. The rarity of ground stone at the site possibly relates to the vagaries of archaeological sampling and also to a slow abandonment process during which precious possessions (including ground stone) were carried away by departing residents (Biskowski 2000, 294; Schiffer 1985, 1987; Cameron 1993).

The distribution of manos and metates at Motul by architectural volumetric rank is detailed in Table 4.2. The distribution appears highly skewed, with more than half of the Motul ground stone excavated in Group D. This may imply that the western structure of this group where most of these were found had a special function tied to food preparation[10] for feasting in this group or in the Main Plaza. Hence, we removed Operation 15 from further calculations. We have calculated densities of ground stone by excavation volume[11] to take into account the different scale of excavation in each residential group. The table shows that Rank 3 groups have the highest density at 0.050 per square meter, with Rank 2 groups close at 0.048, and finally Rank 1 groups at the lowest density of 0.031 (without Group D).

This skewed distribution of ground stone density suggests that royal elite compounds of Rank 1 (with the exception of Group D) processed the least amount of maize than middle status groups of Rank 2, and lower status groups of Rank 3. This is surprising since the Rank 1 groups probably included a larger number of individuals than Ranks 2 and 3, such as the royal family, courtiers, bodyguards, warriors, attached servants, and other specialists. The royal elites were also quite likely involved in more feasting activities that would have required significant quantities of foods and drinks. This suggests that their requirements for processed maize were filled through taxing: commoners processed the food in their own compounds and then brought them to the Rank 1 residents of Groups A, B, C, and D. The surprising discovery of over twenty ground stone fragments in the royal compound of Group D in Operation 15 brings into relief the distinct activities that took place in this group during the Terminal Classic. Such high density of ground stone argues for food production at a more intense or larger scale than in other locales, under the supervision of elites, presumably for feasting purposes.

Another aspect highlighted by the skewed distribution of ground stone is that maize processing did take place within the royal elite compounds

Table 4.2. Distribution of ground stone at Motul de San José

Operation	Group	Ground stone	Density[a]
2	Acropolis	3	0.044
15	Group D	22	0.103
12, 14	Group B	0	0
8, 9	Group A	1	0.026
Total rank 1	**4 groups**	**4 (26 w/ MSJ15); 1.33/ group[b]**	**0.031[c]; (0.076 w/ MSJ15)**
10	Med., Gr.A	0	0
20, 22	Med., Gr. E	1	0.050
29	Med., Gr. E	3	0.071
30	Med, Gr. E	0	0
32	Med, Gr. C	0	0
33	Med, Gr. C	0	0
26	Lg, North Zone	0	0
35	Lg, North Zone	0	0
36	Md, North Zone	1	0.087
39	Lg, North Zone	2	0.195
43	Lg, North Zone	1	0.075
Total rank 2[d]	**11 groups**	**8; 0.73/group**	**0.048**
13,16	Sm., Gr.A	1	0.073
27	Sm, Gr. A	2	0.533
17	Sm, Gr. C	1	0.067
18	Sm, Gr. C	0	0
19	Sm, Gr. C	1	0.138
34	Sm, Gr. C	2	0.444
23,24, 25	Sm, North Zone	0	0
31	Sm, North Zone	0	0
38	Sm, North Zone	0	0
42	Sm. North Zone	2	0.174
45	Sm, North Zone	0	0
Total rank 3	**11 groups**	**9; 0.82/group**	**0.072**
TOTAL		**43**	**0.050[e]**

[a] The density of ground stone is calculated based on volume of excavation. The volume of excavation is estimated by the areal extent of each operation (Table 4.4).

[b] Operation 15 is removed from this calculation.

[c] Operation 15 is removed from this calculation.

[d] Only intensively tested, residential/domestic groups were included here. Some operations had to be excluded because they represented public space (operations 3,4, 11, 28) or nondomestic space (operation 21 in quarry behind the pyramid of Group E; operation 37 in chultun associated with small residential group along the eastern edge of the Motul de San José National Park). Other operations were not intensively tested and had to be excluded: 1, 5, 6, 7, 40, 41, 44.

[e] Operation 15 is removed from this calculation.

Table 4.3. List of excavation units per operation

Operation	# Test units (sq. m)	# Shovel tests (0.25 sq. m)	Totals[a] (sq. m)
RANK 1			
2	68	0	68[b]
15	192	85	213.25
12,14	9	60	24
8,9	7	124	38
Total rank 1			**343.25 sq. m**
RANK 2			
10	5	34	13.5
20,22	2	72	20
29	31.75	41	42
30	4	15	7.75
32	3	47	14.75
33	3	36	12
26	0	33	8.25
35	4	36	13
36	5	26	11.5
39	4	25	10.25
43	2	45	13.25
1	3	0	3
Total rank 2 (w/ 1)			**169.25 sq. m**
Total rank 2 (w/out 1)			**166.25 sq. m**
RANK 3			
13,16	3	43	13.75
27	1	11	3.75
17	5	40	15
7	4	0	4
18	0	17	4.25
19	2	21	7.25
34	0	18	4.5
23,24,25	5	57	19.25
31	21	28	28[c]
38	5	27	11.75
42	5	26	11.5
45	5.5	0	5.5
Total rank 3 (w/ 7)			**128.5 sq. m**
Total rank 3 (w/out 7)			**124.5 sq. m**

[a] Total Excavations = Test Units + ¼ Shovel Units.

[b] Without 2005 excavations.

[c] We screened and analyzed several looter's back piles and these are not included in area excavated.

(although at a lower scale or intensity), as well as in the middle rank groups. It is possible that attached retainer-servants or extended kin within the high-elite and even middle-rank households were used to grind the corn for the production of food within the Rank 1 and 2 households. The distribution of maize processing at Motul de San José contrasts with contemporaneous major Maya cities such as Tikal and Caracol, and the Aztec-period city-state of Otumba in Central Mexico, where little to no food preparation took place within the core of royal courts at the center of each city (Harrison 1999, 195–98; A. Chase and D. Chase 2001, 131; Biskowski 2000, 302). This underscores the direct involvement by the Motul elite in economic matters, rather than relying completely on the tax-tribute system.

Textile Production

Another activity that was basic to pre-Hispanic households was weaving (Clark and Houston 1998; Brumfiel 2006; Hendon 1992a, 1997; McCafferty and McCafferty 2000; Nichols, McLaughlin, and Benton 2000). Halperin (2008) has formulated a typology of spinning tools (spindle whorls and centrally perforated sherd disks) for the Motul de San José region, and has described their distribution across the residential groups at the site. In contrast to the ground stone distribution, Rank 1 or royal elite compounds had the highest density (0.91 per thousand ceramic sherds), with decreasing densities among the Ranks 2 and 3 groups (0.57 per thousand ceramic sherds and 0.52 per thousand ceramic sherds, respectively; see Halperin 2008, table 4). Bone weaving tools (such as needles, awls, and perforators/picks) analyzed by Emery and tallied by Halperin (2008) possessed similar distribution patterns with the highest densities at Rank 1 groups (1.06 per thousand ceramic sherds) and lower densities among Rank 2 and 3 groups (0.05 per thousand ceramic sherds and 0.20 per thousand sherds, respectively). Although the Rank 1 royal houses were more invested in these activities, spinning and weaving were not centralized, but took place among most households of all socioeconomic strata at Motul (ibid.).

Nevertheless, more spinning and weaving occurred in the royal compounds (Rank 1). This is reasonable because royal households are larger and more complex than smaller, lower-status ones. Halperin comments on the higher density of weaving tools in the royal elite and secondary elite groups at Motul: "elite households could devote more time to crafts (more intensity) or mobilize more labor (larger scale) through non-kin networks, such as landless 'client' families or servants, or through extended kin alliances and associations" (2008, 120). Paralleling the evidence from ground stone, this evidence on the textile production also points to a very active and direct involvement by the highest elites in economic production.

Pottery and Stone Tool Production

A third basic household activity is the production of pottery and stone or bone tools for daily use. In contrast to maize processing and spinning/weaving, the evidence for pottery and tool production at Motul de San José is much more restricted, although not necessarily under elite control. Brian (2005) has examined the chert lithic industry at Motul de San José, and has only been able to identify one locus of production within the site: Groups 9M3 and 9M2 (Operations 23, 24, 25) in the North Zone. These groups pertain to Rank 3 and suggest that lithic production was not controlled by the elite. Lawton (2007b) has identified significant lithic specialization approximately 3 kilometers south of Motul in several communities along the north shore of Lake Petén Itzá (Trinidad, Buenavista-Nuevo San José, Las Estrellas or Chak Maman Tok'). These communities along the lake were adjacent to chert quarries and specialized in the extraction of nodules and the production of final tools or large blanks, which were then traded to other sites, like Motul de San José, where they were fashioned into the final tools.

Pottery manufacture has been notoriously hard to identify in the Maya lowlands, leading many scholars to conclude that it was carried out on a small scale by part-time specialists in household "workshops" located in dispersed settlements surrounding larger centers (P. Rice 1985, 1987a; Foias 1996, 2004; Foias and Bishop 1997). Halperin and Foias (this volume) present in detail the evidence for pottery production found in the Acropolis in Group C (Operation 2). Based on the Instrumental Neutron Activation Analysis (INAA) chemical data (Reents-Budet et al. 2007) and the firing wasters found in these deposits, the residents of Str. 8L-9 (or nearby buildings) in the Acropolis (explored in Operation 2) were scribes who crafted polychrome vessels, including the Ik'-style vases, in one or several scribal palace "workshops" like those excavated at Aguateca (Inomata 2001b) and at Buenavista de Cayo (Reents-Budet et al. 2000). The fact that this activity is part of the royal court represented by the Acropolis at Motul de San José suggests that elaborate polychrome production was controlled by royal elites. Unfortunately, we are not able to assess the regional distribution of production of monochromes or unslipped pottery as no other production loci were recognized in the Motul zone. The lack of evidence for potting activity within Motul beyond the Acropolis supports previous interpretations that the elite controlled only the prestige pottery production, whereas other vessels were manufactured in a dispersed pattern beyond the large centers.

Figurine Production

Figurine production has also been studied at Motul de San José by Halperin through the presence of figurine molds, high figurine densities, and figurine paste analyses (Halperin 2007, this volume; Halperin et al. 2009). A figurine mold fragment and a high number of identical figurines (figurines possibly made from the same mold or mold replicas) were found intermixed with the Operation 2 polychrome pottery production midden mentioned above, suggesting that the two media may have been produced in the same royal elite workshop(s) or zone of the site. The coproduction of polychrome pottery and figurines would not be surprising as multicrafting of the two media has been recorded at Tikal (Becker 1973, 2003a) and both involved the application of similar types of paint. A possible figurine mold fragment was also recovered from the largest architectural group at the site of Akte (Yorgey 2005, 58–59). Despite the paucity of direct evidence of figurine production, unusually high figurine densities were present in Motul de San José Rank 1 (Group 8K5&6, called Group B) and Rank 2 Groups (9L7, 8L4, and 10M3). Although relatively inconclusive without other lines of evidence, high densities of finished products often represent production loci (Becker 2003a; Feinman and Nicholas 2000; Lucero 1992). When combined with other figurine molds finds outside the Motul de San José region, these data suggest that figurine production was more likely to be produced by elite and middle-status households than those of the lower echelons of society (Halperin 2007, 259–69).

Other Craft Production Activities

Evidence for the more specialized activity of papermaking and painting was also found at Motul in Group D (Operation 15A): one bark beater was excavated among the wall fall from the southern room of the western palace. Painting activity was also suggested by a concentration of pigments in this structure (several blocks or balls of red and yellow pigments) and a volcanic stone metate. This volcanic stone metate had three small supports, which is distinct from the usual calcite or quartzite metate found in this palace and across the site. It may have been used for the preparation of pigments rather than for maize grinding. However, residue or wear pattern analysis needs to be undertaken to pursue this hypothesis.

Emery's (2003a, this volume) zooarchaeological analysis has also identified the manufacture of bone tools or ornaments in seven residential
groups, from royal compounds (Operations 2, 15) to secondary elite plazas
of Rank 2 (Operations 1, 33, both associated with the Acropolis) to the
smallest groups of Rank 3 (Operations 7, 13, and 31). Thus, the manufacture of tools and jewelry out of animal bone was not centralized under
the elite, although the royal elite clearly participated in this activity within
their palaces (possibly through attached servants or specialists). Emery
notes, though, that finished artifacts were only concentrated among the
royal compounds, and not among smaller groups that had high densities
of production debitage (2003a, 41). These latter groups therefore produced
bone tools and jewelry not for their own consumption, but for the royal
houses (see discussion in Emery, this volume).

Conclusions

The structural and nonstructural excavations carried out at Motul de San
José reveal a complex interplay of economic and political forces. The royal
elites were actively involved in many economic activities, and sometimes
on a larger scale than either middle-status groups of Rank 2 or lower-status
groups of Rank 3. The only manufacturing activities that appear to have
been exclusively controlled by the royal elite is the crafting of elaborate
polychrome vessels, and possibly the creation and painting of paper. Otherwise, activities that were undertaken within the royal compounds (such
as maize processing, spinning and weaving, bone tool manufacture) were
also carried out by Rank 2 and Rank 3 groups.

Based on this evidence for significant production in the elite households, we conclude that the Motul royal elites cannot be seen as parasitic
(although they may have maintained only a supervisory role in many of
these economic undertakings within their compounds). The fact that these
activities were carried out within the royal compounds suggests that the
ruling families were actively interested in them. Taken as a group, the royal
compounds of the Late and Terminal Classic witnessed more maize processing (if Group D is included) and more spinning and weaving than all
other groups. These activities created basic goods (food and cloth) that
could be easily used as payments or gifts. This suggests more economic
power in the hands of the royal families, but not economic centralization
since lower-status households carried out or had access to many of these
productive activities without relying on the royal lineages. Inomata (2007)
describes a similar situation for the royal court at Aguateca in the Pasion

region. Aguateca courtiers were scribes, wood-carvers, stone-carvers, and so on, with these crafting activities undertaken by them or under their supervision in their own compounds in the city core (ibid.).

Consumption and Wealth Indices

Social stratification is founded, in part, on unequal distribution of wealth. To understand wealth distinctions among the social strata at Motul de San José, we have considered the distribution of nonlocal or exotic resources and of hypertrophic or labor-intensive items excavated from the 1998–2001 field seasons.

The Classic Maya city-states obtained a number of nonlocal resources through long-distance trade. Of these, many were probably perishable and did not leave marks in the archaeological record. Among those that preserve, the inhabitants of Motul imported obsidian and volcanic ground stone from the Maya highlands; greenstone, including jade, from the highlands and Motagua drainage; pyrite from the Guatemalan highlands; marine shell and other resources,[12] like stingray spines, from the Pacific and Atlantic Oceans. Table 4.4 presents the distribution of these nonlocal resources at Motul de San José. As the table underscores, all these exotic resources were rare and, with the exception of obsidian, highly restricted at the site during the Late and Terminal Classic.

Obsidian

Obsidian is the resource most broadly available to basically every Motul household. Densities of obsidian were calculated to take into account differences in excavated volume[13] for each operation. Rank 1 groups had a density of 2.10 obsidian per square meter; Rank 2 groups of 2.26 obsidian per square meter; and, finally, Rank 3 of 1.88 obsidian per square meter (Table 4.4). Although obsidian densities are skewed toward the top ranks, they are overall quite similar across the whole population.

It is also important to note, though, that the Terminal Classic residences correlate with the highest densities of obsidian in their ranks. Operations 15 and 29, which continued to be occupied during the Terminal Classic, have the highest concentrations of obsidian in their Ranks 1 and 2, respectively. Similarly, Operation 42 of Rank 3 with a late occupation into the Terminal Classic/Early Postclassic had a high obsidian density. If these Terminal Classic–Early Postclassic occupations are excluded, the densities of obsidian by ranks become more significantly distinct: Rank 1: 3.78 per

Table 4.4. Distribution of nonlocal resources at Motul de San José

Operation	Group	Obsidian & volcanic stone	Marine shell[a] & resources	Greenstone (e.g., jade)	Pyrite
2	Acropolis	444	19	0	1
15	Group D	231	55 (& 51 in tomb[b])	15 (& 30 in tomb)	4 (& 98 in tomb)
12, 14	Group B	23	0	0	0
8, 9	Group A	24	0	0	0
Total rank 1		**722; 180.5/ group; 2.10/sq. m**	**74; 18.5/gr; 0.216/sq. m**	**15; 3.75/gr; 0.044/sq. m**	**5; 1.25/gr; 0.015/sq. m**
10	Med, Gr.A	23	0	0	0
20, 22	Med, Gr. E	23	2	0	0
29	Med, Gr. E	94	2	1	0
30	Med, Gr. E	26	0	0	0
32	Med, Gr. C	16	0	0	0
33	Med, Gr. C	27	0	0	1
26	Lg, North Zn	4	0	0	0
35	Lg, North Zn	34	0	0	0
36	Lg, North Zn	8	0	0	0
39	Lg, North Zn	117	0	0	0
43	Lg, North Zn	4	0	0	0
Total rank 2		**376; 34.2/gr; 2.26/sq. m**	**4; 0.4/gr; 0.024/sq. m**	**1; 0.09/gr; 0.006/sq. m**	**1; 0.1/gr; 0.006/sq. m**
13,16	Sm., Gr.A	5	0	0	1
27	Sm, Gr. A	2	0	0	0
7	Sm, Gr. E	13	1	1	0
17	Sm, Gr. C	32	0	0	0
18	Sm, Gr. C	4	0	0	0
19	Sm, Gr. C	10	0	0	0
34	Sm, Gr. C	34	0	0	0
23,24, 25	Sm, North Zn	7	0	0	0
31	Sm, North Zn	31	1	0	0
38	Sm, North Zn	19	0	0	0
42	Sm. North Zn	75	0	1	0
45	Sm, North Zn	2	0	0	0
Total rank 3		**234; 19.2/gr; 1.88/sq. m**	**2; 0.2/gr; 0.016/sq. m**	**2; 0.17/gr; 0.016/sq. m**	**1; 0.1/gr; 0.008/sq. m**
TOTAL		**1332**	**80**	**17**	**5**

[a] Three other operations produced marine shell (1 each): MSJ4A, which consisted of two test units placed in front of each of the "Twin Pyramids" in the Main Plaza; MSJ44I, which explored Gr. E2I in Chakokot; MSJ44J, which tested Gr. E2J in Chakokot.
[b] The looted royal tomb found in the eastern pyramid of Group D included fifty marine shell artifacts (mostly mosaic pieces and beads) and one fragmented stingray spine.

Table 4.5. Densities of nonlocal resources in Late Classic residences by rank

Rank	Obsidian and volcanic stone	Marine shell and resources	Greenstone (e.g., jade)	Pyrite
1	3.78/sq. m	0.146/sq. m	0	0.008/sq. m
2	2.27/sq. m	0.016/sq. m	0	0.006/sq. m
3	1.36/sq. m	0.017/sq. m	0.009/sq. m	0.008/sq. m

square meter; Rank 2: 2.27 per square meter; Rank 3: 1.36 per square meter (Table 4.5).

Classic period obsidian has been seen by some archaeologists to be under elite control (Aoyama 2001; P. Rice 1987a), and by others as freely traded in marketplaces, although more expensive than chert tools (Sheets 2000; Hirth 1998). Prudence Rice (1987a) also notes that the availability of obsidian increases during the Terminal Classic, and we see the same pattern at Motul. The broad availability of obsidian at Motul during the Late Classic, albeit in small quantities in comparison to chert, supports a market exchange model, although elites clearly had more access to it.

Marine Shell, Greenstone, and Pyrite

In contrast to obsidian, marine shell, greenstone (including jade), and pyrite are almost exclusively royal prerogatives at Motul (Tables 4.4, 4.5). Jade was seen by the Classic Maya as the most precious of substances, as green represented maize, fertility, water, the axis mundi, and even the essence of life (Miller and Taube 1993; Taube 1998, 2005; Kovacevich 2007). Jade objects like figurines, earspools, and ceremonial bars were used to conjure gods or ancestors (Taube 2005). Another precious material, pyrite, was fashioned by the Classic Maya into mirrors. These were also used as ritual equipment for divination, creating smoke or fire, as portals into the supernatural world, or as symbols of several deities (Miller and Taube 1993; Taube 1992; Kovacevich 2007). Spondylus, as the quintessential marine shell with its red or pinkish hues, was also the medium of royal power since the inception of Maya kingship in the Late Preclassic (Freidel, Reese-Taylor, and Mora-Marin 2002). It was associated with the Kan Cross that marked the birthplace of the Maize God (ibid., 66). These three raw materials were charged with great ritual or ideological value and were regarded as highly precious jewels by the Maya from the Late Preclassic on. Therefore, it is not surprising that the distribution of these raw materials was highly restricted at Motul de San José.

Only a few examples of marine shell, jade, and pyrite were found beyond the royal compounds. Net quantities of marine shell were almost forty times as common in royal residences than in Rank 2 groups and almost one hundred times more than in Rank 3 groups.[14] Greenstone was only found in three groups (of Ranks 2 and 3) beyond the royal compounds, and pyrite in two other nonroyal groups (of Rank 2 and 3). The only provenience that had a wealth of these highly restricted materials was the looted royal tomb discovered in the eastern pyramid of Group D. We suspect that there were many other marine shell, greenstone, or pyrite artifacts that were removed by the looters. But even in spite of the looting, the tomb's quantities of these exotic ornaments are a striking contrast to their rarity elsewhere at the site. When the Terminal Classic to Early Postclassic operations are separated (Table 4.5), the higher availability of marine shell to the royal compounds is reiterated and the rarity of greenstone and pyrite across all three ranks is even more apparent.

Other Hypertrophic Objects: Polychromes

Apart from these imported raw materials, the Motul elite also consumed more hypertrophic or labor-intensive objects than lower-rank residents (Table 4.6). These hypertrophic objects included polychromes (especially the elaborately painted vessels) that required more labor to create than monochromes and unslipped wares and finely modeled figurines that were examined by Halperin (this volume).

Although polychromes were widely distributed at Motul, with small to large groups often having above 5 percent, Rank 1 and Rank 2 residential groups had more than Rank 3 groups (Table 4.6). Hence, polychromes were not controlled by the royal elite and were broadly available to all residents of Motul de San José. The broad availability of polychromes underscores that this was not a status symbol. It also suggests that these polychromes could have been distributed via markets (Minc 2005; West 2002; Fry 1979, 1980; Fry and Cox 1974).

In contrast to simple polychromes, elaborately painted vessels were highly restricted (Table 4.6). Elaborate polychromes are characterized by hieroglyphic texts and/or intricate scenes of palaces, rituals and dances, with humans and/or supernaturals. These require specialized or esoteric knowledge of the Classic Maya hieroglyphic writing system and mythology (Reents-Budet 1998; Inomata 2001b). Such elaborate polychromes are very restricted in distribution at Motul, with the great majority found in royal compounds (thirty-six of forty vessels). Rank 2 groups sported

Table 4.6. Distribution of polychromes, elaborate polychromes and polychrome vases at Motul de San José

Operation	Group	Polychrome density[a]	Elaborate polychromes[b]	Polychrome vases
2	Acropolis	14.91%[c]	32	56
15	Group D	10.83	4	29
12, 14	Group B	3.33	0	0
8, 9	Group A	9.67	0	5
Total rank 1		**9.69%/group**	**36; 9/gr; 0.105/sq. m**	**90; 22.5/gr; 0.262/sq. m**
10	Med, Gr. A	10.61%	0	0
20, 22	Med, Gr. E	6.73	3	1
29	Med, Gr. E	8.10	0	4
30	Med, Gr. E	10.30	0	0
1	Med, Gr. C	16.52	0	2
32	Med, Gr. C	5.15	0	0
33	Med, Gr. C	8.17	0	0
26	Lg, North Zn	1.12	0	0
35	Lg, North Zn	10.60	0	2
39	Lg, North Zn	14.60	1	6
Total rank 2		**9.19%/group**	**4; 0.3/gr; 0.024/sq. m**	**15; 1.3/gr; 0.106/sq. m**
13,16	Sm, Gr. A	10.86%	0	2
27	Sm, Gr. A	1.22	0	0
7	Sm, Gr. E	12.88	0	1
17	Sm, Gr. C	8.90	0	11
18	Sm, Gr. C	1.95	0	0
19	Sm, Gr. C	1.46	0	0
34	Sm, Gr. C	2.99	0	1
23,24,25	Sm, North Zn	10.05	0	3
31	Sm, North Zn	16.22	0	1
38	Sm, North Zn	4.56	0	1
42	Sm. North Zn	9.97	0	7
45	Sm, North Zn	4.33	0	0
Total rank 3		**7.12%/group**	**0; 0.000 sq. m**	**27; 2.3/gr; 0.210/sq. m**
TOTAL			**40**	**132**

[a] All ceramic densities were calculated by Melanie Kingsley (Appendix, www.motul-archaeology.williams.edu) who has kindly allowed their inclusion here.
[b] Only rims were included in this analysis of the distribution of polychrome vases and elaborate polychrome designs.
[c] Percentages are based on totals within each operation, excluding indeterminate or eroded pottery.

another four elaborate polychrome vessels, and Rank 3 groups had none. However, pottery slip preservation was much better in the Acropolis than in any other provenience, and so it is very difficult to ascertain whether this skewed distribution was caused by preservation bias. If we assume that preservation did not affect the distribution, the royal elites at Motul and a few of the secondary elites had access to elaborate polychromes.

LeCount (2001) has made the argument that Classic Maya polychrome vases were highly restricted because they were used to serve cacao drinks central to political events or acts at Xunantunich, Belize. The distribution of polychrome vases can therefore hint at the level of political involvement among the residents of Motul de San José. Vases did indeed have a restricted distribution: the royal compounds in Groups C, D, A, and B-E had the highest incidence of this vessel form (with ninety of 132; see Table 4.6). But there were examples from small to large nonroyal households, too, and surprisingly Rank 3 groups averaged 2.3 vases in comparison to Rank 2 groups that averaged only 1.3 vases. Furthermore, the densities of polychrome vases across the three ranks are much closer than expected: Rank 1 or royal groups have a density of 0.262 vases per square meter, with Rank 3 groups coming close at 0.210 vases per square meter; Rank 2 groups have the lowest density of 0.106 vases per square meter.

However, this higher incidence of vases among Rank 3 groups is due to only two operations: Operation 17, which uncovered eleven vases, and Operation 42, which exposed seven. Both of these groups were special in other respects. For example, Operation 17 has the third highest count of pottery at Motul de San José (after Operations 2 and 15) even though the scale of excavations in this group was minor. A possible explanation for this is that Group 8M5 explored by Operation 17 is directly west of Group D, but much reduced in scale and construction volume, and, thus, may represent attached retainer-servants to Group D. The midden that was associated with Operation 17 may represent activities in both this group and in Group D. Similarly, Operation 42 in the North Zone is also special because it has two oddly shaped small platforms that are oriented distinctly in comparison to other Motul plaza groups (see description above and Figure 4.14). It also had a higher density of refuse than other groups of Ranks 2 or 3, in spite of its diminutive size. It is therefore possible that Operation 42 may also represent attached retainers-servants to another nearby elite group. If Operations 17 and 42 are removed from the sample, the Rank 3 average is reduced to 0.9 vases per group or a density of 0.09 vases per square meter (almost a third of the estimated Rank 1 density of 0.262 vases per square meter).

If LeCount (2001) is right that feasting with vases were a means for generating political power, a great deal of the power was concentrated in the hands of the royal families residing in Groups C and D (less for Groups A and B). But, both Rank 2 middle-status and Rank 3 lower-status groups were also political players as Ranks 2 and 3 had comparable net quantities and densities per area, although less than the royal houses once Operations 17 and 42 were excluded. Political power as represented by vases appears to have been relatively similar in the hands of Rank 3 as among Rank 2 groups.

In summary, the distribution of wealth indices at Motul generally paints a highly hierarchical social structure, with the main distinction between the Rank 1 royal elites and everyone else. However, the fact that their compounds were involved in more production than Rank 2 and 3 groups suggests that an important source of wealth, apart from tribute-tax, was "in-house" economic activity, creating an *oikos* or great house as in the royal houses of Sumerian Mesopotamia of the Early Dynastic period in the third millennium BC (S. Pollock 1999).

Conclusions

Architecture, reconstructions of political and economic activities, and artifact distributions at Motul de San José reveal a complex and highly stratified social system in which individuals and groups disproportionately garnered political power, hereditary privilege or estate, and wealth to both produce and maintain their social ranks. We suggest that the covariation between these archaeological indices provides the most pervasive evidence for the identification of ruling elites. At the same time, variability within and between these indices also suggests ways in which groups engaged in "politicking" and wealth accumulation without hereditary status as nobles or, alternatively, ways in which nobles and other elite groups were unable to amass labor and wealth items to the same degree as their peers.

Maya hieroglyphic texts alone indicate that political power must have varied tremendously within the elite "class" of political elites (or nobles, named *ajaw* in the texts) who are identified as filling administrative positions (D. Chase and A. Chase 1992; Schele and Freidel 1990; Inomata and Houston 2001; Foias and Emery, this volume). For example, the political power of the divine rulers (*k'ujul ajaw*) would have been of a different scale and scope than that of a noble who had a small land estate somewhere in the periphery. In addition, the political clout of the divine ruler of Tikal would have been much higher than that of the divine ruler of smaller sites like Motul de San José.

At Motul proper, the greatest divide within architectural group volumes is between Rank 1 and Ranks 2–3, whereas differences between Rank 2 and Rank 3 are better represented as a continuum in which negotiation and social mobility were more likely to have taken place. This on its own would suggest that Rank 1 represents the elite *estate*, and Ranks 2 and 3 represent the nonelite *estate*. Rank 1 patio groups were not only larger and more internally complex (revealing their role as administrative as well as domestic settings), but were also spatially closer to the major temple-pyramid complexes, public plazas, and stelae, such that political power was materialized in spatial arrangements and monumentality (DeMarrais, Castillo, and Earle 1996). These more permanent strategies of political power coincided with repetitive political practices enacted through feasts and drinking parties, as manifested in Rank 1's larger quantity of polychrome vases. Hosting feasts as strategies and displays of power, however, were not restricted to the ruling elites, but were also part of alliance- and prestige-building practices of lower-ranking groups to lesser degrees.

The Motul de San José elites, and especially the Rank 1 royal elites, were actively involved in economic activities. Royal courts and secondary elite houses at other Classic Maya centers have shown similar engagement in the manufacture of social valuables (or prestige goods), such as elaborate polychrome pottery, obsidian eccentrics, paper, shell and greenstone jewelry, pyrite mirrors, or polished greenstone axes (e.g., for Aguateca, see Inomata 2001b; Inomata and Stiver 1998; Inomata and Triadan 2000; Inomata et al. 2002; for Copán, see Andrews and Fash 1992; Hendon 1997; Webster et al. 1998; for Piedras Negras, see Urquizú et al. 1999; for Cancuen, see Kovacevich 2007). But there are distinctions between the major capitals of large-scale states (like Tikal and Caracol) and minor capitals of smaller-scale polities (like Motul, Copán, and Aguateca). The Motul royal elites were involved in basic economic activities such as food and textile production. On the other hand, food production seems to be absent in the royal courts of the larger cities of Tikal and Caracol (Harrison 1999; A. Chase and D. Chase 2001). A. Chase and D. Chase (2001) discuss the limited production that took place within the epicentral palaces of Caracol in comparison to the plentiful evidence for manufacturing activities in the residential groups beyond the core. At Copán, subroyal elites residing in Groups 9N-8, 9M-22, and 9M-24 undertook a variety of productive activities, including food production, but the dominant structures in each patio (presumably the residence of the highest-ranking member of the house or lineage) was associated with more cooking, eating (and feasting), and ritual activities and with little craft production (Hendon 1997, 2003). In addition, Hendon (2003, 224) found that smaller, less wealthy houses (represented by Group 9M-22) were involved in more feasting than larger houses in an attempt to make their wealth more visible and increase their status.

The distribution of construction volume across the Motul landscape shows that Rank 1 royal groups are substantially larger than all other residential groups at Motul. Within Rank 1, the Acropolis, the proposed royal court during the Late Classic, is exceedingly larger than the other three royal groups (Group A, B-E, and D). We want to stress that both architectural volume and consumption patterns underscore that the major socioeconomic distinction was between the royal elite and everyone else. The Maya rulers and their close kin groups were much richer than everyone else in all respects: wealth, social status, prestige, and political power.

Rank 2 groups at Motul de San José were initially hypothesized to be secondary or subroyal elites based on the substantial constructions involved in these plaza groups. The problem is that they are too numerous, representing slightly less than 50 percent of all the groups at Motul proper. Scholars (Webster 1992; Kai Lee, personal communication, 2006) estimate that in preindustrial agrarian societies, elites or nonfarming, tribute-receiving upper "class" can only reach a maximum level of 10 percent of the total population. We can reconstruct an estimate for the population of Motul de San José (the site, not the polity) using settlement densities from the mapping of the core and three transects (Moriarty 2004d, 30): based on contiguous settlement found in the survey transects, the total extent of Motul is estimated at 4.18 square kilometers, with a density of 159.72 structures per square kilometer in the core (based on survey results of 230 structures within an area of 1.44 square kilometers surveyed), and a lower density of 50 structures per square kilometer beyond the core (based on two controlled survey transects to the south and to the northeast of the site). Rice and Culbert (1990) discuss the multiple limiting factors involved in all estimates of archaeological populations and suggest an average of five people per structure and a 30 percent reduction in total structural count due to disuse, noncontemporaneous occupation, hidden structures, and nonresidential function frequencies. Using their figures and the size and density of settlement at Motul, we reach an estimate of 1,200 to 2,000 people within the center, although we suspect that it was close to the lower end of this

range. The point of this exercise is to estimate the number of elites residing at Motul. If preindustrial agrarian societies could maintain at most 10
percent of their total population as elites, the estimated number of elites at
Motul is around 234 individuals. That's about all the monumental groups
of Rank 1 could hold. This suggests that Rank 2 were nonelite. D. Chase and
A. Chase (1992) encountered a similar difficulty at Caracol: they remark
that the middle groups at the latter site "are far more numerous than would
generally be expected of any elite grouping" (314). So, it is hard to categorize the middle group defined by Motul's architectural volumetric data
and consumption patterns as elite or as receivers of tribute.[15] Nevertheless,
if we consider the population of the whole polity controlled by Motul de
San José, this estimate may reach between 13,000 and 27,000 people at its
Late Classic apogee (Foias, forthcoming); of this polity total, elites would
represent 10 percent or 1,300–2,700, and this estimate fits with both Rank
1 and Rank 2 households (and even Rank 3). So, taking into account the
whole Motul polity population, it is possible that Rank 2 encompasses the
secondary elites. However we define them, Motul's Rank 2 groups support
the presence of a middle rank in Classic society, as suggested by the Chases
for Caracol.

We interpret Rank 3 groups as the commoners or lower class. Although
generally the architecture of these groups was simple and small scale,
Group 11N2 explored by Operation 31 revealed a masonry building with
interior stuccoed benches. This was the largest structure of the group, and
hence we suspect that it was the residence of the head of this lineage or
house. The access to, display, and/or consumption of nonlocal or prestige
goods among Rank 3 individuals is also lower than among the royal elite
and middle-rank compounds, but sometimes not significantly. Obsidian
and polychrome pottery were found at basically the same or slightly lower
densities in Rank 3 groups than in Rank 1 groups. Exotic substances (like
jade, marine shell, and pyrite) that have important supernatural associations and highly hypertrophic items (like elaborate polychromes) were
very rare overall at Motul, and appear to be highly controlled by the royal
elites (of Rank 1) and basically only available to them, although a few were
consumed by other ranks (see also Emery, this volume, for a discussion of
shell).

The one unexpected finding was that polychrome vases, seen by LeCount
as a medium for creating and displaying political power, are found across
the three ranks. This suggests some degree of political decentralization
and the possibility that Rank 3 groups functioned as lower-level political

officials, a scenario supported by the discovery of new Classic Maya administrative, but possibly nonelite, titles like *lakam* (Lacadena 2008). The use by a ruling elite of lower socioeconomic echelons as political officials in lieu of the older aristocracy is found among other ancient states and empires, such as in the Early Roman Empire when Augustus begins to rely on Equestrians rather than Senators for his officials (Doyle 1986; Garnsey and Saller 1987; Eisenstadt 1993). Alternatively, cylindrical vases were important in all rituals that involved feasting related to religious, social, or political occasions. All individuals would then have employed such vases, and these would be distributed among all ranks. Then, the distribution of polychrome vases at Motul only suggests that royal compounds were involved in more feasting than lower ranks.

In sum, our examination of architectural volume, construction, and layout, together with artifact distributions indicate that wealth, estate, and political power converged most significantly to distinguish the royal elites (Rank 1) from the remaining social groups (Ranks 2 and 3). Although such a division may imply a two strata system, we suggest that social and political dynamics were much more complex for such a simplified dichotomy (see also Emery, this volume). Incidentally, in his exploration of "eliteness" at the Aztec-period city-state of Otumba, Garraty (2000) finds a similar distribution and comments: this "illustrate[s] the fluidity of wealth and privilege beyond the simple noble-commoner distinctions described by many colonial sources" (fig. 5, 333–34). We could hypothesize that the elite *estate* may have been claimed by Rank 2 (or even some Rank 3) groups as suggested by the substantial architectural investment in Rank 2 groups with their stone masonry and stone roofs, even though not all of them may have had the necessary economic capital or have engaged in political aggrandizing strategies on the necessary scale to convert hereditary privilege into noticeable material gain. In turn, some lower-status groups of Rank 3 without hereditary titles (and hence not of elite *estate*), were successful in acquiring some degrees of wealth or political power beyond the typical means of their commoner *estate*. We contend that these diverse strategies of social mobility are evident in the "messiness" of the archaeological record, especially between Ranks 2 and 3.

5

Figurine Economies at Motul de San José

Multiple and Shifting Modes of Valuation

CHRISTINA T. HALPERIN

Recent archaeological research on craft production (Bayman 2002; Hruby and Flad 2007; Spielmann 2002), goods exchange (Aswani and Sheppard 2003; Bruck 2006), and ritual economy (Wells 2006; Wells and Salazar 2007) have emphasized multiple modes in which goods acquire and take on value. These emphases recognize that the meanings and worth of material objects are contingent on their social and historical contexts. In turn, their valuation is not grounded in "purely" economic, social, political, or ritual terms, but in mutually affecting or combinations of these ontological spheres. Such contextual and mutually affecting sources of valuation are epitomized by recent attention to social valuables, "objects used in ritual performance and social payments" whose "worth" is produced by multiple influences including the exotic, sacred, or cosmological significance of the raw material, their mode of production, distribution, life history, and aesthetics (Spielmann 2002, 198). Unlike prestige goods, these objects may have been, but were not necessarily, controlled by political elites (Bayman 2002; Janusek 1999). In addition, whereas social valuables often marked social difference or heterarchy, they did not always reinforce social hierarchy. As such, they allow for a more inclusive discussion of the social meanings of material goods as they relate to their material acquisition and use. Both social valuables and prestige goods, however, are often considered as inalienable possessions in that they were highly personalized items that embodied their owners; were often unique or rare; and were exchanged only through formal, restricted networks as heirlooms or gifts (Earle 2004; Mills 2004; Weiner 1992).

In this chapter, I examine Late and Terminal Classic figurines from the Motul de San José region in relation to the concepts of social valuables with particular reference to figurine economies as they intersect with figurine imagery and performative use. The model of social valuables is useful in that the social meanings and the economic importance of ceramic figurines were not uniform, but were multiple and shifting. I find that although some ceramic figurines may have functioned as prestige goods and inalienable possessions, most figurines in the Motul de San José region could not be considered as such. Rather, they were widely distributed and used by most if not all households in the region. On the other hand, figurines cannot be characterized as subsistence or utilitarian goods, often the most common forms of alienable possessions. Furthermore, the figurine production and distribution patterns found in the Motul de San José region were not necessarily present at all Maya sites, suggesting that figurine valuation was spatially diverse. In order to explore these nuances in Late Classic figurine economies, I examine figurine (1) manufacturing techniques, (2) contexts of production, and (3) density distributions across the Motul de San José region and compare these patterns to other regions of the Maya area, such as central Belize, Quiriguá and Copan, and Tikal.

Motul de San José Figurine Collection and Contexts of Recovery

The Motul de San José region figurines were recovered by the Proyecto Arqueológico Motul de San José during the 1998–2005 field seasons. Figurines derived primarily from excavations at the site of Motul de San José and five of its satellite sites, the secondary sites of Akte, Chächäklu'um, and Trinidad de Nosotros, and the tertiary sites of Buenavista and Chäkokot (Foias 1998, 1999, 2001; Foias and Castellanos 2000; Moriarty 2002; Moriarty, Castellanos, and Foias 2003; Moriarty et al. 2007). A total of 2,800 figurines (including complete and fragmentary specimens) have been recovered from these investigations to date. This chapter examines only the Late or Terminal Classic period (Tepeu 1–3) figurines (n = 2,767). They consist of a suite of different figurine representations, such as anthropomorphic, supernatural, zoomorphic, and hybrid figures (zoomorphic-supernatural, human-supernatural, zoomorphic-anthropomorphic).

Classic Maya figurines are often associated with domestic rituals because they are frequently recovered from households (Hendon 2003; Moholy-Nagy 2003; Triadan 2007; Willey 1972, 1978). In turn, most of the figurines from the Motul de San José region were recovered in fragmentary condition from household middens and fill.[1] A growing body of evidence from sites throughout the Maya area, however, suggests that it is also productive to consider figurines as part of a more diverse range of practices, including their use within public, civic-ceremonial contexts, caves, and sweatbaths (Halperin 2007, 285–300). Although the Motul de San José Archaeological Project's excavations in public, ceremonial zones were relatively limited in scope, one figurine may have been deposited as an offering on a stela platform in front of Motul's twin-pyramid complex and a large sample (n = 155) of figurines were excavated from a ceremonial feasting midden located at the edge of a ball court at the site of Trinidad.

The presence of figurines in a small sample of Classic period burials throughout the Maya area indicates that they are often found in high-status and low-status, adult and child, as well as male and female interments. Nonetheless, they are more often recovered from those of adult females and children than adult males (Ardren 2002; Halperin 2007, 295–96, table 8.13; Healy 1988; López Bravo 2000; Pina Chán 1996; Ruscheinsky 2003; Sears, Bishop, and Blackman 2004; Welsh 1988). Thus, while figurines may highlight the performative roles of women and children, it is unlikely that they were exclusively used by any single age group or sex group. Because most Late Classic Maya figurines were musical instruments (see below), I consider them as integral to both informal performances (nonstructured parts of large-scale ceremonies, festivals, and spectacles, or small-scale entertainment and play) as well as small-scale formal rituals (Halperin 2007, 334–43). The shift in their performative roles recognizes but also appropriately bisects dichotomies of children and adult as well as play and ritual.

Manufacturing Techniques

One way in which prestige goods and social valuables are assessed is by relatively high levels of skill and labor invested in their production. It is often assumed that more specialized producers manufacture goods with higher levels of skill or labor investment than less specialized producers (Brumfiel and Earle 1987; Costin 1991, 2001; Costin and Hagstrum 1995). In particular, elite and attached specialists can produce prestige goods that involve relatively large labor investments and skill levels because they can afford to devote more time to, and thus acquire more practice (i.e., skill) in, manufacturing activities. In addition, the disposal of their craft goods is guaranteed. Thus, they are not under constraints to be competitive or to improve their productive efficiency (Costin 1991, 38; Costin and Hagstrum 1995; cf. Spielmann 2002). One way to measure labor investments is by using production step indices (Feinman, Upham, and Lightfoot 1981).

This perspective follows a labor theory of value (Clark 2007, 27; Marx 1982, 29–30). In turn, the products of elite or certain revered artisans can be imbued with more prestige or value as a result of the producer's specialized knowledge, social status, or access to the sacred (Inomata 2001b). As Spielmann (2002, 200), Janusek (1999), and others have pointed out, however, specialized, nonelite artisans may also produce social valuables. These artisans do not fit neatly into the dichotomous categorization of attached/elite producers and independent specialists because their products are not necessarily for elite patrons, on the one hand, or for unrestricted mass consumption, on the other.

The skill and labor investment involved in figurine production is examined here in reference to the reliance on molding or modeling techniques as well as the quality of modeling. Based on ethnographic research of pottery production, I suggest that molded and crudely modeled figurines involved less labor investment or skill than finely modeled or partially modeled figurines. Using these criteria and taking into consideration their music-making capacities, I divide the Motul de San José figurine collection into four general manufacturing types (Table 5.1). These manufacturing types are based, in part, on an earlier figurine typology by Ivic de Monterroso (1999, 2002) for the Piedras Negras figurine collection as well as other works describing Classic Maya figurine manufacturing techniques (Goldstein 1979, 52–56; Hammond 1975b, 371–72; Schlosser 1978, 46–51).[2] I then discuss the distribution of these types among different status households and sites in the Motul region. Although the different manufacturing types may reflect some differences in labor and skill levels, they reflect little differences in figurine access and consumption. Rather, what appeared to have been more definitive in marking difference or prestige was the combination of the manufacturing type with the figurines' imagery and musical capabilities.

Ethnographic Research

Ethnographic data suggest that mold technology often reduces production time and requires less skill than many modeling techniques. For example, Arnold's (1985, 1999) research among contemporary Maya potters from Ticul, Yucatán, found that adults with little to no experience in ceramic production could quickly learn how to produce figurines using vertical half molds. He notes that the mold-made products of an amateur were indistinguishable from those of a master ceramicist. In contrast, traditional coiling

Table 5.1. Figurine manufacturing types with description and musical capabilities

Type	Description	n	% (total)	% (identified)	Music characteristics
Appliqué	Modeled appliqué part; could have been attached to any figurine type	556	20.09		
Mold	Mold fragment	2	0.07		
Type 1	Full-figure, one-sided press mold; plainly modeled back and base	1375	49.69	77.73	Ocarina
Type 1a	Molded head and molded body; plainly modeled back and base	2	0.07	0.11	Ocarina
Type 1 or 3	Molded head; unknown body type	68	2.46	3.84	Ocarina
Type 2	Crudely modeled head and body	64	2.31	3.62	Ocarina or whistle
Type 2a	Crudely modeled body (head not present for identification)	98	3.54	5.54	Ocarina or whistle
Type 2b	Crudely modeled head and body; body is the shape of a small tube	2	0.07	0.11	Ocarina
Type 3a	Partly molded; molded heads (some with plugs) attached to modeled bodies (not crudely modeled)	30	1.08	1.70	Some are ocarinas
Type 3b	Molded head with plug (body missing, but presumably plug head was inserted into modeled body)	22	0.80	1.24	Some are ocarinas
Type 3c	Partly molded?; modeled body (neither crudely nor finely modeled) missing head	40	1.45	2.26	Some are ocarinas
Type 4a	Finely modeled head and body	9	0.33	0.51	NA
Type 4b	Finely modeled body; head missing	26	0.94	1.47	NA
Type 4c	Modeled flutes with finely modeled bodies and flat molded faces[a]	17	0.61	0.96	1 chamber flute
Type 4d	Modeled flute	16	0.58	0.90	1, 2, or 3 chamber flute
Indeterminate		440	15.90		
Total		**2,767**	**2,767**	**1,769**	

[a] One of the figurines labeled type 4c (F2669; TRI13E-5-2-2b) is a finely modeled head with two stops and attached to a hollow modeled tube, and another in the type 4c category has a bulbous chamber (F1993; MSJ3A-12-1f) in the form of a goiter flute.

and modeling techniques required "a set of specific motor habit patterns that have been learned over an extended period of time" (Arnold 1999, 64). These skills are best learned during childhood and require extensive training. In addition to the low level of skill involved in making vertical half-mold figurines, Arnold found that they require less fabrication and drying time than modeled types (1985, 205–7).

Ruben Reina and Robert Hill's research in highland Guatemala reveal some of the difficulties associated with producing modeled figurines in comparison to traditional ceramic forms with few protrusions. Because the modeled figurine forms have different wall thicknesses, they must be dried more carefully than ceramic vessels in order to avoid cracking. One of the female potters from Chinautla whom they interviewed remarked:

> [Modeled] Figurine making is free from repetition; each piece is a different work . . . each form we create, how much one needs to think until one succeeds! Just think about making a chicken with all its feathers . . . each single feather is placed on the body, and they must stay on after firing. It requires patience and careful control of the humidity. Firing is a delicate thing. And even as one is finishing an order, one begins to decide what will be the next form. To think and to decide are sometimes very tiring. (1978, 262)

I also conducted an ethnoarchaeological study in March 2006 at the Magaña Art Center in Succotz, Belize, and conducted formal and informal interviews of ceramicists, Davíd and Estrella Magaña. The Magaña Art Center is attached to Davíd and Estrella's house and serves as a full-time crafts workshop. Pottery production is their principal craft, and all of the production steps (clay acquisition at a clay bed in Succotz, clay storage and processing, ceramic forming, drying, and firing) are conducted in their workshop by their extended family. The interviews I conducted also reiterate some of the differences between modeled and molded techniques. Davíd emphasizes the labor over the skill in modeling parts onto molded forms. He stated that "it is not hard [to put on appliqué pieces] it is just the time that takes to do it" (Interview #1 2/4/06). Similarly, Estrella remarked that appliqué techniques were easy. It only gets difficult if one is applying very small and delicate appliqué pieces (personal communication 2/21/06).

Differences in the skill levels between simple molded figurines and more elaborate molded figurines with appliqué parts are also visible in the division of labor of Davíd's brother, an adult ceramicist with many years of experience, and Davíd's nephew, Chepe Magaña, who is less experienced.

David's brother produces effigy pipes and figurines that combine modeled and molded techniques, whereas his adolescent son, Chepe, makes simple, molded bird and turtle whistles. In drawing from these possible differences in skill and labor investment, I assess four general figurine types (see also Ivic de Monterroso 1999, 2002).

Type 1

Type 1 likely required the least amount of labor and skill of all the figurine types because they are almost entirely produced using molds (Figure 5.1). They are completely molded in the front but possess plain, hand-modeled backs and bases. The back is simple and lacks bodily contours. The figurines are hollow and functioned as ocarinas. An ocarina mouthpiece was appliquéd to the back, and a circular base piece outfitted with an airhole was attached to the bottom of the figurine. This flat base piece provides structural stability for the figurine to stand upright. In addition, two stops, placed side by side, were pierced into the figurine back.

The front head and body parts were produced together using a one-sided press mold. At least two examples (designated as Type 1a), however, may have been produced with separate head and body molds. Imprints in the interior of the Type 1 figurines indicate that clay was pressed into the molds using a flat sticklike object rather than the artisan's fingers. Although the bodies were left hollow, the heads were usually solid. In some cases, vertical striations on the back of the head are visible where the artisan had

Figure 5.1. Type 1 figurine, female with hat broken off (probably a broad-brimmed hat), ocarina (ATE2A-1-0-0a; drawing by I. Seyb).

scraped the clay into the mold using a tool with a serrated edge, perhaps by a serrated univalve shell. This manufacturing process is also noted on figurines from Lubaantun (Hammond 1975b, 371). Some of these Type 1 figurines were then adorned with additional appliqué elements (e.g., earspools, hair, headdress elements).[3] Type 1 figurines represent over 77 percent of all identifiable fragments.

These figurines also possess the most diverse figurine representations, including ruler figurines, women with elaborate headdresses and adornment, women with simpler costumes, couple figurines, warrior or warrior performers, ballplayers, musicians, ritual clowns, grotesque or trickster characters, dwarves, owls and other birds, monkeys, felines, dogs, and various other animals. The molded production of the Type 1 figurines also allowed for duplicate figurines with the same image. In other cases, figurine imagery was similar to one another, but did not represent exact duplicates (Halperin 2009).

Type 2

Type 2 figurines are crudely modeled. Their production likely required low skill levels (Figure 5.2). Although the designation of whether a modeling technique was crude or not is a qualitative measure, the Type 2 designation was based primarily on the absence of detailed body and facial features. That is, appendages have few contours and "unrealistic" body proportions. Body parts are composed without the application of reductive techniques (e.g., scraping, shaving) and with minimal shaping techniques (e.g., smoothing, contouring). Thus, arms and legs were stick-shaped and facial features were simple shapes (e.g., plain, circular appendages for eyes). At least four figurines (designated as Type 2b) had small tubular bodies with the ocarina stops located on the ends, and crude feet and head parts protruding from the center of the tube (Figure 5.2b). Like the Type 1 figurines, the Type 2 versions were either ocarinas, which possess two stops, or whistles, which possesses only an air vent for the production of a single-note (T. Lee 1969, 65). In rare cases, they also had suspension holes for hanging by a cord or string (Figure 5.2c). Most of the crudely modeled figurines (77 percent) depicted animals. Of the identifiable Type 2 zoomorphic figurines, 80 percent were birds. Interestingly, in Piña Chán's (1996) documentation of burials from Jaina, Campeche, he mentions the presence of anthropomorphic figurines in both adult and child burials, but only mentions zoomorphic figurines-whistles in reference to burials of children (Entierros 12, 52, 22, 30, 32). In addition, Type 2 figurines from the Motul de San José region are

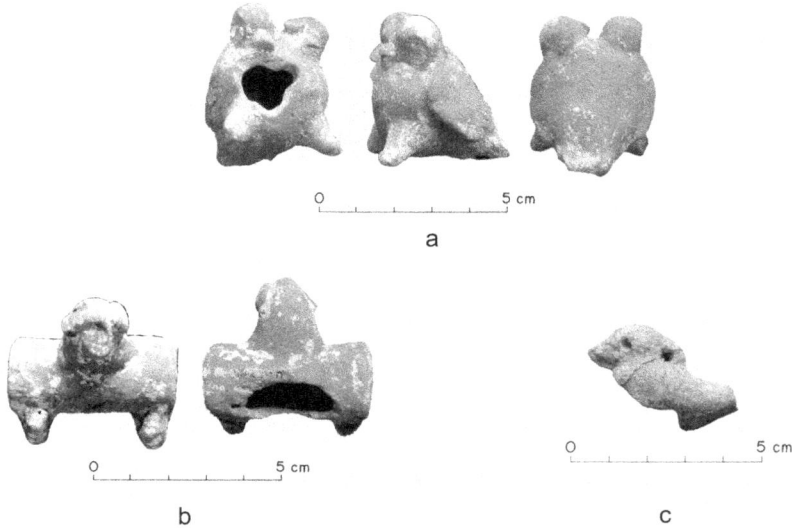

Figure 5.2. Type 2 figurines: (a) Type 2a, bird pair, whistle, or ocarina (MSJ2A-40-4-1e); (b) Type2b, bird, ocarina (MSJ8B-2-5-1a); (c) Type 2a with suspension hole, ocarina (MSJ15A-40-2-4a; photos by C. Halperin).

generally smaller than the other figurines and thus, may have been used, if not produced, by children.

Type 3

The third type identified in the Motul de San José collection is a partially molded technique in which a molded head was attached to a hollow, modeled body (Figure 5.3). Figurine bodies are supported by either four (zoomorphic) or two (anthropomorphic/supernatural) legs unlike the flat clay slabs of Type 1 figurines. Type 3 is divided into three subtypes, Type 3a, 3b, and 3c, some of which may overlap with Type 4. Type 3a consists of molded heads, many with plug appendages, attached to modeled bodies. The plug was located at the neck area where the head was fit into a circular neck hole created at the shoulders of the modeled body (Figure 5.3a). The body fragments were not crudely modeled like in Type 2, and some showed signs of very elaborate details and contours (Figure 5.3b). As such, these figurines likely required higher skill levels than Type 2 figurines and likely higher skill and labor investment levels than Type 1 figurines. Some of these body appendages appeared to have been made with a stick of wood that served as the base around which the clay was formed. The stick burns out during the

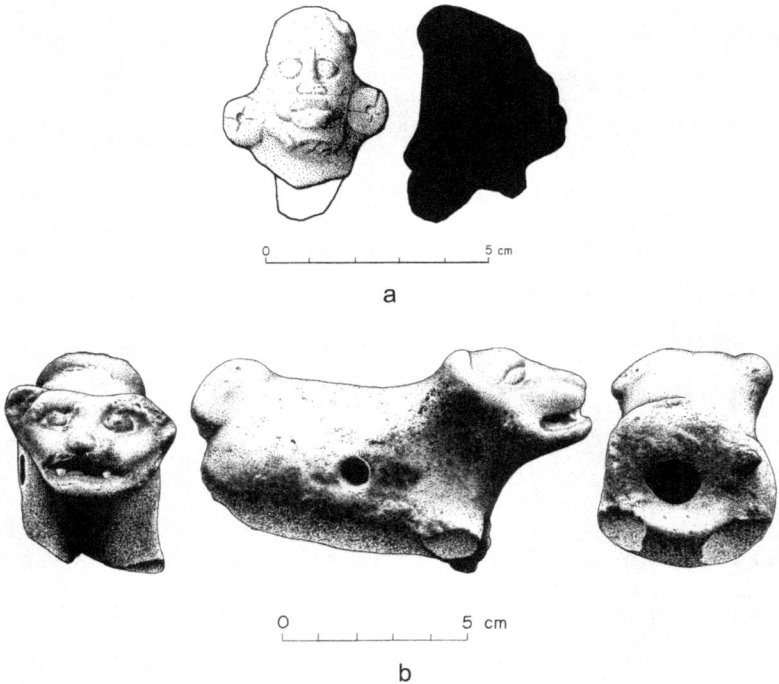

Figure 5.3. Type 3 figurines: (a) Type 3a, "grotesque" head with appendage for insertion into hollow body (MSJ29F-7-2-3a; drawing by Ingrid Seyb); (b) Type 3b, feline, ocarina (TRI6D-9-2-1a; drawing by L. F. Luin).

firing process to form a hollow cylindrical area. Type 3b consists of molded plug heads missing body parts. Presumably, these heads were once attached to modeled bodies. Molded head fragments without plugs or body parts, however, were placed in a miscellaneous Type 1 or 3 category because neither Type 1 nor 3 could be distinguished based on the available remaining portion of the figurine. Type 3c represents modeled body parts that were not crudely modeled like Type 2. Some possessed circular holes at the neck where a head plug could be inserted.

Like Types 1 and 2, many of the more intact Type 3 specimens also served as ocarinas as they were outfitted with stops and mouthpieces. Others possessed stop holes typically found on Type 3a ocarina bodies. Because they were missing their heads, however, it is also possible that they possessed modeled heads as well. Like the Type 1 figurines, Type 3 figurine imagery was diverse, encompassing various anthropomorphic types, dwarves, grotesque or trickster figures, and zoomorphic figures (deer, jaguar, lizard, monkey, turtle).

Type 4

Type 4 figurines are finely modeled and likely overlap in labor investment and skill with Type 3 (Figure 5.4). Although completely modeled figurines are the norm during the Preclassic period, they are less common during the Late Classic period. In fact, these figurines were the least common of all figurine types. Type 4 figurines are divided into flutes and non-music-producing figurines. They include Type 4a, finely modeled heads and bodies, and 4b, finely modeled bodies with missing heads. The bodies had realistic features and contours manufactured using smoothing and reductive techniques to shape details such as the knees, calves, and ankles. The Type 4b figurines consisted primarily of freestanding male legs and torsos (Figure 5.4a, b) and parallel the "semisolid, simply dressed" males in the Altar de Sacrificios collection (Willey 1972, 45–49, fig. 37) and Jaina Group B-F and Jaina Modeled Misc. figurines (Corson 1976). Ivic de Monterroso (2002, 556) also notes that modeled figurines at Piedras Negras tended to represent males whereas a greater number of molded figurines represented females. Although there might be an inclination to categorize these figurines as children's toys or "dolls" because they lack music-making capacities, these figurines are the least likely to have been handled by children as they are the most fragile with their modeled protrusions and the least structurally sound with two modeled feet supports rather than flat bases or four legs.

Type 4c represented effigy flutes whose effigy bodies were finely modeled but whose face alone appears to have been produced with a mold (Figure 5.4c). The molded faces were relatively flat in order to fit without too much protrusion on the circular, modeled flute. The modeled flute walls were uniform and well crafted. They contained stops along the flute cylinder. Some solitary, flat molded faces were also recovered. These faces were probably attached to flutes, although one has two suspension holes on either side of the forehead and may have been turned into a pendant. Although sample sizes were low among this category, no women effigy flutes were present. Only zoomorphic, anthropomorphic males, or supernatural figures with male-gendered clothing were identified. Type 4d represents modeled single, double, or triple chamber flutes (Figure 5.4d). Although all of the specimens were fragmentary and could have possessed a figural effigy

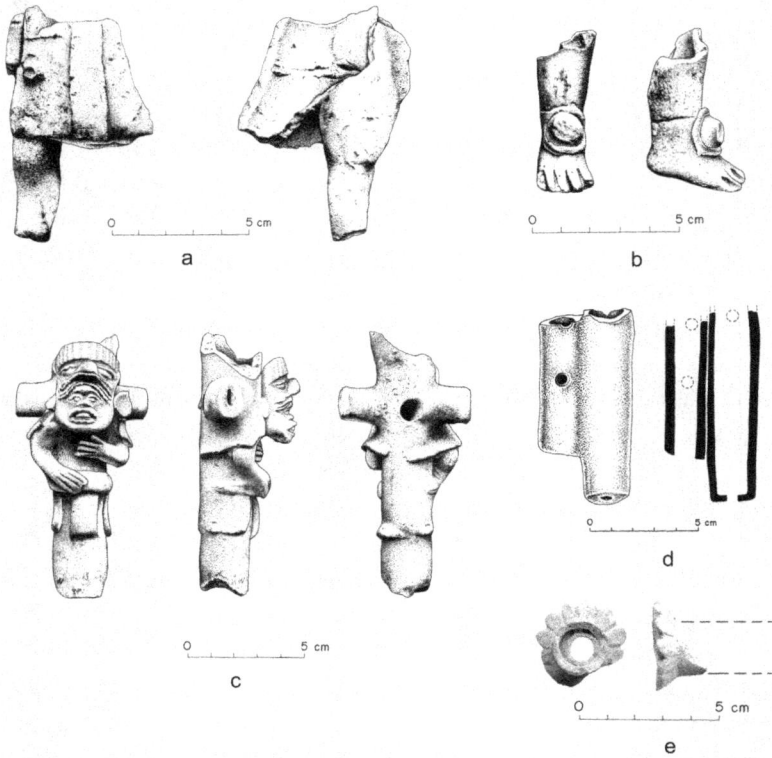

Figure 5.4. Type 4 figurines: (a) Type 4b, hollow, finely modeled anthropomorphic male body (MSJ39G-7-2-1n); (b) Type 4b, hollow, finely modeled anthropomorphic body (MSJ2B-1-4-1j); (c) Type 4c, finely modeled effigy flute, dwarf (TRI13E-5-3-1b); (d) Type 4d, modeled double-chambered flute (MSJ2A-3-12-1a); (e) Type 4d, modeled single-chambered flute with flower on distal end (MSJ46A-1-2-4a; drawings by L. F. Luin; photo by C. Halperin).

attached to them, no effigies were visible. One fragment, however, had a modeled flower at the distal end similar to other flutes found throughout Mesoamerica that appear to cross-reference the sweet scent of flowers with the sound of music (Figure 5.4e; Taube 2000, 114–15, fig. 102; see also K5534 for the depiction of flowers at the distal end of a trumpet and Healy [1988, 30] for a flower design at the end of a flute from Pacbitun). Because the 4d flutes lacked elaborate effigy modeling, labor and skill levels may have been lower than for their 4c counterparts.

Types 4c and 4d contrast with the figurine ocarinas not only in shape, but also in their ability for a greater sound-production range. The flutes had more stops than the ocarinas and came in multiple forms, some with multiple chambers and at least one with a bulbous chamber. In addition, flutes were played as part of formal musical ensembles (Miller 1988) and musicians with flutes are portrayed in a range of iconographic media. Interestingly, despite their greater frequencies in archaeological contexts, ocarinas are relatively absent from any imagery. This inversion of artifact frequencies and iconographic representation is explored further below.

Distribution of Figurine Manufacturing Types

Figurine-manufacturing-type distributions at Motul de San José and Chäkokot reveal that households of different statuses had access to all four figurine types regardless of their architectural volumetric rank (Figure 5.5, Table 5.2; Rank 1 = elite; Rank 2 = lesser elite/middle status; Rank 3 = commoner; see discussion of volumetric rankings in Foias et al., this volume). Type 1 figurines are the most common manufacturing type and are indiscriminately present in all contexts. Some very slight differences from the other manufacturing types, however, were observable. The smaller Volumetric Rank 3 and Rank 2 households had slightly higher percentages of the Type 2 crudely modeled figurines than households of Volumetric Rank 1. In turn, the smaller households possessed comparatively fewer finely

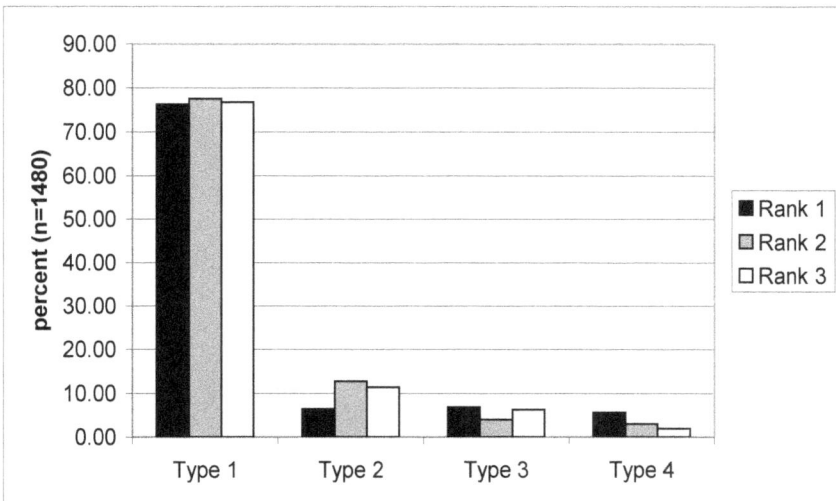

Figure 5.5. Comparison of figurine manufacturing types by volumetrically ranked architectural groups.

Table 5.2. Manufacturing types by volumetrically ranked architectural groups from Motul de San José and the East Transect (MSJ and CHT)

	Volumetric rank 1		Volumetric rank 2		Volumetric rank 3		
	N	%	N	%	N	%	% SD
Type 1	531	76.29	411	77.55	195	76.77	0.63
Type 1a	0	0.00	0	0.00[a]	2	0.79	0.45
Type 1 or 3	33	4.74	14	2.64	7	2.76	1.18
Type 2	14	2.01	26	4.91	14	5.51	1.87
Type 2a	29	4.17	40	7.55	15	5.91	1.69
Type 2b	2	0.29	2	0.38	0	0.00	0.20
Type 3a	16	2.30	7	1.32	5	1.97	0.50
Type 3b	9	1.29	7	1.32	4	1.57	0.16
Type 3c	23	3.30	7	1.32	7	2.76	1.02
Type 4a	6	0.86	2	0.38	0	0.00	0.43
Type 4b	14	2.01	5	0.94	3	1.18	0.56
Type 4c	10	1.44	3	0.57	1	0.39	0.56
Type 4d	9	1.29	6	1.13	1	0.39	0.48
Subtotal	696		530		254		
Appliqué	197	18.73	201	22.46	87	21.59	1.95
Indeterminate	159	15.11	164	18.32	62	15.38	1.78
Total	**1,748**		**1,425**		**657**		

Notes: Percentages of types derive from subtotal. SD = standard deviation.

modeled figurines (Type 4a and 4b) and rare musical instruments, such as flutes (Type 4c), effigy flutes (Type 4d), and tubular ocarinas with crudely modeled faces (Type 2b), than did the larger Rank 1 and 2 households.

Inter-site distributions of the figurine types reveal similar results to the household rank distributions (Table 5.3). Types 1 and 2 molded and crudely modeled figurine ocarinas and whistles were present at all sites except Chächäklu'um whose sample size was small (only three figurines could be identified for manufacturing type). At the tertiary centers of Buenavista and Chäkokot, the Type 2, crudely modeled, figurines were slightly higher than those from Trinidad and Motul de San José. The site of Trinidad, whose sample size of figurines was larger than the other satellite sites, possessed a range of figurines types. Most of the Trinidad Type 4 figurines (87.5 percent) were restricted to an elite residence (Group U, Op. 13E) or a ball court midden (Group F, Op. 10D) with the exception of a single eroded zoomorphic effigy flute, which was excavated from the small residential Group O.

Thus, in comparison to the molded (Type 1) and crudely modeled (Type 2) figurine whistles and ocarinas, ceramic effigy flutes, flutes, and non-music-making figurines (Type 4) appear to be more restricted in distribution (Figure 5.6). These rarer types may also parallel the distribution of other ceramic instruments. For example, excavations during the 2005 field season recovered ceramic drums only from excavations adjacent (nine drums; Op. 2 [Rank 1]) and near (four drums; Op. 46 [Rank 2]) Motul de San José's Acropolis and were absent from excavations of households in the northern periphery (Op. 39 [Rank 3]; Op. 42 [Rank3]) and of households (Op. 44E and 44C [Rank 3]) from Chäkokot. They also appear to parallel the distribution of formal deity figurines from Motul (only six were found; all were from elite contexts) and outside the region (whether made from clay, wood, bone, or stone), where they appear primarily in public ceremonial or elite palace contexts (Coggins 1988; Miller and Martin 2004; Rands, Bishop, and Harbottle 1978; Rands and Rands 1959; P. Rice 1999).

Production Context

Another way in which prestige goods and social valuables are assessed is by examining production context. Prestige goods and social valuables may have been produced in either elite (as attached specialists or as elite artisans) or nonelite contexts (as corvée laborers, embedded specialists, etc.; see Costin 1991, 2001; Costin and Hagstrum 1995; Janusek 1999; Spielmann

Table 5.3. Manufacturing types by sites in the Motul de San José region

	MSJ		TRI		TBV		CHT		ATE		CHA	
	n	%	n	%	n	%	n	%	n	%	n	%
Type 1	1,085	76.52	200	82.99	32	78.05	52	85.25	3	42.86	3	100
Type 1a	2	0.14		0.00				0.00				
Type 1 or 3	54	3.81	13	5.39	1	2.44		0.00				
Type 2	50	3.53	4	1.66	2	4.88	4	6.56	2	28.57		
Type 2a	83	5.85	9	3.73	6	14.63		0.00				
Type 2b	4	0.28		0.00				0.00				
Type 3a	27	1.90	2	0.83			1	1.64				
Type 3b	19	1.34	2	0.83			1	1.64				
Type 3c	36	2.54	3	1.24			1	1.64				
Type 4a	8	0.56	1	0.41				0.00				
Type 4b	21	1.48	4	1.66			1	1.64				
Type 4c	14	0.99	3	1.24				0.00				
Type 4d	15	1.06		0.00			1	1.64				
Total	1,418		241		41		61		5		3	

Note: Excludes appliqué and indeterminate figurine fragments.

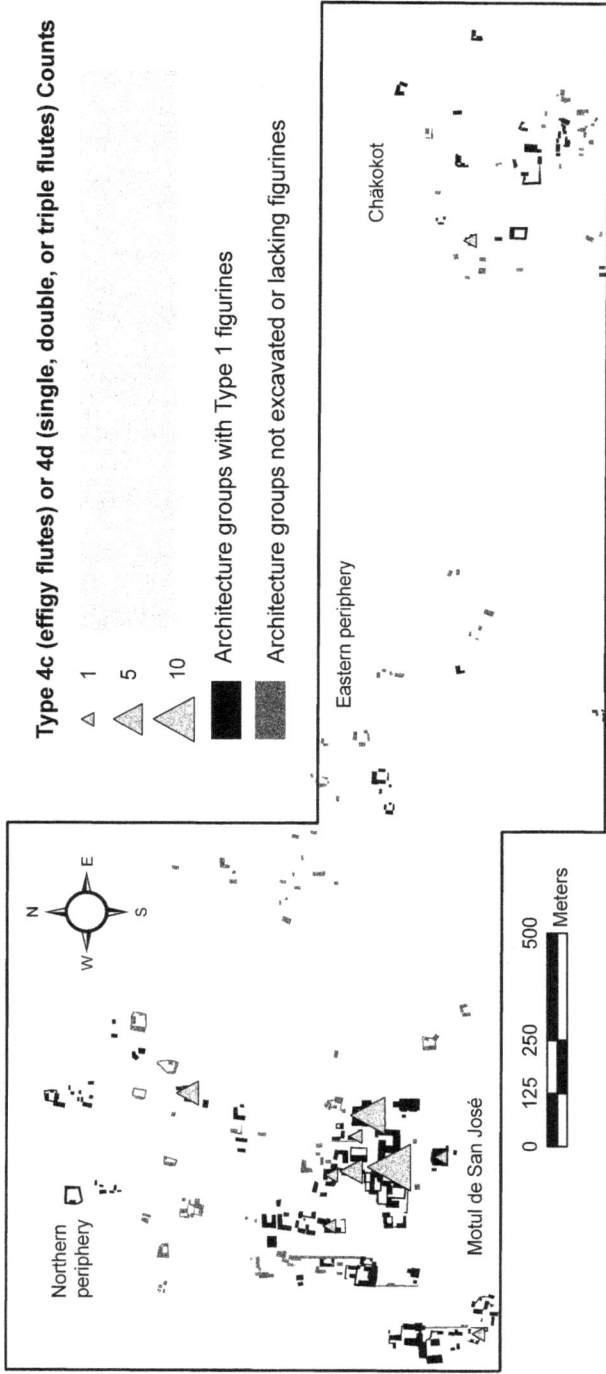

Type 4c (effigy flutes) or 4d (single, double, or triple flutes) Counts

△ 1
◁ 5
◁ 10

■ Architecture groups with Type 1 figurines

▨ Architecture groups not excavated or lacking figurines

Northern periphery

Eastern periphery

Chäkokot

Motul de San José

0 125 250 500

Meters

Figure 5.6. Distributions of Type 4c and 4d figurines in comparison to Type 1 figurines from Motul de San José and the East Transect.

2002; Trubitt 2000). Maya archaeologists, however, have found evidence of highly skilled crafting of prestige goods, such as pyrite mirrors, polychrome ceramics with hieroglyphs, codices, obsidian eccentrics, jade jewelry and sculpture, and marine shell ornaments primarily within the contexts of Maya palaces and elite residences (e.g., Ball 1993; Coe and Kerr 1998; Emery 2003b; Hruby 2007; Inomata 2001b; Inomata et al. 2002; Reents-Budet 1998; Reents-Budet, Bishop, and MacLeod 1994). In some cases, however, initial stages of production of even the most restricted items may have been conducted by nonelites with the final stages and/or use ultimately controlled by elites (Kovacevich 2007). Was Maya figurine production controlled, to some degree, by elite members of society? Was production undertaken as a bottom-up (taking place in periphery settlements and within commoner households) or top-down affair (taking place in urban settlements and in the context of elite or middle-status households)?

One possible site of figurine production at Motul de San José is in or by the Acropolis at Group C, the likely location of the (or one of the) royal palace(s) where a single figurine mold fragment was recovered. As mentioned in Halperin and Foias (this volume), this area of the site also possessed the largest number of figurine matches (n = 15; with four of the matching match mates found from the same operation), and duplicate figurines found in the same context tend to occur close to production areas (Barbour 1975, 118–19; Feinman 1999, 92; Hernández et al. 1999, 77). In addition, a possible figurine mold fragment was also found at the site of Akte (Figure 5.7). It was recovered from a midden associated with the largest, elite residential group of the site (Yorgey 2005, 58–59). Although it is larger in size than the figurine mold fragment from Motul de San José, the interior iconography of the specimen is not discernable.

Figurine molds have been found at the other sites within the Maya area. When examined together, the data indicate that: (1) figurine production occurred both in the core of large centers and in smaller, peripheral sites, although more evidence is available for the former; (2) the contexts of production was likely household-based; and (3) households of a range of different social statuses participated in figurine production although more evidence exists for elite and epicenter contexts of production.

Production within Site Centers

Figurine molds have often been found within elite contexts or centralized areas of settlements, such as at Aguateca, Altar de Sacrificios, El Chal, Ixtonton, Lagatero, Lubaantun, Palenque, and Seibal (Table 5.4). At Lubaantun

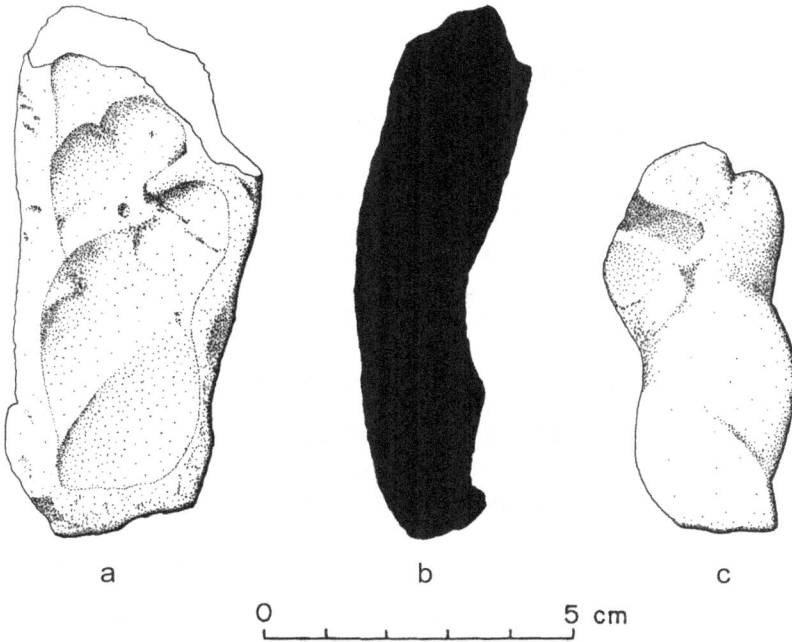

Figure 5.7. Possible figurine mold fragment from Akte (ATE1A-1-6-3): (a) plan;
(b) cross-section; (c) contemporary positive (drawing by I. Seyb).

in southern Belize, for example, Hammond (1975, 373) reports that all of
the molds with known provenience come from an area around Plaza IV
where elite residences and the main ceremonial and administrative structures are located. At Palenque, two of the four figurine molds with known
provenience documented by Schele and Mathews (1979, figs. 902, 903) were
found in the ceremonial precinct of the site, 100 meters west of the Temple
of Inscriptions. Interestingly, the latter two molds portray state symbolism:
one is an architectural replica of a pyramid structure and the other is a
figure with a large feathered headdress. Rands (1967, 143; Rands and Rands
1959, 225) also notes that cache vessels, *incensarios*, serving vessels, and 98
percent of figurine molds and figurines all share the same quartz tempered,
red-brown paste and were probably made locally, at or close to the site.

At Aguateca, figurine molds were recovered in the site epicenter (Inomata 1995, tables 7.12, 7.14; Triadan 2007). Inomata argues that two structures, Str. K7–11 and M8–19, were loci of figurine production because they
possessed both figurine molds and high frequencies of figurines. The structures consisted of low rectangular featureless platforms. He suggests that

Table 5.4. Figurine mold distributions at sites in the Maya area

Site	Citation	No. of molds	Mold recovery locations	Time
Aguateca, Guatemala	Inomata (1995, tables 7.12, 7.114)	8	Site epicenter; Structures K7-11, M6-18, and M8-19.	LC
Akte, Guatemala	Triadan (2007, table 2)	5	Site epicenter; elite domestic structures.	LC
	Yorgey (2005, 58–59)	1	One possible mold fragment found in association with the central, elite residential group of the site.	LC
Altar de Sacrificios	Willey (1972, 72–74, fig. 59, 60)	3	Site center; 1 -Mound 20; 1-Structure A-I; 1-Structure A-II.	LC & TC
Cancuen, Guatemala	Sears (2007)	4	NA	
Comalcalco, Mexico	Gallegos Gómora (2003, 48)	NA	Molds and 480 figurine fragments found from a single residential structure.	LC
Copan, Honduras	Hendon (2003, 32)	1	One mold of an animal whistle figurine was found in the eastern sector of Copan where noble residential compounds were located.	
El Chal, Guatemala	Laporte, Reyes, and Chocon (2004, 343, F-189)	1	Site center; Bs-044 (anthropomorphic head)	TC
Ixtonton, Guatemala	Laporte, Reyes, and Chocon (2004, 303, H033)	1	Site center; Plaza B; Est. Sur (couple figurine mold).	TC
Lagartero, Mexico	Ekholm (1979a, 185)	20	Site center; large ceremonial refuse midden located in the central plaza of the site.	LC
Lubaantun, Belize	Rivero Torres (2002, 47–50)	37	Ball court and associated altars.	LC-EPC
	Hammond (1975b, 373)	NA	All of the molds with known provenience come from the area around Plaza IV where the main ceremonial and administrative structures are located.	LC
Motul de San José, Guatemala	reported here	1	One figurine mold fragment found in a large midden (Op.2A) at the edge of the Acropolis.	LC

Site	Reference	Count	Notes	Period
Palenque, Mexico	Rands and Rands (1959, 225); Rands (1965, 54)	NA	Molds are reported as "fairly numerous at the site."	LC
	Schele and Mathews (1979, figs. 902, 903)	4	Two have no provenience data and two were found 100 meters west of the Temple of Inscriptions.	LC
Piedras Negras, Guatemala	Schlosser (1978, 44)	2	NA	LC
	Ivic de Monterroso (2002, 556, fig. 3)	2	NA	LC
Quirigua, Guatemala	Ashmore (1988, 164; 2007, 121–22, 173, 260, 283, 315)	34	Two molds were found in the Site Core. The remaining molds were found in four loci within Quirigua's Floodplain Periphery (1A-28, one mold; Str. 3C-13, two molds; Group 3E-3, one mold; Mdn. 7C-1, twenty-eight molds).	LC
Seibal, Guatemala	Willey (1978, 9, 37–38, fig. 44)	6	Site center; five molds come from residential structures located adjacent to the main plazas or near the principal causeways; one was found in fill from Temple 5113.	LC
Tikal, Guatemala	Becker (1973, 399; 2003a)	4	Plaza Plan 2 residential Group 4H-1 belonging to "middle-class" inhabitants.	LC
	Haviland (1985, tables 43, 46)	2	Small structure residential Groups 4F-1 and 4F-2 possessed one figurine mold each.	LC
Xunantunich, Belize	LeCount (1996, 427); Briggs Braswell (1998, 696)	3	Three molds found in Structure D-7 in elite residential Group D located in the site center.	TC

Notes: LC = Late Classic period; C = Classic period; TC = Terminal Classic period; EPC = Early Postclassic period.

figurine production was small in scale due to the number of figurines from these loci and the presence of the molds from multiple structures (n = 3; 1995, 551). These combined data from the different sites suggest, as P. Rice (1987a, 79) noted two decades ago, that whereas civic-ceremonial centers were largely consumers of ceramics produced outside the center, some elite wares and specialized ceramic forms, such as figurines, were probably produced within civic-ceremonial centers. In this sense, figurine production conform more to what McAnany (1989, 365) calls a "core model" of production in which manufacture occurs within centers rather than a "ring model" in which manufacturing loci are thought to have been located primarily outside centers.

Household Production

Many of the figurine molds from Maya sites were found, like those from Tikal and Aguateca, in association with household structures. This find supports the general notion that craft production in Mesoamerica was conducted primarily on the scale of the household (Feinman and Nicholas 2000, 2004; McAnany 1989, 1993a). At Motul de San José, the large Op. 2A midden containing evidence of polychrome pottery and possibly of figurine production also included utilitarian vessels, obsidian blades, spindle whorls, and bone tools in addition to the large quantities of polychrome vessels, figurines, and pottery production refuse (see Halperin and Foias, this volume). The unusually high number of molds from the site of Lagatero provides an exception to this trend. They were found in public ceremonial contexts with large numbers of other figurines.[4] The ones recovered by Ekholm in the central plaza of the site were found in a large midden interpreted as a ceremonial refuse dump (Ekholm 1979a, 1979b, 1985, 1990). This deposition pattern, however, does not necessarily imply that figurines were produced in the plaza area itself.

Craft production conducted as part of household economies may have involved inclusive (multiple genders, multiple age-groups) or exclusive (gender-segregated, age-segregated) practices (Gero and Scattolin 2002; Mills 2000). In contemporary Maya villages, women more than men tend to produce pottery (Reina and Hill 1978). Archaeologists have noted from ethnographic data in many regions of the world, however, that the production of pottery requires many tasks and steps and that both male and female members of a household contribute to the overall production process even though only some members may take the credit as having been the producers (P. Rice 1991b; Wright 1991). As mentioned earlier, ethnographic examples also reveal that children were involved in the fabrication of some of the simpler ceramic and figurine forms, and many archaeologists are recognizing the significant contributions of children in household labor (Ardren and Hutson 2006; Crown 1999; Smith 2006). As mentioned earlier, adolescents may have even been responsible for the modeling of some of the crudely modeled zoomorphic figurines (Type 2a) as they required less skill and are often associated with children. Thus, while it is unclear based on the available evidence who were the primary producers in the past, it is productive to examine their manufacture as inclusive practices.

Elite Figurine Production

Many of the examples also demonstrate that molds have been found associated with elite architecture (Altar de Sacrificios, Akte, Copan, Lagartero, Lubaantun, Motul de San José, Seibal, Xunantunich; see Table 5.4). Figurine production, however, may not have been restricted to elite households or site core zones in all cases. For example, at the urban site of Tikal, figurine molds were excavated from three households located in the eastern section of the site. Four molds were recovered from Group 4H-1, a "middle-class" residential group, and one each was found from the small structure Groups 4F-1 and 4F-2 respectively (Becker 1973, 399; 2003a; Haviland 1985, tables 43, 46). In addition, figurine molds from Quiriguá were found both in the site core and in at least four loci in the surrounding Floodplain Periphery (although none were detected from the Wider Periphery; see Ashmore 1988, 164; 2007, 122, 126, 173, 260, 283, 315). Many of the settlement groups associated with the molds belonged to the lower tier of the settlement hierarchy although some of them (e.g., 1A-28) had "relatively elaborate architectural features" (Ashmore 2007, 126). These data suggest that although figurine molds are often found in elite households, they were not necessarily restricted to these contexts. Nonetheless, figurine production was not a "bottom-up" affair in which we would expect to see greater evidence of production in periphery sites and lower-status households.

Figurine Density Distributions

All sites investigated by the Motul de San José Archaeological Project yielded figurines, revealing their occurrence at multiple sites regardless of their settlement rank (e.g., primary, secondary, and tertiary centers). In addition, Motul de San José and Chäkokot households, regardless of social

Table 5.5. Figurine frequencies by volumetrically ranked architectural groups from Motul de San José and the East Transect

Residential structure groups	Mean	Standard deviation	N	95% confidence
Volumetric rank 1	2.14	0.90	5	±0.79
Volumetric rank 2	1.76	1.28	22	±0.55
Volumetric rank 3	1.17	1.10	23	±0.43
Temple pyramid groups	1.16	1.18	2	±1.64

Note: Excludes groups with < 100 sherds.

class, had access to figurines. These distributions do not support the assignment of figurines as prestige goods (Table 5.5).

Despite the fact that almost all households within the Motul de San José region appeared to have possessed figurines, figurine frequency means were positively correlated with household status (Figures 5.8, 5.9, Table 5.5). Figurine mean frequencies and confidence intervals were calculated by the ratio of figurines to one thousand ceramic sherds. These distribution patterns parallel those of simple polychrome serving vessels at many Late Classic period Maya sites where households of all social classes possessed them, but elite households possessed higher frequencies in comparison to commoner or peripherally-located households (Foias 2006, table 6.1; Fry 1979, 496; 1980, 5; Palka 1997, 298). They contrast with exotic (imported) pottery and polychrome vessels with painted figural scenes with hieroglyphs, which tend to be much rarer or absent in commoner contexts than locally made serving vessels or polychromes with simple geometric forms (Foias 2006; Foias and Bishop 1997; LeCount 1999).[5] I suggest elsewhere that one way in which figurines were exchanged were at festival-markets or other large-scale ceremonial occasions (Halperin et al. 2009). This assertion is based on a relatively homogenous distribution of paste types identified by visual, petrographic, and Instrumental Neutron Activation Analysis (INAA) analyses and the depiction of ceremonial pomp and spectacle on the figurines themselves.

Not all sites in the Maya area, however, possessed such widespread figurine distributions across households, indicating that figurines held different social meanings and values depending on their geographical (and perhaps ethnic) region. At Copan, Hendon (2003, 29) notes that 511 whole or partial figurines were found in thirteen high-status residential compounds located in the eastern sector of Copan during the Copan Archaeological Project

**Figurine/1000 Sherd Ratio Means
and 95% Confidence Intervals**
(exluding samples w <100 sherds)

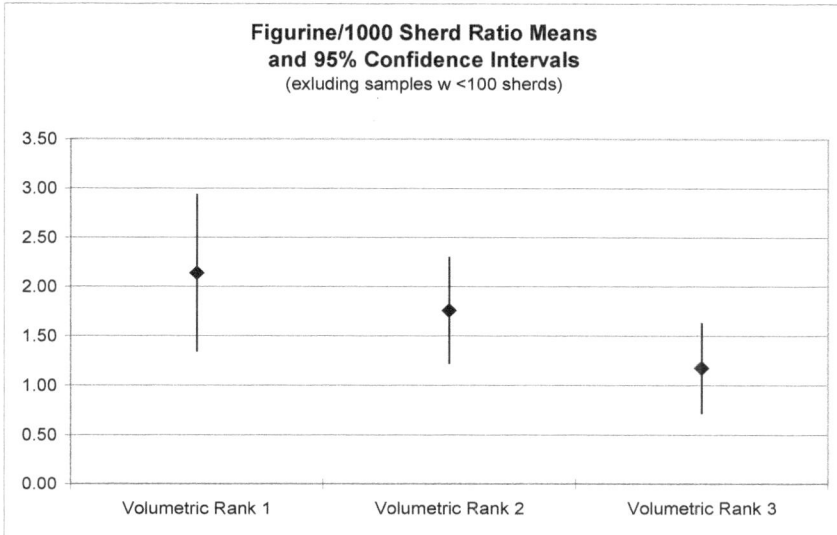

Figure 5.8. Figurine density (figurine to ceramic sherd ratios x 1000) means and 95 percent confidence intervals by volumetrically ranked architectural groups.

Phase II (PAC II) excavations between 1981 and 1984. In contrast, almost no figurines were found in the PAC II investigations of Copan's small rural households (Gonlin 1994). This discrepancy may relate to the finding that most figurines at Copan were imports. Hendon (1991, 909; 2003, 32) notes, for example, that 70 percent came from outside the Copan region, such as the Ulúa Valley where they were produced in large quantities. These distributions contrast with the nearby site of Quiriguá where figurines were recovered from a wide range of households including those from the Acropolis, the Floodplain Periphery, and the Wider Periphery (315 of the 349 figurines reported from the site were found in the site's periphery). Unlike those from Copan, the Quiriguá figurines appear to have been produced locally (Ashmore 2007, 121).

As at Copan, archaeologists working at the site of Xunantunich, Belize, have found restricted distributions of both figurine molds and figurines (LeCount 1996, 427, fig. E.35). Most of them "are representations of kings with large headdresses" (ibid., 427). For example, three figurine molds and fourteen figurines were found in Late Classic II and Terminal Classic contexts at Xunantunich's elite residential Group D. Within the group, these finds were present only from the highest-status households (D-7; the Central Platform Complex; see Briggs Braswell 1998, 288, 696). In contrast,

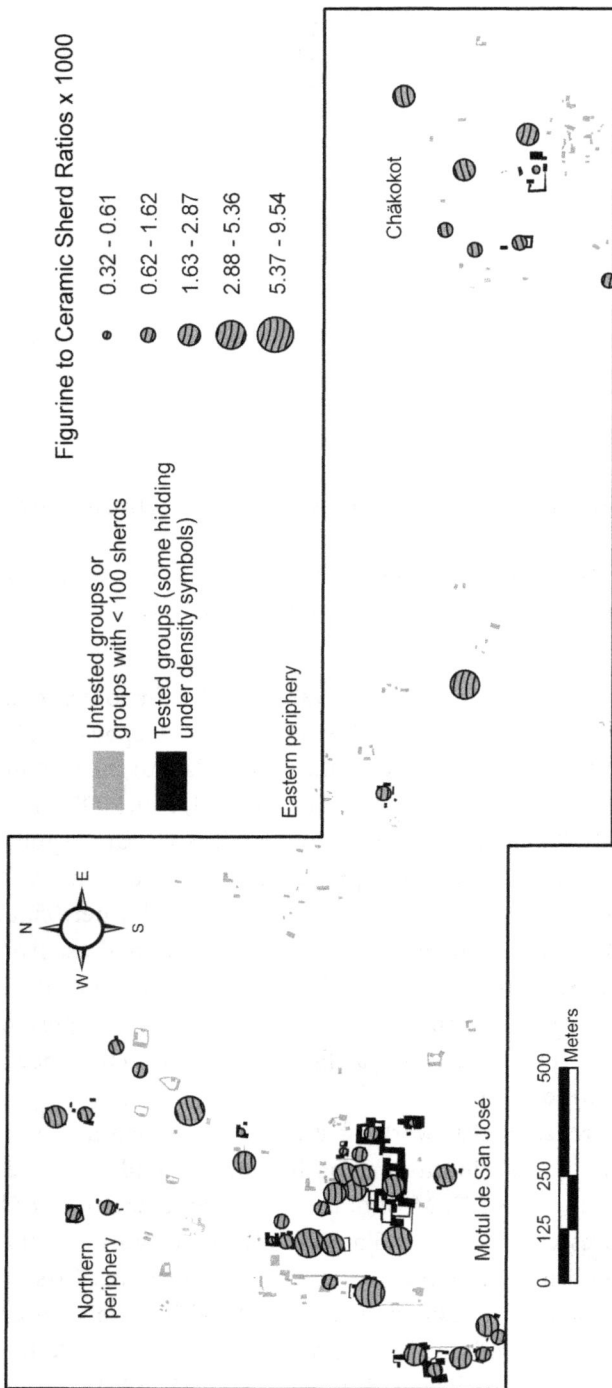

Figure 5.9. Spatial distribution of Motul de San José and East Transect figurine densities.

few figurines were recovered from the center's peripheral settlements. Two anthropomorphic figurine whistles were found with other ritual items (e.g., a bone flute, *incensario* fragments, high frequencies of serving vessels, and faunal remains) from the "public ritual" structure, SL-13 at the outlying community of San Lorenzo (Yaeger 2000, 857–58). None, however, were recovered from the extensive excavations of households throughout the San Lorenzo community. In addition, no figurines were reported from the horizontal and test-pitting excavations at the rural sites of Chan Nòohol and Dos Chombitos Cik'in (Robin 1999). The distinctions between the Copan/Xunantunich figurine finds and those from western and central Maya sites imply that figurines did not have uniform values and uses throughout the Maya area, but may have been considered as prestige goods at some sites and more as social valuables in other regions.

Conclusion

Maya ceramic figurines dating to the Late and Terminal Classic periods are heterogeneous in their social meaning and economic value. Some figurines likely served as prestige goods. In the Motul de San José region, a select group of figurines that required high labor and skill levels (e.g., effigy flutes and finely modeled, non-music-producing figurines) were rarer and more spatially restrictive to elite contexts than many of the other figurine types. Although iconography was not discussed in detail here, formal deity figurines were also highly restrictive in distribution. Thus, although inferred skill and labor investments involved in the production of figurines do not appear to definitively reveal differences in their value by themselves, the combination of these criteria with their function, performative use, and imagery likely created social and economic distinctions in their meaning and worth. These rare figurines and effigy flutes may have been inalienable possessions whose performative value, links to the supernatural, and productive significance were likely intimately tied to their owners (Weiner 1992).

On the other hand, most molded figurines were easily accessible and widely distributed to elite and commoner, as well as capital center and settlement periphery. The limited data available on figurine mold distributions seem to imply that although figurine production was not rigidly controlled by elites, they tend to be produced primarily in site centers rather than periphery settlements. Nonetheless, figurines were not unique or rare social valuables, but a more widespread type of social valuable integral to domestic and nondomestic ritual performance, entertainment, and play. Their easy accessibility and possession may have implicitly or explicitly marked the social and religious activities of a subset of the Maya area, as not all sites participated in the same music-making rituals and performances. In turn, the restricted production and exchange spheres of figurines at sites such as Copan and Xunantunich appear to have reinforced a more prestige-inspired status of the figurines in these regions. In this sense, figurine economies are best examined as situational, fluid, and multiple.

6

Motul de San José Palace Pottery Production

Reconstructions from Wasters and Debris

CHRISTINA T. HALPERIN AND ANTONIA E. FOIAS

The social contexts of Late Classic Maya pottery production have been relatively elusive due to the dearth of archaeologically detected pottery "workshops," areas, or centers. Midden prospecting and test excavations at Motul de San José provide rare evidence of pottery production from a large midden located at the edge of the site's royal and elite residential and administrative structures. Although ceramic kilns and *in situ* production materials were not located, the pottery production debris point to the crafting of polychrome pottery and ceramic figurines by palace artisans.

Motul de San José is known from iconographic studies and chemical sourcing analyses as one of the production centers of the Ik'-style polychromes (Reents-Budet et al., this volume; Reents-Budet, Bishop, and MacLeod 1994; Reents-Budet et al. 2007). These painted, glyphic-bearing vessels vary in design, quality, and chemical signatures. Hence, they were probably produced at different centers in the Motul de San José region for different consumption communities. The finest were reserved for the royal elites, and were gifted among them at ritually charged feasts celebrating rites of passage of the royal dynasties, religious events, and political functions (McAnany 1995; LeCount 1996; Reents-Budet 2000b; Inomata 2001b; Foias 2007). This chapter presents evidence for the recovery of additional Ik'-style pottery vessels as well as direct evidence of pottery production at or near the royal court of Motul de San José uncovered during excavations carried out between 1998 and 2005.

Production Models

Pottery production has garnered a great deal of attention because it has become the focus of multiple debates between divergent views of Maya economic and political systems. Early evolutionary perspectives were concerned with pottery specialization as it correlated with the rise of social and political complexity. The assumption was that economic specialization would increase to meet the needs of a more complex social system and a growing political bureaucracy (Childe 1947, 1951; Service 1975). Archaeological research has since shown, however, that economic specialization and sociopolitical complexity do not always coincide and that specialization was part and parcel of a suite of historical, social, and ecological processes (Earle 2002; Wailes 1996). More recent models have considered agency approaches, which examine the ways in which human actors (whether individuals or groups, factions, communities, etc.) actively used or manipulated economic resources to further their particular social, political, and economic goals (Costin and Wright 1998; Dobres 2000; Dobres and Hoffman 1994; Foias 2007; Inomata 2001b; Schortman and Urban 2004; Wells 2006). In general, these approaches have been extended primarily to the activities and roles of political elites, although increasing research has looked at the active participation of secondary elites and commoners within the economy (Elson and Covey 2006; Iannone and Connell 2003; Lohse and Valdez 2004; McAnany 1993a; Scarborough, Valdez, and Dunning 2003).

One of the most common models of the Classic Maya economy is a two-part system comprising a general economy, which included the manufacture and distribution of utilitarian, everyday goods, and a prestige economy, which revolved around a network of wealth or luxury goods production and circulation (Foias and Emery, this volume; Masson and Freidel 2002; McAnany 1993a; see also Brumfiel and Earle 1987; D'Altroy and Earle 1985; P. Rice 2009a, 2009b). In this two-part system, archaeologists have argued that political elites played a peripheral role in the general economy, but rigidly controlled luxury and wealth goods. An absolute distinction between subsistence/utilitarian goods and prestige/wealth/luxury goods, however, is overly simplistic as objects are not inherently utilitarian or prestige goods, but take on such values and uses in specific historic and social contexts (Clark 2007; Flad and Hruby 2007; Kopytoff 1986). In fact, investigations have increasingly focused on the social practices and meanings embedded within the production process itself as a means to situate economic decisions and processes. These emphases include the political, mythical, and social ideologies surrounding manufacture, ritual practices tied to production, knowledge systems as embodied action, and the role of production in the constitution of social and political identities (Costin and Wright 1998; Hendon 2006; Hruby and Flad 2007; Inomata 2001b; McAnany 2010; P. Rice 2009a; Wells 2006; Wells and McAnany 2008; Wells and Salazar 2007). In order to reconstruct the social, political, and economic contexts of production, however, archaeologists need to focus their attention on discovering the actual "workshops" or areas of production.

Direct and Indirect Evidence of Classic Period Pottery Production in the Maya Lowlands

In Mesoamerica, few ceramic production workshops or areas have been detected (for an example in coastal Southern Belize, see Arnold III, Pool, and Santley 1993; Balkansky, Feinman, and Nicholas 1997; Hernández et al. 1999; Lopiparo 2003; see also Munera Bermundez 1985; Pool 1997; Rattray 1988; Stark 1985; Urban, Wells, and Ausec 1997; Winter and Payne 1976). Archaeologists have therefore opted to investigate ancient ceramic production primarily using indirect evidence (Costin 1991, 2001; Costin and Hagstrum 1995; P. Rice 1991a). This approach focuses on the analysis of finished products through studies of paste composition, skill and labor investment, diversity, and/or standardization. One of the most commonly employed methods involves standardization. Standardization analysis is based on the assumption that large-scale, full-time specialists produce more standardized products than those working in small scale, part-time household workshops (P. Rice 1981, 1991; Longacre et al. 1988; Benco 1988; Foias 1996; Foias and Bishop 1997; Blackman et al. 1993; Costin and Hagstrum 1995; Sinopoli 1988). However, standardization studies have to be carefully used as they may not always correlate directly with the degree of specialization (Costin 1991; P. Arnold 1991; Blackman et al. 1993; P. Rice 1991a, 1996b; Kvamme et al. 1996). Another indirect method used to illuminate ancient pottery manufacture is the production step or labor input studies (Feinman et al.1981; Hagstrum 1988; Costin and Hagstrum 1995; Halperin 2007). This approach quantifies the number of stages involved in the production of each artifact type, as these steps are equivalent to human labor. Production step studies have provided a window into the organization of production and the amount of human labor required by different crafts. For example, those that require exorbitant amounts of labor (what Malinowski calls "hypertrophic" [Clark and Parry 1990]) are seen as indicating attached specialization for high-status patrons, as only these individuals could "afford" such items (see also West 2002; Clark 2007; Flad 2007). Although more rarely used in ceramic analysis, diversity studies are predicated on the assumption that the more producers involved in manufacture, the more diverse the resulting corpus of pottery. Such an approach has been usefully employed to understand pottery production changes at Late Classic Copán (Bill 1997).

Indirect methods are helpful in understanding the broad or relative patterns of a production system, but are less helpful in pinpointing the sociopolitical contexts and spatial organization of production. Direct evidence of production, on the other hand, can shed light on this latter domain. Direct evidence refers to (1) the actual ceramic firing features, such as kilns or firing pits; (2) ceramic debris left over from the manufacturing process, such as wasters (misfired or deformed vessels or sherds, as well as large quantities of broken ceramics), fired and unfired clay clumps, and ash; (3) ceramic production tools, such as figurine and vessel molds, pot stands, smoothing and polishing stones, and manos and metates used to grind temper or paint pigments; or (4) the raw material used for production, such as clays, paint pigments, and tempers. The presence of multiple indicators is recommended to conclusively state that ceramic production occurred at a given locus (Stark 1985; 2007, 152).

Compared with other areas in Mesoamerica, archaeological research in the Maya Lowlands has revealed relatively little direct evidence of production. Some investigations draw primarily on firing debris, ceramic wasters, and tools, which are also the types of remains found in association with the royal Acropolis at Motul de San José. For instance, Becker (1973, 2003a, 2003b) identified polychrome (referred to as "high-quality" polychromes but no ceramic types or descriptions are provided), figurine, and possibly censer production at a "middle-class" residential neighborhood in the eastern sector of Tikal, Guatemala. This identification was based on (1) the presence of enormous waster piles of ceramics (in this case, broken sherds), (2) figurine and censer molds within structural fill and middens, and (3) the close proximity of these finds to clay resources in the surrounding *bajo*.

Ashmore (1988, 164; 2007, 122–23, table 6.1) reported evidence of ceramic production from households in Quiriguá's floodplain periphery (surrounding the site core), but not from its wider periphery (its hinterland). These data included unfired clay found adhering to the inside surfaces of bowls, ceramic figurine molds, concave ceramic stamps, and possible burnishing stones. Like at Tikal, Quiriguá vessels and figurines were apparently produced together in the same production areas. Due to the type of unfired paste from the bowl interiors, she argues that at least the Tipon ceramic group vessels, "minimally decorated" serving wares found commonly throughout the site, were produced in these identified production loci.

Elsewhere in the Maya Lowlands, figurine molds have been recovered from a number of site centers, suggesting that their production often took place within urban settings (Briggs Braswell 1998, 696; Hammond 1975b, 373; Hendon 2003, 32; Inomata 1995, tables 7.12, 7.14; Laporte, Reyes, and Chocon 2004, 303, 343; LeCount 1996, 427; Rands 1965, 54; Rands and Rands 1959, 225; Schele and Mathews 1979, figs. 902, 903; Willey 1972, 72–74; 1978, 37–38; see also Halperin, this volume). Since pottery vessel manufacture did not generally employ easily recognizable molds, evidence of vessel production tools are often more elusive.

Reents-Budet and colleagues (2000) located an elite-oriented or "palace school" polychrome vessel workshop at the site of Buenavista del Cayo, Belize. The materials from this site included paint pots, modeling, smoothing, scraping, and burnishing tools, and a ceramic levigation vat for processing slips. They were recovered from Late Classic period refuse deposits within palace structure fill (ibid., 111). Their chemical testing of polychrome vessels from the site in conjunction with stylistic analysis helped identify the likely products of the workshop: "special-purpose" ceramics with figural scenes painted in the Holmul style (mostly Zacatel Cream-polychrome and Cabrito Cream-polychrome) as well as "general service ware vessels," which included simple polychrome, bichrome, incised monochrome, and unslipped-burnished vessels (Cabrito Cream-polychrome, Benque Viejo Orange-polychrome, Velloso Orange-polychrome, Xunantunich Black-on-orange, Chinos Black-on-cream, and Chaa Creek Composite).

Although analysis of ceramic pastes has suggested that utilitarian vessels may have been produced outside of major centers within rural or smaller community loci (Bishop 1994; Rands and Bishop 1980; Fry 1980; Fry and Cox 1974; West 2002), few cases of direct evidence have confirmed such a pattern. Freter (1996) has identified possible areas for pottery manufacture in Copan's hinterlands (Site 32D-19-1) based on one or more of the following indices: high frequencies of ceramics in some areas, possible pigments, unfired clay, ground stone tools (e.g., small celts and a basalt slab), and misfired or heavily fireclouded sherds. Ceramic production in these rural zones focused primarily on Late Classic period undecorated utilitarian wares (Zico Pasted). In addition, McAnany and Murata (2008) document pottery production at Wits Cah Ak'al, Belize. They find evidence for possible firing features (although some of the firing features appear to have been used for salt production), dense ceramic deposits, a crab claw with red pigment on its end, and ceramic wasters (e.g., fire spalls [small conical sherds] and long, thin pointed sherds thought to have formed from vessel breakage during firing). Ceramic manufacture appears to have been aimed, at least in part, at the production of red-lipped, cream-washed jars used to produce salt, one of the principal activities conducted at the site.

Other archaeological research has uncovered possible ceramic firing facilities, although less is known about the types of ceramics produced there. Masson (2000, 81–87) reports the presence of eight firing features dating to the Early Facet of the Postclassic period at Laguna de On Island in Belize, and suggests that some of them may have been used to produce ceramics. In addition to a diversity of midden materials, these pit features contained relatively large ceramic sherds, large stone slabs, and recycled metates, all three of which, she suggests, may have been used to support or protect ceramics during the firing process. No ceramic production tools or deformed wasters, however, were recovered. At the site of K'axob in northern Belize, archaeologists uncovered a Late Classic period pottery workshop based on the finding of a double-chambered kiln with a chimney, possible single-chambered kilns, lumps of fired clay, possible temper materials, and ceramic production tools, such as reused ceramic sherds and ground stone (López Varela, McAnany, and Berry 2001, 187). Interestingly, despite the kilns and possible tools, no ceramic wasters were found.

As mentioned, chemical provenience studies in the southern Maya Lowlands appear to suggest that most pottery production occurred beyond major centers (see also P. Rice 2009a, 136–39). In contrast, the paste data suggest that ritual or prestige ceramics (such as specialized polychrome vessels, *incensarios*, and some figurines) were more likely to have been produced within major centers (Foias 1996; Fry 1979, 1980; Fry and Cox 1974; Rands and Bishop 1980; Rands, Bishop, and Harbottle 1978; Reents-Budet et al. 2000; P. Rice 1987a). Ritually charged or prestige pottery may have been crafted by elite artists and/or attached lower-rank specialists within elite or royal residential compounds at the core of Maya centers. Ball (1993) has called these "palace schools," and epigraphic and iconographic studies by Reents-Budet, Bishop, and MacLeod (1994) have supported this interpretation with the discovery of possible name tags for "craft workshop" and "apprentice." However, the nature of these "palace schools" is poorly known: were there several apprentices (elite or nonelite) working under an elite master? Were finely painted polychrome vessels the only products of these "palace schools," or were they produced alongside other types of ceramics and/or crafts? The recent research at Motul de San José has found evidence for a similar "palace school" to that found at Buenavista del Cayo and sheds additional light on the nature of these artisans.

Excavations of the Acropolis Middens

Evidence for pottery production at Motul de San José was discovered in the Acropolis of Group C, the largest monumental group in the core of the site, and the presumed residence of the royal court. A series of dense middens were identified immediately north of the Acropolis using a combination of electromagnetic survey by Joel Palka (Emery and Higginbotham 1998), magnetometer survey by Halperin (Halperin and Martinez Salguero 2007a, 2007b), and test-pitting excavations (Figures 6.1, 6.2). These test pits (MSJ2A-3, -5, -40), in addition to horizontal excavations in the nearest structure of Acropolis Court #4 (Str. 8L-9; units MSJ2A-1,2,6–39) and in a building (Op.46A-6, -7, -9, -10, -11) just to the north, uncovered evidence of pottery production tools and debris dating to the Tepeu 2 phase (ca. AD 700–830) of the Late Classic period (Castellanos 2000; Emery and Higginbotham 1998; Guffey, Tonoike, and Castellanos 2000; Halperin and Martinez Salguero 2007; Foias et al., this volume).

The largest concentration of production evidence was located in midden from units 2A-3, -5, -40, -41, and -42. These units were situated on what appeared to have been a single, large platform or terrace (as seen in Figure 6.1). The recovery of low platform retaining walls in units 2A-3, -5, -41, and -42 during excavations, however, suggest that the area comprised a series of smaller platforms set on a larger terrace. Excavations were not extensive enough to map the extent of these low platforms. Both the low platforms and the larger terrace were constructed during the Tepeu 2 phase of the Late Classic period.

The midden context containing the production debris was located primarily within fill, making them secondary or redeposited refuse. In units 2A-3, -5, -41, -42, pottery production debris was found below Floor D where the midden deposit was the most dense and extended over 1 meter deep (Figure 6.2). This part of the units' stratigraphy lacked large concentrations of fill rocks. The secondary midden continued until bedrock, but the size and frequency of the materials decreased after approximately 1.2–1.5 meters below Floor D. Bedrock (at 3.22 meters below surface in unit

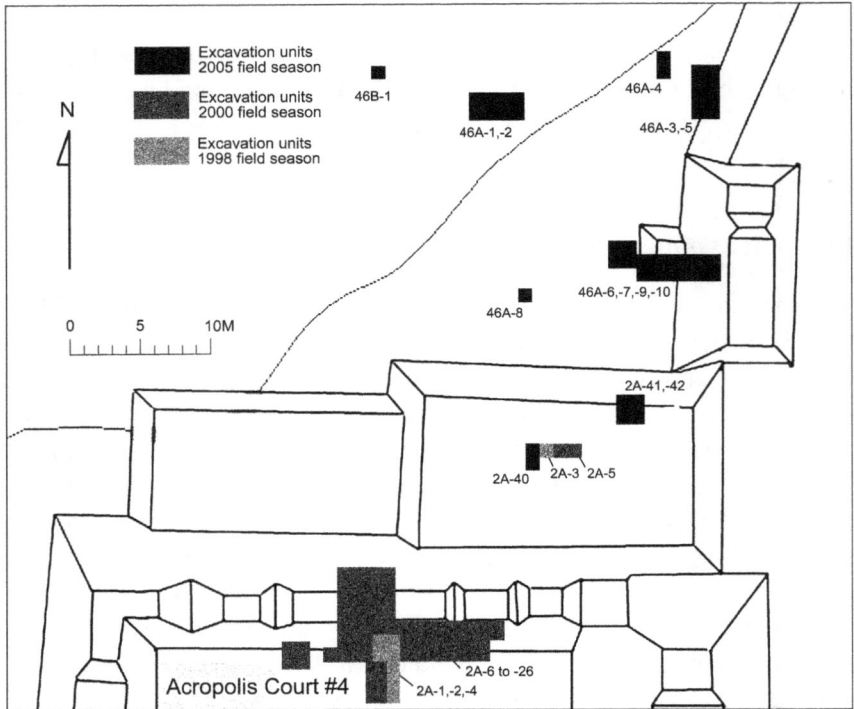

Figure 6.1. Map of northwestern part of Acropolis Court #4 and excavation units from Operations 2 and 46.

3 and 2.7 meters below surface in units 5 and 40) appears to have been leveled out with a dense, clayey soil, and miniscule gravel.

In general, the construction of Floor D and of the fill below it represents a major project. Such a large-scale endeavor speaks to a successful dynasty that had recently (presumably) obtained control over a large labor force (either through immigration of population to Motul or through tribute labor payments of newly integrated communities in the periphery of Motul).

In contrast to the deep stratigraphy of units MSJ2A-3, -5, -40, bedrock was much closer in units MSJ2A-41 and -42, both of which were approximately 8 meters north of MSJ2A-3, -5, -40. Thus, the terrace fill was shallower (bedrock was located about 50–55 centimeters below the surface). It also contained higher frequencies of small rock fill. Nonetheless, like the other three units, secondary refuse from MSJ2A-41, and -42's fill was extremely dense and also contained pottery production debris.

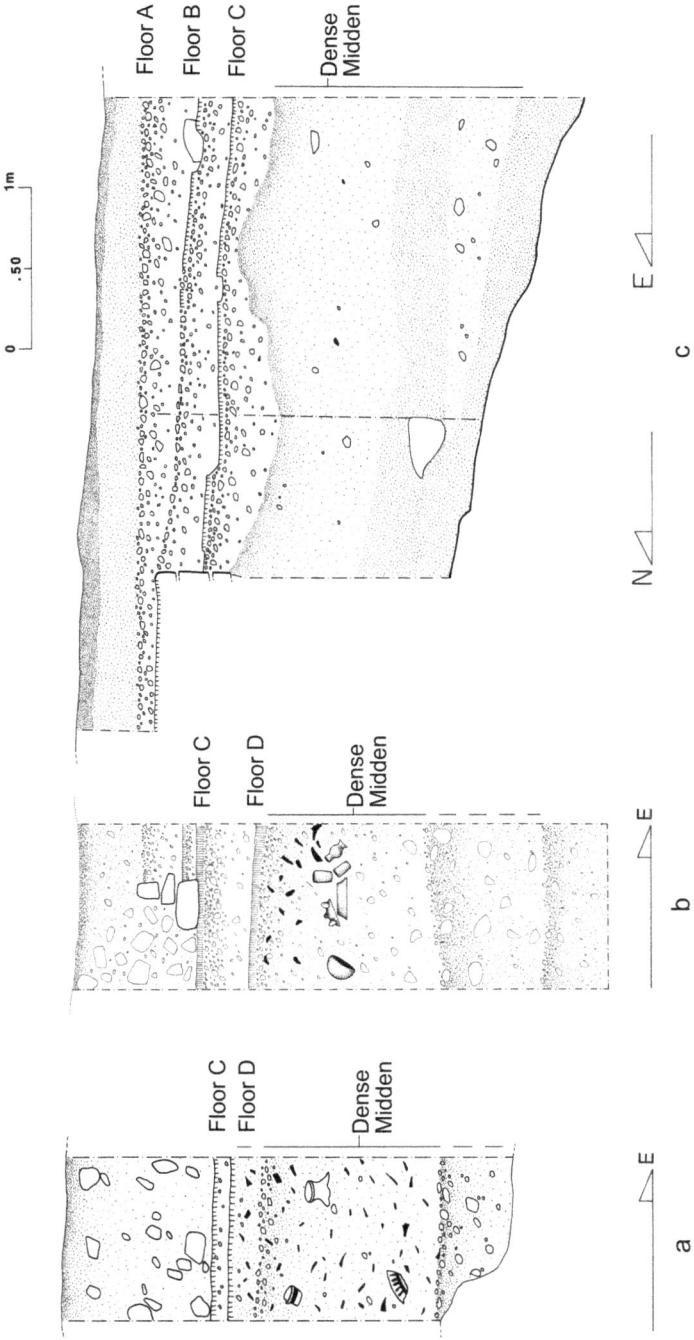

Figure 6.2. Profiles of excavation units showing the location of dense midden concentrations: (a) MSJ2A-40; (b) MSJ2A-3; (c) MSJ2A-5.

One of the unique characteristics of the refuse context from units MSJ2A-3, -5, and -40 (below Floor D) and MSJ2A-41 and -42 is their soft, gray matrix (2.5YR 5/1) containing high concentrations of ash and carbon flecks as well as smaller amounts of burnt clay (Figure 6.3). The burnt clay was gray (10R7/2, 10YR6/3, 10YR5/1, 10YR4/1) in color and lacked temper. Because some of the burnt clay chunks possessed formed, smoothed edges and all were extremely hard, it is possible that they were part of a firing pit, a hearth, or perhaps even a kiln. Burnt clay "lumps" and "roughly rectangular blocks" with smoothed edges have also been found in fill surrounding a ceramic firing feature at the site of K'axob, Belize (López Varela, McAnany, and Berry 2001, 184–85).

Because of the massive scale of both the midden and fill (soil and rocks) materials, we interpret them to have come from nearby, most likely from the elite and royal residents of the Acropolis (Group C) or from other elite residents in the vicinity of this centrally located zone of the city. Although this interpretation is based primarily on its location, it is also supported by the exotic nature of the materials in comparison to other middens at Motul de San José, such as a high frequency of marine shell and ritual faunal remains (e.g., crocodile and jaguar; see Emery 2003a, table 2; Emery, this volume). Furthermore, we found many refits (sherds that pertain to the same vessel), which suggests that the middens were not moved a long distance.

The ceramic production debris was mixed with other evidence of craft production as well as domestic refuse materials. These finds included worked bone tools (e.g., awls, pins, needles, rasps), some of which were likely used for weaving and sewing; spindle whorls and centrally perforated sherd disks likely used for spinning thread; bone-working debris indicating bone tool production; obsidian blade fragments; chert flakes; mano and metate fragments; and broken pieces of shell and shell ornaments (Emery 2003a ; Halperin 2008). Most of the remains, however, were ceramic: elaborate and simple polychrome pottery, monochrome serving, cooking, and storage wares, unslipped utilitarian wares, polychrome drums, figurines, and spindle whorls. The more elaborate polychrome vessels possessed hieroglyphs and figural scenes typical of "palace school" artisans. Some of these were Ik'-style vessels or related to the Ik' style, such as Cat. # 57/ Vessel 7/MSJ104. Three of the vessels (Cat. #51654, #51759, #57) possessed cream slips and were decorated with the characteristic Ik'-style pink glyphs outlined in red (Figure 6.3). Two of these vessels were also decorated with black rim bands whose interiors were scalloped, another diagnostic feature of the Ik' style (Reents-Budet, Bishop, and MacLeod 1994). A number of

Figure 6.3. Polychrome vases from the Acropolis middens that fit within the Ik' style: (a) Cat. #51654 (exterior view showing PSS with pink glyphs outlined in red and interior view showing scalloped black rim band); (b) #51759 (exterior view showing PSS with pink glyphs outlined in red and interior view showing scalloped black rim band); (c) vase with tribute presentation scene (Cat. #57/V#7/MSJ104).

other vessels[1] may also pertain to the Ik' style because of the presence of black scalloping on the interior rim or because of the presence of pink specular hematite. Unfortunately, their eroded exteriors impede conclusive classification.

The diversity of ceramic types and pastes from the middens in units MSJ2A-3, 5, 40, 41, and 42 suggests that at least some of the sherds were the remains of debris used for domestic or ceremonial purposes. Nonetheless, the middens were unusual in their extremely high ceramic sherd densities in comparison to other middens from Motul de San José with the exception of unit MSJ46A-4 (Table 6.1; see Figure 6.1 for location of the latter unit). Ethnographic research indicates that areas of pottery manufacture are often littered with large amounts of ceramics broken during the production process (e.g., some examples report 20–27 percent vessel loss per firing; see P. Arnold 1991; Rye 1981). In addition, many of the vessel sherds could be reconstructed as partial or almost complete vessels, and the figurines from these contexts were less fragmentary than those from other middens at the site. These vessels may be the result of ritual breakage after feasting, but may also be due to accidental breakage at the time of production. On the other

Table 6.1. Ceramic sherd density from units 2A-3, -5, -40, -41, -42 in comparison with other Motul de San José midden excavations

Unit	Ceramic sherd count	Ceramic weight (g)	Excavated volume (m³)	Ceramic sherds/ m³
2A-3	2,363	81,586	2.8	844
2A-5	10,759	270,404.7	5.5	1,956
2A-40	5,345	163,029.1	5.24	1,020
2A-41	1,095	31,062.4	1.48	740
2A-42	1,236	27,111.6	1.55	797
Unit Average	4,159.6	114,638.8		1,071
UNITS WITH MIDDENS FROM 2005 FIELD SEASON				
46A-1	1,128	21,759	3.61	312
46A-2	508	4,433	2.35	216
46A-3	495	7,613	2.53	196
46A-4	2771	49,718	1.91	1,451
46A-6	600	12,410	4.64	129
39A-2	304	2,976	0.84	362
39G-5	374	3,576	1.32	283
39G-7	1690	23,344	3.24	522
42B-2	782	8,185	1.12	698
42G-4	1146	9,733	2.73	420
Unit average	979.8	14,375		459

hand, their partial and reconstructable breakage patterns point against a long-term deposition within a primary midden before being placed in the construction fill. Pieces from the same reconstructable pots were found at varying depths within this deposit, suggesting that the midden, despite its large size, was a cohesive one.

Evidence for Pottery Production

In addition to the possible refuse of a firing feature in the form of ash, carbon, and burnt clay, and the high ceramic densities, more conclusive evidence of ceramic manufacturing activities were encountered in the Acropolis middens in the form of ceramic wasters and tools (Tables 6.2, 6.3).

Wasters

The wasters consisted of over-fired and vitrified sherds, bubbly, spalled, or cracked sherds, a possible unfinished vase (#50980), as well as twisted and warped sherds (Table 6.2). Most of these wasters are polychrome dishes, bowls, and vases, either eroded Late Classic polychromes or Zacatal Cream polychromes (Figure 6.4). At least two of the polychrome vessel wasters contained finely painted figural scenes[2] whereas the others had simpler geometric designs. Unfortunately, decoration on many of these vessels was not always clearly visible due to extensive spalling of their surfaces. Rye (1981) depicts a spalled waster identical to the ones found here. He identifies the cause of this spalling as firing the vessel when its clay was still wet. Although the majority of these wasters are polychromes, one over-fired sherd was identified as a Pantano Impressed monochrome jar (#51778). In a recent review of Late Classic Maya pottery production, Prudence Rice remarks that polychrome pots may have been individually fired in "saggar kilns" made of a larger pot, and that these latter pots will appear over-fired, "clinky," of "striking orange and fuchsia-pink colors" due to their repeated firings (2009a, 121–22). It is possible that the Pantano Impressed over-fired sherd was part of one of these "saggar kilns."

Eight of these wasters were submitted to instrumental neutron activation sourcing analysis (INAA) and of these, seven could be assigned to preliminary chemical Groups A and F1 as defined by Reents-Budet et al. (2007; see also Reents-Budet et al., this volume). Group A is the central group of four main chemical clusters representing pottery production at Motul de San José, and Group F1 is a second cluster more closely associated with figurine producers also at Motul de San José (Reents-Budet et al. 2007).

Table 6.2. List of possible ceramic production debris with context information

Description	Vessel type	Provenience	Catalog no.	INAA #	INAA Gr.[a]
Vessel waster?: twisted & overfired	Eroded Late Classic polychrome	MSJ2A-40-5-3	50552		
Vessel waster: bubbly & spalled	Eroded Late Classic polychrome	MSJ2A-40-5-2	50477	MSJ254	A
Vessel waster?: twisted and warped	Eroded Late Classic polychrome	MSJ2A-42-3-1	51764		
Vessel waster?: unfinished glyph rim	Eroded Late Classic polychrome	MSJ46A-1-2-4	50980		
Vessel waster: spalled	Eroded Late Classic polychrome	MSJ2A-5-6-15	11454		
Vessel waster: spalled	Eroded Late Classic polychrome	MSJ2A-5-6-15	11455-16		
Vessel waster: spalled	Eroded Late Classic polychrome	MSJ2A-5-6-15	11457-8		
Vessel waster: bubbly & spalled	Eroded Late Classic vessel	MSJ2A-40-4-3	50243		
Vessel waster: overfired & vitrified	Eroded Late Classic vessel	MSJ2A-41-3-1	51667	MSJ256	F1
Vessel waster: overfired	Eroded Late Classic polychrome	MSJ2A-5-6-12	11392-2		
Vessel waster: bubbly & deformed	Palmar Orange polychrome	MSJ2A-3-16-1	512-2		
Vessel waster: spalled	Eroded Late Classic polychrome	MSJ2A-3-17-1	430		
Vessel waster?: discolored; overfired; surface cracked	Pantano Impressed (monochrome)	MSJ2A-42-3-1	51778		
Vessel waster: bubbly & spalled	Zacatel Cream polychrome	MSJ2A-40-4-3	50293	MSJ253	F1
Vessel waster: bubbly & spalled	Zacatel Cream polychrome	MSJ2A-40-5-1	50412	MSJ255	
Vessel waster: spalled	Zacatel Cream polychrome	MSJ2A-5-6-4	10265	MSJ127	
Vessel waster: spalled	Zacatel Cream polychrome	MSJ2A-5-6-8	10312		
Vessel waster: spalled	Zacatel Cream polychrome	MSJ2A-5-6-8	10318		
Vessel waster: spalled	Zacatel Cream polychrome; figural scene & glyphs	MSJ2A-3-12-1	55	MSJ090	A
Vessel waster: spalled	Eroded Late Classic polychrome: bowl	MSJ2A-5-6-16	10442		
Vessel waster: spalled	Eroded Late Classic polychrome: jar neck	MSJ2A-3-15-1	620		
Vessel waster: spalled	Eroded Late Classic polychrome: deep bowl	MSJ2A-5-6-14	10363	MSJ128	F1
Vessel waster: bubbly & spalled	Zacatel Cream polychrome; Ik' style with figural scene	MSJ2A-40-5-1,2	50423	MSJ250	F1
Vessel waster: spalled	Eroded body sherd	MSJ2A-3-12-1	37		

[a] INAA Group assignment given in Reents-Budet et al. (2007).

Figure 6.4. Wasters from Op 2A: (a) Zacatel Cream polychrome #50423; (b) photo of Zacatel Cream #55/Vessel 5/MSJ090; (c) Zacatel Cream polychrome #50412 (exterior and interior).

Group A includes the famous vases that depict the best known of the Motul de San José rulers, *Yajawte' K'inich* (Fat Cacique), such as K533 (MS1403), K1463 (MS1418), K3054, K1439 (MS1121), K1452, K2795, and *Lamaw Ek'* (Lord Termination Star), such as K791 (MS1769), K793 (MS1770), K792 (MS1771; see Reents-Budet, Bishop, and MacLeod 1994; Reents-Budet et al. 2007). The master artist who painted many of Fat Cacique's masterpieces signed his name as *T'uubal Ajaw* or the Lord from T'uubal, a site located between Tikal and Naranjo (Reents-Budet et al. 2007, this volume).

Smoothers and Polishers

Seven possible smoother and polisher tools were also recovered (Figure 6.5, Table 6.3). Three are reutilized sherds with smoothed edges and shaped into triangular forms. One of them (MSJ46A-4-2-1), a reused, ash-tempered ceramic sherd, was analyzed under a 100x handheld microscope. The use-wear edge of the sherd shows signs of thin unilinear striations (perpendicular to the length of the tool) and rounding. Its use-wear characteristics are typical of scraping and smoothing ceramic production tools found in the archaeological record at K'axob and of pottery tools made specifically for ceramic replication experiments by López Varela and colleagues (López Varela, van Gijn, and Jacobs 2002, tables 1, 4). The other reutilized smoothers and polishers[3] are two polychrome sherds pertaining to vases painted with elaborate palace scenes and glyphic inscriptions, similar in style to the Ik' style (Figure 6.5c). The fourth ceramic tool (MSJ2A-40-4-1), a polisher, was also manufactured from ash-tempered clay. It, however, was modeled from the clay (before firing) specifically for its use as a tool rather than manufactured from a reused ceramic sherd. It has a half-moon shape and shallow finger grooves on its side (Figure 6.5a). It also shows signs of polishing and rounding on its facet. The other three tools are limestone polishers (Figure 6.5b). Examination of the surfaces of two of these under a 100x handheld microscope revealed evidence of rounding typical of ground stone tools used for polishing (Adams 2002).

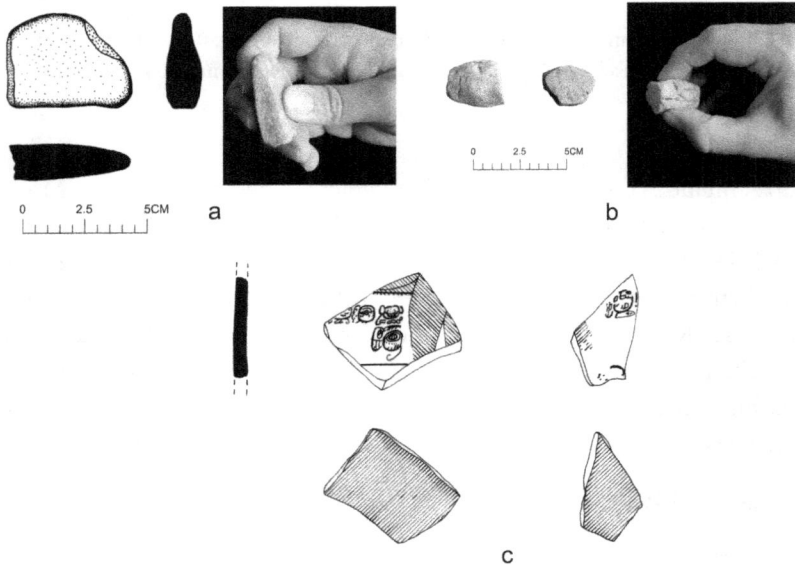

Figure 6.5. Drawings and photograph of smoothers and polishers: (a) ceramic polisher (MSJ2A-40-4-1); (b) limestone polisher (MSJ46A-6-2-1; GR1); (c) two Ik' sherds reutilized as smoothers/polishers (MSJ2A-24-1-1, and 24-2-2; Cat#9910).

Table 6.3. List of possible ceramic production tools

PAINT POTS

Description	Paint	Provenience
Paint pot: miniature jar	Red specular hematite in interior of pot	MSJ2A-40-4-1
Paint pot: miniature jar	Red specular hematite in interior of pot	MSJ2A-40-5-5
Paint pot: miniature jar	Red specular hematite in interior of pot	MSJ2A-5-6-16
Paint pot: miniature jar	Red specular hematite in interior of pot	MSJ2A-5-7-4

FIGURINE MOLD

Description	Figurine	Provenience
Ceramic figurine mold	Feathered headdress?	MSJ2A-5-7-3

POSSIBLE RAW PIGMENT

Description	Color	Provenience
Mineral/pigment for slip or paint	Pink 10R7/8-10R6/6	MSJ2A-40-3-1
Mineral/pigment for slip or paint	Yellow 10YR7/6	MSJ46A-8-2-2
Mineral/pigment for slip or paint	Yellow 10YR8/8-10YR7/8	MSJ2A-41-3-1
Mineral/pigment for slip or paint	Yellow 10YR7/6	MSJ46A-4-3-2
Mineral/pigment for slip or paint	Yellow 10YR7/6	MSJ46A-6-2-4
Mineral/pigment for slip or paint	Red 10R4/6	MSJ2A-5-6-1
Mineral/pigment for slip or paint	Light red 10R6/4-6/6	MSJ2A-5-3-2

CERAMIC SMOOTHERS AND POLISHERS

Description	Modeled or reutilized sherd	Provenience
Ceramic polisher	Modeled ceramic tool (half-moon shaped with finger grooves)	MSJ2A-40-4-1
Ceramic smoother or polisher	Reutilized Late Classic sherd	MSJ46A-4-2-1
Ceramic smoother	Reutilized Ik' style polychrome sherd	MSJ2A-24-1-1/ Cat#9910
Ceramic smoother	Reutilized Ik' style polychrome sherd	MSJ2A-24-2-2/ Cat#9910

GROUND STONE SMOOTHERS AND POLISHERS

Description	Material	Provenience
Ground stone polisher	Limestone	MSJ46A-6-2-1
Ground stone polisher	Limestone	MSJ46A-11-2-1

POSSIBLE BONE PAINTING TOOLS

Description	Paint	Provenience
Bone pin/awl	Traces of red paint on distal end	MSJ2A-40-5-1
Bone pin/awl	Traces of red paint on distal end	MSJ2A-40-5-1
Bone pin/awl	Traces of red paint on distal end	MSJ2A-40-4-4
Bone pin/awl	Traces of red paint on distal end	MSJ2A-40-4-1

Paint Pots

Evidence for painting includes three miniature restricted-neck jars with residues of red specular hematite in their interiors (Figure 6.6a, b, Table 6.3). One was a miniature version of the type Pantano Impressed, whereas the others are simple polychrome. It is noteworthy that both the polychrome vessels and figurines from the middens possessed surfaces painted with red specular hematite. Other miniature jars with polychrome painted exteriors were also recovered in the Operation 2A midden, but no evidence for interior paint was detected. Miniature jars with residues of red pigment have been found at Aguateca in the House of the Scribe (Str. M8-10). Inomata (1995, 708), alternatively, suggests that they were used for facial and body paint. In either case, their small size is indicative of relatively fine-grained detail work and small-scale painting surfaces.

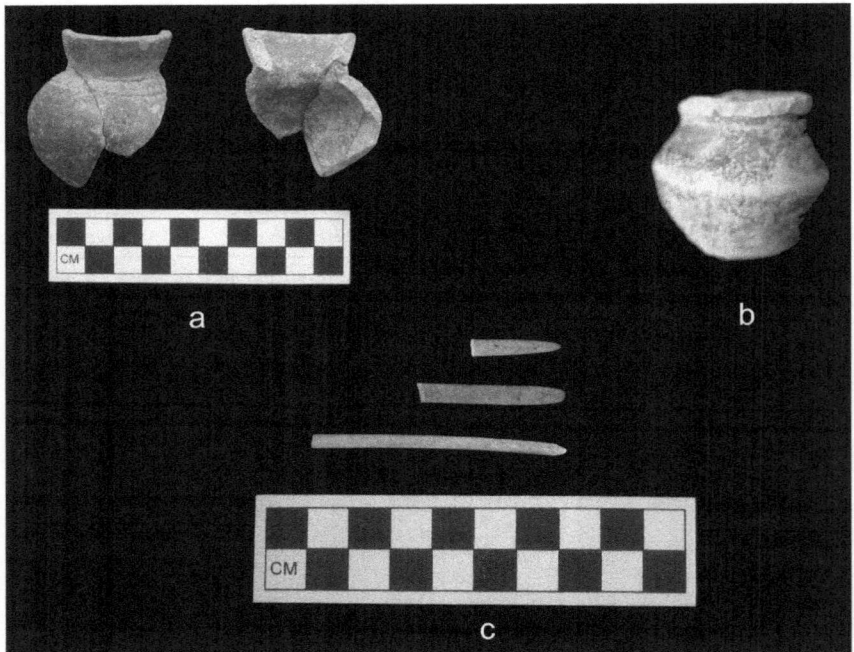

Figure 6.6. Paint pots and bone tools: (a) exterior and interior view of paint pot containing residue of red specular hematite (Cat. #50164); (b) exterior view of paint pot containing residue of red specular hematite (Cat. #10622); (c) bone tools with red paint on proximal ends.

Bone Tools

Some of the bone awls or pins found in these large middens contained traces of red coloring on their proximal ends (Figure 6.6c). Awls and pins are often thought to have functioned as weaving tools or hairpins (Dacus 2005; Halperin 2008; Taschek 1994); however, the residues of red pigment suggest that some may have also been painting tools. The residues were similar to the red specular hematite found in the miniature paint pots, and could have appropriately fit into their necks. The bone tips, where the red coloring was located, were very fine and delicate. Thus, while fur or hair may have been once attached to these ends; their general size, like those of the paint pots, suggests that they were used to paint on small surfaces, such as ceramics, figurines, paper, or the human body (for similar tools, see also Inomata 1995, 588–89, figs. 8.42a, 8.43c; Reents-Budet 1994, 41, figs. 2.13a, 2.13b).

Figurine Mold and Duplicates

A single figurine mold fragment was located among the polychrome vessel wasters and other debris mentioned above (Figure 6.7). In addition, the middens from Operation 2A possessed the largest number (n = 15) of figurine matches (duplicated molded figurines) in the Motul de San José region to date. Although they include matches whose matching mates were found in other areas of the site and other sites in the region, four sets possessed matching mates found within this same operation. Duplicate molded figurines found in the same context tend to occur close to production areas (Barbour 1975, 118–19). For example, duplicates have been recovered in the production debris associated with ceramic pit firing features at the site of Ejutla, Oaxaca (Feinman 1999, 92), and in the production debris associated with an updraft kiln from the site of Tula (Hernández et al. 1999, 77). The close association of figurine production with that of polychrome vessels is further supported in their overlapping paste recipes detected in INAA and petrography analyses (Halperin, this volume; Reents-Budet et al. 2007). Interestingly, one of the matching figurines (Halperin 2007, fig. 6.9c, table 6.7) in a set of three (m05) is chemically sourced to Tikal or its environs and lacks modeled appliqué hair/headdress parts, which are present on the other two matching figurines. It is possible that imported figurines served as the base for the production of locally made mold replicas.

a

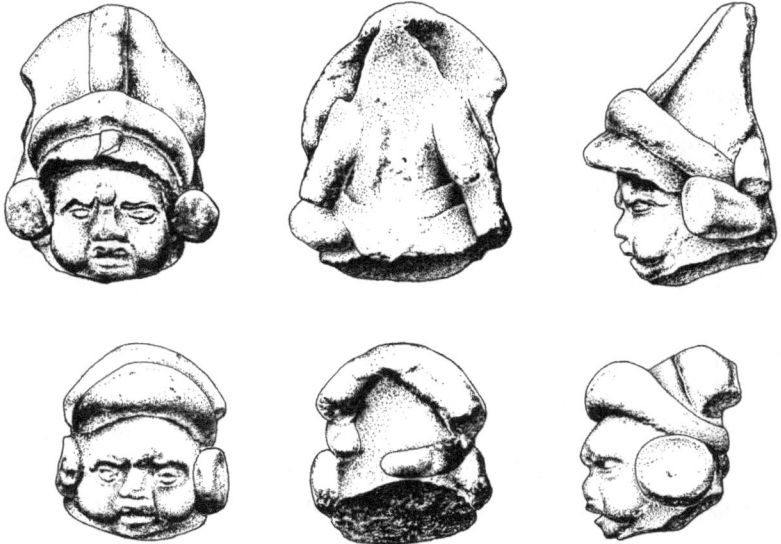

b

Figure 6.7. Figurine production evidence: (a) drawing of figurine mold fragment; (b) drawing of duplicate figurines from the same midden context (molded head is identical, but appliqué headdress varies; MSJ2A-2-7-1a & MSJ2A-40-3-1a).

Pigments

Pink (10R7/8-10R6/6), yellow (10YR8/8-10YR7/8), and red (10R4/6) mineral remains were also detected in the Operation 2A midden with the other production debris as well as in middens just to the north in Operation 46A (units 46A-4, -6, & -8). In the laboratory, we mixed the yellow organic pieces with water. The yellow color from the minerals bled into the water, suggesting that they, indeed, could have been used as a colorant.

Unfinished Cylindrical Vases

Two vases in the Acropolis middens lacked a slip, although they were well smoothed. Although we could argue that they were intended to be left unslipped, their shape, paste, and surface treatment is identical to polychrome vases. If they were meant to have been polychrome vessels as we suspect, polychromes may have underwent two or more firings: the first with a base slip or wash and the second with its final paint. The other cylindrical vase was gauged, but lacked detailing along the rim where glyphs would be located. Therefore, we suspect that these vessels were in the process of production, but for unknown reasons, were thrown away unfinished.

Reconstructing Pottery Production from the Acropolis Middens

Costin (1991, 8) has defined four general parameters to characterize the organization of craft production in ancient societies: (1) context (independent to attached); (2) concentration (dispersed to nucleated); (3) scale (small, kin-based to factory); (4) intensity (part-time to full-time). Flad and Hruby (2007, 6) add a number of other variables: "the *relationship among workers* (kin, convicts, slaves, and so on), the identification of artisans and consumers, the *meaning of production* (religious, secular, and so on)." We consider all of these as important aspects of ancient specialization, as discussed below and throughout this chapter.

The context of production encompasses the sociopolitical arena within which crafting takes place, or put another way, the relationship between producer(s) and the individual(s) that controls the finished product (Costin 1991, 2001; Clark 1995, 2007; Flad 2007; Clark and Parry 1990). Usually the context of production is viewed along a continuum between attached and independent specialization, with attached specialists producing for elite patrons, and independent producers for a general pool of consumers (Brumfiel and Earle 1987; Costin 1991; Costin and Hagstrum 1995; Sinopoli

1988). However, these are oversimplified schemas because the same artisans may sometimes produce for a patron and sometimes for general consumers (Flad 2007, 110; Inomata 2001b). John Clark (1995) has preferred to define context by the relationship between those who produce and those who control the "rights over alienation" of the finished products. Flad has also underscored the variation in attached specialization: attachment "involve[s] some sort of alienation of the product of labor from the producers . . . [it] may be in the form of tribute, taxation, corvée labor, state-sponsored employment, slave labor, distribution monopolies, wage labor, or 'embedded specialization'" (2007, 111).

The dispersion or concentration of production loci is another important feature of craft production as highly dispersed manufacture is much more difficult to control directly than specialists who are concentrated in communities or neighborhoods. On the other hand, concentration does not directly indicate elite control as it may relate with the presence of important raw materials needed by the artisans (D. Arnold 1985; Costin 1991; Nicklin 1979; P. Rice 1981). However, attached specialists tend to be nucleated close to the elite households of their patrons (Morris 1974; Murra 1980; Sinopoli 1988). Archaeologically, the context and concentration of production can be reconstructed through a spatial analysis of the distribution of manufacturing activities. The location of workshops or production loci in association with elite structures indicates attached specialization or "embedded specialization" as defined by Ames (1995; see also Inomata 2001b; P. Rice 2009a). Embedded specialization describes the situation in which a particular craft is pursued by an individual because it is required by his or her social rank or status (Ames 1995; Inomata 2001b). The distribution of manufacturing debris either evenly across the landscape or nucleated in a few locales or sites allows archaeologists to infer the degree of concentration in production.

The scale and intensity of craft production are important parameters as they characterize the degree of craft specialization, a central feature of economic systems. The scale and intensity of production can be reconstructed from the output of excavated workshops, the density of associated manufacturing debris, the size of the production locus and unit, and from the structure or degree of organization in the production space and sequence (Clark 1986; Costin 1991; Peacock 1982; Pool 1990).

The evidence for pottery production in the Motul Acropolis middens speaks to some of these aspects of craft specialization. First, we contend that these massive middens represent the remains of domestic refuse from the elite and royal residences in the Acropolis and the rest of Group C (and possibly from adjacent Groups D and E). But mixed in are also the remains of a "palace school" where fine polychromes were painted by elite priests/ scribes/artists called *ah-kuhun* and *aj tz'ib'* in the Classic period texts (Coe and Kerr 1998 ; Reents-Budet, Bishop, and MacLeod 1994; Reents-Budet 1998; Inomata 2001b; Jackson and Stuart 2001; Zender 2004b). Because these middens are in secondary fill contexts, we cannot pinpoint the exact location of the residence of the scribe/artist, but we suggest that it is the closest structure (Str. 8L-9) to the richest middens found in units 2A-3, 5, 40 following the discovery of two ceramic smoothers/polishers that were reused sherds of Ik'-style vases, on the interior floor of this elite residence (see Figure 6.5c).

Context and Concentration of Pottery Production

The archaeological evidence described above suggests that pottery was produced near or within the royal court of Motul de San José. Although most of the wasters pertain to polychrome pottery, one waster appears to be from a large monochrome red slipped jar. One possibility is that this vessel piece served as a structural element or spacer within the firing pit or kiln. When this evidence is coupled with INAA analyses by Bishop and Reents-Budet (Reents-Budet, Bishop, and MacLeod 1994; Reents-Budet et al. 2007; Reents-Budet et al., this volume), however, it appears that the same pastes were used to produce not only the highest-quality and most elaborate vases painted with palace scenes and fine glyphic texts, but also simpler polychromes with naturalist and/or geometric designs, figurines, and even possibly monochromes. The wasters themselves are not only of vases (that were the recipients of the most complex paintings), but also other serving vessel forms: deep bowls and dishes or shallower bowls that were decorated generally with simpler designs. In other words, the pottery produced in or near the Acropolis "palace school" included both very fine-quality and simpler vessels, as well as figurines.

It is also possible that the clay used by potters of monochrome pottery was supplied to the elite artists who made and painted the finer- and finest-quality polychromes in the Acropolis "Palace School." In this second scenario, only the most elaborate vessels were made in the Acropolis, whereas the simpler polychromes and monochromes were made from the same clays but perhaps in other locations beyond the core of Motul de San José (since no other evidence of pottery manufacture has been discovered within Motul). Reents-Budet (1994, 218–22) describes a separation between the roles of potter and the role of painter-artist for the fine Codex-style polychromes found in North Petén: one individual made the pot, and another painted it. In this case, Reents-Budet argues that the potter and the artist worked together in the same workshop because of the fragility of unfired vessels (ibid.). We suspect this scenario applied to the Motul "palace school."

The location of the production debris and tools next to the Acropolis suggests that polychrome and figurine pottery production took place in the elite residences of the royal court and/or nearby elite groups. Such an association with the high elites is normally seen as attached specialization. We know from epigraphic and iconographic studies that the individuals who painted these vessels were nobles themselves (Coe and Kerr 1998; Reents-Budet, Bishop, and MacLeod 1994), and according to Zender (2004b), some were high priests. To interpret these elite artists as attached specialists is problematic as discussed by Ames (1995) and Inomata (2001b). More likely, the act of painting these vessels may have been integral to their role in society even though they may have been creating them, at times, for particular royal patrons. For example, Reents-Budet (1998) and Inomata (2001b) point out that the production process has been equated to ritual acts of creation and, in most cases, required restricted knowledge related to Maya history, cosmology, and mythology. There is no doubt that many of these vessels were created for specific patrons because the Primary Standard Sequence (PSS), the standard text that is found on most of the elaborate Ik'-style polychromes, includes the name of the patron who sponsored the artist and his work (Reents-Budet, Bishop, and MacLeod 1994). Thus, client–patron networks connected royal (and, possibly subroyal) patrons and scribe-clients. Cross-cultural studies highlight that the patron had clear responsibilities toward his clients and incurred debts toward them when they presented him with gifts (Foias 2007; Schortman and Urban 2004). The act of creating these polychrome masterpieces was also likely one way artisans could gain higher prestige and esteem within the royal courts of Classic Maya society (Inomata 2007; McAnany 2010). The relationship between T'uubal Ajaw, the master painter of many Ik'-style polychromes pertaining to the INAA Group A, and his patron, the Motul de San José divine ruler Yajawte' K'inich (Fat Cacique) may exemplify this relationship between artists and royal elites (see Reents-Budet et al., this volume, for further discussion of these master painters). He is the only known lord-artist who painted for this ruler, while another master painted vases for Yajawte's K'inich's successor, Lamaw Ek' (Reents-Budet et al., this volume).

Scale and Intensity of Polychrome Pottery Production

A second aspect that is illuminated by the Motul excavations is the scale and intensity of polychrome manufacture. Although it is clear that not all of this massive midden deposit was excavated, the overall density of manufacturing debris is quite low: twenty-three wasters, two possible unfinished vases, four paint pots, seven polishers/smoothers, four painting pens/pins, six pigment minerals, a small quantity in comparison to the total ceramic count of 20,798 for the units 2A-3, 5, 40, 41, 42 (see Table 6.1). Although some of these ceramic sherds may have also been by-products of pottery production, the low density of identified waster and manufacturing tools speaks of a low production intensity. It is possible that the production debris were the remains of one or a few elite scribes who painted the vessels, including beautiful masterpieces that depict palace scenes with fancy dancers, bloodletting, feasts, receptions, and tribute payments. Since the highest scribe-artists were also high-level elite priests (Zender 2004b), it is possible that they did not spend all their time in this one activity, but engaged in numerous other responsibilities and duties. Their common depictions on polychrome vessels of the Ik' style in a variety of scenes suggests that they were not only courtiers, but also recorders of tribute (i.e., scribes in the Near Eastern tradition), and diplomats who were sent as messengers or ambassadors to other cities (see also discussion for Aguateca in Inomata 2007, 130; Coe and Kerr 1998; Zender 2004b).

Nonetheless, the production debris from Motul de San José's Acropolis reflects a diversity of production tool and waster types, providing evidence for a range of pottery production stages. Similar to Reents-Budet (1994), we suspect that this diversity speaks to multiple artisans, not just the scribe who was skilled in the painting of glyphic and/or figural imagery. These stages include clay forming stages when the clay is relatively wet (indicated by the mold), the laborious polishing and smoothing stages when vessels were semidry or at the "leather-hard" stage, prefire slipping and painting, tending the firing process, and possibly postfire painting as well. The inclusion of both production errors (wasters) and tools in the same general location suggests that the firing feature may have been located near the area where these earlier stages of production took place. The other producers may have included the elite scribe's relatives (wives, offspring, aunts, etc.), apprentices, or even servants. They likely did not receive the same respect or credit for the vessels as the artisan who painted the glyphs or figural scenes as only single artisans are given credit within glyphic texts.

As mentioned, polychrome vessels also portray deities and elite members of society with their writing utensils, paint pots, and costumes of their trade, but figures responsible for or engaged in forming vessels or other related ceramic production work are noticeably absent. Nevertheless, the diversity of tools from Motul de San José may provide evidence for "invisible" producers that were critical for a successful product (see, for example, discussion in Wright 1991) or, at the very least, processes of production that were not celebrated in vessel texts and iconography. Interestingly, the range of artifacts at Motul de San José is broader than that found at Tikal's middle-class polychrome workshop in Group 4H-1 (Becker 2003a) and the palace at Buenavista del Cayo (Reents-Budet et al. 2000). Is it possible that production stages were either more spatially or socially separate at these latter sites?

Another issue that concerns production scale and intensity is multi-crafting or the engagement of a single household or social unit in diverse types of crafts and economic endeavors. The Acropolis midden included evidence for multiple crafts apart from pottery production: debris from the manufacture of figurines, of bone or shell tools and ornaments were also identified in this massive deposit (see Halperin, this volume; Emery, this volume). Multicrafting appears to be a common feature of pre-Hispanic Mesoamerican economies. In pre-Hispanic Oaxaca, Feinman and Nicholas (2000, 2004) have found that pre-Columbian specialists often had multiple crafts, each practiced on a small scale, but put together, they formed full-time specialization. A similar case for multiple specializations can be made for several Late Classic elite residences at Aguateca excavated by Inomata and colleagues. For example, at Structure M8-10 (House of the Scribe), excavators found evidence for scribal work, shell and bone tool or ornament production, and textile production (Inomata 2001b; Inomata and Stiver 1998). At Structure M8-4 (House of the Mirrors), craft activities included scribal work (stone mortars and pestles), textile production, and pyrite ornament production (Inomata et al. 2002, 311–18; see also discussion in Andrews IV and Fash 1992; Hendon 1997; McAnany and Plank 2001).

Conclusion

Maya scholars have often suggested that finely painted polychrome vessels were manufactured by artisans belonging to or attached to elite households and royal courts. This interpretation derives from the depictions of artisans in the iconography; from hieroglyphic inscriptions detailing the artisans' identity; and from the highly skilled as well as labor-intensive require-ments for their production, their paste composition, and their relatively restricted distributions (Ball 1993; Coe and Kerr 1998; Foias and Bishop 1997; Reents-Budet 1994, 1998; Reents-Budet et al. 2000; P. Rice 1987a). The investigations at Motul de San José complement these data in presenting archaeological evidence for ceramic production in or near the site's royal Acropolis. Because of the secondary nature of the ceramic manufacturing debris, however, we are unable to speculate on the spatial organization of production in relationship to specific architectural features (Costin 2001, 293). In addition, we have difficulty calculating the extent to which broken sherds were errors created during the production process or domestic re-fuse. This problem is not new, however, as debris found at other sites, such as Buenavista and Tikal, have also been found in secondary contexts.

Nonetheless, evidence from the ceramic wasters and tools from Motul de San José provide some clues to the types of products that were made: finely painted polychromes with hieroglyphs and figural scenes, simple geomet-ric polychrome vessels and figurines. Other vessels, such as monochrome wares, may have also been produced in this same context, although fur-ther research is required to confirm this assertion. We suggest that pottery production debris and tools found within the Motul de San José Acropolis may highlight the work of elite priest-scribes and, possibly, the apprentices, relatives, or servants who are ignored in textual sources and iconography (that is, by the very scribes and artisans who finish the last stages of their work). In addition, we find that ceramic production intensity was likely to have been low. But when it is examined in relation to the other activities, it appears that the Motul de San José royal court, similar to those at other Late Classic sites, were engaged in a broad range of prestige goods crafting as well as various subsistence endeavors. It was through the production of these socially and ritually potent materials that the Motul de San José royal court and/or elite residences nearby produced and defined their own Ik' polity identity as well as garnered resources for creating social alliances, fulfilled social and ritual responsibilities, and gained prestige among their peers and subordinates.

7

History, Politics, and Ceramics

The Ceramic Sequence of Trinidad de Nosotros, El Petén, Guatemala

MATTHEW D. MORIARTY

Introduction

Since its inception, the Motul de San José Archaeological Project has focused on testing economic and political models for the Late Classic Maya polity headed by Motul de San José (Foias 2003; Foias and Emery, this volume). Although most project research has emphasized the critical interval in the latter half of the Late Classic period when Motul emerged as a major political center, an equally important aspect of the investigations has been to provide a temporal context for these developments. Culture-historical questions have formed a significant portion of all studies, with stratigraphic excavations at eight different sites (Foias 2003; Foias et al., this volume; Moriarty 2004b, 2005; Castellanos 2007; Spensley 2008). This work has highlighted the length and complexity of occupation in the Motul de San José area, as well as the relative brevity of Motul's local preeminence.

The complexity of diachronic developments in the Motul area prior to Motul's emergence as a political capital is well illustrated by Trinidad de Nosotros. Although five seasons of research at Motul have identified only minor occupation prior to its Late Classic zenith, excavations at Trinidad have documented the longest and most complete record of occupation in the Motul area. Trinidad served as Motul's port and principal secondary center in the Late Classic. During this time, Trinidad's residents enjoyed a degree of access to exotic imports second only to the royal residents of central Motul. Other economic activities at Trinidad included extensive chert tool production (Lawton 2007a, 2007b) and fishing (Thornton and

Emery 2007; Thornton, this volume), with both goods likely distributed throughout the Motul area.

Stretching from the initial ceramic-bearing colonization of El Petén through to the contact and historical eras, Trinidad's ceramic sequence provides a framework for understanding long-term developments in the Motul de San José area. This chapter presents the ceramic sequence defined at this site. Such detailed ceramic chronological studies as described in this chapter are critical to our understanding of Motul's role in the region: the presence of considerable occupation at Trinidad previous to the Late Classic highlights that Motul's florescence during the Late Classic was intrusive to this zone. Furthermore, the nature of integration processes within the Motul polity can be revealed through detailed modal ceramic analyses of subsidiary sites like Trinidad: close integration between Trinidad's and Motul's pottery assemblages during the Late Classic would speak to strong integrative mechanisms (whether political, economic, or social).

The first section of this chapter provides an introduction to the site, the history of research there, and its hypothesized role in the Late Classic Motul polity. This is followed by a brief discussion of the Trinidad ceramic sample, its analysis, and associated radiocarbon dates. The next section provides summaries of each of the ten ceramic complexes that comprise the Trinidad sequence. The final section briefly considers Trinidad's developmental trajectory in comparison with Motul.

Trinidad de Nosotros

The ancient Maya center of Trinidad de Nosotros (*Sik'u'* in Itzaj Maya) is located on the north shore of Lake Petén Itzá, 2.6 kilometers southeast of Motul de San José's principal plaza (Figure 1.4). This location places Trinidad near the east-west midpoint of the lake's northern arm and at one of the best natural access points on the northern shore of the lake, most of which is lined by steep limestone escarpment and narrow rocky beaches. This position also places the site between Motul and trade routes utilizing Lake Petén Itzá, and at the southern terminus of the portage from the lake basin to the Río San Pedro drainage to the northwest. This combination of factors makes Trinidad a natural gateway and a key settlement for the Motul de San José area.

In scale, Trinidad is a modest-sized secondary center, roughly comparable to the "level 7: small major ceremonial center" in the settlement hierarchy proposed for northern Belize by Hammond (1975b). Contiguous settlement covers an area of just over one square kilometer with approximately 150 structures (Figure 7.1). Most structures are organized into thirty distinct architectural groups within a highly nucleated 50-hect-are site center. This central area is bounded to the north and west by an 8-meter-deep *arroyo* and to the south by the lake. The tallest structure (Structure A-1) is a 12-meter-high pyramid, and this is one of only three structures at Trinidad over 4 meters in height (Figure 7.2).

Within the Motul area, Trinidad's scale and architectural complexity place it in the second tier, larger than all but Motul and Chächäklu'um, a site located 5 kilometers to the northeast (Figure 1.4). Motul, the only primate center in the MSJ area, is roughly three to four times more extensive (ca. 4.2 square kilometers, four-hundred-plus structures; Moriarty 2004b, 2005) and much more monumental (see Figure 1.2). Motul's central precinct includes several temples over 15 meters high, and the construction volume of its central acropolis alone exceeds that of all public constructions at Trinidad combined (Foias 2003; Moriarty 2004b).

Trinidad is comparable with Motul only in terms of its central public and ceremonial space. Trinidad's six public plazas (I-VI) cover an area of 19,030 square meters. This total closely approaches that found at Motul (ca. 23,000 square meters) and greatly exceeds that of any other site investigated by the MSJ Project (Table 7.1). The potential capacities of these plazas are also many times greater than Trinidad's peak Late Classic population, which likely numbered no more than 750 inhabitants (Moriarty, Spensley, Lawton, et al. 2008). The extension of public plaza space at Trinidad is notable even at the regional level, falling within the range of centers of vastly greater political importance and population (see Inomata 2006, table 1). This extensive public plaza space may reflect a shared community ethos emphasizing trade, transportation, and public spectacle. Trinidad's central precinct also includes the only ball court in the Motul de San José area (Moriarty and Foias 2007). A multitude of evidence suggests that here, Trinidad's residents hosted elaborate ball game–related feasts and other rituals throughout the Late Classic period (Moriarty and Foias 2007; Moriarty and Thornton 2007; see below).

Trinidad is also remarkable for its harbor. Although small, the harbor features a 70-meter-long breakwater, a roughly 30-by-40-meter loading platform adjacent to the lake, and a 12-meter-long possible dock (see also the stucco evidence in Spensley, this volume). Together these features, along with the natural landscape, form a partially enclosed bay or coastal basin that would have provided a safe area for landing, loading, and unloading canoes, as well as protection from seasonal storms. Local informants report

Figure 7.1. Map of Trinidad de Nosotros, El Petén, Guatemala. Contour intervals equal one meter. Map set to magnetic north (drawing by M. D. Moriarty).

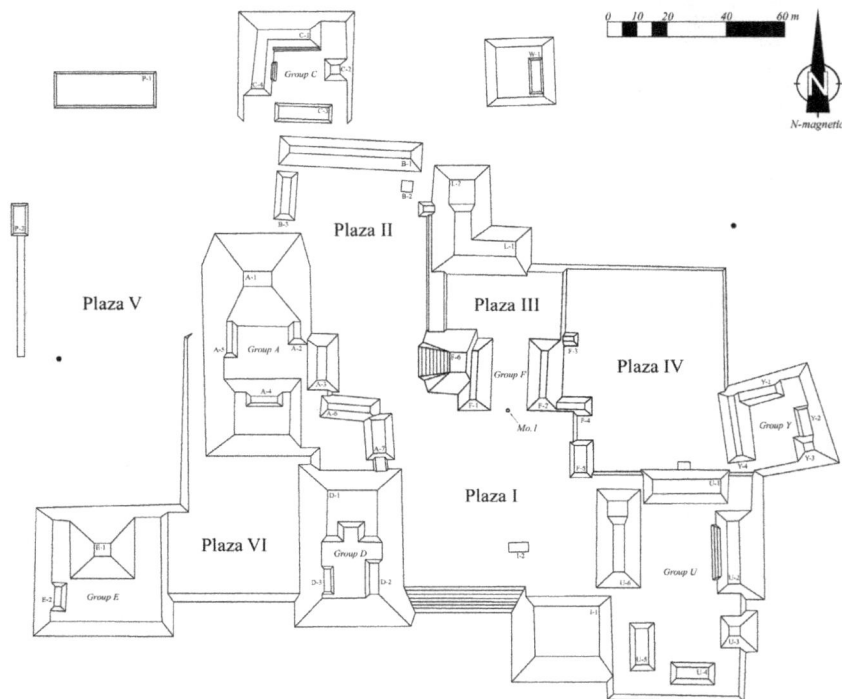

Figure 7.2. Trinidad's central precinct with public plazas and principal architectural groups indicated. Small residential groups not included.

Table 7.1. Public plaza space and plaza capacity estimates for selected sites in the Motul de San José area

		Plaza capacity estimates (no. of people)		
Site	Plaza space (m²)	3.6 m²/ person	1.0 m²/ person	0.46 m²/ person
Motul de San José	23,000	6,389	23,000	50,000
Trinidad de Nosotros	19,030	5,286	19,030	41,370
Chäkokot	4,077	1,133	4,077	8,863
Akte	4,000	1,111	4,000	8,696
Buenavista-Nuevo San José	2,773	770	2,773	6,028
Xilil	1,484	412	1,484	3,226

Source: For a detailed discussion of the figures used to produce these estimates see Inomata (2006, 811–14) and Moore (1996).
Note: Plaza areas calculated using existing MSJ Project maps.

that this area was utilized as a transshipment point during the mid-twentieth-century *chicle*[1] boom, and a similar function can be inferred for earlier periods.

The combination of the site's strategic location, the unusually large amount of public plaza space, and the presence of a harbor suggested that Trinidad may have functioned as a port. Investigations, conducted in 2003 and 2005, were designed to test this hypothesis through systematic test-pitting, midden testing, and harbor and residential excavations (Moriarty, Castellanos, and Foias 2003; Moriarty et al. 2007). These two seasons generated a wealth of data and strongly support the contention that Trinidad played such a special role in the Late Classic Motul polity.

Support for the port hypothesis was found in harbor area excavations and the analysis of obsidian artifacts. Excavation of harbor features and associated high-density middens indicated a long sequence of construction, modification, and use beginning in the Preclassic and extending through the Postclassic, with a peak in activity during the Late Classic (Spensley and Moriarty 2006). Further, obsidian analyses indicate that during the critical Late Classic to Terminal Classic interval Trinidad's residents had access to the greatest number of obsidian polyhedral cores, conserved obsidian least in blade production, and procured obsidian from the broadest array of sources among all centers in the Motul area (Moriarty, Spensley, Lawton, et al. 2008). All in all, various obsidian indices (average blade widths, cutting-edge-to-mass ratios, core to blade ratios, and others) strongly support the proposition that Trinidad had a particularly high level of access to obsidian and played a key role in its distribution (ibid.). This pattern in obsidian procurement and consumption closely resembles the expectations for ancient Maya trading ports (Andrews 1990; McKillop 1989, 1996).

These investigations also provided direct evidence for Trinidad's involvement in the Late Classic ritual economy of the Motul area. The most obvious manifestation of this role came from a series of Late Classic middens encountered adjacent to the ball court's eastern lateral structure. Partial excavation of these deposits yielded more than twenty-one thousand potsherds of which an unusually large percentage came from decorated serving vessels (see below; Moriarty 2009; Moriarty and Foias 2007). The faunal assemblage was also remarkably rich in rare or ritually significant species (Thornton, this volume). Hundreds of exotic artifacts, including obsidian, greenstone, and pyrite were also found in these ball court middens. The festive and musical atmosphere that attended these activities is suggested by fragments from more than a dozen ceramic drums, several bone raspers, and more than 150 whistle figurines. Cumulatively, these deposits represent multiple, large-scale ball game–related feasts within Trinidad's central precinct (Moriarty 2009; Moriarty and Foias 2007).

In summary, current evidence suggests that Trinidad played a multifaceted role within the Late Classic Motul polity. From its position astride long-distance trade routes utilizing Lake Petén Itzá, Trinidad functioned as an economic gateway with an important role in the procurement and distribution of some long-distance trade goods, including obsidian and fish (Thornton, this volume). Further, Trinidad also likely acted as a political gateway to the Motul polity, serving both as a physical intermediary between Motul and the larger lake basin and as a setting for the complex sociopolitical negotiations and interactions required by an emergent polity. The extensive evidence for ball game feasting underscores the importance and highly intertwined nature of these roles (Fash and Fash 2007; J. G. Fox 1996).

The Ceramic Sample and Chronological Research at Trinidad

Two seasons of excavations at Trinidad produced more than 250,000 potsherds. Of these, just over one-third (86,478) were selected for full first-level analysis. This sample was drawn primarily from middens and architectural fill associated with domestic groups and public architecture within the site center. Midden assemblages provided the bulk of the analyzed sample; materials from stratified deposits were useful primarily in assessing temporal concerns. The robust nature of the midden sample from Trinidad was especially helpful in separating the early and late portions of the Late Classic ceramic assemblage at Trinidad.

Ceramic analyses followed type-variety methods as defined by Gifford (1960, 1976) and others (Smith, Willey, and Gifford 1960; Willey, Culbert, and Adams 1967). Specific protocols followed those developed by Foias (1996) and utilized by all Motul de San José Archaeological Project personnel. This allowed for direct comparisons with previously analyzed materials. Due to time constraints, sherds were classified following published descriptions and no formal second-level analysis was conducted.[2] To offset the absence of a full modal analysis, observations were regularly recorded for key attributes on the most common types, and varieties have been left as unspecified for most types to indicate the provisional nature of the identification.

To supplement ceramic analyses, eleven specimens of wood charcoal and deer bone[3] were submitted for AMS radiocarbon analysis to the NSF-Arizona AMS Laboratory at the University of Arizona. Samples were selected to address key points in Trinidad's developmental sequence and were drawn exclusively from contexts where depositional processes could be inferred and postdepositional effects were minimal. Samples represent the Late Classic (five midden samples), the Late Preclassic (four midden, one cache), and the Postclassic (midden). Sample provenience, Δ^{13}C, uncalibrated ^{14}C age determinations, and one- and two-sigma calibrated date ranges are presented in Table 7.2.

The Trinidad de Nosotros Ceramic Sequence

Chronological research at Trinidad revealed a continuous occupation beginning with the initial ceramic-bearing colonization of the central Petén lowlands and extending through to the historical period. On the basis of ceramic analyses, radiocarbon dating, and comparative research, this sequence has been divided into ten named phases with associated ceramic complexes. Complex names are presented in Table 7.3 with associated periods and estimated date ranges. Duration ranges for these complexes follow those proposed for highly similar complexes at Tikal, with a few exceptions (Culbert 2003, table 2.1).

The following sections provide brief synopses for each of Trinidad's ceramic complexes. As a result of space constraints, the discussion focuses primarily on key types and diagnostic attributes for each complex. Form descriptions, where possible, follow the lexicon provided by Sabloff (1975, 22–27). This report follows Forsyth (1993a, 34) and Foias (1996) in adapting type names as originally defined by Smith and Gifford (1966) for modern Spanish usage in Guatemala. Complete sherd counts by ceramic group and type are available in Moriarty (forthcoming) and in digital appendices (available at http://motul-archaeology.williams.edu).

Aj Wo' Pre-Mamom Early Middle Preclassic Complex (800–650 BC)

The earliest pottery recovered at Trinidad dates to the pre-Mamom early Middle Preclassic period. These materials were identified only in very small quantities within a limited number of deposits. The only secure Aj Wo' construction identified at Trinidad consisted of two postholes cut into bedrock beneath Group C, a Late Classic residential group north of Plaza II. The postholes presumably represent the remains of a small perishable structure placed directly atop bedrock during the initial occupation of the site. Moderate quantities of Aj Wo' materials were also recovered mixed with later Ix Cha' Mamom sherds in the fill of a 25-centimeter-high cobble platform 20

Table 7.2. AMS radiocarbon assays from Trinidad: Radiocarbon ages and calibrated date ranges

Lab. No.	Archaeological context (lot)	Phase	Material	$\Delta^{13}C$	^{14}C Age (BP)	Calibrated 2-sigma range(s) (%p)
AA72662	Upper level of high-density midden adjacent to harbor Platform EE (TRI12A6-3-2).	Säk-tunich	Deer bone	-21.6	893 ± 40	AD 1035–1218 (95.4)
AA72660	Burned level within high-density midden adjacent to harbor Platform EE (TRI12A6-3-5).	Sik'u' I-II	Wood charcoal	-26.5	1,236 ± 49	AD 670–891 (95.4)
AA72665	Upper level of high-density midden directly east of Structure F-4 (TRI10D10-3-2).	Sik'u' II	Deer bone	-21.7	1,139 ± 42	AD 779–94 (4.4); AD 798–988 (90.9)
AA72666	Upper level of high-density midden directly east of Structure F-4 (TRI10D10-3-2).	Sik'u' II	Deer bone	-9.6	1,188 ± 42	AD 694–701 (0.7); AD 707–47 (7.3); AD 765–903 (76.1); AD 914–69 (11.2)
AA72663	Lower level of high-density midden directly east of Structure F-4 (TRI10D10-3-5).	Sik'u' I	Deer bone	-20.2	1,270 ± 43	AD 662–830 (88.9); AD 836–68 (6.5)
AA72664	Lower level of high-density midden directly east of Structure F-4 (TRI10D10-3-6).	Sik'u' I	Deer bone	-21	1,287 ± 43	AD 654–783 (87.1); AD 787–824 (5.7); AD 841–61 (2.6)
AA72667	High-density midden atop bedrock beneath Structure C-1 (TRI4A13-6-3).	Chukan	Wood charcoal	-24.4	2,294 ± 41	409–348 BC (54.1); 317–207 BC (41.3)
AA72668	Midden redeposited as fill beneath Structure C-1 (TRI4A13-6-1).	Chukan	Wood charcoal	-26.1	2,144 ± 40	357–280 BC (25.3); 257–245 BC (1.3); 235–52 BC (68.8)

AA72669	High-density midden atop bedrock beneath Group G platform (TRI1G1-6-1).	Chukan	Wood charcoal	−25.5	2,201 ± 40	382–175 BC (95.4)
AA72670	High-density midden atop bedrock beneath Group G platform (TRI1G1-6-2).	Chukan	Wood charcoal	−17.6	2,206 ± 40	383–180 BC (95.4)
AA72671	Charcoal deposited as part of greenstone cache (#2) under Floor 7 beneath ball court playing alley (TRI1F2-8-1).	Chukan	Wood charcoal	−25.4	2,278 ± 40	403–348 BC (44.4); 317–207 BC (51.0)

Note: Dates calibrated using the Calib 5.10 radiocarbon calibration software with the Intcal04 calibration data (see Stuiver and Becker 1986; Stuiver and Reimer 1993; Reimer et al. 2004).

Table 7.3. Ceramic complexes for Trinidad

Complex	Chronological period	Date ranges
Aj B'oj	Contact/Historical	AD 1500–1950
Säk-tunich	Postclassic	AD 950–1500
Yaljob'ach	Terminal Classic	AD 850–950
Sik'u' II	Late Classic	AD 700–850
Sik'u' I	Late Classic	AD 550–700
'Ayim-tun	Early Classic	AD 200–550
P'ich 'Ayim	Terminal Preclassic	AD 150–200
Chukan	Late Preclassic	350 BC–AD 150
Ix Cha'	Middle Preclassic	650–350 BC
Aj Wo'	Middle Preclassic	800–650 BC

Note: All date ranges are approximate.

meters to the east and likewise situated directly atop bedrock. The remaining materials were found in trace quantities within mixed Ix Cha' fill deposits throughout the site center. In general, materials of such an early date were highly fragmentary and only forty slipped sherds could be positively identified. With these limitations in mind, the early Middle Preclassic Aj Wo' complex can be presented in provisional format only.

The Aj Wo' complex consists of four monochrome (red, white, black, and orange) groups and one unslipped group. Unslipped sherds in Aj Wo' collections could not be separated from materials identified as Achiotes Unslipped in the subsequent Ix Cha' complex, and were provisionally identified as such in the present complex. Slipped materials were separated from subsequent Ix Cha' specimens on the basis of slip color, surface treatment, paste, and form attributes. Both the red and white slips of this complex differ significantly in color from the red-orange and cream of later Mamom types. Further, unlike the waxy surface finish that characterizes Mamom and Chicanel sphere materials, slipped monochromes of the Aj Wo' complex have a notably matte finish. In many instances, slips also appear thin and wash-like, an attribute with clear parallels in the Real Xe complex at Seibal (Sabloff 1975, 53). Aj Wo' monochrome pastes, characterized by dark black cores and a high incidence of calcite and other mineral inclusions visible under both low-power (10x) magnification and naked-eye observation, also differ significantly from the more evenly fired and typically grog-tempered Ix Cha' complex monochromes. Indeed, Aj Wo' monochrome pastes appear to have a closer correspondence with unslipped Achiotes group materials than with later monochromes. Form data for the Aj Wo' complex are limited. Only a handful of form diagnostic rim sherds were positively identified, all from the red- and white-slipped groups. The forms identified, however, are consistent with those found in early collections at Seibal (Sabloff 1975, 50), Cahal Pech (Cheetham, Forsyth, and Clark 2003, 633), and Uaxactún (R. Smith 1955, fig. 77).

Aj Wo' complex materials were originally classified using Xe sphere-type designations (R. Adams 1971; Sabloff 1975), and the materials themselves are quite similar to Xe specimens. The small size and eroded nature of the Trinidad sample, however, precluded effective comparison with materials from the Xe or other early complexes (e.g., Ball and Taschek 2003; Cheetham, Forsyth, and Clark 2003, 633; Culbert 1979, 2003; P. Rice 1979a). Aj Wo' complex materials are, of course, most comparable to pre-Mamom materials collected at the nearby site of Buenavista-Nuevo San José by Jeanette Castellanos (2007), and will be classified in a similar manner pending further comparative analyses. A conservative starting date of 800 BC was selected to align with Tikal's Eb complex, although more detailed comparisons are needed.

Ix Cha' Mamom Late Middle Preclassic Complex (650–350 BC)

The onset of the late Middle Preclassic Ix Cha' phase coincides with a notable increase in population and the beginning of complex developments at Trinidad. Ix Cha' Mamom sphere materials were recovered in small quantities in most operations and were well distributed throughout the site center. Ix Cha' packed-earth and plaster floors were identified beneath two Late Classic residential groups, and initial plaza constructions in Plazas I-II, the ball court area, and Group A all date to this phase, suggesting that later developments in Trinidad's central-most precinct derived from a Middle Preclassic template. The only area that failed to produce evidence for an Ix Cha' phase occupation was the harbor area. There, two seasons of excavation produced only a handful of Ix Cha' sherds, suggesting that this area was either unused or that lake levels were significantly higher than at any other point in Trinidad's occupation.

The Ix Cha' complex is characterized by a suite of well-defined Mamom sphere types and consists of five groups of slipped pottery and one group of unslipped pottery (Figure 7.3). Of the monochrome groups, the Juventud group, characterized by its orange to red-orange slip and waxy finish, is the most diagnostic for the Ix Cha' complex. Waxy, black-slipped Chunhinta group materials are second in importance. On the other hand, cream-slipped materials of the Pital group are very limited in distribution. Within

Ix Cha' collections, a small number of sherds were also identified with an orange to red-orange slip and "buff to tan splotches" similar to those described for the Tierra Mojada group at Nakbé (Forsyth 1993a, 39). Mars Orange ware materials, though rare, serve as excellent diagnostics for the Ix Cha' complex. Forty-two additional sherds were characterized by slightly darker pastes and more inclusions than normal for the Savana group (Gifford 1976, 74). These were classified provisionally as "cf. Savana Orange," and presumably constitute local reproductions or alternative production sources. Unslipped Ix Cha' complex materials were dominated by the type Achiotes Unslipped (Figure 7.3). Small quantities of striated body sherds were also recovered in some Ix Cha' lots. A handful of unslipped sherds also included faint daub decoration, particularly around the exterior neck of jar forms, and were classified as Palma Daub.

Typologically, the Ix Cha' complex bears a clear affiliation to the Mamom ceramic sphere with strong resemblances to other Petén Mamom complexes (R. Adams 1971; P. Rice 1979a; Sabloff 1975; R, Smith 1955), particularly the Tzec complex of Tikal (Culbert 1979, 2003). Although incising, chamfering, and certain other decorative techniques are not notably common in Ix Cha' assemblages, particularly when compared to collections from Nakbé (Forsyth 1993a) and Uaxactún (R. Smith 1955), this likely results in part from the limited nature of the Trinidad sample. At the local level, with the exception of the Temchay and Vecanxan groups, which have not been identified at Trinidad, the Ix Cha' appears comparable to the Chunzalam complex of the Tayasal-Paxcamán zone (A. Chase 1983, 28–30).

Chukan Chicanel Late Preclassic Complex (350 BC–AD 150)

During the Late Preclassic period, Trinidad underwent the first of two clear peaks in settlement density and constructional intensity. Late Preclassic Chukan phase constructions were identified in virtually all residential groups, and most of the large basal platforms that characterize Trinidad's site center were first built at this time. All tested public architectural complexes, including all public plazas and the ball court, show evidence for either initial Chukan construction or repaving over earlier Ix Cha' episodes. The Chukan phase also witnessed the first formal modifications in the harbor area, including the construction of a low platform directly adjacent to the lake. Finally, the prolific nature of this phase at Trinidad is best evidenced by the richness and wide distribution of high-density Chukan middens throughout the site center. Virtually all site center excavations encountered Chukan phase middens of medium-density or higher. The large

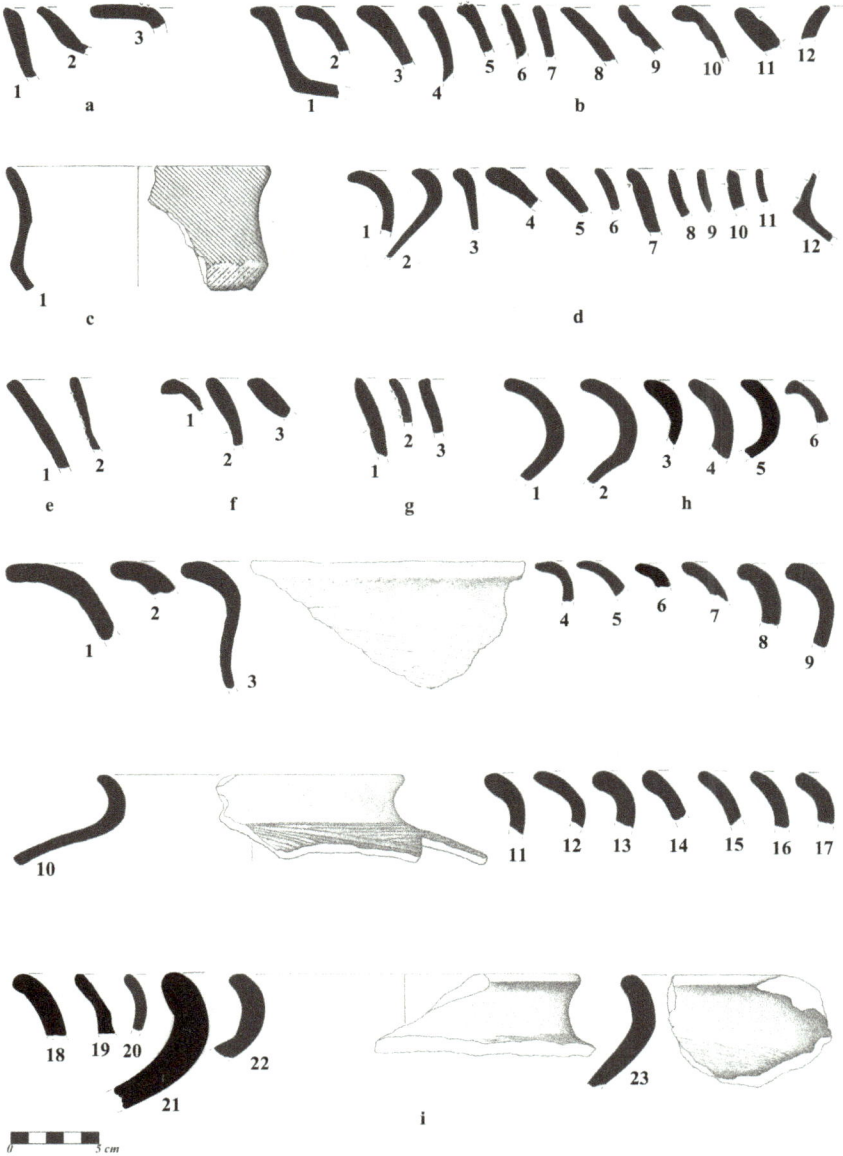

Figure 7.3. Aj Wo' Complex: (A1) Eroded/Group Undesignated; (A2–3) Unnamed White Group. Ix Cha' Complex: (B–C) Joventud Group; (D) Chunhinta Group; (E) Pital Group; (F) Tierra Mojada Group; (G) Savana Group; (H) Achiotes Group. Chukan Complex: (I) Achiotes Group (this and other chapter drawings by I. Seyb and L. F. Luin unless otherwise stated).

sample of ceramics from these deposits permitted clear definition of the Chukan complex, as well as its early and late facets.

The Chukan complex is dominated by a suite of well-defined Chicanel sphere ceramic groups and types found throughout the Maya lowlands (Figure 7.4). The principal monochrome slipped pottery is the Sierra ceramic group, identifiable by its waxy red slip. Pre-slip circumferential grooving on the interior of rims is very common (Figure 7.4: A1–A5, A8). Although labial and medial flanged bowls are also common (Figure 7.4: B1–B4), they appear less frequently than at better-known sites like El Mirador (Forsyth 1989) and Uaxactún (R. Smith 1955), and are more characteristic of the late facet of the Chukan complex. Black-slipped types of the Polvero group are characterized by bowl and jar forms analogous to those of Sierra Red (Figure 7.4: C1–C3). Medial flange bowls are common (Figure 7.4: C4), and appear slightly earlier than similar Sierra group forms. Among cream-slipped Flor group types, this form also appears earlier than in the Sierra group. As with the preceding Ix Cha' complex, unslipped materials of the Chukan complex are dominated by the Achiotes ceramic group. The principal difference between the two complexes lies in the use of striated decoration. During the Late Preclassic, Achiotes Unslipped is largely replaced by the type Zapote Striated (Figure 7.3: I1–I23). This type normally constitutes more than eighty percent of unslipped materials in Chukan collections. The dominant form, a short-necked jar with a slightly out-curved neck, is basically identical to earlier Ix Cha' unslipped jars. Open unslipped forms are very rare during Chukan times, although a few censer forms were classified as Morfín Unslipped.

In composition, the Chukan complex bears an unequivocal affiliation to the Chicanel sphere and shares many of its diagnostic types with Late Preclassic complexes throughout the Maya lowlands. At the local level, the Chukan complex exhibits obvious similarities to the Kax complex of the Tayasal-Paxcamán zone (A. Chase 1983), although the Escobal and Topol groups have not been identified at Trinidad. Affiliations with the Late Preclassic complexes of Tikal are less certain, but may be close. Early and late facets to the Chukan complex, however, have been identified at Trinidad and may correlate to the Chuen and Cauac complexes of Tikal (Culbert 1979, 2003). Early facet Chukan materials frequently exhibit close ties to the preceding Ix Cha' complex, including delicate forms, a more orange slip than typical for the Sierra group, and a lack of medial and labial flanges on red slipped materials. Late facet forms tend to be more robust, Sierra materials exhibit redder slip, and flanges are more common on all slipped

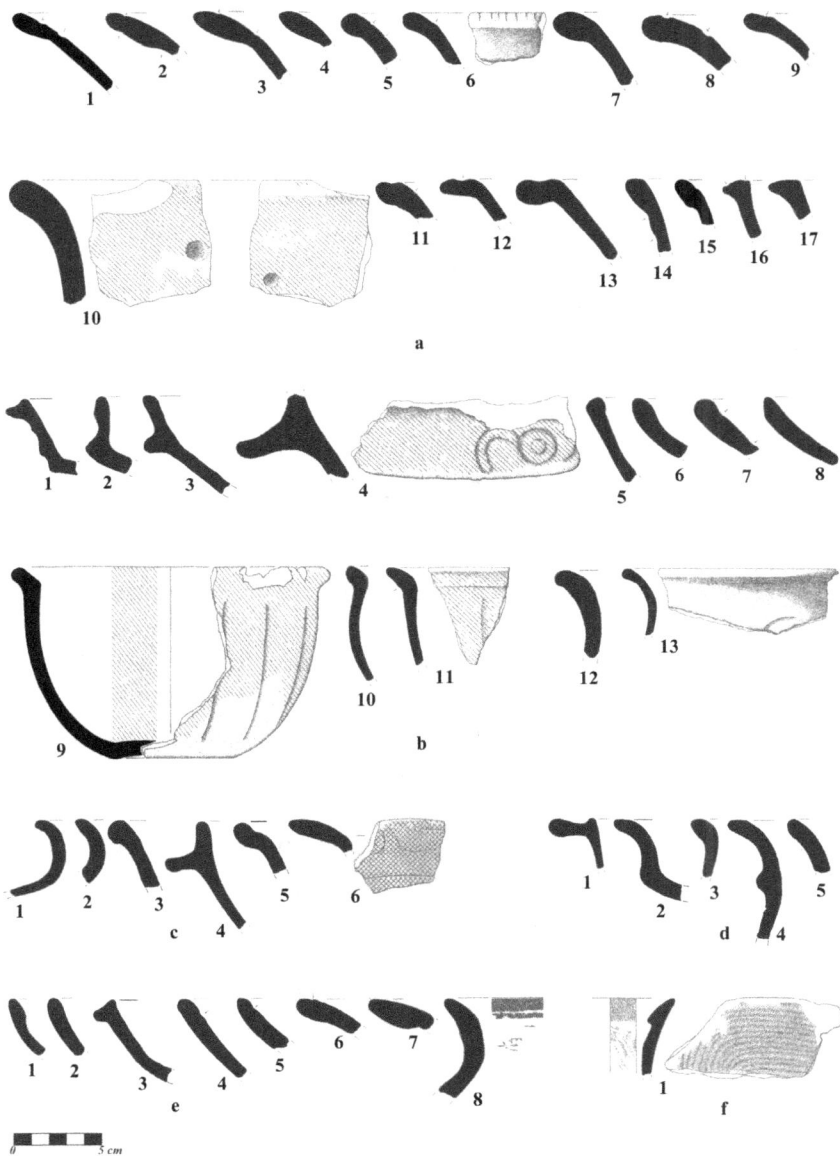

Figure 7.4. Chukan Complex: (A–B) Sierra Group; (C) Polvero Group; (D–E) Flor Group; (F) cf. Iberia Group.

materials. Of the two, the early facet is the most heavily represented in Chukan collections.

P'ich 'Ayim Terminal Preclassic Complex (AD 150–200)

As is the case elsewhere in the Maya lowlands (Brady et al. 1998; Forsyth 1989, 51–59), the end of the Preclassic at Trinidad is marked by a high degree of ceramic variability, the introduction of new types and modes, and the co-occurrence of types more diagnostic of both earlier and later complexes. This situation is complicated by the nature of Terminal Preclassic P'ich 'Ayim deposits at Trinidad. P'ich 'Ayim materials were not well distributed and were encountered almost exclusively in middens and special deposits. Further, only a handful of P'ich 'Ayim fill episodes were identified in the site center, suggesting a nearly complete cessation in construction during the transition from the Preclassic to the Classic. Despite the limited nature of assemblage data, however, the relatively complete inventory of both specialized and mundane forms suggests identification as a discrete ceramic complex, rather than a separate ceremonial subcomplex.

Monochrome pottery of the P'ich 'Ayim complex is dominated by groups that first appeared in Chukan times, in particular the Sierra and Polvero groups. Minority types, especially those characterized by penetrative decoration, occur in much lower frequencies than seen in pure Chukan deposits. Likewise, unslipped materials are dominated by the Achiotes group and by the type Zapote Striated. Although most of the materials recovered in P'ich 'Ayim deposits were highly fragmentary, forms are highly comparable to those found in Chukan assemblages. Among the few clear P'ich 'Ayim diagnostics is the hooked rim mode. At Trinidad, this mode appears most frequently on jars or deep-collared bowls, with a small fillet attached to the inner wall of the rim, just below the lip. This mode has been identified for the type Polvero Black (Figure 7.5: B1, B3) and on unslipped Achiotes group forms (Figure 7.5: B2). In P'ich 'Ayim contexts, this particular form is quite common, although jar forms more typical of the Late Preclassic also occur. Another hooked rim form, similar to that identified for the late Cascabel and Paixbancito complexes of El Mirador (Forsyth 1989, 18S–JJ), is also occasionally present on Sierra and Polvero group materials at Trinidad (Figure 7.4: C5), though it is quite rare and its relationship with the P'ich 'Ayim complex is not clear. All of the P'ich 'Ayim contexts at Trinidad also included a small number of orange-slipped sherds. Most of these could not be separated from later Aguila group types and were classified as such. A small number of sherds, however, had a red-orange slip, reddish paste, and

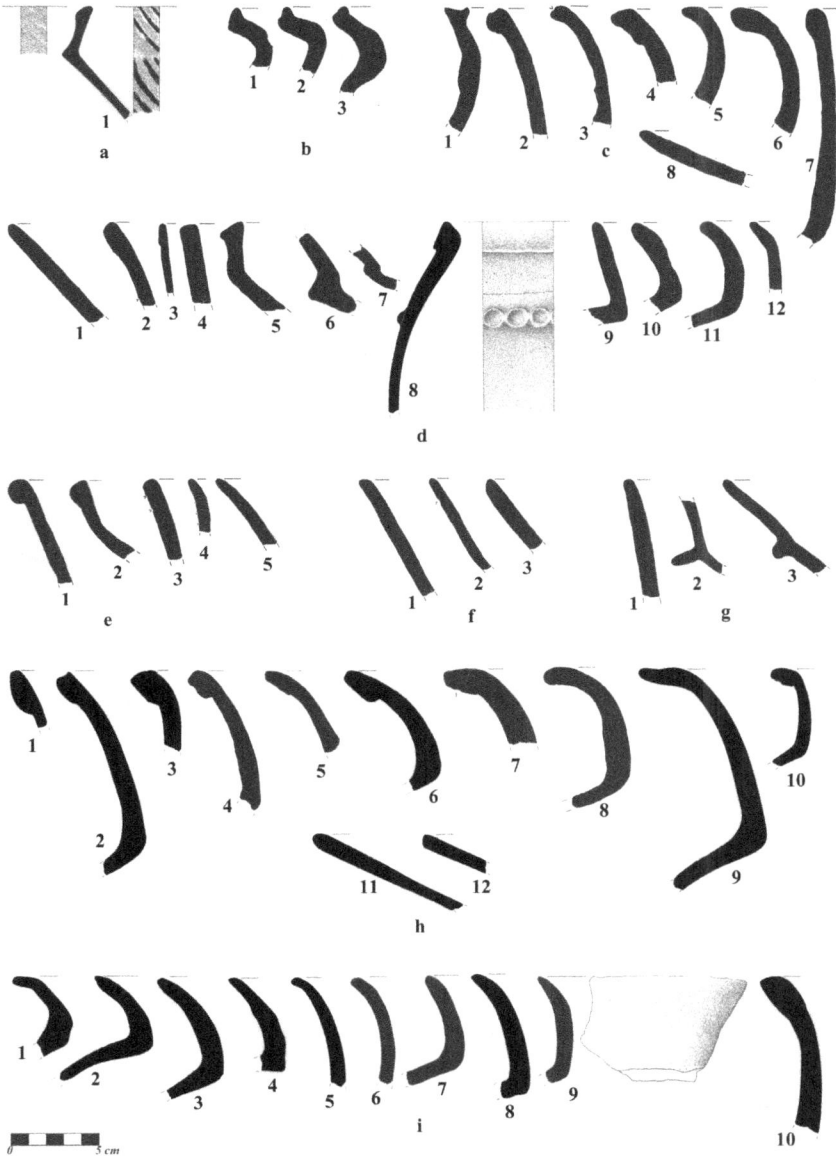

Figure 7.5. P'ich 'Ayim Complex: (A) cf. Iberia Group; (B1, 3) Achiotes Group; (B2) Polvero Group. 'Ayim-tun Complex: (C) Quintal Group; (D) Aguila Group; (E) Balanza Group; (F) Caribal Group; (G) Actuncan-Dos Arroyos Group; Sik'u' I–II and Yaljob'ach Complexes: (H) Cambio Group; (I) Tinaja Group.

a slightly waxy finish and were provisionally classified as Iberia Orange (Sabloff 1975, 90). Similarly, a small number of black- and red-slipped monochromes had lighter pastes and a more lustrous finish than was typical for slipped Chicanel sphere materials and were classified within the Balanza and Caribal groups.

The P'ich 'Ayim complex is also notable for a slight increase in the use of dichromes and the introduction of rare polychromes. Chicanel sphere dichromes such as Repasto Black-on-red, Mateo Red-on-cream, and Matamoro Red-on-black, as well as several other unnamed dichromes have a somewhat greater distribution in P'ich 'Ayim assemblages than in earlier Chukan deposits. Further, although the type Caramba Red-on-orange first appears in Chukan contexts, it was more commonly recovered with P'ich 'Ayim materials (Figure 7.4: F1). The type Sacluc Black-on-orange as a deep-collared bowl with widely flared sides appears exclusively in P'ich 'Ayim assemblages and constitutes a virtual diagnostic for the complex (Figure 7.5: A1). Finally, a small number of eroded and highly fragmentary polychromes were also recovered in P'ich 'Ayim contexts. These were provisionally classified within the Actuncan-Dos Arroyos ceramic group, although the presence of several partial mammiform supports suggests a closer affiliation to Ixcanrio Orange Polychrome and other "Protoclassic" types (R. Adams 1971; Brady et al. 1998).

The absence of well-preserved decorated serving wares makes ceramic sphere affiliation problematic for the P'ich 'Ayim complex. Although available data hint at a peripheral relationship with the Floral Park sphere (Gifford 1976), more detailed form and decoration data are needed. Local comparisons, however, are more productive. In terms of type composition, particularly continuity in the use of key Chicanel types, the P'ich 'Ayim complex is quite similar to the Cimi complex of Tikal (Culbert 1979, 2003). Interestingly, this reliance on Preclassic types is not a notable feature of the Yaxcheel complex of the Tayasal-Paxcamán zone (A. Chase 1983), which may fall slightly later in time than the P'ich 'Ayim.

'Ayim-tun Tzakol Early Classic Complex (AD 200–550)

Following upon the construction downturn that characterized the P'ich 'Ayim, the Early Classic 'Ayim-tun phase constitutes a resurgence in both population and architectural investment. Construction episodes dating to the 'Ayim-tun were noted throughout the site center, particularly in public architectural complexes including the ball court and Plazas I-IV. Residential groups showed less evidence for new construction, but high-density middens associated with several groups indicate extensive activities during this phase. Likewise, though harbor excavations identified little evidence for 'Ayim-tun construction, dense middens indicated heavy use of this area throughout the Early Classic.

The principal 'Ayim-tun complex monochromes are orange-slipped Aguila group materials, followed by the black-slipped Balanza group (Figure 7.5: C-I). Although no clear slab-cylinder vessels were identified in archaeological collections from Trinidad, construction work at Casa Las Americas, a hotel 500 meters east of Trinidad, produced an excellent example of a hollow slab support with carved and incised decoration. Within 'Ayim-tun collections a small quantity of sherds were recovered with lustrous red slips. These materials were assigned to the Caribal group. Polychrome and bichrome materials were identified in very small numbers within 'Ayim-tun collections and were classified to the general Actuncan-Dos Arroyos group. Fragments from thin polychrome scutate lids are quite common in Early Classic collections and constitute a virtual 'Ayim-tun diagnostic. Unslipped Early Classic materials are dominated by types from the Quintal group (Figure 7.5: C).

In terms of type distribution, form, and slip attributes, the 'Ayim-tun complex demonstrates unmistakable membership in the Tzakol sphere, with close affiliations to the Manik complex of Tikal (Culbert 2003) and the Hoxchunchan of the Tayasal-Paxcamán zone (A. Chase 1983). Though more comparative research would be necessary to firmly subdivide the 'Ayim-tun chronologically into separate complexes or subcomplexes, temporal distinctions are apparent in field collections, and later materials (approximately contemporaneous with Tzakol 2–3) appear most numerous. The latter portion of this complex also bears an important relationship to the subsequent Sik'u' I. Many of the richest 'Ayim-tun deposits occurred immediately prior to the beginning of the Late Classic and include a smattering of Sik'u' I types. Similar trends were observed at Tikal (Culbert 2003, 60; Laporte 2003, 300–301) and Altar de Sacrificios (R. Adams 1971, 129).

Sik'u' I-II Tepeu Late Classic Complexes (AD 550–850)

The onset of the Late Classic period marks the beginning of Trinidad's second and principal peak in construction and occupation. Late Classic deposits have been identified in virtually all areas of the site. Major construction episodes are associated with the ball court, the site's principal temples, and Plazas I-IV, with the ceremonial heart of the settlement taking its final form. Virtually all of the residential groups tested by the Motul de

San José Archaeological Project were occupied at this time; most included Late Classic construction and were surrounded by dense Late Classic domestic refuse. The harbor area also underwent significant modification and use during this interval, indicated by the augmentation of key harbor features, maintenance of the protected harbor, and the accumulation of dense harbor middens.

Late Classic materials constituted more than half of all collected sherds, including thousands of well-preserved specimens from midden deposits. The quantity and quality of Late Classic materials at Trinidad and, in particular, the large number of well-preserved polychromes recovered in ball court area excavations (Moriarty 2009; Moriarty and Foias 2007) have permitted the separation of Trinidad's Late Classic ceramics into two highly related complexes. These complexes—Sik'u' I and Sik'u' II—date to the first and second halves of the Late Classic period. In definition, these complexes are closely related to the Ik and Imix complexes of Tikal (Culbert 2003) and the Tepeu 1 and Tepeu 2 complexes of Uaxactún (R. Smith 1955). Further, as with those complexes, definitions for the Sik'u' I and Sik'u' II are largely dependent on the distribution of a few key polychrome types and forms. Monochrome and unslipped pottery is, with a few exceptions, consistent throughout the Late Classic period and constitute a general Sik'u' complex that underlies the Sik'u' I and Sik'u' II complexes (Figure 7.6).

As noted above, the separation of the Sik'u' I and Sik'u' II complexes was based on the distribution of polychromes assigned to the Saxche-Palmar Group. Sik'u' I polychromes include Saxche Orange, Juleki Cream, Sibal Buff, Desquite Red-on-orange, and Uacho Black-on-orange. Sik'u' II polychromes include Palmar Orange, Zacatal Cream, Paixban Buff, and Chinos Black-on-cream, but they tended to be much more eroded than earlier materials and, thus, more difficult to sort to the type level. For this reason, laboratory sorting of these materials, particularly when fragmentary, was often problematic and was based, in large part, on modal attributes of two key form classes: tripod plates and dish/bowls. Sik'u' I tripod plates are widely open and lack a clear angle or division between base and body (Figure 7.7: A1–A16; see also Eberl 2007). Medial and near-basal ridges are quite common and these are occasionally notched to form Ik' symbol cutouts (Figure 7.7: A8). In contrast, Sik'u' II tripod plates are characterized by slightly more restricted orifices than their Sik'u' I equivalents and have a clear angle or division at the base-body junction (Figure 7.8: A1–B1). Further, Sik'u' II plate walls are generally out-flared or slightly outcurved. Basal ridges sometimes appear on Sik'u' II plates (Figure 7.8: B1),

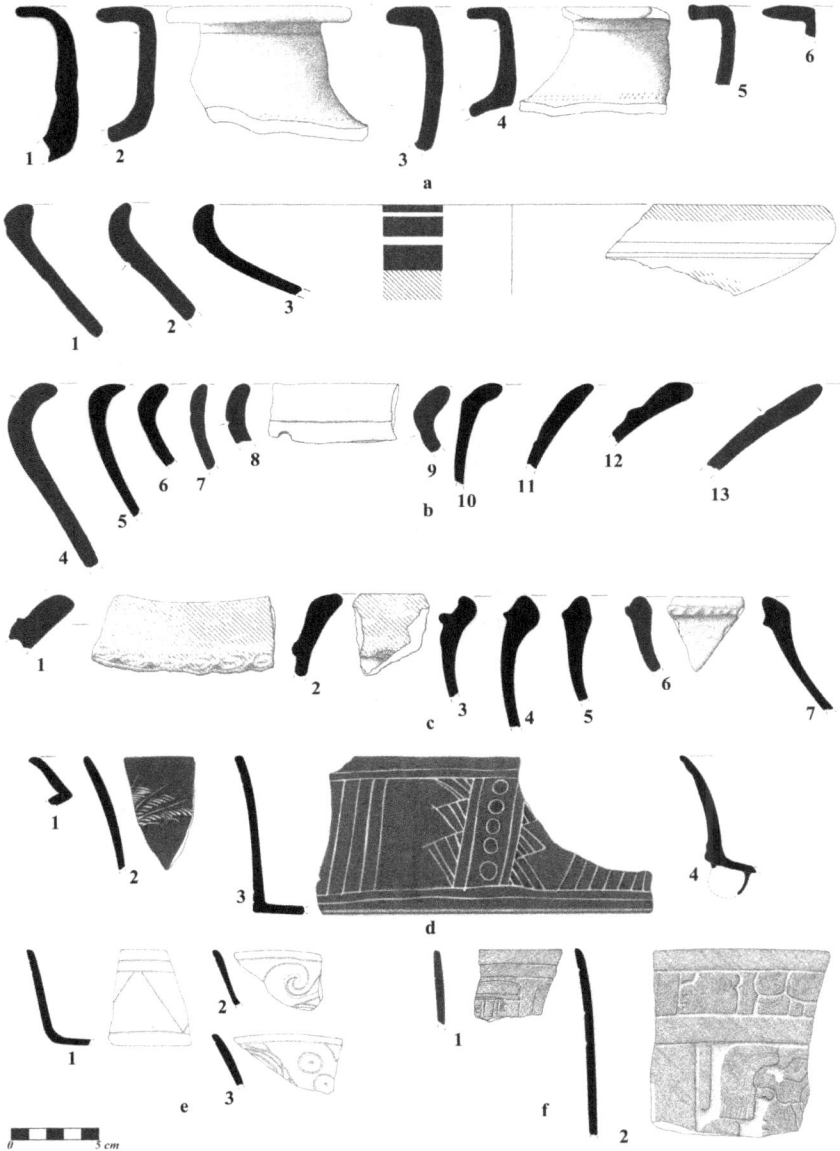

Figure 7.6. Sik'u' I-II and Yaljob'ach Complexes: (A–C) Tinaja Group; (D) Infierno Group; (E) Unnamed White Group; (F) Azote Group.

although they are not as common as those found in Sik'u' I collections. The Sik'u' I dish/bowl class is dominated by deep bowls with rounded walls and slightly incurved rims (Figure 7.7: B1–B6, B10). Decoration on these vessels is highly variable, but wide red rim bands are common and exterior designs are frequently geometric, rather than glyphic or naturalistic. When glyphs do appear on this form, texts frequently appear as simple repetitions of a single glyph (Figure 7.7: B5). Although the Sik'u' I dish/bowl class also includes less restricted forms with simple, rounded or out-flared rims (Figure 7.7: B7–B9), these forms are more characteristic of the Sik'u' II complex. The Sik'u' II dish/bowl class is dominated by shallow bowls or deep dishes with slightly out-curved or out-flared walls and direct rims (Figure 7.8: B2–B12).

Separation of Sik'u' I and Sik'u' II polychromes is also aided by some paste and slip attributes likely related to production. Sik'u' I polychromes are generally much better preserved than Sik'u' II materials, and this relates to differences in paste recipe, slip preparation, and firing methods. Sik'u' I polychrome slips are harder and tend to have a greater overall surface luster than Sik'u' II slips. Sik'u' II slips, in contrast, are thinner and more easily eroded. Some paste differences are also evident. Sik'u' II polychromes are characterized by light yellow to tan pastes with a fine, slightly gritty texture. Such pastes frequently leave a dusty residue behind during analysis. Although Sik'u' I pastes are broadly similar, they include a larger number of varieties both denser in texture and pinker in color than their Sik'u' II equivalents. This situation has some parallels in the distribution of ash and calcite tempered polychromes in the Pakoc and Hobo complexes of the Tayasal-Paxcamán zone (A. Chase 1983, 35–36), although the dichotomy appears to have greater temporal significance at Trinidad.

The Sik'u' I and Sik'u' II complexes constitute unambiguous members of the Tepeu sphere, with close similarities to contemporary complexes throughout the central lowlands. Within this general characterization, however, it is clear that various components of the complex demonstrate slightly different patterns of affiliation. In terms of polychromes, extensive comparative research by the author revealed particularly close ties with the Ik and Imix complexes of Tikal. Sik'u' I and Ik complex materials, in particular, would be difficult to impossible to separate if mixed. The two complexes share the same range of forms and modal attributes, feature closely similar surface treatments, and share many identical decorative motifs. Likewise, Sik'u' II polychromes share many attributes with the Imix complex; however, by this time, Trinidad's polychromes are most closely

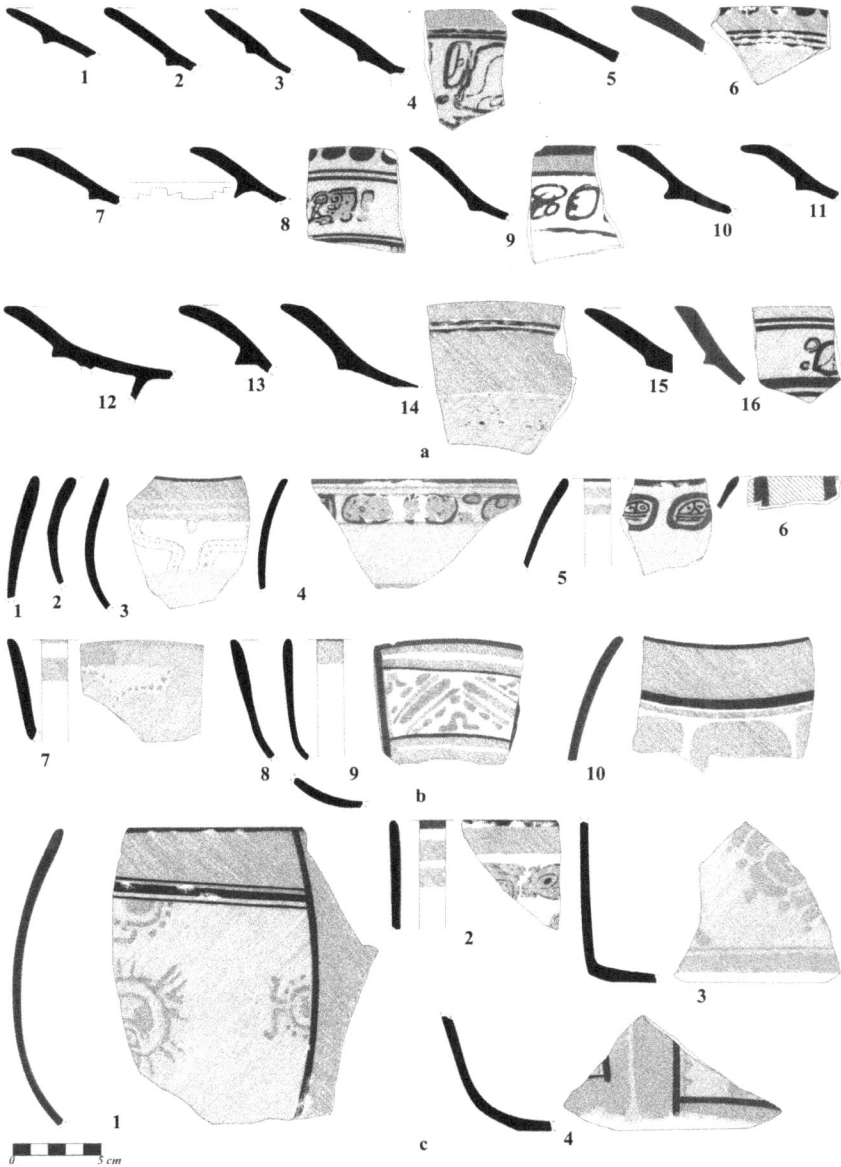

Figure 7.7. Sik'u' I Complex: (A–C) Saxche-Palmar Group (drawings by L. F. Luin).

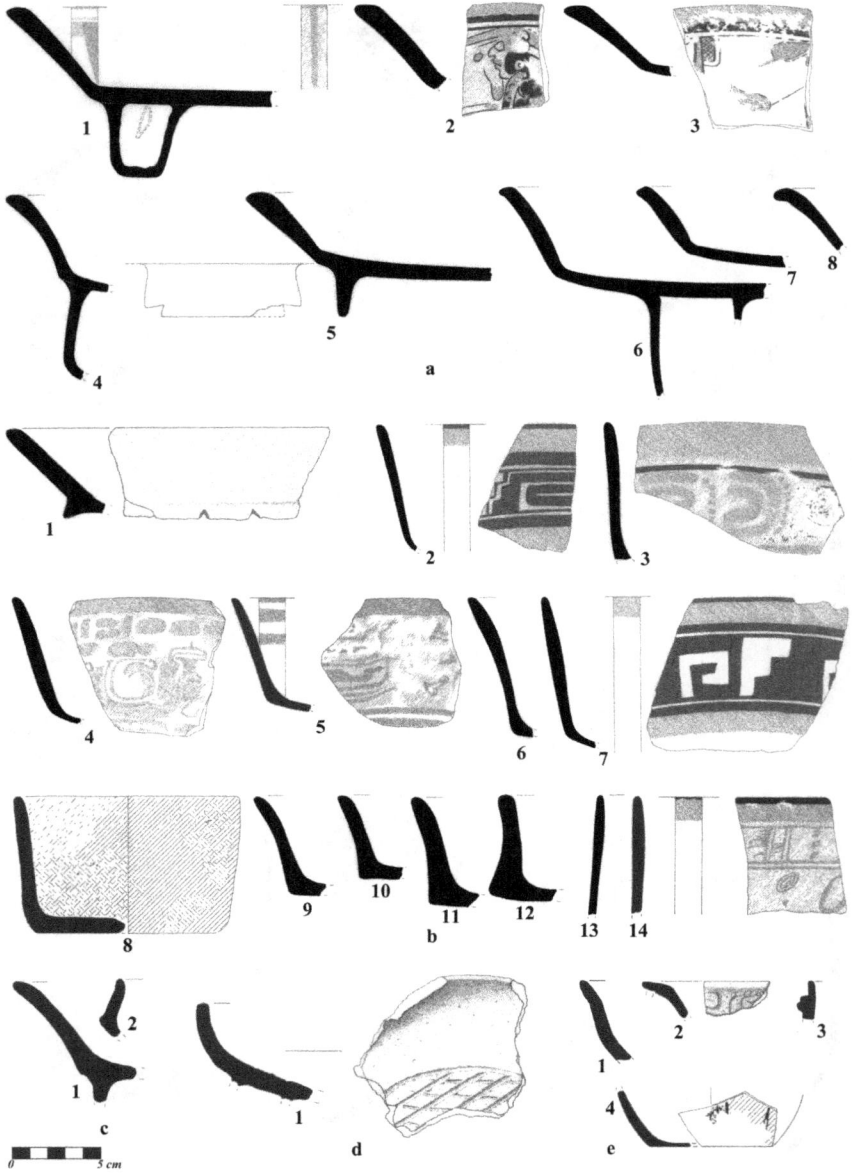

Figure 7.8. Sik'u' II Complex: (A–B) Saxche-Palmar Group. Yaljob'ach Complex:
(C) Tinaja Group; (D) Achote Group; (E1, 2, and 4) Altar Group; (E3) Tres Naciones Group.

affiliated with those of Motul de San José. Although Sik'u' II materials were insufficiently preserved to identify "Ik' corpus" vessels on stylistic or epigraphic grounds (Reents-Budet 1994; Reents-Budet et al., this volume), Sik'u' II polychromes appear highly similar to those of Motul and may have come from the same production sources. Red-slipped monochrome bowls, however, reveal a slightly different pattern of affiliation. Although Chinja Impressed incurved-rim bowls, characteristic of Late Classic complexes to the north (Forsyth 1989, 1993a; R. Smith 1955), are present at Trinidad, they are minority types only. Instead, Subín Red and Chaquiste Impressed dominate this form class at Trinidad, suggesting closer affiliation with sites to the southwest (R. Adams 1971; Foias 1996; Sabloff 1975). Although we should not make too much of subtle differences in decorative technique, the apparent blending of traditions at Trinidad likely results in part from its location within the Lake Petén Itzá basin, intermediate between these and other production zones.

It is useful to discuss in more detail the ceramics recovered from the ball court feasting deposits that pertain to the Sik'u' I-II complexes. The evidence for ball game–related feasting during the Late Classic comes from three dense middens behind the ball court's eastern lateral structure. The Motul de San José Archaeological Project was able to excavate a sample of approximately 15 cubic meters of midden, though the deposits are much more extensive. The excavated inventory of these deposits is extensive. They were rich and diverse in obsidian, with multiple exhausted polyhedral cores and core fragments, as well ovoid scrapers otherwise rare in Motul area Late Classic contexts. Forty-five percent of all figurines from Trinidad were recovered here, together with spindle whorls and carved disks (Moriarty et al. 2008). A large proportion of Trinidad fauna came from here, as well as a majority of ornamental objects of marine shell (Thornton, this volume).

The ball court midden ceramic sample consisted of more than twenty-one thousand potsherds and whole or partially reconstructable vessels weighing more than 268 kilograms. Most of the ceramics were fairly well preserved, albeit highly fragmentary. The ceramic collection is particularly notable for the high frequency of "fancy" decorated wares (Hendon 1987), and polychromes alone account for 23 percent of all sherds. These deposits also include a large number of monochrome vessels featuring incising, fluting, or other penetrative decorative techniques. These deposits are also rich in forms that appear relatively rarely in Late Classic assemblages in the Motul area, including small polychrome jars, ceramic drums, miniatures, and modeled censers. Finally, the middens also produced a large number of vessels with slips, paint, or other attributes that suggest they were not produced locally. While we await the results of Instrumental Neutron Activation Analysis (INAA) testing, stylistic assessments suggest these deposits have a decidedly international character. Type-variety ceramic analyses and four AMS radiocarbon assays date these deposits to at least two separate events occurring in the first and second halves of the Late Classic period.

The distribution of ceramic vessel forms also provides a window into the activities that produced these deposits. All rim sherds were refit during type-variety analysis. Of the 1,401 unique rims recovered, we were able to assign open or closed form for 97 percent by frequency and 99.5 percent by weight. The open-to-closed ratio by weight is 2.35:1 and the ratio by frequency is 4:1. As generalized measures, these ratios are greatly in excess of the minimum 2:1 expectations for deposits produced by feasting (see Clayton, Driver, and Kosakowsky 2005; J. G. Fox 1996; Hageman 2004; LeCount 2001; P. Rice 1987c), and are the highest for any deposit excavated by the Motul de San José Archaeological Project (Moriarty, Spensley, Lawton, et al. 2008). We also estimated the proportions of different, potentially functional, vessel classes, and found that vases, plates, and dish/bowls alone constitute nearly two-thirds (65.5 percent) of the specifically identifiable forms (1,366) in the ball court middens. Both the open-to-closed frequency ratio and the high proportion of clear serving vessels are unmatched elsewhere in the Motul de San José area, even within other deposits interpreted as resulting from feasting, and it appears likely that Trinidad's ball court feasts were unusually lavish, possibly involving high-level political interaction (Moriarty, Spensley, Lawton, et al. 2008).

Yaljob'ach Tepeu 3 Terminal Classic Complex (AD 850–950)

Beginning with the Terminal Classic, the tempo of construction and the extent of occupation at Trinidad began to taper. None of Trinidad's public plazas were modified following the Late Classic, and only two of the public architectural complexes were altered during this interval. This falloff in architectural investment did not, however, correlate to an abandonment of the site. Many of the Late Classic residential groups in the site center continued to be occupied through the Terminal Classic, and humus levels surrounding these groups contained large quantities of Terminal Classic Yaljob'ach refuse. Likewise, though excavations revealed a distinct pause in construction and maintenance within the harbor area, associated refuse deposits indicate continued use of this zone of the site.

As with the preceding Sik'u' complexes, monochrome pottery of the Terminal Classic Yaljob'ach complex is dominated by red-slipped types of the Tinaja group. Within the Tinaja group, the most significant Terminal Classic developments occur in: the preference for horizontally everted jar rims (Figure 7.6: A1–A6), although out-curved-neck forms continue to occur (Figure 7.6: I1–I10); and the preference for simple incurved-rim bowls with one horizontal incised line below the rim (Figure 7.6: B8). The Yaljob'ach complex also marks the appearance of Tinaja Red tripod plate forms (Figure 7.8: C1–C2; see also Sabloff 1975, fig. 380). Most of the minority types found in Sik'u' collections also have some distribution in the Yaljob'ach complex. Black-slipped materials were, with one exception, impossible to separate from those found in Sik'u' collections and were classified within the Infierno ceramic group. The exception was a black-slipped tripod plate with rounded sides and deep incisions on the interior base (Figure 7.8: D1). As this piece was virtually identical to Cubeta Incised "grater bowls" from Seibal (Sabloff 1975, figs. 360, 361) and Uaxactún (R. Smith 1955, figs. F1–F3), it was classified as such at Trinidad. The Azote and Tialipa groups are also present in Yaljob'ach collections, although in insufficient numbers to characterize.

Use of polychrome pottery declines notably during the Terminal Classic, although available specimens indicate strong continuities with the preceding complex. Forms for Yaljob'ach complex Saxche-Palmar group polychromes mirror those of the Sik'u' II complex, with an emphasis on tripod plates with clear angles of division at the base-body junction (Figure 7.8: A1, A6–B1) and dish/bowls with flared walls (Figure 7.6: B8–B12). Vases are very rare in Yaljob'ach collections, although this may be a result of sampling rather than distribution. Polychrome and dichrome slips were also eroded in almost all instances, making it impossible to identify Lombriz Orange Polychrome, Jato Black-on-gray, or other Saxche-Palmar group types characteristic of the Terminal Classic in the central Petén lakes district (A. Chase 1979, 1983, 1984; P. Rice 1987b). The reduction in polychromes during Yaljob'ach times is offset in part by the use of imported fine paste wares. Although unambiguous Fine Orange and Fine Gray ware sherds are comparatively rare in Trinidad collections, they serve as useful markers for the Yaljob'ach complex (Figure 7.8: E1, 2, 4).

Yaljob'ach complex unslipped materials are similar to those found in the general Sik'u' complex. During this period, however, there is some evidence to suggest that local potters were experimenting with new forms. Variants of the standard Cambio group jar were recovered in several Yaljob'ach contexts. The most easily identifiable consists of a deep globular jar with a tall, direct neck and rim, attributes much more commonly found in Postclassic Pozo Unslipped jars. A similar form was identified in the Terminal Classic Romero complex at Macanché and may suggest some continuity between the Cambio and later Pozo groups (P. Rice 1987b, 80).

Toward the end of the Terminal Classic, or perhaps within the first few decades of the subsequent Postclassic, a number of additional wares appear in Trinidad collections. Two Tohil plumbate sherds were recovered in late Yaljob'ach–early Säk-tunich contexts, and most of the possible local imitations ("c.f. Plumbate") were recovered in similar contexts. Further, a handful of Yaljob'ach contexts included small numbers of sherds characterized by waxy slips and, occasionally, by black-on-gray trickled decoration, bearing strong similarities to slate wares produced in Yucatán (R. Smith 1971).

Finally, many of the Terminal Classic deposits excavated at Trinidad also included small quantities of wares normally associated with the Postclassic, including Augustine Red, Paxcamán Red, and Pozo Unslipped (see below). Although in many instances these materials are likely intrusive, some contexts appear to date the transition between the Terminal and Postclassic complexes at Trinidad. Particularly characteristic of these contexts are rounded tripod plates or bowls with hollow, semi-hemispherical feet (Figure 7.9: E11). Deep incising occasionally appears on the interior of these vessels, creating the so-called "grater bowl" form. Although the presence of these and other late markers may more properly place these contexts within the subsequent Postclassic, it is clear that the Terminal and Postclassic complexes at Trinidad are marked by a high degree of continuity.

In type and form composition, the Yaljob'ach complex demonstrates clear affiliation with the Tepeu 3 sphere, with clear parallels in the Eznab complex of Tikal (Culbert 1993, 2003) and the late facet Hobo of the Tayasal-Paxcamán zone (A. Chase 1983). The Yaljob'ach shares many attributes, in particular, with the Eznab complex, including the decline in the use of polychromes, the appearance of red-slipped tripod plates, the presence of fine paste serving vessels in small numbers, and the appearance of what appear to be local imitations of fine paste imports. The continuity observed at Trinidad between the Yaljob'ach and subsequent Säk-tunich complexes is a characteristic with clear parallels throughout the central Petén lakes region (A. Chase 1983; P. Rice 1987b; P. Rice and D. Rice 2004).

Säk-tunich New Town Postclassic Complex (AD 950–1500)

The Postclassic period at Trinidad marks the culmination of a transformation in settlement that began during the Terminal Classic. As with the preceding Yaljob'ach, Postclassic Säk-tunich materials were recovered throughout the site; however, by Postclassic times occupation of the site center was indicated only by a thin veneer of surface deposits, a handful of late modifications to earlier structures, and two possible altars. Evidence for occupation of the harbor area is much more extensive. Though maintenance of the harbor area's principal features had stopped, allowing colluvial and lacustrine processes to choke the principal landing area with sediments and midden, the harbor nonetheless became the principal locus of Postclassic settlement. This area produced copious quantities of well-preserved Postclassic ceramics, as well as the only stratified Säk-tunich deposits at Trinidad. Cumulatively, materials from this area allowed for definition of the Postclassic Säk-tunich complex, as well as the identification of clear early and late facets.

The Säk-tunich complex is dominated by two monochrome wares. The most common is the Volador Dull-slipped ware and its constituent Pax-camán (Figure 7.9: E1–E15, F1–F2), Fulano, and Trapeche (Figure 7.9: D1–D3) groups. At Trinidad the Volador ware is characterized by a dark gray to light brown paste, the frequent occurrence of snail shell inclusions, and a dull matte to low luster finish (Cowgill 1963; P. Rice 1987b, 105, 112). The pastes and slips of the Volador group, however, are marked by a greater degree of variability than any other ware at Trinidad. Slips are, likewise, highly variable and include matte, lustrous, and, occasionally, near "waxy" surface finishes. A few rare slips also feature greenish splotches that may result from unusually high firing temperatures. The second major monochrome ware, Vitzil Orange-red ware, is also common at Trinidad, although it appears to have a much more restricted temporal distribution than Volador ware. Vitzil Orange-red ware materials are easy to separate from the Volador ware on the basis of their characteristic reddish-brown paste with coarse white calcite inclusions (see P. Rice 1987b, 165). The only ceramic group pertaining to this ware is the Augustine group (Figure 7.9: C1–C6). Säk-tunich collections also include a large number of unidentified sherds with paste attributes slightly variant from those defined for Augustine Red or the Vitzil Orange-red ware.

Unslipped Säk-tunich materials were dominated by ceramics pertaining to the Montículo Unslipped and Uapake Unslipped wares. Of the two,

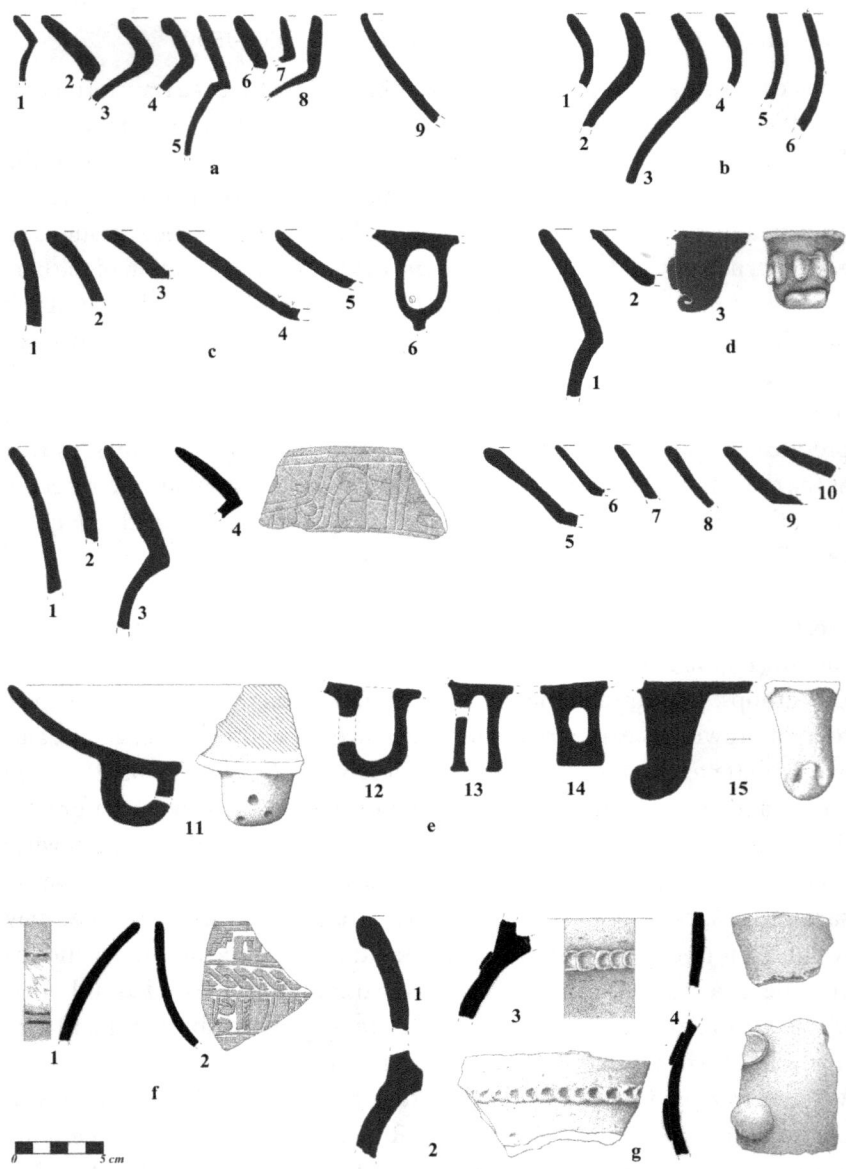

Figure 7.9. Säk-tunich Complex: (A) Pozo Group; (B) Chilo Group; (C) Augustine Group; (D) Trapeche Group; (E–F) Paxcamán Group; (G)Undesignated Censers.

Montículo Unslipped ware and its Pozo group, characterized by light gray pastes with abundant calcite inclusions (P. Rice 1987b, 171), are the most common, accounting for a little less than half of all identified Postclassic sherds. The dominant type for this group is Pozo Unslipped (Figure 7.9: A1–A9). The Uapake Unslipped ware is much less common. Uapake pastes are generally reddish-brown in color and coarse in texture. Surfaces are usually rough and appear "carelessly finished" (P. Rice 1987b, 180). Chilo Unslipped of the Chilo group is the only type from this ware identified at Trinidad (Figure 7.9: B1–B6).

Säk-tunich collections also included a significant number of unslipped censers. Censer forms are quite varied, and effigy, impressed, chambered, and bowl forms are all present (Figure 7.9: G1–G4). Patches of stucco or soft calcareous substances were recovered on many sherds and appear particularly characteristic of these forms. Censer pastes were found to be highly variable and difficult to classify based on published descriptions alone (see also Ball and Taschek 2007, 461–63). For this reason, these materials were classified within a general "Postclassic censer" category.

Säk-tunich collections also included a large number of possible import wares. Both Fine Orange and Plumbate ware sherds were recovered in very small quantities in Postclassic deposits. Many Säk-tunich contexts also included possible slate ware pieces with a nearly "waxy" surface finish and, occasionally, black-on-gray trickle decoration (see also P. Rice 1987b, 167–68). Several sherds were also provisionally identified as part of the Daylight ceramic group (Gifford 1976), although further comparative study will be necessary to confirm this designation. Finally, Säk-tunich deposits also produced several sherds with a cream paste and red slip that were provisionally classified to the Topoxte ceramic group (P. Rice 1987b, 157–59).

Other investigators in central Petén have traditionally divided the New Town Postclassic sphere into two or more separate complexes based on detailed paste analyses and the distribution of key types (A. Chase 1979, 1983, 1984; Cowgill 1963; P. Rice 1979b, 1987b). Although the Säk-tunich complex clearly shares numerous attributes with the local expressions of the New Town sphere, including the Chilcob and Cocahmut complexes of the Tayasal-Paxcamán zone (A. Chase 1983) and the Aura and Dos Lagos complexes of the Central Petén Lakes (P. Rice 1987b), limitations in Postclassic stratigraphy, as well as time constraints in the analysis, precluded formal identification of separate complexes at Trinidad. Nonetheless, early and late facets, approximately corresponding to those complexes in form and type distribution, are evident in Säk-tunich collections.

Aj B'oj Historical Complex (AD 1500–1950)

The historical period is difficult to isolate at Trinidad. Continuities in the use of Säk-tunich complex pottery, including Paxcamán Red and Chilo Unslipped, into the historical era make it particularly difficult to separate the contact period from the late facet Säk-tunich. Further, unlike other sites near Lake Petén Itzá (e.g., A. Chase 1983, 42), investigations at Trinidad produced no true Majolica pottery. Although many of the latest deposits in the harbor area include artifacts indicative of a historical date (e.g., square-cut nails), the potential for mixing with earlier materials made it impossible to delineate discrete Aj B'oj assemblages.

One possible marker for the early Aj B'oj at Trinidad is an unidentified ware characterized by an unusually hard slip. Forms for this ware include short-necked jars, simple plates, and deep bowls. In many respects, this ware has close parallels in the Uapake Unslipped ware. Surfaces were only lightly smoothed and few of the rims could be described as carefully finished. In other respects, however, the unnamed hard slip ware is easily separated from the Uapake ware. Dense red, green, and white slips were identified on many of the 260 examples recovered at Trinidad, and, further, the characteristic hardness of this ware is suggestive of much higher firing temperature than likely utilized for the Chilo Unslipped. These materials may constitute a local earthenware produced in the contact period or, possibly, a precursor to the recent historical wares produced in San José and described by Reina and Hill (1978, 141–45).

The later historical component to the Aj B'oj complex is much more easily separated. A surface refuse deposit in the site center produced three sherds of mid-nineteenth-century English Staffordshire ware and many humus deposits, especially those in the harbor area, produced dark green bottle glass and small lead or iron objects. Many of these objects likely derived from activities associated with a historical household located just to the northwest of the mapped portion of the site, or to camping and other activities associated with Trinidad's modern usage as a port and trailhead by *chicleros*.

Discussion

In summary, investigations at Trinidad de Nosotros produced evidence for a continuous occupation spanning the interval from the early Middle Preclassic period up to the historical era. The principal peaks in this sequence occurred during the Late Preclassic Chukan and Late Classic Sik'u'

I-II phases; both intervals are marked by prolific construction in public and residential architectural complexes and the dense accumulation of refuse across the site. Likewise, both phases are accompanied by upticks in activity within the harbor area. Although these intervals represent the high points of Trinidad's history, other phases are still noteworthy. The late Middle Preclassic Ix Cha', for example, witnessed the establishment of the architectural template for Trinidad's central-most ceremonial precinct. Further, though the Early Classic 'Ayim-tun, Terminal Classic Yaljob'ach, and Postclassic Säk-tunich appear diminished in comparison to the Chukan and Sik'u', they constitute robust occupations for the Motul area during these intervals.

In many respects, the length of Trinidad's occupation may be accounted for by its position with respect to Lake Petén Itzá. Trinidad's proximity to the lake provided preferential access to local and nonlocal resources, with the broader resources of the lake basin serving as a stabilizing feature for Trinidad during periods of political turmoil or shortfall (see also A. Chase 1979, 101). Beginning with its earliest occupation, Trinidad seems to have capitalized on this situation, serving as a port and gateway to the Motul de San José area. Through its involvement in long-distance trade, Trinidad emerged as a key center in the Motul de San José area and likely interacted with major regional centers like Tikal, located just 35 kilometers to the northeast. These interactions may account for long-term patterns in Trinidad ceramic affiliations.

From the late Middle Preclassic Ix Cha' through the Terminal Classic Yaljob'ach, Trinidad's ceramics bear particularly strong affiliations with Tikal, suggesting that Trinidad participated in a larger Tikal interaction sphere. This affiliation is particularly obvious during the early Late Classic when Sik'u' I complex materials are virtually identical to contemporaneous Ik complex specimens. Nevertheless, the Sik'u' II pottery from Trinidad stylistically most resembles Motul de San José rather than Tikal. At the beginning and end of the Trinidad sequence, however, different patterns of affiliation are evident. Although more comparative research is in order, close similarities between the early Middle Preclassic Aj Wo' and Xe sphere materials suggests ties to the southwest rather than the eastern Petén and Belize. Likewise, the Postclassic Säk-tunich and historical Aj B'oj complexes demonstrate participation in the transformed Petén Postclassic interaction spheres (P. Rice and D. Rice 2004), with more tangible links within the Lake Petén Itzá basin.

During the Late Classic period, when Motul de San José reached its apogee as a political center, Trinidad probably functioned as both a material and symbolic gateway to the Motul polity. Its center features substantial public architectural complexes, including plaza space well beyond the needs of its few hundred inhabitants and the only ball court in the Motul area. It is also surprising to find such extensive evidence for ball game feasting and ritual at a center of Trinidad's modest size. During the Late Classic period, Trinidad is unlikely to have been a political player of any magnitude. The nearby centers of Tayasal, Nixtun-Ch'ich', and Motul de San José all dwarf Trinidad physically and almost certainly one of them, possibly Motul, dominated it politically. Under these circumstances, however, Trinidad may have emerged as a neutral ground or boundary settlement where inter-dynastic affairs could be conducted with feasting, the ball game and other rituals providing the necessary social lubricant. The costs of hosting such events in terms of time, labor, and resources would have been enormous. Yet, such a role would have been well in keeping with Trinidad's function as a port, with these costs more than offset by the opportunity for Trinidad's residents to conduct the material transactions that so frequently occur in conjunction with public spectacle. If so, then the ball court deposits at Trinidad constitute a tangible record of the fundamental linkages between ritual and material economies in the Maya lowlands.

Acknowledgments

Investigations at Trinidad de Nosotros were funded by the National Science Foundation (Dissertation Improvement Grant BCS # 0528789), the Foundation for the Advancement of Mesoamerican Studies, Inc. (FAMSI), Tulane University, the Middle American Research Institute, Amherst College, Williams College, Brigham Young University, and various anonymous donors. Radiocarbon analyses were provided by NSF-Arizona AMS Laboratory with the support of Greg Hodgins. All investigations were conducted in collaboration with the Instituto de Antropología e Historia (IDAEH) de Guatemala and the Municipio of San José, El Petén, with the support of Don Julian Tesucún y Tesucún, Lic. Salvador Lopez, Lic. Paulino Morales, Licda. Yvonne Putzeys, and Gustavo Amarra. Special thanks to all Trinidad field and laboratory staff, especially Antonia Foias, Jeanette Castellanos, and Melanie Kingsley, for assistance with ceramic analysis, and Crorey Lawton and Ellen Spensley Moriarty for support during the 2005 field season. Additional thanks to Ellen Spensley, Will Andrews, Kitty Emery, and Antonia Foias for productive comments on the original version of this manuscript.

8

Wealth, Status, and Stucco

Micromorphology Studies at Trinidad, a Secondary Center in the Motul de San José Periphery

ELLEN SPENSLEY MORIARTY

Archaeological Applications of Micromorphology

Micromorphology is a technique used to study sediments, soils, and various types of anthropogenically derived deposits at a detailed level. This technique involves collecting intact blocks of sediment or soil, hardening these blocks with resin, and producing slides to be examined using a petrographic microscope. Since the 1980s, this method has been applied to archaeological sediments to examine a wide variety of issues, including distinguishing the signatures of various kinds of activities, identifying the composition of construction materials, reconstructing past environmental conditions, and characterizing postdepositional disturbances (e.g., Courty, Macphail, and Goldberg 1989; Gé et al. 1993; Goldberg 1983; Goldberg and Macphail 2006; Grave and Kealhofer 1999; Hansen 2000; Matthews 1995; Matthews et al. 1997). The benefits of micromorphology lie in the nature of sample collection and preparation: analyzing intact depositional sequences allows for examination of the component sediments, artifacts, and biological remains in relation to their spatial and temporal contexts (Matthews 1995, 46). These structurally intact samples are especially useful when considered in tandem with standard artifact analyses or ecological data, because they can provide contextual information that is often not visible in the field and/or provide detailed information about both formation and postdepositional processes.

One the most common uses of geoarchaeological micromorphology has been the study of soils and sediments to reconstruct paleoenvironmental and climatic conditions (e.g., Boschian 1997; Macphail 1999; Macphail and Goldberg 2003), often in attempts to determine how environmental changes may have affected humans or the preservation of archaeological sites. Other inquiries investigate past agricultural systems (e.g., Carter and Davidson 1998; Macphail n.d.; Wilson, Simpson, and Currie 2002; Pohl and Bloom 1996), exploring the intensity of labor required to create and maintain various types of systems and their long-term effects on the environment.

More recently, micromorphology has been used to complement artifact-based analyses of activity areas within and surrounding structures. Determining activity area use based on artifacts can be difficult, as items may or may not have been used in the locations where they are recovered and debris may have been cleared away after activities were carried out. Pioneering petrographic work by Wendy Matthews and others (1995; Matthews et al. 1997; Gé et al. 1993) on microdebris and wear patterns at a selection of Near Eastern sites used characteristics such as frequency of floor resurfacing, presence of fiber mats, deposits characteristic of sweeping or trampling, and microartifacts to define distinct areas used for reception, ritual, cooking, and storage within single structures (Matthews 1995; Matthews et al. 1997).

Studies of activity areas have also employed ethnoarchaeological approaches to facilitate the interpretation of thin sections. By sampling deposits such as floors, sleeping areas, hearths, and trash dumps as they are created or modified by living people, observed characteristics may be linked directly to specific activities. Informed conclusions may then be drawn from archaeological samples. This type of work has been carried out in the Near East (Goldberg and Whitbread 1993), Scotland (Davidson, Carter, and Quine 1992), and in the United Kingdom (Macphail and Cruise 2001). Some of these studies have gone beyond an analysis of purely functional activities to examine micromorphological characteristics resulting from ritual behaviors (for India, see Boivin 2000).

Thus, micromorphology may be used to investigate questions ranging in scale from interregional to intra-structure, and to analyze materials from soils to plasters, making it an extremely useful and powerful technique. Despite a theoretically widespread applicability, however, micromorphology has most commonly been used to study soils from archaeological sites in the Old World. In the New World, micromorphology has been applied at several Paleo-Indian or prehistoric sites in North America (e.g., Goldberg and Sherwood 1994; Doucette 2003; Rinck 2007) but has been employed in only a few instances in Mesoamerica (Wilson 2002; Pohl and Bloom 1996), and rarely to examine anthropogenic materials produced by complex societies (but cf. Hansen 2000).

In this chapter, I present the results of a micromorphological study of plaster floors from the site of La Trinidad de Nosotros (Trinidad), the port of Motul de San José on the shore of Lake Petén Itzá (Figure 1.4). Plaster is one of the most ubiquitous construction materials encountered at Maya sites, and yet it is rarely studied in detail. After briefly reviewing previous studies of plaster in the Maya area, I examine several samples from a variety of structures (both residential and public) and plazas, to outline temporal, functional, and status-related trends in plastering at Trinidad. As plaster requires resources and human labor, the details of its production and modification form an index of the degree of economic control by the elite vis-à-vis the nonelite. The use of thick or multiple layers of stucco would suggest significant investment by individuals in conspicuous consumption, and if these individuals were elites, it would imply more centralization of economic resources in the hands of the upper group of Maya society. Changes in the technology of stucco production may also show trends toward more conservation of resources and energy, or incrementing desire for conspicuous consumption.

Plasters in the Lowland Maya Area

The use of lime plaster by the Maya has an extremely long history. Its earliest appearance in Mesoamerica coincides with the first settled villages, where it was used to coat low platforms (e.g., McAnany 2004; Hammond and Gerhardt 1991). Plaster production increased as structures became larger and more elaborate and the landscape more densely settled. During later periods, plaster was used not only to construct floors, but also to coat inner and outer walls and benches and to model decorative features.

Composition and Preparation

The plaster used in the lowland Maya area was a carbonate-based product. Most often the base material used was calcium carbonate ($CaCO_3$) in the form of limestone. In some coastal areas, however, the carbonate base was derived from marine shells and magnesium ions substituted for calcium, resulting in different chemical signatures (Littmann 1957; MacKinnon and May 1990). To form plaster, the limestone or shell is broken into pieces and heated to a temperature of at least 800 degrees Celsius to drive off carbon dioxide (CO_2), leaving quicklime (CaO) powder (Morris 1931; Russell and Dahlin 2007; for a discussion of heating methods, see Wernecke 2008). The next step, slaking, occurs when water is added to the quicklime, changing the chemical composition to Ca $(OH)_2$ (Roys 1934, 97). The addition of enough water to "slake" the lime (change the chemical composition), however, does not actually result in a workable paste; additional water must be added to achieve a workable "putty" (Hansen 2000, 66). When the putty is exposed to air, excess water escapes and carbon dioxide is reabsorbed, converting the Ca $(OH)_2$ to $CaCO_3$. The final product is chemically the same as the limestone it originated from; essentially, the process of producing plaster is analogous to re-creating rock in a specific shape, and the end product is often harder than the original (Roys 1934, 97).

Various products may be added to plaster during production. Aggregate material is added either to the quicklime powder or the wetted lime to prevent cracking and minimize shrinkage while the plaster dries (Hansen 2000, 66). Aggregate may include various types of rock fragments, soil, shell, pottery, recycled plaster, and a decomposed limestone known as *sascab*. Finally, organic extracts have been noted as important additives (Morris 1931, 240). These extracts are derived from tree barks, including *Chucum* (*Pithecolobium albicans*), *Chacté* (*Caesalpinia platyloba*), *Jabín* (*Pescidia communis*), and *Chacah* (*Bursera simaruba*). Laboratory tests by Edwin Littmann (1960b) demonstrated that adding extracts made from these tree barks did, to varying degrees, alter the finished product. Plaster samples to which these products were added not only showed color change; they had smoother surfaces and exhibited lustrous, glossy finishes. The chemistry behind these effects is not understood at present.

Previous Studies of Lowland Maya Plasters

A substantial body of work exists on the topic of Maya plasters, though most of these studies have not been undertaken at a microscopic level (but cf. Hansen, Hansen, and Derrick 1995; Hansen, Rodriguez-Navarro, and Hansen 1997; Hansen 2000). Ancient Maya plasters have been conceptualized within three general frameworks: composition/construction patterns, energetics, and activity areas. Most studies have focused on the first of these three; a recurring theme within the study of Maya buildings is a need for specific definitions of their most basic components (mortar, stucco, plaster, etc.). Early studies of plaster (Roys 1934) focused on defining such categories.

This work was continued by Edwin Littmann, who throughout the late 1950s and 1960s surveyed a suite of Maya sites studying the composition and uses of lime-based products (Littmann 1957, 1958, 1959a, 1959b, 1960a, 1960b, 1962, 1967). By comparing the use of mortars and plasters at several sites including Tikal, Palenque, Uaxactún, and Uxmal, Littmann identified a systematic construction process generally followed throughout the Maya area. In terms of the study of plaster floors, two components defined by Littmann (1957, 136) are of direct relevance and are defined here:

> *Plaster*: burned lime, may be mixed with sascab and other types of aggregate material. Often denser and more finely grained than mortar, this material is used as a flat external coat over a monolithic mass. The plaster may be protective or provide a base for paintings.
> *Wash Coat*: a thin, inclusion-free coat of plaster applied as a slurry, the final surfacing layer.

Some microscopic work with Maya plaster has been undertaken by Eric Hansen (Hansen, Hansen, and Derrick 1995; Hansen, Rodriguez-Navarro, and Hansen 1997; Hansen 2000), mainly from the site of Nakbe in northern Guatemala. Concerned with the composition of burnt-lime products, these analyses examined technical details of floor plasters and stucco used for modeling, and how these attributes changed through time. Mercedes Villegas and her colleagues (1995) also investigated changes in plaster technology during the Late Classic period at Palenque; both Hansen and Villegas were able to correlate changes in plaster production with political shifts or developments at their respective sites.

A different perspective on plaster is gained through the energetics studies of Elliot Abrams. Abrams seeks to quantify the labor invested in various structures at the site of Copan, Honduras, by calculating both the cost of materials and the amount of time needed for building and maintenance (Abrams 1994). To this end, he considers the amount of plaster used in a building, rather than the specific qualities of plaster and its use. Although such estimates may be useful for estimating varying degrees of wealth, these types of analysis may be too simplistic. For example, Abrams notes that plaster containing a higher percentage of pure lime is of higher quality and more expensive to produce (1996, 198), but does not figure such variations into his energetic analysis. Additional factors such as the type of aggregate material included in a plaster may be indicative of the wealth of the commissioners. These subtle qualities, however, are often not apparent in the field, and must be investigated at a microscopic level.

Chemical analyses have also been employed to investigate Maya plasters. Since trash was often not allowed to accumulate in residential and public structures, determining what activities took place in a building often depends on analyzing artifacts found outside of it. As in other parts of the world and of Mesoamerica, chemical analysis has been used in the Maya area to test for both organic and inorganic residues on plaster floors, in many cases revealing potential activities that took place on top of them (Emery 2003a; Fernández et al. 2002; Hutson and Terry 2006; Terry et al. 2004).

Methods

Sample Selection

The plaster samples discussed here were collected during the 2003 field season at Trinidad. To investigate potential variations in plastering techniques in different parts of the site, samples were collected from a variety of structures, including residences, ritual edifices such as the ball court, port-related features adjacent to the lakeshore, and open plazas. Clearing excavations of two structures (C1 and G1) in the site center provided ample opportunity for plaster collection from interior and exterior floors and wall and bench coatings. The remaining samples were collected from floors exposed in test units excavated in plazas and platforms throughout the site (Figure 8.1). A total of twenty-four plaster samples, ranging from the Middle Preclassic to the Postclassic, are presented here (Table 8.1).

Sample Preparation

Samples were removed as intact blocks from floors or other plaster surfaces after excavation, drawing, and photographing were completed. In most cases, a piece could be carefully cut away from the floor or peeled off a wall using a trowel or machete. Samples were immediately wrapped in toilet paper and sealed with packing tape to maintain structural integrity. In the micromorphology lab at Boston University, each sample was unwrapped as much as possible and dried in a convection oven at 60 degrees Celsius for at least one week. Once dry, the samples were impregnated with a mixture of polyester resin, styrene, and methyl ethyl ketone peroxide and placed in a fume hood to cure. In most instances, the resin hardened to a gel-like consistency within one and a half weeks. At this point, the samples were returned to the convection oven for twenty-four hours. Once completely

Figure 8.1. Map of Trinidad and locations of plaster samples (drawn by M. Moriarty).

Table 8.1. Plaster sample numbers, contexts, and dates; dates are based on type-variety analysis of related ceramics

Sample ID	Unit	Ceramic phase	Context description
TRI 041	1F1	Middle Preclassic (B'itzil)	Floor 2 (ca. 90 cmbd)
TRI 031	5A9	Late Preclassic (Chukan)	Facing of Substructure
TRI 001	1A1	Late Preclassic (Chukan)	Floor 2 (ca. 95 cmbd)
TRI 005	1B1	Late Preclassic (Chukan)	Floor 1 (ca. 63 cmbd)
TRI 003	1C1	Late Preclassic (Chukan)	Floor 3 (ca. 136 cmbd)
TRI 004	1I1	Late Preclassic (Chukan)	Floor 2 (ca. 76 cmbd)
TRI 010	1P2	Late Preclassic (Chukan)	"Floor 1" (ca. 63 cmbd)
TRI 039	4A13	Late Preclassic (Chukan)	Floor 2-sub (200 cmbd)
TRI 038	4A13	Late Preclassic (Chukan)	Floor 3-sub (203 cmbd)
TRI 037	4A13	Late Preclassic (Chukan)	Floor 4-sub (264 cmbd)
TRI 028	5A7	Late Preclassic (Chukan)	Floor 3 (ca. 98 cmbd)
TRI 027	5A7	Late Preclassic (Chukan)	Floor 4 (ca. 114 cmbd)
TRI 030	5A8–5A9	Late Preclassic (Chukan)	Bench #2
TRI 022	2A5	Early Classic or Postclassic	Floor 1 (ca. 29 cmbd)
TRI 040	4A13	Late Classic (Sik'u I)	Floor 1 (106 cmbd)
TRI 033	4A1	Late Classic (Sik'u)	Exterior Terrace 1 (73 cmbd)
TRI 013	2A4	Late Classic (Sik'u')	Floor 2 (60 cmbd)
TRI 032	4A	Late Classic (Sik'u')	North Wall (Interior)
TRI 034	4A2	Late Classic (Sik'u')	Exterior Terrace 2
TRI 035	4A3	Late Classic (Sik'u')	Exterior Terrace 3
TRI 011	2A4	Postclassic (Sak-tunich)	Floor 1 (ca. 42 cmbd)
TRI 012	2A4	Postclassic (Sak-tunich)	Floor 1 Fill (ca. 42–60 cmbd)
TRI 021	2E3	Postclassic (Sak-tunich)	Floor 1 (ca. 35 cmbd)

hardened, each sample was sliced, trimmed, and sent to Quality Thin Sections in Tucson, Arizona, for thin sectioning.

Analysis

Petrographic analysis is accomplished using a polarizing microscope. A polarizing microscope utilizes either one or two filters to restrict the plane(s) within which light rays can vibrate. One filter (the polarizer) is located below the microscope stage, and is always in place, transmitting light vibrating in a n–s direction. A second, removable filter (the analyzer) is located in the tube above the stage, and transmits light vibrating in an e–w direction. Together, the filters are called polars. When only the polarizer is used, light is said to be plane polarized, and when both the polarizer and analyzer are used, light is said to be cross polarized (Klein and Hurlbut Jr. 1993, 293–94). Different minerals transmit light differently under each of these conditions, providing the basis for compositional determinations. Plaster attributes analyzed under both plane- and cross-polarized light included composition of the matrix material and added aggregate; the morphological relationships of these two components; degree of aggregate sorting, porosity, layering, wear patterns; and surface treatments—all qualities invisible to the naked eye. Each thin section was described following standardized terminology, and percentages were estimated using comparative charts (Bullock et al. 1985).

Results

All of the plasters at Trinidad were composed of a $CaCO_3$, limestone-derived matrix. Carbonaceous material is readily abundant in the area, and limestone for plaster production would have been easily acquired. Dolomite was used in some floors as an aggregate material, and is also present in the area. *Sascab*, a decomposed, powdery limestone, was also noted as both a matrix and aggregate material; modern inhabitants of the Motul area note that sascab is still used in house and floor construction (Moriarty n.d.). Previous studies indicate that the use of immediately available products for building construction was a common trend in Mesoamerica; for example, at coastal sites, shells and beach sands were used as construction materials (Abrams 1996; Bain 1985; Mackinnon and May 1990). Conversely, in highland terrains, pumice and other volcanic products were incorporated in floor construction (Houston et al. 2003; Hyman 1970).

Despite the fact that all plasters at Trinidad have broadly similar matrix compositions, significant variation exists in the composition and amount of aggregate materials, internal microstructure (presence or absence of fine layering), and surfacing layers. This variation likely relates to a number of factors, three of which are examined below: date, function, and status.

Temporal Trends

Two plastering trends with a clear temporal aspect are evident in the floor samples of the Trinidad data set, and relate to composition and physical structure. Although the samples range from Middle Preclassic to Late Postclassic, the single Middle Preclassic floor sample is omitted from discussion here.

One temporal trend in the composition of the stucco at Trinidad is the amount of sascab included: sascab tends to make up a higher percentage of the total aggregate material in Late Preclassic floors. Though the percent of sascab varies between approximately 10 and 100, as a group the Late

Preclassic floors have more sascab aggregate when compared to floors from other time periods (Table 8.2, Figure 8.2). A series of vertically superposed Late Preclassic floors from a structure in the site center further highlights the diminishing use of sascab throughout this period: the oldest floor contains 100 percent sascab aggregate, the middle floor contains 20 percent sascab aggregate, and the most recent has only 1 percent. The second-most common aggregate materials in the Late Preclassic are limestone fragments and single grains of calcite, and together with sascab these comprise almost all of the Late Preclassic aggregate. Only minor quantities of dolomite, quartz, and soil were noted.

As a group, floor plasters of the Late Classic period not only contain less sascab, but also have a more diverse array of products included as aggregate, such as greater quantities of limestone and single calcite grains, and soil, dolomite, quartz, and highly heated (or calcined) grains of calcite (Table 8.3, Figure 8.3). Although at a smaller scale, these results support a trend noted by Eric Hansen (2000, 229), whereby Late Classic plasters from sites such as Tikal, Yaxchilan, and Nakbé were more diverse at the intersite level than those of the preceding Preclassic. Hansen acknowledges that some of this variation may be due to geographic location, but also suggests that as rulership became more individualized during the Late Classic, greater investment was placed in individual technological styles, perhaps with attached plaster specialists creating recipes for construction and decorative materials unique to certain sites (ibid.). At Trinidad, which peaked in

Figure 8.2. Preclassic floor with sascab aggregate material highlighted. Slide scan, 7.5-by-5.0 centimeters.

Table 8.2. Composition of Late Preclassic floors

% material	TRI001 L.1[a]	TRI001 L.2	TRI003	TRI004	TRI005 L.1	TRI005 L.2	TRI028 L.1	TRI028 L.2	TRI027	TRI037	TRI038	TRI039
Sascab	15	50	100	100	32	100	20	20	5	100	20	1
Calcite	0	0	0	0	32	0	10	8	50	0	56	5
Limestone	0	0	0	0	0	0	20	70	40	0	20	45
Calcined grains	0	0	0	0	0	0	0	0	5	0	0	0
Soil	85	0	0	0	0	0	50	0	0	0	4	4
Shell	0	0	0	0	0	0	0	1	0	0	0	0
Dolomite	0	50	0	0	32	0	0	0	0	0	0	0
Quartz	0	0	0	0	0	0	0	0	0	0	0	0
Micrite	0	0	0	0	0	0	0	0	0	0	0	45
Charcoal	0	0	0	0	0	0	0	1	0	0	0	0

[a] Layers within the same floor are indicated L.1, L.2, etc.

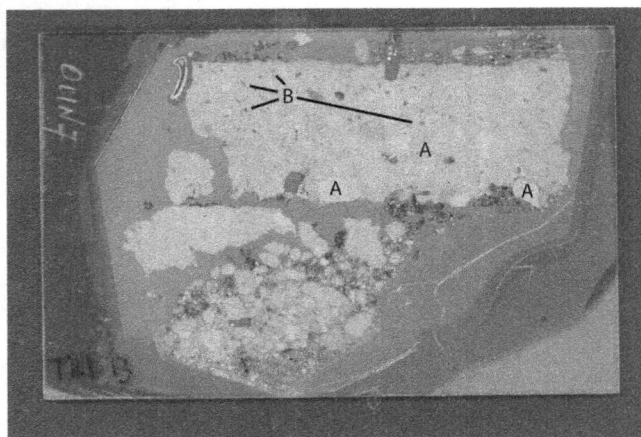

Figure 8.3. Late Classic floor: a. Calcined (highly heated) calcite grains; b. soil aggregates. Slide scan, 7.5-by-5.0 centimeters.

size during the Late Classic (see Moriarty, this volume), the more diverse set of floor plasters could be related to a similar trend, with certain households or elite groups developing personal plastering preferences. Furthermore, the use of less sascab and higher temperatures hints that Late Classic stucco production required more labor investment than previously.

Finally, as a group, Postclassic floor plasters are also distinctive in terms of composition. Sascab is absent as an aggregate, and calcined grains are prevalent (ranging between 45 and 65 percent of the total aggregate in each sample). Additional aggregate materials include limestone, dolomite, soil, quartz, and charcoal (Table 8.4, Figure 8.4). A distinctive structural trend is also noted in Postclassic plaster floors at Trinidad. These floors are notable for the presence of one or more extremely thin, dense surfacing layers, visible only at the microscale (Figure 8.5) and much finer than the internal layering observed in other, earlier, floors at Trinidad. This trend may be linked, however, to function, as all of the Postclassic samples were extracted from the harbor area. This possibility is discussed in greater detail below.

Interestingly, although plasters show clear compositional change through time at Trinidad, decorative techniques appear to have remained fairly constant. Two finishing techniques were noted among the plaster samples at Trinidad: a thin coat of very dark red paint and/or a very flat "razor" edge (Figure 8.6). Traces of red paint were identified under both plane- and cross-polarized light from samples dating from the Late Preclassic to the Postclassic, and from a variety of contexts throughout the site.

Table 8.3. Composition of Late Classic floors

% material	TRI013 L.1[a]	TRI013 L.2	TRI033	TRI034	TRI035 L.1	TRI035 L.2	TRI035 L.3
Sascab	20	0	5	20	0	100	100
Calcite	70	40	25	5	0	0	0
Limestone	0	0	60	40	100	0	0
Calcined grains	10	58	0	20	0	0	0
Soil	0	0	5	0	0	0	0
Shell	0	0	0	0	0	0	0
Dolomite	0	2	0	0	0	0	0
Quartz	0	0	2	0	0	0	0
Micrite	0	0	0	10	0	0	0
Charcoal	0	0	0	0	0	0	0

[a] Layers within the same floor are indicated L.1, L.2, etc.

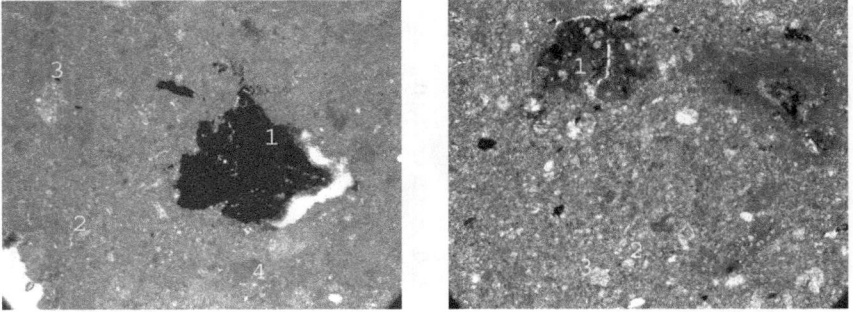

Figure 8.4. Postclassic floors: a. Sample TRI011. (1) charcoal; (2) calcined grains of calcite; (3) rock fragment. Microphoto taken under plane-polarized light, field of view ten millimeters. b. Sample TRI012: (1) soil aggregate; (2) cluster of calcined calcite grains; (3) calcite grains. Photo taken under plane-polarized light, field of view five millimeters.

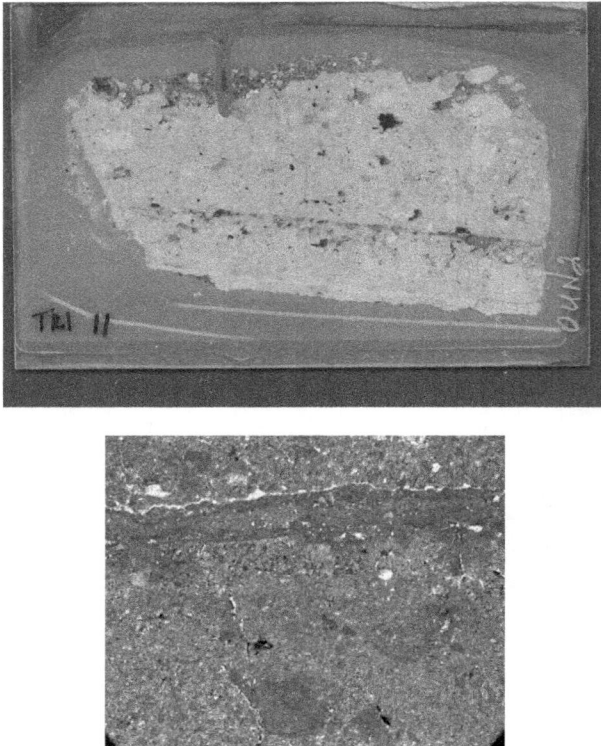

Figure 8.5. Layering in Postclassic floors: a. Slide scan of TRI011. Slide measures 7.5-by-5.0 centimeters. b. Microphoto of layering in TRI012. Photo taken under plane-polarized light, field of view five millimeters.

Table 8.4. Composition of Postclassic floors

% material	TRI011	TRI012	TRI021	TRI022
Sascab	0	0	0	0
Calcite	0	0	50	10
Limestone	25	25	5	8
Calcined grains	65	65	45	80
Soil	1	1	0	2
Shell	0	0	0	0
Dolomite	5	5	0	0
Quartz	1	1	0	0
Micrite	0	0	0	0
Charcoal	3	3	0	0

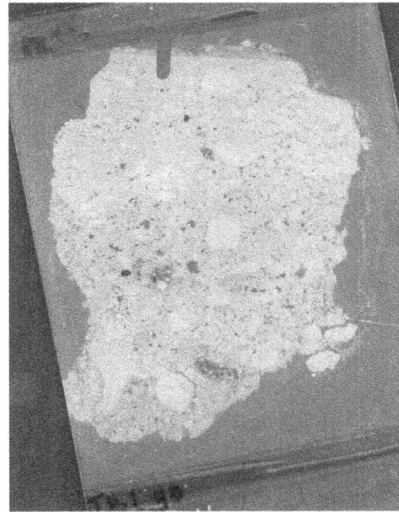

Figure 8.6. Interior floor from structure C-1 (TRI 040) showing a razor edge upper surface (darker material at very top of sample is soil). Slide scan, 7.5-by-5.0 centimeters.

Samples showing a "razor" edge range from the Middle Preclassic to the Late Classic, and were again recovered throughout the site.

Functional Trends

Though locally available materials were used to construct floor, bench, and wall plasters at Trinidad, different mixtures were used for various types of plasters. In general, floors throughout the site incorporate rock fragments as the primary aggregate component. The aggregate used in wall and bench plasters, however, was composed primarily of single calcite grains or small soil aggregates, with the uniformly small size of these particles indicating that a more exhaustive aggregate sorting process took place. As more energy would be expended in such a process, either by hand sorting, sieving, or flotation (Hansen 2000), and only a small proportion of aggregate was added to "stretch" the plaster, these plasters may be seen as more costly both in time and materials.

The specific properties of these plasters may be related to functional requirements of application. For example, the addition of siliceous materials has been noted as a significant developmental step in the stucco used for modeling at Palenque (Villegas et al. 1995), and in preparation of the plaster used to support murals at Teotihuacan (Magaloni et al. 1992). Hansen, Rodriguez-Navarro, and Hansen (1997) note the presence of finely grained, well-sorted aggregate within sculptural stucco elements at Nakbe in contrast to more coarsely grained floor plasters, concluding that the finer, well-sorted aggregate would have resulted in a more plastic material. The wall and bench plasters at Trinidad also incorporate both soil and clay particles in higher percentages than do the floor plasters (Figure 8.7).

Finally, plaster recipes and floor construction techniques at Trinidad varied depending on location within the site. Specifically, the plasters used within the harbor area are distinct from those located within the site core. A significant proportion of the aggregate used in these floors consisted of calcined grains of limestone, and charcoal was also present. Collectively, the port floors appear to have been exposed to higher temperatures than many other plasters at Trinidad. These floors were surfaced with multiple thin plaster layers, a unique finishing process (see Figure 8.5). One possible reason for different preparation processes could be that heating lime to higher temperatures helped to protect the floors from erosion. Carefully constructed, very dense surfacing layers may also have served a similar function. In an area in close proximity to the lake, where floors were likely often wet and heavily trafficked, a special preparation technique may have

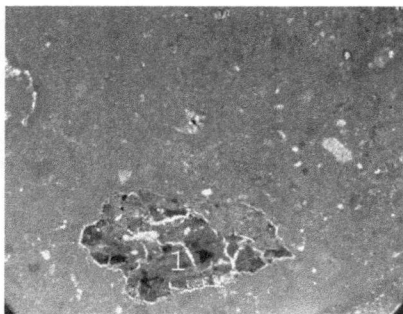

Figure 8.7. Bench plaster (TRI003) with very dense structure and fine aggregate material. (1) soil aggregate. Photo taken under plane-polarized light, field of view ten millimeters.

been necessary. Indeed, plaster floors were discovered in features around the lakeshore where preservation seemed highly unlikely. This strongly supports Moriarty's proposal that Trinidad was a port with a highly trafficked lakeshore harbor (this volume).

Status-Related Trends

A third goal in the analysis of Trinidad plasters was to assess the possibility that plasters from different locations around the site might be indicative of the relative social status of those commissioning construction.

To this end, Late Preclassic floors from two residences (C1 and G1) in the site center were compared, as were Late Preclassic plaza floors from Plazas A and B, also in the site center (see Figure 8.1). Indications about the relative status of people living in, or having access to, these areas was suggested by excavation and artifact analysis; the direct analysis of construction materials, however, avoids the often problematic method of inferring status differences by correlating artifacts and architecture that may or may not be in primary context or directly associated (Sharer 1993, 94), and can highlight just how deeply status differences were expressed.

Relative labor investment in plaster production has been correlated with several factors, including the degree to which aggregate material was sorted, the degree to which charcoal was removed from a finished plaster (Hansen 2000, 63), and the amount of time taken to slake the burned lime (Barger 1995, 394; Morris 1931, 239). In addition to the physical preparation of slaked lime-paste, the manner in which it is applied can also indicate relative labor investment. The careful application of plaster in thin layers has been noted as a reflection of preparation time, level of skill involved, and wealth of those commissioning construction (Hansen 2000, 202; Littmann 1959b; Roys 1934, 97).

The amount of aggregate added to a plaster has also been noted as an expression of wealth; aggregate adds bulk to pure lime plaster, and thus may be used to "stretch" the material (Abrams 1996; Littmann 1962; Goren and Goldberg 1991; Hansen 2000). Although some aggregate is necessary to prevent cracking or excessive shrinkage, wealthy elites presumably would not have needed to conserve lime.

A comparison of Late Preclassic floors from Plazas A and B provides an excellent example of the level of detail that micromorphological analysis may add to archaeological interpretation. Plaza A is located directly south of the principal structure at Trinidad, a 12-meter-high pyramid that faces Lake Petén Itzá (see Figure 8.1). A reasonable assumption, based on this association, would hold that the plaster used for floors in this area would be of high quality. Plaza B is also centrally located, but was more highly restricted from general access (also called Plaza II; see Figure 8.1). Notable variation, however, exists between the plasters used to pave these two plazas. Although layered construction was visible in both locations, the Plaza A floor incorporated a large amount of poorly sorted aggregate (mostly rock fragments). In contrast, Plaza B was paved with a pure lime material that appeared to be more highly heated (Figure 8.8). One way to interpret these differences is that the plaster of Plaza B was more carefully and expensively made, with greater resources focused in this area. This focus on Plaza B seems to have been maintained for some time, as it was resurfaced at least three times during the Late Classic while a single floor in Plaza A may have been maintained by patching (Matthew Moriarty, personal communication, 2003).

Residences at Trinidad also show significant differences in their plasters. Excavation of Structure C1 revealed that the last preserved phase of this centrally located building was vaulted and incorporated well-cut stones (Moriarty 2004a). Excavation of Structure G1, set to one side of the site center (see Figure 8.1), demonstrated that this smaller structure had foundation-brace walls and no evidence of vaulting (Halperin and Hernández Véliz 2004). In both cases, the clearing excavations delineated Late Classic phases of each building, with C1 clearly the higher-status residence. Deep test units were excavated through each structure, revealing several earlier construction phases extending into the Middle and Late Preclassic periods. Even though it was not possible to conduct clearing excavations to reveal

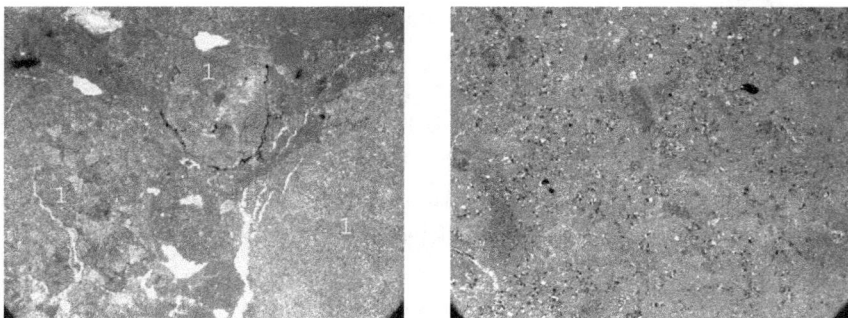

Figure 8.8. Comparison of aggregate material in floors from Plazas A and B: a. Floor from Plaza A. 1 indicates large rock fragments. Photo taken under plane-polarized light, field of view ten millimeters; b. Floor from Plaza B, containing no aggregate material. Photo taken under plane-polarized light, field of view ten millimeters.

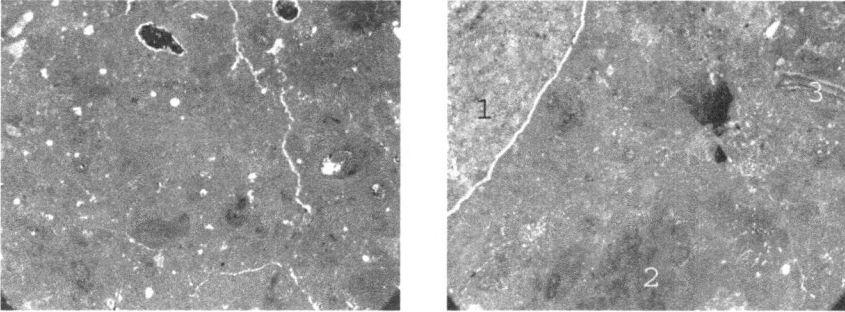

Figure 8.9. Comparison of aggregate material in floors from structures C-1 and G-1: a. Preclassic interior floor from C-1 (TRI 038) with almost no aggregate. Photo taken under plane-polarized light, field of view ten millimeters; b. Preclassic interior floor from G-1 (TRI 028). (1) rock fragment; (2) sascab; (3) shell. Photo taken under plane-polarized light, field of view ten millimeters.

the Late Preclassic phases of these buildings, micromorphological samples were extracted and are used here to investigate status differences of these earlier phases.

Ethnographic evidence from Yucatán suggests that creating a dense plaster layer is a time-consuming process, achieved through tamping floor surfaces for "hours on end" with wooden mauls (Morris 1931, 240). The Late Preclassic floors from C1 showed a subtle layered construction, with the uppermost surface exhibiting an extremely dense texture. In contrast, the floors from Structure G-1 appear to have been laid as single layers with no surface compression. The aggregate incorporated in the interior floor plasters of C-1 also generally shows a better degree of sorting, with a smaller maximum size tolerated (Figure 8.9), suggesting that a relatively higher amount of time and energy was channeled into the creation of these materials. Micromorphological analysis of floors from these two structures thus not only illustrates the degree to which fine social differences may be defined, but suggests that these differences were maintained over several centuries from the Late Preclassic into the Late Classic period.

Discussion and Conclusions

Although the sample of plasters from Trinidad is small, the utility of micromorphological analysis of this type of material is clear, and several intriguing diachronic and synchronic trends have been identified. The clearest temporal trend noted in Trinidad plasters is a general decrease in the use of sascab as an aggregate material through time, and a corresponding increase in a variety of other products. Thus, it would seem that residents of Trinidad moved away from using one of the most expedient of aggregate materials during the Late Classic and Postclassic periods. Plasters composed primarily of sascab have been noted as lacking strength (Hansen 2000, 155), and an increasing reliance on more durable and potentially more time-intensive materials may be linked to the general growth of an elite class at the site (as Trinidad became linked to Motul de San José) and their ability to commission relatively more expensive plasters. The increasing diversity of plasters during the Late Classic may also be related to the dramatic growth of Trinidad and nearby Motul de San José during this period, with various households of occupational specialists within an increasing population creating distinctive plaster recipes and application techniques. These temporal trends intimate that more economic resources were in the hands of Late Classic elites at Trinidad, even though it was a secondary-level site in Motul's polity; wealth appears to have moved down the political hierarchy without trouble, possibly suggesting a more integrative political system.

Even though there were clear temporal changes in plaster technology at Trinidad, some decorative elements appear to have remained constant from the Late Preclassic through the Postclassic. Specifically, two finishing techniques, neither visible to the naked eye, were identified in several samples: red pigment and extremely fine surfacing, resulting in a very flat "razor" edge (Figure 8.6). Traces of pigment were noted on floor, wall, and bench plasters from several locations around the site, as were "razor"-sharp upper surfaces. The consistency of these finishing techniques demonstrates some constant in the aesthetic preferences of inhabitants of Trinidad over an extremely long period of time.

In contrast to diachronic trends that highlight technological changes or continuity, synchronic trends speak more to differences in function and the relative status of residents and users of plazas at Trinidad. A main functional distinction may be drawn between plaster floors from structures and plazas in the site core and those in the harbor area. In terms of function, whereas site core floors are more porous and contain less highly heated lime, the port floors are extremely dense and show evidence for extensive heating of materials. As there is some temporal overlap between both of these groups of floors, I suggest that the unique harbor floors were specially designed to resist heavy traffic and frequent wetting. A second major functional distinction may be drawn between plasters used for floors and those used to coat walls and benches. The extremely fine-grained nature of nonfloor plasters and the addition of siliceous soil/clay materials as aggregate are both qualities noted in sculptural plasters elsewhere in the Maya area and Mesoamerica (Hansen, Rodriguez-Navarro, and Hansen 1997; Magaloni et al. 1992; Villegas et al. 1995) and clearly seem to be related to a difference in the application process.

Finally, status-related differences may be deduced from comparisons of floors from two Preclassic residential structures and two Preclassic plazas at Trinidad. Compositional and structural differences suggest that the elite inhabitants of Structure C-1 and users of the highly restricted-access Plaza B were less conservative in their use of pure lime or other more costly materials, and also devoted more energy to careful floor construction. Presumably, these inhabitants of Trinidad were not concerned with "stretching" their resources, either in terms of raw materials or time needed to complete the job. In the case of the residential structures, micromorphology results fit well with what was already known about the relative status of their inhabitants. In the case of the open plazas, however, micromorphology revealed subtle details that would not have necessarily been inferred during excavation or mapping.

Future work with plasters from the Motul area will continue to investigate the temporal, functional, and status-related plastering trends discussed here. Plaster samples from several additional residential structures and plazas throughout the core of Trinidad will improve spatial and temporal coverage and represent a range of socioeconomic levels. Plaster samples from other nearby sites in the area, including Motul de San José and smaller tertiary settlements, will also be investigated to determine if similar trends are present and whether or not distinctive differences in plastering exist at an intersite level. A wealth of information may be gleaned from the microscopic analysis of Maya plasters, and the application of micromorphology to other anthropogenic materials and deposits should certainly be encouraged throughout the Maya area.

9

Akte

Settlement, Chronology, and Monuments at the Minor Ceremonial Center Akte in the Motul de San José Periphery

SUZANNA C. YORGEY AND MATTHEW D. MORIARTY

Introduction

The Motul de San José Archaeological Project has tested a number of models of the economic and political integration of the Motul de San José polity through multidisciplinary investigations at this center and surrounding sites. In designing a regional investigation program, the project adopted an explicitly heterarchical perspective, utilizing multidisciplinary research to explore which aspects of intersite relationships were hierarchical and which were unranked, and how these shifted through time (Foias 1998, 2003; Hahn et al. 2003; Moriarty 2004b). The goals of the Motul de San José Archaeological Project are discussed in greater detail in Foias and Emery (this volume), Foias (2003), Emery (2003a), and Moriarty (2004d).

In pursuit of these goals, the project has been working to reconstruct the basic settlement history of the Motul area. In the course of establishing a program of regional investigations, we first undertook a program of regional reconnaissance in 2001 (Moriarty and Wyatt 2001). Preliminary investigations conducted at Akte at this time identified high-quality architecture, five stelae or monuments, and extensive storage capacity in the form of numerous *chultunes* associated with the principal group, leading Moriarty to hypothesize that the site functioned as an outlying royal manor or rural administrative center for the Motul polity (see Taschek and Ball 2003). This hypothesis was supported by Akte's strategic location atop a high, and presumably defensible, ridge near the confluence of drainages feeding into the Río Akte. From this position, Akte was well positioned to monitor travel and communication to the northwest of Motul.

With the goal of exploring Akte's social and economic role within the region, Moriarty returned to Akte in 2002 to conduct a six-week field season to map the site and to establish a preliminary site chronology (Moriarty 2002). During the 2002 field season, the project discovered two additional monuments, bringing the total number of possible monuments at the site to seven (Drapkin and Moriarty 2002), further underscoring the fact that Akte does not fit easily into traditional site hierarchies that emphasize settlement size and architectural complexity (i.e., Bullard 1960; Hammond 1975b). Intrigued by these findings, Moriarty and Halperin returned to the site for an additional week in 2003 to investigate the context of the Akte monuments (Moriarty and Halperin 2003). Although these investigations were limited in scale, the results highlight the complexities involved in assessing political and economic relationships of minor sites in the Motul area.

Location and History of Research

The ancient Maya center of Akte is located in Guatemala's department of El Petén, approximately 11 kilometers north of the town of San Andrés and 7.2 kilometers northwest of Motul de San José (Figure 1.4; Latitude 17° 04′ 31″, Longitude 89° 56′ 20″). The site is located near the northeastern end of a line of karstic uplands that separate the Lake Petén Itzá basin from the Río San Pedro drainage to the northwest. The site overlooks the nearby confluence of the Río K'änte't'u'ul and other drainages forming the Río Akte, and Akte's occupants would have been able to monitor movements along both rivers. Although the Río K'änte't'u'ul is currently a seasonal waterway, local informants suggest that the river was large enough to be navigated by canoe in the recent past. If it was also navigable during the pre-Columbian period, then it could have provided an important transportation and trade link between the lake basin and sites to the west and northwest (Moriarty 2004d, 22).

The alluvial soils along both rivers would have provided the opportunity for arboriculture and gardening. The riverbanks near Akte are currently being used by local inhabitants to grow fruit trees. A detailed soil analysis has not yet been undertaken in the area surrounding Akte, but we identified chalky red Chächäklu'um soils under the central platform at the site. Chächäklu'um soils are normally found in raised plateaus covered by grasslands, and their presence suggests that some of the site was once covered by savannah (Jensen et al. 2007; Moriarty 2001; see also Bair and Terry, this volume). Current residents of the area consider Chächäklu'um soils to be somewhat risky for *milpa* agriculture, but nonetheless utilize them heavily due to land pressure. They also note that, as with the local drainages, savanna soils are relatively productive for certain kinds of arboriculture (Jensen et al. 2007; Webb et al. 2007).

Although the zone to the northwest of the Lake Petén Itzá basin is poorly known archaeologically, Akte has long been recognized as a center with carved monuments. Ian Graham visited the site in the 1960s, photographed two monuments, and included Akte as a site with inscriptions on his map of the central Maya lowlands (I. Graham 1982). Although Karl Herbert Mayer published photographs of Stela 1 (2000b), no additional research was conducted at the site until members of the Motul de San José Archaeological Project initiated investigations in 2001.

Settlement and Site Organization

Akte is a relatively small site with fifty to sixty structures. The site center consists of thirty-five structures (Figure 9.1), which are situated atop a steep, 40-meter-high ridge that appears to have been modified significantly along its eastern edge to increase the steepness of the slope (Morales, Drapkin, and Moriarty 2002, 6). From the ridge summit, the Río Akte is clearly visible to the south and a small spring-fed tributary can be seen half a kilometer to the east. Peripheral residential groups are located within sight several hundred meters to the south and southeast, with a second large cluster of buildings, including a pyramid, 8–10 meter-high, approximately half a kilometer to the north. Additional residential groups may be located directly west of the site center, but this area was not investigated by the Motul de San José Archaeological Project (Morales, Drapkin, and Moriarty 2002).

The principal complex of Akte's site center is a large platform group with three distinct patios (Platform A-B; see Figure 9.1). The northern patio (Patio A) is bounded to the north and west by low range structures and to the east by a tall, square structure, interpreted as a temple or oratorio. This layout is characteristic of Plaza Plan 2 as defined at Tikal by Becker (2003b, 259; MSJ Type VI, see Moriarty 2004b). The southern patio (Patio B) layout is typical of the residential groups in the Motul area, with a large L-shaped structure forming the north and west sides and a lower range structure to the east. A third, lower patio (Patio C), with a single large structure on its south side, is attached to the western edge of the platform. A line of five *chultunes* is located just off the platform's northwestern corner, with an additional single *chultun* located just south of the platform's southern end and within Plaza E (Morales, Drapkin, and Moriarty 2002, 9).

Multiple joined patios like those seen on Platform A-B are frequently interpreted as elite residential groups (see Arnold and Ford 1980; Haviland 1981; D. Rice 1988). To date, this type of multi-patio arrangement has been identified in the Motul de San José area only within the central precinct of Motul itself (Moriarty 2004b; Spensley and Foias 2001). The layout of Akte Platform A-B, with a Plaza Plan 2 patio to the north and a simple patio group to the south, closely mirrors that of two high-status residential groups at Motul de San José (MSJ Groups 7J1–7J2 or Group A and 10L2–10L3 in Figure 1.2; see also Moriarty 2004b, fig. 2). These similarities, as well

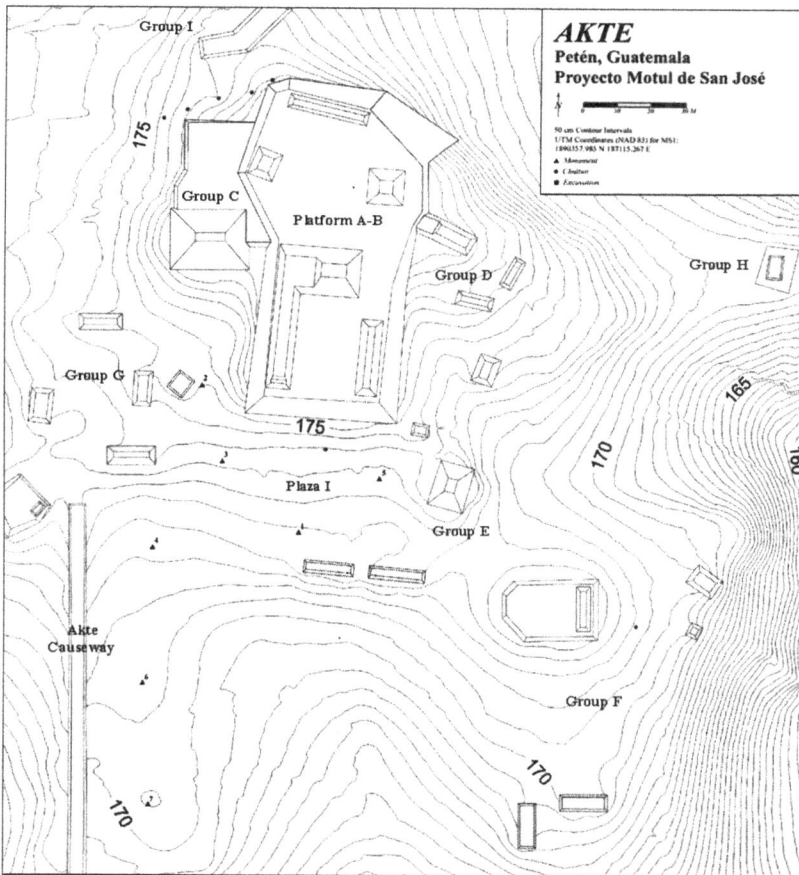

Figure 9.1. Preliminary map of Akte, El Petén, Guatemala (from Moriarty 2004b, fig. 9.7).

as the substantial volume of storage provided by the six nearby *chultunes*, suggest that the residents of Akte's Platform A-B may have enjoyed a high-level elite status within the Motul area, potentially corresponding with that of upper level residential groups at Motul itself, such as Groups A and D.

Smaller patio groups are located to the east, southeast, and southwest of Platform A-B. Most consist of two to four low, rectangular structures organized around small formal or informal patios (Groups D, F, G, H, and J). Two consist of a single structure atop a low basal platform with a small attached courtyard (Groups G and H). Both patio layouts are common in the Motul area and appear frequently at all levels of settlement (Moriarty 2004b).

The central public and ceremonial space at Akte is framed by Plaza E (or Plaza I), a 100–by-40-meter space located directly south of Platform A-B. This plaza is also the setting for five of the Akte's monuments. To the east, Plaza E is bounded by Structure E-1, a pyramidal temple structure 5 to 6 meters tall that has been destroyed by looters. The southern edge of the plaza is formed by two low (ca. 50 centimeters high) range structures. To the west, Plaza E ends at the northern terminus of the Akte Causeway. The five-meter-wide causeway runs south for approximately 115 meters before disappearing near the modern road on the southern edge of the site center (Morales, Drapkin, and Moriarty 2002, 8). For most of its length, the causeway rises only 50 to 75 centimeters above the ground; however, near its southern end the causeway was raised 2 to 3 meters above a section of lower terrain. A 15-meter section of the causeway also appears to have been leveled recently, probably by an earlier version of the modern road that passes through the site. The overall layout of public space (Plaza I or Plaza E) to the south of the more private space (Platforms A-B) is similar to the core of Motul de San José where the Acropolis (the probable Late Classic royal court) is situated north of the Main Plaza (or Plaza I; see Figure 1.2).

As with many of the sites in the region, Akte has been heavily looted. Virtually all of the structures in the central portion of the site have been illegally excavated and many of the largest buildings have been trenched or tunneled several times. Several of these trenches revealed intact walls several meters high. Notable sections of wall with carefully constructed facades were identified within looters trenches in Structures A-2, B-1, and C-1, all of which are at risk of collapse. Other buildings have been essentially destroyed by repeated excavation. Structure E-1, for example, has been tunneled and trenched to such an extent that its final form can only be guessed at. Local informants also report that a small carved monument and possible monument fragments were removed from the site by looters. The cultural patrimony destroyed by these excavations is incalculable and will seriously impede future research at the site.

Ceramics and Chronology

MSJAP investigations in 2002 and 2003 included test excavations in Platform A-B, Plaza I, the Akte Causeway, and Groups A-G (see Moriarty 2002; Moriarty and Halperin 2003; Yorgey 2005). Additional materials were collected from excavations surrounding the stelae, as well as the looters' spoil piles near Structure C-1 and other surface collections. In total, these excavations produced 8,278 potsherds and one complete vessel. Although the ceramic sample from Akte is relatively small in comparison to Motul and Trinidad (see Moriarty, this volume), it provides the framework for a brief discussion of Akte's chronological development. These materials were analyzed by Yorgey as part of her master's research (Yorgey 2005), where additional details regarding the methods and results are provided.

The Akte ceramic collection has several critical limitations. Although excavators located some moderate density middens, most materials from Akte were recovered in fill contexts. The problems with reconstructing settlement chronology from the results of excavations in structural stratigraphy are well known (i.e., Gifford 1976; Phillips, Ford, and Griffin 1951). Further, the small size of the collection and the fragmentary nature of most recovered sherds limited the extent of comparisons that could be made. The Akte ceramic sequence is, therefore, preliminary in nature and constrained to general periods only.

Middle Preclassic

The earliest ceramics recovered at Akte pertain to the Mamom ceramic sphere. The Akte excavations did not identify any pure Mamom contexts, and the number of Mamom ceramics identified was quite small (n = 69). Most Mamom materials came from mixed-fill deposits in the Group A-B Platform and in Group F (Yorgey 2005).

The principal diagnostics included the Juventud, Chunhinta, and Pital Groups, all of which exhibited the classic waxy slip and vessel forms of the Mamom ceramic sphere (Figure 9.2a). One of the key problems in the identification of Mamom ceramics is the difficulty in separating Mamom and Chicanel period body sherds because of similarities in the qualities of the waxy slip (Forsyth 1989, 7). Within the Akte collection, Mamom ceramics could be separated from later Chicanel materials only when the

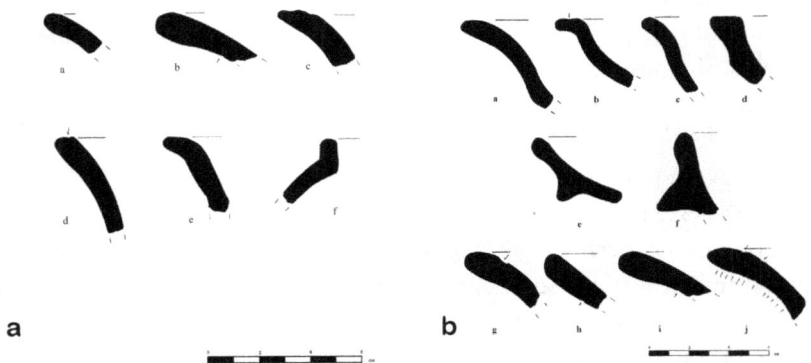

Figure 9.2a. Mamom ceramic materials from the Akte collection (adapted from Yorgey 2005, fig. 5.1); b. Chicanel ceramic sphere rims from the Akte collection (adapted from Yorgey 2005, fig. 5.2).

sample included diagnostic rim sherds. These diagnostics included either the forms (bowls with flaring wall and direct or everted rims and cuspidors) or the surface treatments (chamfering, fluting and pre-slip incising) common throughout the Mamom ceramic sphere (Forsyth 1993a, 1993b, 1996; Willey et al. 1967). Even allowing for potential underreporting caused by these factors, however, Mamom ceramics were relatively rare at Akte.

The Akte collection included a single sherd of Tierra Mojada, which has been noted as an excellent horizon marker in the Petén (1993a, 39) as it occurs in small numbers at Uaxactún (R. Smith 1955, 60), Tikal, Altar de Sacrificios (R. Adams 1971, 85), and Seibal (Sabloff 1975, 71–74). Finally, the Akte collection also included a single sherd of Palma Daub. Forsyth (1992, 1993a) has noted that the distribution of daub decoration may indicate a separation between the central and east Petén and the area surrounding the Central Petén Lakes. Daub decoration is common at Nakbé (Forsyth 1993a, 40), Uaxactún (R. Smith 1955), and Tikal (Forsyth 1993a, 40), whereas very few examples have been identified in the north-central Petén or in the area directly surrounding the Central Petén Lakes (A. Chase and D. Chase 1983, 78; Foias 1996, 63; Forsyth 1996, 7). Consistent with this pattern, Palma Daub is rare throughout the Motul de San José area. Limited Middle Preclassic ceramics have been located at the site of Motul de San José, but recent excavations at the site of Trinidad de Nosotros and Buenavista de Nuevo San José have identified an extensive Middle Preclassic occupation (Moriarty, this volume; Castellanos 2007). Analysis of the

Trinidad ceramics is ongoing, but only a small number Palma Daub sherds have been identified to date (see Moriarty, this volume).

Late Preclassic

The first major occupation at Akte occurred during the Late Preclassic. Easily recognizable Chicanel period ceramics were recovered in all test pits in Groups A through G, suggesting that most areas of the site were occupied during this period. An early phase of the central platform at the site, the Group A-B Platform, appears to have been built at this time. Testing of the Akte causeway also revealed two episodes of construction, with the earliest dating to the Late Preclassic (Yorgey 2005).

The Late Preclassic ceramics at Akte demonstrate the vessel forms and waxy red slip that define the Chicanel sphere ceramics throughout the Maya Lowlands (Willey, Culbert, and Adams 1967, 308). The Chicanel ceramics identified at Akte include unslipped types from the Achiotes Group as well as slipped types from the Sierra, Polvero, and Flor Groups (Figure 9.2b). The most common forms in the collection included everted rim bowls, sometimes with incision or grooving; bowls with flared walls; and short- to medium-necked bowls. Although labial, medial, and lateral flanges are diagnostic of the Chicanel ceramic sphere throughout the Petén (Forsyth 1993a), very few were identified in the Akte collection. Medial breaks or lateral angles were also rare in the Akte collection, although this may be due to the small size of many of the recovered sherds.

Early Classic

Clearly identifiable Early Classic materials were relatively rare at Akte (Figure 9.3). Although many sites in the Petén region experienced an apparent population decline during the Early Classic (Foias 1996; Forsyth 1989; Sabloff 1975), some sites in the central area, including Tikal and Uaxactún, do show significant concentrations of Tzakol sphere ceramics interpreted as high-population densities (Culbert 2003; R. Smith 1955). In the case of Akte, it is difficult to say whether the decrease in ceramic densities reflects a decline in population or problems with the ceramic typologies currently in use (Foias 1996; Kosakowsky 2005; Lincoln 1985). Although Mayanists have recognized problems with current ceramic typologies for this time period for some time (Foias 1996; Kosakowsky 1987; Pring 2000), recent research in the Three Rivers Region of Belize suggests that Late Preclassic ceramic traditions may have persisted during the Early Classic period (Kosakowsky 2005; Sullivan 2005). Although additional research will be needed to clarify

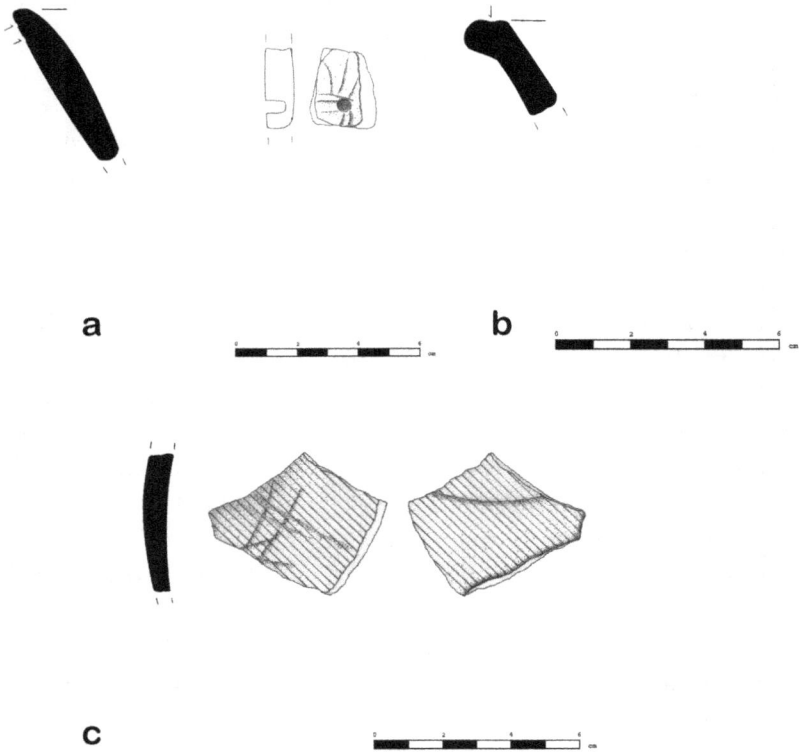

Figure 9.3. Early Classic ceramic rim profiles from the Akte collection (adapted from Yorgey 2005, figs. 5.7–5.9): a. Lucha Incised; b. Quintal Unslipped; c. Mahogany Creek Incised.

this pattern further, a growing body of evidence suggests that the transition from Late Preclassic to Early Classic differed regionally (Brady et al. 1998; Pring 2000; Willey and Mathews1985), further complicating the interpretation of these ceramics. In the Akte collection, Early Classic sherds were identified in mixed-fill contexts across the site, with several low concentrations located at the central platform (Platform A-B) at the site (Yorgey 2005). Additional research, both at Akte and throughout the region, may be required to clarify the site's occupation during this period.

Late Classic

The second major peak in occupation at Akte occurred in the Late Classic, with Late Classic ceramics recovered from all sections of the site. Additional construction was undertaken across the site during this period,

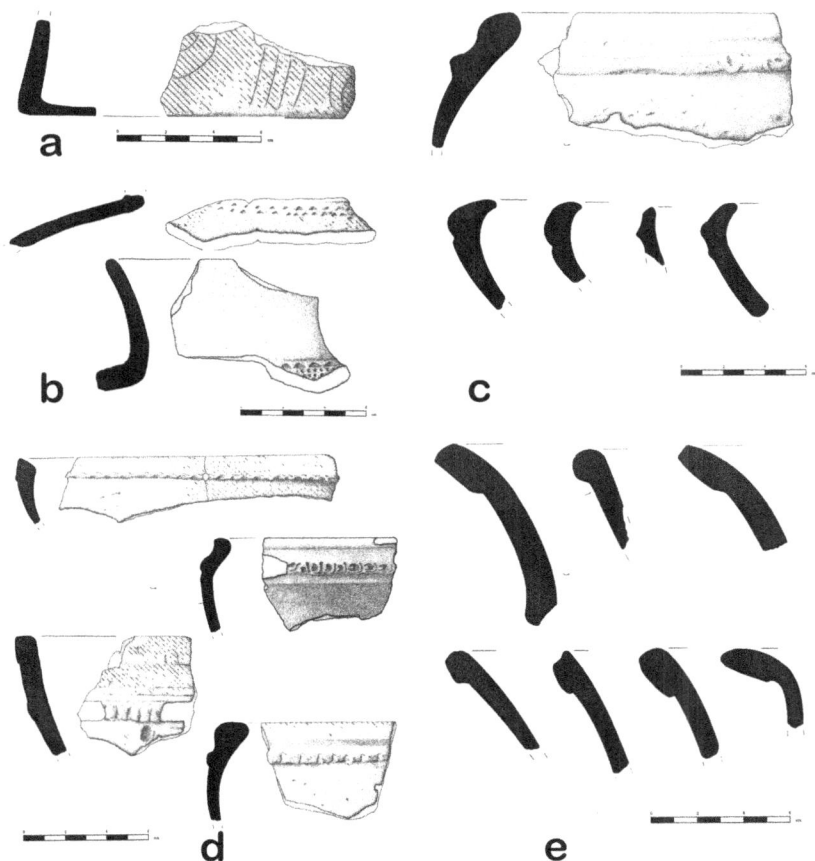

Figure 9.4. Late Classic ceramic rim profiles from the Akte collection (adapted from Yorgey 2005, figs. 5.10–5.14): a. Corozal Incised; b. Pantano Impressed; c. Subin Red; d. Chaquiste Impressed; e. Cambio/Encanto jars.

including a final phase of construction on both the Akte causeway and the Group A-B Platform. The available information suggests that Plaza E was constructed during this period, and at least one of the monuments can be dated stylistically to this period (Yorgey 2005).

The Late Classic monochrome ceramics at Akte are dominated by the Tinaja Group (n = 516; Figure 9.4). A vessel from the Saxche/Palmar Group was identified under a series of large stones in a probable Late Classic burial in Platform A-B (Kerns et al. 2002, 12; Yorgey 2005, 39–43). As with most of the sherds from the Saxche/Palmar Group, the vessel was badly eroded and could not be classified to the type level. The only well-preserved polychrome samples in the collection were recovered from the looter's tunnels in Structure C-1.

Terminal Classic

Terminal Classic horizon markers are rare in the Akte collection, suggesting that Akte may have experienced a population decline in the Terminal Classic. The Terminal Classic remains poorly understood throughout the region, however, and interpretation is further complicated by the fact that Late Classic slipped types continued to be used in the Terminal Classic (Foias 1996, 224; P. Rice 1987b) and by an overall pattern of microregional variability (Chase 1979, 94–95; Culbert 1973, 81–82; P. Rice 1987b, 59–60). Additional excavation, both at Akte and the surrounding sites, will be needed before a clear picture of the Terminal Classic at Akte can be reconstructed. Trade wares (i.e., Plumbate, slate wares, modeled-carved pottery, and Fine Orange) are rare at Akte. Only one piece of Fine Orange and five pieces of an apparent local copy were identified. Several pieces of eroded Tohil Plumbate were recovered during surface collection, all of which exhibited the characteristic Plumbate surface of vitrified greenish gray (Shepard 1948, 135).

Postclassic

Although recent studies have significantly expanded our understanding of the Postclassic in Petén (A. Chase and D. Chase 1983; D. Rice 1986; P. Rice 1980, 1986), analysis of the ceramics remains problematic, since Petén Postclassic sites often have poor stratigraphy and reflect localized ceramic traditions (P. Rice and D. Rice 1985). Postclassic ceramics were rare at Akte, accounting for only 2 percent of the identifiable sherds in the collection. Although pure Postclassic contexts were not found in any excavation units, Moriarty identified a possible Postclassic structure on top of structures E-3a and E-3b on the northern side of Akte's central plaza. This area has not yet been excavated, however, and additional research would be required to confirm this identification. The Akte collection contained Postclassic ceramics from the Pozo, Paxcamán, and Chilo Groups (Figure 9.5). The diagnostic right-angled rim of the Pozo Unslipped Type was relatively easy to identify, but the identification of the Chilo Group was more problematic. As defined by Bullard (1973) and formalized by P. Rice (1987b, 179), the Chilo definition is difficult for sherd analysis since it hinges on temper and quality of vessel construction. This is particularly troubling for the Akte collections, since many of sherds are heavily eroded, however, and many

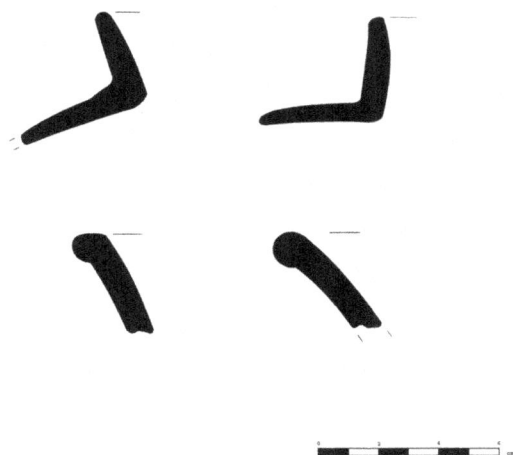

Figure 9.5. Postclassic ceramic rim profiles from the Akte collection (adapted from Yorgey 2005, figs. 5.15).

of the Chilo sherds could not be identified to the type level. Identification of the red-slipped Paxcamán Group was also difficult, as there are significant differences in the group as defined by Cowgill (1963), Bullard (1970) and P. Rice (1987b), particularly in relation to the Trapeche and Augustine Groups. We identified a small number of sherds from the Paxcamán Group (n = 18), including both the yellow ash tempered and the grey snail inclusion paste varieties (P. Rice 1987b, 105–9), but did not identify any examples of the Trapeche or Augustine Groups.

Akte Site Ceramic Collection

Although Spensley is currently undertaking research that will provide ceramic samples from a number of smaller sites within the Motul de San José region (Spensley 2008), the only comparative materials that are currently available are those from the larger sites of Motul de San José and Trinidad de Nosotros. The Akte ceramic complexes clearly fall within the ceramic tradition exhibited at these sites; however, the materials from Akte are substantially less well preserved than ceramic materials from either of the larger sites. The differential preservation may be partially due to drainage and weathering patterns, as many areas of both Motul de San José and Trinidad de Nosotros have extensive overburden likely to protect ceramics used in construction fill. The heavy erosion may also be a function of the resources utilized in local ceramic production at Akte. Field personnel reported that the spring located near the site had a high mineral and salt content, and use of this water for ceramic production may have contributed to weak, easily eroded vessels. This may also suggest that Akte controlled its own pottery production, rather than obtaining ceramics from Motul de San José.

Preliminary analysis, however, clearly indicates that the Akte collection contains notably fewer exotics than either the Motul de San José or Trinidad de Nosotros collections. The relatively low numbers of exotics in the Akte collection contrasts sharply with the number of stelae at the site, again suggesting the heterarchical nature of the political, social and economic connections between Akte and the surrounding sites.

Obsidian

Although investigations at Akte were designed to address chronological issues, they nonetheless provided some data useful for assessing other aspects of Akte's occupation. Some of the more interesting results came from the analysis of obsidian carried out by Moriarty. A total of 127 obsidian artifacts were recovered during two seasons of research at Akte. Of these, 109 came from Late Classic or Terminal Classic contexts including fill, midden, and especially substela caches (see below). The vast majority of these were broken prismatic bladelets (n = 101), although two polyhedral core fragments and various utilized and unutilized flakes and shatter were also recovered. Although the Akte sample was relatively small, it was sufficient to provide a preliminary characterization of obsidian consumption at Akte during the interval associated with Motul's regional ascendancy.

The analysis of MSJAP obsidian focused on basic indices designed to assess treatment of obsidian as a scarce resource. Two of the most widely applied indices included in this analysis were cutting-edge-to-mass (CE/M) ratios and average blade widths (McKillop 1996; Rovner 1976; Sheets 1978; Sheets and Muto 1972; Sidrys 1979). Both indices serve as useful analytical tools for intersite comparisons as they provide a rough measure of conservation in blade production: high average blade widths and low CE/M ratios correlate with less conservation (and more access to obsidian), and low average blade widths and high CE/M ratios correlate with greater conservation (and less access to obsidian). The distribution of obsidian cores is also thought to correlate with access to obsidian (McKillop 1989, 1996), and relative core frequencies were tabulated for each site as an index of cores recovered per one hundred bladelets (cores/bladelets × 100). These indices were applied to the MSJAP sample of materials from Late to Terminal

Classic contexts (n = 2,577) drawn from six sites (Motul, Trinidad, Akte, Chäkokot, Buenavista, and Xilil).

Suggestively, the Akte sample of prismatic bladelets produced the lowest average blade width (0.95 centimeters) and the highest CE/M ratio (4.06) of all sites. By comparison, none of the other sites produced average blade widths lower than 1.05 centimeters or CE/M ratios higher than 3.29 (Moriarty, Spensley, Lawton, et al. 2008). These results indicate that, among investigated sites in the Motul de San José area, Akte's inhabitants exhibited far and away the greatest degree of conservation in prismatic blade production. Likewise, although Akte was one of only four tested sites (Motul, Trinidad, Buenavista, and Akte) where cores were recovered, Akte's core frequency score of 1.98 was by far the lowest of that group. From these results, we infer that Akte's residents had the lowest level of access to obsidian in the Motul area.

Monuments

As outlined above, Akte was selected for inclusion in the Motul de San José Archaeological Project in part due to the identification of numerous monuments, which raised questions regarding the role of the site within the Motul polity or as a potential competitor to the royal lineage at Motul. Although "minor ceremonial centers" do not usually have stelae (Bullard 1960), Akte is not the only minor center in the area to have carved monuments. Several other minor sites in the San Pedro drainage basin have carved monuments, including B'alumtun (Mayer 1995) and Wakutal (Graham 1982, 186; Mayer 2000a). Although only one monument has been found at each of these sites, extensive mapping programs, like that which located the remains of Stelae 3–7 at Akte, have not been undertaken at either site.

At least one of the Akte monuments can be dated stylistically to the Late Classic, but research throughout the Lowlands has shown that monuments were not always carved and erected simultaneously (Folan, Kintz, and Fletcher 1983, 81; I. Graham 1978, 107; Hammond and Bobo 1994, 26; Jones and Satterthwaite 1982; Martin 2000; H. Pollock 1919; Satterthwaite 1958, 75–76; Thompson 1932, 131–33). Field personnel had also noticed an apparent concentration of Postclassic ceramics around the monuments during initial investigations, suggesting that the monuments could have been moved from another site and re-set at Akte during the Postclassic period. Motul de San José Archaeological Project personnel returned to the site in 2003 in order to explore this possibility. During the limited 2003 field season, Moriarty directed the cleaning and turning of several of the monuments, as well as excavations surrounding three of the Akte monuments (Stelae 1, 3, and 4) with the goal of identifying any artifactual materials associated with the erection of these monuments (Moriarty and Halperin 2003; Yorgey 2005).

Stela 1, the most complete monument at Akte, is located on the southern edge of Plaza E (Figure 9.6). The stela, which measures approximately 230 centimeters tall, 136 centimeters wide, and 50 centimeters deep, was originally identified by Ian Graham in the 1970s (1982). The photographs Graham took at Akte are currently stored in the Corpus for Maya Hieroglyphic Inscriptions at the Peabody Museum of Archaeology and Ethnology at Harvard University and have not yet been published. Graham graciously provided us with copies of his photographs of the front and back of Akte Stela 1 (see Yorgey 2005). Graham noted that the monuments at Akte were heavily eroded when he visited the site (personal communication, 2004) and the stelae appear to have suffered from additional erosion and frequent burnings since that time.

The front of Stela 1 clearly portrays a standing figure with the typical Late Classic costume of divine rulership, including a backrack, a manikin scepter, and a small shield (Proskouriakoff 1950, 1993). Unfortunately the top of the stela is missing and no evidence of a headdress has been preserved. Four glyph blocks (A1–B3) are located above the head of the

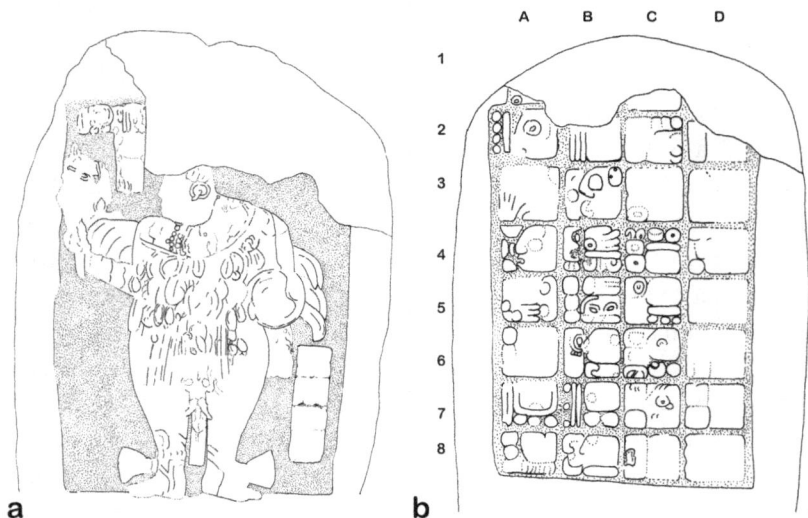

Figure 9.6a. Stela 1, front (preliminary drawing based on field sketches and photographs); b. Stela 1, back (drawing based on field sketches and photographs).

figure in an inverted *L* shape. The first two glyph blocks (A1–B1) contain calendrical information, including a clear Ahau glyph. During the early investigations at the site in 2001, Stela 1 was resting on its left side (Moriarty and Wyatt 2001). In 2003, the project conducted several excavations in the surrounding area and turned Stela 1 to examine its back.[1] During the final preparation for turning Stela 1, excavators found a wooden plank underneath the monuments, apparently left under the monument when it was turned at an earlier point in time. Since Stela 1 was clearly moved previously, the underlying stratigraphy may also have been disturbed (Moriarty and Halperin 2003).

After turning the monument, MSJ personnel identified four incised glyph blocks on the left side of the stela and a text of at least thirty-two glyph blocks on the back of the stela (Figure 9.6b). Although the glyphs in columns A and B were buried and partially protected, the glyphs in column C and D were exposed and are heavily eroded. A reading for these Calendar Round dates has been suggested elsewhere (Mayer 2000b), but Graham's photographs of the back of Stela 1 provide additional details of glyph blocks A2–A4 and B2–B4 that are no longer visible. Utilizing both Graham's photograph and the photographs taken during the 2003 field season, we were able to compile a list of possible dates carved on the stela. Graham's photographs suggest that the Long Count date can be read as 9.15.?.?.0, placing the date between 9.15.0.0.0 (August 20, AD 731) and 9.15.19.17.0 (April 17, AD 751). Stylistic analysis supports this date, but the possibilities can be narrowed by utilizing all of the fragmentary information preserved on the monument. Although the *tun* coefficient cannot be clarified, Graham's photographs suggest that the *uinal* coefficient (B3) is 1, 2, 3, or 0. MSJAP photographs from 2003, however, show a Calendar Round date that includes an Ahau with a coefficient of either 5 or 10 (A7) and an illegible glyph with a coefficient of either 8 or 13 (at B7). The 2003 photographs show that B7 has a lower element, which narrows the possible glyphs that could fill this position. After combining all of the information described above, the possible Long Count dates are limited to a brief period of time as follows:

- 9.15.5.0.0   10 Ahau 8 Chen   AD 736
- 9.15.8.1.0   5 Ahau 13 Chen   AD 739
- 9.15.16.0.0   5 Ahau 13 Xul   AD 747

Tokovinine and Zender (this volume) support the third date for this stela, and suggest that it was raised by an Akte lord after Late Classic Motul ruler Yajawte' K'inich suffered defeat at the hands of the Dos Pilas king.

Since Stela 1 is the only Akte stela with legible calendrical information, Motul de San José Archaeological Project personnel conducted additional excavations in the surrounding area to explore the chronology of the original erection of the stela and any relationship with the adjacent plaza (Moriarty and Halperin 2003, 152). A unit placed directly south of the stela identified a series of eight irregularly shaped rocks that may have been used to brace the base of the stela. The recovered ceramics suggest that that these rocks were placed on top of a layer of Preclassic fill, followed by additional layers of Late Classic fill. Eight Postclassic sherds were also recovered from the top two levels, but these may have been integrated from the surface, either when the stela fell from its base or when it was later turned (Yorgey 2005, 64–67).

The second monument identified by Graham, Stela 2, is located approximately 40 meters northwest of Stela 1, just east of a low platform (Structure G-3). Because at least four of the monuments at Motul de San José were originally set in platforms, we suspect that this structure may have had a similar function. Two large fragments of Stela 2 were identified. The largest of the two shows at least two columns of glyphs, each one with at least three glyphs (Figure 9.7). Two partially legible glyphs remain. Block B1 contains the prefix "ya-" (T126) and block B2 contains an anthropomorphic head which can be read as "K'awiil" (T1030; see Drapkin and Moriarty 2002, 24).

Figure 9.7. Stela 2, largest piece (photograph provided by M. D. Moriarty).

Although we cannot be certain, this may be a reference to the Dos Pilas ruler who defeated Motul at this time (K'awiil Chan K'inich). Although a number of additional fragments were located in the area, Stela 2 was too fragmented to be reconstructed (ibid.). The identifiable pieces do not appear to represent an entire monument, and Moriarty has suggested that this may not be the original location of Stela 2. Excavations were not carried out in this area, and additional pieces may still be buried.

Prior to the MSJAP investigations, Stelae 1 and 2 were the only two monuments that had been identified. In the course of the 2001 reconnaissance and the subsequent field seasons, the MSJAP identified an additional five possible monuments (Moriarty 2002; Moriarty and Halperin 2003; Moriarty and Wyatt 2001). Three of the five can be identified as monuments with a reasonable degree of certainty. Extensive carving was identified on two of these (Monuments 4 and 7), whereas a third (Monument 3) was likely blank when erected. The remaining two possible monuments (Monuments 5 and 6) have not yet been examined in detail. As reflected on the site map (Figure 9.1), all five additional monuments are located within the public center of the site. Three of these (Monuments 4, 6, and 7) were found along the eastern edge of the Akte Causeway. Another monument (Monument 3) was identified in Plaza I, with a final possible monument (Monument 5) located on the eastern end of the same plaza, approximately 10 meters west of Structure E-1.

Monument 4, which measures 220 by 110 centimeters, is located at the northern end of the Akte Causeway. Moriarty had identified faint traces of shallow carving on the exposed sections of the monument (Drapkin and Moriarty 2002, 24). In 2003, we turned the monument and discovered a text of at least forty-five small glyph blocks carved in shallow relief (Figure 9.8). Another small fragment contained eight additional glyph blocks. After reviewing the fragments, Moriarty and Halperin suggested that the back of Monument 4 originally had a text containing at least sixty to eighty small glyph blocks (2003, 159), although none of the text is legible due to the extreme erosion. A nearby test pit identified the remains of a decomposing floor on top of a layer of Late Classic fill; however, the available evidence does not allow us to associate the floor with Monument 4 (Yorgey 2005).

Monument 7, consisting of three fragments of varying sizes, was identified at the southern end of the Akte Causeway. The back of the largest fragment measures approximately 85 by 60 centimeters and contains an eroded text with two parallel columns of three glyph blocks each (Figure 9.9a). The front of the fragment has a text of six glyph blocks, which appears to

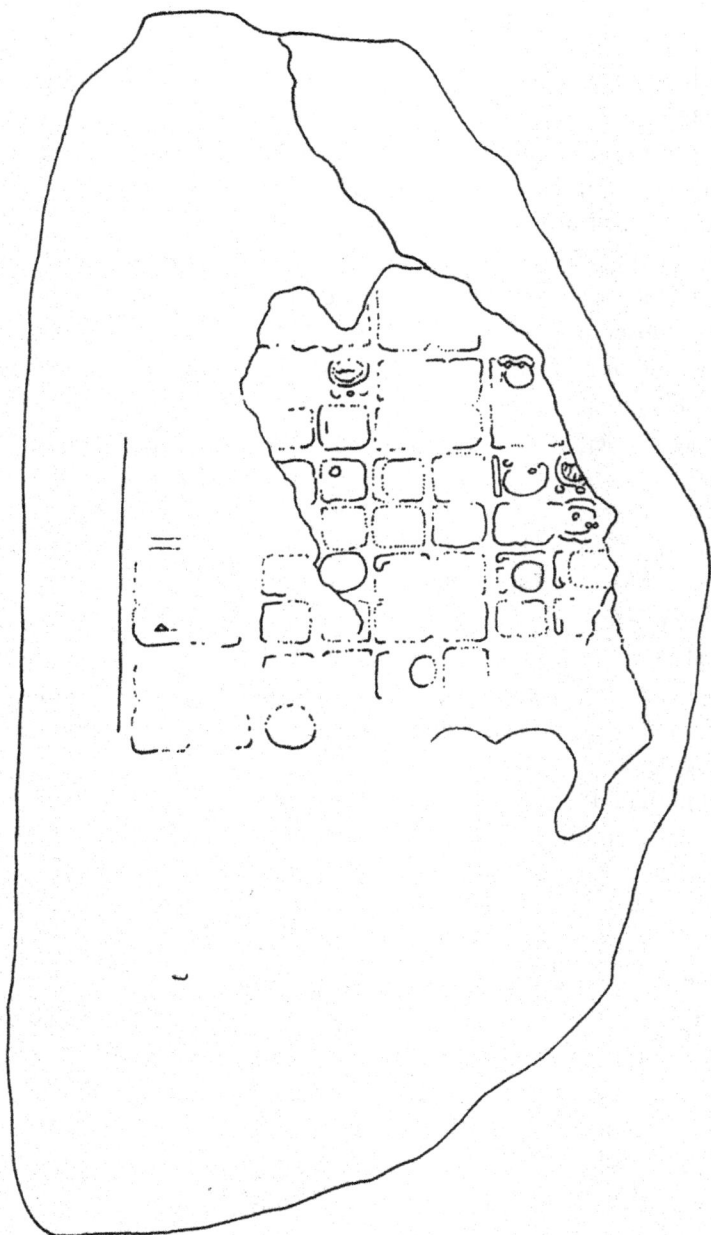

Figure 9.8. Stela 4, largest fragment (drawing based on field sketches and photographs).

differ stylistically from those on other Akte stelae. The text could not be reconstructed, but Moriarty identified a female prefix (*ix*) and a zoomorphic head at A2 and B2. Although the fragments of Monument 7 are thicker than any of the other Akte stelae (45 centimeters), they fall in the range of carved stelae thickness at Tikal (Jones and Satterthwaite 1982, 119). The upper right edge of the monument has an incised circular element that measures approximately 30 centimeters in diameter, but no evidence of glyphs or other elements could be identified on the edges of the monument (Figure 9.9b).

Between Monuments 4 and 7, Motul de San José personnel identified a collection of buried stone fragments that have been provisionally identified as Monument 6. At least one of these fragments appears to be worked stone, but no evidence of carving could be identified from the surface (Drapkin and Moriarty 2002). Although additional research would be required to determine the source of these fragments, they were provisionally identified as the remains of a stela base due to their position between, and in line with, Monuments 4 and 7 along the eastern side of the Akte causeway.

The remaining two monuments were identified in Plaza E. Monument 3 is located in the northwest corner of Plaza E. The top section of the monument, which fell toward the east, is largely intact, but the base of the monument is fragmented into numerous small pieces. Although MSJAP personnel turned all of the pieces during the 2003 field season, no evidence of carving could be identified (Moriarty and Halperin 2003, 157). A test pit placed around the monument identified a level of fill covering a depression in the bedrock that may have been created as a base for Monument 3. High artifact concentrations were also recovered from this area, including a probable substela cache consisting of sixty-six small pieces of obsidian (Figure 9.10). The ceramic fill from the surrounding area included both Late Preclassic and Late Classic materials, suggesting that Late Classic fill was packed around the monument when it was erected (Yorgey 2005). We identified six additional large-stone fragments along the eastern edge of Plaza E, which have been provisionally identified as Monument 5. The fragments, which were found on the surface, do not exhibit evidence of carving (Drapkin and Moriarty 2002). Additional research will be needed to determine whether these fragments are the remains of a stela; alternatively they might constitute the remains of a vault stone or other architectural element removed from Structure E-1 by looters. It is also possible that the remaining fragments might have been created by the trimming of another carved monument; local informants suggest that looters recently carried off a small carved monument in a truck.

Figure 9.9a. Stela 7, back (photograph provided by M. D. Moriarty); b. Stela 7, side (photograph provided by M. D. Moriarty).

Figure 9.9. *Continued*

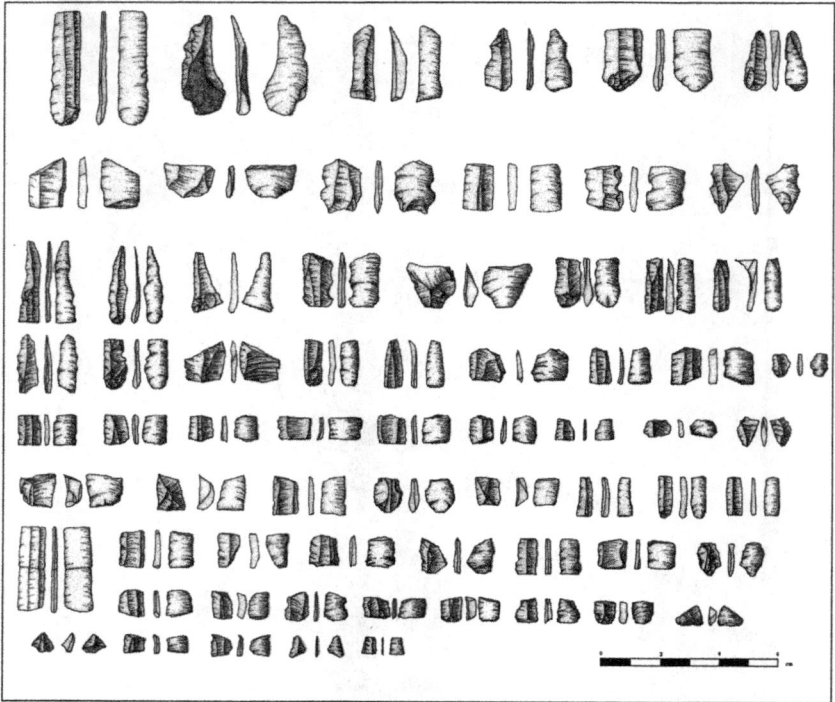

Figure 9.10. Substela cache located below Monument 3 (Yorgey 2005, fig. 4.5).

Conclusions: Rural Complexity in the Central Petén Lowlands

In scale, composition, and organization, the site of Akte is dwarfed by both Motul de San José (Foias and Emery, this volume; Foias et al., this volume), and by Motul's principal port, Trinidad de Nosotros (Moriarty, this volume). In the context of these two much larger sites, Akte would clearly be defined as a minor site. However, the presence of certain diagnostic criteria (including monuments, causeway, storage facilities, and high-quality architecture) suggests that Akte participated in the social and economic networks of the region in a variety of ways.

While ongoing research throughout the Maya Lowlands has demonstrated that traditional site hierarchies can rarely encompass the true variety of archaeological settlements, site size hierarchies continue to form the basis for many models of political and economic organization throughout the area. The results of the MSJAP investigations at Akte, as well as the preliminary results of ongoing research at other minor sites in the area (see Moriarty, this volume; Spensley and Garrido Lopez 2008), emphasize the variability among minor sites within the region and suggest the need for alternative models to address this diversity.

Although the use of heterarchical models in Maya archaeology remains in its early stages (see Becker 2004; Brumfiel 1995; Crumley 1995; Iannone and Connell 2003; King and Shaw 2003; Scarborough, Valdez Jr., and Dunning 2003), heterarchical frameworks provide the flexibility required to conceptualize relations between sites diachronically, as they explicitly recognize the likelihood of temporal and spatial variability in economic and sociopolitical relations among sites (Crumley 1995, 4). As King and Shaw note, the use of heterarchical models is most compelling "where the political systems appear to be vertically aligned but other systems do not align" (2003, 67), since they allow for the interaction of ranked and unranked elements.

As with all Maya builders, the architects of the site of Akte utilized a "flexible vocabulary of spatial expression that allowed them to make statements of varying degrees of grandeur and pretension" (Ashmore 1992, 173). Although the form and the function of the site were quite likely shaped by its strategic location, the site layout suggests that the occupants sought to associate themselves with the elites of the regional sociopolitical system. Akte's multiple plaza layout and stelae placement is unique among the small sites in the Motul de San José area. This participation in the regional elite sphere of interaction does not, however, appear to be reflected in the site's artifactual collections, which suggest that Akte had limited access to local trade networks. Thus, we see it more as a frontier settlement that possibly protected the northwestern flanks of the Motul de San José polity through its ability to view movement along the water route of Rio Akte, which through its tributary Rio K'änte't'u'ul connected Motul de San José with the San Pedro Martir drainage (see Figure 1.4).

Since carved monuments functioned fundamentally as commemorations of political authority (Ashmore 1992, 173), the presence of multiple stelae at Akte may reflect local political tensions or the need to reaffirm political power. In a recent review of monuments located outside large sites, Simon Martin suggested that stelae could serve either to emphasize ties to a central authority or to reflect a high degree of local autonomy (2000a, 51). If the Akte stelae are in their original positions, we must consider the possibility that Akte lies outside the Motul de San José polity or on its edge. However, the poor preservation of these monuments impedes us from making final conclusions. Furthermore, the limited scope of the excavations at the site also does not permit more detailed comparative statements.

Akte's site layout is similar to Motul de San José in several respects and may hint to the site's inclusion or participation in the Motul de San José polity at least at some point in time (Yorgey 2005, 110). Nevertheless, further excavations are warranted and worth pursuing in spite of the extensive looting. Additional work currently under way at other minor sites within the Motul zone will provide further comparative information which may allow us to reassess the role of Akte within the region.

Throughout the Maya Lowlands, the exploration of rural complexity has provided a surprising variety of data regarding sophisticated sociopolitical and socioeconomic functions (see, for example, Scarborough, Valdez Jr., and Dunning 2003, Iannone and Connell 2003). Preliminary results of investigations at other minor sites in the Motul de San José area also emphasize differences that are not addressed by site size hierarchies, including significant distinctions in site planning. In combination with the general characteristics of the Motul de San José area, which includes a broad range of sites with divergent developmental patterns in varied microenvironments, the differences in site planning suggest that heterarchical analysis may be particularly valuable in the Motul de San José area to explore multiple and variable economic, political and social connections between pre-Hispanic settlements.

10

Preliminary Investigations in Macro- and Microbotany at Motul de San José

ANDREW R. WYATT, DAVID M. JARZEN, LIZZY HARE,
AND KITTY F. EMERY

From its inception, the Motul de San José Archaeological Project has integrated a systematic regime of archaeobotanical sampling (Emery 2003a). This sampling strategy includes macrobotanical remains (large plant parts identified primarily with the naked eye or through low-power magnification) and microbotanical remains (small plant parts identified through high-power magnification). These complementary data sets require different recovery and analytical techniques, and they are the primary means used by archaeologists to identify economic plant species and their cultivation, distribution, and use.

Reconstructing the distribution of botanical products within households and communities and across the landscape of the Motul de San José polity is intrinsic to understanding the ancient economics of this polity capital—how these materials were acquired, used, and traded by the ancient residents. This chapter details the preliminary archaeobotanical work of the Motul de San José Project, and discusses our research on appropriate field recovery and laboratory extraction methods for both macro- and microbotanical archaeological remains. We emphasize the value of archaeobotanical collection and curation in all archaeological field projects since these remains become a resource for ongoing and future research.

The long-term interests of the Motul de San José Project lie in tracking whether plant resources were acquired locally or through trade; comparing potential agricultural and nonagricultural lands to determine where plants might have been grown, what plants were grown where, and how they were grown; and understanding whether agricultural fields and therefore plant resources were managed by local farmers or distant elites (see also Bair and Terry, this volume; Webb and Schwarcz, this volume). We ultimately aim to situate the productive resources and capacities of Motul de San José within the regional economic system of the central Petén and the Lake Petén Itzá area, and to understand the relationships linking the residents of Motul, both elite and nonelite, to the local economy. Our short-term goals, presented in this chapter, are to understand the benefits and utility of comparative micro- and macrobotanical approaches to evaluating plant remain distributions. We investigate best-practice in archaeobotanical recovery and processing in the Maya lowland context, and discuss the potential for archaeobotanical remains to reveal information important to studies of ancient Maya economics.

The Ecology Subproject of the Motul de San José Archaeology Project included broad sampling of all deposits for archaeobotanical testing, initial analysis, and future considerations (Emery 1998b). Researchers systematically sampled excavations as part of coordinated archaeological and ecological testing so that excavated deposits would have comparable data available for all material types. Wyatt conducted all macrobotanical flotation sampling tests in the field at the campsite of Motul de San José. An initial test of microbotanical remains recovery was conducted in the Paleobotany and Palynology Laboratory of the Florida Museum of Natural History by volunteer Adam Dubbin under the direct supervision and instruction of Jarzen. Subsequent processing was done by Hare at the University of Missouri Paleoethnobotany Laboratory in the summer of 2010 under the supervision of Dr. Deborah Pearsall. All field samples and processed materials are curated by Emery in the collections of the Environmental Archaeology Program at the Florida Museum of Natural History, Gainesville, Florida.

Our initial archaeobotanical work with these samples included experimental recovery of both macro- and microbotanical remains from various deposits across the site of Motul de San José with a focus on comparing several different deposit types and preservational situations. These activities provide a baseline for considering future field recovery strategies and post-field laboratory methods. Our strategy of sample collection from the Motul de San José project has made available a full complement of archaeobotanical samples from all excavations areas, and represents a valuable corpus of materials for later study. Our experiments in field and laboratory recovery also provide important information on best practices to guide later archaeobotanical research in the Motul de San José polity and elsewhere in the Maya area.

Macrobotany

Macroremains include plant fragments that can be identified with the naked eye or with the aid of low-power magnification, although the increasing use of scanning electron microscopy (SEM) has enabled the identification of extremely small and fragmentary remains (Hastorf, Whitehead, and Johannessen 2005). Macrobotanical analysis provides valuable information on diet, agriculture, and the role of plants in ancient economics (e.g., Hastorf and Popper 1988). For example, the ubiquitous but differential archaeological distribution of maize remains in elite and commoner Maya households demonstrate its role as a dietary staple also embedded in politics, economics (Lentz 1999; Turner II and Miksicek 1984), and ritual (Taube 1989, 1985). An increased focus on the rarer archaeological remains of other economically important food crops—such as squash and gourd (*Cucurbitaceae*); beans (*Phaseolus sp.*; Cliff and Crane 1989; Lentz 1991; Miksicek, Wing, and Scudder 1991); fruits (Folan, Fletcher, and Kintz 1979; McKillop 1994); and root crops (Bronson 1966; Hather 1994)—will also reveal differences in use among community members and clarify the role of these in ancient economics.

Macrobotanical assemblages have recently provided a unique perspective on ancient Maya ritual activities, now understood to have been intrinsic to economics, particularly in the Late Classic (Wells 2006). Morehart's (2002) archaeobotanical cave research has focused on the ritual use of various plants, including woods such as pine (*Pinus sp.*), copal (*Protium copal*), and balché (*Lonchocarpus violaceus*), and domesticated crops such as maize, beans, and cacao (*Theobroma cacao*). Lentz and colleagues' (2005) broad study of pine remains recovered at Belize River Valley sites revealed that the regional economic system restricted access to pine to the elite class. Analysis of the distribution of economically valuable tree species at the site of Cobá also concluded that elites had greater access to these important resources (Folan, Fletcher, and Kintz 1979). Studies of archaeobotanical remains clearly can provide a unique insight into economic systems, resource management, and ritual.

However, plant macroremains, due to their fragile structure, can suffer severe degradation over time. Plant remains quickly decay in the tropical environment of the southern Maya lowlands, limiting study, in most cases, to carbonized remains, except in special circumstances such as dry caves, sealed tombs, or wetland environments (Morehart 2002; Turner 1983). The generally shallow soils in the lowland Maya area expose plant remains to the elements and to bioturbators such as tree roots, earthworms, rodents, and especially humans. The activities of bioturbators quickly break down plant remains and mix modern materials with archaeological ones.

Recovery and analysis is further complicated by the fact that some of the most important Maya plants and plant parts are differentially preserved. Maize cobs and kernels, for example, are durable and well represented in macrobotanical assemblages, whereas remains of other economically important plants, such as beans or cacao, are fragile or entirely consumed during use; thus, their importance to the ancient Maya is underrepresented.

Motul de San José Macrobotany Sampling Strategy

During the Motul de San José field excavations, soil samples for macrobotanical testing were taken from all special deposits, occupation surfaces, and middens as revealed by the extensive Motul de San José test-pitting program and general excavation (see Foias et al., this volume), as well as infield soil phosphate testing for organic residue (see Emery 2001). Composite soil samples made up of small amounts of soil taken from the entire excavation locus were taken from all selected contexts. This strategy of "blanket sampling" (Pearsall 2000, 66) from each context assures that the sample represents the entire context. In the first year of excavations, five-liter soil samples were taken from all contexts for macrobotanical analysis; however, in subsequent years the amount of soil was raised to ten liters after flotation recovered scant carbonized remains. Ten-liter soil samples are quite heavy and bulky and are a burden to transport, but the number of charred plant remains recovered in flotation was substantially greater (see below).

Soil samples from most contexts were taken below depths of 20 centimeters from the ground surface to avoid the bioturbation effects of contemporary agricultural practices. The slash-and-burn farming practiced by Maya modern farmers leaves a great deal of charred material on the surface, and manual planting works this material into the top layer of soil, making archaeological material difficult to distinguish from modern material. However, no plows or other mechanical agricultural tools are used in the Motul de San José region, so at depths of 20 centimeters and below carbonized remains are most likely archaeological.

Macrobotanical Processing Methods

Soil samples were collected and placed in plastic mesh bags to dry the soil and facilitate the flotation process. Samples from the first field season were processed using a manual IDOT-style flotation system (Pearsall 2000, 30).

This flotation apparatus is a wooden box measuring 10 inches x 10 inches to a side, 15 inches deep, and covered on the bottom and two sides with 0.011 inch screen. A removable screen on the top collected the heavy fraction.

For the second season we used an SMAP-type flotation system powered with a 5.5 horsepower gasoline powered water pump to draw water from the lake. This system consisted of a fifty-five-gallon plastic barrel fitted at the bottom with a plastic plumbing fixture to regulate the flow of water into the barrel, and perforated PVC tubing inside the barrel that agitated and "frothed" the soil to break up the matrix and release the plant remains. A metal insert in the barrel with a fine 0.011-inch screen collected the heavy fraction, and a metal outflow chute at the top directed the light fraction for collection with a fine 0.002 inch copper mesh.

The SMAP-type system was superior to the IDOT-type system in most respects. The mechanical agitation and frothing action provided by the water pump separated more plant remains from the soil matrix, particularly in the more clayey soils. We were also able to process the larger ten-liter soil samples, which would not have been possible with the hand-operated IDOT-type system. However, cleaning the SMAP-type system was much more difficult, requiring that we empty, clean, and refill the barrel every five to seven soil samples. In a circumstance without easy water access, we would have had to modify the flotation system to recycle water.

Macrobotanical Identification and Quantification

Although complete analysis of the macrobotanical remains is pending, a total of 190 macrobotanical samples were taken and 75 percent were found to contain carbonized remains, with amounts ranging from many small carbon flecks to large pieces of carbon. Many of these carbon-laden samples also contained significant quantities of ceramics, lithic debitage, obsidian fragments, bone, and shell. Preliminary analysis indicates that the larger soil samples collected in the second year were more effective for recovering carbon (an average of 0.052 grams of carbon in the larger samples from the second year, as compared with 0.037 grams in samples from the first year).

Initial identification of the macrobotanical remains was conducted by Hare (supervised by Wyatt) in the Paleobotany (Jarzen) and Environmental Archaeology (Emery) laboratories of the Florida Museum of Natural History. This preliminary study concentrated on fifty-nine samples from economically important contexts such as the proposed Plaza II marketplace (see Bair and Terry, this volume) and household middens (see Tables 10.1–10.4 for details).

Table 10.1. Distribution of plant taxa found in Motul de San José botanical samples recovered in and near Plaza II (30 samples)

Taxa	Macrobot		Microbot		Both	
	N	%	N	%	N	%
Poaceae	0	0.00	143	67.77	143	51.62
Aracaceae	7	10.61	0	0.00	7	2.53
Hardwood	51	77.27	0	0.00	51	18.41
Asteraceae	0	0.00	44	20.85	44	15.88
Pinus sp.	8	12.12	0	0.00	8	2.89
Heliconia sp.	0	0.00	10	4.74	10	3.61
Zea mays	0	0.00	9	4.27	9	3.25
Annonaceae	0	0.00	2	0.95	2	0.72
Musa sp. (leaf)	0	0.00	2	0.95	2	0.72
Cucurbita pepo	0	0.00	1	0.47	1	0.36
Totals	**66**		**211**		**277**	

Table 10.2. Distribution of plant taxa found in Motul de San José botanical samples recovered from household middens (37 samples)

Taxa	Macrobot		Microbot		Both	
	N	%	N	%	N	%
Poaceae	0	0.00	5	12.20	5	3.55
Aracaceae	80	80.00	0	0.00	80	56.74
Hardwood	0	0.00	0	0.00	0	0.00
Asteraceae	0	0.00	35	85.37	35	24.82
Pinus sp.	18	18.00	0	0.00	18	12.77
Heliconia sp.	0	0.00	1	2.44	1	0.71
Zea mays	2	2.00	0	0.00	2	1.42
Annonaceae	0	0.00	0	0.00	0	0.00
Musa sp. (leaf)	0	0.00	0	0.00	0	0.00
Cucurbita pepo	0	0.00	0	0.00	0	0.00
Totals	**100**		**41**		**141**	

Ten of the samples studied contained carbonized plant remains that could be confidently classified as archaeological based on the presence of pine, which does not grow locally at the site now, and almost certainly did not during the time of the site's occupation. This verifies the utility of sampling below 20 centimeters depth to avoid modern contaminants where possible.

To date, thirty-two samples have recovered identifiable remains. Seven plant taxa have been identified, including general hardwoods, pine wood,

Table 10.3. Distribution of plant taxa found in Motul de San José botanical samples recovered from transects (15 samples)

Taxa	Macrobot N	Macrobot %	Microbot N	Microbot %	Both N	Both %
Poaceae	0	0.00	69	86.25	69	56.10
Aracaceae	3	6.98	0	0.00	3	2.44
Hardwood	35	81.40	0	0.00	35	28.46
Asteraceae	0	0.00	6	7.50	6	4.88
Pinus sp.	3	6.98	0	0.00	3	2.44
Heliconia sp.	0	0.00	4	5.00	4	3.25
Zea mays	2	4.65	1	1.25	3	2.44
Annonaceae	0	0.00	0	0.00	0	0.00
Musa sp. (leaf)	0	0.00	0	0.00	0	0.00
Cucurbita pepo	0	0.00	0	0.00	0	0.00
Totals	**43**		**80**		**123**	

Table 10.4. Total distribution of plant taxa found in Motul de San José botanical samples (82 samples)

Taxa	Macrobot N	Macrobot %	Microbot N	Microbot %	Both N	Both %
Poaceae	0	0.00	217	65.36	217	40.11
Aracaceae	90	43.06	0	0.00	90	16.64
Hardwood	86	41.15	0	0.00	86	15.90
Asteraceae	0	0.00	85	25.60	85	15.71
Pinus sp.	29	13.88	0	0.00	29	5.36
Heliconia sp.	0	0.00	15	4.52	15	2.77
Zea mays	4	1.91	10	3.01	14	2.59
Annonaceae	0	0.00	2	0.60	2	0.37
Musa sp. (leaf)	0	0.00	2	0.60	2	0.37
Cucurbita pepo	0	0.00	1	0.30	1	0.18
Totals	**209**		**332**		**541**	

palm (*Aracaceae*), and maize. Seeds from the *Fabaceae* (legume family), *Vitaceae* (grape family), and *Chenopodiaceae* (goosefoot family—includes the cultivated chia and several weedy taxa) families were recovered, but were uncarbonized, indicating the presence of modern intrusions in some of the macrobotanical samples. The diversity of plant species recovered in the macrobotanical samples is low, most likely as a result of poor preservation. The primary taxa, not surprisingly, represent the robust hardwoods, which are relatively resistant to postdepositional degradation; however, these hardwood fragments were too small to identify more specifically.

Of particular importance to our understanding of economics at Motul de San José is the recovery of pine remains in ten of the samples. Because pine would not have been locally grown, its presence likely indicates long-distance acquisition or trade. Pine may have been present in the poor, acidic soils of the savannas south of Lake Petén Itzá near present-day Poptún approximately 35 kilometers away, although an even more distant source in the highlands or in the Maya Mountains of Belize cannot be ruled out. The presence of hardwoods in nearly half (n = 27) of the macrobotanical samples analyzed may suggest that the residents of Motul de San José had access to forested areas, although the very small size of the remains is suggestive of smaller trees, possibly secondary and disturbance species.

An initial and cursory analysis of several flotation samples from the site of La Trinidad de Nosotros (Trinidad) provides comparative evidence of the valuable data that can be recovered from the Motul de San José area. Samples from a midden behind the Trinidad ball court representing a potential feasting event (see Moriarty, this volume, and Thornton, this volume) were informally sorted, revealing abundant economic species, including pine, maize, and the much more rare finding of chile pepper (*Capsicum annuum*). Although the Trinidad samples await formal study, these samples indicate that preservation in sites throughout the Motul de San José polity allows for the recovery of numerous plant remains with important economic implications.

Microbotany

Microbotanical remains, defined as those that must be viewed through a microscope, include pollen and spores, phytoliths, starch grains, and other residues (e.g., small plant cell parts, calcium oxalate crystals, and diatoms). Pollen and spores, plant reproductive cells, are taxonomically distinct, often identifiable to the genus and sometimes to the species level. If well preserved and carefully interpreted with an eye to plant biology, pollen can reveal plant use patterns in and between communities (Traverse 2007). Phytoliths are inorganic deposits that form from groundwater silica in the cell walls and interstitial spaces of all plant tissues (Piperno 2006). These can be differentiated between plant taxa, plant individuals growing under different environmental conditions, and plant parts, and so provide a wealth of information about habitats, agricultural practices, and various plant uses (for tropical examples, see various case studies in Hather 1994). Over the past decades, there has been a rapid increase in the study of these materials and experimental work to improve methods for their recovery, processing, and analysis (Lentfer and Boyd 1998; Pearsall 2000; Powers and Gilbertson 1987).

As with macrobotanicals, microbotanicals are affected by preservation processes. Pollen grains and spores, composed of the durable sporopollenin, and phytoliths, composed of silica, can be subject to chemical and physical degradation (Piperno 2006). They are subject to disturbance by bioturbators and modern activities, are differentially preserved among taxa, and can be highly variable in rate of production and extent of dispersion. Pollen from maize and from trees in the Moraceae family (including the disturbance species *Brosimum alicastrum* or *ramón*) are produced in abundance and are widely dispersed, whereas cacao and many high-canopy tree species produce little pollen or their dispersal is highly local (for further discussion of Moraceae and its effects on interpretations of the ancient Maya forest, see Ford and Nigh 2009).

The Motul de San José Project has been particularly interested in the use of microbotanical remains in reconstructing resource economics at several levels. At the household level, microbotanicals can provide information on where plants were used, prepared, eaten, and stored. This is the case even in the absence of macrobotanical evidence because the microfossils can be preserved in the plaster and dirt of floors where macrofossils are exceedingly rare (Manzanilla and Barba 1990). Middens are often too shallow or exposed to allow for the preservation of macrobotanical remains, but microbotanicals from middens could potentially reveal differences in the use of plants between community groups (families, occupational groups, status groups).

Microbotanical Field Sampling Strategy

Soil samples for microbotanical specimen recovery were collected using standardized methods in all appropriate deposits including transects, middens, and occupation surfaces (Emery 1998a, 1998b). Two one-hundred-milliliter samples were taken at 50-meter intervals along all transects and across the center of the site core. Samples were drawn with a cleaned LaMotte soil corer from a depth of approximately 20 centimeters below surface and were deposited immediately into Whirlpak bags and labeled with transect sample number, map location, excavator/collector, and collection date.

All settlement deposits defined as middens (by location or accumulation of artifactual materials or soil characteristics indicative of high organic content) were sampled from clean scraped surfaces from each cultural level below the humus, taking great care to avoid contamination from upper or adjacent levels. Sample size was a minimum of one hundred milliliters of unscreened soil. All occupation surfaces with well-preserved stucco (plaster) including room floors, terrace surfaces, bench surfaces, plazas, and the like, were also sampled. A soil corer fitted with a plastic collection tube was used to collect samples across the entire surface at 25-centimeter intervals. Cores were taken to the known base of the plaster floor to avoid mixing with earlier floor surfaces.

Microbotanical Laboratory Methodology

The Motul de San José microbotanical studies have included two preliminary tests of preservation and laboratory processing methods. Our first study, designed and supervised by Jarzen (for the palynological laboratory techniques) and Emery (for the sample selection and preparation and archaeological guidance), was carried out by Dubbin under Jarzen's supervision. Various sample types were included to allow us to evaluate the specific problems presented by highly calcareous soils (Fredlund 1986), particularly in occupation surface plasters, and in the clay soils so typical of the lowland Maya area (Lentfer and Boyd 1999). These included: (1) soils from an area of potential agricultural activity in the outlying area of the site, (2) midden soils from close to an elite household, and (3) plaster from the floor of a palace located in the main Acropolis of the site. Samples were chosen from areas with elevated phosphate levels, locations where organic remains would most likely be recovered (see Bair and Terry, this volume; Emery 1998a; Jensen, Johnson, and Terry 2001; Jensen et al. 2003).

To assure maximum conservation of the microfossils (Coil et al. 2003; Lentfer and Boyd 2000), the laboratory procedure employed both a palynological (digestion, oxidation, acetylation, and sieving) and a hybridized phytolith procedure involving heavy liquid separation (for a detailed description, see Hare and colleagues, forthcoming). Standard palynological methods as outlined by Jarzen (2006) were used. However, the standard use of hydrofluoric acid (HF) following the HCl treatment was omitted to avoid destruction of silica based microfossils, such as phytoliths. Additionally two tests of heavy liquid separation were done, one with sodium polytungstate and the other with zinc iodide (Madella, Powers-Jones, and

Jones 1998; Six et al. 1999), to test the utility of these in combined separation of light (biogenic) fraction from the heavy (inorganic) materials. The results were similar, but zinc iodide, although recyclable, is very expensive and should be prepared fresh for each use. After most steps, samples were visually inspected for microfossil presence or degradation to evaluate the process and keep sample destruction to a minimum. If at any point along the staged processing path the samples appeared to have lost microfossils, the processing was stopped and the point at which the procedures required modification was determined.

Our second microbotanical test was done by Hare in 2010. Soil samples were processed in the University of Missouri Paleoethnobotany Laboratory[1] following their Soil Processing Procedure (Pearsall and Duncan 2005). More detailed descriptions of the full methods can be found in Hare and colleagues (forthcoming). Some procedure modifications were made under the guidance of Dr. Deborah Pearsall and PhD candidate Neil Duncan because of the high concentration of carbonate, organic, and clay materials in the soil samples. To produce the best possible extraction of phytoliths, this study did not include simultaneous processing for pollen. As in the first microbotanical test, samples were selected from plaster floors, archaeological transects, and the proposed marketplace area in Plaza II.

The most important modification to the standard procedures was the use of larger, two-hundred-milliliter Nalgene bottles as opposed to fifty-milliliter centrifuge tubes. This allowed space for the strong reactions of the highly carbonate and organic samples to the processing chemicals. Many reactions, such as with the dilute acid, the strong acid, and organic removal, were repeated several times to completely remove carbonate and organic matter that would otherwise have interfered with the extraction and identification of phytoliths. Highly organic samples benefited from the use of both standard organic removal, using hydrogen peroxide, and removal using twenty milliliters of Schultze's solution (twenty grams KCl dissolved in 150 milliliters of nitric acid on a warming plate) following addition of twenty milliliters of nitric acid. Color changes indicated organic matter breakdown, following which samples were rinsed with distilled H_2O and centrifuged, and then returned to the step of organic removal using hydrogen peroxide. It is recommended that the samples alternate between hydrogen peroxide and Schultze's solution to achieve the most complete removal of organic material.

In samples with high clay contents, the additional step of sedimentation facilitated complete removal of clays, as rinsing and centrifuging with

Alconox™ was insufficient and impeded the heavy liquid flotation process. Lithium metatungstate, standard in the University of Missouri Paleoethno-botany Lab, was used for heavy liquid floatation as it is relatively inexpensive and less toxic than the alternatives.

Microbotanical Identification and Quantification

Preliminary Test of Processing Methods

Soils for our preliminary microbotanical test of preservation and processing techniques (see Hare et al., forthcoming) were selected on the basis of sample type and evidence for elevated phosphate levels, an indication of organic materials. Samples from the first microbotanical test of plaster floors from Operation MSJ 2A, a residential range structure in Court 4 of the Main Acropolis (in Group C) and part of the royal court during the Late Classic (Foias et al., this volume; Halperin and Foias, this volume) indicated the presence of many categories of microfossils: pollen, spores, charcoal, and phytoliths. Samples from middens were highly variable with some very limited in organic inclusions (for example, the samples from unit MSJ 10D-20, behind the west structure of elite Late Classic Group 7J4), and some very organic with humic inclusions that may indicate contamination from surface plants (such as those from unit MSJ 8F-7 at the corner of west and north structures of Group 7J2 within major Group A). Even midden soils with low organics suggested by phosphates included pollen, spores, charcoal, and possible parasite ova. Soils from transects were highly organic and composed primarily of clay with high moisture content and both organic and pebble inclusions. These required drying and physical processing and were often poorly revealed because of the difficulty in breaking down soil constituents in these samples. Those that could be viewed contained high quantities of biogenics including pollen, spores, phytoliths, and insect and plant parts.

Overall, in six of the subsamples analyzed from three archaeological matrix types, the experimental combined procedures successfully isolated large quantities of both pollen and spores, including some fungal spores and mycelia (or vegetative part of a fungus), as well as silica structures that are most likely phytoliths (final identification awaits study with appropriate comparative materials). The samples also included other microscopic plant remains such as helical thickenings, sieve plates, charcoal, and wood chips.

Unfortunately, the experimental methods attempted here did not yield completely unobscured samples, making it difficult to quantify the relative proportions of the microfossils. This is in part because soils from middens and transects include highly bonded clays that involve very complex soil chemistry that requires further evaluation. Soils from plaster floors also present a very different set of challenges inasmuch as the plaster is formed of limestone calcium. The high variation in miscellaneous debris inclusions (plant tissue, insect parts, etc.) between subsamples from each soil sample is also problematic because this variation tends to obscure any actual differences between the samples.

Test of Phytolith Preservation and Processing

The second test of phytolith recovery (by Hare) found that processing for phytoliths alone did indeed result in much less obstructed slides, with visible organic matter absent from most slide. Twenty-four samples were processed for phytolith extraction including twelve from the Plaza II area, a potential marketplace (see Bair and Terry, this volume); six from transects; and six from household middens (see Tables 10.1–10.4 for details).

Samples from the Plaza II area included the highest proportion of phytoliths that were not eroded and could be identified. Eighteen percent of the Plaza II sample phytoliths could be identified, versus 9 percent from the transect samples and 5 percent from midden samples. Unfortunately, relatively few identifiable phytoliths were recovered overall, with the plaza area averaging eighteen identifiable phytoliths per slide and the midden samples averaging only three identifiable phytoliths per slide. Midden samples that contained large amounts of carbonate material, such as a plaster floor mixed with midden, were particularly low in phytoliths, with one sample only containing twenty-four phytoliths, none of which could be identified. This may be due to the physical degradation that occurs in these carbonate matrices.

Phytoliths identified from all three contexts included members of the Poaceae (grasses), Asteraceae (daisy family), Musaceae (banana family), Annonaceae (custard apple family), and Cucurbitaceae families. All of these families contain plants economically important to the ancient Maya, including maize (Poaceae), sunflowers (Asteraceae), cherimoya (*Annona cherimola*), guanabana (*A. muricata*), custard apple (*A. squamosa*), and squash and gourds (Cucurbitaceae). Phytoliths representing common domesticates (maize and squash) were found in six of the twenty-four samples, and of these, five were from the Plaza II area, with one sample from the transect. Squash, Annonaceae, and Musaceae were found exclusively in the Plaza II area, and disturbance taxa Poaceae and Asteraceae were fairly ubiquitous across samples.

A greater diversity of taxa were found in the Plaza II area samples (seven taxa) than in the transect samples (four), and the least diverse samples were from the household middens (three). The relative abundance and diversity of phytoliths in Plaza II may, however, suggest some recent (postcontact) agricultural or trash deposition activity in the plaza area, since this is also where the Musaceae (which were introduced to Mesoamerica from the Old World) were found.

Processing for phytoliths alone is highly recommended, and is worth the extra expense and time. In the Maya lowlands area, archaeological sediments are too rich in carbonates, clays, and organic material to result in clear and easily analyzed slides when processed using a multiple-recovery procedure. Since processing for phytoliths requires the use of only ten grams of soil, separate processing of pollen and phytoliths in the laboratory should not require any modifications to the field collection procedures. As phytolith researchers continue to develop comparative collections, more specific and confident identifications will be possible.

Conclusions

In summary, a total of eighty-three archaeobotanical samples have been analyzed to date, yielding twelve taxonomic identifications, with only one species overlapping between the macrobotanical and microbotanical remains. By including both data sets, we have doubled our number of identifiable taxa from the site, which highlights the differential preservation of microbotanical remains and macrobotanical remains, especially when nonorganic microbotanical materials (such as phytoliths) are considered. Of the taxa identified from Motul de San José, four taxa are almost certainly modern intrusions (Chenopodiaceae, Fabaceae, Vitaceae, Musaceae), whereas two are certainly domesticates (maize and squash). Pine is clearly an imported product, indicating an affiliation with long-distance trade networks. The ubiquity of taxa that favor disturbed or secondary-growth habitats, along with the small size of many of the hardwood fragments, may suggest a landscape that included highly managed forests and/or the use of resources from fields in advanced stages of fallow (Ford 2008).

Recommendations for Maya Archaeobotany

On the basis of our work at the Motul de San José sites, we offer the following recommendations for archaeobotanical sample collection and research in the Maya area and elsewhere.

Research Design: Archaeologists must consider the utility of all archaeo-botanical materials with as much care as they do other material remains. These finds are valuable and irreplaceable once excavation is complete. Archaeological projects should include consultation with an archaeobotanist from the planning stages, and consider archaeobotanical sampling, preparation, storage, and eventual identification and analysis of the materials as part of the research design of the project.

Recovery Methods: Archaeobotanical and other paleoenvironmental materials can easily be recovered and sampled as part of routine fieldwork, with very little added cost or personnel time. One important consideration is the addition of data on sediment type, grain size (standard geological charts), color (Munsell), and biogenic structures (tissue, seeds, fragments, animal parts). Recording pH is useful because the variable pH of lowland Petén soils (Beach et al. 2003) affects potential recovery. Pollen and spores are best preserved in slightly acidic soils, in soils with pH greater than 6.0, recovery may be low and palynomorphs degraded (Dimbleby 1957). Phytoliths are vulnerable to highly alkaline soils (Piperno 2006).

Sample size is also important. Most microbotanical sample preparations require only twenty-five to thirty grams of sediment, although the actual need depends on the type of sediment. A dark, rich, well-compacted soil sample will require less material for testing than a loosely consolidated, lighter colored, sandier soil. Most microbotanists overcollect to allow for reprocessing if necessary or future analyses as techniques change. For macrobotanical sampling, samples of at least ten liters ensure recovery of fragmentary plant remains in open contexts.

Curation and Bulk Processing: The storage of archaeobotanical samples should not be considered a barrier to archaeobotanical collection for later research. Soil and sediment samples for later micro- and macrobotanical processing are compromised by the growth of fungus, which contaminates the ancient materials. A recommended method is to dry the samples at low temperatures in a lab or in a sheltered area with shade and minimal air movement to reduce contamination or sudden drying that shatters carbonized samples. Samples must be thoroughly dry before storing to prevent mold growth (several days). Light and dry fractions must be packaged separately.

Microbotanical laboratory processing reduces the sediment samples to a set of slides and residues. Residues of processed materials can be stored in one-dram vials (or similar storage vessels) for later restudy. It is worthwhile to process a few samples from each sediment/soil/context type early in a field project, to determine whether the samples are likely to be palynomorph-rich or not, and which contexts are most suitable for further research.

Many archaeological projects in the Maya lowlands have limited funding and time to reach their stated goals. Deciding which of many investigative procedures are appropriate is difficult and archaeobotanical analysis is often set aside in favor of more established studies. Archaeologists should think as carefully about discarding archaeobotanically laden soils during excavation as they would about discarding ceramics simply because they had no project ceramicist to look at them or funds to immediately complete their analysis. However, we suggest that archaeobotanical sampling, well integrated with traditional excavation regimes, can provide valuable information on the role of plants in ancient subsistence, economic, political, and ritual life. These remains are easily gathered and can be curated with very little effort until funds allow their processing and analysis. They are only available in context at the time of excavation and it is therefore imperative that standard excavation methods include their recovery regardless of whether funds are available for their immediate analysis.

11

The Motul de San José Animals in an Economic Perspective

Within any society there is no doubt that higher-ranked community members have preferential access to higher-valued animal resources. This cross-cultural standard has been fundamental to most interpretations of animal use by elite and nonelite residents of ancient Maya sites. The Maya elite are presumed to have had more meat, more highly valued animal species, higher-quality meat cuts, and a greater diversity of animals from both local and exotic sources (Masson 1999, 2008; Pohl 1985a, 1985b, 1994). In some studies evidence has been found to support these suggestions, but in others, the evidence has suggested a more complicated picture that involves animal use as food, medicine, tool, adornment, and ritual actor by different community members with different goals (Emery 2002). The Motul de San José faunal assemblage allows us to explore this more complex relationship between rank, wealth, and access to animal resources from a single site as it varied over time.

In this analysis of animal remains from the site of Motul de San José, capital center of the Motul de San José polity, I review the distribution of faunal remains, taxa, and crafting products among residences of different time periods and ranks. I attempt to provide a history of animal use by residents of the site and periphery, and to define how, by whom, and where animals were acquired, prepared, consumed, and discarded. This unraveling of the exchange network allows us to evaluate political and social relationships within the community and between this capital and its satellite centers.

Methods

This chapter presents the analysis of animal remains from Motul de San José, capital of the Motul de San José polity, and the area of most intense archaeological and ecological research during the first phase of the Motul de San José Archaeological Project (MSJAP), directed by Foias and Emery. For the purposes of this study of the economics and politics of animal use, I also include small assemblages excavated from the small satellite center of Chäkokot a few kilometers east of the Motul de San José site core along the Motul de San José Eastern Transect, and possibly a rural outlier closely allied to the main capital site. Animal remains were recovered from all excavations, those from occupation surfaces and middens using one-quarter-inch screens, and those from special deposits using either flotation (one-sixteenth-inch heavy fraction screen) or fine gauge screen sampling (nested quarter-, eighth-, and sixteenth-inch screens). All chronological, spatial, functional, and status rankings used in this analysis have been provided by Foias (Foias and Emery, this volume; Foias et al., this volume).

All Motul de San José animal remains were identified using the Florida Museum of Natural History Environmental Archaeology Program comparative collections, either by me or under my supervision (by UF/FLMNH students Erin Thornton, Lisa Tromley, and the 2004 Environmental Archaeology class). Standard methods of identification and analyses were used for all assemblages (e.g., Reitz and Wing 2008), and are described in detail elsewhere (Emery 1998a, 2003a). Taxonomic nomenclature follows ITIS.gov (www.itis.gov) and the FLMNH Invertebrate Zoology Database (www.flmnh.ufl.edu/scripts/dbs/malacol_pub.asp, last accessed December 2009). The assemblage includes unmodified remains and artifacts of both vertebrates and invertebrates. All calculations are based on number of identified specimens (NISP).[1]

Results

Distribution of Animal Remains

The animal remains examined in this analysis were recovered from several site areas (Table 11.1). Nineteen groups in the site center provided most of the animal remains (NISP = 3658, 92 percent). Smaller samples were collected from seven groups in the northern zone (NISP = 178, 4 percent—a region slightly less densely populated but contiguous with the center), two groups and two chultunes in the eastern zone (NISP = 82, 2 percent—a lightly populated area separated by low-lying terrain from the site center and northern zone), and seven groups from the neighboring hamlet of Chäkokot (NISP = 72, 2 percent).

Table 11.1. Spatial distribution of animal remains as %NISP of total assemblage and density per unit of excavated soil

Site area	Rank	Operation	NISP	As % of total site NISP	Density
Site center	1	3	1	0.03	1
Site center	1	4	6	0.15	1.5
Site center	1	2	1,365	34.21	20.07
Site center	1	15	1,775	44.49	8.32
Site center	1	8,9	2	0.05	0.05
Subtotal rank 1		**N = 5**	**3,149**	**78.92**	**6.19**
Site center	2 (Large)	46	90	2.26	2.5
Site center	2 (Medium)	10	23	0.58	1.7
Site center	2 (Medium)	1	19	0.48	6.33
Site center	2 (Medium)	32	24	0.6	1.63
Site center	2 (Medium)	33	10	0.25	0.83
Site center	2 (Medium)	34	81	2.03	18
Site center	2 (Medium)	29	115	2.88	2.74
Site center	2 (Medium)	30	17	0.43	2.19
Site center	2 (Medium)	7	23	0.58	5.75
Site center	2 (Medium)	20,22	8	0.2	0.4
Subtotal rank 2		**N = 10**	**410**	**10.28**	**4.21**
Site center	3	13,16	44	1.1	3.2
Site center	3	17	31	0.78	2.07
Site center	3	18	2	0.05	0.47
Site center	3	19	22	0.55	3.03
Subtotal rank 3		**N = 4**	**99**	**2.48**	**8.77**
Total site center		**N = 22**	**3,658**	**91.68**	**19.17**
North zone	2 (Large)	35	10	0.25	0.77
North zone	2 (Large)	26	4	0.1	0.53
North zone	2 (Large)	39	73	1.83	7.12
North zone	2 (Large)	43	8	0.2	0.6
Subtotal rank 2		**N = 4**	**95**	**2.38**	**2.26**
North zone	3	31	15	0.38	0.54
North zone	3	23	2	0.05	0.1
North zone	3	42	66	1.65	5.74
Subtotal rank 3		**N = 3**	**83**	**2.08**	**2.12**
Total north zone		**N = 7**	**178**	**4.46**	**4.38**
East zone	3	41B	2	0.05	2
East zone	3	41G	1	0.03	1
East chultun	3	37B	78	1.95	6.5
East chultun	3	37A	1	0.03	0.08
Subtotal rank 3, total east zone		**N = 4**	**82**	**2.06**	**2.4**
East transect, Chäkokot	3	44C	1	0.03	1
East transect, Chäkokot	3	44D	44	1.1	44

(*continued*)

Table 11.1. (*Continued*)

Site area	Rank	Operation	NISP	As % of total site NISP	Density
East transect, Chäkokot	3	44E	2	0.05	2
East transect, Chäkokot	3	44G	1	0.03	1
East transect, Chäkokot	3	44H	12	0.3	12
East transect, Chäkokot	3	44I	8	0.2	8
East transect, Chäkokot	3	44J	4	0.1	4
Subtotal rank 3, total east transect		**N = 7**	**72**	**1.8**	**10.29**
COUNT OF RANKED GROUPS					
Total rank 1		N = 5	3,149	78.92	6.19
Subtotal rank 2 large		N = 5	185	4.64	2.31
Subtotal rank 2 medium		N = 10	320	8.02	4.4
Total rank 2		N = 15	505	12.66	6.7
Total rank 3		N = 18	336	8.42	5.37
Site totals and averages[a]		N = 38	3,990	100	6.09

[a] NISP and %NISP represent sums, density represents average.

Although the proportions of remains are quite different across the site area, the density of remains relative to volume of excavated soil varies much less. The remains from the site center were the most densely distributed (nineteen remains per square meter of excavated soil), but the variation in density of remains in these deposits was also high—ranging from 0.05 to greater than twenty remains per unit of excavated soil in the high-density middens of the acropolis (Operation 2). In fact, only two deposits in the site center contained greater densities of remains than those found in the eastern periphery site of Chäkokot (ten remains per square meter), and only six deposits had densities greater than those found in the northern zone (four remains per square meter).

Most of the remains were recovered from five Rank 1 or high-elite residential and ritual groups containing 79 percent of the site NISP.[2] Only two of these can be immediately defined as nonresidential deposits, including a stela cache excavated in the front of the twin temples (Operations 3/4) and the looted tomb of a Late Classic site ruler in the temple of Group D (Operation 15F). Other deposits might represent the remains of feasting or other ritual activities, but they are found within residential contexts and are considered residential in this analysis. The remainder is from residential deposits including occupational surfaces, middens, and fill. These are all located in the site center and the majority of the remains are from the Acropolis palace or Operation 2 and the Group D palace or Operation 15A-E (79 percent of site NISP). Another large proportion of the remains came from Rank 2 or middle-status groups (fifteen groups, 13 percent of site NISP). Finally, a small proportion of the remains were recovered from Rank 3 or commoner deposits (eighteen groups, 8 percent of site NISP). Despite the variation in relative proportion of remains, the absolute density of animal remains between rank groups was again similar (average Rank 1 density was six per square meter, Rank 2 density was seven per square meter, Rank 3 density was five per square meter).

Animal remains were recovered from most periods of site occupation, in proportions relative to the extent of residency during these periods (see Foias and Emery, this volume, for more detail on the chronology of the site). Most of the remains were found in deposits from the Late Classic, the period of greatest population and political power of the polity. A still appreciable number of remains were found in Terminal Classic deposits when the site was still active though less politically dominant in the region. Smaller numbers of remains were found in Preclassic and Postclassic deposits.

We find high variability in proportion of animal remains across site areas, ranks, and periods but similarity in overall density of remains. This indicates that variation in proportions between the assemblages from different groups represent differences in excavation volume. Therefore, NISP proportions (percent) within each assemblage act as effective comparative values between assemblages. This finding also indicates that the differences in proportion of remains across the Motul de San José site and peripheries are the result of variable excavation volume and not, as has been suggested elsewhere (Moholy-Nagy 1994; Teeter 2004), that the actual availability or use of animal resources was significantly less in more peripheral site areas or in site areas with lower-status residential groups.

Taxonomy of the Motul de San José Animal Remains

Overall: In this section I begin with an overview of the animal groups or taxa that were recovered during excavations of Motul de San José and its periphery (Table 11.2). All scientific names are given in the tables. Ranked in order of frequency in the archaeological record, the favored Motul animal species included the white-tailed deer, the two freshwater gastropods jute and apple snail, the large river clam, and the Central American river turtle. Mammals (58.42 percent) and mollusks (19.47 percent) dominate the sample. Only 4 percent of the mollusks are marine, the majority being freshwater species from either the nearby rivers (jute and river clam) or slower-moving waters, lakes, and aguadas (apple snail). Smaller proportions of other animals were recovered, including reptiles (7.49 percent, predominantly turtles at 5.16 percent, but also including crocodiles, lizards, and snakes); birds (0.82 percent including galliforms such as quail, turkey, and chachalaca, 0.31 percent in total, and perching songbirds); fish (0.46 percent); and amphibians (0.08 percent). The white-tailed deer is clearly the favorite mammal, but dogs, armadillos, brocket deer, rabbits, peccaries, cats, agoutis, and pacas were also fairly common. Opossums, tamandua, gray fox, pocket gopher, and squirrels were all found in smaller quantities.[3] Bats and very small rodents were likely intrusive elements.

Distributions by Rank: It is clear that these species would have been available to the different residents of the Motul de San José site in different proportions because some were considered favorites, better food species, important ritual species, and the like (Tables 11.3 and 11.4). I explore the proportions of these groups in each of the three ranked subsections of the Motul de San José community.

White-tailed deer and Central American river turtle are considered by the San José residents today to be the highest-status foods and are the most common species in elite deposits at most Maya sites (Emery 2007a). Other Maya favorites include large-bodied species such as peccary, brocket deer, the larger tapir,[4] and the large galliform birds.

Whitetails are very common in Rank 1 deposits, particularly when considered as a subset of all the remains identified only as artiodactyl (79 percent). The proportion of white-tailed deer in Rank 2 deposits is considerably smaller (2 percent or 48 percent of all artiodactyls). Surprisingly the proportion of white-tailed deer in Rank 3 deposits was also very high (6 percent or 91 percent of all artiodactyls). This suggests that the abundance of these favored species is either not correlated to rank or is correlated at both the level of acquisition and eventual consumption (Rank 3 hunters, for example, may have acquired and butchered deer, providing prepared portions to Rank 1 elite). In contrast, Rank 2 deposits have higher proportions of large mammals than do either Rank 1 or Rank 3 deposits,

Table 11.2. Chronological distribution of the Motul de San José archaeological animals

Taxon	Common name	Preclassic		Late Classic		Terminal Classic		Postclassic		Undated		Total	
		NISP	%	NISP	%	NISP	%	NISP	%	NISP	%	NISP	%
Mollusca	Mollusks	0	0.00	5	0.19	0	0.00	0	0.00	1	0.39	6	0.15
Mollusca, marine	Marine mollusks	0	0.00	12	0.45	29	4.76	0	0.00	0	0.00	41	1.03
Gastropoda, marine	Marine gastropods	1	0.83	14	0.52	3	0.49	1	0.31	0	0.00	19	0.48
Olividae	Olive	1	0.83	1	0.04	0	0.00	0	0.00	0	0.00	2	0.05
Oliva sayana	Lettered olive	1	0.83	2	0.07	2	0.33	0	0.00	1	0.39	6	0.15
Olivella perplexa	Dwarf olive	0	0.00	11	0.41	1	0.16	0	0.00	0	0.00	12	0.30
Olivella/prunum	Dwarf olive/prunum	0	0.00	11	0.41	0	0.00	0	0.00	0	0.00	11	0.28
Prunum apicinum	Common Atlantic marginella	0	0.00	1	0.04	12	1.97	0	0.00	1	0.39	14	0.35
Jenneria pustulata	Jenner's pustulate cowry	0	0.00	1	0.04	0	0.00	0	0.00	0	0.00	1	0.03
Strombidae	Conchs	0	0.00	50	1.86	3	0.49	0	0.00	1	0.39	54	1.35
Strombus alatus	Florida fighting conch	0	0.00	1	0.04	0	0.00	0	0.00	0	0.00	1	0.03
Strombus gigas/costatus	Queen/milk conch	0	0.00	0	0.00	1	0.16	0	0.00	0	0.00	1	0.03
Dentaliidae	Tusk shell	2	1.65	0	0.00	0	0.00	0	0.00	0	0.00	2	0.05
Pachychilus glaphyrus	"Spiny" jute	0	0.00	5	0.19	0	0.00	0	0.00	1	0.39	6	0.15
Pachychilus indiorum	"Smooth" jute	1	0.83	33	1.23	9	1.48	109	33.96	17	6.69	169	4.24
Pomacea flagellata	Apple snail	58	47.93	92	3.43	33	5.42	55	17.13	15	5.91	253	6.34
Spondylus	Thorny oysters	0	0.00	7	0.26	0	0.00	0	0.00	0	0.00	7	0.18
Unionidae	River clams	1	0.83	4	0.15	0	0.00	0	0.00	0	0.00	5	0.13
Psoronaias	River clam	0	0.00	142	5.29	18	2.96	1	0.31	6	2.36	167	4.19

(continued)

Table 11.2. (Continued)

Taxon	Common name	Preclassic		Late Classic		Terminal Classic		Postclassic		Undated		Total	
		NISP	%	NISP	%	NISP	%	NISP	%	NISP	%	NISP	%
Vertebrata	Vertebrates	4	3.31	360	13.41	101	16.58	14	4.36	13	5.12	492	12.33
Rajiformes/ myliobatiformes	Ray	0	0.00	1	0.04	0	0.00	0	0.00	0	0.00	1	0.03
Osteichthyes	Bony fish	0	0.00	15	0.56	0	0.00	0	0.00	0	0.00	15	0.38
Cichlidae	Cichlid fishes	0	0.00	0	0.00	0	0.00	2	0.62	0	0.00	2	0.05
Tetrapoda	Tetrapods	10	8.26	26	0.97	0	0.00	0	0.00	0	0.00	36	0.90
Bufo/rana	Toad/frog	0	0.00	3	0.11	0	0.00	0	0.00	0	0.00	3	0.08
Reptilia/amphibian	Reptile/amphibian	0	0.00	2	0.07	0	0.00	0	0.00	0	0.00	2	0.05
Reptilia	Reptile	0	0.00	4	0.15	0	0.00	0	0.00	0	0.00	4	0.10
Squamata	Lizards/snakes	0	0.00	9	0.34	0	0.00	0	0.00	0	0.00	9	0.23
Squamata, small	Small lizards/snakes	0	0.00	3	0.11	0	0.00	0	0.00	0	0.00	3	0.08
Iguanidae	Arboreal lizards, chuckwallas, iguanas	0	0.00	1	0.04	0	0.00	0	0.00	0	0.00	1	0.03
Corytophanidae	Helmet lizards	0	0.00	2	0.07	0	0.00	0	0.00	0	0.00	2	0.05
Serpentes	Snakes	0	0.00	6	0.22	3	0.49	0	0.00	4	1.57	13	0.33
Viperidae	Vipers	0	0.00	0	0.00	0	0.00	2	0.62	1	0.39	3	0.08
Crocodylus	Crocodiles	0	0.00	3	0.11	0	0.00	0	0.00	0	0.00	3	0.08
Testudines	Turtles	0	0.00	31	1.15	14	2.30	5	1.56	5	1.97	55	1.38
Kinosternon	Small mud/musk turtles	0	0.00	7	0.26	0	0.00	0	0.00	1	0.39	8	0.20
Staurotypus triporcatus	Giant musk turtle	0	0.00	7	0.26	1	0.16	1	0.31	0	0.00	9	0.23
Dermatemys/staurotypus	Giant musk turtle/CA river turtle	0	0.00	6	0.22	0	0.00	0	0.00	0	0.00	6	0.15

Taxon												
Dermatemys mawii Central American river turtle	0	0.00	124	4.62	3	0.49	0	0.00	0	0.00	127	3.18
Emydidae Pond turtles, terrapins	0	0.00	6	0.22	0	0.00	0	0.00	1	0.39	7	0.18
Trachemys scripta Common slider	0	0.00	15	0.56	0	0.00	0	0.00	34	13.39	49	1.23
Aves Birds	0	0.00	7	0.26	1	0.16	0	0.00	2	0.79	10	0.25
Aves, large Large birds (hawk/turkey sized)	0	0.00	3	0.11	0	0.00	0	0.00	0	0.00	3	0.08
Aves, intermediate Intermediate birds (parrot, jay size)	0	0.00	2	0.07	0	0.00	0	0.00	0	0.00	2	0.05
Aves, small Small birds (perching bird size)	0	0.00	5	0.19	0	0.00	0	0.00	0	0.00	5	0.13
Galliformes, small Fowl, smaller than turkey, not quail	0	0.00	1	0.04	1	0.16	0	0.00	0	0.00	2	0.05
Phasianidae Pheasants, quail, turkey	0	0.00	1	0.04	0	0.00	0	0.00	0	0.00	1	0.03
Colinus nigrogularis Yucatan bobwhite	0	0.00	1	0.04	0	0.00	0	0.00	0	0.00	1	0.03
Meleagris Turkey	0	0.00	5	0.19	1	0.16	0	0.00	0	0.00	6	0.15
Passeriformes Perching bird	0	0.00	2	0.07	0	0.00	0	0.00	0	0.00	2	0.05
Mammalia Mammal	4	3.31	428	15.95	88	14.45	44	13.71	44	17.32	609	15.26
Mammalia, very large Very large mammal (tapir size)	0	0.00	2	0.07	1	0.16	0	0.00	0	0.00	3	0.08
Mammalia, large Large mammal (peccary/deer size)	28	23.14	457	17.03	132	21.67	42	13.08	46	18.11	705	17.67
Mammalia, large/intermediate Large/int mammal (small peccary, brocket deer size)	0	0.00	60	2.24	69	11.33	2	0.62	2	0.79	133	3.33
Mammalia, intermediate Int. Mammal (dog size)	6	4.96	148	5.51	7	1.15	1	0.31	24	9.45	186	4.66

(continued)

Table 11.2. (Continued)

Taxon	Common name	Preclassic		Late Classic		Terminal Classic		Postclassic		Undated		Total	
		NISP	%	NISP	%	NISP	%	NISP	%	NISP	%	NISP	%
Mammalia, small	Small mammal (rodent size)	1	0.83	42	1.56	7	1.15	1	0.31	5	1.97	56	1.40
Didelphidae	Opossum	0	0.00	9	0.34	0	0.00	0	0.00	3	1.18	12	0.30
Tamandua mexicana	Northern tamandua	0	0.00	0	0.00	0	0.00	0	0.00	5	1.97	5	0.13
Dasypus novemcinctus	Nine-banded armadillo	0	0.00	40	1.49	0	0.00	3	0.93	1	0.39	44	1.10
Chiroptera	Bats	0	0.00	2	0.07	0	0.00	0	0.00	0	0.00	2	0.05
Carnivora	Carnivores	0	0.00	4	0.15	0	0.00	0	0.00	0	0.00	4	0.10
Canidae	Coyotes, dogs, foxes	0	0.00	3	0.11	0	0.00	0	0.00	0	0.00	3	0.08
Canis lupus familiaris	Domestic dog	0	0.00	42	1.56	2	0.33	0	0.00	3	1.18	47	1.18
Urocyon cinereoargenteus	Gray fox	0	0.00	1	0.04	0	0.00	0	0.00	0	0.00	1	0.03
Felidae	Cats	0	0.00	2	0.07	0	0.00	0	0.00	0	0.00	2	0.05
Felidae, large	Large cat (jaguar, puma)	0	0.00	4	0.15	0	0.00	0	0.00	0	0.00	4	0.10
Puma concolor	Puma	0	0.00	1	0.04	0	0.00	0	0.00	0	0.00	1	0.03
Panthera onca	Jaguar	0	0.00	2	0.07	0	0.00	0	0.00	0	0.00	2	0.05
Leopardus pardalis	Ocelot	0	0.00	2	0.07	0	0.00	0	0.00	0	0.00	2	0.05
Artiodactyla	Even-toed ungulates	0	0.00	12	0.45	0	0.00	0	0.00	0	0.00	12	0.30
Tayassuidae	Peccaries	0	0.00	7	0.26	1	0.16	2	0.62	1	0.39	11	0.28
Cervidae	Deer	0	0.00	10	0.37	3	0.49	14	4.36	0	0.00	27	0.68
Odocoileus virginianus	White-tailed deer	1	0.83	229	8.53	56	9.20	13	4.05	2	0.79	301	7.54
Mazama	Brocket deer	0	0.00	23	0.86	4	0.66	8	2.49	0	0.00	35	0.88
Agouti paca	Paca/tepezcuintle	0	0.00	3	0.11	2	0.33	0	0.00	0	0.00	5	0.13
Dasyprocta punctata	Agouti	0	0.00	3	0.11	0	0.00	1	0.31	1	0.39	5	0.13

Taxon	Common name	n	%	n	%	n	%	n	%	n	%	n	%
Rodentia, intermediate	(pocket gophers, squirrels)	1	0.83	0	0.00	0	0.00	0	0.00	0	0.00	1	0.03
Rodentia, small	(mice, rats)	1	0.83	57	2.12	1	0.16	0	0.00	7	2.76	66	1.65
Sciuridae	Squirrels	0	0.00	0	0.00	0	0.00	0	0.00	1	0.39	1	0.03
Muridae/heteromyidae	Mice/rats, pocket mice	0	0.00	23	0.86	0	0.00	0	0.00	0	0.00	23	0.58
Cricetinae	Mice	0	0.00	1	0.04	0	0.00	0	0.00	1	0.39	2	0.05
Sigmodon	Cotton rats	0	0.00	4	0.15	0	0.00	0	0.00	0	0.00	4	0.10
Geomyidae	Pocket gopher	0	0.00	0	0.00	0	0.00	0	0.00	2	0.79	2	0.05
Orthogeomys hispidus	Giant pocket gopher	0	0.00	1	0.04	0	0.00	0	0.00	1	0.39	2	0.05
Sylvilagus	Rabbits	0	0.00	12	0.45	0	0.00	0	0.00	1	0.39	13	0.33
Total counts		121	100.00	2684	100.00	609	100.00	321	100.00	254	100.00	3990	100.00
Number of independent taxa		8		43		19		12				46	

Table 11.3. Rank distribution of the Motul de San José archaeological animals

Taxon	Common name	Rank 1		Rank 2		Rank 3	
		NISP	%	NISP	%	NISP	%
Mollusca	Mollusks	3	0.10	1	0.20	2	0.60
Mollusca, marine	Marine mollusks	40	1.27	0	0.00	1	0.30
Gastropoda, marine	Marine gastropods	9	0.29	7	1.39	3	0.89
Olividae	Olive	0	0.00	2	0.40	0	0.00
Oliva sayana	Lettered olive	5	0.16	1	0.20	0	0.00
Olivella perplexa	Dwarf olive	6	0.19	5	0.99	1	0.30
Olivella/prunum	Dwarf olive/marginella	2	0.06	8	1.58	1	0.30
Prunum apicinum	Common Atlantic marginella	14	0.44	0	0.00	0	0.00
Jenneria pustulata	Pustulate cowry	1	0.03	0	0.00	0	0.00
Strombidae	Conchs	53	1.68	1	0.20	0	0.00
Strombus alatus	Florida fighting conch	1	0.03	0	0.00	0	0.00
Strombus gigas/costatus	Queen/milk conch	1	0.03	0	0.00	0	0.00
Dentaliidae	Tusk shell	0	0.00	0	0.00	2	0.60
Pachychilus glaphyrus	"Spiny" jute	4	0.13	2	0.40	0	0.00
Pachychilus indiorum	"Smooth" jute	152	4.83	13	2.57	4	1.19
Pomacea flagellata	Apple snail	142	4.51	48	9.50	63	18.75
Spondylus	Thorny oysters	6	0.19	1	0.20	0	0.00
Unionidae	River clams	1	0.03	3	0.59	1	0.30
Psoronaias	River clam	144	4.57	14	2.77	9	2.68
Vertebrata	Vertebrates	452	14.35	27	5.35	13	3.87
Rajiformes/myliobatiformes	Ray	1	0.03	0	0.00	0	0.00
Osteichthyes	Bony fish	15	0.48	0	0.00	0	0.00
Cichlidae	Cichlid fishes	2	0.06	0	0.00	0	0.00

Tetrapoda	Tetrapods	7	0.22	19	3.76	10	2.98
Bufo/rana	Toad/frog	2	0.06	1	0.20	0	0.00
Reptilia/amphibian	Reptile/amphibian	2	0.06	0	0.00	0	0.00
Reptilia	Reptile	2	0.06	1	0.20	1	0.30
Squamata	Lizards/snakes	9	0.29	0	0.00	0	0.00
Squamata, small	Small lizards/snakes	2	0.06	1	0.20	0	0.00
Iguanidae	Arboreal lizards, chuckwallas, iguanas	1	0.03	0	0.00	0	0.00
Corytophanidae	Helmet lizards	2	0.06	0	0.00	0	0.00
Serpentes	Snakes	6	0.19	3	0.59	4	1.19
Viperidae	Vipers	2	0.06	0	0.00	1	0.30
Crocodylus	Crocodiles	3	0.10	0	0.00	0	0.00
Testudines	Turtles	31	0.98	17	3.37	7	2.08
Kinosternon	Small mud/musk turtles	6	0.19	2	0.40	0	0.00
Staurotypus triporcatus	Giant musk turtle	7	0.22	2	0.40	0	0.00
Dermatemys/staurotypus	Giant musk turtle/CA river turtle	5	0.16	0	0.00	1	0.30
Dermatemys mawii	Central American river turtle	108	3.43	8	1.58	11	3.27
Emydidae	Pond turtles, terrapins	4	0.13	2	0.40	1	0.30
Trachemys scripta	Common slider	10	0.32	1	0.20	38	11.31
Aves	Birds	6	0.19	0	0.00	4	1.19
Aves, large	Large birds (hawk/turkey size)	3	0.10	0	0.00	0	0.00
Aves, intermediate	Intermediate birds (parrot, jay size)	2	0.06	0	0.00	0	0.00
Aves, small	Small birds (perching bird size)	5	0.16	0	0.00	0	0.00
Galliformes, small	Fowl, smaller than turkey, not quail	2	0.06	0	0.00	0	0.00
Phasianidae	Pheasants, quail, turkey	1	0.03	0	0.00	0	0.00
Colinus nigrogularis	Yucatan bobwhite	1	0.03	0	0.00	0	0.00
Meleagris	Turkey	5	0.16	0	0.00	1	0.30
Passeriniformes	Perching bird	2	0.06	0	0.00	0	0.00
Mammalia	Mammal	545	17.31	29	5.74	35	10.42

(*continued*)

Table 11.3. (Continued)

Taxon	Common name	Rank 1		Rank 2		Rank 3	
		NISP	%	NISP	%	NISP	%
Mammalia, very large	Very large mammal (tapir size)	2	0.06	0	0.00	1	0.30
Mammalia, large	Large mammal (peccary/deer size)	504	16.01	146	28.91	55	16.37
Mammalia, large/intermediate	Large/int mammal (small peccary, brocket deer size)	98	3.11	29	5.74	6	1.79
Mammalia, intermediate	Int. Mammal (dog size)	133	4.22	43	8.51	10	2.98
Mammalia, small	Small mammal (rodent size)	41	1.30	11	2.18	4	1.19
Didelphidae	Opossum	7	0.22	1	0.20	4	1.19
Tamandua mexicana	Northern tamandua	0	0.00	0	0.00	5	1.49
Dasypus novemcinctus	Nine-banded armadillo	30	0.95	11	2.18	3	0.89
Chiroptera	Bats	2	0.06	0	0.00	0	0.00
Carnivora	Carnivores	4	0.13	0	0.00	0	0.00
Canidae	Coyotes, dogs, foxes	3	0.10	0	0.00	0	0.00
Canis lupus familiaris	Domestic dog	40	1.27	6	1.19	1	0.30
Urocyon cinereoargenteus	Gray fox	1	0.03	0	0.00	0	0.00
Felidae	Cats	2	0.06	0	0.00	0	0.00
Felidae, large	Large cat (jaguar, puma)	3	0.10	1	0.20	0	0.00
Puma concolor	Puma	1	0.03	0	0.00	0	0.00
Panthera onca	Jaguar	2	0.06	0	0.00	0	0.00
Leopardus pardalis	Ocelot	2	0.06	0	0.00	0	0.00
Artiodactyla	Even-toed ungulates	5	0.16	7	1.39	0	0.00
Tayassuidae	Peccaries	10	0.32	0	0.00	1	0.30
Cervidae	Deer	23	0.73	3	0.59	1	0.30
Odocoileus virginianus	White-tailed deer	268	8.51	12	2.38	21	6.25
Mazama	Brocket deer	32	1.02	3	0.59	0	0.00

		Count	%	Count	%	Count	%
Agouti paca	Paca/tepezcuintle	5	0.16	0	0.00	0	0.00
Dasyprocta punctata	Agouti	5	0.16	0	0.00	0	0.00
Rodentia, intermediate	Int.-size rodent (pocket gophers, squirrels)	0	0.00	1	0.20	0	0.00
Rodentia, small	Small-size rodents (mice, rats)	63	2.00	0	0.00	3	0.89
Sciuridae	Squirrels	0	0.00	0	0.00	1	0.30
Muridae/heteromyidae	Mice/rats, pocket mice	13	0.41	10	1.98	0	0.00
Cricetinae	Mice	0	0.00	1	0.20	1	0.30
Sigmodon	Cotton rats	4	0.13	0	0.00	0	0.00
Geomyidae	Pocket gopher	0	0.00	0	0.00	2	0.60
Orthogeomys hispidus	Giant pocket gopher	0	0.00	0	0.00	2	0.60
Sylvilagus	Rabbits	11	0.35	1	0.20	1	0.30
Total counts		3,149	100.00	505	100.00	336	100.00
Number of independent taxa		42		22		19	

Table 11.4. MSJ rank and chronological distributions of selected taxa and taxonomic groups

	Total[a]		Rank 1[b]		Rank 2		Rank 3	
	NISP	%	NISP	%	NISP	%	NISP	%
HIGH-VALUE FAUNA								
White-tailed deer	301	7.54	268	8.00	12	2.00	21	6.00
(as % of artiodactyl)		78		79		48		91
Preclassic	1	0.83	1	9.00	0	0.00	0	0.00
Late Classic	229	8.00	202	9.00	10	3.00	17	13.00
Terminal Classic	56	9.00	54	10.00	2	2.00	0	0.00
Postclassic	13	4.00	9	3.00	0	0.00	4	25.00
Large mammals	1,065	26.69	818	26	169	33	78	23
Preclassic	29	23.97	3	27.27	3	27.27	23	23.23
Late Classic	724	26.97	586	27.09	99	25.58	39	29.10
Terminal Classic	192	31.53	125	24.41	67	69.79	0	0.00
Postclassic	71	22.12	56	18.86	0	0.00	15	93.75
CA turtle	127	3.18	108	3.00	8	2.00	11	3.00
(as % of turtle)		62		77		53		22
Preclassic	0	0.00	0	0.00	0	0.00	0	0.00
Late Classic	124	5.00	105	5.00	8	2.00	11	8.00
Terminal Classic	3	0.49	3	0.59	0	0.00	0	0.00
Postclassic	0	0.00	0	0.00	0	0.00	0	0.00
Galliform birds	0	0.25	9	0.29	0	0.00	1	0.30
(as % of bird)		31		33		0		17
Preclassic	0	0.00	0	0.00	0	0.00	0	0.00
Late Classic	8	0.30	7	0.32	0	0.00	1	0.75
Terminal Classic	2	0.49	2	0.39	0	0.00	0	0.00
Postclassic	0	0.00	0	0.00	0	0.00	0	0.00

LOWER-VALUE FAUNA

Freshwater mollusks	600	15.04	443	14.07	80	15.84	77	22.92
Preclassic	60	50.00	7	64.00	6	54.00	47	47.00
Late Classic	276	10.00	201	9.00	51	13.00	24	18.00
Terminal Classic	60	10.00	48	9.00	12	12.00	0	0.00
Postclassic	165	51.00	157	53.00	8	100.00	0	0.00
Large rodents	15	0.38	10	0.32	1	0.20	4	1.19
Preclassic	1	0.83	0	0.00	1	9.00	0	0.00
Late Classic	7	0.26	6	0.28	0	0.00	1	0.75
Terminal Classic	2	0.33	2	0.39	0	0.00	0	0.00
Postclassic	1	0.31	1	0.39	0	0.00	0	0.00
Armadillo	44	1.10	30	0.95	11	2.18	3	0.89
Preclassic	0	0.00	0	0.00	0	0.00	0	0.00
Late Classic	40	1.50	26	1.20	11	3.00	3	2.00
Terminal Classic	0	0.00	0	0.00	0	0.00	0	0.00
Postclassic	3	0.93	3	1.00	0	0.00	0	0.00

SPECIAL-VALUE FAUNA

Total marine mollusks	171	4.29	138	4.38	25	4.95	8	2.38
Preclassic	5	4.00	1	9.00	1	9.00	3	3.00
Late Classic	11	4.00	83	4.00	23	6.00	5	4.00
Terminal Classic	51	8.00	50	10.00	1	1.04	0	0.00
Postclassic	1	0.31	1	0.34	0	0.00	0	0.00
Total dogs	51	1.28	44	1.40	6	1.19	1	0.30
Preclassic	0	0.00	0	0.00	0	0.00	0	0.00
Late Classic	46	1.70	39	1.80	6	1.50	1	0.75
Terminal Classic	2	0.33	2	0.39	0	0.00	0	0.00

(continued)

Table 11.4. (*Continued*)

	Total[a]		Rank 1[b]		Rank 2		Rank 3	
	NISP	%	NISP	%	NISP	%	NISP	%
Postclassic	0	0.00	0	0.00	0	0.00	0	0.00
Total Cats	2	0.28	1	0.32	1	0.20	0	0.00
Preclassic	0	0.00	0	0.00	0	0.00	0	0.00
Late Classic	11	0.41	10	0.46	1	0.26	0	0.00
Terminal Classic	0	0.00	0	0.00	0	0.00	0	0.00
Postclassic	0	0.00	0	0.00	0	0.00	0	0.00

[a] Totals for each taxon include specimens from undated assemblages (Preclassic NISP = 121, Late Classic NISP = 2684, Terminal Classic NISP = 609, Postclassic NISP = 321; Total site NISP = 3,990). Total taxon %NISP represents taxon as percent of all specimens from MSJ. Total period taxon %NISP represents taxon as percent of all specimens from that period. Total period taxon %NISP represents taxon as percent of all specimens from that period.

[b] Rank %NISP represents taxon as percent of all specimens from that rank in total or rank and period.

suggesting a higher diversity of large-bodied mammals and less emphasis on the highest-ranking white-tailed deer (summed proportions of all large mammals: Rank 1 n = 818, 26 percent; Rank 2 n = 169, 33 percent; Rank 3 n = 78, 23 percent).

Among other high-status foods, the Central American turtle is found in approximately equal proportions in all ranked deposits, but when considered as a proportion of all turtles, it is clear that Rank 1 residents obtain and use/consume the highest proportion of these favored turtles (Rank 1 = 77 percent of all turtles, Rank 2 = 53 percent, Rank 3 = 22 percent). Similarly, Rank 1 residents used and discarded high proportions of galliform birds and the highest proportion when galliforms are considered as a percent of total birds (33 percent). But the remains of these birds were also found in Rank 3 deposits (17 percent of total birds), whereas none were apparently used by Rank 2 residents.

Taxa generally considered food species of lesser status include such intermediate-size mammals as armadillo, the large-bodied rodents (paca, agouti, pocket gopher, squirrels), and freshwater mollusks. Freshwater mollusks and large-bodied rodents are found in highest proportions in Rank 3 households and lowest proportions in Rank 1 households. The proportion found in Rank 2 households is lower than in Rank 1, but not appreciably. Armadillo remains are found in highest proportions in Rank 2 groups, indicating perhaps that this animal was either a slightly higher-ranked food than mollusks and rodents or that it served additional purposes for Rank 2 residents.

Several taxa deserve special consideration because of their role in ritual and expression of status and prestige. Dogs are known to have been not only an important source of food, but also highly symbolically valued, sacrificed, and included in burials and caches and possibly eaten in ritualized feasts (for examples, see Clutton-Brock and Hammond 1994; Valadez, Paredes, and Rodríguez 1999; White et al. 2004; Wing 1978). Cats were considered specific markers of high status, and are generally considered to have been used primarily in ritual and ceremony (Ballinger and Stomper 2000; Benson 1988). Both of these taxa are found in highest proportions among Rank 1 households and lowest in Rank 3 households; cats are not found at all in Rank 3 households. Marine mollusks are linked primarily with status displays and ceremony but, as will be discussed later, are also one of the basic raw materials for crafting. These remains are found in very similar proportions in Rank 1 and Rank 2 deposits, but surprisingly, are also fairly frequent in deposits of the lowest-status group at the site.

Distribution by Time Period: The proportion of animals varies somewhat over the periods of occupation of the Motul de San José site and periphery (Preclassic NISP = 121, Late Classic = 2,684, Terminal Classic = 609, Postclassic = 321).[5] The highest number of taxa is found in the Late Classic deposits (forty-three), the least in the Preclassic (eight). Very few species are ubiquitous (appearing in all periods) with the exception of olive shells, smooth jute, apple snail, river clam, large turtles, artiodactyls, and large rodents. Therefore, for the most part, the rank comparison is based heavily on proportions represented in the Late Classic period. In this next section, I tease the rank and chronology information apart to give a more detailed view of animal use.

During the Preclassic period, highly valued species are rare. Marine shell is found in all rank groups, white-tailed deer only in Rank 1. Lower-valued species are more common, including sixty freshwater mollusks found primarily in Rank 3 deposits. In combination this suggests a low differentiation between status groups in terms of animal use and a low overall emphasis on high-value species.

The picture is quite different during the Late Classic period. During this period, white-tailed deer represent 8 percent of the overall assemblage (and 81 percent of all artiodactyls, 32 percent of all large mammals for the period), 9 percent of the Rank 1 assemblage, 3 percent of Rank 2, and a surprising 13 percent of Rank 3. CA turtles represent 5 percent of the overall Late Classic assemblage, 5 percent of the Rank 1, 2 percent of the Rank 2, and 8 percent of the Rank 3 assemblage. Galliform birds follow the same trend by representing 0.3 percent overall and of Rank 1 and 0.75 percent of Rank 3 (none are found in Rank 2 deposits). Special-value species do not show this same trend. Dogs and cats are most abundant in Rank 1 deposits (dogs 2 percent, cats 0.46 percent), less so in Rank 2 deposits (dogs 1.5 percent, cats 0.26 percent), and even less abundant in Rank 3 deposits (dogs 0.75 percent, cats 0 percent). Marine mollusks, however, represent 4 percent of Rank 1 assemblages, 6 percent of Rank 2 assemblages, and 4 percent of Rank 3 assemblages. Lower-value animals generally used as food show the opposite patterns. Freshwater mollusks and large rodents are least frequent in Rank 1 deposits, and armadillos are also least frequent in Rank 1 deposits (1 percent) though most frequent in Rank 2 deposits (3 percent). Taken together, Late Classic high-value food species are found primarily at Ranks 1 and 3, low-value food species are found primarily at Rank 3, and special-value species are found primarily at Rank 1. This suggests that the hypothesized acquisition and distribution pattern from Rank 3 groups to Rank 1 groups might have held true for all the high-value food species during the Late Classic, but that Rank 1 groups had direct access to special-value fauna such as dogs and cats.

Terminal Classic use of high- and special-value animals appears quite different. The highest proportions of white-tailed deer, which represents 87 percent of artiodactyls at this point and 29 percent of all large mammals, are found in Rank 1 deposits (10 percent), less so in Rank 2 (2 percent), and not at all in Rank 3 (the only Terminal Classic Rank 3 remain was a single mammal bone). Similarly, the Central American turtle and galliform birds are found only in Rank 1 deposits of the Terminal Classic. Rank 1 deposits held all the special-value fauna either exclusively (dogs 0.39 percent) or primarily (marine mollusks 10 percent versus 1 percent in Rank 2 and none in Rank 3). No cats are found at all in Terminal Classic deposits. Freshwater shells are relatively frequent in both Rank 1 (9 percent) and Rank 2 (12 percent) deposits. Rank 1 residents during this period may have had exclusive rights to most high-value species, but the lack of Rank 3 specimens makes this suggestion difficult to confirm.

Postclassic assemblages are quite small in all ranks. No dogs or cats are found in any rank, but marine mollusks continue to be found in at least Rank 1 assemblages, representing 0.34 percent of the total assemblage at that rank and date. No Central American turtles or galliform birds are found during this period, but the final high-value species, white-tailed deer, is found in both Rank 1 (3 percent) and Rank 3 assemblages (25 percent), representing 35 percent of artiodactyls and 18 percent of all large mammals overall during this period. Lower-ranked species are more common. Freshwater mollusks and armadillo represent large proportions of the Rank 1 and 2 assemblages (mollusks equal 100 percent of the Rank 2 assemblage and 53 percent of the Rank 1 assemblage). Armadillos and rodents fill out the Rank 1 assemblage, but do not appear in Rank 2 deposits.

Crafting

Overall: The evaluation of crafting evidence in bone and shell is a second valuable route to understanding the economics of animal resource use (Emery 2009; Emery and Aoyama 2007). At the site of Motul de San José and its peripheries, a total of 433 remains, or 11 percent of the total modified and unmodified assemblage, were artifactually modified (this count includes remains from all deposits whether chronologically dated or not; see Table 11.5 for all details). These included adornments and instruments (n = 253, 58 percent of all artifacts), utilitarian artifacts (n = 101, 23 percent), and those for which function was unknown. Note that even fine perforators were classified as utilitarian given their probable role in textile production, but they may also have been used to fasten clothes and adorn hair (modern women of the Guatemalan highlands use weaving implements as hair adornments when they are not in use). But whereas all utilitarian artifacts were vertebrate (all but one mammalian) in origin, most of the adornments (85 percent of adornments/instruments) were molluscan (equal proportions freshwater and marine).

Where production stage was known (n = 414, 96 percent of artifacts), most were finished artifacts, but an appreciable proportion were production debris in comparison to other sites (for comparison with other sites, see Emery 2010). Over half of the finished artifacts were molluscan, in approximately equal proportions of marine and freshwater. The majority of the vertebrate finished artifacts were mammalian (mostly deer, with some dogs, cats, pacas, and rabbits), with a very few examples made of elements from reptiles (turtle) and birds. Artifacts in production were mainly mammalian (74 percent of production debris, those including 38 percent deer and 4 percent cat, the others not identifiable beyond class). However, some 26 percent of the production materials were from shell, almost half of which was marine as opposed to freshwater.

Chronological and Spatial Distributions: The details of production and ownership are revealed in an analysis of the distributions of these remains among the ranked groups within each time period. In this discussion only deposits with clear chronological context are included.

I begin with a summary of differences in crafting between time periods. Most artifacts recovered from the Motul de San José deposits from all time periods were adornments as opposed to utilitarian objects. During the Preclassic period, most of those adornments were manufactured of marine products, indicating a healthy trade relationship with the coast even during this earliest period of occupation. During the subsequent periods the proportions of shell adornments from marine versus freshwater sources was approximately equivalent except during the Postclassic when no freshwater shell was used. (Marine adornments: 83 percent marine versus 17 percent freshwater in the Preclassic, 42 percent marine versus 45 percent in the Late Classic, 41 percent versus 32 percent in the Terminal Classic, 50 percent versus 0 percent in the Postclassic.) However, the proportion of vertebrate

Table 11.5. Motul de San José artifacts of animal bone and shell listed by artifact type and production stage

	Adorno/ instrument (%NISP)	Utilitarian (%NISP)	Unknown type (%NISP)	Production (%NISP)	Finished (%NISP)	Unknown stage (%NISP)	Total artifacts (%NISP)	Total counts (%NISP)[a]
PRECLASSIC								
Gastropoda, marine	16.67	0.00	0.00	0.00	11.11	0.00	11.11	100.00
Olividae	33.33	0.00	0.00	0.00	22.22	0.00	22.22	100.00
Dentaliidae	33.33	0.00	0.00	0.00	22.22	0.00	22.22	100.00
Pomacea flagellata	16.67	0.00	0.00	0.00	11.11	0.00	11.11	1.72
Mammalia (large, intermediate)	0.00	100.00	0.00	0.00	33.33	0.00	33.33	8.82
TOTAL NISP (sum)	6	3	0	0	9	0	9	121
TOTAL NISP (% of period artifacts)	66.67	33.33	0.00	0.00	100.00	0.00	100.00	7.44
LATE CLASSIC								
Mollusca, marine	1.83	0.00	0.00	0.00	1.34	0.00	1.07	33.33
Gastropoda, marine	3.20	0.00	0.00	1.69	2.01	0.00	1.87	50.00
Olividae	9.59	0.00	0.00	1.69	6.69	0.00	5.61	150.00
Prunum apicinum	0.46	0.00	0.00	0.00	0.33	0.00	0.27	100.00
Jenneria pustulata	0.46	0.00	0.00	0.00	0.33	0.00	0.27	100.00
Strombidae	22.83	0.00	0.00	0.00	16.39	6.67	13.37	98.04
Psoronaias	44.75	0.00	1.54	8.47	28.76	40.00	26.47	69.72
Spondylus	3.20	0.00	0.00	1.69	2.01	0.00	1.87	100.00
Aves (all)	0.00	1.11	0.00	0.00	0.33	0.00	0.27	3.70
Mammalia (large, intermediate)	7.76	77.78	63.08	33.90	34.45	40.00	34.22	19.25

(continued)

Table 11.5. (Continued)

	Adorno/instrument (%NISP)	Utilitarian (%NISP)	Unknown type (%NISP)	Production (%NISP)	Finished (%NISP)	Unknown stage (%NISP)	Total artifacts (%NISP)	Total counts (%NISP)[a]
Canis familiaris	1.37	0.00	0.00	0.00	1.00	0.00	0.80	7.14
Felidae (all)	0.91	1.11	3.08	5.08	0.67	0.00	1.34	45.45
Cervidae (both)	2.28	20.00	32.31	47.46	4.68	13.33	11.76	16.79
Agouti paca	0.46	0.00	0.00	0.00	0.33	0.00	0.27	33.33
Sylvilagus	0.91	0.00	0.00	0.00	0.67	0.00	0.53	16.67
TOTAL NISP (sum)	219	90	65	59	299	15	374	2,684
TOTAL NISP (% of period artifacts)	58.56	24.06	17.38	15.78	79.95	4.01	100.00	13.93
TERMINAL CLASSIC								
Gastropoda, marine	9.09	0.00	0.00	10.00	5.88	0.00	6.67	66.67
Olividae	9.09	0.00	0.00	0.00	11.76	0.00	6.67	66.67
Prunum apicinum	13.64	0.00	0.00	0.00	17.65	0.00	10.00	25.00
Strombidae	9.09	0.00	0.00	20.00	0.00	0.00	6.67	50.00
Psoronaias	31.82	0.00	0.00	60.00	5.88	0.00	23.33	38.89
Testudines	0.00	0.00	33.33	0.00	0.00	33.33	3.33	7.14
Aves (all)	4.55	0.00	0.00	0.00	5.88	0.00	3.33	33.33
Mammalia (large, intermediate)	9.09	100.00	66.67	10.00	35.29	66.67	30.00	4.33
Canis lupus familiaris	9.09	0.00	0.00	0.00	11.76	0.00	6.67	100.00
Cervidae (both)	4.55	0.00	0.00	0.00	5.88	0.00	3.33	1.59
TOTAL NISP (sum)	22	5	3	10	17	3	30	609
TOTAL NISP (% of period artifacts)	73.33	16.67	10.00	33.33	56.67	10.00	100.00	4.93

Gastropoda, marine	50.00	0.00	0.00	50.00	0.00	0.00	20.00	100.00
Mammalia (large, intermediate)	50.00	0.00	100.00	50.00	66.67	0.00	60.00	6.67
Cervidae (both)	0.00	100.00	0.00	0.00	33.33	0.00	20.00	2.86
TOTAL NISP (sum)	2	1	2	2	3	0	5	321
TOTAL NISP (% of period artifacts)	40.00	20.00	40.00	40.00	60.00	0.00	100.00	1.56
TOTAL RANK 1								
Mollusca, marine	1.89	0.00	0.00	0.00	1.39	0.00	1.13	10.00
Gastropoda, marine	2.36	0.00	0.00	3.51	1.05	0.00	1.41	55.56
Olividae	5.66	0.00	0.00	0.00	4.18	0.00	3.39	109.09
Prunum apicinum	2.36	0.00	0.00	0.00	1.74	0.00	1.41	35.71
Jenneria pustulata	0.47	0.00	0.00	0.00	0.35	0.00	0.28	100.00
Strombidae	25.00	0.00	0.00	5.26	17.07	9.09	14.97	96.36
Psoronaias	45.75	0.00	0.00	14.04	30.31	18.18	27.40	67.36
Spondylus	2.83	0.00	0.00	0.00	2.09	0.00	1.69	100.00
Testudines	0.00	0.00	6.78	0.00	1.39	0.00	1.13	12.90
Aves (all)	0.47	0.00	0.00	0.00	0.70	0.00	0.56	7.41
Mammalia (large, intermediate)	6.13	80.72	59.32	28.07	32.40	63.64	32.49	15.65
Canis lupus familiaris	2.36	0.00	0.00	0.00	1.74	0.00	1.41	12.50
Felidae (all)	0.47	1.20	3.39	5.26	0.35	0.00	1.13	40.00
Cervidae (both)	2.83	16.87	30.51	43.86	4.18	9.09	10.73	11.76
Agouti paca	0.47	0.00	0.00	0.00	0.35	0.00	0.28	20.00
Sylvilagus	0.94	0.00	0.00	0.00	0.70	0.00	0.56	18.18
TOTAL NISP (sum)	212	83	59	57	287	11	354	1,462
TOTAL NISP (% of rank artifacts)	59.89	23.45	16.67	16.10	81.07	3.11	100.00	24.21

(continued)

Table 11.5. (Continued)

	Adorno/ instrument (%NISP)	Utilitarian (%NISP)	Unknown type (%NISP)	Production (%NISP)	Finished (%NISP)	Unknown stage (%NISP)	Total artifacts (%NISP)	Total counts (%NISP)[a]
TOTAL RANK 2								
Gastropoda, marine	10.71	0.00	0.00	7.69	5.56	0.00	5.45	42.86
Olividae	42.86	0.00	0.00	7.69	30.56	0.00	21.82	75.00
Psoronaias	21.43	0.00	5.88	23.08	2.78	25.00	12.73	50.00
Spondylus	3.57	0.00	0.00	7.69	0.00	0.00	1.82	100.00
Testudines	0.00	0.00	5.88	0.00	0.00	25.00	1.82	5.88
Mammalia (large, intermediate)	17.86	100.00	76.47	46.15	58.33	25.00	50.91	12.84
Felidae (all)	3.57	0.00	0.00	0.00	2.78	0.00	1.82	100.00
Cervidae (both)	0.00	0.00	11.76	7.69	0.00	25.00	3.64	11.11
TOTAL NISP (sum)	28	10	17	13	36	4	55	292
TOTAL NISP (% of rank artifacts)	50.91	18.18	30.91	23.64	65.45	7.27	100.00	18.84
TOTAL RANK 3								
Gastropoda, marine	23.08	0.00	0.00	0.00	16.67	0.00	12.50	100.00
Olividae	15.38	0.00	0.00	0.00	11.11	0.00	8.33	100.00
Dentaliidae	15.38	0.00	0.00	0.00	11.11	0.00	8.33	100.00
Pomacea flagellata	7.69	0.00	0.00	0.00	5.56	0.00	4.17	1.59
Psoronaias	23.08	0.00	0.00	0.00	0.00	100.00	12.50	33.33
Mammalia (large, intermediate)	15.38	37.50	66.67	33.33	33.33	0.00	29.17	9.86
Cervidae (both)	0.00	62.50	33.33	66.67	22.22	0.00	25.00	27.27
TOTAL NISP (sum)	13	8	3	3	18	3	24	172
TOTAL NISP (% of rank artifacts)	54.17	33.33	12.50	12.50	75.00	12.50	100.00	13.95

TOTAL ALL RANKS

Mollusca, marine	1.58	0.00	0.00	1.17	0.00	0.92	9.76
Gastropoda, marine	4.35	0.00	4.11	2.35	0.00	2.54	57.89
Olividae	10.28	0.00	1.37	7.33	0.00	6.00	83.87
Prunum apicinum	1.98	0.00	0.00	1.47	0.00	1.15	35.71
Jenneria pustulata	0.40	0.00	0.00	0.29	0.00	0.23	100.00
Strombidae	20.95	0.00	4.11	14.37	5.56	12.24	94.64
Dentaliidae	0.79	0.00	0.00	0.59	0.00	0.46	100.00
Pomacea flagellata	0.40	0.00	0.00	0.29	0.00	0.23	0.40
Psoronaias	41.90	1.27	15.07	25.81	33.33	24.71	64.07
Spondylus	2.77	0.00	1.37	1.76	0.00	1.62	100.00
Testudines	0.00	6.33	0.00	1.17	5.56	1.15	9.09
Aves (all)	0.40	0.00	0.00	0.59	0.00	0.46	6.25
Mammalia (large, intermediate)	7.91	63.29	31.51	35.19	44.44	34.64	14.65
Canis lupus familiaris	1.98	0.00	0.00	1.47	0.00	1.15	10.64
Felidae (all)	0.79	2.53	4.11	0.59	0.00	1.15	45.45
Cervidae (both)	2.37	26.58	38.36	4.69	11.11	10.62	12.67
Agouti paca	0.40	0.00	0.00	0.29	0.00	0.23	20.00
Sylvilagus	0.79	0.00	0.00	0.59	0.00	0.46	15.38
TOTAL NISP (sum)	**253**	**79**	**73**	**341**	**18**	**433**	**2,141**
TOTAL NISP (% of rank artifacts)	**58.43**	**18.24**	**16.86**	**78.75**	**4.16**	**100.00**	**20.22**

[a] NISP of all remains, modified and unmodified, and % artifacts of all remains.

material displayed as ornaments varied from 0 percent (of adornments) in the Preclassic to 14 percent in the Late Classic (including dogs, cats, deer, paca, and rabbits); 23 percent in the Terminal Classic (birds, dogs, and deer); and 50 percent (species unknown) in the Postclassic.

The production or crafting of animal products in situ at the site varied considerably over the periods of occupation. No evidence for production was found in the Preclassic period, but production debris represented ever-increasing proportions as compared to finished artifacts over time, rising from 16 percent of all artifacts in the Late Classic to 40 percent in the Post-classic. Crafting activities appear to have been particularly important in the Terminal and Postclassic periods. The proportion of crafting that involved exotic materials also varied over time. Although only a small proportion of the total crafted material was marine shell in the Late Classic (most was mammalian), 30 percent of the crafted material was marine shell in the Terminal Classic and 50 percent (a very small assemblage) was marine shell in the Postclassic, with no representatives of freshwater shell.[6]

In sum, we see a picture of continuous use of marine exotics as adornments, but an emphasis on crafting those exotics alongside local freshwater shell and mammalian bone from the Late Classic period on, intensifying in the Terminal Classic and Postclassic both in terms of production activities but also in terms of emphasis on crafting marine shell.

Artifact Distributions among Ranked Groups: This view of changing rates of production and crafting of exotic products is best understood from the perspective of different activities among the community members during each period. Therefore, here I compare crafting evidence from each of the three ranked subgroups in each time period.

During the Preclassic, only a single finished molluscan shell adornment was found, and that in a Rank 1 nonresidential cache. From Preclassic deposits in Rank 2 groups came another finished molluscan shell ornament and three utilitarian mammalian artifacts, all finished. Rank 3 groups contained four finished shell adornments in Preclassic deposits—one a freshwater shell, the others all marine. Despite the small size of the assemblage, it is clear that both the Motul de San José and periphery residents had strong connections to the coast during this period since exotic mollusks account for 56 percent of the total artifact assemblage for the period. There is no evidence of in situ production of artifacts in this period, although the sample is very small for any conclusions.

In the Late Classic period animal remains were modified and artifacts were used by community members from all ranks and areas of the site.

Rank 1 materials are represented by remains from two groups (Operations 2 and 15) and include a total of 312 artifacts. Rank 2 materials include remains from ten groups and include forty-two artifacts. Rank 3 materials, from six groups, include twenty artifacts. In all Late Classic deposits, adornments/ instruments were the dominant artifact type over utilitarian artifacts. Of those, the majority in all ranks were molluscan in origin (Rank 1 n = 165, 87 percent molluscan; Rank 2 n = 17, 81 percent molluscan; Rank 3 n = 7, 78 percent molluscan). However, marine mollusks were found in quite different proportions of the adornments among the ranked groups with the highest proportion of these exotic resources found in Rank 2 deposits and the lowest proportion actually found in Rank 1 deposits.[7] Further information is found in a review of production remains. These are found in approximately equal proportions among all ranks. However, what is being crafted differs significantly between ranks. Rank 1 residents crafted far fewer marine exotics than did residents of the Rank 2 groups, and crafted somewhat more mammalian remains (primarily as perforators for textile production). Rank 3 households crafted no molluscan materials at all. Many of the freshwater adornments crafted in Rank 1 households may have been nacreous "sparklers" for textile decoration, suggesting in-house production of the tools and adornments for textile working in Rank 1 households, and the crafting of elite exotic adornments in Rank 2 households.[8]

Terminal Classic artifacts are found in deposits from both Rank 1 and Rank 2 residences. The majority of the artifacts from Rank 1 and Rank 2 deposits are adornments versus utilitarian objects. In both Rank 1 and 2 deposits, most of the adornments were molluscan (Rank 1 n = 12, 75 percent; Rank 2 n = 4, 67 percent). In Rank 1 deposits, however, around half of these were from marine mollusks with the other half from freshwater clam, whereas in Rank 2 deposits, only one was marine and the majority was freshwater clam. The remainder of the adornments in both ranks were primarily mammals (Rank 1 n = 8, 49 percent; Rank 2 n = 6, 67 percent). All the utilitarian artifacts were mammalian in both Rank 1 and Rank 2 deposits. This suggests a difference in the quality of materials displayed as adornments by these two ranks. Rank 1 residents displayed a high proportion and diversity of marine shell adornments. Rank 2 residents also displayed shell adornments but of primarily freshwater origin.

Another important observation is in the differences between production debris. Although most of the Rank 1 remains were finished artifacts, the Rank 2 remains were predominantly production debris. This suggests more crafting in the Rank 2 residences than in the Rank 1 residences although crafting was still high in those areas too. The majority of the production debris in both ranks was molluscan (Rank 1 n = 5, 100 percent; Rank 2 n = 4, 80 percent) but again the proportions of marine to freshwater shell differed. Rank 1 production debris was 40 percent marine mollusks, whereas that from Rank 2 deposits was only 20 percent marine. Although samples are small, this suggests that although crafting of marine shell occurred in both residential ranks, the Rank 1 residents crafted with higher-quality materials.

Finally, in the Postclassic, only five artifactually modified remains are found, all from the Rank 1 Group D (Operation 15). These include one marine shell artifact of unidentified gastropod in production and four mammalian long bone artifacts, including one in production and three finished products. As a relative proportion of the total Postclassic remains, this is a fairly high proportion of both modified exotics (n = 1, 20 percent) and production debris (n = 2, 40 percent) of total worked assemblage. However, it is interesting that the exotics are not as diverse or numerous as in prior periods, and the production debris, now of mammalian instead of exotic materials, is a greater proportion of the materials. Although the sample size is too small for conclusions, this might suggest that Rank 1 crafters at this point in the site's occupation were manufacturing primarily low-value local materials.

Discussion

Summary: This review of the taxa of the Motul de San José animal remains has highlighted some of the economic relationships between the community members of the Motul de San José site and its peripheries. Here it is informative to think about the animal findings in terms of the cycle of resource economics—acquisition, distribution, consumption, and discard. The taxonomic findings suggest that, at least during the apogee of the Late Classic, Rank 3 residents had equal or greater access to several very high-value species, including white-tailed deer, the Central American turtle, and turkeys and their allies. It is possible that as providers of their own household meat, they were able to acquire these favored species at similar rates to the Rank 1 highest elite, and at rates far greater than the Rank 2 middle-status groups. However, an alternative suggestion is that these hunters may have been providing both for their own tables and for the tables of the rulers. Rank 2 residents were not lacking for animal resources and in fact had the highest diversity and proportion of large game with the exception of the most highly valued species. Perhaps they were also provided with game by the lower-ranking residents of the site, or perhaps they were provisioned by their own family members who had access to species other than the white-tailed deer. This hypothesis could be tested with a study of body portion since it should show that Rank 3 deposits had the lower-quality portions of the high-ranked species, and higher-quality/full body of low-ranked species. Special-value species such as dogs and cats are also found in close correlation with rank, with the highest-ranked groups having the largest proportions. Lower-value species such as freshwater mollusks, armadillos, and large rodents are found in highest proportions in the lower-ranked deposits. This picture therefore suggests that "ceremonial" species were the exclusive right of the highest elite, whereas high-value food species were the primary right of the Rank 1 rulers, but were acquired and presumably processed by the Rank 3 residents. One exception to these distributions is the marine molluscan assemblage. These are more frequently found in Rank 2 assemblages than in Rank 1 assemblages, but this distribution may have more to do with crafting and marine shell adornment production than final ownership and use of these materials.

These findings reflect predominantly the Late Classic situation since those remains are the most frequent. But viewing the dated assemblages separately reveals that chronological patterns vary significantly. The finding that in the Preclassic highly valued species were rare in comparison to lower-status taxa, and that the distribution between was quite even, suggests a low differentiation between ranks in terms of animal use and a low overall emphasis on high-value species at this time. The patterns revealed during the Terminal Classic are again quite different from those seen in the Late Classic assemblages. Rank 1 residents during this period appear to have had exclusive rights to most high-value species, including the white-tailed deer, galliforms, and large game as well as the ritual species, dog and cats. However, the lack of specimens from the Rank 3 households makes it difficult to hypothesize about whether this indicates a shift in the pattern of resource acquisition and movement within the site or simply a lack of evidence for Rank 3 activities. I suspect, given the presence of materials in other deposits from these residences, that in fact, the nonelite community members were restricted in their access to high-status foods and ceremonial goods during this period. During the Postclassic, as in the Preclassic, special-value and high-value species are limited to white-tailed deer and marine mollusks. Lower-value species predominate and the absence of many of the status-marker species suggests these might have been eradicated around the site, or that their value for marking either status or ceremony was diminished at this point. However, again, our Postclassic sample is quite small as the general focus of the Motul research was on the Late Classic period.

To fully understand the movement of animal goods through the Motul de San José community, it is important to consider the use of animal materials in crafting as well as in direct consumption for food or as ritual commodities. We begin with the crafting itself. An appreciable proportion of production debris was found in most periods at the site compared to other sites, suggesting that the crafting of animal materials into both adornments and utilitarian objects was an important part of the site economy. Much of the production debris was shell, much of that marine in origin, suggesting that marine shell was transported into the site and modified there to create adornments (no marine shell was used in the production of utilitarian objects), presumably for use by the Motul elite given the high proportions of finished artifacts in the Rank 1 deposits.

The production or crafting of animal products in situ at the site varied considerably over the periods of occupation. No evidence for production was found in the Preclassic period, but production debris represented ever-increasing proportions as compared to finished artifacts over time, rising from 16 percent of all artifacts in the Late Classic to 40 percent in the Postclassic. Crafting activities appear to have been particularly important in the Terminal and Postclassic periods. The proportion of crafting that involved exotic materials also varied over time. Although only a small proportion of the total crafted material was marine shell in the Late Classic (most was mammalian), 30 percent of the crafted material was marine shell in the Terminal Classic; 50 percent (a very small assemblage) was marine shell and 50 percent mammalian in the Postclassic, with no representatives of freshwater shell.

Consumption or use is the final stage of the economic process before discard. The distribution and materials of the Motul de San José artifacts provide insight to this stage. It is intriguing that shell adornments were exclusively marine in the Postclassic and Preclassic, whereas during the Late and Terminal Classic they were equivalent proportions of marine and freshwater (nacreous river clam). However, that result needs to also be viewed alongside the finding that whereas no adornments were made of bone (presumably local) during the Preclassic, the proportion of mammalian materials used for adornments rose through all periods to reach a peak in the Postclassic. Does this indicate that the diversity of adornment materials and types was increasing or that the proportion of shell available for crafting adornments was decreasing? As well, an important observation is that although residents of the Rank 1 and 2 groups had many more adornments than utilitarian artifacts, and the most molluscan adornments, the highest proportion of marine molluscan adornments was found in Rank 2 deposits, followed by Rank 3 deposits, Rank 1 coming last. Were the adornments found in these deposits for use or for eventual redistribution?

The clue perhaps lies in what was being crafted by different ranks during the different periods. Late Classic Rank 1 residents crafted far fewer marine exotics than did residents of the Rank 2 groups, and crafted somewhat more mammalian remains (primarily as perforators for textile production). Rank 3 households crafted no molluscan materials at all. Many of the freshwater adornments crafted in Rank 1 households may have been nacreous "sparklers" for textile decoration, suggesting in-house production of the tools and adornments for textile working in Rank 1 households, and the crafting of elite exotic adornments in Rank 2 households. In the Terminal Classic as well, most artifacts from Ranks 1 and 2 are adornments, most made of mollusks, and most finished, suggesting the Rank 1 residents were adorned in marine shell. But at this point, Rank 2 artifacts were primarily production debris and almost exclusively of freshwater shell. The Rank 2 residents appear to have been crafting freshwater shell adornments, probably not primarily for their own use.

How then should we interpret the movement of animal resources through the Motul de San José community? Research presented here and elsewhere (Emery 2003a) indicates that initial acquisition of animal resources was, for the most part, quite local to the Motul polity region. A majority of the animals were likely acquired at milpa field edges either opportunistically (associated with farming) or intentionally (through maintenance of high-diversity agricultural field edges and old-field systems to lure edge-browsing prey). However, at a more detailed level, the taxa used by the Motul residents were not always directly local to the site itself (Emery 2003a). Several savannah-loving species (such as armadillos and rabbits, for example) indicate procurement from areas nearer the sites of Akte and Chachaklum, whereas the large-bodied water species (the large turtles, large fish, crocodile, etc.) indicate procurement near Trinidad, directly on the edge of the Lake Petén Itzá. These were obtained either directly by Motul hunters/fishers at unsettled lake edges or indirectly either by trade or tribute from these communities. Work by Thornton (this volume) suggests that the latter is the most likely explanation.

The Motul de San José animal remains reveal another level of complexity. Certainly, the wealthy members of the community had greater access to the large-bodied food species in general, including most large mammals. Earlier research also indicated that the highest-ranking individuals also had and used more of the heavy meat-bearing body portions generally considered of highest food value (Emery 2003a). However, the analysis presented here suggests that initial procurement and processing of certain large-bodied and "high-value" species, such as white-tailed deer, large river turtle, and galliform birds, may have been at the lowest-ranked levels. This raises several questions. Were the Rank 3 community members local farmer/hunters who had access to high- and low-value species and procured, processed, and consumed them independently from the highest elite, or were these Rank 3 folk in fact procuring all resources and processing them in-house (leaving debitage in their middens), but sending the high-value animals as tribute or tax to the highest nobility? I prefer the latter explanation because most of the high-quality meat cuts are found in the deposits of the Rank 1 structures, suggesting that they consumed high-value meat cuts of high-value species. However, some of these species, specifically the large turtle, were primarily available at the lake and not within the immediate bounds of the Motul site catchment. This then begs the question of whether the lower-rank hunters also procured these species directly from more distant areas or indirectly as part of an even more complex system of trade with residents from Trinidad and other lakeside communities.

Other species, those of ceremonial value (dogs, cats, crocodiles, etc.), are found primarily among Rank 1 structures and are not found in the middens of the Rank 3 communities. This suggests that these species were at least processed and used only by the highest elite (to leave debitage in the middens and on floors). They may also have been procured only by the highest elite, although there would be no archaeological record if they were procured by other ranks and brought as complete carcasses to the Rank 1 households. I favor an explanation of exclusive procurement, processing, and use rights among the highest elite.

Intriguingly, the most "valuable" commodity, marine shell, was found in all ranks, and was not most frequent in the homes of the highest ruling elite, but in the homes of the middle-ranked residents. Although the ruling nobility were clearly adorned in marine shell, the middle-status folk were likely the ones crafting many of the shell adornments. An exception appears to be the crafting of pearly nacreous "sparklers" from river clam, which is most common in Rank 1 residences. This finding and the very high proportion of perforators found in these residences (see also Halperin 2008) suggest that textile production might have been accompanied by textile decoration using these shells.

The residents of Motul de San José and its outliers were linked together in a complex economic network that included specialized animal procurement and processing, as well as specialized animal-product crafting. Elite residents had preferential access to high-value species and body portions, but as the hunters, so too did Rank 3 residents. Noble residents crafted alongside the secondary elite, but in different craft specialties. As this study highlights, however, even those relationships were not stable through the occupation of the site. Not surprisingly, as political power centralized in the capital site of the polity, resource access also became more centralized in the hands of the nobility (and it is perhaps at this point that the animal-based economic ties were most complex). During earlier and later periods the resources appeared to have been more equitably distributed and locally acquired.

12

Animal Resource Use and Exchange at an Inland Maya Port

Zooarchaeological Investigations at Trinidad de Nosotros

ERIN KENNEDY THORNTON

This chapter discusses patterns of animal resource use, acquisition, distribution, and exchange at the site of Trinidad de Nosotros (hereafter Trinidad), an important subsidiary site in the Motul polity. The site is located approximately 2.6 kilometers south of the site of Motul de San José and is situated directly on the northern shore of Lake Petén Itzá. Excavation of the site, under the auspices of the larger Motul de San José Archaeological Project, was directed by Matt Moriarty (Tulane University) between 2003 and 2005 (Moriarty, this volume). Based on the site's location, Moriarty has interpreted Trinidad as a Maya port, which likely participated in coastal-inland trade moving east to west across the lake, and farther into the interior of the Petén (Moriarty 2004c). Artificially constructed dock facilities, as well as quantities of exotic goods including obsidian, marine shell, and nonlocal chert and ceramics, have been uncovered at Trinidad, thus supporting the site's interpretation as a trade port (Moriarty 2004d; Moriarty et al. 2004; Spensley 2007a).

Zooarchaeological investigations into the spatial and temporal distribution of animal remains at Trinidad considered how animal products were used as dietary, utilitarian, ornamental, ceremonial, and prestige goods throughout the site's occupation from the Middle Preclassic (ca. 600–300 BC) through the Postclassic (AD 950–1500). These results then address environmental questions regarding how Trinidad's inhabitants used various habitats for natural resource acquisition and economic questions related to exchange and the differential access to resources both within and between regional sites.

Based on Trinidad's lacustrine location, one environmental topic of particular interest was the contribution of aquatic resources to the prehistoric inhabitants' diet. Although species such as turtles and freshwater mollusks appear in many Maya faunal assemblages, freshwater fish remains are much less common, and subsistence patterns at inland Maya sites (especially during the Late Classic period) are generally assumed to be terrestrial-based. Through the use of fine-screen recovery methods, a significant quantity of small fish remains was recovered at Trinidad. Without the use of the fine-screen recovery techniques, only a small fraction of these remains would have been recuperated. The Trinidad faunal assemblage therefore allows us to reexamine aquatic resource use and to explore whether the contribution of freshwater fish to prehistoric Maya diets has been underestimated at other sites due to recovery method bias.

Economic analysis of the Trinidad faunal remains focuses on preferential elite use of particular animal resources for subsistence and ceremonial purposes, as well as on its role within the Motul polity. These topics have been addressed through ceramic and lithic analyses at sites within the Motul region (see Foias et al., this volume; Halperin, this volume; Moriarty, this volume), and this chapter is intended to complement these studies by addressing how animal resources fit into the local and regional economy and exchange networks. One primary question is how Trinidad's possible role as a trade port influenced its residents' overall status and access to resources. To date, few faunal assemblages from inland ports have been identified. This study therefore allows us to examine whether Trinidad's strategic harbor location on the lakeshore and involvement in long-distance exchange of ceramic and lithic artifacts affected both its access to exotic animal resources and its role in providing freshwater aquatic resources to the broader Motul polity. Within this economic framework, I also consider patterns of elite animal use since a large portion of the Trinidad faunal assemblage was recovered from three high-status residential groups and a dense midden associated with the site's ball court. Artifactual and unmodified remains found in these contexts provide information about possible feasting activities and the differential access to certain species, cuts of meat, and bone and shell artifacts.

Study Site: Trinidad de Nosotros

Trinidad is the subject of several chapters in this volume (Moriarty, this volume; Spensley, this volume), but several features of this site are important to reiterate to contextualize the faunal analysis. Moriarty's extensive research has revealed that Trinidad is the largest secondary center within the Motul de San José region (Figure 1.4). Except for the site's harbor facilities, most of the site's architectural features are clustered on top of a high ridge overlooking Lake Petén Itzá. Within the site's epicenter, the prehistoric inhabitants constructed a 12-meter-high radial pyramid, five public plazas, several residential groups, and a ball court. As Moriarty notes, the presence of a ball court at Trinidad is noteworthy because no ball courts have yet been identified at the much larger site of Motul de San José. Trinidad is also unique in the amount of plaza space the site has, considering its overall size and rank as a secondary center (Moriarty 2004d, 33).

Moriarty's survey and excavation of Trinidad's harbor identified a series of artificial terraces and platforms, as well as port facilities consisting of a dock, breakwater, and modified interior harbor wall. The use of Trinidad as a harbor or port site is not surprising considering its location. The site is situated along one of the most accessible stretches of Lake Petén Itzá's northern shoreline, and at the closest point of the lake to major rivers flowing northwestward or westward out of the Petén Lakes region (Moriarty 2004c).

Ceramic analysis data and radiocarbon dates compiled by Moriarty indicate that Trinidad had a long history of precolonial occupation running from the Middle Preclassic through the Postclassic (Moriarty 2004d, 2005, this volume; Moriarty et al. 2007). Trinidad was therefore occupied both before and after the fairly rapid Late Classic florescence of the site of the Motul de San José. Trinidad appears to have expanded during the Late Classic period, but there is also evidence for substantial construction and occupation activity at the site during the Preclassic and Postclassic periods (Moriarty, this volume).

The site's environmental setting on the shore of the Lake Petén Itzá would have given the residents direct access to a diversity of lake taxa, including freshwater mollusks, crabs, fish, turtles, and wading birds or waterfowl. Terrestrial habitats surrounding Trinidad may have been a patchwork of milpas and secondary forest in various stages of regeneration due to the conversion of mature primary forest to agricultural plots (Binford 1983; Deevey et al. 1979; Leyden 2002; Vaughn and Deevey 1985; Wiseman 1985). Isolated pockets of savanna habitats with lower growth and highly weathered soils are also found in the Petén Lakes region both north and east of Trinidad. Mature forest habitats were also probably present in the area, but their extent and distance from the site is unknown.

Background to the Study

Maya Port Sites and Trading Centers

Identification of Maya trading centers is frequently based on the presence of large quantities of exotic materials or on a site's location between resource zones and along known trade routes (Andrews 1990; Dahlin et al. 1998; McKillop 1996). To date, the majority of published research on Maya trading centers has focused on coastal ports of trade (Andrews 1990; Andrews et al. 1988; Dahlin et al. 1998; Guderjan and Garber 1995; McKillop 1996; McKillop and Healy 1989; Sabloff and Freidel 1975), whereas inland trade centers have received much less attention. Discussions of trading center economies are therefore biased toward their function within coastal trade networks.

Over the years, several different interpretations of trading centers have been proposed. Early models of trading centers as politically neutral places where foreign traders met to engage in the exchange of elite luxury goods (Chapman 1957) have been rejected based on evidence for less restricted distributions of exotic resources (Hammond 1972) and the potential use of trading ports as outposts for larger Maya centers (Andrews 1990; Berdan 1978). Other interpretations of Maya trading centers emphasize their utility as transshipment ports where long-distance trade goods are accumulated and then diverted inland for distribution (Andrews et al. 1988; Guderjan, Garber, and Smith 1989; McKinnon 1989). This model has only been applied to coastal trade ports, but similar roles can be inferred for inland sites like Trinidad, which may have served to distribute trade goods away from major riverine or lacustrine transportation routes. Besides their important function as distribution hubs, Maya trading centers may also have been established for the extraction or production of trade commodities, including faunal resources (D. Chase and A. Chase 1989; McKillop 1996). In northern Belize, excess processing of marine fish for exchange has been identified at the sites of Cerros (Carr 1986); Northern River Lagoon (Masson 2004; Mock 1997); and Isla Cerritos (Masson 2004). Remains at Caye Coho also suggest specialized production of marine shell artifacts for export (Masson 2002).

Status and Ceremony: Patterns of Elite Maya Animal Use

Demand for specific animal resources for dietary consumption, artifact production, and ritual or ceremonial use by the upper classes undoubtedly impacted the distribution of animal remains at Maya archaeological sites. In general, Pohl (1990, 1985b) has suggested that faunal samples from higher-status groups are characterized by high species diversity. Although the greater number of species identified in elite deposits could be a product of preservation bias, it may also reflect greater dietary breadth among the elite and the use of rare species or suites of species for ceremonial or ornamental purposes. Particular species favored by the Maya elite include the white-tailed deer (*Odocoileus virginianus*), peccary (*Pecari tajacu* and *Tayassu pecari*), domestic dog (*Canis lupus familiaris*), turkey (*Meleagris* sp.), and the giant Central American river turtle (*Dermatemys mawii*; see Carr 1985; Emery 2007a; Giddens Teeter 2004). Additional species that are found almost exclusively in high status and ritual deposits include: rabbit (*Sylvilagus* sp.), quail (*Colinus* sp.), large felids (*Puma concolor* and *Panthera onca*), and marine fish and shellfish when found at inland sites (Beaubien 2004; Carr 1985; Moholy-Nagy 1985, 2004; Pohl 1983, 1990).

Maya elites may also have had preferential access to particular skeletal elements or cuts of meat. At some sites elite deposits contain more major meat-bearing elements (e.g., bones of the fore and hind limbs) of preferred game species (Pohl 1983, 1985b, 1990). In particular, Pohl has suggested that elites may have had much greater access to deer hind limbs, which have been identified in codices and from ethnohistoric accounts as a form of elite tribute (Tozzer 1941; Tozzer and Allen 1910). Although they are not major meat-bearing elements, crania may also be overrepresented in elite or ritual deposits due to their use in ceremonial costumes or their deposition in ritual contexts (Brown 2001, 2005; Pohl 1983, 1981). Preferential use of left body portions in elite and ceremonial contexts has also been previously reported though it does not appear to be consistent (Emery 2004a; Pohl 1983, 1990; Pohl and Pohl 1983; Pohl 1985b; Savage 1971).

A final characteristic that may distinguish elite and ceremonial animal use in the Maya area is presence of juvenile or subadult individuals. The remains of young animals are relatively uncommon in Maya faunal assemblages as a whole, but they are found in much higher frequency in elite and ritual deposits (Carr 1996; Emery 2003b, 2004a; Emery and Thornton 2008a; Pohl 1983, 1981; Thornton 2008; Wing and Scudder 1991). This may be a feature of improved preservational conditions in the larger limestone structures of the elite and ritual core, but may also reflect the special role of juvenile individuals as high-status or ritual commodities. Certain species that tend to be represented by subadult individuals include deer, peccaries, dogs, and felids, although young birds, turtles, crocodiles, and mollusks have also been found in cache deposits (Emery and Thornton 2008a). Favored selection of young individuals may have been based on culinary preference or on the association of juvenile individuals with symbols of renewal or rebirth if the animals were used for ceremonial purposes (Pohl 1981, 1983).

Methods

Field Methods and Sample Recovery

During general excavation directed by Moriarty, faunal remains were recovered by processing excavated soil through 1/4-inch mesh screens. All faunal remains, including possible intrusive species such as small rodents and terrestrial gastropods, were collected. However, when large accumulations of terrestrial gastropods were encountered, a subsample of the representative species was often taken to conserve excavation time.

Since it is generally accepted that fine-screen sieving methods (e.g., 1/8- or 1/16-inch mesh) are the most effective means of recovering zooarchaeological materials (James 1997; Shaffer and Sanchez 1994; Wake 2004), a series of five- to ten-liter soil samples was also water-screened through nested 1/4-, 1/8-, and 1/16-inch mesh screens to quantify the effects of recovery method procedures on the zooarchaeological sample. A total of 116 soil samples (749 liters) from a variety of contexts including floor surfaces, middens, burials, and fill deposits were gently water-screened through the nested sieves by Thornton between 2004 and 2006, following protocols developed by Emery. The faunal remains recovered from the fine-screen tests are compared to those recovered through general excavation to evaluate the effects of fine-screen recovery procedures on the site's faunal assemblage composition.

Methods of Zooarchaeological Analysis

I conducted the faunal identifications under the supervision of Dr. Kitty Emery (Florida Museum of Natural History) primarily at the Florida Museum of Natural History (FLMNH) Environmental Archaeology Laboratory (Gainesville, Florida). At FLMNH, faunal remains were identified using modern comparative collections housed in the museum's Environmental Archaeology collection.[1] All faunal remains including intrusive and nonintrusive species were analyzed, but potentially modern rodents and terrestrial gastropods have been omitted from the current analysis. Small rodents were deemed to be intrusive when the skeletal remains appeared to be much better preserved than those found in the same or nearby contexts. It was much more difficult to determine whether the remains of other burrowing species such as armadillos were archaeological or intrusive, but the same process of visual preservation assessment was applied.

Standard zooarchaeological procedures were used to analyze the faunal assemblage (see Grayson 1984; Reitz and Wing 2008). Data collected for each specimen include: closest taxonomic identification, element, element side, portion/completeness, pathology, and age and sex characteristics. Cultural and natural modification of the remains was also noted, including observations of butchery, artifactual modification, burning, rodent or carnivore gnawing, root etching, and extensive weathering.

The zooarchaeological assemblage was quantified according to the number of identified specimens (NISP). Although NISP tallies have the potential to overestimate the contribution of species with large numbers of identifiable elements, such as turtles and armadillos, other derived quantification measures, including the minimum number of individuals, tend to overestimate the contribution of rare species that may only be represented in the assemblage by one or two specimens (Grayson 1984; Lyman 2008; Reitz and Wing 2008). Whenever possible, fragments of the same element were refit and counted as a single specimen. When large numbers of armadillo scutes or very small fragments of mollusk shells were recovered from a single context, these remains were also tallied conservatively in terms of NISP. Although this method is slightly subjective, it prevents the overcounting of remains from a single but highly fragmented element or individual.

Sample Description

The Trinidad faunal assemblage contains 10,687 vertebrate and invertebrate faunal remains (Table 12.1). A total of 3,823 bone and shell fragments were recovered during general excavation, whereas the remaining 6,864 fragments were recovered in the soil samples processed through a series of fine-mesh screens. The remains were recovered from 237 excavation units ranging between 0.5 and 8.0 square meters (average = 1.0 square meter) in size.

Although preservation varied greatly across the site, the faunal remains were fairly well preserved overall. Extensive weathering, root etching, and rodent gnawing was observed on only a small number of specimens (less

Table 12.1. Animal taxa identified in the Trinidad de Nosotros faunal assemblage quantified by the number of identified specimens (NISP)

Scientific name	Common name	General excavation		Fine screen		Total	
		NISP	%	NISP	%	NISP	%
Vertebrata	Vertebrate (unidentified)	494	12.9	2,929	42.7	3,423	32
MAMMALS							
Mammalia	Mammal	37	1	460	6.7	497	4.7
Mammalia (very large)	Mammal (e.g., deer, tapir)	17	0.4	—	—	17	0.2
Mammalia (large)	Mammal (e.g., deer)	602	15.7	218	3.2	820	7.7
Mammalia (medium/large)	Mammal (e.g., deer, dog)	118	3.1	649	9.5	767	7.2
Mammalia (medium)	Mammal (e.g., dog)	67	1.8	4	0.1	71	0.7
Mammalia (small/medium)	Mammal (e.g., dog, agouti)	66	1.7	8	0.1	74	0.7
Mammalia (small)	Mammal (e.g., rodent)	—	—	13	0.2	13	0.1
Didelphidae	Opossum	1	0	0	0	1	0
Didelphis sp.	Opossum	5	0.1	1	0	6	0.1
Dasypus novemcinctus	Armadillo	217	5.7	20	0.3	237	2.2
Rodentia	Rodent	—	—	9	0.1	9	0.1
Sciuridae	Squirrel	—	—	1	0	1	0
Muridae	Mouse/rat	—	—	27	0.4	27	0.3
Sylvilagus sp.	Rabbit	10	0.3	—	—	10	0.1
Orthogeomys hispidus	Pocket gopher	1	0	1	0	2	0
Agouti/Dasyprocta sp.	Paca/agouti	4	0.1	—	—	4	0
Agouti paca	Paca	4	0.1	—	—	4	0
Dasyprocta punctata	Agouti	6	0.2	—	—	6	0.1
Eira barbara	Tayra	1	0	—	—	1	0
Bassariscus sumichrasti	Cacomistle	2	0.1	—	—	2	0
Nasua narica	Coati	—	—	1	0	1	0

(continued)

Table 12.1. (Continued)

Scientific name	Common name	General excavation		Fine screen		Total	
		NISP	%	NISP	%	NISP	%
Canis lupus familiaris	Domestic dog	21	0.5	—	—	21	0.2
Urocyon cinereoargenteus	Gray fox	1	0	—	—	1	0
Leopardus pardalis	Ocelot	1	0	—	—	1	0
Puma concolor	Puma	2	0.1	—	—	2	0
Artiodactyla	Artiodactyl	2	0.1	—	—	2	0
Tayassuidae	Peccary	17	0.4	—	—	17	0.2
Cervidae	Deer	11	0.3	—	—	11	0.1
Mazama sp.	Brocket deer	20	0.5	1	0	21	0.2
Odocoileus virginianus	White—tailed deer	104	2.7	—	—	104	1
BIRDS							
Aves	Bird	1	0	—	—	1	0
Aves (large)	Bird (e.g., turkey)	18	0.5	—	—	18	0.2
Aves (medium/large)	Bird (e.g., turkey, duck)	6	0.2	—	—	6	0.1
Aves (medium)	Bird (e.g., duck)	5	0.1	—	—	5	0
Meleagris ocellata	Ocellated turkey	4	0.1	—	—	4	0
Colinus nigrogularis	Quail	3	0.1	—	—	3	0
REPTILES/AMPHIBIANS							
Anura	Frog/toad	—	—	9	0.1	9	0.1
Reptilia/Amphibia	Reptile/amphibian	—	—	2	0	2	0
Reptilia	Reptile	2	0.1	1	0	3	0
Crocodylus sp.	Crocodile	1	0	—	—	1	0
Lacertilia	Lizard	—	—	3	0	3	0
Iguanidae	Iguana	1	0	—	—	1	0
Testudines	Turtle	45	1.2	3	0	48	0.4

Taxon	Common name						
Testudines (medium/large)	Turtle (medium)	48	1.3	—	—	48	0.4
Testudines (small/medium)	Turtle (small/medium)	2	0.1	—	—	2	0
Testudines (small)	Turtle (small)	3	0.1	—	—	3	0
Cheloniidae	Sea turtle	2	0.1	—	—	2	0
Chelydra serpentina	Snapping turtle	1	0	—	—	1	0
Kinosternidae	Mud/musk turtle	7	0.2	2	0	9	0.1
Kinosternon sp.	Mud/musk turtle	5	0.1	—	—	5	0
Kinosternon acutum	Tabasco mud turtle	1	0	—	—	1	0
Kinosternon leucostomum	White-lipped mud turtle	1	0	—	—	1	0
Staurotypus triporcatus	Giant musk turtle	13	0.3	—	—	13	0.1
Dermatemys mawii	Central American river turtle	17	0.4	—	—	17	0.2
Emydidae	Emydid turtle	6	0.2	1	0	7	0.1
Rhinoclemmys areolata	Furrowed wood turtle	7	0.2	—	—	7	0.1
Trachemys scripta	Slider turtle	16	0.4	—	—	16	0.1
Serpentes	Snake	2	0.1	6	0.1	8	0.1
Crotalus sp.	Rattlesnake	—	—	1	0	1	0
FISH							
Rajiformes	Stingray	—	—	1	0	1	0
Osteichthyes	Fish	4	0.1	1,269	18.5	1,273	11.9
Atractosteus tropicus	Gar	—	—	13	0.2	13	0.1
Siluriformes	Catfish	—	—	3	0	3	0
Ariidae	Catfish	—	—	1	0	1	0
Rhamdia sp.	Catfish	—	—	1	0	1	0
Synbranchidae	Swamp eel	—	—	19	0.3	19	0.2
Cichlidae (2 species)	Cichlid	1	0	156	2.3	157	1.5
Cichlosoma sp.	Cichlid	—	—	1	0	1	0
Cichlosoma urophthalmus	Cichlid	—	—	1	0	1	0
Petenia splendida	Blanco	1	0	1	0	2	0

(*continued*)

Table 12.1. (Continued)

Scientific name	Common name	General excavation		Fine screen		Total	
		NISP	%	NISP	%	NISP	%
INVERTEBRATES							
Decapoda	Crab	5	0.1	1	0	6	0.1
Mollusca	Mollusk	1	0	402	5.9	403	3.8
Gastropoda	Gastropod	1	0	413	6	414	3.9
Pachychilus sp.	Jute	3	0.1	2	0	5	0
Pachychilus glaphyrus	Jute	9	0.2	1	0	10	0.1
Pachychilus indiorum	Jute	331	8.7	7	0.1	338	3.2
Pomacea flagellata	Apple snail	1,088	28.5	172	2.5	1,260	11.8
Bivalvia	Bivalve	4	0.1	4	0.1	8	0.1
Unionidae	Freshwater mussel	203	5.3	4	0.1	207	1.9
Lampsilis sp.	Freshwater mussel	11	0.3	—	—	11	0.1
Nephronaias sp.	Freshwater mussel	2	0.1	—	—	2	0
Psoronaias sp.	Freshwater mussel	52	1.4	—	—	52	0.5
Psoronaias percompressus	Freshwater mussel	1	0	—	—	1	0
Psoronaias semigranosus	Freshwater mussel	6	0.2	—	—	6	0.1
Mollusca (marine)	Marine mollusk	6	0.2	11	0.2	17	0.2
Gastropoda (marine)	Marine gastropod	4	0.1	—	—	4	0
Dentaliidae	Tusk shell	1	0	1	0	2	0
Strombus sp.	Conch	16	0.4	—	—	16	0.1
Strombus pugilis	Fighting conch	1	0	—	—	1	0
Oliva sp.	Olive shell	14	0.4	—	—	14	0.1
Oliva sayana	Lettered olive	3	0.1	—	—	3	0
Olivella sp.	Olivella shell	—	—	8	0.1	8	0.1

Prunum sp.	Marginella	1	0	—	—	1	0
Prunum apicinum	Marginella	—	—	1	0	1	0
Columbella mercatoria	Common dove shell	1	0	—	—	1	0
Spondylus sp.	Spondylus	1	0	1	0	2	0
Asaphis deflorata	Gaudy sanguin	1	0	—	—	1	0
Arca zebra	Turkey wing	1	0	—	—	1	0
Dinocardium robustum	Cockle	1	0	—	—	1	0
Donax denticulatus	Donax	1	0	—	—	1	0
Total		**3,823**	**100**	**6,864**	**100**	**10,687**	**100**

than 1 percent of the sample). Sample preservation may also be assessed through the number of specimens identified to a particular taxonomic level, since highly weathered and fragmented assemblages contain more remains that cannot be identified below the level of taxonomic class. Within the Trinidad faunal assemblage, approximately 59 percent of the general excavation remains were identified to the level of taxonomic family or below, and 41 percent of the remains were only identifiable to the level of class or above. In contrast, only 6 percent of the fine-screened remains were identifiable to family or below, and 94 percent were identified to the level of class or above. Differences in the size of fragments recovered through general excavation and fine screened samples accounts for much of this variation. However, the fine-screen samples also contained a large number of well-preserved fish remains, which were not identified below the level of taxonomic class due to a lack of appropriate comparative specimens at FLMNH. A greater percentage of the remains would have been identified to a lower taxonomic level if more modern skeletal specimens had been available.

Taxonomic Composition of the Assemblage

The Trinidad faunal assemblage contains a total of fifty-eight taxa spread across eight classes (mammals, birds, reptiles, bony fishes, cartilaginous fishes, bivalves, gastropods, and crustaceans; see Table 12.1). According to NISP tallies, mammals are the most commonly identified animals in the assemblage (42 percent), followed by freshwater mollusks (30 percent), and fish (23 percent; see Figure 12.1). The remaining 5 percent of the assemblage is composed of reptiles (3 percent), birds (1 percent), and marine mollusks (1 percent).

Apart from the NISP tallies, the taxonomic composition of the assemblage differs between the general excavation and fine-screened samples (Figure 12.2). More than 50 percent of the general excavation remains are freshwater mollusks, and fish account for less than 1 percent of the sample. In contrast, 47 percent of the fine-screened animal remains are fish, and a much smaller percentage (6 percent) is freshwater mollusks. These results emphasize the importance of using fine-screen recovery methods within the Maya region, especially at sites located near major lakes and rivers. Without the fine-screen sample, the dietary contribution of small fish at Trinidad would have been greatly underestimated. Additional taxa that

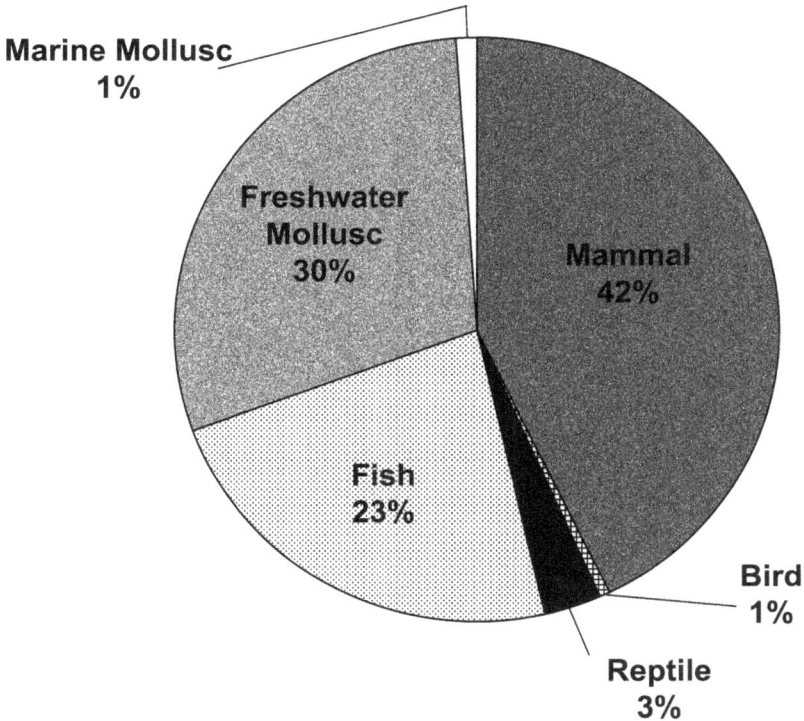

Figure 12.1. Taxonomic composition (percent NISP) of the Trinidad faunal assemblage.

would not have been identified in the sample without fine-screen recovery techniques include: coati (*Nasua narica*), squirrel (Sciuridae), rattlesnake (*Crotalus* sp.), frog/toad (Anura), stingray (Rajiformes), and small olivella shells (*Olivella* sp.).

Mammals

The remains of eighteen separate species of mammals were identified in the Trinidad assemblage. The most commonly identified animals include armadillo (*Dasypus novemcinctus*), white-tailed deer, domestic dog, brocket deer (*Mazama* sp.), and peccary (Tayassuidae). Other species present in the assemblage, but represented by ten or fewer specimens, include: opossum (*Didelphis* sp.), squirrel, rat (Muridae), rabbit, pocket gopher (*Orthogeomys hispidus*), paca (*Agouti paca*), agouti (*Dasyprocta punctata*), tayra (*Eira barbara*), cacomistle (*Bassariscus sumichrasti*), coati, fox (*Urocyon cinereoargenteus*), ocelot (*Leopardus pardalis*), and puma.

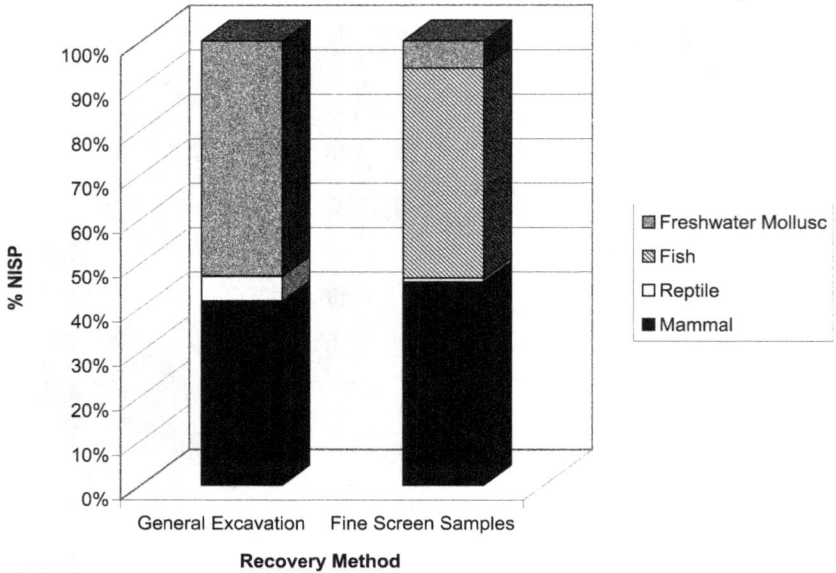

Figure 12.2. Comparison of the taxonomic composition of the general excavation and fine-screen samples.

Birds

The majority of avian remains in the assemblage were unidentifiable long bone shaft fragments of large-bodied species. Based on the size and thickness of the long bones, they likely come from turkeys or other large birds such as the curassow, guan, or chachalaca, although other large taxa including wading birds and raptors cannot be ruled out. Well-preserved and more complete remains of turkey and quail were identified in an elite midden context associated with the site's ball court.

Reptiles and Amphibians

Over 85 percent of the site's reptilian remains are turtle carapace and plastron fragments. Common terrestrial and aquatic turtle species in the assemblage include: the musk turtle (*Kinosternon* sp.), slider turtle (*Trachemys scripta*), furrowed wood turtle (*Rhinoclemmys areolata*), Central American river turtle, giant musk turtle (*Staurotypus triporcatus*), and snapping turtle (*Chelydra serpentina*). Surprisingly, two fragments of sea turtle (Cheloniidae) plastron were identified in a Postclassic fill deposit within the site's port area. This animal represents a long-distance trade item transported into the site from either the Atlantic or Pacific coast. A small number of remains of frog/toad, crocodile (*Crocodylus* sp.), small lizard, iguana, and rattlesnake were also present. Snake remains of species other than the rattlesnake were found, but they were not identifiable to family, genus, or species. The presence of rattlesnake at Trinidad suggests at least some use of savanna habitats for animal resource acquisition (J. Lee 2000).

Fish

A single stingray tail spine fragment was recovered along with several obsidian blades in a Postclassic cache deposit near the site's port facilities (platform GG, cache #4). All of the other fish remains recovered at the site are from small freshwater species, which would have been abundant in nearby Lake Petén Itzá. Several species of cichlids (including *Petenia esplendida* and *Cichlasoma uropthalmus*), gars (*Atracosteus tropicus*), swamp eels (Synbranchidae), and catfish (*Rhamdia* sp.) were the most common species in the assemblage. Since many of the fish at Trinidad are very small, they were likely cooked whole in soup rather than being filleted or smoked. Unfortunately, a portion of the freshwater fish remains identified in the site's port/harbor area may be modern rather than archaeological due to periodic inundation of the site's low-lying areas. The distinction between archaeological and potentially modern fish remains is considered in more detail in the discussion below.

Invertebrates

Locally abundant apple snails (*Pomacea flagellata*) are the most common freshwater mollusks in the assemblage, followed by jute (*Pachychilus* sp.) and several species of river clams (Unionidae: *Lampsilis*, *Nephronais*, and *Psoronaias* sp.). Apple snails could have been obtained along the shores of Lake Petén Itzá, but the jute and river clams may have come from nearby rivers, like Rio Kantetul, since these taxa prefer aquatic habitats with fast-moving water (Goodrich and van der Schalie 1937).

Eleven species of marine mollusks were also found at Trinidad. They include small species (e.g., *Olivella* sp., *Prunum* sp., *Columbella mercatoria*, and Dentaliidae), which were probably used as beads, as well as larger species (e.g., *Strombus* sp., *Oliva* sp., *Dinocardium robustum*, and *Spondylus* sp.), which were used as larger artifacts such as pendants, tinklers, shell disks, and other adornments.

Spatial Distribution of Animal Remains at Trinidad

These faunal remains were recovered from 237 excavation units spread across twenty-one operations (Figures 7.1, 8.1). A large percentage of the faunal remains from Trinidad was recovered in the site's harbor area (46 percent). Significant quantities of archaeological bone and shell were also recovered from Group G (26 percent), a middle-status residential platform located southwest of the ceremonial precinct; Group A (8 percent), which includes the site's principle structure; the site's ball court (7 percent); Group C (6 percent) and Group Y (3 percent), two high-elite residential groups connected to Trinidad's ceremonial core; and Group O (2 percent), a low- to middle-status residential group located on the western side of Plaza V. Excavations in the remaining proveniences yielded less than one hundred fragments per group. The following paragraphs discuss areas of the site with significant faunal assemblages and compare status groups occupying the site's ceremonial precinct and more peripheral areas. Full descriptions of the faunal remains recovered from each architectural group are available as part of this volume's digital appendix on the web (http://motul-archaeology.williams.edu/).

Group F—Ball Court (Operations 1F and 10)

Excavations directly behind Trinidad's eastern ball court structures (F-2, 3, and 4) uncovered several rich middens containing well-preserved animal remains. Moriarty and Foias (2007) have argued that these middens are the result of feasting associated with the ball game. Therefore, it is not surprising that, in comparison to other Late Classic faunal samples at Trinidad, the Group F middens have greater taxonomic diversity and a greater portion of exotic species and bone and shell artifacts.

Thirty-three taxa were identified in the sample including: opossum, agouti, rabbit, armadillo, domestic dog, peccary, deer, turkey, quail, fish, jute, apple snail, river clam, and four species of turtle. Several of these species have been suggested as preferred sacrificial or feasting animals including the turkey, deer, dog, rabbit, and quail (Pohl 1983, 1985b). It is therefore significant that with the exception of the dog, all of these species are either exclusively present or present in much greater quantities in the ball court middens than in other Late Classic deposits at Trinidad. Additional species are only represented in the ball court middens as modified artifactual remains. These include the puma and cacomistle (which are represented by perforated teeth) and various species of marine mollusks such as conch

(*Strombus* sp.), spondylus (*Spondylus* sp.), and tusk (Dentallidae), and olive shells (*Oliva* sp.).

The Group F middens are also distinct in terms of skeletal element and age class distributions. In the ball court middens, hind limb elements are present in much greater-than-expected frequencies, whereas cranial, axial, and distal elements are all underrepresented in the sample. However, the difference is not statistically significant for cranial and distal regions. It is also interesting to note that all but one of the artiodactyl (deer and peccary) hind limb elements come from the left side of the body. Few subadult animals were identified in the Trinidad assemblage, but nearly all of them were found in the ball court middens. Young individuals of white-tailed deer, peccary, agouti/paca, and two species of emydid turtle were among those identified.

Although browned, blackened, and calcined remains are not common across the site as a whole, a larger percentage (6 percent) of the faunal remains from Group F showed evidence of burning. Most of the burned remains were found in a high-density midden located east of Str. F-4. Many of the bones were burned on both the interior and exterior surface or on the interior surface only. This indicates that the bones were burnt after being defleshed and deposited as trash, instead of being burnt as part of the food-preparation process.

Artifactually modified faunal remains are also more common in the ball court middens than in any other deposit at the site. A majority of bone and shell artifacts (greater than 60 percent) from these deposits are ornamental objects such as tinklers, earplugs, and beads—many of which were made from exotic marine shells. Smaller quantities of bone and shell debitage were also identified in the sample along with a pair of bone rasps and utilitarian items such as bone needles, picks, and fragments of worked antler. Significantly, few other utilitarian bone or shell implements were found in other areas of the site.

Group G (Operations 1G and 5)

A large faunal sample was also obtained from excavations in Group G, a middle-status residential platform located southwest of the site's public plazas and monumental core. Group G consists of a 2.8-meter-high basal platform, which supports three structures surrounding an interior plaza. The western structure (G-1) is the largest in the group. Based on ceramic analysis, the group had a long occupation history spanning from the Middle Preclassic to Postclassic (Moriarty et al. 2004). The residents of the group may have been involved in chert artifact production during the Classic period, and to a lesser extent in the production of obsidian artifacts during the Middle Preclassic (Halperin and Hernández Véliz 2004).

This group is unique because fine-screening recovered a large quantity of well-preserved small freshwater fish remains. This represents the greatest concentration of fish remains outside the harbor area. Many of the fish are small species of cichlids, but swamp eel and gar were also present. Some of the fish remains were recovered from a high-density Preclassic midden buried in the interior plaza east of the group's main structure, but the majority of fish bones came from an interior floor surface within structure G-1. Based on stratigraphy and associated ceramics, they likely date to a Late Preclassic occupation.

Other taxa identified in the Group G faunal sample include apple snail, jute, freshwater clam, domestic dog, rabbit, agouti, armadillo, deer, peccary, bird, frog/toad, snake, and turtle. All of the jute found in the Group G middens show evidence of butchery by having the spire lopped off. Three species of nonlocal marine shells were also identified. All of the marine shells were artifactually modified into tinklers, perforated shell pendants, beads, or other types of ornaments. An isolated spire of a conch shell that was cut and removed from the body whorl is the only evidence for possible on-site shell artifact production in Group G. Other bone and shell artifacts found in Group G include two fragments of polished mammal bone and two perforated freshwater clamshells. One of the perforated clamshells was a very large individual identified as *Psoronaias percompressus*.[2] This shell was associated with a Middle Preclassic burial placed beneath the group's interior plaza floor.

Harbor (Operations 2 and 12)

The harbor area at Trinidad contains port facilities and architectural structures that may have been used to facilitate transportation, for aquatic resource extraction, or for ceremonial purposes. Although ceramic fishing weights were found scattered across the site, the majority of them were found within and around architectural features near Trinidad's harbor (Spensley 2003, 2007a). This suggests that the area was an important site for fishing, fish processing, or net production.

Excavations in the harbor produced a large (n = 4,943) and highly diverse faunal sample (greater than thirty taxa). Many of the harbor remains were recovered from dense midden deposits located near Structure EE, which forms the interior wall of Trinidad's harbor. Some of the middens near Structure EE appear to have been burned (Moriarty, personal communication 2007). Similar to Group F, the faunal remains were burned after disposal, rather than during cooking. There is some indication that the burning may have been associated with termination rituals occurring between the Late Classic and Postclassic occupation of this structure (Moriarty, personal communication).

Core versus Periphery: Diet, Crafting, Ritual, and Differential Access to Resources

Comparison of animal remains found in the site's ceremonial core and more peripheral zones can provide information about the differential access to resources across status boundaries and activity areas. For this analysis, I have divided the site into three broad zones: the ceremonial core, peripheral core, and harbor. The ceremonial core includes those architectural groups and features directly connected to the main plazas. This area encompasses the site's ball court, main pyramid structures, and elite residential units. The peripheral core includes the slightly smaller residential groups surrounding, but not attached to, Trinidad's ceremonial precinct. Based on the degree of architectural elaboration, these groups are generally interpreted as slightly lower status than those in the ceremonial core. The harbor area is considered separately due to its greater distance from the site's architectural core and the different types of activities that might have been carried out in this area. The following comparisons are also limited to well-dated Late Classic deposits. Although this reduces the sample sizes, it controls for temporal variation in animal use.

At the peak of the Motul polity, the residents of Trinidad's ceremonial core had preferential access to birds, turtles, and various mammalian taxa including deer, peccary, dog, agouti/paca, armadillo, and rabbit (Figure 12.3). Many of these species were likely selected as preferred dietary resources by the Trinidad elite, but other nondietary uses cannot be ruled out. For example, perforated puma and cacomistle teeth, bone pins and needles, and a pair of white-tailed deer metapodial rasps in the ball court middens indicate the secondary use of animal remains as adornments, utilitarian tools, and musical instruments. A large portion of the molluscan remains (20 percent) from the ceremonial core also represent adornments rather than dietary resources. The artifactually modified shells are primarily marine species and freshwater clams, both of which are most common in the ceremonial core during all time periods.

Residents of the slightly lower-status peripheral core had less access to mammals, birds, and turtles, and instead used fish and freshwater mollusks

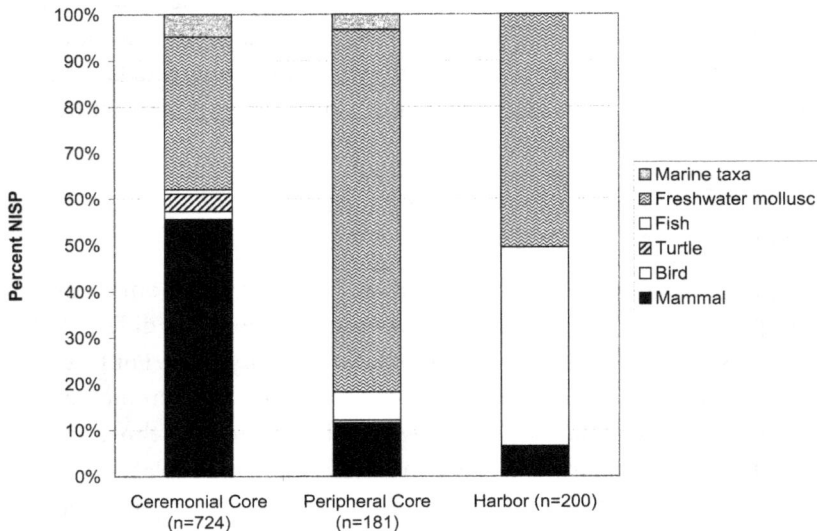

Figure 12.3. Distribution of major taxonomic groups across spatial and status boundaries at Trinidad.

to a greater extent (Figure 12.4). Freshwater jute shells are particularly abundant in the peripheral core middens, and nearly all of the shells show evidence of butchery by having their spires chopped off. In certain archaeological contexts, jute have been suggested to be ritual or feasting resources (Halperin et al. 2003; Healy, Emery, and Wright 1990). However, since most of the jute at Trinidad are found in residential middens and within the peripheral core, rather than in the ceremonial core, this suggests that jute were being used primarily as dietary rather than ritual resources. Moreover, jute are uncommon in the site's burials, caches, and ball court middens.

Small numbers of exotic marine shells were also found dispersed across several of the peripheral core residential groups, but the quantities are small in comparison to the ceremonial core. Since most of the architectural groups in the peripheral core appear to be residential in nature, it is likely that the remains reflect more domestic and mundane activities than the middens in the ceremonial precinct, which contain a mixture of elite residential and ceremonial refuse.

Late Classic animal use in Trinidad's harbor is focused on freshwater fish and shellfish. It is not unexpected that the refuse in this area primarily comes from aquatic taxa, but the lack of turtles is surprising. Jute and freshwater clams are also much less common in the harbor than in the

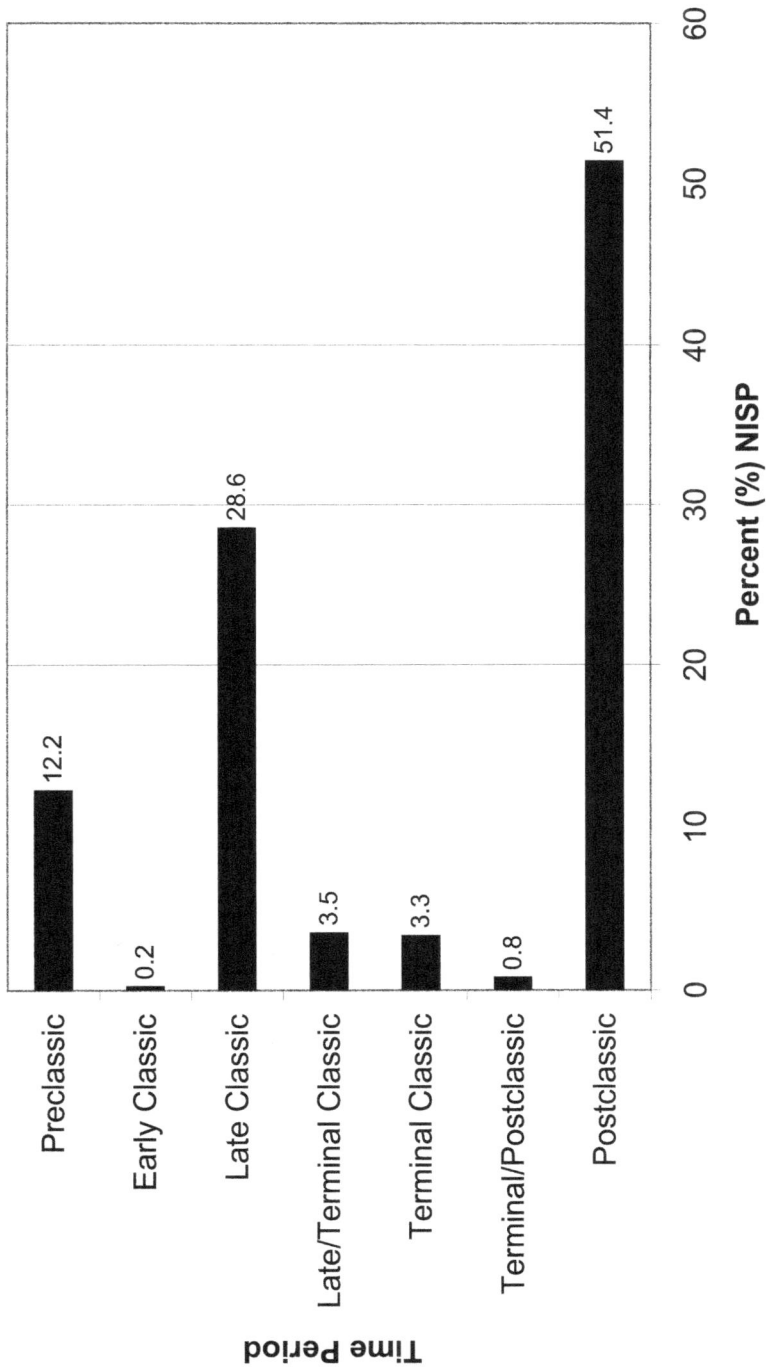

Figure 12.4. Temporal distribution of Trinidad faunal remains datable to a particular time period. Remains from undated or mixed deposits are not included in the percentages.

ceremonial and peripheral core areas, whereas apple snails are more common. The nature and use of the Late Classic structures in the harbor are not entirely clear, but it is possible that the area was used to some extent for fishing and shellfish collection or fish and shellfish processing.

There is little evidence across the site of Trinidad for the production of bone and shell artifacts. However, the fragments of faunal debitage found at the site suggest that artifact production primarily took place in the ceremonial core. Bone and marine shell working activities are particularly limited to the ceremonial core, whereas freshwater shell modification occurred more evenly across the site. This pattern is especially pronounced in the Late Classic period before bone working increased slightly in the harbor area during the Postclassic. Crafting took place in elite and subelite residential groups across the entire site (ceremonial core, peripheral core, and harbor). However, the largest quantities of bone and shell debitage were found in nonresidential contexts, including middens associated with the site's ball court and interior harbor wall.

Temporal Distribution of Animal Remains

Considering the long history of human occupation at Trinidad from the Middle Preclassic through Early Postclassic, we also need to consider how the faunal remains are temporally distributed (Figure 12.4). Approximately 30 percent of the site's zooarchaeological assemblage comes from either mixed or undated deposits. However, the remaining 70 percent may be assigned to a time period based on a combination of ceramic, stratigraphic, and carbon-14 dating techniques. In the following discussion, only remains from securely dated deposits are considered. Faunal remains dating to the Early Classic are also not discussed due to an extremely small sample size (NISP = 10).

The earliest faunal remains at Trinidad date to the Middle and Late Preclassic (12 percent of the dated assemblage). Since the number of remains that can be firmly dated to the Middle Preclassic is very small, the entire Preclassic sample is considered here as a single assemblage, which primarily represents Late Preclassic animal use. A majority (76 percent) of the Preclassic fauna come from Group G with smaller quantities coming from Groups C (14 percent), A (3 percent), and F (3 percent). Therefore, the Preclassic sample largely represents animal use in a middle-status residential context, although elite residential and ceremonial contexts are also represented to a much lesser extent. Small freshwater fish account for 68 percent of the Preclassic remains, and mammals (17 percent), freshwater mollusks

(14 percent), and turtles (less than 1 percent) are less common (Figure 12.5). This indicates heavy dependence on local aquatic resources obtained from Lake Petén Itzá or other nearby bodies of water. Only 1 percent of the Preclassic remains are from non-local taxa such as marine mollusks, but this accounts for 12 percent of all of the nonlocal taxa identified at the site across all time periods.

A large portion of the Preclassic terrestrial faunal remains are unidentifiable long bone shaft fragments of large and medium-bodied mammals, but remains of armadillo, rabbit, squirrel, dog, brocket deer, and white-tailed deer were also identified. Unlike other Preclassic assemblages in Mesoamerica (e.g., Blake et al. 1992; Carr 1985; Emery et al., in press; Masson 2004; Shaw 1991; Wing 1978; Wing and Scudder 1991), dogs were not common at Trinidad during this time period. However, this may be due to the fact that the Trinidad Preclassic remains come primarily from a middle-status residential complex. Recent research suggests that dogs are much more common in Preclassic elite administrative, residential, and ceremonial contexts than in peripheral or lower-status areas (Emery 2002; Emery et al., in press; Rosenswig 2007).

The Late Classic faunal sample is larger (29 percent of the dated assemblage) and more taxonomically diverse than the Preclassic assemblage (Figure 12.5). Freshwater fish are much less common in the Late Classic (10 percent); instead the sample is dominated by mammals (43 percent)

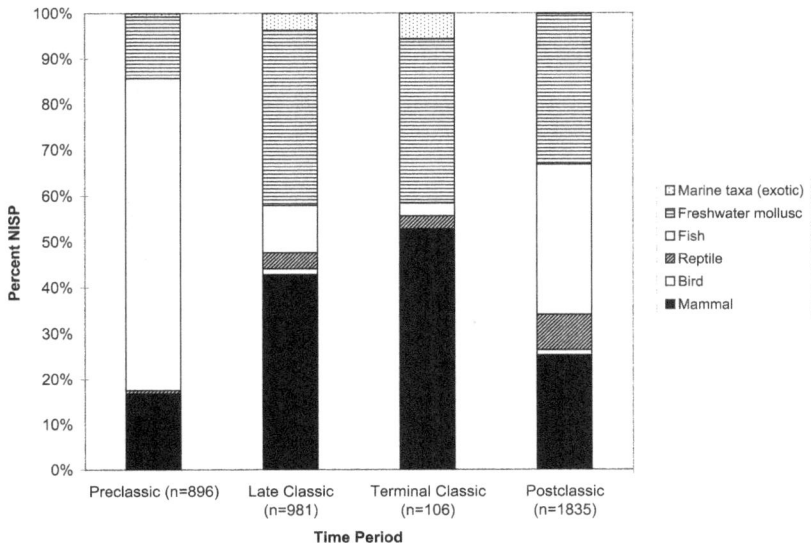

Figure 12.5. Chronological variation in animal use at Trinidad (by percent NISP).

and freshwater shellfish (28 percent). The Late Classic deposits also contain more birds (1 percent) and turtles (4 percent) than the Preclassic sample, but these still only account for relatively small portions of the entire assemblage. In terms of spatial distribution, a large portion of the Late Classic remains come from the site's ball court (46 percent) and harbor (24 percent), with smaller quantities from elite residential groups such as Groups Y (10 percent), C (4 percent), and U (4 percent), and middle- or lower-status residential areas including groups G, KK, and S (2 percent each). Zooarchaeological remains recovered in the harbor area from this time period are primarily freshwater fish and mollusks, although a small number of deer and armadillo elements are also present. Consequently, the predominance of mammals in the Late Classic is largely due to the greater presence of mammalian taxa in the ball court and elite residential middens than in other Late Classic contexts across the site (Figure 12.6). Access to nonlocal marine shells also peaks during the Late Classic period. Approximately 4 percent of the Late Classic remains are from nonlocal marine taxa, which represents 50 percent of all the nonlocal marine resources identified at the site.

The Terminal Classic assemblage is relatively small in comparison to the other time periods (3 percent of the dated assemblage), and the remains are primarily concentrated in elite residential units within the site's ceremonial core (Group C: 58 percent; Groups U/Y: 39 percent; Group A: 3 percent).

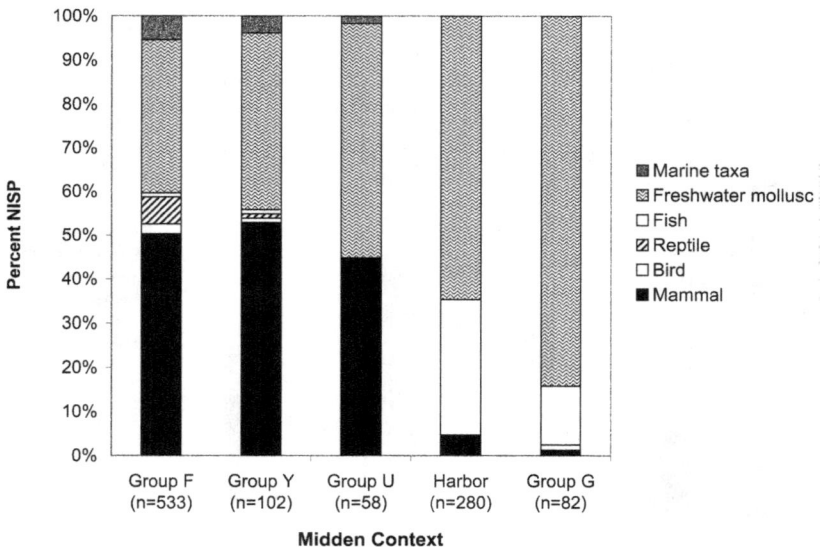

Figure 12.6. Comparison of Late Classic middens at Trinidad by taxonomic class.

Similar to the Late Classic, mammals are the most common taxa (Figure 12.5), but the diversity of mammals is greatly reduced. Species identified in the Terminal Classic include deer, armadillo, turtle, freshwater fish and shellfish, and marine mollusks.

Surprisingly, the largest faunal sample at Trinidad dates to the Postclassic period (51 percent of the dated assemblage). Remains from this period were overwhelmingly recovered in the harbor area (97 percent), with a much smaller quantity found in Group G (3 percent). Aquatic taxa dominate the sample with almost 75 percent of the assemblage being composed of freshwater turtles, fish, and shellfish (Figure 12.5). Although mammals only represent 25 percent of the Postclassic assemblage, the diversity of mammalian taxa identified is similar to that found in the Late Classic sample. This contrasts sharply with the Preclassic and Terminal Classic periods, which are characterized by lower mammalian diversity. Despite the large size of the Postclassic assemblage, only four examples of nonlocal marine resources were found. These include two marine shell artifacts, an incomplete stingray tail spine, and one large fragment of sea turtle plastron.

Although these general observations are intriguing, it is difficult to draw solid conclusions about changes in habitat and species use over time at Trinidad due to the unequal distribution of faunal remains from each time period across status and functional boundaries. For example, the Preclassic sample overwhelmingly reflects animal use within a middle-status residential group, whereas the Late Classic sample primarily comes from middens adjacent to the site's ball court, which may contain large quantities of feasting and ceremonial refuse (Moriarty and Thornton 2007; Moriarty and Foias 2007). The status level and types of animal use activities recorded in these deposits are likely very different. It is tempting to draw general conclusions about the greater use of aquatic taxa during the Preclassic and Postclassic periods, but this observation may be skewed by the fact that the Late and Terminal Classic deposits preferentially represent ceremonial, administrative, and high-elite residential contexts within the site's architectural core.

Discussion

Habitat Use and the Effects of Recovery Methods on Zooarchaeological Interpretations

Considering Trinidad's location on the shores of Lake Petén Itzá, it is not surprising that local aquatic resources played an important role in subsistence during all periods of the site's occupation. Even during the Late and Terminal Classic when the use of large- and medium-bodied mammals increases, aquatic taxa still account for at least 40 percent of the faunal assemblage. This pattern may be contrasted with that observed at the nearby but inland site of Motul de San José, which relied primarily on terrestrial fauna during all time periods (Emery 2003a, this volume). This suggests that animal use at both sites was largely determined by the availability of local habitats and resources surrounding each center. However, status differences between the two sites should also be considered. Late and Terminal Classic elite administrative/residential deposits at Trinidad contain greater quantities of terrestrial fauna. It is therefore possible that elite preference, rather than simple habitat availability, influenced the greater use of terrestrial resources at the primary, higher-status center of Motul de San José.

Terrestrial versus aquatic habitat use patterns at Trinidad and Motul would have appeared more similar if fine-screen recovery methods had been employed at both sites. This is because fish remains would have been almost completely absent from the Trinidad sample, thus causing the contribution of freshwater taxa to be greatly underestimated. Only six fish bones were found during general excavation and 1/4-inch mesh-screening. Instead, fish remains were almost exclusively recovered while water-screening through 1/16-inch mesh. Since only a subsample of all excavated contexts were fine-screened, it is likely that the dietary contribution of fish is still underestimated in the Trinidad assemblage. The recovery of a large number of small fish remains at Trinidad emphasizes the need to employ fine screen recovery methods at Maya sites located near extensive aquatic resource zones (both freshwater and marine). Although water-screening or flotation can be time-consuming, these methods may yield a much more accurate picture of the subsistence economy.

Elite Animal Use: Diet, Ceremony, and
the Differential Access to Resources

The large Late Classic middens found in association with Trinidad's ball court and elite residential groups provide perspective into elite animal use during the peak occupation of the Motul polity. In particular, the zooarchaeological remains from the ball court middens may contain evidence of feasting activities (Moriarty and Thornton 2007). Although no distinct zooarchaeological signature for feasting activities has been identified within the Maya area, these deposits allow us to explore how feasting assemblages may differ from other types of faunal assemblages in terms of species composition, element distribution, and age classes. However, based on the size of the middens, the presence of utilitarian artifacts, and the long period over which they may have accumulated, it is likely that refuse from other ceremonial and mundane activities was also deposited in this area. The observations may therefore reflect broader patterns of elite animal use for various purposes including, but not exclusive to, feasting.

Compared to other Late Classic deposits across the site, the ball court middens contain greater numbers of species suggested to be preferred for sacrifices or feasts (Pohl 1983, 1985b). Although not common at the site overall, younger animals are also overrepresented in the ball court sample. These observations conform to previous descriptions of elite and ceremonial faunal assemblages from the Maya area (e.g., Carr 1985; Emery 2003b, 2004a, 2006, 2007a; Giddens Teeter 2004; Hamblin and Rea 1985; Pohl 1990; Thornton 2008).

As a whole, the Late Classic residents of Trinidad's elite ceremonial core had greater access to large-bodied, meat-bearing species such as mammals, large birds, and turtles, whereas the residents of the peripheral core and harbor relied more on fish and freshwater shellfish. These differences likely reflect dietary divisions according to status, but the number of contexts in the ceremonial core that cannot be easily classified as either residential or ceremonial suggests that many of the faunal remains in and around the main plazas were chosen for more than just gustatory reasons. Therefore, the core versus periphery comparisons drawn from the Trinidad faunal assemblage may largely reflect differences in ceremonial versus domestic deposits, rather than dietary differences between social strata.

Caution in interpreting the differential access to resources is also needed because the majority of faunal remains recovered from Maya archaeological sites often come from elite contexts within the site epicenter or core (Emery 2004c, 2004e). The relatively small faunal assemblages recovered from nonelite, peripheral contexts therefore make it difficult to accurately compare animal use patterns across social classes at any particular site. This is in fact the case at Trinidad, where over 65 percent of the Late Classic remains come from inside the ceremonial precinct. Moreover, the division of the Trinidad sample into only two status-based categories likely glosses over more subtle differences in rank and occupation that may occur within or between architectural groups. However, the relatively small size of the Trinidad faunal assemblage precluded status comparisons at the household or group level.

Trade, Site Status, and Intrapolity Economics

Exotic marine shells, stingray tail spines, and sea turtle remains provide evidence for long-distance trade between Trinidad and coastal areas during the site's entire occupation from the Preclassic through the Postclassic. Not surprisingly, access to nonlocal animal commodities at Trinidad peaked during the height of the Motul polity between the Late and Terminal Classic. Based on Trinidad's role as a harbor or trade port, and its access to significant quantities of other nonlocal resources such as obsidian (Moriarty 2004c, 2005), we would expect the site to also have used its trade connections and possible elevated economic position to obtain more high-status nonlocal marine resources. However, this does not appear to be the case, and Trinidad in fact has far fewer marine resources than the site of Motul de San José (see Emery, this volume). Trinidad's strategic port location and involvement in long-distance exchange networks therefore does not appear to have substantially increased its access to exotic or other high-status faunal resources.

Moreover, despite Trinidad's proximity to Lake Petén Itzá, the site's residents appear to have had less access to some of the largest and meatiest resources found in this habitat. Crocodiles, giant Central American river turtles, and very large fish are all more common at the inland site of Motul de San José than at the lacustrine site of Trinidad. This could suggest the preferential distribution of favored aquatic species to the Motul elite through tribute or intrapolity exchange, using Trinidad as a specialized extraction site for aquatic species. However, direct procurement of these resources by Motul hunters cannot be ruled out.

Conclusions

Analysis of the Trinidad faunal assemblage represents an important contribution to our understanding of prehistoric Maya animal use. First of all, the site's lacustrine location allows us to address issues regarding the importance of aquatic resources in the prehistoric Maya diet. Aquatic vertebrate and invertebrate taxa appear to have been important dietary resources throughout the site's occupation, despite a rise in use of terrestrial mammals during the Late and Terminal Classic. This pattern may be contrasted with that observed at the nearby site of Motul, which relied much more heavily on terrestrial fauna. This difference suggests that animal use patterns may be largely determined by the availability of local habitats. The results of the fine-screening of Trinidad soil samples also emphasize the need to use this recovery technique to accurately estimate the contribution of aquatic resources in ancient Maya diet. The small size of the fish remains recovered at Trinidad prevented them from being recovered during general excavation. Without the fine-screen samples, use of this important and abundant natural resource would have been greatly underestimated.

Potential feasting and ritual midden deposits found in association with Trinidad's ball court also provide insight into patterns of elite animal use at the height of the Motul polity's power. As suggested by other zooarchaeological studies, the Trinidad elites appear to have preferentially used large-bodied mammals, birds, and turtles rather than the fish and freshwater shellfish that are more common in slightly lower-status residential contexts. Younger, subadult animals were also preferentially used in the feasting or other ceremonial activities taking place in association with the site's ball court. Patterns of elite and ceremonial animal use may therefore be determined to a lesser extent by resource availability and more by cultural ideas about what species are imbued with high status and ritual meaning.

The results of this study also provide information regarding whether Trinidad's role as a trade port resulted in greater access to nonlocal or high-status resources. In comparison to the larger site of Motul de San José, the residents of Trinidad had more restricted access to preferred meat resources and ritual and exotic commodities. Trinidad's proposed role as a trade port and involvement in long-distance exchange therefore did not elevate its access to exotic faunal resources such as marine shell and stingray tail spines. However, this conclusion needs to be further assessed through a comparison of Trinidad with other inland trade ports and sites of similar size and status.

Acknowledgments

I would like to thank Dr. Antonia Foias (Williams Collage), Dr. Kitty Emery (Florida Museum of Natural History), and Matt Moriarty (Tulane University) for assistance in the field and lab, and for granting permission to study the Trinidad de Nosotros faunal remains. I also thank the Guatemalan Instituto de Arqueología e História for the additional permission to export and study the remains. Appreciation is extended to the Florida Museum of Natural History (Gainesville, Florida) for allowing access to the modern comparative collections used to identify the archaeological assemblage.

Funding for this research was generously provided by the National Science Foundation (grant #0622805 to Emery and Thornton), and the Foundation for Advancement of Mesoamerican Studies, Inc. (FAMSI) (grant #06027 to Thornton). I am particularly grateful to Dr. Kitty Emery, who provided comments that greatly improved the quality of this manuscript.

13

In Search of Markets and Fields

Soil Chemical Investigations at Motul de San José

DANIEL A. BAIR AND RICHARD E. TERRY

Human society is highly dependent on natural resources, and none of these is more important than fertile soils for agricultural societies. In addition, control over good soils leading to agricultural food surplus was the most important source of economic wealth among ancient complex societies like the Classic Maya. Some of the most important goals of the Motul de San José Archaeological Project were to understand the distribution of fertile soils across the landscape, determine its use for agriculture, and attempt to understand who controlled these agricultural systems through their association with human settlements. Although all of these are long-term goals, our research has taken several steps toward attaining them.

Soil chemical investigations were conducted at Motul de San José, Guatemala, between 1998 and 2002, and at sites within the Motul de San José polity during the 2001, 2002, and 2005 field seasons. The soil research aimed to understand the general soil characteristics of the area (in relation to possible agricultural production), to identify evidence of ancient agriculture (either intensive or extensive), and to define activity areas within structures and plazas at these sites. In 2001, specific field studies involved the excavation and description of sixteen soil profiles, stable carbon isotope analyses to determine the ancient agricultural use of these soils, phosphate prospection at outlying rural mound groups, and an ethnoarchaeological study of Itzaj traditional soil classifications. The results of these investigations were presented in Jensen and colleagues (2007), Webb and colleagues (2007), and Moriarty 2001 (see also Webb and Schwarcz, this volume). In this chapter, we present results of the latest studies that took place between 2002 and 2005. In 2002, project members collected over one hundred surface samples from Plaza II in Motul's core (see location in Figure 1.2), to determine its ancient use through the geospatial concentrations of elements within the plaza. In 2005, Halperin and Martinez Salguero (2007a) collected additional surface samples from the southeast corner of this plaza and from the adjacent north platform of the Acropolis. Soil investigations were also expanded that year to explore the soil resources of a local savanna, a specific ecozone of some importance in the periphery of Motul.[1] Three soil profiles were collected at Sabana Chächäklu'um, a peripheral site located in a savanna approximately 6 kilometers east of Motul de San José. The geochemical study of Motul's Plaza II and the soil study at Sabana Chächäklu'um deepen our understanding of the environmental and economic resources underwriting Motul's political power.

Stable Isotope Analyses and the Vegetation History of Ancient Maize Agriculture

Numerous studies have used $\delta^{13}C$ ratios (ratios of ^{13}C to ^{12}C isotopes) contained in the soil organic matter (SOM) as indicators of historic and prehistoric changes in vegetation (see also discussion in Webb and Schwarcz, this volume). Changes in climate from the end of the Pleistocene to the interglacial period of the Holocene have resulted in vegetation changes in many parts of the world. The changes in $\delta^{13}C$ in soil profiles that result from the shifts of C_3 forest vegetation to C_4 or mixed C_3/C_4 savanna vegetation serve as useful proxies for both vegetation and climate changes (Huang et al. 2001; Kelly, Yonker, and Marino 1993).

Soil profile studies in the Caribbean and in Mesoamerica have reported the carbon isotope signatures of C_4 vegetation associated with ancient maize agriculture, sandwiched between the C_3 signatures of forest prior to and following ancient settlement because maize is one of the principal C_4 crops of prehistoric Mesoamerica. Lane and colleagues (2008) recently reported the isotopic signature of C_4 vegetation in lake sediments, against a background of C_3 forest vegetation, as a highly sensitive proxy for prehistoric maize agriculture in a small watershed in the Dominican Republic.

Stable carbon isotope enrichment of the SOM has been used at several lowland Maya sites as a proxy for the shift from C_3 forest vegetation to C_4 plants associated with land clearance for maize agriculture. Polk, van Beynen, and Reeder (2007) found evidence of changes in vegetative history in the Maya area in the $\delta^{13}C$ values of sediments deposited in a sinkhole cave in the Vaca Plateau of Belize. They reported that the isotopic signature of ancient Maya agriculture was greatest during the Preclassic population maximum around 2500 cal yr BP (500 BC) with a decline during the Maya Middle Classic hiatus about 1500 cal yr BP (AD 500). Maya agriculture again imparted the $\delta^{13}C$ signature of C_4 crops and weeds to the sediment organic matter (OM) corresponding to the Classic occupation. In areas of the Maya Lowlands that are currently under C_3 forest vegetation, carbon isotope analyses have successfully delineated soils with vegetative histories that reflect ancient maize (C_4) agriculture (Beach et al. 2008a,b; Fernández et al. 2005; Johnson et al. 2007; Johnson, Wright, and Terry 2007; Sweetwood et al. 2009; Webb, Schwarcz, and Healy 2004; Webb et al. 2007; Wright, Terry, and Eberl 2009). Several soil profiles were shown to have significant ^{13}C enrichment within ancient root zones.

This technique was applied by Webb and colleagues (2007; Webb and Schwarcz, this volume) in combination with soil physical character analysis (Jensen et al. 2007) in a study of the Motul de San José East Transect to identify ancient agricultural practices between the capital site and its outlier Chäkokot. We discuss these studies briefly here as background to similar work we carried out at the site of Chächäklu'um, presented in detail here. Soil resources along this East Transect from the site center of Motul de San José to the rural site of Chäkokot were studied through sixteen soil test pits. Samples from each soil horizon were collected and characterized (Jensen et al. 2007). All sixteen profiles were classified as Mollisols with surface horizons nearly neutral in pH, and organic C contents of approximately 2.8 percent. The soils in and around Motul de San José were deemed suitable for maize and other crops, although shallow soil depth and nutrient deficiencies are limitations of some profiles. Stable carbon isotope studies of these profiles were conducted by Webb and colleagues (2007). They reported differences in $\delta^{13}C$ between the surface SOM derived from C3 forest vegetation and the SOM of the 45- to 75-centimeter-deep root zone horizons of greater than 3.5 per mil in eight of the sixteen profiles. Changes in $\delta^{13}C$ within some profiles ranging from 4.7 to 7.7 per mil provided strong evidence that C_4 plants (like maize) replaced C_3 (forest) vegetation in the nearly level hillcrests, foot slopes, and toe slopes surrounding Motul de San José and the neighboring site of Chäkokot. The relative enrichment in the heavier ^{13}C isotope observed in the deep root zones were the result of SOM formed from maize and other C_4 vegetation associated with forest clearance for ancient agriculture. The stable carbon isotopes provided evidence that ancient agricultural areas reverted to C_3 forest vegetation following Maya abandonment at the end of the Classic period (after 1000 cal yr BP).

The Savanna Site of Chächäklu'um

The lowland Maya area encompasses zones of dense tropical forest, perennial and seasonal wetlands, upland karst hills, river floodplains, lakeshores, and seacoasts. One type of ecological niche that has been consistently understudied, however, is the savanna. There are localized savannas scattered throughout the Petén region. The savanna Chächäklu'um is located north of Lake Petén Itzá and approximately 6 kilometers east of the site of Motul de San José (Spensley 2007b). Excavations at Chächäklu'um consisted of three 1–by-1-meter test units placed by members of the Motul de San José Project during the 2005 field season. The test excavations revealed repeated construction episodes beginning at least as early as the Late Preclassic and continuing through the Late Classic.

Soil Properties and Vegetative History

We used carbon isotope analysis to search for areas of ancient maize agriculture at Chächäklu'um, extending the previous study of the distribution of agriculture at Motul and its environs along the East Transect (Jensen et al. 2007; Webb et al. 2007). Daniel Bair and Matt Moriarty collected three soil profiles from the spaces between mound groups at Chächäklu'um for soil characterization (Figure 13.1). Samples were collected with the aid of a bucket auger (AMS, American Falls, ID) at 15-centimeter depth intervals. Soil properties included Munsell color, horizon depth, total nitrogen, total carbon, organic carbon, carbonate, and stable nitrogen and carbon isotope

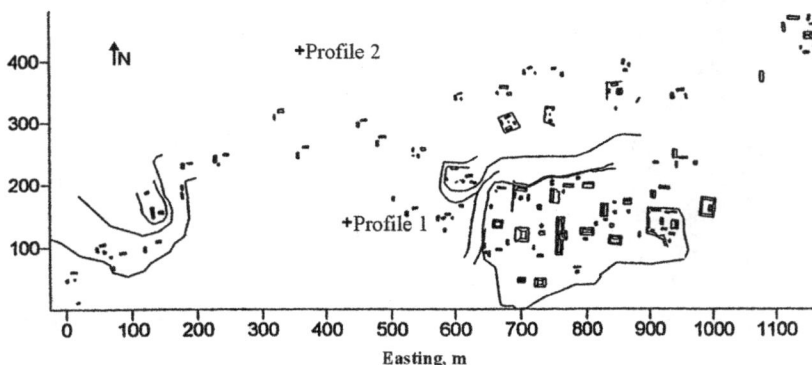

Figure 13.1. Map of Chächäklu'um approximately six kilometers east of Motul de San José. The location of soil profiles 1 and 2 are shown.

ratios, following procedures outlined by Johnson et al. (2007) and Wright, Terry, and Eberl (2009). Sabana Chächäklu'um soil characteristics and the stable isotopic ratios of the SOM are shown in Table 13.1.

The three Chächäklu'um profiles belong to the soil order Mollisols and are characterized by their dark, organic matter rich, mollic surface horizons (Soil Survey Staff 2006, 7). The subsurface horizons contained redoximorphic features that included mottling and manganese concretions. The Chächäklu'um profiles were much deeper than the soil profiles collected by Jensen and colleagues (2007) at Motul and in its east periphery. In addition, the Chächäklu'um profiles belonged in a different suborder called Aquolls. The heavy clay horizons of those Aquolls act as aquitards to slow drainage and promote occasional ponding of water after rainfall. Mollisols of the Petén region have been described as generally fertile (Fernández et al. 2005; Johnson et al. 2007; Olson 1977; Wright, Terry, and Eberl 2009) as they contain high cation exchange capacity, high base saturation, and nearly neutral pH. The Chächäklu'um savanna soils would have been particularly useful in maize agriculture as they are level and have deep root zones of more than 50 centimeters.

The $\delta^{13}C$ of the SOM of the various horizons in the Chächäklu'um profiles ranged from –14.07 to –21.60 per mil. These isotopic signatures reflect long-term mixed C_3 and C_4 vegetation in the savanna. The pattern of increased ^{13}C in the SOM in the rooting zone is similar to soil profiles in and around Motul de San José that were likely used in ancient maize agriculture (Webb et al. 2007). The changes in $\delta^{13}C$ of three Chächäklu'um profiles are plotted alongside profile KJ8 from the Motul de San José site center (Webb et al. 2007; see Figure 13.2). The carbon isotopes of the surface horizon of profile KJ8 (–25.4 per mill) reflect the old-growth forest vegetation that has prevailed in the area since the Terminal Classic abandonment. The change in $\delta^{13}C$ from A1 horizon to the buried Ab horizon of KJ8 was 6.6 per mil. This isotopic signature confirms the shift in ancient vegetative history to C_4 plants associated with ancient agriculture against the isotopic background of subsequent C_3 forest vegetation. The $\delta^{13}C$ of the surface A1 horizons of Chächäklu'um profiles 1, 2, and 3 (–17.7, –16.4, and –18.1 per mil, respectively) reflect the long vegetative history of mixed C_3/C_4 plants in the savanna (i.e., some tree stands among savanna grasses). However, the changes in the $\delta^{13}C$ with depth in these profiles provide evidence of significant prehistoric changes in the C_3/C_4 vegetative histories of this site.

Table 13.1. The physical, chemical, and stable isotopic properties of Chächäklu'um savanna soil profiles

Soil horizon	Depth interval (cm)	Moist color	pH	Clay	Total N	Total C (%)	Carbonate C	Organic C	$\delta^{15}N$ (parts per mil)	$\delta^{13}C$ (parts per mil)	Portion of SOC derived from C4 (%)
PROFILE 1											
A1	0–30	5Y 2.5/1	7.4	75.4	0.24	6.62	4.26	2.36	5.89	−17.50	63
A2	30–45	2.5Y 3/2	7.6	65.4	0.12	7.41	6.23	1.18	5.91	−15.42	77
B	45–60	10YR 5/3	7.6	43.6	0.05	12.72	9.88	2.84	6.81	−14.07	86
C	60–90	10YR 6/4	—	—	0.03	11.08	10.08	1.00	2.38	−20.79	41
	105–20	5Y 5/8	—	—	0.02	11.00	10.39	0.61	2.84	−19.07	53
PROFILE 2											
A1	0–15	10YR 2/1	5.8	86.7	0.18	2.26	0.52	1.73	7.33	−16.44	70
A2	15–30	10YR 3/1	5.6	90.8	0.1	0.89	0.24	0.64	6.52	−16.31	71
AB	30–45	2.5Y 4/2	6.3	88.5	0.08	0.59	0.51	0.08	6.54	−16.91	67
B	45–60	2.5Y 6/4	—	—	0.03	7.42	6.99	0.43	3.43	−15.95	74
	60–75	2.5Y 6/4	—	—	0.03	7.91	7.39	0.52	−0.99	−19.50	50
C	75–90	10YR 6/6	—	—	0.02	8.80	8.40	0.40	−1.94	−19.96	47
	90–105	10YR 6/4	—	—	0.02	10.04	9.25	0.79	3.90	−16.62	69
PROFILE 3											
A1	0–15	2.5Y 2.5/1	5.5	89	0.16	2.15	0.17	1.98	5.62	−18.12	59
	15–30	2.5Y 2.5/1	5.0	—	0.10	1.10	0.39	0.71	4.54	−18.56	56
A2	30–45	2.5Y 3/1	5.7	95.1	0.07	0.71	0.36	0.34	3.60	−21.60	36
B	45–75	2.5Y 5/2	—	89.3	0.05	0.35	0.31	0.04	2.71	−20.94	40
C	75–120	5YR 5/4	—	—	0.02	7.00	6.66	0.34	2.74	−16.30	71

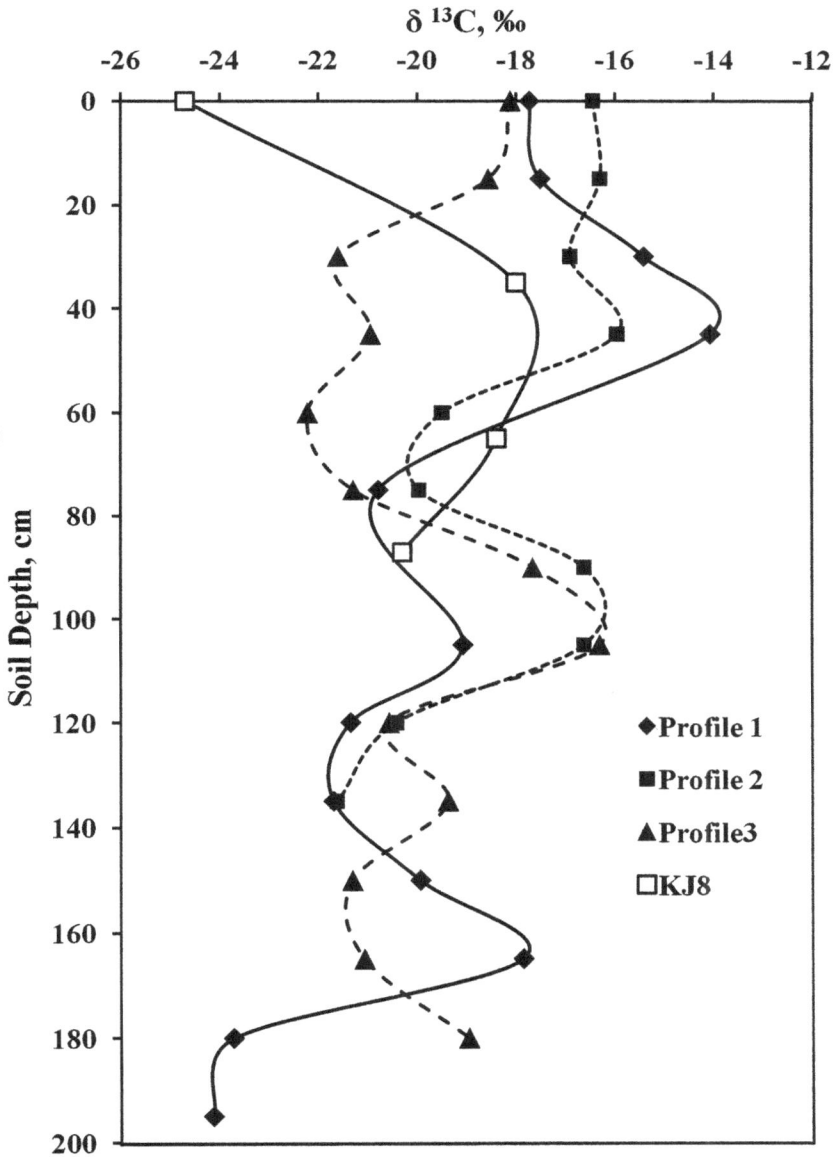

Figure 13.2. The change in $\delta^{13}C$ of the SOM within the savanna Chächäklu'um Profiles and Motul de San José Plaza II Profile KJ8.

The proportion of C_4 plants in the landscape that was deposited as soil organic carbon (SOC) can be calculated by the following equation (Nordt 2001, 423; Fernández et al. 2005, 2031):

$$\text{Percent SOC derived from } C_4 \text{ plants } (C_{C4}) = 100 \; * \; (\delta^{13}C_{SOC} - \delta^{13}C_{C3})/ (\delta^{13}C_{C4} - \delta^{13}C_{C3})$$

With the assumptions that $\delta^{13}C_{C3}$ = -27 per mil and $\delta^{13}C_{C4}$ = -12 per mil (Ehleringer 1991; Liu et al. 1997), proportions of C_4 carbon in the SOC were estimated and presented in Table 13.1. The majority of the SOC in the 0-to-60-centimeter depths of profiles 1 and 2 (as much as 86 percent) was derived from C_4 savanna vegetation. Just over half of the SOC of the A1 horizon (0 to 30 centimeters) of profile 3 originated from C_4 plants. A shift in vegetation to more than 50 percent C_3 forest trees and vines is seen at the 60- to-90-centimeter depths of profiles 1 and 2 and at depths of 30 to 75 centimeters in profile 3. We can conclude from this that in the past, the site had many more trees than at the present time. The isotopic enrichment of C_4 vegetation within ancient root zones of nearby Motul profiles were discovered at the 45- to 75-centimeter depths (Webb et al. 2007). The root zone horizons of the savanna profiles contain SOM derived from ancient C_4 vegetation when compared to lower horizons. The SOM of the 75- to 90-centimeter depths of the three Chächäklu'um profiles was derived mainly from C_3 vegetation. The changes in $\delta^{13}C$ of more than 4 per mil contained in the SOM of the surface to 45-centimeter depths of these profiles reflect a significant vegetation shift to mostly C_4 vegetation associated with ancient maize agriculture and with modern savanna vegetation. There is evidence of another shift in vegetation from mostly C_3 (forest and/or tree) plants to mostly C_4 (maize and other grasses) vegetation at the 105- to 120-centimeter depths in profiles 2 and 3. We do not have radiocarbon dates for these horizons so we cannot estimate the timing of this earlier vegetation shift.

In summary, the three soil profiles from the savanna of Chächäklu'um have provided new information about this ecological zone and its agricultural uses in the pre-Hispanic period. First, the savanna soils are classified as Aquolls, with dark, SOM-rich surface horizons and redoximorphic features that are evidence of occasional ponding of water on these level, clay-textured soils. Second, the comparison of the mixed C_3/C_4 vegetation signature of carbon isotopes contained in the SOM of the surface Chächäklu'um horizons with the $\delta^{13}C$ of deeper root zone horizons does not provide a difference of more than 3.5 per mil. Therefore, the signature of ancient maize agriculture is not readily apparent in these upper levels that seem to correlate with soil deposition at Motul de San José. Neverthe-less, the isotopic signature of ancient agriculture does appear when the root zone SOM is compared to horizons deeper than 60 centimeters. These soil profiles contain carbon isotopic evidence of several vegetative shifts from mostly C_3 trees and vines to mostly C_4 grasses of the savanna during the thousands of years of soil formation.

The soil studies of this important savanna ecological zone in the periph-ery of Motul de San José suggests a complicated use history for these soils, which probably incorporated both arboriculture and some maize agricul-ture. However, Carbon-14 dating of the vegetative shifts found in the deep soil profiles in this savanna is needed to better correlate land use with pre-Hispanic Maya population. Although the vegetative shifts suggest that in the Classic period, the zone did incorporate more high trees (forest or fruit) than it does today. This supports the hypothesis that Motul de San José re-lied on a variety of food sources and agricultural systems, with secondary centers partly specialized in such and other economic pursuits.

Geochemistry of Ancient Human Activities

Archaeologists deduce social and cultural patterns of past human activities based on a variety of architectural and artifactual evidences. Unfortunately, much of ancient material culture was made of organic materials that de-composed and are absent from the traditional archaeological record (Ca-vanagh 1988). In addition, many artifacts were disturbed or removed from their loci of use by people in both ancient and modern times; therefore, artifact distribution does not always correspond to areas of ancient activi-ties (Terry et al. 2004). In the case of plazas that were swept clean of debris in ancient times, there may be few if any artifacts remaining to suggest an-cient activities (Dahlin et al. 2007). Fortunately, phosphorus (P) and some metallic elements related to ancient human activity remain fixed on the surfaces of soil particles and leave persistent chemical traces. Geochemical distributions can then be mapped on archaeological surfaces to define areas where particular activities occurred in the past. Application of geochemical techniques to contemporary soil surfaces (such as modern Maya houses or modern Guatemalan marketplaces) have also been used to interpret the ancient human activity patterns of archaeological surfaces (Fernández et al. 2002; Terry et al. 2004; Wells 2004).

Geochemical analysis of soils in archaeology extends back to the early 1930s when Arrhenius (1931) reported the relationship between elevated soil phosphate levels and sites of previous human occupation. More recently, Barba, Manzanilla, and their colleagues demonstrated that earthen and stucco floors in domestic compounds at the ancient Maya city of Coba in Yucatán and the site of Teotihuacan in Central Mexico trapped chemical compounds derived from specific activities that were repeatedly performed in given locales (Barba et al. 1987; Barba and Manzanilla 1987; Manzanilla and Barba 1990). Their work along with other geochemical studies have helped identify areas for food preparation and consumption, storage, refuse, sleeping quarters, workshop activities, and for ritual and funerary activities (Barba and Ortiz 1992; Fernández et al. 2002; see also Barba et al. 1995; Pierrebourg 1999; Terry et al. 2000; Wells et al. 2000).

Anthropogenic P originates from plant and animal materials gathered for food and brought to settlements for consumption. Activities associated with high soil P concentrations include gardening, food preparation and consumption, waste disposal, animal pens, and sweeping, which pushes organic material to the patio peripheries. As food wastes are disposed, the P constituents released from the OM are readily fixed or adsorbed on the surface of soil particles where they remain for centuries (Barba and Ortiz 1992; Parnell, Terry, and Golden 2001; Parnell, Terry, and Nelson 2002; Parnell, Terry, and Sheets 2002). Metals including iron (Fe), copper (Cu), manganese (Mn), lead (Pb), and zinc (Zn) originate from various minerals and pigments attributed to ritual, workshop, and painting activities (Parnell, Terry, and Nelson 2002; Parnell, Terry, and Sheets 2002; Wells et al. 2000). Many of the metallic ions remain stable in soils for long periods in the form of adsorbed and precipitated ions on clay surfaces, and as insoluble oxides, sulfates, and carbonates (Lindsay 1979; see also Wells et al. 2000). Many of the pigments used by the pre-Hispanic Maya contained metallic bases, such as hematite, ochre, and cinnabar (Goffer 1980, 167–73; for examples, see also Vásquez Negrete and Velázquez 1996a, 1996b); thus, elevated values of trace metals in soils may help to identify areas where pigments were processed or applied and where craft workshops were located.

Geochemical analysis of soil phosphate prior to excavation has been used to identify waste middens and other important features (Parnell, Terry, and Golden 2001; Terry et al. 2000). Phosphate and heavy metal analyses of occupational surfaces of both contemporary and ancient households have been successfully used to identify specific activity areas (e.g., Manzanilla and Barba 1990; Barba et al. 1996; Fernández et al. 2002; Parnell, Terry, and

Nelson 2002; Parnell, Terry, and Sheets 2002; Terry et al. 2004). Ceremonial, feasting, and marketplace activities in open plazas have recently been identified by chemical analyses of gridded soil samples (Dahlin et al. 2007, 2009; Wells 2004).

Phosphorus Prospection in the Motul de San José Zone

In 2001, as part of a broad study (Moriarty 2001) of soils and settlement across the Motul de San José East Transect Jensen, Johnson, and Terry (2001) sampled soils from the surface of a small plazuela group, Group E2E[2], located in the agricultural area outside of the Motul de San José archaeological park boundary. The group features four very low mounds and does not show any signs of significant architecture. The sample collection and phosphate extraction procedures described by Terry et al. (2000) and Parnell, Terry, and Golden (2001) were used to delineate food preparation and waste disposal areas at this small rural mound group. A 5-meter grid system was established and soil samples were collected from the mounds and surrounding areas. Phosphate analyses were conducted at the field camp with Mehlich II extraction solution and Hach reagents (Hach Co., Loveland, Colorado). Solutions were measured for relative phosphate concentrations using a Hach DR 700 spectrophotometer. The percent transmittance readings were then compared to a standard curve and converted to milligrams per kilogram (parts per million) concentrations of phosphorus (Parnell, Terry, and Golden 2001; Terry et al. 2000). This procedure has been successfully tested at other Maya sites (Hutson and Terry 2006; Hutson et al. 2007; Parnell, Terry, and Golden 2001; Parnell, Terry, and Nelson 2002; Parnell, Terry, and Sheets 2002; Terry et al. 2000) and in ethnoarchaeological contexts (Fernández et al. 2002; Terry et al. 2004).

The results of the soil P prospection in Group E2E are shown in Figure 13.3. The background P level of 9.1 milligrams per kilogram in the mound group was calculated from the average of the 10 percent of samples lowest in P concentration. The samples highest in P concentration (13 milligrams per kilogram) were found in a small drainage east of the mound group, suggesting waste disposal at that location. Later excavations in the group revealed low artifact density (Moriarty et al. 2001; Halperin and Martinez Salguero 2007a). Both the low level of soil P and low artifact density are likely a result of short-term occupation. The group may represent field houses used seasonally during planting, maintenance, and harvesting of milpa cultivation plots.

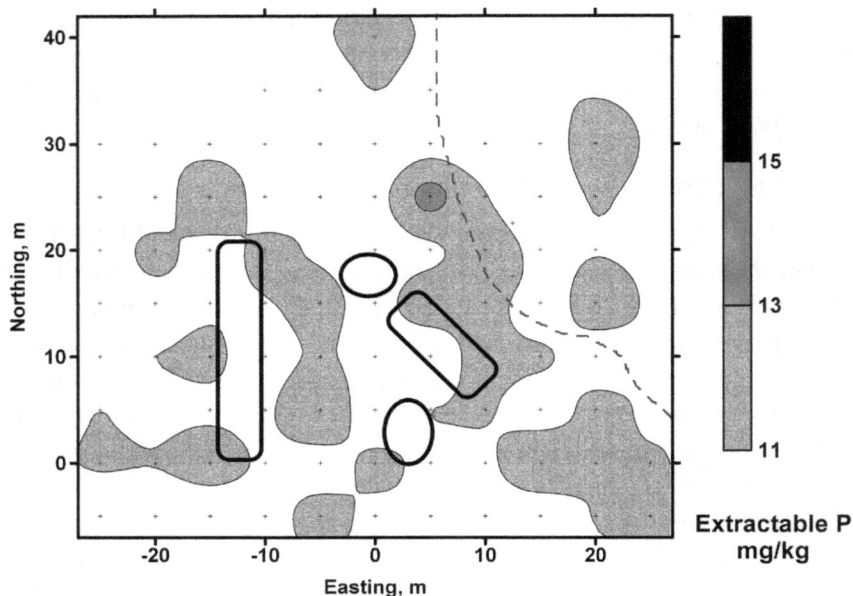

Figure 13.3. The spatial distribution of extractable P (mg/kg) within the rural house mound group E2E. Black outlines are platforms.

Chemical Analysis of Stucco Floor Samples

Activity area analyses of architecture, artifacts, and geochemical residues were conducted on the stucco floors of two elite residences in the site center of Motul de San José. We analyzed the geochemical residues in the stucco floors with the aim of identifying ancient activity areas. Geochemical studies like the ones described here are critical in assisting excavators in reconstructing the type of activities that took place within residential spaces that were maintained very cleanly, with few or no artifacts or ecofacts left behind.

Samples were collected over 25- to 50-centimeter grids across all well-preserved stucco, following protocols designed by Emery and Higginbotham (1998). At the Brigham Young University soil analysis laboratory, the samples were air-dried and the aggregates were crushed to pass a 2-millimeter sieve. Extractable P concentrations in the floor samples were determined with the same Mehlich II extraction procedure listed above. Trace metal analysis was conducted by a chelate extraction procedure using 0.5 molar DTPA (diethylenetriaminepentaacetic acid) solution buffered at pH 7.3 (Fernández et al. 2002; Hutson et al. 2007; Lindsay and Norvell 1978;

Parnell, Terry, and Nelson 2002; Parnell, Terry, and Sheets 2002; Terry et al. 2004). Heavy metal concentrations were then determined on a Thermo ICPAES. Metals analyzed were copper (Cu), iron (Fe), manganese (Mn), lead (Pb), and zinc (Zn). The Mehlich II and DTPA extraction procedures remove portions of precipitated and adsorbed P and trace metals from the surfaces of soil particles. Quality-control samples are analyzed with each run. Background values of soils and floors are based on the average extractable element concentration in 10 percent of the samples lowest in concentration (Parnell, Terry, and Nelson 2002; Terry et al. 2004; Hutson and Terry 2006; Dahlin et al. 2007).

The first structure (Str. 8M-10) that we explored was located in Group D, a royal monumental group directly north of the Main Plaza of the site. The stucco floors of this elite building were uncovered in 2000 and 2001 by Foias and colleagues in Operation 15A (Foias, Foster, and Spensley 2000; Alvarez, Castillo, and Foias 2001; Foias et al., this volume). P concentrations in the floor of structure 8M-10 are shown in Figure 13.4a. The background P levels in the floor were about 4.8 milligrams per kilogram. The highest P concentration of 12.1 milligrams per kilogram was in front of the west bench and somewhat lower concentrations were present in front of the east bench. It is likely that food was consumed at these locations. The metallic ions, including Cu, Fe, Mn (Figure 13.4b-d), and Pb (data not shown), were highest in concentration just north of the west column supporting an exterior covered patio (see Foias et al., this volume). These metals could indicate paint on the front of the structure or ritual use of pigments at that location. Elevated concentrations of P and Cu (Figure 13.4a–b) were at the base of the east bench of the structure. Residues of P in the floor samples suggest food consumption or preparation, but the combination with Cu suggests that mineral pigments or workshop items may have been used on this floor. The chemical patterning is supported by the excavation of a partial metate and mano adjacent to the face of the eastern bench (Alvarez, Castillo, and Foias 2001). In addition, the presence of elevated concentrations of metallic ions (Figure 13.4b–d) suggests the preparation or use of pigments, and this is paralleled by the finding of a bark beater and several pigment balls or bricks in the adjacent building (Str. 8M-11; see Foias et al., this volume).

We also carried out geochemical residue analysis in a second elite structure (Str. 8L-9) located in the Acropolis that probably functioned as the royal court during the Late Classic. Emery and Higginbotham (1998) began the excavation of this Acropolis elite residence in 1998 (Operation 2A).

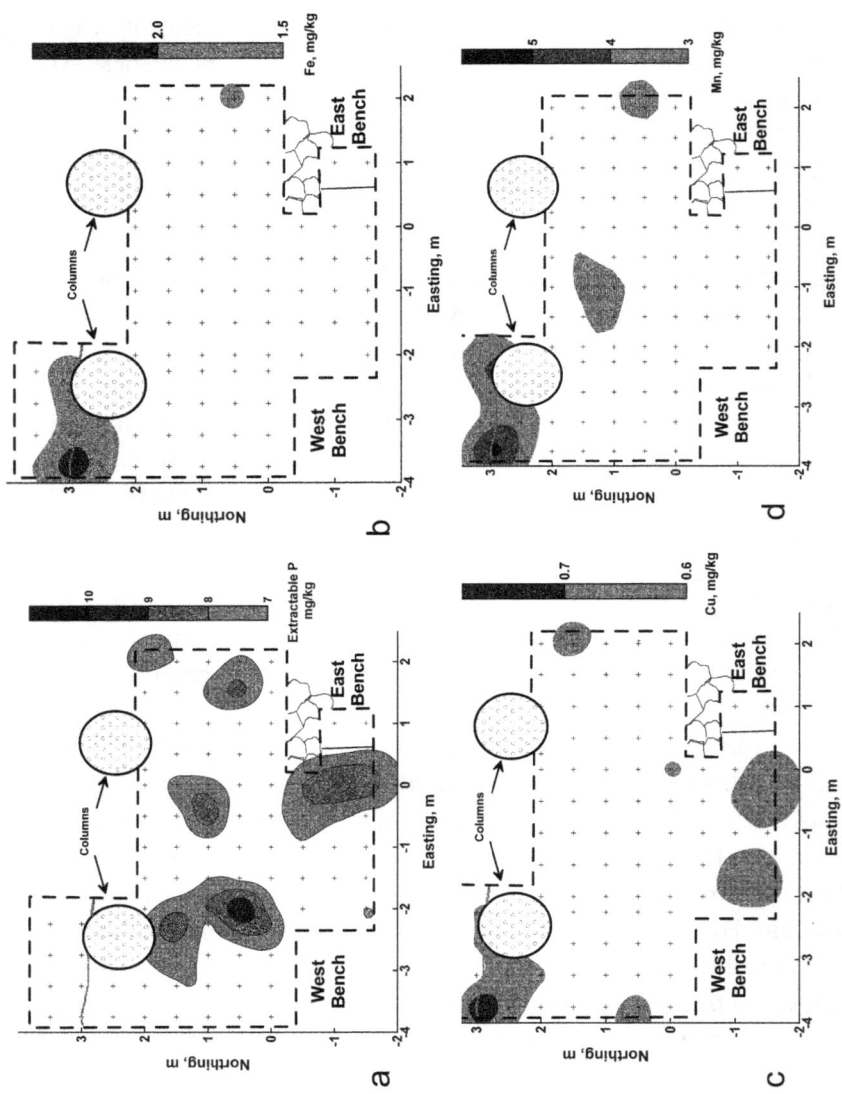

Figure 13.4. The areas of elevated extractable P (a), DTPA extractable Cu (b), Fe (c), Mn (d) (all in mg/kg) in samples of stucco floors from southern palace in Group D.

Directly behind this palace, units 3, 5, 40, 41 uncovered the richest midden yet found at Motul (Figures 1.2, 6.1; see Halperin and Foias, this volume). Because of the high midden density and the clear evidence of pottery production, additional units 8–12, 20, and 21 were opened in Str. 8L-9 in the hopes of discovering additional evidence of scribal activity or pottery production. Disappointingly, the floors of the residence were very clean with few artifacts and ecofacts left behind. Nevertheless, two sherds were discovered that had clear post-breakage use and wear very similar to sherds used in polishing vessels before firing, according to experiments done by Lopez Varela, van Gijn, and Jacobs (2002; see also Foias 2003; Halperin and Foias, this volume). Stucco floor samples from the 4×8 meter excavation of the interior floor surface of the central room of this three-room palace were taken on a 0.25- to 0.5-meter grid for geochemical analysis. Extractable P and metal concentrations are shown in Figure 13.5 and listed in Table 13.2. The concentrations of extracted elements were near background levels, indicating that the floor was kept clean in ancient times. P and Zn concentration just above background were found in samples along the north end of the massive interior bench in this room (Figure 13.5a–b). Elevated levels of Cu Fe, Mn, Pb, were found at the center of the room in front of the bench and in the doorway (Figure 13.5c–d). This may be due to either painting of the walls and benches of the palace or to scribal use of mineral pigments.

The floors of the two excavated elite residences described here contained relatively few artifacts and generally very low levels of P and heavy metals. Terry and colleagues (2004) reported very low concentrations of these elements in the central rooms of elite residences of Aguateca. Adjacent rooms that contained artifacts related to workshop or kitchen activities exhibited much greater elemental concentrations. Central rooms of the Aguateca structures and the Motul elite residences were likely swept and kept clean for the hosting of visitors. Therefore, P and metals associated with food and crafting materials did not accumulate in these floors. In the two cases described here, the geochemical residue analysis has supported the artifactual and ecofactual evidence that these residential spaces had social, administrative, or political functions that did not involve major food consumption or crafting practices. These activities were probably carried out in adjacent spaces (likely, both interior and exterior).

Geochemical Analysis of Ancient Plaza Activities

In 2002, a geochemical survey targeted Plaza II in central Motul de San José, located directly north of the Acropolis in Group C (Figure 1; Halperin and

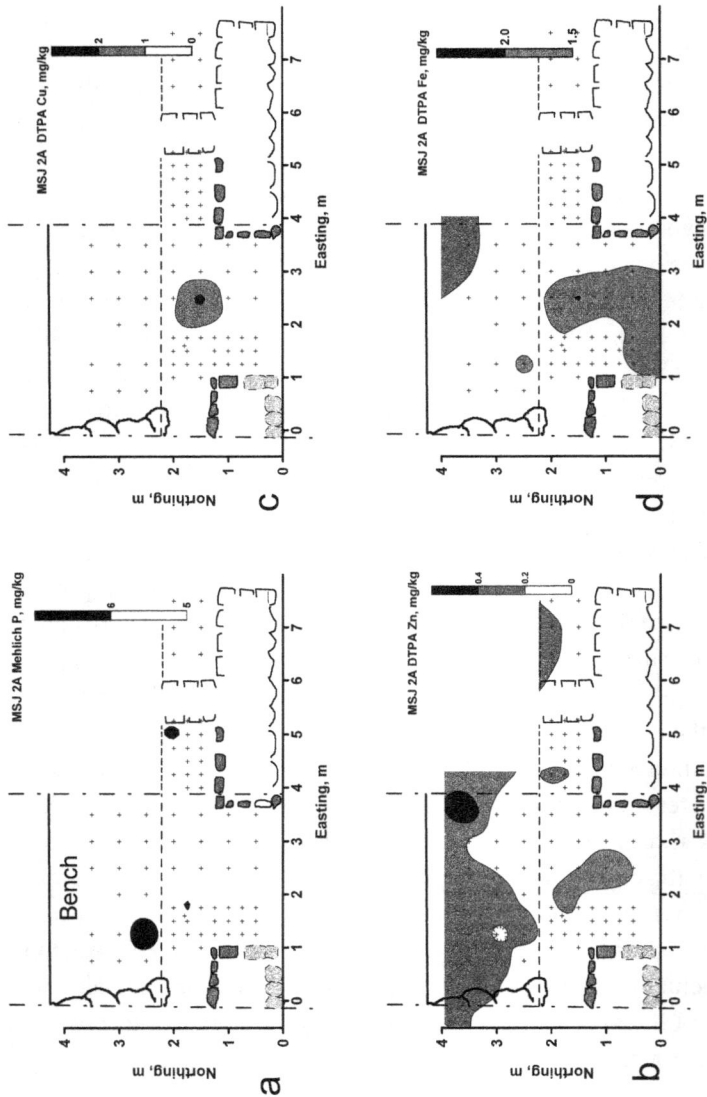

Figure 13.5. The areas of elevated Mehlich II extractable P (a), DTPA extractable Zn (b), Cu (c) and Fe (d) (all mg/kg) in samples of stucco floors from northern elite residence in Group 8L6 in the Acropolis.

Table 13.2. The background, average, maximum, and minimum concentrations of P and heavy metals extracted from surface soils of Plaza II

| | | | | | Extracted element concentrations | | |
	P (mg/kg)	Cu (mg/kg)	Fe (mg/kg)	Mn (mg/kg)	Pb (mg/kg)	Zn (mg/kg)
GROUP E2E						
Background[a]	9.1	n.d.	n.d.	n.d.	n.d.	n.d.
Average (n = 88)	10.8	n.d.	n.d.	n.d.	n.d.	n.d.
Maximum	15.6	n.d.	n.d.	n.d.	n.d.	n.d.
Minimum	8.4	n.d.	n.d.	n.d.	n.d.	n.d.
STRUCTURE 8L1I, OP. MSJ15A						
Background	4.8	0.4	0.7	1.2	0.7	0.04
Average (n = 88)	6.6	0.5	1.1	2.4	1.1	0.2
Maximum	12.1	0.9	2.9	7.2	2	0.6
Minimum	4.3	0.3	0.6	0.6	0.6	0.02
STRUCTURE 8L6, OP. MSJ2A						
Background	4.3	0.4	0.7	1.7	0.7	0.1
Average (n = 75)	5.5	0.6	1.3	3.2	0.9	0.2
Maximum	8.7	2.4	2.7	6.4	1.3	0.5
Minimum	3.9	0.4	0.6	1	< .02	< .02
PLAZA II SAMPLED IN 2002						
Background	16.9	0.6	1.6	30.2	0.7	0.7
Average (n = 106)	73.6	2.5	19.2	60.2	1.5	1.9

(continued)

Table 13.2. (*Continued*)

				Extracted element concentrations			
	P (mg/kg)	Cu (mg/ kg)	Fe (mg/kg)	Mn (mg/ kg)	Pb (mg/ kg)	Zn (mg/ kg)
Maximum	351.8	7	193.9	165.3	4.3	9.7
Minimum	15.1	0.5	1.3	27.8	0.6	0.6
SE CORNER OF PLAZA II AND ACROPOLIS PLATFORMS SAMPLED IN 2004 OP. MSJ2A						
Background	9.5	0.4	1.9	17.5	0.6	0.7
Average (n = 77)	36.8	1	4.8	28.9	0.9	1.9
Maximum	155	2.4	14.7	83.2	1.5	4.2
Minimum	8.4	0.3	1.5	16	0.5	0.4

[a] Background concentrations are based on the average of the 10 percent of samples lowest in concentration.

Martinez Salguero 2007a). Plaza II was not originally considered a public space, but rather a refuse deposition zone associated with the Acropolis (explored by Operation MSJ2A) and surrounding residential groups to the north (Operation MSJ19), to the northeast (Operation MSJ33), to the west (Operation MSJ29), and to the east (Operation MSJ46). In 2005, Halperin explored the southeast corner of this open area, including the north platform of the Acropolis in hopes of discovering additional middens. Instead, Halperin reported substantial stone-built structures facing north and west (Halperin and Martinez Salguero 2007a). The elaborate construction and orientation of these structures confirmed the public nature of this space (see Figure 1.2).

In the years 1997 through 2005, several units of Operation 2A were excavated along the low platform at the north end of the Acropolis and south edge of Plaza II (Emery and Higginbotham 1998; Foias 2000a; Guffey, Tonoike, and Castellanos 2000; Halperin and Martinez Salguero 2007a; see also Halperin and Foias, this volume). Foias, Foster, and Spensley (2000) reported a dense midden of elite materials including polychrome and hieroglyphic adorned vases and other ceramics, monochrome and unslipped pottery, bone refuse, lithic tools, and so on, in this zone. It is likely that the midden originated from an elite ceramic workshop as well as from residential activities in the Acropolis (see Halperin and Foias, this volume). These midden materials suggest that Motul de San José was a center of prestige ceramic production and exchange (Foias, Foster, and Spensley 2000; Halperin and Foias, this volume).

Extensive shovel tests and test pits around major groups surrounding Plaza II were conducted in 1999 and 2000 (Yorgey et al. 1999; Ramirez, Sanchez, and Alvarado 2000). Posthole tests in Operation 19B on a minor domestic group (Gr.8L1) located at the north end of the plaza revealed plaza fill at approximately 20 to 30 centimeters of depth. A low platform of this group extended into the Plaza II and surface soil samples were collected atop the platform and to the south and west sides. Posthole tests in Operation 19A explored the area north of the low platform of this group, just outside of our surface sampling of the plaza (Yorgey et al. 1999, fig. 3.1). The archaeologists reported a well-preserved floor and a dense midden consisting of ceramics, lithics, and animal bones (Yorgey et al. 1999, 25–26). The lithic and bone materials in the midden suggest that crafting, food processing, and consumption activities took place at the north end of Plaza II.

Operation 29 explored Group 8L2 along the west edge of Plaza II, with test pits and shovel tests on the edges of the structures (Ramirez, Sanchez, and Alvarado 2000, 16–19). Test pit 29D-1 in the central structure of Group 8L2 revealed an eroded plaza floor at 0.2 to 0.4 meters. About 0.5 meters below the floor was a north-south-oriented drainage channel that was excavated anciently into the bedrock. The channel would have directed drainage to the west side of Plaza II. The test pits and shovel tests around Group 8L2 confirmed the presence of patio and plaza floors, ceramic, and lithics associated with an elite Classic household. Excavations and shovel tests by Ramirez, Sanchez, and Alvarado (2001, fig. 3.1) on the northeast side of Plaza II, just outside Group 8L3, revealed stucco floors and fill material with few Late Classic artifacts. All these excavations confirm that the plaza was artificially filled and leveled for public activities and that substantial residential activities occurred in the structures surrounding it.

Jensen et al. (2007) examined soil profile KJ8 located at the edge of the Acropolis north platform and within Plaza II. The foot slope profile was classified as Typic Argiudolls. The A1 and A2 horizons (0–65 centimeters) were formed in midden materials using plaza fill. A 22-centimeter-deep buried Ab horizon (Ab designates a relic surface horizon that was subsequently buried) beneath the plaza fill was free of artifacts. The Ab horizon was once the surface horizon before it was buried by plaza fill. Webb et al. (2007) used the stable carbon isotope signatures of the profile SOM to identify vegetative shifts associated with the Maya occupation of this area. The $\delta^{13}C$ of the A1 horizon (0–35 centimeters) was -24.7 per mil, reflecting the C_3 forest vegetation that has prevailed since the Terminal Classic abandonment. The $\delta^{13}C$ of the A2 (35–65 centimeters) and buried Ab (65–87 centimeters) horizons were -18.0 and -18.4 per mil, respectively. The vegetation that that decomposed to form the SOM in these two horizons consisted of at least 57 percent C_4 plants. The Ab horizon atop the C horizon of weathered limestone was likely the soil surface encountered by the earliest farmers in the area. The carbon isotopic signature of the Ab horizon reflects ancient maize agriculture that likely occurred at this location prior to establishment and artificial leveling of Plaza II and the north platform of the Acropolis. The $\delta^{13}C$ of the buried Ab horizon represents a shift of 6.3 per mil within the profile. The A2 horizon material that was brought into the plaza as fill (see Halperin and Martinez Salquero 2007a) also contained a strong signature of ancient C_4 vegetation. Many years of ancient maize agriculture contributed to the C_4 vegetation signature in the SOM of the original soil surface and the plaza fill.

A 10-meter grid covering Plaza II was set up in the 2002 season for the geochemical survey. Soil surface samples were collected at grid intersections to a depth of 10 centimeters. Samples were transported to Brigham Young University for P and heavy metal extraction and analysis (Terry et al. 2000; Parnell, Terry, and Golden 2001; Parnell, Terry, and Nelson 2002). Spatial analyses of the P and trace metal concentrations of 183 samples from the 2002 survey and from the 2005 sampling of the southeast corner and Acropolis north platforms were plotted with Surfer software (Golden Software, Golden, Colorado). The extracted element concentrations were subjected to principal components and cluster analyses with the NCSS statistical package (NCSS, Kaysville, Utah). Background concentrations of each element were determined by averaging the 10 percent of samples lowest in concentration.

The distribution of P in Plaza II of Motul de San José is shown in Figure 13.6a. The levels of P vary from 15 to 352 milligrams per kilogram (Table 13.2). The background P level was determined to be 17 milligrams per kilogram. This background is much higher than background P levels of 9.1 milligrams per kilogram in the E2E mound group and 4.8 milligrams per kilogram in the floor of Str. 8L-10. Background P levels in Plazas II through V at nearby Trinidad de Nosotros were approximately 6 milligrams per kilogram (Bair 2009). Similarly, the average soil surface P level of the sixteen soil profiles from areas within the park boundaries and rural and urban areas outside the park along the East Transect was 10.2 milligrams per kilogram (Jensen et al. 2007, table IV). High levels of human activity and importation of large quantities of organic materials to Plaza II would have been required to elevate the background P concentration to 17 milligrams per kilogram. In addition, the greatest P concentration in the plaza floor was twenty-one times the background level.

The elevated concentrations of P found in the middle of Plaza II range from 80 to 352 milligrams per kilogram and are not associated with visible mounds. These concentrations form two intersecting linear patterns that are in line with possible ancient entryways into the plaza. The areas of P concentration are not adjacent to the household structures that surround the plaza so it is unlikely that the high P concentrations in the plaza center were the result of kitchen middens. Soils around the low platform of Group 8L1 at the north end of the plaza contained very high levels of P, up to 315 milligrams per kilogram. The low platform is not of the size or significance to have generated such quantities of household trash. It is more likely that the P concentrations at the platform and the plaza center resulted from large inputs of OM attributable to market exchange of foodstuffs and/or to feasting activities.

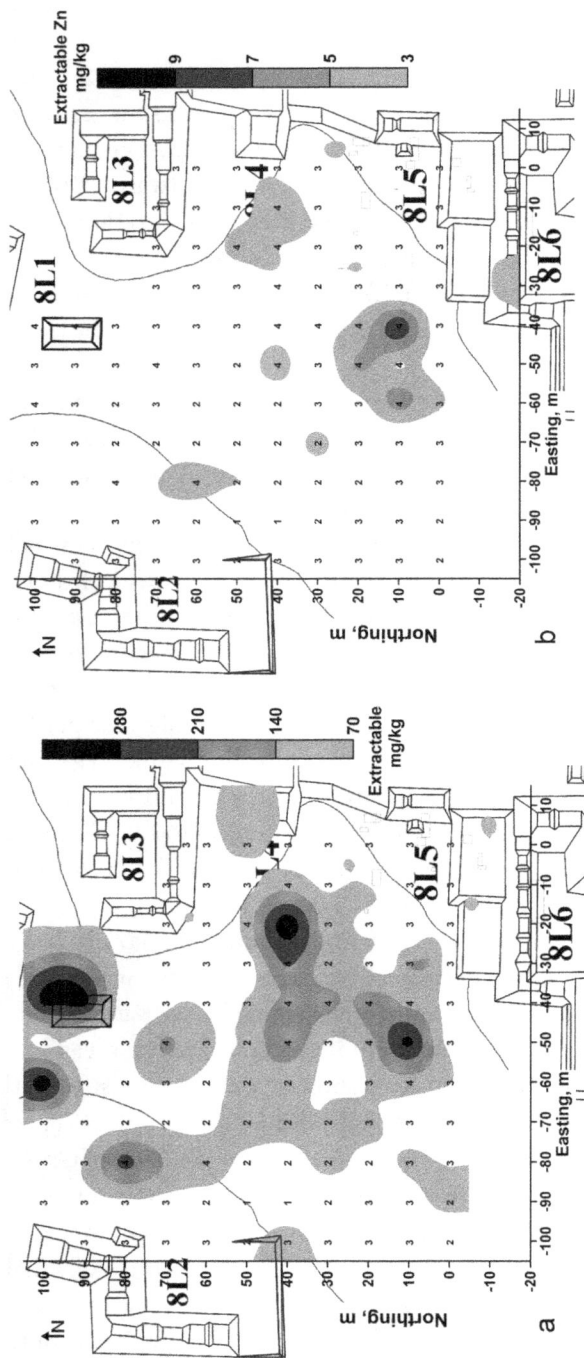

Figure 13.6. The concentration isopleths of extractable P (a) and DTPA extractable Zn (b) in the surface soils of Plaza II. The gridded numbers denote the sample locations and the cluster to which each sample belongs. Numbers of structures identify plaza group names.

Background levels and minimum and maximum concentrations of each of the trace metals in the soils of Plaza II are presented in Table 13.2. Extracted Zn concentrations (Figure 13.6b) are significantly correlated with levels of P ($r = 0.34$, $p < .01$). The correlation between extractable P and Zn has been discovered in soils associated with contemporary marketing of fruits, vegetables, and prepared foods at the Antigua, Guatemala, marketplace (Dahlin et al. 2007). Parnell, Terry, and Nelson (2002) also reported a significant correlation between P and Zn in the floors of an ancient domestic structure at Piedras Negras. High levels of extractable Fe (Figure 13.7a), Cu (Figure 13.7b), Mn (Figure 13.8a), and Pb (Figure 13.8b) were encountered near a large platform attached to elite residential Group 8L2 on the west side of the plaza. Elevated concentrations of these metals radiate out to the center of the plaza. Increased metal concentrations have been attributed to workshop and ceremonial use of mineral pigments, paints, and pyrite mirrors (Cook et al. 2006; Parnell, Terry, and Nelson 2002; Parnell, Terry, and Sheets 2002; Terry et al. 2004; Wells et al. 2000). There is no pyramid or recognizable shrine near the platform, so ceremonial use of pigments is not a likely explanation. The high concentrations and radial distribution of the metals suggests workshop and market distribution of craft minerals from the Gr. 8L2 platform.

To better understand the distribution of these phosphates and heavy metals, Principal Component Analysis (PCA) was applied to the element concentration data of the Plaza II samples. The first three principal components or factors produced through PCA account for 87.79 percent of the variance within the data set. Factor 1 accounts for 53.9 percent of the variance with high loadings for Cu, Mn, Fe, and Pb (Table 13.3). Factor 2 accounts for an additional 22.8 percent of the variance with high loadings for Zn and P. Factor 3 accounts for 11.3 percent of the variance with a high positive loading for P and negative loading for Zn.

The loadings of each sample on the three discriminant factors produced from the PCA were then subjected to cluster analysis to determine plaza areas with similar element concentrations. The gridded numbers within the plaza shown in Figures 13.6–13.8 not only indicate the locations where samples were taken, but also identify the cluster that each sample belongs to. Cluster 1 is comprised of two samples located at the edge of the 8L2 platform, highest in all the metals except Zn. The high metal concentrations suggest workshop activities (i.e., craft-derived waste with heavy use of mineral-based pigments) or paint residues from structure 8L2. However, the second explanation seems unlikely because these two samples are far removed from the structures of

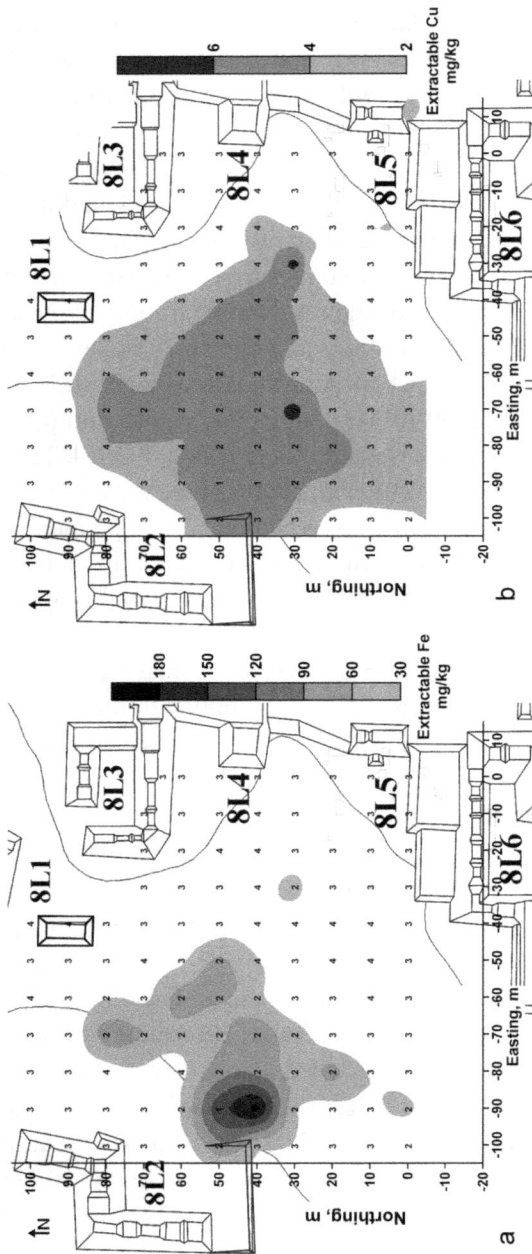

Figure 13.7. The concentration isopleths of DTPA extractable Fe (a) and Cu (b) in the surface soils of Plaza II. The gridded numbers denote the sample locations and the cluster to which each sample belongs. Numbers of structures identify plaza group names.

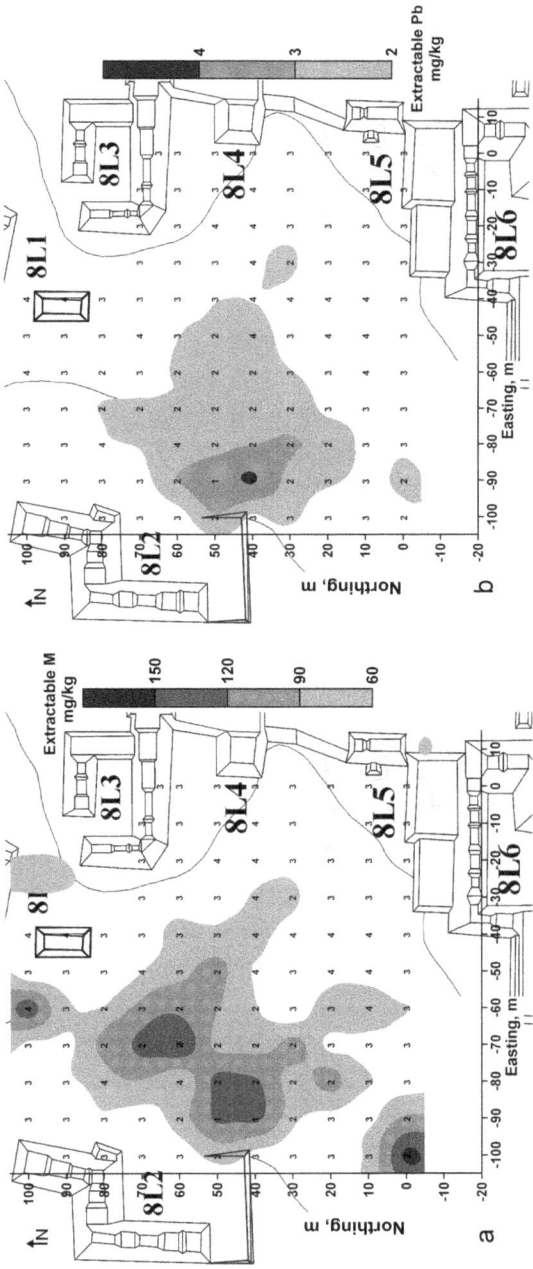

Figure 13.8. The concentration isopleths of DTPA extractable Mn (a) and Pb (b) in the surface soils of Plaza II. The gridded numbers denote the sample locations and the cluster to which each sample belongs. Numbers of structures identify plaza group names.

Table 13.3. Principal component analysis of extractable element concentrations in Plaza II

Eigenvectors elements	Factor 1	Factor 2	Factor 3
P	0.03	0.70	0.68
Cu	0.51	0.07	−0.07
Fe	0.50	−0.16	−0.04
Mn	0.45	0.02	0.18
Pb	0.53	−0.05	0.01
Zn	0.07	0.69	−0.70

Group 8L2. Cluster 2 samples are medium in P concentration but high in metals. These areas mark the transition of activities with foodstuffs to areas where mineral craft materials were used or marketed. Cluster 3 samples are all low in P and metals and likely mark the ancient pathways through the plaza or the use of nonfood, nonpigment goods. Cluster 4 samples are high in both P and Zn but low in other metals. Very high levels of vegetable matter would have increased the P content of Cluster 4 samples.

Several authors have listed attributes or lines of evidence that should exist at ancient Mesoamerican marketplaces (Bair and Terry 2009; W. Coe 1967; Dahlin et al. 2007, 2009; Tourtellot 1988; Wurtzburg 1991). Some of these attributes were described by Cortez and others at the time of the conquest (Diaz del Castillo 1956; Tozzer 1941). Other attributes are visible in contemporary marketplaces (Dahlin et al. 2007; Cook and Diskin 1976). Based on these accounts, marketplace attributes include (Dahlin et al. 2007, 2009; Wurtzburg 1991):

1. location of the urban center along trade routes and artifactual evidence of trade;
2. designated open space for a marketplace adjacent to transportation arteries;
3. proximity to public structures (e.g., palace, acropolis, ball court, or sweatbath structures);
4. specific areas for the exchange of different classes of goods and postholes or stone alignments to denote assignment of market spaces or kiosks; and
5. regular patterns in the chemical concentrations of P and metallic ions aligned with pathways (low concentrations), areas of foodstuff distribution (high levels of P), and the marketing of workshop or craft materials (high levels of metal ions).

Several of these market attributes can be ascribed to Plaza II. First, the plaza is located at the urban center of Motul de San José, which was a significant political and likely a trading center during the Classic period (see Foias and Emery, this volume). A rich pottery midden was excavated at the southern edge of Plaza II and was suspected to be the product of a polychrome workshop (Foias 2002, 2003; Halperin and Foias, this volume). These elaborate ceramics were exchanged over much of the Maya lowlands. Second, the plaza is about 4 hectares in size with two main entryways located at the north and south ends and may be at the upper size limit of ancient Mesoamerican marketplaces as proposed by Dahlin et al. (2009). Third, Plaza II is centrally located near public structures. Administrators of plaza activities likely lived in the elite residences and the royal palace surrounding the plaza. Lastly, patterns of chemical concentrations across the plaza indicate an influx of foodstuffs and craft-derived materials, suggesting possible marketplace activities. In all, Plaza II of Motul de San José meets four of the five attributes listed above. A future surface survey of Plaza II might confirm attribute 4, the existence of stone alignments or other markers of market kiosks, giving further credence to the marketplace hypothesis.

In conclusion, soil chemical analyses in conjunction with architectural and artifactual data exposed hidden clues as to the ancient use of Plaza II. Patterns of elevated P, Zn, Mn, Pb, Fe, and Cu concentrations delineate areas within the plaza where both organic goods and workshop/painting materials could have been sold or traded. Although multiple use of the plaza for other activities including festivals, ceremonies, and feasting could also have contributed to the pattern of element concentrations, these patterns suggest the arrangement of stalls within defined areas of the plaza where specific goods would have been marketed.

The probable use of Motul Plaza II as a marketplace impacts our perspective of the role of Classic Maya political centers. As discussed by Foias and Emery (this volume), Classic Maya centers are generally described as regal-ritual cities (in sensu R. Fox 1977). Although several scholars have suggested that Tikal, Caracol, Sayil, and a few other cities had functioning marketplaces in their cores, archaeological evidence in support of markets has been hard to come by. The new line of geochemical soil studies described in this chapter has afforded the opportunity to gain such evidence (see similar studies in Dahlin et al. 2007, 2009), and we can now say that many Maya centers probably had marketplaces. Specifically, Motul Plaza II had such a role. Its location next to the Late Classic royal court, but not next to the highest temple-pyramids (around Plaza I), suggests that the elites had a primary concern in the affairs of the marketplace, but that these economic pursuits were separate from the more politico-ritual ones that took place in Plaza I (or Main Plaza). The activities that took place in the Plaza II marketplace would have been supervised in some manner by the royal elites residing next to it, and would have provided another economic resource to underwrite their political ambitions.

Conclusions

Soil studies in the Motul de San José zone have encompassed the characterization of soil resources, the assessment of their utility for agriculture, and their use in pre-Hispanic times. Soil profile characterization and stable carbon isotope analysis of the SOM of Savanna Chächäklu'um soils confirmed that the agricultural resources of this specific environmental zone in the periphery of Motul, the savanna, were generally productive Aquolls with isotopic evidence of ancient vegetative shifts related to pre-Hispanic maize agriculture. Previous studies of the agricultural resources of Motul have confirmed the presence of productive Mollisols in and around the site and isotope analysis of the SOM confirmed that many of those soils were once cleared of forest for maize agriculture (Jensen et al. 2007; Webb et al. 2007).

Geochemical prospection and activity area analysis of elite residential structures and a public plaza (Plaza II) at Motul de San José have provided important data that enhance archaeological interpretation of ancient Maya lives. Phosphate prospection at the rural group E2E and the paucity of artifacts suggest that the group was occupied briefly. Artifactual and geochemical evidence from the stucco floors of two elite residences in the epicenter of Motul suggest that the rooms were swept and generally kept clean. This was a likely expectation because both of the rooms that underwent geochemical residue analysis were the main rooms of these palaces. Low concentrations of P and heavy metals in those floors suggest some food consumption and mineral pigment use did take place there in Classic times.

Geochemical soil analysis has also allowed us to suggest that one of the main public spaces in the epicenter, Plaza II, may have functioned as a marketplace. Plaza II is a 4-hectare open space with evidence of leveling to support public activities at the center of Motul de San José. Elite residences and the Acropolis surround the plaza. The patterns and concentrations of P and Zn in the central portion of the plaza suggest the use or trade of large quantities of food stuffs. Low levels of P and metals at the southwest and northwest corners of the plaza suggest the location of swept and cleaned entrances and pathway into the plaza. Significant concentrations of heavy metals (Cu, Fe, Mn, and Pb) just east of the Group 8L2 suggest that substantial mineral workshop materials and mineral pigments were processed, used, or traded on the west central portion of the plaza. Nevertheless, additional architectural evidence of marketing spaces or kiosks are needed to support this marketplace hypothesis.

Acknowledgments

Funds for the geochemical research were provided in part by a Mentoring Environments Grant from Brigham Young University. Thanks go to Drs. Antonia Foias and Kitty Emery, codirectors of the Motul de San José Archaeological Project, as well as the other members of this project. Special thanks are also given to Christopher Jensen, Kristofer Johnson, and Matthew Moriarty for the field sampling. The excellent laboratory analysis by Carmen Lopez, Travis Thomason, Amy Dawson, Rachel Bair, Michael Shurtz, Todd Robinson, and Joshua Steffen is acknowledged gratefully.

14

Stable Carbon Isotope Evidence of Ancient Maize Cultivation on the Soils of Motul de San José

ELIZABETH A. WEBB AND HENRY P. SCHWARCZ

One of the central goals of this volume is to shed light on the organization of Classic Maya economy and its intersection with political power at the Central Petén site of Motul de San José in northern Guatemala. The ancient Maya population of Motul de San José was supported by its agricultural system, which produced maize in addition to other fruits and vegetables. Two critical questions rise to the forefront in reconstructions of Classic Maya agriculture: Which areas were used for agriculture, and in particular for maize agriculture? And who owned these agricultural lands (elites or nonelites)? Maya archaeologists have wrestled with these issues of land use and ownership for a long while. New stable carbon isotope soil studies hold great promise to reveal where maize agriculture was practiced prehistorically. The Motul de San José Archaeological Project employed this new line of soil studies in the hopes of understanding if the residents of Motul practiced maize agriculture within the confines of the settlement or whether they depended on maize production from outside the site limits.

Agricultural residues from maize crops may linger in the soil and can be identified by their ^{13}C-enriched carbon-isotope signatures that are distinct from the isotopic compositions of the native vegetation that is the primary source of the soil organic matter (SOM). The naturally labeled ^{13}C-enriched organic matter can be used to identify the regional extent of cultivation and soil types that were selected by the ancient Maya for maize agriculture. However, intermittent use of this area for milpa agriculture, including the growth of maize, from the end of the peak Maya population (AD 600–830) until the present has also added modern ^{13}C-enriched carbon to the soil, effectively obscuring the ancient maize isotope signal. Fortunately, the different fractions of the soil humus have varying turnover rates and each preserves different amounts of ancient versus modern carbon. At Motul de San José, an ancient ^{13}C-enriched maize signal was observed in the humin fraction, whereas modern maize imparted ^{13}C-enriched carbon to the humic acid fraction. An analysis of the humic fractions from sixteen soil profiles along the 2.5-kilometer East Transect between Motul de San José and the neighboring settlement of Chäkokot revealed that ancient maize agriculture was primarily distributed around the neighboring settlement rather than within the limits of Motul de San José proper (Webb et al. 2007; see also Jensen et al. 2007). Furthermore, there appears to be little correlation with either soil type or topographic slope (ibid.). Here, we pursue the implications of these studies further. For example, the lack of a correlation between soil type and the practice of agriculture may suggest that the distribution of agricultural fields was influenced by politics and population growth rather than soil fertility.

Evidence for Ancient Agriculture

Anthropogenic landscape modification can result in rapid ecosystem shifts from forested areas to agricultural land for grazing or cropping. As population density increases over time and larger areas of land are dedicated to food production, there will be a greater capacity for soil erosion on a landscape-wide scale and less opportunity for fields to lie fallow and replenish nutrients (Beach et al. 2006). Often, the landscape is progressively modified in an effort to reduce environmental degradation and increase agricultural yields. This pattern is exemplified by the development of agricultural systems that supported the ancient Maya populations in the lowlands of Belize and Guatemala. In some areas trenches and raised fields were carved out of wetland areas to produce flat, nutrient-rich, agricultural land (Turner II and Harrison 1981; Scarborough et al. 1995; Dunning et al. 2002). In areas with more pronounced topography, land clearance for agriculture and settlement resulted in significantly increased rates of soil erosion (e.g., Curtis et al. 1998; Beach et al. 2006). In many regions, soil erosion was reduced and even reversed by the construction of terrace systems on hill slopes (Healy et al. 1983; Beach et al. 2002). These visible landscape modifications provide evidence that the ancient Maya knew how to manipulate their environment to their advantage (Dunning and Beach 2000; Ford and Emery 2008).

However, in areas like the Motul de San José polity in Guatemala, where agricultural development was not inhibited by saturated soils or over-steepened slopes (Jensen et al. 2007), these adaptations are absent, so agricultural activities are more difficult to trace. In addition, sustainable Maya agricultural activity also took advantage of economic native tree species in combination with milpa agriculture to create forest-gardens in some areas, making it more difficult to identify agricultural activity from landscape modification alone (Ford 2008).

Soils used for agriculture can sometimes be identified based on changes in soil chemistry that occur as a result of decreases in the quality and quantity of litter input to the soil during cultivation. For example, it has been demonstrated that prolonged cultivation in modern systems depletes the underlying soil of nutrients and carbon and nitrogen contents are reduced (Murty et al. 2002; Lemenih, Karltun, and Olsson 2005; Lal 2009). It is widely accepted that the ancient Maya prepared forest areas for agriculture through slash-and-burn practices, using fire to help remove forest vegetation. Burning of vegetation can also change the texture and chemistry of the underlying soil by altering mineralogy, reducing organic carbon and nitrogen in surface soils and contributing charcoal in organic-rich soils (Fynn, Haynes, and Conner 2003; Ketterings, Bigham, and Laperche 2000; Michelsen et al. 2004).

Ancient Maya agriculture can also be identified by the chemical changes in the soil and organic residues that result specifically from the growth of maize. Archaeobotanical quantification of dietary products from archaeological sites confirms that maize was the dominant crop (Lentz 1999), whereas palynological research verifies the extent of corn production over time and space (Pohl et al. 1996; Leyden 2002). Stable isotope analyses of bone preserved from the Maya indicate that maize was a staple of their diet (White and Schwarcz 1989; Wright and White 1996). Evidence of ancient maize growth in soils can therefore be used as an indicator of the extent of maize agriculture in a given region and also serve as an identifier of former agricultural fields that may have been used for other crops as well. The introduction of maize to an ecosystem can have a profound effect on soil properties. This species uses massive amounts of nutrients, which depletes soils after only a few years, resulting in reduced crop yields (Turner II, Klepeis, and Schneider 2003; Lemenih, Karltun, and Olsson 2005). It has also been demonstrated in some systems that tropical grasses such as maize contribute a larger proportion of decay-resistant organic matter, with higher carbon to nitrogen (C/N) ratios, to the underlying soil (Mahaney, Smemo, and Gross 2008).

Carbon Isotopes in Soil as an Indicator of Maize Cultivation

Plants take up carbon dioxide from the atmosphere via the processes of photosynthesis. During diffusion of carbon dioxide into the stomata of the leaves and throughout biochemical conversion to simple sugars and more complex organic molecules, the plant preferentially incorporates the light carbon isotope ^{12}C. Variations in the abundances of the carbon isotopes are expressed in the δ notation, where $δ^{13}C$ is the extent to which the carbon-12/carbon-13 ratio of a material deviates from a universal standard (VPDB). The differences are given in per mil (‰). Because the isotope ratio of all organic matter is lower than that of VPDB, all $δ^{13}C$ values for plants, soil, and so on, are negative (see Sharp 2007 for further details).

The majority of plants incorporate carbon dioxide though a series of chemical reactions known as the Calvin cycle, initially creating a sugar with three carbon atoms. These plants, referred to as C_3 plants, have $δ^{13}C$ values ranging from −23‰ to −34‰, with a mean value of −27‰. Some tropical grasses evolved to incorporate carbon dioxide at lower ambient concentrations, which allows them to thrive under hotter conditions by closing stomatal pores on the leaves to reduce water loss (Teeri and Stowe 1976; Glaser 2005). These plants, called C_4 plants, initially convert carbon dioxide into an organic molecule (aspartate or malate) containing four carbon atoms. The C_4 plants have $δ^{13}C$ values ranging from −9‰ to −17‰, with an average value of approximately −12‰ (Smith and Epstein 1971). Stable isotope analysis can measure differences in $δ^{13}C$ of as little as 0.02‰. Therefore, the much larger 15‰ difference in stable isotope composition between C_3 and C_4 plants should provide a readily detectible natural isotopic label for the source of vegetation contributing to soil organic matter in regions that have supported both C_3 and C_4 vegetation.

The primary input of carbon into soils is from the vegetation that the soils support. As such the organic matter content of a soil and its fertility are related to the quantity and quality of plant litter inputs. The stable isotope composition of soil organic matter is established by the type of decaying vegetation input to the soil over time. Because many tropical grasses utilize a unique chemical pathway for photosynthesis, they acquire an isotopic signature that is distinct from approximately 90 percent of the rest of global vegetation, including trees and shrubs. Hence, stable isotopes have proven to be a useful tool to identify changes in vegetation input to the soil in certain areas where the dominant vegetation has shifted between forest and grassland biomes (e.g., Roscoe et al. 2000; Webb, Schwarcz, and

Healy 2004, Johnson et al. 2007). Most importantly for this study, because maize is a C_4-plant, the residual organic matter transferred to the soil has an isotopic composition that is distinct from the primarily C_3 forest plants that dominate the temperate rain forest ecosystems of the Maya lowlands.

If long periods of time have elapsed since the termination of agriculture in an area, the ^{13}C-enriched chemical fingerprint of maize agriculture will only be preserved under ideal conditions. In accretionary soils that build in depth over time, ancient chemical signals may be preserved in deeper layers that were surface soils at some time in the past (e.g., de Freitas et al. 2001). However, in the shallow soils that have developed over limestone bedrock in the Maya lowlands, soils are continually mixed by the root systems of new vegetation. This provides new organic matter and oxygen to all layers of the soil, which promotes mixing, microbial breakdown of organic matter, and a rapid cycling of nutrients. In addition, intense tropical rainfall can cause rapid soil erosion in these areas wherever soils are not anchored by overlying vegetation (e.g., Beach et al. 2006). In a previous study of the carbon isotope composition of terraced soils from the Maya site of Caracol, Webb, Schwarcz, and Healy (2004) demonstrated that the prolific modern forest vegetation has diluted the ^{13}C-enriched maize organic matter in the soils, and mixing via roots and soil fauna has displaced this signal to the deeper layers of the soil. In the area of Motul de San José, soils have accumulated at an approximate rate of 0.091 millimeters per year and 3 to 10 centimeters of topsoil has been deposited since the most prominent Maya occupation in the Late Classic, based on studies from neighboring regions (Beach 1998; Fernández 2002). This means that chemical changes in surface soils that occurred during cultivation of these lands may have been preserved as they were buried by subsequent soil layers. Nevertheless, the high productivity of these soils and pervasive root systems of rain forest plant species means that significant mixing has likely occurred.

As vegetation decays naturally with the help of microbes, organic tissues are broken down into smaller and smaller molecules, which are recombined into new organic complexes referred to collectively as humic substances. Fulvic acid, humic acid, and humin are all different classifications of humic substances that are difficult to define because they are comprised of associations of different organic molecules held together in loose configurations and thus can vary between different soils with different vegetative inputs in different climates (Krosshavn et al. 1992; Stevenson 1994; Spaccini et al. 2000; Hayes and Clapp 2001; Tan 2003).

The different classifications of humic substances see these as heterogeneous mixtures defined only by their behavior in acid and base systems. Fulvic acids are soluble at any pH, humic acids are only soluble in basic solutions, and humin is classified as the material that is not soluble at any pH and therefore remains associated with the mineral matter during laboratory extraction. Carbon-14 dating has demonstrated that humin, the highest molecular weight fraction of humic substances, is generally older than humic acid and fulvic acid extracted from the same soils (Balesdent 1987; Pessenda, Gouveia, and Aravena 2001; Rethemeyer et al. 2005). The large size of these molecules and their close association with the mineral matter of the soil protects these organics from further decay. Prolonged preservation and continual accretion ensure that the humin fraction represents an assemblage of the most resilient and oldest organics in the soil. In contrast, fulvic acids and humic acids are comprised of more recent organic matter and tend to be more mobile within the soil profile owing to their greater solubility (Rethemeyer et al. 2005). A comparison of the stable carbon isotope compositions of different humic substances can provide information about more recent versus more ancient vegetation contributing organic matter to the soil. As humin contains more ancient organic matter, its $\delta^{13}C$ values will represent an earlier phase of vegetation. Humic acid contains younger carbon and its $\delta^{13}C$ values will represent more recent vegetation stored in the same layer of soil (Lichtfouse et al. 1995). Hence, at a site like Motul de San José, we can use the stable isotope composition of separate humic fractions to distinguish between modern and ancient contributions of C_4 vegetation to the soil.

Study Area and Methods

In the current study, we examined the stable carbon isotope signal of soil organic matter from soils collected from a 2.5-kilometer survey transect between the site of Motul de San José and the neighboring community of Chäkokot located approximately 2 kilometers east (see Figures 1.3 and 1.4). Motul de San José was an ancient Maya site that was settled continuously from 600 BC onwards, with its zenith occurring in the Late Classic Period (600–AD 850). Although the area surrounding Lake Petén Itzá has been sparsely populated since this time, population has increased to approximately five hundred thousand today and the area is heavily cultivated by modern Maya agriculturalists who utilize traditional swidden farming practices. None of the soils in this study currently support primary forest assemblages. The sampling area is partly within a protected reserve, but the rest is still used by locals for agriculture. All sites sampled for this study had been cleared for farming in the last five to twenty years and currently support secondary growth forest comprised of C_3 plants. An interview of locals in the area indicates that at least some of the recent cultivation was for maize (Jensen et al. 2007). At one of the locations tested along the East Transect (KJ3; see Jensen et al. 2007), the soil was currently being cultivated in modern milpas for maize (R. Terry, personal communication, 2001). This potentially can contribute modern ^{13}C-enriched organic matter to the soil, which may cloak the ancient signal. To circumvent this problem, soil organic matter was fractionated into its humic components.

The carbon isotope composition was determined for bulk carbon, humin, and humic acid fractions of the soils from depths of 0–100 centimeters (see also Webb et al. 2007; Jensen et al. 2007). The soil profiles were collected by Christopher Jensen and Kristopher Johnson (Brigham Young University). Chris Jensen classified the soils according to the classification used by the local Itzaj Maya farmers as defined by Matt Moriarty's (Tulane University) research on indigenous soil classification in the region (Jensen et al. 2007; also see Moriarty, Chapter 7; Moriarty 2001). The soil profiles were chosen to represent variations in topography and soil type. Comparisons were done among these variables to determine if a ^{13}C-enriched signal, indicative of the former presence of maize cultivation, would be correlated with slope of the landscape or soil fertility as perceived by the Maya. The analytical details of humic separation, isotope analyses, and a detailed interpretation of the data are described in Webb et al. (2007). In the preindustrial era the average $\delta^{13}C$ values for C_3 and C_4 plants would have been closer to –25 and –10‰, respectively, because of higher $\delta^{13}C$ values of CO_2 before the addition of fossil fuel emissions to the atmosphere. This shift has been factored into the data interpretation.

Results and Discussion

The $\delta^{13}C$ values of all soil profiles were dominated by a strong C_3 organic matter signal. This is not surprising given that all of the samples were collected to represent soil types that develop under forest vegetation (e.g., *Säkni'is*, *Ek'lu'um*, and *Ek'luk*, according to the Itzaj Maya classification system, see discussion below; Moriarty 2001; Emery and Foias, this volume). The Itzaj Maya term for soils that develop under savannah vegetation

(*Chächäklu'um*) did not apply to any of the soils collected in this study as this environmental zone is located beyond the survey transect (but see recent analyses from this zone in Bair and Terry, this volume). C_3 plants are the native forest vegetation in the area and even where maize cultivation did occur, the amount of C_4 carbon added to the soil would be less than that contributed by the forest. There are two reasons for this. First, during harvest, it is likely that at least some if not all of the aboveground plant material was removed from the soils as it is by modern milpa farmers (Reina 1967). Second, fresh organic matter is preferentially consumed by the microbial biomass so it takes a long time to replace old soil organic matter with new vegetative inputs (e.g., Balesdent, Wagner, and Mariotti 1988). Nevertheless, the soil profiles examined in this study can be grouped into three categories: (1) those that have no evidence of ^{13}C-enriched C_4 organic matter; (2) those that have evidence of ancient C_4 organic matter preserved in the older humin fractions of the soil organic matter; and (3) those that contain ^{13}C-enriched organic matter from both modern and ancient maize cultivation.

The $\delta^{13}C$ values of the soil organic matter in the surface layers were varied (-19.1 to –26.8‰). All sixteen soil profiles were close to the range of $\delta^{13}C$ values reported for C_3 plants, but slightly more enriched in ^{13}C relative to average C_3 plants. This suggests that carbon from C_3 vegetation has been the dominant input to the soil. As remarked above, this is not surprising since the natural vegetation in this area is comprised of C_3 plants. Despite the use of this area for modern agriculture, most of the soils in this study had been supporting secondary growth forest for five to twenty years prior to sample collection. The large range in $\delta^{13}C$ values for bulk carbon of the surface soils reflects partial contribution of C_4 maize carbon from recent agriculture in some profiles. For example, the organic matter in the surface soil at testing location CJ6 had a $\delta^{13}C$ value of –19.1 ‰ (the location of these soil profiles is discussed in detail in Jensen and colleagues (2007) and Webb and colleagues (2007); for the exact location of this unit on the eastern slopes of Chäkokot, see Webb et al. 2007, fig.1). The locations that have relatively ^{13}C enriched values (> –23‰) for the bulk carbon of the surface soils likely contain carbon contributed from modern maize cultivation that occurred on these soils over the last one hundred years. To provide evidence that this ^{13}C-enriched signal is from recent carbon inputs requires a closer examination of the $\delta^{13}C$ values of the different humic fractions. Humic acid should contain a greater proportion of carbon from recent vegetation than the humin or bulk carbon. Indeed, the humic acids of these soils are more enriched in ^{13}C than the bulk carbon or humin as can be observed in profiles CJ5 and CJ6 in Figure 14.1. This suggests that the contribution of C_4 (maize) carbon to the soil was recent.

When examining the deeper soils in each profile several trends in the stable isotope compositions can be identified. In six soil profiles, particularly those that lie in the intersettlement area between Motul de San José and Chäkokot and one location within the Motul de San José center, there is very little variation in δ^{13}C values of bulk carbon, humin, or humic acid with depth. This suggests that little or no ancient maize cultivation took place in these locations. An example of this trend is shown for profiles KJ3[1] and KJ5 in Figure 14.2 (for the location of these at transect midpoint and western edge of MSJ, respectively, see Webb et al. 2007, fig. 1). The average δ^{13}C values for the bulk carbon, humin, and humic acid of each fraction was less than –23‰, well within the expected values when C_3 plants contribute 100 percent to the organic matter. The general trend in δ^{13}C values of bulk carbon, humic acid, and humic fractions of these profiles was a slight increase from values of approximately –27 to –25‰ at the surface to values of –24‰ in the C-horizon (50–100 centimeters depth). This degree

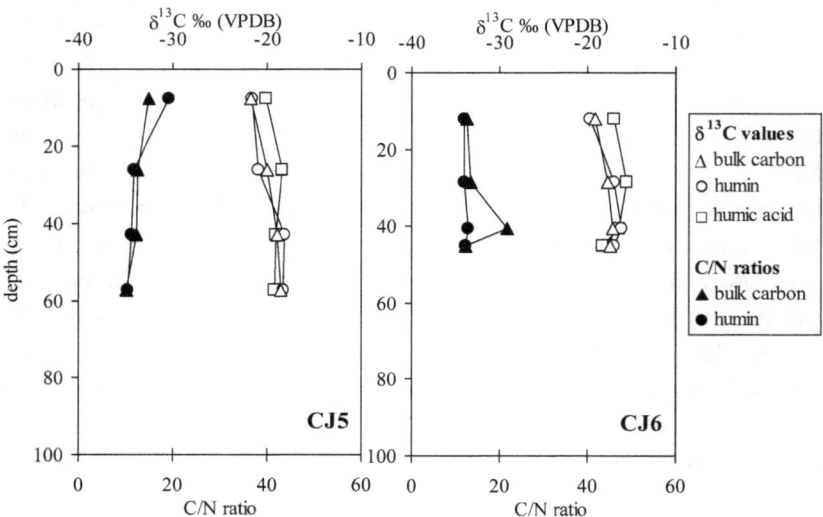

Figure 14.1. The δ^{13}C values and C/N ratios of organic matter from soil profiles collected at Motul de San José, Guatemala, within the neighboring settlement of Chäkokot (CJ5 and CJ6). These soil profiles are examples of soils with ^{13}C-enrichment of the soil organic matter resulting from ancient maize cultivation (within the humin fraction) and modern maize cultivation (within the humic acid fraction).

of ^{13}C-enrichment with depth reflects the incorporation of ancient organic tissues produced with preindustrial CO_2 (2‰ enriched in ^{13}C compared to modern atmospheric CO_2) and is within the limits of natural fractionation that may occur during the decay of organic matter in the soil (+4‰). Over time, organic matter in the soils, including the humic substances are processed by microbes. During this process the microbial biomass becomes progressively enriched in the heavier ^{13}C atoms (Šantrucková, Bird, and Lloyd 2000; Boström, Comstedt, and Ekblad 2007). Hence, with repeated processing over time soil organic matter will increase in microbial biomass and δ^{13}C values by a few parts per thousand. Organic matter in deeper soil layers is older and more processed; therefore, we observe slight ^{13}C enrichment with depth in these profiles (Figure 14.2). This process is sometimes accompanied by an increase in the C/N ratio of soil organic matter as the proportion of nitrogen-rich labile components declines (Yoshida and Kumada 1978). An increase in C/N ratios of the organic matter with depth is also observed in most soil profiles in this study and this pattern is more pronounced for the older, more processed humin fraction (Figure 14.2). The absence of ancient maize agriculture at both locations KJ3 and KJ5 is

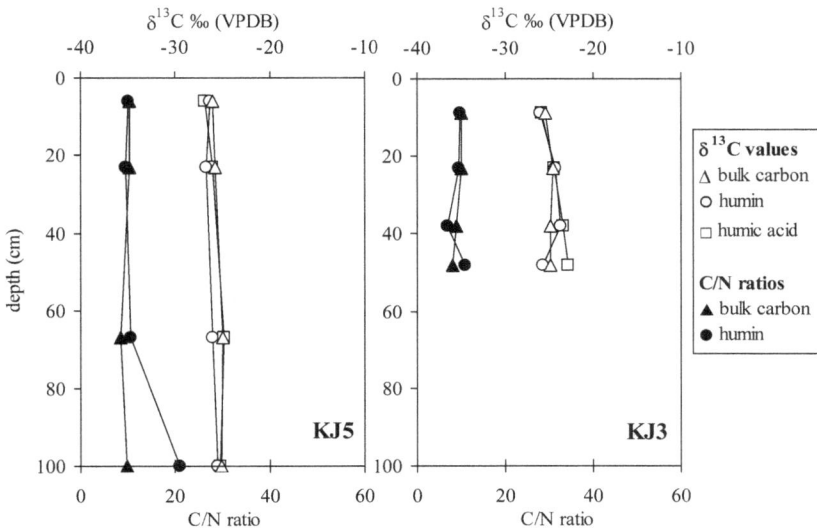

Figure 14.2. The δ^{13}C values and C/N ratios of organic matter from soil profiles collected at Motul de San José, Guatemala, in the peripheral area between the site core and the neighboring settlement of Chäkokot (KJ3 and KJ5). These soil profiles are examples of soils showing no evidence of ^{13}C-enrichment of the soil organic matter from ancient or modern maize cultivation.

surprising because these lands are close to the core of Motul, and have quite fertile soils, according to Jensen and colleagues (2007). One possible explanation is that the zones were maintained as forest reserves by the Motul political elites, possibly as hunting parks (R. Terry, personal communication, 2009).

Half of the profiles collected from the settlement of Chäkokot (four of eight profiles), and two profiles from within the site core of Motul (KJ6 and KJ8) show a significant increase in $\delta^{13}C$ values of bulk carbon, humic acid and/or humin with depth (Figure 14.3). The organic matter in the surface layers of the soil have average $\delta^{13}C$ values of –27 to –24‰ that increase to –24 to –18‰ in the C-horizon (50 to 80 centimeters depth) for the bulk carbon, humin, and humic acid fractions. In most cases individual humic fractions all showed an increase in $\delta^{13}C$ values of more than 4‰ with depth. In two of the soils, this degree of ^{13}C enrichment with depth was only observed in the oldest, humin fraction of the soil organic matter (e.g., profile CJ7, Figure 14.3). This degree of ^{13}C enrichment is greater than expected for microbial recycling or from the contribution of ^{13}C-enriched preindustrial CO_2 incorporated into ancient vegetation. The ^{13}C-enriched carbon in these soils most likely represents the contribution of C_4 carbon to the soil. To determine whether or not this is modern or ancient maize we look again at the $\delta^{13}C$ values of the humic acid versus the humin. For all but one of these profiles, the $\delta^{13}C$ values of the humin displays the greatest degree of ^{13}C enrichment with depth. This means that the oldest carbon in the soil has the greatest percentage of C_4 carbon, indicating that this represents pre-Hispanic maize cultivation. In these profiles, the depths that contain the most ^{13}C-enriched humic fractions also have the highest C/N ratio reflecting the advanced decomposition of the organic matter at these depths (Figure 14.3).

The third pattern concerns the soil profiles where the surface soils were already enriched in ^{13}C relative to values typical for C_3 vegetation in the area. These four soil profiles, which comprise half of those collected from the site of Chäkokot, appear to contain modern maize carbon in the upper layers of the soil. However, they also have high $\delta^{13}C$ values with depth (see Figure 14.1). To determine if the ^{13}C enrichment is from either modern or ancient maize growing on these soils requires a closer examination of the carbon isotope behavior of the humic substances. Near surface soils have humic acid $\delta^{13}C$ values that are more enriched in ^{13}C than humin (e.g., profiles CJ6 and CJ7 in Figure 14.1). This indicates that the ^{13}C-enriched organic matter is a fairly recent addition to the soil since humic acid has a

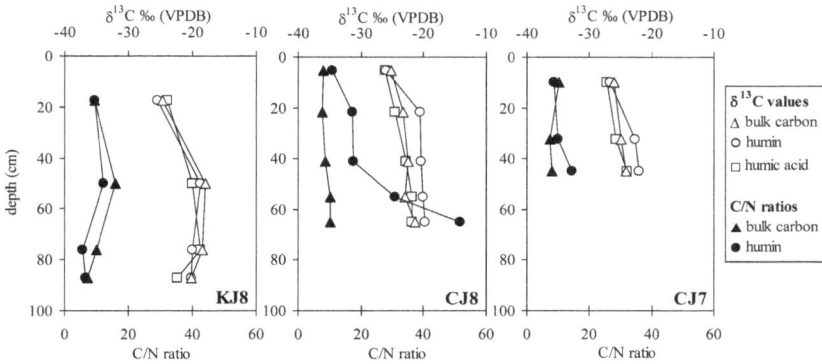

Figure 14.3. The $\delta^{13}C$ values and C/N ratios of organic matter from soil profiles collected at Motul de San José, Guatemala, within the site core (KJ8) and within the neighboring settlement of Chäkokot (CJ7 and CJ8). These soil profiles are examples of soils that were used for ancient maize agriculture evident in the ^{13}C-enrichment in the deeper (older) soils and humin (older) fraction of the soil organic matter.

faster turnover rate than humin. Below a depth of 20–40 centimeters, the pattern reverses and the humin $\delta^{13}C$ values are greater than for humic acid (see Figure 14.1). The older soils at depth in these profiles have preserved ^{13}C-enriched organic matter in the oldest humin fraction of the soil, indicating that this is likely from pre-Hispanic maize agriculture. Although humic acids may be translocated downward in the soil owing to their smaller atomic size and greater solubility, this process is minimized in soils that have not been tilled (Rethemeyer et al. 2005).

This limited data set suggests that maize was grown within and in the near periphery of both the settlements of Chäkokot and Motul de San José. All the soil profiles from Chäkokot and two of three profiles within Motul showed evidence of ancient maize agriculture. The majority of the samples taken from Chäkokot were placed on the outskirts of the village, but two samples (CJ1 and CJ2) are from among the residential plaza groups, suggesting that maize was also grown in smaller gardens among the house compounds within the village. In contrast, almost none of the soil profiles between these two settlements had stable-isotope evidence of ancient maize agriculture.

We did not find any soil profiles that showed evidence of modern maize inputs that lacked ancient maize signatures. This may indicate that soils that the ancient Maya found to be the most suitable for agriculture are still considered fertile today. However, the number of soil profiles analyzed for this study was small and it is difficult to make final conclusions. Therefore, we also assessed factors that may have influenced choices for agricultural fields, such as topography and soil type among the profiles that show evidence of ancient maize agriculture.

Soil types throughout Motul de San José and its periphery were classified by Matthew Moriarty based on his interviews with local modern Itzaj Maya farmers (Moriarty 2001, 2004d; Jensen et al. 2007; Webb et al. 2007; Emery and Foias, this volume). *Säkni'is* soils are comprised of black soil with common white tiny pebbles and have a high nutrient content. They are suitable for short-term milpa agriculture, but may be productive for longer periods of time if bio-intensive methods are used for fertilization. *Ek'lu'um*, or "black earth," soils commonly occur on uplands and hill tops. They are generally considered to be among the most fertile of all the soils in the region and are suitable for long-term milpa agriculture. A third soil type, called *Tierra Mezclada*, is a mixture of a number of different soils (Moriarty 2001, 2004d; Jensen et al. 2007; Emery and Foias, this volume). The fertility of *Tierra Mezclada* soils is highly variable depending on the mixture of the soils. However, it is generally believed that mixtures of Säkni'is and Ek'lu'um soils are ideal for long-term agriculture. *Ek'luk* or black clay soils are thick soils that accumulate at the base of slopes or in low-lying areas (*bajos*) and contain well-developed soil horizons. They are considered to be suitable for maize agriculture only under very specific circumstances, such as favorably wet conditions. Although the modern Itzaj Maya population generally feel that the Ek'lu'um soils are the most fertile, they note that the choice of fields to work is primarily based on political ownership and other factors such as drainage, exposure to sunlight, and altitude (Reina 1967).

There was no correlation between the soil types in these Itzaj Maya classification and the presence of ^{13}C-enriched organic matter from ancient or modern agriculture (see also Webb et al. 2007). The ten out of sixteen profiles that displayed evidence of ancient maize cultivation occurred in all of the soil classification types. There was slightly higher occurrence of a ^{13}C-enriched signal in the Säkni'is and Ek'lu'um soil types, but there were almost an equal number of samples taken from these soil types that showed no evidence of modern or ancient cultivation. This does not mean that the ancient Maya did not take soil fertility into consideration when choosing their fields, but further work is clearly necessary to determine whether the ancient perception of soil fertility has been maintained to the present day. It is also likely that ancient populations experienced pressure for land development and may have also been influenced by landownership or stewardship issues.

Soils that showed evidence of ancient maize agriculture were then compared to hillslope location. It is possible that in an area without terracing, flatter areas of land would be more productive and experience less soil erosion than midslope regions. The profiles in this study were collected from toe slope, foot slope, back slope, and hillcrest locations (see also Webb et al. 2007). There was no significant correlation between hillslope location and the presence of an ancient maize signal in the soil organic matter. However, the majority of base-slope soils did show evidence of cultivation, but this may be an artifact caused by erosion of soils from higher on the slope.

Conclusions

Ten of the sixteen profiles collected along the Eastern Transect between the epicore of Motul de San José and the adjacent village of Chäkokot (some 2 kilometers east) contained ^{13}C-enriched carbon in the humin fraction of the soil organic matter, which is evidence of ancient maize cultivation on these soils (see further details in Webb et al. 2007). The contribution of maize carbon to the soils that resulted from modern agriculture can be differentiated by the preservation of the ^{13}C-enriched signal in the younger humic acid fraction of the soil. There was no significant correlation between the occurrence of ancient maize carbon and soil type or hillslope location. Although the sample size is small, this data set indicates that perception of soil fertility and topography was not the controlling factor in decisions of where to cultivate maize. However, all soil profiles that contained traces of modern maize carbon also had evidence of ancient maize carbon preserved in the humin fraction. This might indicate that the distribution of agriculture in the past and present may be based on similar criteria, such as land stewardship, but does not rule out continuity in and awareness of soil fertility or drainage issues.

Overall 80 percent of the soils that contained ^{13}C-enriched carbon as evidence of ancient maize cultivation (eight profiles) occurred around the village settlement of Chäkokot. The other two profiles occurred in the urban center of Motul de San José. Based on this data set, it appears that corn cultivation occurred primarily at or near the residential areas with minimal agricultural activity taking place in the peripheral zone between the two sites. Proximity to residential structures could therefore have been a key factor in deciding where to plant. Jensen and colleagues (2007), based on

Moriarty's settlement correlations, note that these house groups are also situated on soils that are most suitable for milpa agriculture and garden plots (*Säkni'is* and *Ek'lu'um*) and propose that soil fertility potential may have contributed, in part, to the decision to settle these areas. Modern farmers in the area often maintain small fields in the vicinity of their settlements with larger fields at greater distances (Reina 1967). This pattern may also reflect the degree of preservation of carbon in the soils. If cultivation began close to residential areas, then, even as agriculture expanded and radiated outward, those soils closest to the home would experience a longer period of C_4 carbon input. This overall longer history of maize cultivation would mean that a greater amount of C_4 carbon would exist in the soil and, perhaps at current rates of decay, still be present today.

The stable carbon isotope analysis of soil organic matter is a useful tool to identify ecosystem changes where the dominant vegetation has shifted between forested (C_3) and grassland (C_4) or agriculture systems. However, preservation of ancient organic matter can be highly variable in tropical climates with high amounts of precipitation and pervasive rooting systems of the modern vegetation. Assessing changes in the carbon isotope composition of the humic substances within the soil organic matter provides more information about the relative timing and degree of preservation of ancient vegetation shifts. The stable isotope analyses of soils around Motul de San José have provided critical information about the distribution of ancient maize cultivation in the center and its periphery. The rather limited maize cultivation in the outskirts of Motul de San José contrasts with the broad incidence of ancient maize cultivation in the nearby village of Chäkokot. This has significant implications for the political economy of the Motul de San José realm and argues that the residents of Motul obtained agricultural products from villages like Chäkokot, possibly through tribute-tax systems or through market exchange.

15

Landscape, Economies, and the Politics of Power in the Motul de San José Polity

KITTY F. EMERY AND ANTONIA E. FOIAS

This monograph has examined, from a number of different perspectives, the nature of political, economic, and social organization of the small Classic Maya polity of Motul de San José located in the Central Petén Lakes region of northern Guatemala. This represents the first phase of our long-term research in the region, and to date our investigations have primarily targeted the capital center itself. However, we have also surveyed and tested smaller subsidiary centers and intersite regions along transects between sites. We have explored the interactions between sites and communities and, on a more specific scale, the possible interactions between members of the Motul communities and families.

In this chapter we reflect on a decade of archaeological research at Motul de San José and its contribution to the debates on Classic Maya economics and politics. We review the cultural and environmental landscape of the Motul de San José polity and discuss aspects of political and economic scale, structure, and integration.

Landscape, History, and Settlement of Motul de San José

The Motul de San José polity is located on the northern shore of the Lake Petén Itzá. The area was first settled probably in the eighth century BC as suggested by early Mamom pottery at Buenavista-Nuevo San José (Castellanos 2007) and Trinidad (Moriarty, this volume), and populations pushed inward during the following centuries, flourishing in the Late Preclassic, especially at Trinidad (and secondarily at Motul de San José; see Moriarty, this volume). This first peak of settlement in this region is followed by an apparent decline during the Early Classic. The most important peak in population occurs during the Late Classic at both Motul and Trinidad, although Motul dwarfs Trinidad by this time. The smaller sites that were tested, although with some Preclassic occupation, also flourished during the Late Classic. During the Terminal Classic, Motul diminished in influence, whereas Trinidad and other sites closer to the lakes began to expand in the Postclassic while Motul de San José was basically abandoned (Foias and Emery, this volume; Foias 2003). Trinidad continued as a successful port through Historical times (Moriarty, this volume).

The largest site, and the one with the most massive and elaborate architecture, is the capital of Motul de San José, lying 3 kilometers from the shore of Lake Petén Itzá (Figure 1.4). Surrounding that capital are a series of medium-size and smaller satellites. Trinidad de Nosotros (Trinidad), the second largest of the Motul de San José polity sites, lies 2 kilometers southeast of Motul, directly on the lake edge on the only northern egress from the lake and beside a small river outlet that during the Late Classic likely joined up with the Rio K'änte't'u'ul to the north (Moriarty, this volume).

Three additional midsize centers lie approximately equidistant from Motul de San José: to the east some 5.5 kilometers, upland and off a branch of Rio K'änte't'u'ul, is the site of Chächäklu'um; to the northeast 8 kilometers from Motul de San José and on the highest rise of land in the area is El Guineo (a site almost as large as Motul itself; see Moriarty 2001); and, approximately 7 kilometers to the northwest on a hilltop overlooking the confluence of Rios Akte and K'änte't'u'ul is the smaller site of Akte (Yorgey and Moriarty, this volume). To what extent these sites are part of the Motul polity is open to debate, but their locations equidistant from the capital site and surrounding the smaller sites is suggestive of possible frontier settlements (see further discussion in Yorgey and Moriarty, this volume).

A matrix of small satellite centers lies closer to Motul de San José. Directly to the south of Motul de San José are three small sites, Chakalte (at about 1 kilometer south); Buenavista-Nuevo San José (Buenavista, at about 2.25 kilometers south); and Chak Maman Tok or Las Estrellas (about 2.5 kilometers south). Buenavista and Chak Maman Tok lie slightly upland. Other small sites are found on upland rises throughout the zone: Xilil, 4 kilometers southeast, and San Pedro, 6.80 kilometers southeast; Chäkokot, 2 kilometers east; Jobonmo' 2.5 kilometers northeast; Tikalito, 3.5 kilometers north; and K'änte't'u'ul, 2.5 kilometers northwest (Moriarty et al. 2001; Moriarty 2004d; Moriarty, this volume; Yorgey and Moriarty, this volume; Castellanos 2007). Of these, only Chäkokot, Trinidad, Buenavista, and

Akte have been sufficiently tested to allow us to discuss them in any detail here. We plan to test the other minor centers in the future.

That the Motul de San José polity commanded the northern shore of the largest permanent water body in the central lowlands is vitally important in an area where settlement has been challenged by a general lack of surface water. The rulers of Motul de San José may have intentionally linked themselves to the Lake Petén Itzá or the region around it. As Tokovinine and Zender (this volume) suggest, the toponym of the site, Ik'a', literally "Windy Water," aptly describes the lake, and they suggest it may have referred to both the lake and the ancient city. This is no surprise considering the importance of this water system as a source of basic resources and a communication link into the eastern and northern regions of the Petén.

The Petén Itzá Lake basin has been interpreted as a "crossroads" (P. Rice and D. Rice 2004) for ideas and populations between south Petén, north Petén, the San Pedro drainage, and East Petén-Belize, and a water bridge[1] for overland trade crossing the southern spine of the Maya lowlands (Guderjan 1995). The success of this small polity can be attributed, at least partially, to its landscape setting at a trade and travel nexus, adjacent to the largest standing water body in lowland Petén.

Paleoenvironmental research in the Central Petén Lakes basin and elsewhere indicates that Preclassic and Late Classic climatic conditions were significantly wetter than in the Terminal and Postclassic periods than they are today. Rates of precipitation were higher and, in the Late Classic, more predictable (Anselmetti et al. 2007; Brenner et al. 2002; Ford and Nigh 2009; Hodell, Brenner, and Curtis 2000). This is confirmed by zooarchaeological research at the Motul de San José polity sites that indicates higher proportions of both lake and seasonal swamp species during these periods (Emery and Thornton, press). Survey with local informants (Emery 1998a; Moriarty 2004d) and by other experts in neighboring regions (Fialko, personal communication, 2000; Scarborough, Valdez Jr., and Dunning 2003) suggests that surface water may have been available at most sites in the polity. The region would likely have been crisscrossed by flowing rivers[2] that would have ameliorated the seasonality of rainfall and lack of water during the dry seasons, as well as providing important riverine and lacustrine resources and transportation routes.

Access to these water sources may have dictated the placement of several sites as will be discussed below (Figure 1.3). However, the presence of highly fertile agricultural lands, suitable topographies, and the location of other resources was also pivotal. The Motul de San José polity rests within a low-lying area characterized by a rolling topography (Figure 1.4) and large areas of highly fertile soil with relatively good drainage (no permanent bajos or swamps are found in the Motul de San José area; see Moriarty 2001).

Agricultural potential was perhaps the most significant factor in settlement of the region, though the elevated uplands were preferentially settled throughout the area (Ford 1996; Moriarty 2001). Soil physical and chemical analysis by Terry and students combined with indigenous soils research and local topographic analysis by Moriarty indicates rich agricultural potential throughout the region (Bair and Terry, this volume; Jensen et al. 2007; Moriarty 2001). Soils considered by both studies to be of highest value (Ek'lu'um) were found primarily within the Motul de San José capital (Jensen et al. 2007), which might explain why the Motul de San José site area, fairly distant from the lake, was initially preferred for settlement and later for political control (Moriarty 2001). Säkni'is soils, highly favored by the modern Itzaj for their diverse milpas despite their susceptibility to erosion, were consistently associated with archaeological settlements (Moriarty 2001), and were found particularly around the small Motul de San José satellite centers of Chäkokot and K'änte't'u'ul (Jensen et al. 2007). Carbon isotopic analysis of these soils indicated these had been used in the past for maize agriculture (Webb and Schwarcz, this volume; Webb et al. 2007), although they were likely also used for many other crops (see Wyatt et al., this volume).

Many of the animal species found in the faunal records of Motul de San José and Trinidad are those attracted to secondary forest or disturbed habitats, and are the species opportunistically hunted today by farmers visiting their milpas. Ethnographic research reveals that the highly diverse milpa, also known as forest garden, intentionally duplicates the most productive forest zones to maintain multiple resources including domestic and wild plants and wild animals (see Ford and Emery 2008). This was undoubtedly the pattern in the Motul de San José polity as well (Emery 2003a).

The Motul area soils of least agricultural potential (Ek'luk) were found in topographic depressions between sites and particularly between Motul de San José and its eastern satellites, Chäkokot and Jobonmo', and never in association with permanent settlement (Bair and Terry, this volume; Moriarty 2001). Isotopic work did not find any evidence of corn agriculture in these soils (Webb and Schwarcz, this volume). These intersite lowland regions may have been a valued source of clay resources. Itzaj informants noted that these clayey, poorly drained soils were sought for clay and pigments (Moriarty 2001). For example, one clay sample taken between Motul de San José and Trinidad was chemically comparable to the main pottery group excavated at Motul de San José according to Instrumental Neutron Activation Analysis (INAA) analysis (Halperin et al. 2009; Bishop, personal communication, 2006). It is also possible that these areas between settlements might have functioned as natural reserves for animals and wild products as proposed by Bair and Terry (this volume) and also suggested by the predominance in the zooarchaeological record of animal species that prefer high or less disturbed forest (Emery, this volume; Thornton, this volume; Emery and Thornton, 2008).

Another environmental type may have provided yet another important set of resources: these are several raised plateaus characterized by savanna-type vegetation (Brenner et al. 1990; P. Rice and D. Rice 1979), savanna animal species such as armadillos and rabbits (Emery 2003a), and a characteristic soil type, Chächäklu'um, used today for arboriculture (Moriarty 2001). Two sites likely part of the Motul de San José polity, Chächäklu'um and Akte, have savanna-type characteristics and may have been the source of fruits (Moriarty 2001; Yorgey and Moriarty, this volume) and savanna animals (Thornton, this volume). Soil tests by Bair and Terry (this volume) at the site of Chächäklu'um found only limited ancient maize signatures, suggesting that, as today, these areas were not preferentially used for corn agriculture.

Chert was another vital resource that was used throughout the region for stone tools and is ubiquitous in all deposits. However, the resource appears to be limited to a band along the western part of the northern shore of the Lake. The sites of Buenavista, Chak Maman Tok', and Trinidad lie along this band and the first two were loci of intensive chert quarrying and tool production (Lawton 2007b; Moriarty et al. 2007).

Political Structure and Integration at Motul de San José

With this brief summary of the landscape and cultural context of the Motul de San José polity, we now explore insights from our research on questions of scale, structure, and integration of the Motul de San José polity, as well as the role of community members, both the rulers and the ruled, in polity economics and politics.

First, in terms of scale, it is of interest that the Motul de San José polity was at all times very small in comparison to other Maya polities and global estimates for archaic states. The site of Motul may have held between 1,200 and 2,000[3] people, and we suggest that the territory it controlled at its Late

Classic height (AD 650–830) may have extended between 5 and 7 kilometers around the site.[4] This places the reconstructed scale of the Motul de San José polity between 78.5 square kilometers and 153.9 square kilometers. Therefore, at its apogee, the Motul polity was quite small in comparison to the average size of Classic Maya polities (2,500 square kilometers as calculated by Mathews 1991). It is closer to the minimum scale in population and territory reconstructed for archaic states (ca. twenty-five hundred people and 625 square kilometers or a radius of ca 14.1 kilometers; see Renfrew 1975, 1982; Feinman 1998). Nevertheless, it is comparable to the average size of Central Mexican city-states (or *altepetl*) during the Late Postclassic of 90 square kilometers (M. Smith 2008; Chase, Chase, and Smith 2009).

Structure at the Superstate Level

This small size does not necessarily correlate with small political clout, as Motul lays claim to one of only thirty known Emblem Glyphs suggesting its political parity with other, larger capitals (Mathews 1991; Grube 2000; Stuart and Houston 1994; Houston and Stuart 1996). Its princesses were worthy of marriage into the Yaxchilán dynasty, and its Emblem Glyph was included in the famed Seibal Stela 10 and the Altar de los Reyes Altar 3, which lists thirteen famous dynasties (Tokovinine and Zender, this volume). However, the very small size of the Motul polity argues that even those city-states identified by Emblem Glyphs would have varied greatly in political capital because of their highly divergent sizes and resources.

We turn then to a discussion of political structure to understand the Motul polity. Beginning with the role of the Motul de San José polity in external systems, the southern lowland hieroglyphic corpus relates Motul's alliances or wars with Tikal, Calakmul, Dos Pilas, Yaxchilán, and so on. Alliances between Motul and the San Pedro Martir River polities of Hix Wits (Zapote Bobal-El Pajaral) and Namaan (La Florida) may have allowed "confrontation of more powerful neighbors, or perhaps the control of trade routes along the Rio San Pedro to the Lake Petén Itzá" (Tokovinine and Zender, this volume).

The *y-ajaw* expression in the hieroglyphic text on Motul de San José Stela 1 indicates that Motul was one of the vassal states of the Tikal hegemony (Foias 2000b; Tokovinine and Zender, this volume), though a member at the lowest levels of this superstate (Grube 2000; Martin and Grube 1995, 2000). Tikal appears to have sponsored the earliest rulers of the Motul polity at the end of the seventh century AD and Motul de San José might well have paid tribute to this larger hegemony as suggested by

Grube (2000, 550). But in the beginning of the eighth century AD, the capital site of Motul de San José, and other sites within its polity such as Trinidad and Akte, appear to have had a number of liberties, including the right to raise stelae and substantial temple-pyramids and palaces, suggesting a more dispersed form of political power. This supports Grube's (2000, 550) interpretation of the superstate hegemonies as decentralized with no military occupation or central administration of the vassal states. Motul de San José could also be interpreted as a Tikal border center following Chase, Chase, and Smith (2009) since it is located some 30 kilometers distant and seems to have switched alliances several times between Tikal, Calakmul, and Dos Pilas (Tokovinine and Zender, this volume).

Structure at the Polity Level

We have also gained a window into the internal political structure of this small polity. Within the Motul de San José polity, the minor centers identified by regional reconnaissance between 2 and 5 kilometers from Motul range in size from the very small (Chäkokot) to the substantial (Trinidad). These subsidiary centers generally consist of one major temple-pyramid, a major residential plaza group, and a dozen (more or less) small plazuela groups, exceeding 10 hectares in settlement (Moriarty 2004d, 32–37), but they are otherwise quite variable. Some insight is provided by a brief review of the findings at the largest subsidiary site, Trinidad, and at several of the smaller sites including Akte, Chäkokot, and Buenavista.

Trinidad de Nosotros is much larger than the other subsidiary centers, and may be the first among these. The site comprised only thirty to forty households (Moriarty, this volume) and has no structures taller than 12 meters, but it likely functioned as an inland trading port and stopping point on the traverse between the two major lake ports at Ixlu (east) and Nixtun-Ch'ich (west), providing a distribution point for products into the Motul de San José polity and possibly further into the Maya inlands north and west (Moriarty and Thornton 2007). Preferential access to obsidian at Trinidad in volumes greater even than that found at Motul de San José proper suggests a fairly indirect control of exotic products through the polity by the Motul de San José rulers (Moriarty, this volume). This is confirmed by the fact that the Trinidad elite (though not nonelite) had access to the same animals enjoyed by the Motul elite, including dietary species like deer and turtle and exotics like marine shell (Thornton, this volume; Thornton and Emery 2007). However, evidence for craft production at Trinidad is limited. Although plaster production was highly specialized, materials were local (Spensley, this volume). Likewise, ceramics were produced using local recipes and materials, although they were decorated with Motul de San José iconography indicating affiliation with the polity (Moriarty and Spensley 2009). The site lies above a rich chert source and a diverse array of tools were produced but not on a scale indicating community specialization (Lawton 2007b). Bone and shell crafting was dispersed across the site, also suggesting local production for domestic consumption (Thornton, this volume). Moriarty et al. (2008) notes that although agricultural tools were common in household middens, because the site lacked prime agricultural soils, agricultural production was intended only for household consumption and tribute to the Trinidad elite. However, Thornton (this volume) reveals that the site provided lacustrine animals to the residents of Motul de San José proper (this volume), and possibly the highest value of those directly to the elite of that site (Thornton, this volume; Emery, this volume).

Trinidad, clearly the economic gateway into the Motul de San José polity, may also have functioned as an ideological gateway. The site contains the only ball court in the Motul de San José polity and it is characterized by extremely large public spaces, much larger than required to hold the small resident population (Moriarty, this volume). Moriarty has identified a large midden associated with the Trinidad ball court as a feasting deposit based on ceramic, figurine, and animal evidence (Moriarty, this volume; Moriarty, Halperin, et al. 2008). Intriguingly, he and his colleagues suggest that these may be the remains of ball game–associated polity-wide ceremonies officiated, at least in the Late Classic, by the Motul de San José polity elite (ibid.). The implications of these features will be discussed in more detail below.

The site of Akte is substantially smaller than Trinidad but it was strategically located in the northeastern uplands at the confluence of the Rios K'änte't'u'ul and Akte (Figure 1.4) that perhaps linked the Motul de San José polity with sites to the west and northwest (Yorgey and Moriarty, this volume). Akte had the lowest access to obsidian among Motul de San José sites (ibid.), and its ceramics, locally made, were among the most poorly preserved probably because of the poor local clays (Yorgey 2005). The limited evidence of wealth suggests Akte was not a prime mover within the polity, but the presence of several interesting features, including causeways, high-quality architecture, and seven carved stelae, suggest otherwise. The site may have acted as a northern gateway or border community for the polity (Yorgey 2005; Yorgey and Moriarty, this volume).

Smaller sites seem also to have had important roles in economic production and distribution. The small sites of Buenavista and Chak Maman

Tok' (each holding only five or six households) are located adjacent to rich chert quarries and initial surveys indicate that at least Chak Maman Tok' was a chert production site with high debitage densities on the scale of 1.5 million flakes per cubic meter (Lawton 2007b). Excessive volumes of chert flakes (Castellanos 2007) and chert bifaces (Moriarty, Halperin, et al. 2008) revealed at Buenavista suggest its residents were specialized in the extraction of nodules and production of final tools or large blanks, which were likely then traded to other sites, like Motul de San José, where they were fashioned into final tools (Lawton 2007b).

Chäkokot, a still smaller site located close to Motul de San José proper, may have been heavily involved in agricultural production and the acquisition of wild animals. The soils here are highly fertile (Moriarty 2001) and isotopic signatures of ancient maize are strong in interhousehold soils (Webb and Schwarcz, this volume; Webb et al. 2007). The many general utility bifaces recovered at the site were likely used in agriculture (Moriarty, Halperin, et al. 2008). The Chäkokot residents had access to the most highly valued animals species, but not the most highly valued body portions of these animals, hinting that the Chäkokot residents were responsible for hunting and butchering the animals, not perhaps consuming all of the meat from them (Emery, this volume). The site was not a wealthy one, as indicated by a general lack of large architecture (only one small temple-pyramid) and scarce high-status resources (very limited obsidian access, for example; see Moriarty and Thornton 2007). However, the presence of several marine shell artifacts (Emery, this volume), indicates that the residents were not depauperate.

In sum then, the sizes and placements of the Motul de San José polity sites suggest a hierarchical political organization, but on a limited scale with perhaps only two ranks. The few subsidiary political titles in the Classic texts of Motul de San José supports the model of a small, unspecialized administrative cadre more typical of decentralized political systems (Inomata 2001a; Houston and Stuart 2001; Sharer and Golden 2004; Parmington 2003; Foias 2003, forthcoming). Although texts at major centers like Palenque refer to at least three levels of priestly/administrative offices below the k'uhulajaw or divine lord (ti'sakhuun, sajal, and ajk'uhuun; see Zender 2004b), the Motul texts (mostly on Ik'-style polychrome vases) show only the lower levels, and in most cases these are shown reporting directly to the k'uhulajaw. These scenes only once name a Motul de San José sajal who brings tribute directly to the Motul de San José ruler, but more often depict the ruler with one or two ajk'uhuuns (Tokovinine and Zender, this volume) and once with three *lakams* (Lacadena 2008), possibly a rank below *ajk'uhuun*. The secondary centers might be the residences of subsidiary elites with political administrative functions. Perhaps the smaller centers, with less evidence of wealth, were the residences of the nonelite, not part of the administrative organizations except as tax/tribute providers.

Structure at the Community Level

Finally, intensive work at the site of Motul de San José has told us much about economic and political structure at the community level and of the status and occupational groups within it. Within the community, much depends on the comparison of different status groups, and at Motul, Foias and colleagues (this volume) used architectural volumetrics to define three ranks: Rank 1, occupying the monumental compounds (Group A-E), were royal elites; Rank 2, occupying stone-vaulted masonry buildings in substantial groups, were likely middle "class" but not elite; Rank 3, occupying mostly non-stone-vaulted buildings in smaller groups, were likely commoners.

Overall, it is clear that the Motul de San José capital was a wealthy settlement, one that does not fit the suggestion that premodern polities were exploitative. Most households at Motul had stone architecture and sustained access to polychrome pottery and obsidian (Foias et al., this volume). Nevertheless, the distribution of other wealth indices at Motul generally paints a hierarchical social structure, with the main socioeconomic distinction between the Rank 1 royal elites and everyone else (Ranks 2 and 3). The details of production and distribution of resources are important for understanding the roles and integration of the various groups within the community.

High maize signatures in soils used prior to the Late Classic (used as Late Classic fill) indicate that the Motul de San José core area was farmed during the Preclassic (Webb et al., this volume; Bair and Terry, this volume). However, in the Late Classic and later periods, isotopic signatures reveal that little agriculture was taking place in Motul proper even though its soils remained the most fertile in the region (Jensen et al. 2007; Webb et al. 2007). This suggests that agricultural[5] products were brought into the capital center from outlying sites such as the neighboring satellite of Chäkokot. Manos and metates, prime markers of corn flour production, were more rare in Rank 1 groups than Ranks 2 and 3, implying that the royal elites prepared much less corn flour than did other households (Foias et al., this volume), and that prepared corn flour was supplied through taxes from the commoners (Rank 3 and possibly also Rank 2).

Our work on craft production presents a less sharply defined picture. Chert tools likely entered Motul proper as complete tools or as blanks for limited further reduction within households (Brian 2005; Lawton 2007b). Only a single locus of chert tool production has been identified at Motul, in a North Zone Rank 3 Group (9M3, 9M2—Operations 23–25; see Brian 2005), suggesting this was a low-rank craft specialty. Bone and shell production debitage is found widely distributed across Motul de San José, although shell crafting is limited to Ranks 1 and 2 and the production of utilitarian bone implements is more evenly distributed throughout the site (Emery 2003a, this volume).

Obsidian tools present a different scenario as an exotic resource that came exclusively from outside the Motul de San José region. Foias and colleagues (this volume) show that obsidian was somewhat limited, but broadly available to all households at Motul de San José (although densities were highest in Rank 1 and 2 households). The distribution of exotic marine shell is similarly broad across all households although with much greater proportions available to Ranks 1 and 2. This evidence supports a market exchange model (cf. Sheets [2000] and Hirth [1998], although contrary to Aoyama [2001] and P. Rice [1987a], who suggest elite control), although elites clearly had preferential access (see Foias et al., this volume).

The production of textiles was also basic to pre-Hispanic Maya households (Clark and Houston 1998; Hendon 1992a, 1997; McAnany 2010). Items used presumably as weaving tools (including whorls, needles, awls, etc.) were most densely distributed in Rank 1 households, and much less so (but almost equivalently) in households of Ranks 2 and 3 (Halperin 2008). Textile production was therefore more predominant in households of the royalty and may have been done by the royal family members or supervised by them in their royal compounds.

In addition, Rank 2 residents crafted more marine shell and Rank 1 residents used/displayed more finished marine shell adornments (many of which were fashioned for attachment to clothing). Rank 1 residents, on the other hand, crafted more freshwater pearly nacre shell, predominantly into thin rings perhaps used as "sparklers" on clothing (Emery, this volume). Based on this evidence, royal households at Motul were more heavily invested in crafting fancy textiles than were Rank 2 and 3 households.

The production of pottery has been problematic in understanding Maya economies. The Motul de San José excavations have revealed a rare pottery production workshop in or near the Acropolis Group C (Foias 2003;

Halperin and Foias, this volume). As Halperin and Foias (this volume) describe, the evidence suggests that the residents of Str. 8L-9 in the Acropolis (or nearby compounds) were scribes who crafted polychrome vessels, including the Ik'-style vases, in a scribal palace workshop(s). The restriction of evidence for the production of elaborate polychrome vessels (defined by intricate painted scenes) indicates that these activities were controlled by royal elites. Different paste recipes have been found in nonelaborate polychromes and general wares at the various sites within the Motul polity suggesting that production of these ceramics was local but dispersed (Reents-Budet and Bishop, this volume; Reents-Budet et al. 2007; Halperin et al. 2009), and the elite controlled only the prestige pottery production. The distribution of polychromes is also telling in that the elaborate polychromes are entirely restricted to Rank 1 residences whereas other polychromes are dispersed through the ranks, indicating that these could have been distributed via markets (Foias et al., this volume). Halperin (2007, this volume) reveals coproduction of figurines and polychrome pottery in the Acropolis pottery workshop. High densities of finished figurines from Motul de San José Rank 1 and 2 residences suggest that production of figurines might have been centered in these ranks (Halperin 2007, 259–69). However, Halperin (this volume) also finds that figurines were manufactured at the household level and most likely were used by all residents of the site including women, men, adults, and children. On a regional scale, a figurine mold fragment at Akte (Yorgey 2005, 58–59) and another at Motul's Acropolis (Halperin and Foias, this volume) suggest that, as with other ceramics, figurines were produced locally but were formed according to Motul polity ideologies and concerns.

A final important productive activity would have been painting and scribing. Foias and colleagues (this volume) note papermaking and paint-making evidence from Group D (Operation 15), including a bark beater, pigment balls of red and yellow, and a distinct volcanic stone metate that may have been used for grinding pigments. Halperin and Foias (this volume) suggest that some of the bone awls or pins found in the Operation 2 middens with red coloring on the proximal ends were painting tools used with miniature paint pots also found in this locus that contained red specular hematite. Scribal activities are generally presumed to have been part of the elite households only, and the Motul de San José information supports this interpretation. Not only is evidence for papermaking and fine painting limited to the Rank 1 structures, but so too are the finished painted products such as fine polychromes with scenes.

Integration

The structure and mechanisms of integration of these political, social, and occupational strata within such Maya communities as Motul remain among the most intriguing questions in Maya political archaeology. Our excavations in the Motul zone have shown some functional redundancy between Motul and the smaller subsidiary centers, including a dispersed production of both clay and plaster products (Spensley, this volume; Halperin and Foias, this volume; Halperin et al. 2009). However, functional variability is more characteristic: some rural sites appear to have specialized in the extraction of the nearby chert sources (Buenavista, Chak Maman Tok', and Trinidad) whereas central Motul may have been partly dependent for agricultural foodstuffs and perhaps animal products on peripheral villages and secondary centers like nearby Chäkokot (Emery, this volume; Moriarty, this volume; Thornton, this volume; Webb and Schwarcz, this volume; Jensen et al. 2007; Webb et al. 2007).

In addition, our work suggests that site size is not well correlated with political importance either for the polity as a whole (see earlier discussion of scale versus external relationships) or within the polity. Trinidad is larger than all other minor centers within the Motul de San José polity, and was the lakeshore port of Motul (Moriarty, this volume). Akte, a tiny site, has as many hieroglyphic stelae as Motul (Yorgey and Moriarty, this volume). Furthermore, complexities in religious power are also evident as no ball court was found at Motul de San José; instead, a ball court is located at Trinidad, which also boasts very large public plazas and evidence of feasting, likely in association with ball game–related polity-wide rites (Moriarty, this volume).

This lack of centralization of religious and economic activities at Motul speaks against the highly centralized state model. Nevertheless, the presence of partial specialization in economic activities across the Motul realm does suggest that activities of integration were needed, and the Motul elite may have fulfilled such roles.

The mechanisms of such integration still remain opaque, and here we can only make a few suggestions. We suggest three mechanisms by which the specialized satellite centers were integrated into the polity-wide economy: tribute-tax, palace and estate production and redistribution, and market exchange. We also explore here the means by which the ruler and ruled of the Motul de San José communities participated in such means of integration.

Specialized goods and foodstuffs produced elsewhere may have reached elites at Motul proper and at other subsidiary centers in the Motul realm through tribute-taxes. Several glyphs associated with tribute have been deciphered: *patan* (tribute), *u-tohol* (his payment), and *yubte'* (tribute mantle; see Stuart 1995; Reents-Budet, Bishop, and MacLeod 1994; Foias 2002), and some of these glyphs are found on Ik'-style polychromes. Elsewhere, Foias (2002) suggests that such tribute would have included both valuables and subsistence goods: textiles, corn, turkeys, beans (cacao and/or regular beans), feathers, pelts, and jade (see also McAnany 2010, 269–304). The low density of grinding tools in high-rank versus commoner households at Motul (Foias et al., this volume) suggests that taxes/tribute within Motul consisted at least in part of corn flour. Combined faunal and archaeological evidence indicates that agricultural produce, meat, and other animal products (and possibly chert tools) may have also been part of the tax/tribute system. It is interesting that in terms of both corn flour production and animal products, the Rank 2 and Rank 3 groups were quite similar, suggesting that taxes and tribute were due only to the ruling families of Rank 1.

Another venue in the integration of capital and hinterland could have been markets. We have found intriguing evidence pointing to two markets located within Motul and Trinidad (Halperin 2007; Moriarty, forthcoming; Dahlin et al. 2009; Bair and Terry, this volume). The long debate on the presence of markets and their location in the Classic period Maya lowlands has been renewed by new discoveries at Calakmul (Simon Martin, personal communication, 2007), Chunchucmil, and Trinidad (Dahlin et al. 2007, 2009). Geochemical analysis in the Motul Plaza II (located in the center of the Motul de San José site, directly adjacent to the Operation 2 elite ceramic workshop) by Bair and Terry (this volume) strongly supports the marketplace model and also provides more detail about marketplace activities, such as crafting (see also Dahlin et al 2007, 2010). Halperin's (2007, this volume) figurine analysis also intriguingly highlights market activity, both in the finding of many figurines wearing what has been described as "market hats" and also in her iconographic and paste evidence that figurines may have been exchanged at festival-markets or other large-scale, ceremonial occasions (Halperin et al. 2009). The Motul and Trinidad markets suggest multifunction spaces where, as today, various community activities such as rituals, crafting, and exchange were carried out. That markets are found at both the capital site and the harbor port indicates that they may have been quite widespread and not isolated only to the "ruling" capitals.

A third method for integrating these semispecialized communities could be through elite estates dispersed across the Motul polity where needed goods and foodstuffs were produced and then brought into the capital. The presence of estates is suggested by the identification of residences that were used by rulers as their "summer" palaces and elite manors (Ball and Taschek 2001; Taschek and Ball 2003; Tourtellot et al. 2003), similar to those used by aristocrats in Medieval Europe. Good candidates for such country estates are the tiny sites of Chakalte and Xilil,[6] but further investigations are needed at both to confirm this function. These estates would serve as a nexus of interaction between the center and periphery of Motul, bringing together the ruling families or their representatives with the populations that lived full-time in such agricultural villages as Xilil or Chäkokot.

We next must question how well integrated the Motul political system was, and therefore we must know more about the people who ruled and were ruled. Until recently, scholarship on political organization focused on the role of leaders. But recent evidence points to the agency of all groups in human societies, albeit with different degrees of influence (Blanton and Fargher 2008; Pauketat 2007). This brings into focus the importance of examining both leaders and their political ideologies, and also collective action, and the role of negotiation among rulers and the ruled. We must look at various media produced and used by both the ruler and the ruled to express and materialize their political legitimacy and power.

Halperin contrasts expressions of political power in ruler figurines and stone stelae with those depicted on polychrome vases (like the Ik' style) where the rulers are generally much more simply dressed and with small headdresses (2007, 224). On these vessels, the rulers (via the scribes) understate their wealth and political clout probably in an attempt to create a common elite identity in contrast to the stela imagery where the ruler is portrayed in the larger-than-life role as a divine being. The depiction of the rulers with their important courtiers (with few differences in accoutrements) not only created a common elite identity, but also enhanced the position of these elites and bound them to the ruler (Foias, forthcoming). In contrast, we see Motul rulers arrayed in the complex symbols of divine power in the various carved stelae at the capital site: headdresses decorated with different gods, the God K scepter, heavy jade pectorals, and so on. Interestingly, we also see these depictions in other media that would have been used and displayed by the other members of the Motul communities: one of the more common anthropomorphic figurine types at Motul depicts rulers (or high-status elites) wearing large, fan-shaped War Serpent headdresses, as they are also immortalized on stelae, and so, obviously eulogizing official state rituals (Halperin 2004b, 2007). This indicates a penetration of public ideology into the private household context. Nevertheless, as Halperin (this volume, 2007) discusses, Motul de San José figurines included many other images not necessarily tied into state ideology.

Although we do not discuss these aspects in detail here (see Foias, forthcoming), to understand how these complex communities of diverse people were maintained, we must also consider the performances of political power or political rituals (Inomata 2006). One method proposed to legitimate rulership and promote community integration may have been through community-shared rituals such as feasting (Yaeger 2003; Inomata 2006; Pauketat 2007). At Motul we have important evidence for the production of large quantities of corn flour, perhaps for feasting rituals, in the royal palace of Group D (Operation 15; see Foias et al., this volume). These may have been more exclusive to royal groups, but may have included the Motul de San José community. Certainly, feasting conducted in at least one group on the periphery of Plaza II (the proposed Motul marketplace; see Bair and Terry, this volume) and in the large plazas and community spaces at Trinidad (Moriarty, this volume; Dahlin et al. 2009) were likely to have included site-wide and even polity-wide communal groups. These may easily have promoted polity involvement in economic and political integration and polity-wide acceptance of Motul's overlordship.

Conclusions

The Motul de San José Archaeological Project has provided a glimpse into the Late Classic relationship between human settlement, natural resources, and political power on the north and northwest shores of Lake Petén Itzá in the Central Petén Lakes region of northern Guatemala. During the Late Classic peak of settlement, this region was likely crisscrossed by flowing rivers that provided resources and transportation, locating Motul at the crossroads between a west–east route and a north–south one. Motul de San José was a tiny polity during its heyday in the Tepeu 2 Late Classic years, but this small size belies its level of political influence as recorded in texts across the Maya lowlands (Tokovinine and Zender, this volume). Although the realm's size may have fluctuated with the fortunes of its Late Classic rulers, its core would have been the zone extending some 5–7 kilometers around the site itself. As a small polity, Motul may have not needed an extensive hierarchy to administer its diminutive territory. Settlement work clearly shows that political organization was hierarchical, likely with two levels. The presence of a ring of minor centers at 2–3 kilometers away from the capital of Motul de San José suggests that these functioned as secondary administrative centers, each with one or several pyramids, and with resident elites with political administrative functions (e.g., *sajals*; see Moriarty, this volume, 2004d; Yorgey and Moriarty, this volume).

However, the variation in size and sociopolitical rank among these subsidiary sites, and significant resource specialization, also suggests heterarchical elements. The partial religious and economic specialization of these subsidiary centers speaks against a highly centralized state model. For example, Motul's control over exotics entering through Trinidad's port was limited, though it is likely that the Motul elite officiated at Trinidad's festivals (Moriarty, this volume; Moriarty, Halperin, et al. 2008). Buenavista and Chak Maman Tok' located along the north shore of Lake Petén Itzá had easy access to chert sources and appear to have specialized in the production of blanks and tools.

This partial specialization of the subsidiary sites implies that a system of integration was also at work, possibly through marketplaces at both Motul and Trinidad (Bair and Terry, this volume; Dahlin et al. 2009; Moriarty, this volume). Another mechanism that would serve to integrate the Motul polity would be through its political elite that could have resided full-time or part-time in the secondary centers or in their own "country estates" as well as in the capital.

Turning to the capital of Motul de San José, it becomes clear that this was a wealthy settlement, with a complex socioeconomic and political hierarchy. The royal elite of Rank 1 supported itself through dual spheres of the political economy: (1) the palace economy in which Rank 1 and Rank 2 residents were critical and (2) the tax/tribute system, in which Rank 2 but especially Rank 3 residents were critical (Foias et al., this volume; Emery, this volume).

Rather than viewing political power as static, modern perspectives construe it as built on contestations between different competitors and factions. Discourses and ideologies depicted in different art media hint at such political contestations and concerns. Although there are differences between the "public transcripts" of the divine and richly attired rulers on Motul's stelae, the "intra-elite transcript" on painted Ik'-style vessels that record multiple nobles arrayed around the simply attired ruler, and the "hidden transcripts" of the tiny figurines that display both elaborately clothed rulers and many different animals and supernaturals, there is also a common concern with both state ideology and ritual running through all of them (Halperin 2007, this volume; Foias, forthcoming). In sum, Classic Maya society at Motul de San José was both heterarchical and hierarchical and partly, but unevenly, integrated.

16

Control without Controlling

Motul de San José and Its Environs from an Outsider's Perspective

ELIZABETH GRAHAM

In their introduction to this volume, Foias and Emery construct a framework for reporting the results of the investigations at Motul de San José by drawing on existing debates about the nature of Maya political organization during the Classic period. Most debates have been concerned with whether forces of centralization or decentralization were at work among Maya polities or whether there existed multiple trajectories of expansion and contraction (e.g., Chase and Chase 1996; Demarest 1992; 1996; Houston 1993; J. Marcus 1973, 1998; see Lucero 1999, 212–16). Other approaches have attempted to identify the nature of the tensions between organizational structures, such as those between kinship and kingship, that could have given rise to forces of centralization and decentralization (Iannone 2002; McAnany 1995). Foias and Emery observe that centralization and decentralization are generalized concepts that are not particularly informative about the dynamics of power or, in their words, about the "mechanisms used by . . . political actors and/or factions to gain more power" or "to pursue their agendas within their individual polities." They also make the point—in my view the most important factor driving the research represented in the volume—that power, however political, was tied to economic matters.

If we accept that links between economy and power were inextricable, then dichotomies such as kinship versus kingship can be misleading because neither term serves to describe or explain the dynamics behind dispersal (kinship) or concentration (kingship) of power and authority (Iannone 2002, 74; McAnany 1995, 131). Power and authority are actualized through differential access to wealth and resources and can take a number of forms the dynamics of which need not be dependent on replacing factions based on kinship with those that are not. Competition was important, but we cannot assume that factions were based (solely) on kinship or that the role of kinship was necessarily diminished with the institution of kingship. The critical element in these deliberations is how the economy functioned. Who had access to what, how much, and how? In answering these questions, interpolity relationships reflect much about the reach and limits of Maya centers and the economic practices of their leaders, but how wealth was distributed *within* Maya polities, such as Motul de San José, is also an important indicator of power because whatever decentralizing or centralizing forces existed would have affected internal as much as external relationships.

Discovering the mechanisms used by actors to gain power or to effect control may be archaeologically as elusive as evidence for whether or not an ancient Maya authority distributed administrative functions. Nevertheless, in the research on Motul de San José and its environs, the emphasis placed by Foias, Emery, and their colleagues on the range of ways agendas were pursued and goals achieved as reflected in material culture—and on the kinds of productive activities that existed and where they were carried out—has provided highly valuable new insights into Maya state organization. Evidence from Motul de San José and from sites such as Trinidad de Nosotros and Akte, as well as Chäkokot, shows that both a range of products and productive activities crosscut the ranks of society. Differential distributions of ground stone, spindle whorls, chert and bone tool debris, figurines, fragmented vessels, pottery wasters, faunal remains, and chemical traces in soils all highlight that different social strata were involved in distinct activities at different scales and intensities (see the specific chapters in this volume). Although economic power was concentrated in the hands of the royal or noble families, lower-status households had access to many of these productive activities and indeed engaged in production on their own, a feature of complex societies that is by no means unique to Maya economy (Baines and Yoffee 1998, 227–28; E. Graham 2002; Lucero 1999, 231, 234–36).

Owing to the preservation of stone stelae and polychrome pottery, our picture of Maya society is crowded with the images and activities of the uppermost echelon. We are fortunate to have this information, but the complexities of elite machinations are only part of the picture. Evidence over the years from Belize tells us that ancient cities such as Lamanai and the towns and villages along the coast and cayes with which Lamanai was connected through trade comprised households engaged in a variety of production activities—procuring fish and shellfish for subsistence and export; processing salt, which in the Late Classic was destined predominantly for export; and acting as ports and way stations for goods as part of circum-peninsular trade but also to move products such as dried fish, shells, pottery, and obsidian to inland locations (E. Graham 2011). None of these households, with the possible exception of a few families at Lamanai, seems to represent the uppermost stratum of elites, and even in the Lamanai case, the preserved material culture of the uppermost echelon is relatively depauperate in comparison to the material culture associated with ruling families of the cities of the Petén lakes. Nevertheless, the material culture is rich and varied, the sites represent cosmopolitan communities, and perhaps most important, these communities continued to thrive throughout the period of the Maya collapse.

Centralization and Decentralization

One conclusion of Foias and her colleagues on the basis of the investigations at Motul de San José is that the evidence indicates political decentralization. Certainly the state control over economy envisaged by some researchers is not borne out by the Motul de San José evidence, but the nature of the political system and how it might have operated remains clouded.

The concepts of centralization and decentralization are useful at one level of understanding. They imply either that an individual or small group of individuals is attempting to increase the range of decision-making for which they are responsible by holding office or title (centralization) or that decision-making is distributed and left in the hands of many individuals (decentralization). A political system can, however, be centralized and decentralized at the same time. In the United States, federal taxes represent a feature of political centralization whereas state and city taxes reflect a level of decentralization. With regard to economy, U.S. dynamics are even more difficult to characterize. Holding a political or administrative office can provide an individual with greater access to economic resources or opportunities than he would otherwise have had, but economic control in which community resources are openly and publicly funneled to the individual is generally not part of the mandate of office. It is also significant that most of those who control the greatest amount of wealth not only in the United States but throughout the world hold no political offices. The upshot is that in describing any state system, terms such as *centralization* and *decentralization* may not only reflect fluctuation of political trends over time (J. Marcus 1998), but also concurrent and competing practices (Iannone 2002).

Although the modern world is not the Maya world of the first millennium AD, we can still learn a great deal from thinking about how systems work today. I do not mean to imply identity but rather to build on dynamics with which we are familiar and we know are complex and difficult to describe. When we then proceed to extrapolate from an understanding of these dynamics in all their complexity, we are less likely to simplify the dynamics of the past. If we take modern Cuba as an example of a state in which both political and economic power are centralized, the most telling evidence—and such evidence is potentially detectable archaeologically—is the relative dearth of open local markets and commerce and the comparatively limited range of material goods that can be found in households. At the same time, all households can be found to have access to a basic range of foods and materials as the result of state controls and distribution. Skeletal indicators should also reflect the accessibility of excellent health care.

Even a cursory review of sites in the Maya area, including Motul de San José and the sites in its environs, does not produce evidence of a high degree of control. Skeletal health varies a great deal both in space and in time, and households display considerable variety in material goods. In terms of food intake, results from both Motul de San José (Emery, this volume) and Trinidad de Nosotros (Thornton, this volume) show a rather broadly distributed access to high-value species such as white-tailed deer and turtle. This does not mean that elites might not have got the best cuts or monopolized particular kinds of products such as marine shell made into jewelry, but only that access to species seems not to have been restricted according to rank.

The most telling argument against centralized control in the Maya lowlands is, however, the evidence for lively and extensive commerce and exchange—seaborne, riverine, and overland—that extends back to Preclassic times (Andrews 1990; Andrews and Mock 2002; E. Graham 1989, 1994; McKillop 1996, 2002) and, more recently, the evidence for markets (Carrasco Vargas et al. 2009; Dahlin et al. 2007, 2009). The time-depth and importance of trade and exchange are strongly in evidence at Motul de San José in the variety of goods available to its inhabitants, in the engagement of a range of people in both the subsistence and prestige economy, and in the probable presence of a market plaza (Blair and Terry, this volume). Nearby communities such as Trinidad de Nosotros and Akte have the additional feature of being positioned to take advantage of waterborne travel and trade (Moriarty, this volume; Yorgey and Moriarty, this volume). Whereas only minor occupations prior to Late Classic florescence have been found at Motul de San José, excavations at Trinidad de Nosotros on Lake Petén Itzá have documented the longest and most complete record of occupation in the Motul de San José region. Such continuity seems more likely to be a feature of a society in which a number of groups or strata were involved in accessing, distributing, and exchanging goods. It can also be said that the ability of diverse groups to adjust readily to changing conditions would not be likely under conditions of centralization in which elites controlled economic infrastructure.

There are other kinds of centralization in which the political power of a central authority can affect the economy. For example, European countries such as Sweden, France, and Germany have lively economies but the state extracts high taxes (which we can see as a kind of tribute), controls health care, and to some extent controls wealth distribution, at least to a greater extent than is the case in the United States (see Wilkinson and Pickett 2010). It therefore seems misleading to use a single term (*centralized* versus *decentralized*) to characterize state organization and activity.

I made the point above that wide-ranging commerce and exchange initiatives would be limited under conditions of centralization such as exist in Cuba. On the other hand, it is worth noting that the more equitable distribution of wealth such as exists in Cuba reflects greater controls by a state apparatus. In Western democracies, studies show that the existence of strong trade unions and successful social democratic parties correlates with greater wealth equality as regards income distribution (Stephens 1979). Thus, rather counterintuitively, more equitable wealth distribution is correlated with centralization: political centralization in the case of Western Europe and both political and economic centralization in the case of Cuba. I say "counterintuitively" because the general belief in democracies is that minimal state control fosters the widest economic opportunities. In the United States, which defines itself as a democracy, statistics show that wealth[1] is highly concentrated in a relatively few hands (Domhoff 2010; Wilkinson and Pickett 2010). In 2007, the top 1 percent of households owned 34.6 percent of privately held wealth; the next 19 percent, which comprised managerial, professional, and small business strata, had 50.5 percent. This means that 20 percent of the people owned 85 percent of the wealth, leaving 15 percent of the wealth for the remaining 80 percent. In terms of financial wealth,[2] the top 1 percent of U.S. households controlled an even larger share of 42.7 percent (Domhoff 2010).

Wealth can therefore be centralized even in cases in which decentralization characterizes the economic and to some extent the political system. We could describe the top 1 percent who have 30–35 percent of the wealth, or the top 20 percent who have 84 percent of the wealth, as elites (see Foias et al., this volume, for definitions of "elites") and the rest as nonelites or commoners. In terms of wealth distribution, this has validity and indeed represents an important dynamic in the study of social change. On closer inspection, however, we would find that the nonelites include bankers, businessmen, corporate executives, corporate employees, merchants, IT executives, stockbrokers, butchers, bakers, plumbers, politicians, teachers, university professors, civil service employees, police, firemen, waitresses, maids, laborers, and those on the dole. Clearly there is a level of analysis (or several levels) at which the elite versus commoner distinction, although "true," is not helpful; this is especially the case if we are interested in the productive activities of society across the board, which includes the majority—either the 99 percent or the 84 percent who are not elite, depending on the chosen criteria of wealth. Although I have used the United States as an example, my point—which is that we need to think in terms of different levels of analysis and define our terms accordingly—is applicable to the elucidation of Maya social stratification.

Do the top 20 percent or top 1 percent wealthiest in the United States have power? It is theoretically possible for someone to have power over others and be poor,[3] but most studies tell us that distribution of wealth is a good indicator of power (Domhoff 1990, 2010). Despite the modern worldwide concentration of wealth in the hands of the few (Shah 2010), most of us would characterize the United States or the UK or Mexico or France or Belize as open societies—economically decentralized with varying degrees of political centralization or devolvement—and not as states in which political or economic power is concentrated in the hands of one person or a small group. We elect local officials; we have rights to (own) houses or flats or land; some of us cultivate land and raise animals; we exchange our income for subsistence and utilitarian and luxury goods; we present gifts to each other; we have families both nuclear and extended; we raise children who can be sons, daughters, or nieces or nephews or fictive kin; some of our sons and daughters become soldiers who go to war to "keep the world safe"; we dine out at restaurants or go to pubs with friends and family (feasting); we travel; some of us pray and venerate deities or ancestors; others of us do not think much about life after death; all of us die and are buried and decay, or we are cremated. Our allegiances are to the neighborhood or barrio, to the city or township, to the state or county, to the region, or to the country, but we do not generally think of ourselves as controlled by a centralized state. Yet in economic terms there is a real question as to whether those of us who are not part of the economic elite in the United States or UK or France or Mexico or Belize exercise much power at all. It remains true, however, that if we believe we exercise power via participation in particular levels of political expression or through opportunities for some level of economic involvement, the world system with its elite monopoly is safe and will be reproduced.

These complex dynamics suggest that the forces represented by centralization and decentralization are perceived in different ways both by those characterizing a state and by those within the state. Foias and Emery (this volume) observe that researchers correlate political centralization among the Maya with elite control over economic infrastructure whereas they correlate decentralization or weak centralization with a lack of elite involvement in economic matters of production and exchange beyond the tribute system. This seems to make sense, but closer inspection of operating systems reveals a blurred image. Political centralization can be correlated with control over economic infrastructure, as in the case of modern Cuba, but a number of Western European nations provide examples of political centralization in which wealth distribution is controlled to some extent (through taxation) but productive activity (the generation of wealth) is not. Weak centralization can theoretically be associated with lack of elite involvement in economic matters of production and exchange beyond the tribute system, but as the evidence from Motul de San José and its environs suggests, all segments of Maya society, including elites, seem to have been involved in economic matters of production and exchange. This suggests that the state, through its officeholders (the *kaloomte'* or *baahkab* or *sajal*), made no attempt to control economy *directly* through the power of political office. Yet it is interesting from a historical point of view that such "weak" systems nevertheless result in a small percentage of the population controlling most of the wealth. What seems to be the case, perhaps a bit like Annette Weiner's keeping-while-giving (1992), is that we have elites, both ancient and modern, who control by not controlling.

Tribute, Wealth, and Power

Tribute was a major vehicle by which wealth was appropriated but there is no reason to believe that the generation of products and labor that were diverted to tribute constituted a separate economy. It is highly likely that productive activities overlapped and that goods generated for tribute also circulated more widely, and goods that might initially have been restricted locally (e.g., particular processed foods or the products of a particular ceramics workshop) worked their way rapidly into the tribute system. Nevertheless, the desire for expansion of tribute networks is most likely to have been an important stimulus behind the appropriation of (and possibly qualitative changes in) political power, a matter I will discuss shortly.

As noted above, the evidence from Motul de San José, Trinidad de Nosotros, and Akte tells us that those with the highest status in Maya society had access to a good deal of wealth and power. Outside of this group, as indicated by the variability within and between archaeological indices such as architecture, artifact distributions, and political and economic activities (Foias et al., this volume), there is likely to have been a mix in which some people of lower status had local political positions but a modicum of wealth whereas others, perhaps merchants and traders, had a chunk of wealth but less or no political power and perhaps a status appropriate to their station.

Conditions such as these are not in accord with the centralized state model in which the largest Maya cities are said to be characterized by rulers who amassed and concentrated considerable political power. Rulers do indeed seem to have wielded power, but whether or not this involved attempts to increase central authority is a critical question. If, as I suggest, the economic infrastructure of Maya city-states evolved outside of elite control, then any attempt to centralize or alter the nature of political power could potentially have destabilized the economy. Before we consider this, let us turn again to evidence from Motul de San José and its environs.

Even when the epigraphic record indicates that Motul or Tikal or Calakmul experienced conflict and challenged other centers or their leaders militarily, this need not have meant that individuals who ruled a polity were seeking direct political control or authority over other polities (Martin and Grube 2008, 20–21). It is important to note that when in the literature archaeologists talk about "Motul" or "Tikal" waging war on another "polity" that the vision conjured up is of a bounded group attempting to increase the perimeters of its territory. But successful intercity warfare as recorded in the hieroglyphic texts does not seem to have resulted consistently in increases in territory or even in political administration. The evidence assembled by Tokovinine and Zender (this volume) from the Ik'a' vase paintings gives no indication of expansion of governors or other administrative officials under Tayel Chan K'inich's reign (sometime between AD 711 and

734). During the tenure of K'inich Lamaw Ek', however, who acceded to power between 763 and 767, *sajal* officials at court constituted an additional level of subordinates. One wonders whether the emergence of *sajalob* represents an attempt at increased political control (more territory, so more people are needed to administer it), or increased economic power (more tribute, so more people are needed to keep track of it), or a relatively safe method of absorbing proliferating nobility.

The epigraphic and pictorial records suggest strongly that one of the major concerns of ruling elites was the appropriation of wealth by the expansion of access to tribute (Martin and Grube 2008, 21). This can be seen in interpolity marriage alliances, in the attention given to hierarchical relationships, in the depiction of tribute on vases, and in the frequent depiction of captives who almost certainly had their rights to tribute appropriated. I have argued (E. Graham 2006, 2011, 29–58) that the drive behind captive-taking was not to kill people in temples ("sacrifice") but to increase income, because capturing an individual in war gave the captor rights to his captive's tribute. Hence, in addition to expanding tribute through marriage alliances, tribute was increased by wars that were fought to allow the taking of captives and appropriation of their tribute rights. Such wealth appropriation can be highly successful and can reinforce the wealth of elites even under conditions in which the state (rulers, officials, nobles) makes no attempt politically—via territorial expansion or by changing the nature and obligations of the political office—to control the economy.

To some extent the Maya world system and the subsequent Aztec world system—the latter often described as a hegemonic empire (Berdan et al. 1996; Hassig 1985, 92)—were not entirely different from the modern world system in that they were driven, as are modern states, by an emphasis on appropriation of resources rather than on territorial expansion (see also Hassig 1985, 90–94). Yet evolutionary scenarios would have us believe that the direction of progress is from a hegemonic state to a territorial one. As the Motul de San José project framework makes clear, many if not most of the critical things we need to know about the Maya "state" or "states" lie beyond evolutionary issues. States based on gobbling up territory to gain access to resources can be shorter lived and less stable than states that are seen to be fragmented but have an integrated economic infrastructure (Smith 1986).

If Maya leaders were not driven toward political centralization, this need not be seen as a weakness and hence something we have to grasp at straws to explain; it may have been what made their world system startlingly modern in its mechanisms for achieving economic strength and resilience. In other words, as long as elite individuals of all cities and communities were able to control a range of resources through the tribute system—through warfare or marriage or various forms of negotiation—annexing territory was unnecessary and a waste of time and energy. In the same way, as long as elites in the United States and the UK and Saudi Arabia share rights to oil and hence stand to gain by reinforcing each other's social status and economic position, territorial expansion is unnecessary and a waste of resources.

In conditions such as these, we would expect that a great deal of attention would have been devoted to cementing or expanding interpersonal relationships and obligations, particularly where tribute obligations were involved. As families grew, marriages were negotiated, wars were fought, and trade and commerce expanded, the goods involved and the flow of tribute would have fluctuated. Making clear who owed what to whom—and who was obligated to whom—was essential. Evidence from Motul de San José (Reents-Budet et al., this volume; Tokovinine and Zender, this volume) suggests that the scenes on polychrome vases are just such statements of important hierarchical relationships. Unlike stelae, which were public statements, the audience for the vases was an in-group. As M. Smith (1986) argues for the Aztecs, elites were constantly juggling among themselves for power but at the same time were heavily invested in the system of which they were all a part. Each lord or ruler or noble was not seeking to destroy the system but only to partake of a bigger share of it. Among the Maya, polychrome vases represent the system at its finest.

The nature of hierarchical relationships seems to be a major theme on the vessels. Each person depicted holds a particular stylized position and displays a range of gestures that are to be read in terms of where he or she falls in relation to the others who are depicted. Yet the broadcasting of political position per se does not seem to have been the driving force behind such display. It is true that the depictions generally make the titles and offices clear within naming statements, but no vessel begins and ends with a single person. The vessel scenes illustrate *what people's positions entail* with respect to others, and there seems to be a significant concern with who is subordinate to whom, and by implication who owes what to whom. Tribute scenes appear on vases, and the importance of the painter or scribe is consonant with the role of the scribe as recorder of and witness to important transactions (especially in view of such a "witnessing" role for elites in Contact period Yucatán, see Restall 1997).

It is also worth considering that if the direction and flow of tribute constituted the major dynamic of power, Taj Yal Chan K'inich (Reents-Budet et al., this volume; Tokovinine and Zender, this volume) could have been a *kaloomte'* and received tribute in his own right at the same time that—through warfare or as a consequence of a marriage alliance—he paid tribute to a lord at Dos Pilas. What we would call kingdoms or polities seem to have been places to which particular families had historical rights, and no Maya ruler could annex or occupy (conquer) a place to which he or his family had no historical ties. He could, however, take captives, which would enable him to access the resources of the place from which the captives came. This would explain why, as Reents-Budet and colleagues observe, "there are no known instances of sub-lords of one kingdom offering tribute or kneeling in obeisance to the lord of a foreign kingdom, unless as captives."

Where Maya city-states may have erred in the Late Classic is in the use by some rulers of traditional political offices as vehicles for legitimizing wars the outcome of which stood only to increase (through tribute) the wealth of their families and vassals. The political system as it existed in the Late Classic did not survive, or at least it did not survive intact. The fact that Motul de San José was still functioning in AD 849 as the seat of one of four prominent dynasties, mentioned on Seibal Stela 10, suggests that not all rulers used their political positions for economic aggrandizement. The presence of several Emblem Glyphs in the Ik' ceramic corpus and the monumental inscriptions does suggest, as Reents-Budet and colleagues (this volume) observe, that alliances among local families gave strength to what became the Ik' polity, but such alliances must almost certainly have entailed intermarriages. This would have kept tribute and the rights to the products of the land in the hands of a number of related individuals.

Akte is an interesting case in that it is set in agriculturally marginal savanna land (although fruit trees such as cashew, kinep, and calabash thrive in such soils), but the presence of stelae suggests strongly that there was some connection to Motul de San José, albeit a predominantly reactive one in which Akte's rulers were attempting to carve out their own political and economic niche during a time of intense competition among noble families in the region. Tokovinine and Zender (this volume) describe a stela with an unfamiliar Emblem Glyph erected by a local lord at Akte in AD 747. At this time, the Ik'a' lord at Motul de San José, Yajawte' K'inich, had suffered a defeat at the hands of K'awiil Chan K'inich of Dos Pilas and may well have been funneling resources to Dos Pilas via tribute.

Historically, Motul de San José families and others in the region would already have had access (through tribute rights) to the products of agriculturally viable land in their vicinity. Hence the use of marginal land for a settlement such as Akte suggests a degree of land pressure as the result of elite competition and the proliferation of nobility in the Late Classic (Tokovinine and Zender, this volume). One possibility is that the presence of Akte reflects a marriage alliance between a noblewoman from Motul de San José and a lord who was not from Motul de San José, or vice versa, which could explain Akte's distinctive architectural style and planning. By this I mean that the non–Motul de San José individual would have had access to a different kind of tribute network with resource bases and patterns of culture outside the Motul de San José cultural sphere. Yet Akte is close enough to Motul de San José that any rights to local tribute (e.g., the distinctive local pottery as well as local products and the rights to cultivate land) would have been likely to come through the local families—hence my suggestion that some familial connection to Motul de San José is probable.

Akte would have had its own identity, but the evidence suggests strongly that it, like many towns and cities of the period, was perched precariously between balancing alliances with the major local power and at the same time seeking to increase wealth by expanding both tribute networks and commercial ties. The relatively limited access to obsidian suggests that times got tough.

The possible relocation of the Motul de San José court to Tayasal or Flores in AD 869 suggests that there were mechanisms by which cities and dynasties survived and tribute continued to flow, although in these cases, as must have also been the case at Lamanai, the political structure had altered. Such changes seem to have engendered an economic boom in circum-peninsular trade and commerce. Trinidad de Nosotros with its harbor clearly benefited, and if the Motul de San José court did indeed shift to Tayasal or Flores, the move can be seen as motivated by the desire to be positioned on a lakeshore to key into bustling trade routes, and a new era would have begun.

Notes

Chapter 1. Politics and Economics

1. Mathews (1991) describes in detail the nature of Emblem Glyphs. These are titles of the rulers of independent polities. The superfixes, postfixes, and prefixes are identical in all Emblem Glyphs and can be loosely translated as *k'ujul ahaw* or divine ruler. The main element of each Emblem Glyph is different for each independent state and is generally a place-name associated with the capital center of that state (Mathews 1991).

2. P. Rice (2004) has recently restated a more ritual model for Maya political structure in which Maya cities rotated hosting the *may* cycle of 256 years, based on Edmonson's original formulation for Postclassic Yucatán.

3. Emic definitions of political power among the Classic Maya (i.e., indigenous conceptions of power and legitimacy) appear to have focused on their exclusive control over access to the supernatural spheres (Schele and Freidel 1990) and need to be explored further.

4. Social power is also discussed by Blanton under the rubric of intermember power (1998, 145).

5. The twin pyramids of Motul de San José are found on the same platform and are quite distinct from the Twin Pyramid Complexes defined at Tikal. They are more comparable to the double pyramids of the Yucatán Peninsula. Although they are impressive at 18 meters in height, they both sport roof combs that add substantially to their height.

Chapter 2. Lords of Windy Water

1. Much of the central caption on the monument was already gone even when Maler photographed it over a hundred years ago. The remaining section can be read as "[. . .] **yi-ta-ji 1-TSAK-TOOK' K'UH-i-tsa-AJAW** [. . .] **u-ti-ya-IK'-a**, or . . . *y-itaaj juun tsak took' k'uh[ul] itsa' ajaw . . . u[h]tiiy ik'a',*" and translated as " . . . Juun Tsak Took', holy Itsa' lord, accompanied him . . . it happened [at] Ik'a'."

2. One of the three carvers' signatures on Stela 2 gives his name as **ch'o-ko a-IK'-AJAW** *ch'ok ik'a' ajaw* "young Ik'a' lord"; the other name (its context is somewhat unclear) on Stela 4 is largely illegible except for the last two signs, **a-IK'-a** 4-T544.501-**ni**, which can be read as *aj-ik'a'* "man of Ik'a'" and an undeciphered title that seem to designate regional groups of lords and nonroyal individuals (Tokovinine 2008, 263–64).

3. The statement **u-to-ma 9-AJAW 18-SUUTS'**, or *utoom [ta] waxak ajaw waxaklajuun[te'] suuts'*, can be translated as "it shall happen on 9 Ajaw 18 Zotz'." Such prophetic statements usually refer to future period endings, in which case the Long Count of 9.12.10.0.0 seems to be the best possible reconstruction.

4. The name of this ruler is written as **SAK-?-ni**, where the undeciphered sign is clearly a raptorial bird with traits suggesting both **O'** and **CH'E'N**. Unfortunately, the final -**ni** complement does not correspond to either; nor does the bird have the characteristic traits of **MUWAAN** "hawk" (to which -**ni** would make an appropriate complement). It is possible that the -**ni** cues **MUWAAN** in some kind of conflation with **O'** or **CH'E'N**, but we cannot discount the possibility of a previously unknown bird sign. Therefore, we propose to use the translation "White Bird" until the situation becomes clearer.

5. Reents-Budet et al. (this volume) suggest that the name of the owner of the Dallas vase recorded in its dedicatory inscription (also known as the Primary Standard Sequence or PSS) (**?-ni TI' K'AWIIL ?K'UH-HIX-WITS-AJAW** . . . *ti' k'awiil k'uh[ul] hix wits ajaw* " . . . Ti' K'awiil, holy Hix Wits lord") offers a clue to the chronological placement of White Bird's reign. A Hix Wits lord with an identical name arrived at Yaxchilán in AD 732 (9.15.0.15.3) according to the text in blocks C7–D7 on the tread of the fifth step of Yaxchilán Hieroglyphic Stairway 3 (I. Graham 1982, 171; Mathews 1997, 146; Martin and Reents-Budet 2010, 5). Epigraphic research by Martin and Reents-Budet (2010) suggests that the Hix Wits ruler Janaab Ti' O' reigned at least between AD 685 and 691. If we assume that there was a single line of Hix Wits lords, then the reign of the Dallas vase owner was probably later, closer to the date in the Yaxchilán inscription. However, we believe that there is still not enough evidence for such reconstruction. The history of the Hix Wits dynasty associated with the archaeological sites of El Pajaral, La Joyanca, and Zapote Bobal remains largely unknown despite new discoveries (Stuart 2003, 2008; Fitzsimmons, Gámez, and Forné 2006; Tunesi 2007; Martin and Reents-Budet 2010). The individual mentioned at Yaxchilán might have been a namesake of the Dallas vase owner or one of many Hix Wits lords associated with different sites. For example, another Hix Wits lord Janaab Ti' O' is mentioned on an unprovenanced monument in connection with an event that happened between AD 731 and 736 (Tunesi 2007; Martin and Reents-Budet 2010).

6. Unfortunately, the published photographs do not allow us to confirm the proposed reading of the caption on the El Peru vessel.

7. The inscription on the unprovenanced vase (MVD:K2573) features another unique version of his name: **ta-ye-le ni-CHAN-na-K'INICH** (Figure 2.7c). Here, the -**ni** may just be a displaced complement for **K'INICH**. However, we would caution that this inscription is rather unusual, and the vase's rim text is purely pseudoglyphic.

8. Another Calendar Round associated with Tayel Chan K'inich, unfortunately too eroded to be read, appears on an unprovenanced vase in the National Gallery of Victoria, Melbourne, Australia (Miller and Martin 2004, plate 7).

9. This vase appears to be heavily repainted, but Tayel Chan K'inich's name and titles are still discernible.

10. Although **wa** is never added in local inscriptions, we prefer to transliterate the name as K'inich Lamaw Ek' because of a namesake at Rio Azul whose name is spelled on two unprovenanced vases (MVD:K5022 and K7720) as **K'INICH-LAM-EK'** and **K'INICH-ni la-ma-wa-EK'**, respectively. As is often the case with logographic versus syllabic spellings (see Zender 2004b, 224n83), the **LAM** spelling abbreviates the fuller form **la-ma-wa**. Further, names of this type usually involve agent-focused antipassives (Grube 2002), and what is known of the verb *lam* suggests that *lamaw* would be the appropriate form (Wichmann 2004).

11. Although the identification of this particular logogram in the Emblem Glyph as **MAAN** is problematic (Stephen Houston, personal communication, 2008), there are some examples of this allograph in unequivocal contexts on painted vessels when it is provided with both **na-** and **-ni** syllabic complements (Lopes n.d.). For the time being, then, we consider that it is likely to comprise another instance of the Namaan emblem.

12. The form of the **MUT** logogram in her name is rather unusual. Dmitri Beliaev (personal communication, 2009) suggested that it could be a form of the **YOOTS** sign. If so, then this woman belonged rather to a royal family from northeastern Petén known from a number of unprovenanced painted vases and inscriptions at Naranjo (Boot 1999).

13. It appears as a name of the ancestor's head on the belt of Sihyaj Chan K'awiil depicted on Tikal Stela 31.

14. Bernal Romero (2006) first presented the inscription on El Palma Stela 5, but mistakenly identified the site with another Emblem Glyph in the region. More recently, David Stuart (2007) has presented evidence that the monument was in fact dedicated by a Lakamtuun lord also mentioned on Itzan Stela 17.

15. This sacrifice is reported on Step 7 of Hieroglyphic Stair 2 at Yaxchilán (I. Graham 1982, 160).

16. This vessel's dedicatory text has long eluded a firm attribution. This is largely due to the abbreviated nominal sequence, the interpenetration of iconographic elements into the hieroglyphs, and, not least, a misguided postexcavation attempt at restoration that has unfortunately obscured several key hieroglyphic signs. Nonetheless, the clearly visible nominal element **CHAK-EL** and the probable *UHX-*LAJUUN K'UH title that follows are both directly comparable to other known name phrases of Yajawte' K'inich (see Figure 2.6b–d)

17. See Yaxchilán Lintels 5, 15, 38, and 41 (and see Table 2.1 for dates and events).

18. Juun Tsak Took' evidently had a contemporaneous namesake: the Lakamtuun lord mentioned on El Palma Stela 5 and Itzan Stela 17.

19. **K'INICH K'UH IK' ja-wa** . . . *k'inich k'uh[ul] ik'[a'] [a]jaw.*

20. This figure is often but erroneously identified as a *chilam* "speaker" (e.g., Coe and Kerr 1997, 95). But the hieroglyphic spelling interpolates a clear **ji** sign, and *chilam* is in any case not the canonical form of the Colonial title. Rather, as J. Thompson (1970, 169) long ago observed, "n becomes m before b, hence Chilam Balam." In any context apart from a following bilabial consonant, *chi'lan* is the expected form (see Zender 2004b, 88n21 for further details).

21. We do not see any difficulty with the consideration that the scribe's title ("lord of Tubal") would then imply his membership in the royal family. At least one carver's signature on Motul de San José Stela 2 (Figure 2.2b) identifies the carver as a "young Ik'a' lord" (*ch'ok ik'a' ajaw*), indicating that at least some local artists were of royal blood.

22. Baakal lords resided at Palenque, Tortuguero, and Comalcalco. The court of Kanuul kings was at Calakmul and Dzibanche. The [T1008.552] title is attested only in the names of Edzna rulers (EDZ St 18, St 21, St 22, HS 1). The Chachtahn people lived in Calakmul and Nakbe. Lords of [T579] made pilgrimages to the cave of Naj Tunich (NTN Dr 65) and attended events at Nim Li Punit (NMP St 2), but the location of their court remains unknown. The protagonist of the inscription on a jade plaque found in Tomb B-4/6 at Altun Ha seems to carry the title of "holy [[T579]-ni] lord," so this dynasty could be located in Belize, at Altun Ha or further south, closer to Naj Tunich and Nim Li Punit.

Chapter 3. Identity and Interaction

1. The pictorial and hieroglyphic imagery of the Ik'-style corpus almost exclusively is concerned with publicizing the sociopolitical exploits of its elite patrons and supporters. The imagery constitutes a potent decorative scheme for food service and gift vessels used during politically charged feasts whose goals included boosting the power and prestige of the host, both locally and on the extra-polity political stage. Artists, too, were active participants, their unique painting styles and high technical and aesthetic skills augmenting the stature of the host via the value of the vessel as gift. The pottery tells a tale of social development and political expansion during the eighth century, and also intimates the Ik' polity's deterioration as Maya society fell into socioeconomic decline and political chaos at the end of the Classic period. The Maya Ceramics Project was created in 1968 at Brookhaven National Laboratory with subsequent support by the Museum of Fine Arts Boston; the project moved to the Smithsonian Institution in 1983 (Blackman and Bishop 2007).

2. *Workshop* is a highly loaded term of scant specificity in the field of ancient Maya studies. In this chapter *workshop* refers to a spatially and socially discrete work area where artisans exercised specialized skills to produce distinctive, nonutilitarian ceramic artifacts imbued with patterned aesthetic characteristics (see Helms 1993, 6; Rice 2009b). They maintained a formal personnel structure involving more than one individual, with investments in the relatively permanent, workplace facilities that were physically discrete from daily living areas (Arnold 1971, 1985; Costin 1991; Peacock 1981; P. Rice 1987c). Whether or not the artisans worked full- or part-time is not pertinent to the issues at hand, although the level of artifice (i.e., technical skill, specialized knowledge, and personal talent) indicates focused training and practice of some duration.

3. *Outliers* may refer to individual vessels that do not belong to any of the chemically identified groups, such as a carbonate tempered example being compared against groups of pottery with volcanic ash temper. *Outliers* also may represent an imported sample from a site or subregion for which we have no comparative chemical data, or they may be members of an insufficiently represented group of related wares. Further, *outliers* may simply represent an idiosyncratic paste preparation within the core production area or even arise due to measurement error during the scientific analysis. Outliers can cause major problems for many pattern recognition techniques, and when identified, they are best removed from the analytical process and considered separately.

4. MS0031 has been repainted in modern times, although prerestoration images are available in the Nicholas Hellmuth Photographic Archive at Dumbarton Oaks, Washington DC (LC-cb2-449). Differences in brushstroke technique, hieroglyphic contours, and figural forms suggest that an artist other than the Tuubal Ajaw painted the vase. Alternatively, but less likely, it could be the work of this renowned painter but a less carefully painted vase or one done later in life when artistic faculties had dwindled.

5. Many of these vessels have suffered surface damage and some have been repainted in modern times. We thus urge caution when interpreting the vessels' imagery, especially the hieroglyphic texts. When available, we have used prerestoration images for our research.

6. Vase K1453 portrays an otherwise unattested lord named Siyaj K'awiil seated upon a throne, conversing with a group of courtiers. He is sometimes included in king lists of the

Ik' polity (see Tokovinine and Zender, this volume), but it should be noted that a series of titles intervenes between Siyaj K'awiil and the Ik' Emblem Glyph on this vase. These could well state that Siyaj K'awiil was a vassal of the king, and not the king himself. The title *(u) waxaktal yoon k'uhul ik' ajaw*—"the eighth yoon (of) the Ik' lord"—in fact, also shows up on an Ik' vase found in a tomb at the site of Tamarindito (Valdés 1997, fig. 11). The name preceding this title on the Tamarindito vase, while damaged, is certainly not Siyaj K'awiil and ends with a clear K'inich. There are thus at least two names associated with the "eighth yoon" title in this kingdom. It should also be noted that Vase MS0071 portrays a noble of Tikal, Chak Tahn Moow, who bears the full Tikal Emblem Glyph but was clearly not a king, as he is shown kneeling before Jasaw Chan K'awiil I, who is seated upon a throne in this scene, receiving tribute from Calakmul. It is thus clear that lords bearing a full Emblem Glyph are not necessarily reigning sovereigns. Thus, Siyaj K'awiil could be a nonroyal elite from the Ik' polity or possibly the child name of one of the kingdom's better-known rulers. There is simply not enough evidence to decide which, if any, of these hypotheses is correct. Future discoveries may clarify his identity, but we prefer at this time not to include Siyaj K'awiil in the official king list of the Ik' polity.

7. Although this name is very similar to that of Tayel Chan K'inich, it is important to note that these are not alternative spellings for a single person's name. In the name Tayel Chan K'inich the *tayel* part is spelled out syllabically **ta-ye-le**, whereas in the name Taj Yal Chan K'inich the name is spelled out as **ta-YAL[CHAN]-na K'INICH**. In addition, the vessel's text and archaeological context demonstrate that Taj Yal Chan K'inich must have been ruling prior to 726, whereas a vessel naming Tayel Chan K'inich was found in archaeological context dating to the late eighth century (at the earliest) at the site of El Perú-Waká. Therefore, the complementary data sets clearly indicate that we are dealing with two separate individuals with similar names ruling at opposite ends of the eighth century.

8. This ruler's name cannot be securely deciphered at this time because the second element, a bird's head complemented with syllabic -ni, does not include the feathers or bird claws within the mouth that normally signal the reading **MUWAAN**. Zender (2004a) has read this name as Sak Ch'een, but it should be noted that the logogram **CH'EEN** is otherwise never suffixed with -**ni**, and in any event Zender is no longer advocating this reading (see Tokovinine and Zender, this volume). Since the name Sak Muwaan (Sac Muan in the older orthography) is well established in the extant literature on these vases (e.g., Reents-Budet 1994; Tokovinine 2002; Barrois and Tokovinine 2005), we prefer not to complicate the situation by introducing new nicknames, especially when these are neither more accurate nor precise. For this reason we continue to refer to this ruler as Sak Muwaan with the caveat that this is a nickname and not the ancient pronunciation of the ruler's moniker.

9. MS1847/K1004 may also be the work of the Tuubal Ajaw, a vessel in the collection of the Museum of Fine Arts Boston (1988.1175). Its PSS text records the vase's patron/owner as Yajawte' K'inich, the k'uhul ahaw of Ik'. However, its paste composition is radically different from all sampled Classic Maya ceramics, and instead recalls the composition of pottery from the Middle East. Clearly this is impossible. The explanation lies in the fact that the base, from which the sample was taken, is modern repair. Thus the NAA sample is that of restoration fill material rather than the ancient clay body. The vase currently is under investigation by Pamela Hatchfield and Richard Newman of the Conservation Department, Museum of Fine Arts Boston.

10. MS0031 cannot be assigned with certainty either to Motul Group 1 or Group 2, although its compositional profile asserts that it was made at the site. The compositional ambiguity is reflected in the equally curious combination of stylistic features. The barrel shape and three nubbin supports comprise a form typically associated with late Tepeu II (AD 800–830) and especially Tepeu III pottery (AD 830–880; see Culbert 1991; R. Smith 1955, vol. 2, figs. 2bp, 42b8, 44, 50a). Yet its imagery features Yajawte' K'inich and his associates, here rendered in a mid-eighth-century event recalling those painted on MS1121/K1439, MS1403/K533, DPCS25, and K3054. The Ik' data would suggest the barrel-shaped cylinder vase is not exclusive to Tepeu 3 pottery.

11. We thank Dr. Bryan Just, Princeton Art Museum, for sharing with us a prerestoration rollout photograph of the vase.

12. Stephen Houston and David Stuart suggested that the Ik' Emblem Glyph was used by various centers in the Motul de San José region, its relatively wide distribution being evidence for several capitals within the same polity (Foias 1999, 7). Our research supports Houston and Stuart's hypothesis.

13. At Calakmul, the same artist painted a "pseudo-codex-style" vase and a polychrome plate found in the tomb of Yuknoom Yich'aak K'ak' (Carrasco Vargas et al. 1999). Their highly similar chemical composition intimates production from the same paste recipe, thus indicating production in the same workshop and at the same time. The plate's owner is noted as Yuknoom Yich'aak K'ak' whereas the vase names the previous ruler Yuknoom Ch'een II as its patron/owner (Reents-Budet and Bishop, in press; Reents-Budet et al., in press [English version at www.mayavase.com]).

Chapter 4. Architecture, Volumetrics, and Social Stratification

1. The social organization of the ancient Maya has also engendered a great deal of debate (McAnany 1995; Gillespie 2000; Hageman 2004; Hutson, Magnoni, and Stanton 2004; Freter 2004; Manahan 2004; Becker 2004; Chase and Chase 2004; Kintz 2004; Watanabe 2004). However, it is not the goal of this chapter to engage these controversial issues.

2. Elson and Covey (2006) use the term *noble* to refer to estate only, and therefore keep nobles distinct from political or economic elites.

3. A parallel debate on Aztec social stratification also centers on the presence of two or three classes (Smith and Schreiber 2005, 205). Smith and Schreiber (ibid.) point to two classes as recorded by ethnohistorical documents. Other scholars, though, point to the presence of three classes based on archaeological evidence and theoretical principles (Sanders 1992; Hicks 1999). In our humble opinion, the debates surge at least in part from distinctions between emic and etic definitions of class and also likely between distinctions in social ideals and actual practices as they manifested on the ground level (Bourdieu 1977, 1990). The Postclassic Mexica and Mayas may have recognized only two classes in their societies (nobles versus commoners) based on kinship and descent or what Garraty (2000) has called "estate." However, materially, nobles and commoners differed tremendously in wealth and power, leading to many distinctions in the socioeconomic pyramid visible archaeologically (see discussion in A. Chase and D. Chase 1992, 7–8; Tourtellot, Sabloff, and Carmean 1992, 85; D. Chase and A. Chase 1992).

4. Burials are another body of evidence on ancient social stratification (M. Smith 1987; Haviland and Moholy-Nagy 1992; Gillespie 2000). However, the excavation program at Motul de San José did not expressly target burials, and so we only encountered nine interments, one of which is Preclassic. This sample is too limited and will not be discussed here.

5. Although the major groups at the site have received the letters A through E, the formal mapping of the site has also assigned names to these monumental groups based on a standard grid plan.

6. Stela 1 has an additional large fragment next to it that was originally believed to be a highly eroded altar. However, more recent examinations of this fragment have reinforced its rectangular shape and is now marked as Stela #7 (see Figure 1.2).

7. Ethnoarchaeological and experimental studies of stucco production at El Mirador have underscored the heavy labor investments and possible environmental impacts of Maya monumental construction from the Preclassic onward (E. Hansen 2000; Hansen, Rodriguez-Navarro, and Hansen 1997).

8. Several lines of evidence support this late date, although the structures were built and occupied from earlier on. First, Str. 8M-10 (the southern building) is faced by a patio that sported two round columns, an architectural feature that appears in the Terminal Classic. Second, pottery types discovered on the exterior terrace between the western and southern structures are diagnostic of the Terminal Classic (including Fine Orange Pabellon Modeled-carved, Tumba Black-on-orange, and incurved "grater" tripod bowls). Third, two AMS radiocarbon dates of animal bones found in this structure produced the years AD 670 and AD 890, ranging between AD 640 and 990, using two standard deviations (Foias 2003, 21, table 1).

9. With one exception: in Operation 15, the termination ritual assemblage found between the western and southern structures is included in this analysis as we assume that this refuse was redeposited from an adjacent area that represented midden deposition from the Group D itself.

10. Deal's (1998) ethnographic study of household potters in the Tzeltal community of Chanal in highland Chiapas found that potting households had almost twice as many metates and manos than nonpotting ones. However, in the absence of pottery-manufacturing debris in all Motul operations except Operation 2A, we can suggest that ground stone distribution is correlated with food production rather than pottery manufacture.

11. Excavated volume was estimated through the total areal extent of each operation (see Table 4.3).

12. The marine shell and marine resources data were kindly provided by Kitty Emery (also see Emery 2003a, 40, table 2; Emery, this volume).

13. Excavated volume was estimated through the total areal extent of each operation (see Table 4.3).

14. See Emery (this volume) for a more detailed discussion of the distribution of marine shell at the site.

15. Nevertheless, it is possible that they are elite if our sample is biased toward the upper end of the socioeconomic hierarchy and if most of the commoners resided beyond Motul proper.

Chapter 5. Figurine Economies at Motul de San José

1. Although some have argued that the presence of figurines within middens relate to a mundane rather than sacred or ritual role of figurines, other "ritual" items (ceramic *incensarios*, ceramic drums) are also found within household midden contexts.

2. These types are also described in an earlier study (Halperin 2004b) although sample sizes of this study were based only on figurines recovered from the 1998–2003 field seasons. An expanded 2005 sample from commoner loci have shifted the results slightly. Figurines from other Maya regions include forms with musical capacities not detected at Motel de San José (e.g., figurine rattles, three-part bulbous chambers).

3. In addition, some figurines, regardless of manufacturing type, were painted (with red, blue, and yellow pigments) and possessed incisions for eye slits, fingers, toes, or other decorative work. I suspect that most of the figurines were painted directly on the clay (no slips were used), with the paint having eroded off in all but the better-preserved specimens. In some cases, remnants of paint are visible with the aid of a polarizing microscope. Ellen Spensley's petrographic analysis on a sample of sixty-nine Motul de San José region figurines was not conducted specifically to look for surface treatment; however, she coincidentally found evidence of paint (that was not identifiable to the naked eye) on at least nine of the samples.

4. It is not clear from the publication whether the figurine molds from the ball court were found in structure fill or primary midden contexts.

5. These types are very rare in some southern Lowland sites, such as in Belize (LeCount 1999).

Chapter 6. Motul de San José Palace Pottery Production

1. Vessel #9806 has black scallops in its interior rim. Vessels #11,117–16 and 10144–46 have pink glyphs. Vessel #11081 pertains to Group 3 of the Ik' style (see description of these groups in Reents-Budet, Bishop, and MacLeod 1994).

2. These are #50423 and #55/Vessel 5/MSJ090.

3. These two Ik'-style sherds reutilized as polishers and/or smoothers were found in the elite structure adjacent to these middens (that was also partially explored by Operation MSJ2A).

Chapter 7. History, Politics, and Ceramics

1. *Chicle* is a natural sap obtained from the sapodilla tree (*Manilkara zapota*) of Central and South America. It is used in the production of chewing gum.

2. However, Ellen Spensley Moriarty is undertaking the second level modal ceramic analysis of the Trinidad collection as part of her PhD dissertation.

3. All bone identifications were done by Erin Thornton (this volume).

Chapter 9. Akte

1. Following excavation, cleaning, and drawing, Stela 1 was completely buried to protect it from further damage. During a follow-up visit to the site in 2004, however, the

monument was found in approximately the same position it was in prior to the Motul de San José investigations, apparently re-excavated and reset by unknown parties.

Chapter 10. Preliminary Investigations in Macro- and Microbotany

1. We are indebted to Deborah Pearsall and her laboratory for generously hosting Hare and aiding with the processing and identification of phytoliths. Hare's research in the Missouri lab was funded by a University of Florida Center for Latin American Studies Field Research Grant.

Chapter 11. The Motul de San José Animals in an Economic Perspective

1. This method overrepresents species such as turtles and armadillos with more than standard numbers of bony elements, the minimum number of individual and other modified counts are more likely to be affected by sample size, which is fairly small in all assemblages reviewed here.

2. Status or group rank has been determined for the Motul de San José site using a combination of volumetric architecture estimates (as a measure of relative labor investment) and architectural and artifactual "wealth" measured in terms of both exotic and labor-intensive sumptuary goods (see discussion in Foias et al., this volume).

3. Because not all the deposits were fine-screened, we can assume that proportions of fish, birds, and small species were probably higher than is recorded in these assemblages of primarily 1/4-inch screened material.

4. not specifically identified in this assemblage but may be represented in the few remains classified only as "very large mammals less than one hundred kilograms."

5. Not all deposits could be accurately dated, so this discussion compares only assemblages from dated deposits. Only one specimen was identified to the Early Classic period, so this period is not considered in any comparative analysis.

6. Exotic Production: 0 percent in the Preclassic, 5 percent marine versus 8 percent freshwater (+86 percent mammals) in the Late Classic, 30 percent versus 60 percent (+10 percent mammals) in the Terminal Classic, 0 percent versus 50 percent (+50 percent mammals) in the Postclassic.

7. Rank 1 n = 73, 39 percent marine versus n = 92, 49 percent freshwater; Rank 2 n = 14, 67 percent marine versus n = 3, 14 percent freshwater; Rank 3 n = 4, 44 percent marine versus n = 3, 33 percent freshwater.

8. Rank 1 n = 12 percent marine versus n = 5, 10 percent freshwater (+n = 42, 87 percent mammal); Rank 2 n = 2, 25 percent marine versus 0 percent freshwater (+n = 6, 75 percent mammal); Rank 30 percent marine or freshwater mollusks versus n = 3 (100 percent mammal).

Chapter 12. Animal Resource Use and Exchange

1. More specialized identifications were made using the museum's Ornithology, Malacology, and Mammalogy collections with the assistance of Dr. David Steadman, John Slapcinsky, and Candace McCaffery, respectively.

2. Species identification was made by Dr. Fred Thompson (Curator of Non-Marine Malacology, Florida Museum of Natural History).

Chapter 13. In Search of Markets and Fields

1. Moriarty (2001) and Emery and Foias (this volume) note that savanna soils are known today by local Itzaj farmers to be of low maize agricultural potential but high potential for arboriculture. Motul consumed many animal species that are native to such savanna environments: armadillos and rabbits (Emery 2003a; Emery and Foias, this volume).

2. The numbering of the groups identified on the East Transect follows the pattern of name of transect (in this case E for east); number of the kilometer in which it is located (in this case, second kilometer); and a sequential letter designation based on the order in which the group was found (in this case, letter E, because groups A–D were found previously in the second kilometer).

Chapter 15. Landscape, Economies, and the Politics of Power

1. D. Rice (1996) has found evidence for canals connecting Lake Petén Itzá with the smaller lakes toward the east.

2. Including Riachuelo K'änte't'u'ul that probably drained into Akte River, which then connected via Rio Seco into the west-flowing Rio San Pedro Martir (see Moriarty 2004d; Jones 1998, map 3; P. Rice and D. Rice 2009, map 1.3).

3. See discussion of this estimate in Foias and colleagues (this volume). We suspect that 2,000 is the ceiling for the population of Motul, and that it's more likely that it only reached half of this. Nevertheless, the polity's population must have been over twenty-five hundred people, considering the identification of many secondary and tertiary centers and intersite residences (Moriarty 2004d). If we use a conservative settlement density of 50 structures per square kilometer (taken from the density of the southern transect of 56 structures per square kilometer and of the northeastern transect of 52 structures per square kilometer) and the estimate for the areal extent of Motul's territory, we obtain a range for the total polity population between thirteen thousand and twenty-seven thousand people.

4. This territorial estimate is based on the presence of the very large site of Nixtun-Ch'ich approximately 10 kilometers south of Motul de San José. There is no doubt that this site was independent of Motul, so Motul's territory came short of it, and probably only encompassed the low-lying pocket that is clearly identifiable in Figure 1.4a.

5. Animal products were probably also brought into the capital from Chakokot (Emery, this volume).

6. Although most groups at Xilil are small, and probably would pertain to Rank 3 commoner households, Group B is more elaborate in scale. The largest structure in this group, Str. B1, was heavily looted and produced beautifully drawn polychromes, with the usual palace scenes we find on the Ik'-style vases; however, in this case, they are on tripod plates.

Chapter 16. Control without Controlling

1. "Wealth" is generally defined as the value of everything a person or family owns, minus debts. The statistics provided here are based on wealth distribution, for which economists define "wealth" in terms of marketable assets such as real estate, stocks, and bonds and exclude consumer durables not readily converted into cash. A person's net worth is derived once all debts are subtracted from the value of all marketable assets (Domhoff 2010; Wolff 2004, 4–5). Income, which is what we earn from work or dividends, interest, rent, or royalties, is distinguished by economists from wealth. According to Domhoff, those who own a great deal of wealth in theory may or may not have high incomes, but in reality those at the top of wealth distribution generally have the most income.

2. This is defined by economists as net worth minus net equity in owner-occupied housing. It reflects the resources that would be immediately available for consumption or other investments (Domhoff 2010; Wolff 2004, 5; Wolff 2010).

3. Such as Jesus Christ or Buddha, both poor but with significant power.

Bibliography

Abrams, E. M.

1989 Architecture and Energy: An Evolutionary Perspective. In *Archaeological Method and Theory*, edited by M. B. Schiffer, 47–87. University of Arizona Press, Tucson.

1994 *How the Mayas Built Their World: Energetics and Ancient Architecture*. University of Texas Press, Austin.

1996 Evolution of Plaster Production Techniques and the Growth of the Copán Maya State. In *Arqueología Mesoamericana: Homenaje a William T. Sanders II*, edited by A. G. Mastache de Escobar, 193–208. Instituto Nacional de Antropología e Historia, Mexico City.

Adams, J. L.

2002 *Ground Stone Analysis: A Technological Approach*. University of Utah Press, Salt Lake City.

Adams, R. E. W.

1963 A Polychrome Vase from Altar de Sacrificios. *Archaeology* 16(2): 90–92.

1970 Suggested Classic Period Occupational Specialization in the Southern Maya Lowlands. In *Monographs and Papers in Maya Archaeology*, edited by W. Bullard, 487–98. Papers of the Peabody Museum No. 61. Harvard University, Cambridge, Massachusetts.

1971 *The Ceramics of Altar de Sacrificios*. Papers of the Peabody Museum of Archaeology and Ethnology, Vol. 63, No. 1. Harvard University, Cambridge, Massachusetts.

1977 Comments on the Glyphic Texts of the "Altar Vase." In *Social Process in Maya Prehistory: Studies in Honour of Sir Eric Thompson*, edited by N. Hammond, 409–20. Academic Press, London.

1986 Rio Azul. *National Geographic* 169:420–51.

Adams, R. E. W., and W. D. Smith

1981 Feudal Models for Classic Maya Settlement. In *Lowland Maya Settlement Patterns*, edited by W. Ashmore, 335–49. University of New Mexico Press, Albuquerque.

Adams, R. McC.

1965 *Land behind Baghdad: A History of Settlement on the Diyala Plain*. University of Chicago Press, Chicago.

1966 *The Evolution of Urban Society: Early Mesopotamia and Prehispanic Mexico*. Aldine, Chicago.

1981 *The Heartland of Cities: Surveys of Ancient Settlement and Land Use on the Central Floodplain of the Euphrates*. University of Chicago Press, Chicago.

Agoos, Z. A. F.

2007 *Ik' Site Ceramics: Courtly Pottery of the Ancient Maya*. Undergraduate thesis, Department of Anthropology, Brown University.

Akerman, J.

1962 A Theory of Style. *The Journal of Aesthetics and Art Criticism* 20:227–37. The American Society for Aesthetics. The Cleveland Museum of Art, Cleveland.

Alvarez, M. J., P. R. Castillo, and A. E. Foias

2001 Excavaciones en el Grupo D: Operacion MSJ15A. In *Proyecto Arqueologico Motul de San José Informe Preliminar # 4: Temporada de Campo 2001*, edited by A. Foias, 35–56. Report submitted to the Institute of Anthropology and History, Guatemala City. Williams College, Williamstown, Massachusetts.

Ames, K. M.

1995 Chiefly Power and Household Production on the Northwest Coast. In *Foundations of Social Inequality*, edited by T. D. Price and G. M. Feinman, 155–87. Plenum Press, New York.

Amiguet, V., J. Arnason, P. Maquin, V. Cal, P. Vindas, and L. Poveda

2005 A Consensus Ethnobotany of the Q'eqchi' Maya of Southern Belize. *Economic Botany* 59(1): 29–42.

Andrews, A. P.

1990 The Role of Trading Ports in the Maya Civilization. In *Vision and Revision in Maya Studies*, edited by F. S. Clancy and P. D. Harrison, 159–67. University of New Mexico Press, Albuquerque.

Andrews, A. P., and S. B. Mock

2002 New Perspectives on the Prehispanic Maya Salt Trade. In *Ancient Maya Political Economies*, edited by Marilyn A. Masson and David A. Freidel, 307–34. AltaMira Press, Walnut Creek, California.

Andrews, A. P., T. G. Negron, F. R. Castellanos, R. C. Palma, and P. C. Rivero

1988 Isla Cerritos: An Itza Trading Port on the North Coast of Yucatan, Mexico. *National Geographic Research* 4:196–207.

Andrews IV, E. W., and C. R. Bill

2005 A Late Classic Royal Residence at Copán. In *Copán: The History of an Ancient Maya Kingdom*, edited by E. W. Andrews and W. L. Fash, 293–314. School of American Research and James Currey, Santa Fe and Oxford.

Andrews IV, E. W., and B. W. Fash

1992 Continuity and Change in a Royal Maya Residential Complex at Copán. *Ancient Mesoamerica* 3:63–88.

Anselmetti, F. S., D. A. Hodell, D. Ariztegui, M. Brenner, and M. F. Rosenmeier

2007 Quantification of Soil Erosion Rates Related to Ancient Maya Deforestation. *Geology* 35(10): 915–18.

Aoyama, K.

2001 Classic Maya State, Urbanism, and Exchange: Chipped Stone Evidence of the Copán Valley and Its Hinterland. *American Anthropologist* 103(2): 346–60.

2007 Elite Artists and Craft Producers in Classic Maya Society: Lithic Evidence from Aguateca, Guatemala. *Latin American Antiquity* 18(1): 3–26.

Ardren, T.

2002 Death Became Her: Images of Female Power from Yaxuna Burials. In *Ancient Maya Women*, edited by T. Ardren, 68–88. AltaMira Press, Walnut Creek, California.

Ardren, T., and S. R. Hutson (editors)

2006 *The Social Experience of Childhood in Ancient Mesoamerica*. University Press of Colorado, Boulder.

Arnold, D. E.

1971 Ethnomineralogy of Ticul, Yucatán Potters: Etics and Emics. *American Antiquity* 36(1): 20–40.

1985 *Ceramic Theory and Cultural Process*. Cambridge University Press, New York.

1999 Advantages and Disadvantages of Vertical-Half Molding Technology: Implications for Production Organization. In *Pottery and People: A Dynamic Interaction*, edited by J. M. Skibo and G. M. Feinman, 81–98. University of Utah Press, Salt Lake City.

Arnold, D. E., H. Neff, and R. L. Bishop

1991 The Compositional Analysis of Pottery: An Ethonarchaeological Approach. *American Anthropologist* 93:70–90.

Arnold, D. E., H. A. Neff, R. L. Bishop, and M. D. Glascock

1999 Testing Interpretative Assumptions of Neutron Activation Analysis: Contemporary Pottery in Yucatán, 1964–1994. In *Material Meanings: Critical Approaches to the Interpretation of Material Culture*, edited by E. S. Chilton, 61–84. Foundations of Archaeological Inquiry, University of Utah Press, Salt Lake City.

Arnold, J. E., and A. Ford

1980 A Statistical Examination of Settlement Patterns at Tikal, Guatemala. *American Antiquity* 45(4): 713–26.

Arnold III, P. J.

1991 *Domestic Ceramic Production and Spatial Organization: A Mexican Case Study in Ethnoarchaeology*. Cambridge University Press, Cambridge.

Arnold III, P. J., C. A. Pool, and R. Santley

1993 Intensive Ceramic Production and Classic-Period Political Economy in the Sierra de los Tuxtlas, Veracruz, Mexico. *Ancient Mesoamerica* 4:175–91.

Arrhenius, O.

1931 Die bodenanalyse im dienst der archäologie. *Zeitschrift für Pflanzenernährung, Düngung und Bodenkunde Teil B* 10:427–39.

Ashmore, W.

1988 Household and Community at Classic Quirigua. In *Household and Community in the Mesoamerican Past*, edited by W. Ashmore and R. R. Wilk, 153–69. University of New Mexico Press, Albuquerque.

1992 Deciphering Maya Architectural Plans. In *New Theories on the Ancient Maya*, edited by E. C. Danien and R. J. Sharer, 173–84. University Museum of Archaeology and Anthropology, University of Pennsylvania, Philadelphia.

1997 Monumentos Politicos: Sitio, Asentamiento y paisaje alrededor de Xunantunich, Belize. In *Anatomia de una Civilizacion; Aproximaciones Interdisciplinarias a la Cultura Maya*, edited by A. Ciudad Ruiz, Y. Fernandez Marquinex, J. M. Gardia Campillo, M. J. Iglesias Ponce de Leon, A. L. Gardia-Gallo, and L. T. Sanz Castro, 207–52. Sociedad Española de Estudios Mayas, Madrid.

2007 *Settlement Archaeology at Quiriguá, Guatemala*. University Museum Monograph 126. University of Pennsylvania Museum of Archaeology and Anthropology, Philadelphia.

Aswani, S., and P. Sheppard

2003 The Archaeology and Ethnohistory of Exchange in Precolonial and Colonial Roviana: Gifts, Commodities, and Inalienable Possessions. *Current Anthropology* 44:51–78.

Atran, S.

1993 Itza Maya Tropical Agro-Forestry. *Current Anthropology* 34:633–700.

2003 Anthropogenic Vegetation: A Garden Experiment in the Maya Lowlands. In *The Lowland Maya Area: Three Millennia at the Human-Wildland Interface*, edited by A. Gomez-Pompa, M. F. Allen, S. L. Fedick, and J. J. Jimenez-Osornio, 517–32. Food Products Press, New York.

Atran, S., D. Medin, N. Ross, E. Lynch, J. Coley, E. U. Ek', and V. Vapnarsky

1999 Folkecology and Commons Management in the Maya Lowlands. *Proceedings of the National Academy of Sciences* 96:7598–603.

Bain, R. J.

1985 Petrography of Mayan Mortar, Isla Mujeres, Quintana Roo, Mexico. *Geological Society of America: Abstracts with Programs* 17:517.

Baines, John, and Norman Yoffee

1998 Order, Legitimacy, and Wealth in Ancient Egypt and Mesopotamia. In *Archaic States*, edited by Gary M. Feinman and Joyce Marcus, 199–260. School of American Research Press, Santa Fe.

Bair, D. A.

2009 *The Dirt on Ancient Maya Marketplace Activities*. MS thesis, Department of Anthropology, Brigham Young University.

Bair, D. A., and R. E. Terry

2009 Estudios geoquímicos de suelo en Mayapán, temporada 2008. In *Proyecto Los Fundamentos Del Poder Económico De Mayapán, Temporada 2008*, edited by M. A. Masson, C. Peraza Lope, and T. S. Hare, 377–84. SUNY, Albany.

Balee, W.

2006 The Research Program of Historical Ecology. *Annual Review of Anthropology* 35: 75–98.

Balee, W., and C. L. Erickson (editors)

2006 *Time and Complexity in Historical Ecology: Studies in the Neotropical Lowlands*. Columbia University Press, New York.

Balesdent, J.

1987 The Turnover of Soil Organic Fractions Estimated by Radiocarbon Dating. *Science of the Total Environment* 62:405–8.

Balesdent, J., G. H. Wagner, and A. Mariotti

1988 Soil Organic Matter Turnover in Long-Term Field Experiments as Revealed by Carbon-13 Natural Abundances. *Soil Science Society of America Journal* 52:118–24.

Balkansky, A. K., G. M. Feinman, and L. M. Nicholas

1997 Pottery Kilns of Ancient Ejutla, Oaxaca, Mexico. *Journal of Field Archaeology* 24(2): 139–60.

Ball, J. W.

1993 Pottery, Potters, Palaces, and Politics: Some Socioeconomic and Political Implications of Late Classic Maya Ceramic Industries. In *Lowland Maya Civilization in the Eighth Century A.D.*, edited by J. A. Sabloff and J. S. Henderson, 243–72. Dumbarton Oaks, Washington, D.C.

Ball, J. W., and J. T. Taschek

1991 Late Classic Lowland Maya Political Organization and Central Place Analysis: Insights from the Upper Belize Valley. *Ancient Mesoamerica* 2:149–65.

1992 *Economics and Economies in the Late Classic Maya Lowlands: A Trial Examination of Some Apparent Patterns and Their Implications*. Paper given at the symposium "The

Segmentary State and the Classic Lowland Maya," Cleveland State University, Cleveland.

2001 The Buenavista-Cahal Pech Royal Court: Multi-Palace Court Mobility and Usage in a Petty Lowland Maya Kingdom. In *Royal Courts of the Ancient Maya*, vol. 2, *Data and Case Studies*, edited by T. Inomata and S. Houston, 165–200. Westview Press, Boulder.

2003 Reconsidering the Belize Valley Preclassic: A Case for Multiethnic Interactions in the Development of a Regional Cultural Tradition. *Ancient Mesoamerica* 14:179–217.

2007 Sometimes a "Stove" *Is* "Just a Stove": A Context-Based Reconsideration of Three-Prong "Incense Burners" from the Western Belize Valley. *Latin American Antiquity* 18(4): 451–70.

Ballinger, D. A., and J. Stomper

2000 The Jaguars of Altar Q, Copán, Honduras: Faunal Analysis, Archaeology, and Ecology. *Journal of Ethnobiology* 20(2): 223–36.

Barba, L., B. Ludlow, L. Manzanilla, and R. Valadez

1987 La vida doméstica de Teotihuacan: Un estudio interdisciplinario. *Ciencia y Desarrollo* 77:21–33.

Barba, L., and L. Manzanilla

1987 Estudio de areas de actividad. In *Coba, Quintana Roo Analysis De Dos Unidades Habitacionales Mayas*, edited by L. Manzanilla, 69–115. Universidad Nacional Autonoma de Mexico, Mexico City.

Barba, L., and A. Ortiz

1992 Análisis químico de pisos de ocupación: un caso etnográfico en Tlaxcala, Mexico. *Latin American Antiquity* 3:63–82.

Barba, L., A. Ortiz, K. Link, L. Lopez Lujan, and L. Lazos

1996 Chemical Analysis of Residues in Floors and the Reconstruction of Ritual Activities at the Templo Mayor, Mexico. In *Archaeological Chemistry: Organic, Inorganic, and Biochemical Analysis*, edited by M. V. Orna, 139–56. American Chemical Society, Washington, D.C.

Barba, L., F. Pierrebourg, C. Trejo, A. Ortiz, and K. Link

1995 Activities humaines refletees dans les sols d'unites d'habitation contemporaine et Prehispanique du Yucatan, Mexico: Etudes chimiques, ethonoarcheologiques et archeologiques. *Revue d'Archeometrie* 19:79–95.

Barbour, W. D. T.

1975 *The Figurines and Figurine Chronology of Ancient Teotihuacán, Mexico*. PhD dissertation, Department of Anthropology, University of Rochester.

Barger, M. S.

1995 Materials Characterization of Natural Adobe Plasters: New Approaches for Preservation Strategies Based on Traditional Practice. In *Issues in Art and Archaeology IV*, edited by P. B. Vandiver, J. R. Druzik, J. L. Galvan Madrid, I. C. Freestone, and G. Segan Wheeler, 389–94. Materials Research Society, Pittsburgh.

Barrois, R. R., and A. Tokovinine

2005 El inframundo y el mundo celestial en el Juego de Pelota Maya. In *XVIII Simposio de Investigaciones Arqueológicas en Guatemala, 2004*, edited by J. P. Laporte and B. Arroyo y H. Mejía, 27–38. Museo Nacional de Arqueología y Etnología, Guatemala City.

Barthel, T.

1968 El complejo emblema. *Estudios de cultura maya* 7:159–93.

Bayman, J. M.

1999 Craft Economies in the North American Southwest. *Journal of Archaeological Research* 7:249–99.

2002 Hohokam Craft Economies in the North American Southwest. *Journal of Archaeological Method and Theory* 9:69–95.

Beach, T.

1998 Soil Cantinas, Tropical Deforestation and Ancient and Contemporary Soil Erosion in the Petén, Guatemala. *Physical Geography* 19:378–405.

Beach, T., N. Dunning, S. Luzzadder-Beach, D. E. Cook, and J. Lohse

2006 Impacts of the Ancient Maya on Soils and Soil Erosion in the Central Maya Lowlands. *Catena* 65:166–78.

Beach, T., N. Dunning, S. Luzzadder-Beach, and V. Scarborough

2003 Depression Soils in the Lowland Tropics of the Northwestern Belize: Anthropogenic and Natural Origins. In *Lowland Maya Area: Three Millennia at the Human-Wildland Interface*, edited by A. Gomez-Pompa, M. Allen, S. L. Fedick, and J. Jiménez-Osornio, 139–74. Haworth Press, Binghamton, New York.

Beach, T., S. Luzzadder-Beach, N. Dunning, and D. Cook

2008a Human and Natural Impacts on Fluvial and Karst Depressions of the Maya Lowlands. *Geomorphology* 101:308–31.

Beach, T., S. Luzzadder-Beach, N. Dunning, J. Hageman, and J. Lohse

2002 Upland Agriculture in the Maya Lowlands: Ancient Maya Soil Conservation in Northwestern Belize. *Geographical Review* 92:372–97.

Beach, T., S. Luzzadder-Beach, and J. C. Lohse

2008b Landscape Formation and Agriculture in the Wetlands of Northwestern Belize. In *Classic Maya Political Ecology*, edited by Jon C. Lohse, 97–140. University of Colorado Press, Boulder.

Beaubien, H.

2004 Excavation and Recovery of a Funerary Offering of Marine Materials from Copán. In *Maya Zooarchaeology: New Directions in Method and Theory*, edited by K. F. Emery, 45–54. Institute of Archaeology, UCLA Press, Los Angeles.

Beaudry, M.

1984 *Ceramic Production and Distribution in the Southeast Maya Periphery: Late Classic Painted Serving Vessels.* BAR International Series 203. Archaeopress, Oxford.

Becker, M. J.

1973 Archaeological Evidence for Occupational Specialization among the Classic Period Maya at Tikal, Guatemala. *American Antiquity* 38(4): 396–406.

1979 Priests, Peasants, and Ceremonial Centers: The Intellectual History of a Model. In *Maya Archaeology and Ethnohistory*, edited by N. Hammond and G. R. Willey, 3–20. University of Texas Press, Austin.

1999 *Tikal Report no. 21, Excavations in Residential Areas of Tikal: Groups with Shrines.* University Museum Monography 104. University Museum, University of Pennsylvania, Philadelphia.

2003a A Classic Period Barrio Producing Fine Polychrome Ceramics at Tikal, Guatemala. *Ancient Mesoamerica* 38:396–406.

2003b Plaza Plans at Tikal: A Research Strategy for Inferring Social Organization and Processes of Culture Change at Lowland Maya Sites. In *Tikal: Dynasties, Foreigners,*

& *Affairs of State*, edited by J. A. Sabloff, 253–80. School of American Research Press, Santa Fe, New Mexico.

2004 Maya Heterarchy as Inferred from Classic-Period Plaza Plans. *Ancient Mesoamerica* 15:127–38.

Beliaev, D. D.

2000 Wuk Tsuk and Oxlahun Tsuk: Naranjo and Tikal in the Late Classic. In *Sacred and the Profane: Architecture and Identity in the Maya Lowlands*, edited by P. Robert-Colas, 63–81. Verlag von Flemming, Berlin.

Benson, E. P.

1988 The Eagle and the Jaguar: Notes for a Bestiary. In *Smoke and Mist: Mesoamerican Studies in Memory of Thelma D. Sullivan*, edited by J. K. Josserand and K. Dakin, 161–72. BAR International Series 402(i). Archaeo Press, Oxford.

Berdan, F. F.

1978 Ports of Trade in Mesoamerica: A Reappraisal. In *Cultural Continuity in Mesoamerica*, edited by D. L. Browman, 179–98. Mouton Publishers, Chicago.

2007 Material Dimensions of Aztec Religion and Ritual. In *Mesoamerican Ritual Economy: Archaeological and Ethnological Perspectives*, edited by E. C. Wells and K. L. Davis-Salazar, 245–66. University Press of Colorado, Boulder.

Berdan, F. F., R. E. Blanton, E. H. Boone, M. G. Hodge, M. E. Smith, and E. Umberger

1996 *Aztec Imperial Strategies*. Dumbarton Oaks, Washington, D.C.

Bernal Romero, G.

2006 Pomoy: una de las ciudades perdidas de los mayas. *Arqueología Mexicana* 4(79): 10.

Bezdek, J. C.

1981 *Pattern Recognition with Fuzzy Objective Function Algorithms*. Plenum Press, New York.

1993 Probabilistic, Fuzzy and Neural Models for Pattern Recognition. *Journal of Intelligent and Fuzzy Systems* 1(1): 1–25.

Bill, C. R.

1997 *Patterns of Variation and Change in Dynastic Period Ceramics and Ceramic Production at Copán, Honduras*. PhD dissertation, Department of Anthropology, Tulane University, New Orleans, Louisiana.

Binford, M. W.

1983 Paleolimnology of the Petén Lake District, Guatemala: I. Erosion and Deposition of Inorganic Sediment as Inferred from Granulometry. *Hydrobiologia* 103:199–203.

Bishop, R. L.

1994 Pre-Columbian Pottery: Research in the Maya Region. In *Archaeometry of Pre-Columbian Sites and Artefacts*, edited by D. A. Scott and P. Meyers, 15–65. The Getty Conservation Institute, Los Angeles.

2003 Five Decades of Maya Fine Orange Ceramic Investigation by INAA. In *Patterns and Process: A Festschrift in Honor of Dr. Edward V. Sayre*, edited by L. Van Zelst, 80–91. Smithsonian Center for Materials Research and Education, Suitland, Maryland.

2008 Archaeological Ceramics and Scientific Practice. In *Actas: VII Congreso Ibérico de Arqueometría*, edited by S. R. Llorens, M. García-Heras, M. G. Moret, and I. M. Ruiz, 236–49. Consejo Superior de Investigaciones Científicas (CSIC). Madrid, Spain.

Bishop, R. L, and H. Neff
1988 Compositional Data Analysis in Archaeology. In *Archaeological Chemistry IV*, edited by R. O. Allen, 57–86. Advances in Chemistry Series 220. American Chemical Society, Washington, D.C.

Bishop, R. L., and R. L. Rands
1982 Maya Fine Paste Ceramics: A Compositional Perspective. In *Excavations at Seibal: Analysis of Fine Paste Ceramics*, edited by J. A. Sabloff, 283–314. Memoirs of the Peabody Museum of Archaeology and Ethnology, vol. 15, no. 2. Harvard University Press, Cambridge.

Bishop, R. L., R. L. Rands, and G. R. Holley
1982 Ceramic Compositional Analysis in Archaeological Perspective. In *Advances in Archaeological Method and Theory*, vol. 5, edited by Michael B. Schiffer, 275–330. Academic Press, New York.

Biskowski, M.
2000 Maize Preparation and the Aztec Subsistence Economy. *Ancient Mesoamerica* 11(2): 293–306.

Blackman, M. J., and R. L. Bishop
2007 Smithsonian–NIST Partnership: Application of Instrumental Neutron Activation Analysis to Archaeology. *Archaeometry* 49(2): 321–43.

Blackman, M. J., G. J. Stein, and P. B. Vandiver
1993 The Standardization Hypothesis and Ceramic Mass Production: Technological, Compositional, and Metric Indexes of Craft Specialization at Tell Leilan, Syria. *American Antiquity* 58(1): 60–80.

Blake, M., B. S. Chisholm, J. E. Clark, and K. Mudar
1992 Non-Agricultural Staples and Agricultural Supplements: Early Formative Subsistence in the Soconusco Region, Mexico. In *Transitions to Agriculture in Prehistory*, edited by A. B. Gebauer and T. D. Price, 133–51. Prehistory Press, Madison, Wisconsin.

Blanton, R. E.
1994 *Houses and Households: A Comparative Study*. Plenum Press, New York.
1998 Beyond Centralization: Steps toward a Theory of Egalitarian Behavior in Archaic States. In *Archaic States*, edited by G. M. Feinman and J. Marcus, 135–72. School of American Research, Santa Fe, New Mexico.

Blanton, R., and L. Fargher
2008 *Collective Action in the Formation of Pre-Modern States*. Springer, New York.

Blanton, R. E., G. M. Feinman, S. A. Kowalewski, and P. N. Peregrine
1996 A Dual-Processual Theory for the Evolution of Mesoamerican Civilization. *Current Anthropology* 37(1): 1–14.

Boivin, N.
2000 Life Rhythms and Floor Sequences: Excavating Time in Rural Rajasthan and Neolithic Çatalhöyük. *World Archaeology* 31:367–88.

Boot, E.
1999 A New Naranjo Area Toponym: yo:tz*. *Mexicon* 21(2): 39–42.
2005 Portraits of Four Kings of the Early Classic? An Inscribed Bowl Excavated at Uaxactún and Seven Vessels of Unknown Provenance. *Mesoweb*. www.mesoweb.com/articles/boot/UaxactunBowl.pdf.

Boschian, G.

1997 Sedimentology and Soil Micromorphology of the Late Pleistocene and Early Holocene Deposits of Grotta dell'Edera (Trieste Karst, NE Italy). *Geoarchaeology* 12:227–49.

Boström, B., D.Comstedt, and A. Ekblad

2007 Isotope Fractionation and [13]C Enrichment in Soil Profiles during the Decomposition of Organic Matter. *Oecologia* 153:89–98.

Bourdieu, P.

1977 *Outline of a Theory of Practice*. Cambridge University Press, Cambridge.

1990 *The Logic of Practice*. Stanford University Press, Stanford, California.

Brady, J. E.

1996 *Studies in Mesoamerican Cave Use, Publication 1: Sources for the Study of Mesoamerican Cave Use*. Department of Anthropology, George Washington University, Washington, D.C.

Brady, J., and W. Ashmore

1999 Mountains, Caves, Water: Ancient Maya Ideational Landscapes. In *Archaeologies of Landscape: Contemporary Perspectives*, edited by W. Ashmore and A. B. Knapp, 124–48. Blackwell Publishers, Oxford.

Brady, J. E., J. W. Ball, R. L. Bishop, D. C. Pring, N. Hammond, and R. A. Housley

1998 The Lowland Maya "Protoclassic": A Reconsideration of Its Nature and Significance. *Ancient Mesoamerica* 92(1): 17–38.

Brady, J. E., and K. M. Prufer

2001 Caves and Crystalmancy: Evidence for the Use of Crystals in Ancient Maya Religion. *Journal of Anthropological Research* 55:129–44.

Brenner, M., B. W. Leyden, and M. W. Binford

1990 Recent Sedimentary Histories of Shallow Lakes in the Guatemalan Savannas. *Journal of Paleolimnology* 4:239–52.

Brenner, M., M. F. Rosenmeier, D. A. Hodell, and J. H. Curtis

2002 Paleolimnology of the Maya Lowlands: Long-Term Perspectives on Interactions among Climate, Environment, and Humans. *Ancient Mesoamerica* 13:141–57.

Brian, S. V.

2005 *Lithic Analysis at Motul de San José*. Paper given at the Annual Meetings of the Society for American Archaeology, Salt Lake City, Utah.

Briggs Braswell, J.

1998 *Archaeological Investigations at Group D, Xunantunich, Belize*. Unpublished PhD dissertation, Department of Anthropology, Tulane University.

Bronson, B.

1966 Roots and the Subsistence of the Ancient Maya. *Southwestern Journal of Anthropology* 22:251–79.

Brown, L. A.

2001 Feasting on the Periphery: The Production of Ritual Feasting and Village Festivals at the Ceren Site, El Salvador. In *Feasts: Archaeological and Ethnographic Perspectives on Food, Politics and Power*, edited by M. Dietler and B. Hayden, 368–90. Smithsonian Institution Press, Washington, D.C.

2005 Planting the Bones: Hunting Ceremonialism at Contemporary and Nineteenth-Century Shrines in the Guatemalan Highlands. *Latin American Antiquity* 16(2): 131–46.

Bruck, J.
2006 Death, Exchange, and Reproduction in the British Bronze Age. *European Journal of Archaeology* 9(1): 73–101.

Brumfiel, E. M.
1980 Specialization, Market Exchange, and the Aztec State: A View from Huexotla. *Current Anthropology* 21:459–78.

1987 Elite and Utilitarian Crafts in the Aztec State. In *Specialization, Exchange and Complex Societies*, edited by E. Brumfield and T. Earle, 102–18. Cambridge University Press, Cambridge.

1994 Factional Competition and Political Development in the New World: An Introduction. In *Factional Competition and Political Development in the New World*, edited by Elizabeth M. Brumfiel and John W. Fox, 3–13. Cambridge University Press, Cambridge.

1995 Heterarchy and the Analysis of Complex Societies: Comments. In *Heterarchy and the Analysis of Complex Societies*, edited by R. M. Ehrenreich, C. L. Crumely, and J. E. Levy, 125–31. Archaeological Papers 6. American Anthropological Association, Arlington, Virginia.

2006 Cloth, Gender, Continuity, and Change: Fabricating Unity in Anthropology. *American Anthropologist* 108(4): 862–77.

Brumfiel, E. M., and T. K. Earle
1987 Specialization, Exchange, and Complex Societies: An Introduction. In *Specialization, Exchange, and Complex Societies*, edited by E. M. Brumfiel and T. K. Earle, 1–9. Cambridge University Press, Cambridge.

Brumfiel, E. M., and J. W. Fox
1994 *Factional Competition and Political Development in the New World*. Cambridge University Press, Cambridge.

Bryant, V. M. J.
2009 Pollen Analysis of Samples from Madera Quemada Pueblo. In *Madera Quemada: Archaeological Investigations of a Fourteenth Century Jounada Mogollon Pueblo*, edited by M. R. Miller and T. B. Graves, 273–90. Fort Bliss Cultural Resources Report No. 03–12. Geo-Marine, El Paso, Texas.

Bullard, W. R.
1960 Maya Settlement Pattern in Northeastern Petén, Guatemala. *American Antiquity* 25(3): 355–72.

1964 Settlement Pattern and Social Structure in the Southern Maya Lowlands during the Classic Period. In *XXXV Congreso Internacional de Americanistas*, vol. 1, edited by A. Jiménez Nuñez, 279–87. Mexico City, Editorial Libros de México.

1970 Topoxté: A Postclassic Maya Site in Petén, Guatemala. In *Monographs and Papers in Maya Archaeology, Papers of the Peabody Museum of Archaeology and Ethnology*, vol. 61, edited by W. R. Bullard Jr., 245–308. Harvard University, Cambridge, Massachusetts.

1973 Postclassic Culture in Central Petén and Adjacent British Honduras. In *The Classic Maya Collapse*, edited by T. P. Culbert, 225–42. University of New Mexico Press, Albuquerque.

Bullock, P., N. Fedoroff, A. Jongerius, G. Stoops, and T. Tursina
1985 *Handbook for Soil Thin Section Description*. Waine Research, Wolverhampton.

Burgoa, Fray Francisco de

[1674] 1989 *Geográfica Descripción*, vol. 1. Editorial Porrúa, Mexico City.

Byland, B. E., and J. D. Pohl

1994 *In the Realm of 8 Deer: The Archaeology of the Mixtec Codice*s. University of Oklahoma Press, Norman.

Cameron, C. M.

1993 Abandonment and Archaeological Interpretation. In *Abandonment of Settlements and Regions: Ethnoarchaeological and Archaeological Approaches*, edited by C. M. Cameron and S. A. Tomka, 3–7. Cambridge University Press, Cambridge.

Cannon, M. D.

1999 A Mathematical Model of the Effects of Screen Size on Zooarchaeological Relative Abundance Measures. *Journal of Archaeological Science* 26(2): 205–14.

Canuto, M. A., and J. Yaeger (editors)

2000 *The Archaeology of Communities: A New World Perspective*. Routledge, New York.

Carmack, R. M.

1981 *The Quiché Maya of Utatlan: The Evolution of a Highland Guatemala Kingdom*. University of Oklahoma Press, Norman.

Carmean, K.

1991 Architectural Labor Investment and Social Stratification at Sayil, Yucatan, Mexico. In *Latin American Antiquity* 2:151–65.

Carr, H. S.

1985 Subsistence and Ceremony: Faunal Utilization in a Late Preclassic Community at Cerros, Belize. In *Prehistoric Lowland Maya Environment and Subsistence Economy*, edited by M. Pohl, 115–32. Peabody Museum of Archaeology and Ethnology, Harvard University, Cambridge, Massachusetts.

1986 *Faunal Utilization in a Late Preclassic Maya Community at Cerros, Belize*. PhD dissertation, Tulane University.

1996 Precolumbian Maya Exploitation and Management of Deer Populations. In *The Managed Mosaic: Ancient Maya Agriculture and Resource Use*, edited by S. Fedick, 251–61. University of Utah Press, Salt Lake City.

Carrasco Vargas, R., S. Boucher, P. Alvarez, V. Tiesler Blos, V. García Vierna, R. García Moreno, and J. Vásquez Negrete

1999 A Dynastic Tomb from Campeche, Mexico: New Evidence on Jaguar Paw, A Ruler of Calakmul. *Latin American Antiquity* 10(1): 47–58.

Carrasco Vargas, R., V. A. Vásquez López, and S. Martin

2009 Daily Life of the Ancient Maya Recorded on Murals at Calakmul, Mexico. *Proceedings of the Natural Academy of Science* 106(46): 19245–49.

Carter, S. P., and D. A. Davidson

1998 An Evaluation of the Contribution of Soil Micromorphology to the Study of Ancient Arable Agriculture. *Geoarchaeology* 13:535–47.

Castellanos, J.

2000 Excavaciones en la Estructura Norte (el Palacio) en la Plazuela Noroeste de la Acropolis del Grupo C. In *Proyecto Arqueológico Motul de San José Informe #3: Temporada de Campo 2000*, edited by A. Foias and J. Castellanos, 53–66. Report submitted to the Institute of Anthropology and History, Guatemala City. Williams College, Williamstown, Massachusetts.

2007 *Buenavista-Nuevo San José, Petén, Guatemala: Otra Aldea del Preclásico Medio (800–400 A.C.)*. Report submitted to the Foundation for the Advancement of Mesoamerican Studies, Inc. www.famsi.org/reports/05039es/index.html.

Cavanagh, W. G., S. Hirst, and C. D. Litton
1988 Soil Phosphate, Site Boundaries, and Change Point Analysis. *Journal of Field Archaeology* 15:67–83.

Cecil, L. G.
2001 *Technological Styles of Late Postclassic Slipped Pottery from the Central Petén Lakes Region, El Petén, Guatemala*. PhD dissertation, Department of Anthropology, Southern Illinois University.

Cecil, L. G., and H. Neff
2006 Postclassic Maya Slips and Paints and Their Relationship to Socio-Political Groups in El Petén, Guatemala. *Journal of Archaeological Science* 33(10): 1482–91.

Chang, K. C.
1986 *The Archaeology of Ancient China*. 4th ed. Yale University Press, New Haven, Connecticut.

Chapman, A. C.
1957 Port of Trade Enclaves in Aztec and Maya Civilizations. In *Trade and Market in Early Empires: Economies in History and Theory*, edited by K. Polanyi, C. M. Arensberg, and H. W. Pearson, 114–53. Free Press, Glencoe, IL.

Chase, A. F.
1979 Regional Development in the Tayasal–Paxcaman Zone, El Petén, Guatemala: A Preliminary Statement. *Ceramica de Cultura Maya et al.* 11:87–115.

1983 *A Contextual Consideration of the Tayasal-Paxcaman Zone, El Petén, Guatemala*. PhD dissertation, Department of Anthropology, University of Pennsylvania.

1984 Ceramic Complexes of the Tayasal–Paxcaman Zone, Lake Petén, Guatemala. *Ceramica de Cultura Maya* 13:27–41.

1985 Contextual Implications of Pictorial Vases from Tayasal, Petén. In *Fourth Palenque Round Table, 1980*, edited by E. P. Benson, 191–200. Pre-Columbian Art Research Institute, San Francisco.

1992 Elites and the Changing Organization of Classic Maya Society. In *Mesoamerican Elites: An Archaeological Assessment*, edited by D. Z. Chase and A. F. Chase, 30–49. University of Oklahoma Press, Norman.

Chase, A. F., and D. Z. Chase
1983 *The Ceramics of the Tayasal-Paxcaman Zone, El Petén, Guatemala*. Department of Anthropology, University of Pennsylvania, Philadelphia.

1992 Mesoamerican Elites: Assumptions, Definitions and Models. In *Mesoamerican Elites: An Archaeological Assessment*, edited by D. Z. Chase and A. F. Chase, 1–17. University of Oklahoma Press, Norman.

1996 More than Kin and King: Centralized Political Organization among the Late Classic Maya. *Current Anthropology* 37(5): 803–10.

2001 The Royal Court at Caracol, Belize: Its Palaces and People. In *Royal Courts of the Ancient Maya*, vol. 2, *Data and Case Studies*, edited by T. Inomata and S. Houston, 102–37. Westview Press, Boulder.

Chase, A. F., D. Z. Chase, and M. E. Smith
2009 States and Empires in Ancient Mesoamerica. *Ancient Mesoamerica* 20:175–82.

Chase, D. Z.
1986 Social and Political Organization in the Land of Cacao and Honey: Correlating the Archaeology and Ethnohistory of the Postclassic Lowland Maya. In *Late Lowland Maya Civilization*, edited by J. Sabloff and W. Andrews, 347–77. University of New Mexico Press, Albuquerque.

Chase, D. Z., and A. F. Chase
1989 Routes of Trade and Communication and the Integration of Maya Society: The Vista from Santa Rita Corozal, Belize. In *Coastal Maya Trade*, edited by H. McKillop and P. F. Healy, 19–32. Trent University Occasional Papers in Anthropology, Peterborough, Ontario.
1992 An Archaeological Assessment of Mesoamerican Elite. In *Mesoamerican Elites: An Archaeological Assessment*, edited by D. Z. Chase and A. F. Chase, 303–17. University of Oklahoma Press, Norman.
2004 Archaeological Perspectives on Ancient Maya Social Organization from Caracol, Belize. *Ancient Mesoamerica* 15(1): 139–47.

Chase, D. Z., A. F. Chase, and W. A. Haviland
1990 The Classic Maya City: Reconsidering the Mesoamerican Urban Tradition. *American Anthropologist* 92:499–506.

Cheetham, D., D. W. Forsyth, and J. E. Clark
1985 Contextual Implications of Pictorial Vases from Tayasal, Petén. In *Fourth Palenque Round Table, 1980*, edited by E. P. Benson, 191–200. Pre-Columbian Art Research Institute, San Francisco.
1992 Elites and the Changing Organization of Classic Maya Society. In *Mesoamerican Elites: An Archaeological Assessment*, edited by D. Z. Chase and A. F. Chase, 30–49. University of Oklahoma Press, Norman.
2003 La Cerámica Pre-Mamom de la Cuenca del Río Belice y del Centro de Petén: Las Correspondencias y sus Implicaciones. In *XVI Simposio de Investigaciones Arqueológicas en Guatemala, 2002*, edited by J. P. Laporte and H. Mejía, 615–34. Museo Nacional de Arqueología y Etnología, Guatemala City.

Childe, V. G.
1947 Archaeological Ages as Technological Stages. *Journal of the Royal Anthropological Institute* 74:7–24.
1951 *Social Evolution*. Watts, London.

Ciudad Ruiz, A.
2001 El Sistema Politico Hegemonico en el Sur de las Tierras Bajas Mayas a finales del Postclasico. *Anales de la Academia de Geografia e Historia de Guatemala* 76:191–238.

Claessen, H. J. M.
1984 The Internal Dynamics of the Early State. *Current Anthropology* 25(4): 365–79.

Clark, J. E.
1986 From Mountains to Molehills: A Critical Review of Teotihuacan's Obsidian Industry. In *Research in Economic Anthropology, Supplement 2: Economic Aspects of Prehispanic Highland Mexico*, edited by B. L. Isaac, 23–74. JAI Press, Greenwich, Connecticut.

1995 Craft Specialization as an Archaeological Category. *Research in Economic Anthropology* 16:267–94.

1997 The Arts of Government in Early Mesoamerica. *Annual Review of Anthropology* 26:211–34.

2007 In Craft Specialization's Penumbra: Things, Persons, Action, Value, and Surplus. In *Rethinking Craft Specialization in Complex Socities: Archaeological Analyses of the Social Meaning of Production*, edited by Z. X. Hruby and R. K. Flad, 20–36. Archaeological Papers of the American Anthropological Association, No. 17, Arlington, Virginia.

Clark, J. E., and S. Houston

1998 Craft Specialization, Gender, and Personhood among the Postconquest Maya of Yucatan. In *Craft and Social Identity*, edited by Cathy L. Costin and Rita Wright, 31–46. Archaeological Papers of the American Anthropological Association No. 8, Washington, D.C.

Clark, J. E., and W. J. Parry

1990 Craft Specialization and Cultural Complexity. In *Research in Economic Anthropology*, vol. 12, edited by B. Isaac, 289–346. JAI Press, Greenwich, Connecticut.

Clayton, Sarah C., W. David Driver, and Laura J. Kosakowsky

2005 Rubbish or Ritual? Contextualizing a Terminal Classic Problematical Deposit at Blue Creek, Belize: A Response to "Public Architecture, Ritual, and Temporal Dynamics at the Maya Center of Blue Creek, Belize." *Ancient Mesoamerica* 16:119–30.

Cliff, M. B., and C. J. Crane

1989 Changing Subsistence Economy at a Late Preclassic Maya Community. In *Prehistoric Maya Economies of Belize*, edited by P. A. McAnany and B. L. Isaac, 295–324. JAI Press, London.

Clutton-Brock, J., and N. Hammond

1994 Hot Dogs: Comestible Canids in Preclassic Maya Culture at Cuello, Belize. *Journal of Archaeological Sciences* 21:819–26.

Coe, M. D.

1973 *The Maya Scribe and His World*. The Grolier Club, New York.

1978 *Lords of the Underworld: Masterpieces of Classic Maya Ceramics*. Princeton University Press, Princeton.

Coe, M. D., and J. Kerr

1998 *The Art of the Maya Scribe*. Harry N. Abrams, New York.

Coe, W. R.

1965a Tikal, Guatemala and the Emergent Maya Civilization. *Science* 147:1401–19.

1965b Tikal: Ten Years of Study of a Maya Ruin in the Lowlands of Guatemala. *Expedition* 8(1): 5–56.

1967 *Tikal: A Handbook of the Ancient Maya Ruins*. University Museum, University of Pennsylvania, Philadelphia.

1990 *Excavations in the Great Plaza, North Terrace and North Acropolis of Tikal*. Tikal Report 14. The University Museum, University of Pennsylvania, Philadelphia.

Coggins, C. C.

1975 *Painting and Drawing Styles at Tikal: An Historical and Iconographic Reconstruction*. PhD dissertation, Harvard University.

1988 The Manikin Scepter: Emblem of Lineage. *Estudios de Cultura Maya* 17:123–58.

Coil, J., M. A. Korstanje, S. Archer, and C. A. Hastorf
2003 Laboratory Goals and Considerations for Multiple Microfossil Extraction in Archaeology. *Journal of Archaeological Science* 30:991–1008.

Cook, D. E., B. Kovacevich, T. Beach, and R. L. Bishop
2006 Deciphering the Inorganic Chemical Record of Ancient Human Activity Using ICP-MS: A Reconnaissance Study of the Late Classic Soil Floors at Cancuen, Guatemala. *Journal of Archaeological Science* 33:628–40.

Cook, S., and M. Diskin
1976 The Peasant Market Economy of the Valley of Oaxaca in Analysis and History. In *Markets in Oaxaca*, edited by Scott Cook and Martin Diskin, 6–25. University of Texas Press, Austin.

Corson, C.
1976 *Maya Anthropomorphic Figurines from Jaina Island, Campeche. Ballena Press Studies in Mesoamerican Art, Archaeology and Ethnohistory No. 1.* Ballena Press, Ramona, California.

Cortés, H.
1962 *Five Letters of Cortez to the Emperor.* Norton and Company, New York.

Costin, C. L.
1991 Craft Specialization: Issues in Defining, Documenting, and Explaining the Organization of Production. In *Archaeological Method and Theory*, vol. 3, edited by M. B. Schiffer, 1–56. University of Arizona Press, Tucson.
2001 Craft Production Systems. In *Archaeology at the Millennium: A Sourcebook*, edited by G. M. Feinman and T. D. Price, 273–344. Kluwer Academic/Plenum Publishers, New York.

Costin, C. L., and M. B. Hagstrum
1995 Standardization, Labor Investment, Skill, and the Organization of Ceramic Production in Late Prehispanic Highland Peru. *American Antiquity* 60(4): 619–39.

Costin, C. L., and R. P. Wright (editors)
1998 *Craft and Social Identity.* Archaeological Papers of the American Anthropological Association, No. 8, Arlington, Virginia.

Courty, M.-A., R. Macphail, and P. Goldberg
1989 *Soils and Micromorphology in Archaeology.* Cambridge University Press, Cambridge.

Cowgill, G. L.
1963 *Postclassic Period Culture in the Vicinity of Flores, Petén, Guatemala.* PhD dissertation, Department of Anthropology, Harvard University.

Crown, P. L.
1999 Socialization in American Southwest Pottery Decoration. In *Pottery and People: A Dynamic Interaction*, edited by J. M. Skibo and G. M. Feinman, 25–43. University of Utah Press, Salt Lake City.

Crown, P. L., and S. K. Fish
1996 Gender and Status in the Hohokam Pre-Classic to Classic Transition. *American Anthropologist* 98(4): 803–17.

Crumley, C. L.
1979 Three Locational Models: An Epistemological Assessment of Anthropology and Archaeology. In *Advances in Archaeological Method and Theory*, vol. 2, edited by M. B. Schiffer, 141–73. Academic Press, New York.

1995 Heterarchy and the Analysis of Complex Societies. In *Heterarchy and the Analysis of Complex Societies*, edited by R. M. Ehrenreich, C. L. Crumely, and J. E. Levy, 1–6. Archaeological Papers 6. American Anthropological Association, Arlington, Virginia.

2003 Alternative Forms of Societal Order. In *Heterarchy, Political Economy, and the Ancient Maya: The Three Rivers Region of the East Central Yucatan Peninsula*, edited by V. Scarborough, F. J. Valdez, and N. Dunning, 136–45. University of Arizona Press, Tucson.

Culbert, T. P.

1973 The Maya Downfall at Tikal. In *The Classic Maya Collapse*, edited by T. P. Culbert, 63–92. University of New Mexico Press, Albuquerque.

1979 *The Ceramics of Tikal: Eb, Tzec, Chuen, Cauac, Cimi, and Manik Complexes*. Manuscript on file, Department of Anthropology, University of Arizona, Tucson.

1988a The Collapse of Classic Maya Civilization. In *The Collapse of Ancient States and Civilizations*, edited by N. Yoffee and G. Cowgill, 69–101. University of Arizona Press, Tucson.

1988b Political History and the Decipherment of Maya Glyphs. *Antiquity* 62:135–52.

1991 Polities in the Northeast Petén, Guatemala. In *Classic Maya Political History: Hieroglyphic and Archaeological Evidence*, edited by T. P. Culbert, 128–46. Cambridge University Press, New York.

1993 *The Ceramics of Tikal: Vessels from Burials, Caches, and Problematical Deposits*. Tikal Report No. 25, Part A. University Museum Monograph 81. University of Pennsylvania Press, Philadelphia.

2003 The Ceramics of Tikal. In *Tikal: Dynasties, Foreigners & Affairs of State*, edited by J. A. Sabloff, 47–82. School of American Research Press, Santa Fe, New Mexico.

Culbert, T. P., and D. S. Rice (editors)

1990 *Precolumbian Population History in the Maya Lowlands*. University of New Mexico Press, Albuquerque.

Culbert, T. P., and L. A. Schwalbe

1987 X-Ray Fluorescence Survey of Tikal Ceramics. *Journal of Archaeological Science* 14:635–57.

Curtis, J. H., M. Brenner, D. A. Hodell, R. A. Balser, G. A. Islebe, and H. Hooghiemstra

1998 A Multi-Proxy Study of Holocene Environmental Change in the Maya Lowlands of Petén, Guatemala. *Journal of Paleolimnology* 19:139–59.

Dacus, C.

2005 *Weaving the Past: An Examination of Bones Buried with an Elite Maya Woman*. Unpublished master's thesis, Southern Methodist University.

Dahlin, B. H., A. P. Andrews, T. Beach, C. Bezanilla, P. Farrell, S. Luzzadder-Beach, and V. McCormick

1998 Punta Canbalam in Context: A Peripatetic Coastal Site in Northwest Campeche, Mexico. *Ancient Mesoamerica* 9:1–15.

Dahlin, B. H., D. Bair, T. Beach, M. Moriarty, and R. Terry

2009 The Dirt on Food: Ancient Feasts and Markets among the Lowland Maya. In *Pre-Columbian Foodways: Landscapes of Creation and Origin*, edited by J. E. Staller and M. B. Carrasco, 191–232. Springer, New York.

Dahlin, B. H., C. T. Jensen, R. E. Terry, D. R. Wright, and T. Beach

2007 In Search of an Ancient Maya Market. *Latin American Antiquity* 18(4): 363–85.

D'Altroy, T. N., and T. K. Earle
1985 State Finance, Wealth Finance, and Storage in the Inka Political Economy. *Current Anthropology* 26:187–206.

Davidson, D. A., S. P. Carter, and T. A. Quine
1992 An Evaluation of Micromorphology as an Aid to Archaeological Interpretation. *Geoarchaeology* 7:55–65.

Deal, M.
1998 *Pottery Ethnoarchaeology in the Central Maya Highlands.* University of Utah Press, Salt Lake City.

Deevey, E. S.
1978 Holocene Forests and Maya Disturbance Near Quexil Lake, Petén, Guatemala. *Polskie Archivum Hydrobiologii* 25:117–29.

1984 Stress, Strain, and Stability of Lacustrine Environments. In *Lake Sediments and Environmental History*, edited by E. Y. Haysworth and J. W. G. Lund, 203–29. Leicester University Press, Leicester.

Deevey, E. S., M. Brenner, and M. Binford
1983 Paleolimnology of the Petén Lake District, Guatemala. III. Late Pleistocene and Gamblian Environments of the Maya Area. *Hydrobiologia* 103:211–16.

Deevey, E. S., D. S. Rice, P. M. Rice, H. H. Vaughn, M. Brenner, and M. S. Flannery
1979 Mayan Urbanism: Impact on Tropical Karst Environment. *Science* 206:298–306.

de Freitas, H. A., L. C. R. Pessenda, R. Aravena, S. E. M. Gouveia, A. S. Ribeiro, and R. Boulet
2001 Late Quaternary Vegetation Dynamics in the Southern Amazon Basin Inferred from Carbon Isotopes in Organic Matter. *Quaternary Research* 55:39–46.

De Gruijter, J. J., and A. B. McBratney
1988 A Modified Fuzzy K-Means Method for Predictive Classification. In *Classification and Related Methods of Data Analysis*, edited by H. H. Bock, 97–104. Elsevier, Amsterdam.

Demarest, A. A.
1992 Ideology in Ancient Maya Cultural Evolution: The Dynamics of Galactic Polities. In *Ideology and Pre-Columbian Civilizations*, edited by A. A. Demarest y G. Conrad, 135–58. School of American Research Press, Santa Fe, New Mexico.

1996 Closing Comment to Forum on Theory in Anthropology, the Maya State: Centralized or Segmentary? *Current Anthropology* 37(5): 821–24.

1997 Vanderbilt Petexbatún Regional Archaeological Project, 1989–1994: Overview, History, and Major Results of a Multidisciplinary Study of the Classic Maya Collapse. *Ancient Mesoamerica* 8(2): 209–27.

Demarest, A., H. Escobedo, J. A. Valdés, S. Houston, L. Wright, and K. Emery
1991 Operación DP6A: Excavaciones en la Estructura L5-1 y la Tumba del Gobernante 2 de Dos Pilas. In *Proyecto Arqueológico Regional Petexbatún: Informe Preliminar #3, Tercera Temporada*, edited by A. Demarest, T. Inomata, J. Palka, and H. Escobedo, 37–68. Report submitted to the Institute of Anthropology and History, Guatemala City. Vanderbilt University, Nashville.

DeMarrais, E., L. J. Castillo, and T. Earle
1996 Ideology, Materialization and Power Strategies. *Current Anthropology* 37:15–31.

Deter-Wolf, A., and J. Charland

1998 Excavaciones de Prueba en el sitio Motul de San José. In *Proyecto Arqueológico Motul de San José Informe #1: Temporada de Campo 1998*, edited by A. Foias, 30–62. Report submitted to the Institute of Anthropology and History, Guatemala City. Williams College, Williamstown, Massachusetts.

Diaz del Castillo, B.

1956 *The Discovery and Conquest of Mexico, 1517–1521*. Farrar, Strauss and Cudahy, New York.

Dietler, M.

1996 Feasts and Commensal Politics in the Political Economy: Food, Power and Status in Prehistoric Europe. In *Food and the Status Quest*, edited by P. Wiessner and W. Shieffenhovel, 87–125. Berghahn Books, Providence, Rhode Island.

Dimbleby, G. W.

1957 Pollen Analysis of Terrestrial Soils. *New Phytologist* 56:12–28.

Dobres, M.-A.

2000 *Technology and Social Agency*. Blackwell, Oxford.

Dobres, M.-A., and C. R. Hoffman

1994 Social Agency and Dynamics of Prehistoric Technology. *Journal of Archaeological Method and Theory* 1:211–58.

Domhoff, G. W.

1990 *The Power Elite and the State: How Policy Is Made in America*. Aldine de Gruyter, Hawthorne, New York.

2010 Who Rules America: Wealth, Income, and Power. Webpage: www2.ucsc.edu/whorulesamerica/power/wealth.html.

Doucette, D. L.

2003 *Unraveling Middle Archaic Expressions: A Multidisciplinary Approach towards Feature and Material Culture Recognition in Southeastern New England*. PhD dissertation, Harvard University.

Doyle, M. W.

1986 *Empires*. Cornell University Press, Ithaca, New York.

Drapkin, J., and M. D. Moriarty

2002 Descripciones de los Monumentos de Akte. In *Proyecto Arqueologico Motul de San José Informe #5: Temporada de Campo 2002*, edited by M. D. Moriarty, 23–25. Report presented to the Institute of Anthropology and History, Guatemala. Department of Anthropology, Tulane University, New Orleans.

Drennan, R. D.

1984a Long-Distance Movement of Goods in the Mesoamerican Formative and Classic. *American Antiquity* 49:27–43.

1984b Long-Distance Transport Costs in Pre-Hispanic Mesoamerica. *American Anthropologist* 86:105–12.

Driver, W. D., and J. F.Garber

2004 The Emergence of Minor Centers in the Zones between Seats of Power. In *The Ancient Maya of the Belize Valley: Half a Century of Archaeological Research*, edited by J. F. Garber, 287–304. University Press of Florida, Gainesville.

Dunning, N. P.

1993 Ancient Maya Anthrosols: Soil Phosphate Testing and Land Use. In *Proceedings of the First International Conference on Pedo-Archaeology*, vol. 93–03, edited by John E. Foss,

M. E. Timpson, and M. W. Morris, 203–11. University of Tennessee Special Publication, Knoxville.

Dunning, N. P., and T. Beach

2000 Stability and Instability in Prehispanic Maya Landscapes. In *Imperfect Balance*, edited by D. Lentz, 179–202. Columbia University Press, New York.

2010 Farms and Forests: Spatial and Temporal Perspectives on Ancient Maya Landscapes. In *Landscapes and Societies*, edited by I. P. Martini and Ward Chesworth, 369–89. Springer-Verlag, Amsterdam.

Dunning, N. P., S. Luzzadder-Beach, T. Beach, J. G. Jones, V. Scarborough, and T. P. Culbert

2002 Arising from the *Bajos:* The Evolution of a Neotropical Landscape and the Rise of Maya Civilization. *Annals of the Association of American Geographers* 92:267–83.

Dunning, N., V. Scarborough, F. Valdez Jr., S. Luzzadder-Beach, T. Beach, and J. John

1999 Temple Mountains, Sacred Lakes, and Fertile Fields: Ancient Maya Landscapes in Northwestern Belize. *Antiquity* 73(281): 650–60.

Dwyer, P. D.

1996 The Invention of Nature. In *Redefining Nature: Ecology, Culture, and Domestication*, edited by R. F. Ellen and K. Fukui, 157–86. Berg, Oxford.

Earle, T.

1977 Reappraisal of Redistribution: Complex Hawaiian Chiefdoms. In *Exchange Systems in Prehistory*, edited by T. Earle, 213–29. Academic Press, New York.

1987 Specialization and the Production of Wealth: Hawaiian Chiefdoms and the Inka Empire. In *Specialization, Exchange, and Complex Societies*, edited by E. M. Brumfiel and T. K. Earle, 64–75. Cambridge University Press, Cambridge.

1997 *How Chiefs Come to Power: The Political Economy in Prehistory*. Stanford University Press, Stanford.

2001 Institutionalization of Chiefdoms: Why Landscapes are Built. In *From Leaders to Rulers*, edited by J. Haas, 105–24. Kluwer Academic/Plenum, New York.

2002 Commodity Flows and the Evolution of Complex Societies. In *Theory in Economic Anthropology*, edited by J. Ensminger, 81–104. AltaMira Press, Walnut Creek, California.

2004 Culture Matters in the Neolithic Transition and Emergence of Hierarchy in Thy, Denmark, Distinguished Lecture. *American Anthropologist* 106(1): 111–25.

Eberl, M.

2007 *Community Heterogeneity and Integration: The Maya Sites of Nacimiento, Dos Ceibas, and Cerro de Cheyo (El Petén, Guatemala) During the Late Classic*. PhD dissertation, Department of Anthropology, Tulane University.

Ehleringer, J. R.

1991 $^{13}C/^{12}C$ Fractionation and Its Utility in Terrestrial Plant Studies. In *Carbon Isotope Techniques*, edited by D. C. Coleman and B. Fry, 187–200. Academic Press, San Diego, California.

Ehrenreich, R. M., C. L. Crumley, and J. E. Levy (editors)

1995 *Heterarchy and the Analysis of Complex Societies*. Archaeological Papers of the American Anthropological Association No. 6. American Anthropological Association, Washington, D.C.

Eisenstadt, S. N.

1993 *The Political Systems of Empires*. 2nd ed. Transaction Publishers, New Brunswick.

Ekholm, S. M.

1979a The Lagartero Figurines. In *Maya Archaeology and Ethnohistory*, edited by N. Hammond and G. R. Willey, 172–86. University of Texas Press, Austin.

1979b The Significance of an Extraordinary Maya Ceremonial Refuse Deposit at Lagartero, Chiapas. *Proceedings of the International Congress of Americanists* 8(8): 147–59.

1985 The Lagartero Ceramic "Pendants." In *The Fourth Palenque Round Table, 1980*, vol. 7, edited by M. G. Robertson and E. P. Benson, 211–19. Pre-Columbian Art Research Institute, San Francisco.

1990 Una Ceremonia de Fin-de-Ciclo: el gran basurero ceremonial de Lagartero, Chiapas. In *La Epoca clásica—nuevo hallazgos, nuevas ideas*, edited by A. Cardós de Méndez, 455–67. Museo Nacional de Arqueología, Mexico City.

Elson, C. M., and R. A. Covey (editors)

2006 *Intermediate Elites in Pre-Columbian States and Empires*. University of Arizona Press, Tucson.

Emerson, T. E.

1997 *Cahokia and the Archaeology of Power*. University of Alabama Press, Tuscaloosa.

Emery, K. F.

1998a Investigaciones Ecologicas de 1998: Ecología y Medioambiente de Motul de San José: Estudios Preliminares y Futuros. In *Proyecto Arqueológico Motul de San José Informe #1, Temporada de Campo 1998*, edited by A. E. Foias, 64–75. Report presented to the Institute of Anthropology and History, Guatemala City. Williams College, Williamstown, Massachusetts.

1998b *Proyecto Motul de San José, Sub-Proyecto de Ecologia: Protocol for Environmental Sampling*. SUNY, Potsdam. Manuscript on file with the author.

2001 Investigaciones ecologicas preliminares del medioambiente antiquo de Motul de San José. In *Proyecto Arqueológico Motul de San José Informe # 4: Temporada De Campo 2001*, edited by A. E. Foias, 108–35. Report presented to the Institute of Anthropology and History, Guatemala City. Williams College, Williamstown, Massachusetts.

2002 Evidencia temprana de explotación animal en el altiplano de Guatemala. *Utz'ib* 3(2): 1–16.

2003a Natural Resource Use and Classic Maya Economics: Environmental Archaeology at Motul de San José, Guatemala. *Mayab* 16:33–48.

2003b The Noble Beast: Status and Differential Access to Animals in the Maya World. *World Archaeology* 34(3): 498–515.

2004a Animals from the Maya Underworld: Reconstructing Elite Maya Ritual at the Cueva de los Quetzales, Guatemala. In *Behaviour behind Bones: The Zooarchaeology of Religion, Ritual, Status and Identity*, edited by S. Jones O'Day, W. Van Neer, and A. Ervynck, 101–13. Oxbow Books, Oxford.

2004b Environments of the Maya Collapse: A Zooarchaeological Perspective from the Petexbatún. In *Maya Zooarchaeology: New Directions in Method and Theory*, edited by K. F. Emery, 81–95. Institute of Archaeology, UCLA Press, Los Angeles.

2004c In Search of Assemblage Comparability: Methods in Maya Zooarchaeology. In *Maya Zooarchaeology: New Directions in Method and Theory*, edited by K. F. Emery, 15–34. Institute of Archaeology, UCLA Press, Los Angeles.

2004d In Search of the "Maya" Diet: Is Regional Comparison Possible in the Maya Area? *Archaeofauna* 13:37–56.

2004e Maya Zooarchaeology: In Pursuit of Social Variability and Environmental Heterogeneity. In *Continuity and Contention: Maya Archaeology at the Millennium*, edited by C. Golden and G. Borgstede, 217–41. Routledge Press, New York.

2006 Definiendo el aprovechamiento de la fauna por la elite: evidencia en Aguateca y otros sitios de Petexbatún, Guatemala. *Utz'ib* 4(1): 1–16.

2007a Aprovechamiento de la fauna en Piedras Negras: dieta, ritual y artesanía del periodo Clásico Maya. *Mayab* 19:51–69.

2007b Assessing the Impact of Ancient Maya Animal Use. *Journal of Nature Conservation* 15(3): 184–95.

2009 Maya Bone Crafting: Defining the Nature of a Late/Terminal Classic Maya Bone Tool Manufacturing Locus. *Journal of Anthropological Archaeology* 28:458–70.

2010 *Dietary, Environmental, and Societal Implications of Ancient Maya Animal Use in the Petexbatún: A Zooarchaeological Perspective on the Collapse.* Vanderbilt University Press, Nashville.

Emery, K. F., and K. Aoyama

2007 Bone Tool Manufacturing in Elite Maya Households at Aguateca, Guatemala. *Ancient Mesoamerica* 18(2): 69–89.

Emery, K. F., and L. A. Brown

2008 *Ethnoarchaeological Studies of Animal Material Disposal Patterns in the Southern Maya Lowlands and Implications for Maya Zooarchaeology.* Paper presented at the Society for American Archaeology Meetings, Vancouver, B.C.

Emery, K., and G. Higginbotham

1998 Excavaciones en una Plazuela Elite del Epicentro. In *Proyecto Arqueológico Motul de San José Informe #1: Temporada de Campo 1998*, edited by A. Foias, 16–29. Report submitted to Institute of Anthropology and History, Guatemala. Williams College, Williamstown, Massachusetts.

Emery, K. F., and E. K. Thornton

2008a *Reporte Preliminar Sobre los Restos Animales Procedente del Sitio de La Joyanca, Petén, Guatemala.* Report submitted to the Institute of Anthropology and History, Guatemala City. Florida Museum of Natural History, University of Florida, Gainesville, Florida.

2008b Zooarchaeological Habitat Analysis of Ancient Maya Landscape Changes. *Journal of Ethnobiology* 28(2): 154–79.

In press Tracking Climate Change in the Ancient Maya World through Zooarchaeological Habitat Analyses. In *The Great Maya Droughts in Cultural Context*, edited by G. Iannone. University Press of Colorado, Boulder.

Emery, K. F., E. K. Thornton, N. C. Cannarozzi, S. Houston, and H. Escobedo

In press Ancient Animals of the Southern Maya Highlands: Zooarchaeology of Kaminaljuyu. In *Archaeology of Ancient Mesoamerican Animals*, edited by C. Götz and K. F. Emery. Lockwood Press, Atlanta.

Eppich, K.

2007 Death and Veneration at El Perú-Waka': Structure M14–15 as Ancestor Shrine. *PARI Journal* 8(1): 1–16.

Estrada Belli, F., A. Tokovinine, J. Foley, H. Hurst, G. A. Ware, D. Stuart, and N. Grube

2009 A Maya Palace at Holmul, Petén, Guatemala and the Teotihuacan "entrada": Evidence from Murals 7 and 9. *Latin American Antiquity* 20(1): 228–59.

Fash, B. W., and W. L. Fash

2007 The Roles of Ballgames in Mesoamerican Ritual Economy. In *Mesoamerican Ritual Economy: Archaeological and Ethnological Perspectives*, edited by E. C. Wells and K. L. Davis-Salazar, 267–84. University Press of Colorado, Boulder.

Fash, B., W. Fash, S. Lane, R. Larios, L. Schele, J. Stomper, and D. Stuart

1992 Investigations of a Classic Maya Council House at Copán, Honduras. *Journal of Field Archaeology* 19:419–42.

Fash, W. L.

1991 *Scribes, Warriors and Kings: The City of Copán and the Ancient Maya*. Thames and Hudson, London.

Fedick, S. (editor)

1996 *The Managed Mosaic: Ancient Maya Agriculture and Resource Use*. University of Utah Press, Salt Lake City.

Fedick, S., and A. Ford

1990 The Prehistoric Agricultural Landscape of the Central Maya Lowlands: An Examination of Local Variability in a Regional Context. *World Archaeology* 22(1): 18–33.

Feinman, G. M.

1998 Scale and Social Organization: Perspectives on the Archaic State. In *Archaic States*, edited by G. M. Feinman and J. Marcus, 95–133. School of American Research, Santa Fe, New Mexico.

1999 Rethinking our Assumptions: Economic Specialization at the Household Scale in Ancient Ejutla, Oaxaca, Mexico. In *Pottery and People: A Dynamic Interaction*, edited by J. M. Skibo and G. M. Feinman, 81–98. University of Utah Press, Salt Lake City.

Feinman, G. M., and L. M. Nicholas

2000 High-Intensity Household-Scale Production in Ancient Mesoamerica: A Perspective from Ejutla, Oaxaca. In *Cultural Evolution: Contemporary Viewpoints*, edited by G. M. Feinman and L. Manzanilla, 119–42. Kluwer Academic/Plenum Publishers, New York.

2004 Unraveling the Prehispanic Highland Mesoamerican Economy: Production, Exchange, and Consumption in the Classic Period Valley of Oaxaca. In *Archaeological Perspectives on Political Economies*, edited by G. M. Feinman and L. M. Nicholas, 167–88. University of Utah Press, Salt Lake City.

Feinman, G. M., S. Upham, and K. G. Lightfoot

1981 The Production Step Measure: An Ordinal Index of Labor Input in Ceramic Manufacture. *American Antiquity* 46(4): 871–84.

Feldman, L.

1985 *A Tumpline Economy: Production and Distribution Systems in the 16th-Century Eastern Guatemala*. Labyrinthos, Culver City, California.

Fernández, F. G.

2002 *Chemical and Physical Properties of Anthrosols in Rural Areas near the Ancient Maya City of Piedras Negras, Guatemala*. Unpublished master's thesis, Brigham Young University.

Fernández, F. G., K. D. Johnson, R. E. Terry, S. Nelson, and D. Webster

2005 Soil Resources of the Ancient Maya at Piedras Negras, Guatemala. *Soil Science Society of America Journal* 69:2020–32.

Fernández, F. G., R. E. Terry, T. Inomata, and M. Eberl

2002 An Ethnoarchaeological Study of Chemical Residues in the Floors and Soils of Q'eqchi' Maya Houses at Las Pozas, Guatemala. *Geoarchaeology* 17:487–519.

Fitzsimmons, James L., Laura Gámez, and Mélanie Forné

2006 Epigrafía y arqueológia de Hix Witz: Investigaciones en Zapote Bobal, La Libertad, Péten. In *XX Simposio de Investigaciones Arqueologicos en Guatemala*, edited by J. P. Laporte and B. Arroyo, 293–306. Museo Nacional de Arqueología y Etnología, Guatemala City.

Flad, R. K.

2007 Rethinking the Context of Production through an Archaeological Study of Ancient Salt Production in the Sichuan Basin, China. In *Rethinking Craft Specialization in Complex Socities: Archaeological Analyses of the Social Meaning of Production*, edited by Z. X. Hruby and R. K. Flad, 108–28. Archaeological Papers of the American Anthropological Association, No. 17, Arlington, Virginia.

Flad, R. K., and Z. X. Hruby

2007 "Specialized" Production in Archaeological Contexts: Rethinking Specialization, the Social Value of Products, and the Practice of Production. In *Rethinking Craft Specialization in Complex Socities: Archaeological Analyses of the Social Meaning of Production*, edited by Z. X. Hruby and R. K. Flad, 1–19. Archaeological Papers of the American Anthropological Association, No. 17, Arlington, Virginia.

Foias, A. E.

1996 *Changing Ceramic Production and Exchange Systems and the Classic Maya Collapse in the Petexbatún Region, Petén, Guatemala.* PhD dissertation, Department of Anthropology, Vanderbilt University.

1998 (editor) *Proyecto Arqueológico Motul de San José Informe Preliminar #1: Temporada de Campo 1998.* Report submitted to the Institute of Anthropology and History, Guatemala City. Williams College, Williamstown, Massachusetts.

1999 Introduccion: Entre la Politica y Economia: Proyecto Arqueologico Motul de San José. In *Proyecto Arqueológico Motul de San José Informe # 2: Temporada De Campo 1999*, edited by A. E. Foias, 1–16. Report submitted to the Institute of Anthropology and History, Guatemala City. Williams College, Williamstown, Massachusetts.

2000a Entre la Politica y Economia: Resultados Preliminares de las Primeras Dos Temporadas del Proyecto Arqueologico Motul de San José. In *XIII Simposio de Investigaciones Arqueologicas en Guatemala*, edited by J. P. Laporte, H. L. Escobedo, A. C. de Suasnavar, and B. Arroyo, 945–73. Ministerio de Cultura y Deportes, IDAEH, Associacion Tikal, Guatemala City.

2000b *History, Politics, and Economics at Motul de San José.* Paper presented at the 2000 Maya Hieroglyphic Meetings (Linda Schele Hieroglyphic Weekend), University of Texas, Austin, Williamstown, Massachusetts.

2001 (editor) *Proyecto Arqueológico Motul de San José Informe Preliminar # 4: Temporada de Campo 2001.* Report submitted to the Institute of Anthropology and History, Guatemala City. Williams College, Williamstown, Massachusetts.

2002 At the Crossroads: The Economic Basis of Political Power in the Petexbatún Region. In *Ancient Maya Political Economies*, edited by M. Masson and D. Freidel, 223–48. AltaMira Press, Oxford.

2003 Perspectivas Teóricas en las Dinámicas del Estado Clasico Maya: Resultados Preliminares del Proyecto Arqueológico Motul de San José 1998–2001. *Mayab* 16:15–32.

2004 The Past and Future of Maya Ceramic Studies. In *Continuities and Changes in Maya Archaeology: Perspectives at the Millennium*, edited by Charles Golden and Greg Borgstede, 143–75. Routledge Press, New York.

2007 Ritual, Politics and Pottery Economies in the Classic Maya Southern Lowlands. In *Mesoamerican Ritual Economy: Archaeological and Ethnological Perspectives*, edited by E. Christian Wells and Karla L. Davis-Salazar, 167–94. University of Colorado Press, Boulder.

Forthcoming *Ancient Maya Political Dynamics*. University Press of Florida, Gainesville.

Foias, A. E., and R. L. Bishop

1997 Changing Ceramic Production and Exchange in the Petexbatún Region, Guatemala: Reconsidering the Classic Maya Collapse. *Ancient Mesoamerica* 8:275–91.

2005 Fine Paste Wares and the Terminal Classic in the Petexbatún and Pasion Regions, Petén, Guatemala. In *Geographies of Power: Understanding the Nature of Terminal Classic Pottery in the Maya Lowlands*, edited by S. L. López Varela and A. Foias, 23–40. British Archaeological Reports (BAR) International Series No. 1447. Archaeopress, Oxford.

2007 Pots, Sherds, and Glyphs: Pottery Production and Exchange in the Petexbatún Polity, Petén, Guatemala. In *Pottery Economics in Mesoamerica*, edited by C. A. Pool and G. J. Bey III, 212–36. University of Arizona Press, Tucson.

Foias, A. E., and J. Castellanos (editors)

2000 *Proyecto Arqueológico Motul de San José Informe #3: Temporada de Campo 2000*. Report submitted to the Institute of Anthropology and History, Guatemala City. Williams College, Williamstown, Massachusetts.

Foias, A., M. Foster, and E. Spensley

2000 Excavaciones en la Estructura Oeste del Groupo D: Operacion MSJ15A. In *Proyecto Arqueológico Motul de San José Informe #3: Temporada de Campo 2000*, edited by A. Foias and J. Castellanos, 29–52. Report submitted to the Institute of Anthropology and History, Guatemala City. Williams College, Williamstown, Massachusetts.

Foias, A. E., C. Ryan, E. Spensley, C. Warren, A. Lapin, and T. Morales

1999 Excavacion de una Residencia Elite en el Grupo D. In *Proyecto Arqueológico Motul de San José Informe Preliminar # 2: Temporada de Campo 1999*, edited by A. Foias, 35–46. Report submitted to the Institute of Anthropology and History, Guatemala City. Williams College, Williamstown, Massachusetts.

Folan, W. J., L. A. Fletcher, and E. R. Kintz

1979 Fruit, Fiber, Bark, and Resin: Social Organization of a Maya Urban Center. *Science* 204(4394): 697–701.

Folan, W. J., J. D. Gunn, and M. del Rosario Dominguez Carrasco

2001 Triadic Temples, Central Plazas and Dynastic Palaces: A Diachronic Analysis of the Royal Court Complex, Calakmul, Campeche, Mexico. In *Royal Court of the Ancient Maya, Volume 2: Data and Case Studies*, edited by T. Inomata and S. D. Houston, 223–65. Westview Press, Boulder, Colorado.

Folan, W. J., E. R. Kintz, and L. A. Fletcher

1983 *Cobá: A Classic Maya Metropolis*. Academic Press, New York.

Ford, A.

1986 *Population Growth and Social Complexity: An Examination of Settlement and Environment in the Central Maya Lowlands*. Anthropological Research Paper No. 35. Arizona State University, Tempe.

1991 Economic Variation of Ancient Maya Residential Settlement in the Upper Belize River Area. *Ancient Mesoamerica* 2:35–46.

1992 The Ancient Maya Domestic Economy: An Examination of Settlement in the Upper Belize River Area. In *Memorias del Primer Congreso Internacional de Mayistas: Mesas Redondas, Arqueologia, Epigrafia*, edited by S. Reyes Coria, 143–56. UNAM, Instituto de Investigaciones Filologicas, Mexico City.

1996 Critical Resource Control and the Rise of the Classic Period Maya. In *The Managed Mosaic: Ancient Maya Agriculture and Resource Use*, edited by S. L. Fedick, 297–303. University of Utah Press, Salt Lake City.

2004 Integration among Communities, Center, and Regions: The Case from El Pilar. In *The Ancient Maya of the Belize Valley: Half a Century of Archaeological Research*, edited by J. F. Garber, 238–56. University Press of Florida, Gainesville.

2008 Dominant Plants of the Maya Forest and Gardens of El Pilar: Implications for Paleoenvironmental Reconstructions. *Journal of Ethnobiology* 28:179–99.

Ford, A., and K. F. Emery

2008 Exploring the Legacy of the Maya forest. *Journal of Ethnobiology* 28:147–53.

Ford, A., and R. B. Nigh

2009 Origins of the Maya Forest Garden: A Resource Management System. *Journal of Ethnobiology* 29(2): 213–36.

Forsyth, D. W.

1989 *The Ceramics of El Mirador, Petén, Guatemala. El Mirador Series, Part 4*. Papers of the New World Archaeological Foundation, No. 63. Brigham Young University, Provo, Utah.

1992 Un Estudio Comparativo de la Cerámica Temprana de Nakbe, Petén. In *IV Simposio de Investigaciones Arqueológicas en Guatemala, 1990*, edited by J. P. Laporte, H. Escobedo, and S. Brady, 38–49. Museo Nacional de Arqueología y Etnología, Guatemala City.

1993a The Ceramic Sequence at Nakbe, Guatemala. *Ancient Mesoamerica* 4(1): 31–53.

1993b Cerámica arqueológica de Nakbe y El Mirador. In *III Simposio de Investigaciones Arqueológicas en Guatemala, 1989, Museo Nacional de Arqueología y Etnología*, edited by J. P. Laporte, H. Escobedo, and S. Villagrán, 85–112. Ministerio de Cultura y Deportes, Instituto de Antropología e Historia, Guatemala City.

1996 La Secuencia Cerámica de la Isla Flores, Petén. *Mayab* 10:5–14.

Foucault, M.

1979 *Discipline and Punish: The Birth of the Prison*. Translated by Alan Sheridan. Vintage Books, New York.

1991 Governmentality. In *The Foucault Effect: Studies in Governmentality*, edited by G. Burchell, C. Gordon, and P. Miller, 87–104. University of Chicago Press, Chicago.

Fox, J. G.

1996 Playing with Power: Ballcourts and Political Ritual in Southern Mesoamerica. *Current Anthropology* 37(3): 483–509.

Fox, J. W.

1987 *Maya Post-Classic State Formation: Segmentary Lineage Migration in Advancing Frontiers*. Cambridge University Press, Cambridge.

1989 On the Rise and Fall of "Tulans" and Maya Segmentary States. *American Anthropologist* 91:656–81.

Fox, J. W., G. W. Cook, A. F. Chase, and D. Z. Chase
1996 Questions of Political and Economic Integration: Segmentary versus Centralized States among the Ancient Maya. *Current Anthropology* 37(5): 795–801.

Fox, R. G.
1977 *Urban Anthropology: Cities in their Cultural Settings.* Prentice Hall, Englewood Cliffs, New Jersey.

Fradkin, A., and H. S. Carr
2003 Middle Preclassic Landscapes and Aquatic Resource Use at Cuello, Belize. *Bulletin of the Florida Museum of Natural History* 44:35–42.

Fredlund, G.
1986 Problems in the Simultaneous Extraction of Pollen and Phytoliths from Clastic Sediments. In *Plant Opal Phytolith Analysis in Archaeology and Paleoecology*, vol. 1, edited by I. Rovner, 102–10. Occasional Papers of the Phytolitharien, Raleigh, North Carolina.

Freidel, D. A.
1981 The Political Economics of Residential Dispersion among the Lowland Maya. In *Lowland Maya Settlement Patterns*, edited by W. Ashmore, 371–82. University of New Mexico Press, Albuquerque.
1986 Maya Warfare: An Example of Peer Polity Interaction. In *Peer Polity Interaction and Socio-Political Change*, edited by C. Renfrew and J. F. Cherry, 93–108. Cambridge University Press, Cambridge.

Freidel, D. A., K. Reese-Taylor, and D. Mora-Marin
2002 The Origins of Maya Civilization: The Old Shell Game, Commodity, Treasure and Kingship. In *Ancient Maya Political Economies*, edited by M. Masson and D. Freidel, 41–86. AltaMira Press, Oxford.

Freidel, D. A., and J. A. Sabloff
1984 *Cozumel: Late Maya Settlement Patterns.* Academic Press, New York.

Freter, A. C.
1996 Rural Utilitarian Ceramic Production in the Late Classic Period Copán Maya State. In *Arqueologia Mesoamericana: Homenaje a William T. Sanders*, vol. 2, edited by G. Mastache, M. C. Sera, J. Parsons, R. Santley, and R. Diehl, 209–29. INAH, Mexico City.
2004 Multiscalar Model of Rural Households in Late Classic Copan Maya Society. *Ancient Mesoamerica* 15(1): 93–106.

Fried, M. H.
1967 *The Evolution of Political Society: An Essay in Political Anthropology.* Random House, New York.

Fry, R. E.
1979 The Economics of Pottery at Tikal: Models of Exchange for Serving Vessels. *American Antiquity* 44(3): 494–512.
1980 Models of Exchange for Major Shape Classes of Lowland Maya Pottery. In *Models and Methods in Regional Exchange*, edited by R. E. Fry, 3–18. SAA Papers No. 1, Washington, D.C.
1981 Pottery Production—Distribution Systems in the Southern Maya Lowlands. In *Production and Distribution: A Ceramic Viewpoint*, edited by H. Howard and E. Morris, 145–67. BAR International Series 120, Oxford.

Fry, R. E., and S. C. Cox

1974 The Structure of Ceramic Exchange at Tikal, Guatemala. *World Archaeology* 6:209–25.

Fynn, R. W. S., R. J. Haynes, and T. G. O. Conner

2003 Burning Causes Long-Term Changes in Soil Organic Matter Content of a South African Grassland. *Soil Biology and Biochemistry* 35:677–87.

Gallegos Gómora, M. J.

2003 Mujeres y hombres de barro: Figurillas de Comalcalco. *Arqueologia Mexicana* 11(61): 48–51.

Gámez, L. L.

2006 Salvamento Arqueológico en el Area Central de Petén: Nuevos Resultados sobre la Conformación y Evolución del Asentamiento Prehispánico en la Isla de Flores. In *XX Simposio de Investigaciones Arqueológicas en Guatemala, 2006*, edited by J. P. Laporte, B. Arroyo, and H. E. Mejia, 229–39. Ministerio de Cultura y Deportes, IDAEH, Asociacion Tikal, NWAF, Guatemala City.

Garraty, C. P.

2000 Ceramic Indexes of Aztec Eliteness. *Ancient Meoamerica* 11:323–40.

Gé, T., M.-A. Courty, W. Matthews, and J. Wattez

1993 Sedimentary Formation Processes of Occupation Surfaces. In *Formation Processes in Archaeological Context*, edited by P. Goldberg, D. T. Nash, and M. D. Petraglia, 149–63. Prehistory Press, Madison, Wisconsin.

Geertz, C.

1980 *Negara: The Theater State in Nineteenth-Century Bali*. Princeton University Press, Princeton.

Gero, J. M., and M. C. Scattolin

2002 Beyond Complementarity and Hierarchy: New Definitions for Archaeological Gender Relations. In *In Pursuit of Gender: Worldwide Archaeological Approaches*, edited by S. M. Nelson and M. Rosen-Ayalon, 155–71. AltaMira Press, Walnut Creek, California.

Giddens, A.

1979 *Central Problems in Social Theory: Action, Structure, and Contradiction in Social Analysis*. University of California Press, Berkeley.

1984 *The Constitution of Society*. University of California Press, Berkeley.

Giddens Teeter, W.

2004 Animal Utilization in a Growing City: Vertebrate Exploitation at Caracol, Belize. In *Maya Zooarchaeology: New Directions in Method and Theory*, edited by K. F. Emery, 177–91. Institute of Archaeology, UCLA Press, Los Angeles.

Gifford, J. C.

1960 The Type-Variety Method of Ceramic Classification as an Indicator of Cultural Phenomena. *American Antiquity* 25(3): 341–47.

1976 Prehistoric Pottery Analysis and the Ceramics of Barton Ramie in the Belize Valley. *Memoirs of the Peabody Museum of Archaeology and Ethnology*, vol. 18. Harvard University, Cambridge, Massachusetts.

Gillespie, S. D.

2000 Rethinking Ancient Maya Social Organization: Replacing "Lineage" with "House." *American Anthropologist* 102(3): 467–84.

Glaser, B.

2005 Compound-Specific Stable-Isotope ($\delta^{13}C$) Analysis in Soil Science. *Journal of Plant Nutrition and Soil Science* 168:633–48.

Goffer, Z.

1980 *Archeological Chemistry*. John Wiley and Sons, New York.

Goldberg, P.

1983 Applications of Micromorphology in Archaeology. In *Soil Micromorphology*, edited by P. Bullock and C. P. Murphy, 139–50. Academic Publishers, Berkhamstead.

Goldberg, P., and S. C. Sherwood

1994 Micromorphology of Dust Cave Sediments: Some Preliminary Results. *Journal of Alabama Archaeology* 40:57–65.

Goldberg, P., and R. I. Macphail

2006 *Practical and Theoretical Geoarchaeology*. Blackwell, Malden, Massachusetts.

Goldberg, P., and I. Whitbread

1993 Micromorphological Study of a Bedouin Tent Floor. In *Formation Processes in Archaeological Context*, edited by Paul Goldberg, David T. Nash, and Michael D. Petraglia, 165–88. Prehistory Press, Madison, Wisconsin.

Golden, C., and G. Borgstede (editors)

2004 *Continuities and Changes in Maya Archaeology: Perspectives at the Millennium*. Routledge, New York.

Goldstein, M. M.

1979 *Maya Figurines from Campeche, Mexico: Classification on the Basis of Clay Chemistry, Style and Iconography*. PhD dissertation, Department of Anthropology, Columbia University.

Gómez-Pompa, A., and A. Kaus

1990 Traditional Management of Tropical Forests in Mexico. In *Alternatives to Deforestation: Steps towards Sustainable Use of the Amazon Rain Forest*, edited by A. Anderson, 45–64. Columbia University Press, New York.

Gonlin, N.

1993 *Rural Household Archaeology at Copán, Honduras*. PhD dissertation, Pennsylvania State University.

1994 Rural Household Diversity in Late Classic Copán, Honduras. In *Archaeological Views from the Countryside: Village Communities in Early Complex Societies*, edited by G. M. Schwartz and S. E. Falconer, 177–97. Smithsonian Institution Press, Washington, D.C.

Goodrich, C., and H. van der Schalie

1937 *Mollusca of Petén and North Alta Vera Paz, Guatemala*. University of Michican Museum of Zoology Miscellaneous Publications, No. 34. University of Michigan Press, Ann Arbor.

Gordon, E. A.

1993 Screen Size and Differential Faunal Recovery: A Hawaiian Example. *Journal of Field Archaeology* 20:453–60.

Goren, Y., and P. Goldberg

1991 Petrographic Thin Sections and the Development of Neolithic Plaster Production in Northern Israel. *Journal of Field Archaeology* 18:131–38.

Graham, E.

1987 Resource Diversity in Belize and Its Implications for Models of Lowland Trade. *American Antiquity* 52:753–67.

1989 Brief Synthesis of Coastal Site Data from Colson Point, Placencia, and Marco Gonzalez, Belize. In *Coastal Maya Trade*, edited by Heather McKillop and Paul F. Healy, 135–54. Occasional Papers in Anthropology, No. 8. Trent University, Peterborough, Ontario.

1998 Metaphor and Metamorphism: Some Thoughts on Environmental Metahistory. In *Advances in Historical Ecology*, edited by W. Balee, 119–37. Columbia University Press, New York.

1999 Stone Cities, Green Cities. In *Complex Polities in the Ancient Tropical World*, edited by E. A. Bacus and L. J. Lucero, 185–94. Archaeological Papers of the American Anthropological Association No. 9. Arlington, Virginia.

2002 Perspectives on Economy and Theory. In *Ancient Maya Political Economies*, edited by Marilyn A. Masson and David A. Freidel, 398–418. AltaMira Press, Walnut Creek, California.

2006 An Ethnicity to Know. In *Maya Ethnicity: The Construction of Ethnic Identity from Preclassic to Modern Times*, vol. 19, *Acta Mesoamerica*, edited by Frauke Sachse, 109–24. Verlag Anton Saurwein, Markt Schwaben, Germany.

2011 *Maya Christians and Their Churches in 16th-Century Belize*. University Press of Florida, Gainesville.

Graham, I.

1978 *Corpus of Maya Hieroglyphic Inscriptions*, vol. 2, *Part 2: Naranjo, Chunhuitz, Xunantunich*. Peabody Museum of Archaeology and Ethnology, Harvard University, Cambridge, Massachusetts.

1982 *Corpus of Maya Hieroglyphic Inscriptions*, vol. 3, *Part 3: Yaxchilan*. Peabody Museum of Archaeology and Ethnology, Harvard University, Cambridge, Massachusetts.

1996 *Corpus of Maya Hieroglyphic Inscriptions*, vol. 7, *Part 1: Seibal*. Peabody Museum of Archaeology and Ethnology, Harvard University, Cambridge, Massachusetts.

Grave, P., and L. Kealhofer

1989 Assessing Bioturbation in Archaeological Sediments using Soil Morphology and Phytolith Analysis. *Journal of Archaeological Science* 26:1239–48.

Grayson, D. K.

1984 *Quantitative Zooarchaeology: Topics in the Analysis of Archaeological Faunas*. Academic Press, Orlando, Florida.

Gronemeyer, Sven

2010 A Painted Ceramic Vessel from San Miguel Tayasal, El Petén, Guatemala; Museo Arqueológico Santa Barbara, Flores. *Mexicon* 32(6): 145–47.

Grube, N.

1992 Classic Maya Dance: Evidence from Hieroglyphs and Iconography. *Ancient Mesoamerica* 3:201–18.

2000 The City-States of the Maya. In *A Comparative Study of Thirty City-State Cultures*, edited by M. H. Hansen, 547–65. The Royal Danish Academy of Sciences and Letters, Copenhagen.

2002 Onomástica de los gobernantes mayas. In *La organización social entre los mayas prehispánicos, coloniales y modernos. Memoria de la Tercera Mesa Redonda de Palenque*, vol. 2, edited by V. Tiesler Blos, R. Cobos, and M. Greene Robertson, 321–53. INAH, Mexico City.

2008 Monumentos esculpidos: epigrafía e iconografía. In *Reconocimiento arqueológico en el sureste del estado de Campeche, México: 1996–2005*, edited by I. Sprajc, 177–231. BAR International Series. Archaeopress, Oxford.

Grube, N., and L. Schele

1996 The Last Two Hundred Years of Classic Maya History: Transmission, Termination, Transformation. In *Notebook for the XIX Maya Hieroglyphic Workshop at Texas*, edited by L. Schele and N. Grube, 87–211. University of Texas at Austin, Institute of Latin American Studies, Austin.

2002 Onomástica de los gobernantes mayas. In *La organización social entre los mayas prehispánicos, coloniales y modernos. Memoria de la Tercera Mesa Redonda de Palenque*, vol. 2, edited by V. Tiesler Blos, R. Cobos, and M. Greene Robertson, 321–53. INAH, Mexico City.

Guderjan, T. H.

1995 The Setting and Maya Maritime Trade. In *Maya Maritime Trade, Settlement, and Populations on Ambergris Caye, Belize*, edited by T. H. Guderjan and J. F. Garber, 1–8. Labyrinthos Press, Lancaster, California.

Guderjan, T. H., and J. F. Garber

1995 *Maya Maritime Trade, Settlement, and Populations on Ambergris Caye, Belize*. Maya Research Program and Labyrinthos, San Antonio, Texas.

Guderjan, T. H., J. F. Garber, and H. A. Smith

1989 Maritime Trade on Ambergris Caye, Belize. In *Coastal Maya Trade*, edited by H. McKillop and P. F. Healy, 123–33. Trent University Occasional Papers in Anthropology, Peterborough, Ontario.

Guffey, F., Y. Tonoike, and J. Castellanos

2000 Un Basurero Elite Asociado con la Acropolis. In *Proyecto Arqueologico Motul de San José Informe #3, Temporada de Campo 2000*, edited by A. E. Foias and J. Castellanos, 67–75. Report submitted to the Institute of Anthropology and History, Guatemala City. Williams College, Williamstown, Massachusetts.

Gurnsey, P., and R. Saller

1987 *The Roman Empire: Economy, Society, and Culture*. University of California Press, Berkeley.

Hageman, J. B.

2004 The Lineage Model and Archaeological Data in Late Classic Northwestern Belize. *Ancient Mesoamerica* 15(1): 63–74.

Hageman, J. B., and J. C. Lohse

2003 Heterarchy, Corporate Groups, and Late Classic Resource Management in Northwestern Belize. In *Heterarchy, Political Economy, and the Ancient Maya: The Three Rivers Region of the East-Central Yucatán Peninsula*, edited by V. L. Scarborough, F. Valdez Jr., and N. P. Dunning, 109–21. University of Arizona Press, Tucson.

Hahn, W. L., M. D. Moriarty, E. Kerns, F. Oeur, J. Drapkin, and T. Morales

2003 *In the Land of the Ik Lords? Recent Investigations at Akte, Petén, Guatemala*. Paper presented at the Annual Meetings of the Society for American Archaeology, Milwaukee.

Halperin, C. T.

2004a *Las Figurillas de Motul de San José: Produccion y Representacion*. Paper presented at the XVIII Simposio de Investigaciones Arqueologicas en Guatemala, Guatemala City.

2004b Realeza Maya y Figurillas con Tocados de la Serpiente de Guerra de Motul de San José, Guatemala. *Mayab* 17:45–60.

2007 *Materiality, Bodies, and Practice: The Political Economy of Late Classic Figurines from Motul de San José, Petén, Guatemala.* Unpublished PhD dissertation, Department of Anthropology, University of California.

2008 Classic Maya Textile Production: Insights from Motul de San José, Petén, Guatemala. *Ancient Mesoamerica* 19:111–25.

2009 Figurines as Bearers of and Burdens in Late Classic Maya State Politics. In *Mesoamerican Figurines: Small-Scale Indices of Large-Scale Phenomena*, edited by C. T. Halperin, K. A. Faust, R. Taube, and A. Giguet, 378–403. University Press of Florida, Gainesville.

Halperin, C. T., R. L. Bishop, E. Spensley, and M. J. Blackman

2009 Late Classic (A.D. 600–900) Maya Market Exchange: Analysis of Figurines from the Motul de San José Region, Guatemala. *Journal of Field Archaeology* 43(4): 457–80.

Halperin, C. T., and J. Deckard

2001 Excavaciones en el Grupo E: Operacion MSJ29. In *Proyecto Arqueológico Motul de San José Informe Preliminar # 4: Temporada de Campo 2001*, edited by A. Foias, 57–66. Report presented to the Guatemalan Institute of Anthropology and History. Williams College, Williamstown, Massachusetts.

Halperin, C. T., and A. E. Foias

2010 Pottery Politics: Late Classic Maya Palace Production at Motul de San José, Petén, Guatemala. *Journal of Anthropological Archaeology* 29(3): 392–411.

Halperin, C. T., S. Garza, K. Prufer, and J. E. Brady

2003 Caves and Ancient Maya Ritual Use of Jute. *Latin American Antiquity* 14:207–20.

Halperin, C. T., and Y. Hernández Véliz

2004 Excavaciones en el Grupo G: Operaciones 5A–E y 1G. In *Proyecto Arqueológico Motul de San José Informe #6: Temporada de Campo 2003*, edited by M. Moriarty, J. Castellanos, and A. Foias, 61–74. Report presented to the Institute of Anthropology and History, Guatemala. Department of Anthropology, Tulane University, New Orleans.

Halperin, C., C. Luin, E. McCracken, A. Wyatt, and T. Morales

2001 Programa de Excavaciones de Sondeo. In *Proyecto Arqueológico Motul de San José Informe Preliminar # 4: Temporada de Campo 2001*, edited by A. Foias, 18–34. Report presented to the Guatemalan Institute of Anthropology and History. Williams College, Williamstown, Massachusetts.

Halperin, C. T., and G. Martinez Salguero

2007a Estudios magnetometricos, pruebas de fosfato y excavaciones en tres areas de Motul de San José. In *Proyecto Arqueologico Motul De San José; Informe #7 Temporada de Campo 2005–2006*, edited by M. D. Moriarty, E. Spensley, J. Castellanos, and A. Foias, 37–74. Report presented to the Institute of Anthropology and History, Guatemala. Department of Anthropology, Tulane University, New Orleans.

2007b Localizando evidencia de basureros y producción cerámica por medio de reconocimiento geofísico en Motul de San José, Petén. In *XX Simposio de Investigaciones Arqueologicas de Guatemala*, edited by J. P. Laporte, B. Arroyo, and H. E. Mejia, 1073–83. Ministerio de Cultura y Deportes, IDAEH, Asociacion Tikal, NWAF, Guatemala City.

Hamblin, N. L., and A. M. Rea

1985 Isla Cozumel archaeological avifauna. In *Prehistoric Lowland Maya Environment and Subsistence Economy*, edited by M. Pohl, 175–92. Peabody Museum of Archaeology and Ethnology, Harvard University, Cambridge, Massachusetts.

Hammond, N.

1972 Obsidian Trade Routes in the Mayan Area. *Science* 178:1092–93.

1975a *Lubaantun: A Classic Maya Realm.* Peabody Museum Monographs, No. 2. Harvard University, Cambridge, Massachusetts.

1975b Maya Settlement Hierarchy in Northern Belize. In *Studies in Ancient Mesoamerica, II,* edited by J. A. Graham, 40–55. Contributions of the University of California Archaeological Research Facility No. 27. University of California Press, Berkeley.

1981 Settlement Patterns in Belize. In *Lowland Maya Settlement Patterns,* edited by W. Ashmore, 157–86. University of New Mexico Press, Albuquerque.

1985 (editor) *Nohmul, A Prehistoric Maya Community in Belize: Excavations 1973–1983.* British Archaeological Reports International Series 250. Archaeopress, Oxford.

1991 Inside the Black Box: Defining Maya Polity. In *Classic Maya Political History,* edited by T. P. Culbert, 253–84. Cambridge University Press, New York.

Hammond, N., and M. R. Bobo

1994 Pilgrimage's Last Mile: Late Maya Monument Veneration at La Milpa, Belize. *World Archaeology* 26(1): 19–34.

Hammond, N., and J. Cartwright Gerhardt

1991 Early Maya Architectural Innovation at Cuello, Belize. *World Archaeology* 21:461–81.

Hansen, E. F.

2000 *Ancient Maya Burnt-Lime Technology: Cultural Implications of Technological Styles.* PhD dissertation, University of California, Los Angeles.

Hansen, E. F., R. D. Hansen, and M. R. Derrick

1995 Resultados Preliminares de Los Estudios de los Metodos Y Materiales de Producción. In *VIII Simposio de Investigaciones en Guatemala, 1994,* edited by J. P. Laporte and H. Escobedo, 543–60. Ministerio de Cultura y Deportes, Instituto de Antropología e Historia, and Asociación Tikal, Guatemala City.

Hansen, E. F., C. Rodriguez-Navarro, and R. D. Hansen

1997 Incipient Burnt-Lime Technology: Characterization and Chronological Variations in Preclassic Plaster, Stucco and Mortar at Nakbe, Guatemala. In *Materials Issues in Art and Archaeology V,* edited by P. B. Vandiver, J. R. Druzik, J. F. Merkel, and J. Stewart, 207–16. Materials Research Society, Pittsburgh.

Hansen, R. D., R. Bishop, and F. Fahsen

1991 Notes on Maya Codex-Style Ceramics from Nakbé, Petén, Guatemala. *Ancient Mesoamerica* 2(2): 225–43.

Hare, E., A. Wyatt, D. M. Jarzen, and K. Emery

Forthcoming Methods in the Recovery, Processing, and Analysis of Archaeobotanical Remains from the Motul de San José Site. motul-archaeology.williams.edu.

Harris, M.

1968 *The Rise of Anthropological Theory.* Thomas Y. Crowell, New York.

Harrison, P.

1999 *The Lords of Tikal: Rulers of an Ancient Maya City.* Thames and Hudson, London.

Hassig, R.

1985 *Trade, Tribute, and Transportation: The Sixteenth-Century Political Economy of the Valley of Mexico.* University of Oklahoma Press, Norman.

1992 *War and Society in Ancient Mesoamerica.* University of California Press, Berkeley.

Hastorf, C. A., and V. S. Popper (editors)
1988 *Current Paleoethnobotany: Analytical Methods and Cultural Interpretations of Archae-ological Plant Remains*. University of Chicago Press, Chicago.
Hastorf, C. A., W. T. Whitehead, and S. Johannessen
2005 Late Prehistoric Wood Use in an Andean Intermontane Valley. *Economic Botany* 59(4): 337–55.
Hather, J. G. (editor)
1994 *Tropical Archaeobotany: Applications and New Developments*. Routledge, New York.
Haviland, W. A.
1981 Dower Houses and Minor Centers at Tikal, Guatemala: An Investigation into the Identification of Valid Unites in Settlement Hierarchies. In *Lowland Maya Settlement Patterns,* edited by W. Ashmore, 89–117. University of New Mexico Press, Albuquerque.
1985 *Tikal Report No. 19 Excavations in Small Residential Groups of Tikal: Groups 4F-1 and 4F-2*. University Museum Monographs 58. The University Museum, University of Pennsylvania, Philadelphia.
1992 Status and Power in Classic Maya Society: The View from Tikal. *American Anthropologist* 94:937–40.
1997 On the Maya State. *Current Anthropology* 38:443–45.
Haviland, W. A., and H. Moholy-Nagy
1992 Distinguishing the High and Mighty from the Hoi Polloi at Tikal, Guatemala. In *Mesoamerican Elites: An Archaeological Assessment*, edited by D. Z. Chase and A. F. Chase, 50–60. University of Oklahoma Press, Norman.
Hayes, M. H. B., and E. C. Clapp
2001 Humic Substances: Considerations of Compositions, Aspects of Structure, and Environmental Influences. *Soil Science* 166:723–37.
Healy, P. F.
1988 Music of the Maya. *Archaeology* 41(1): 24–31.
Healy, P. F., K. F. Emery, and L. E. Wright
1990 Ancient and Modern Maya Exploitation of the Jute Snail (Pachychilus). *Latin American Antiquity* 1:170–83.
Healy, P. F., J. D. H. Lambert, J. T. Arnason, and R. J. Hebda
1983 Caracol, Belize: Evidence of Ancient Maya Agricultural Terraces. *Journal of Field Archaeology* 10:397–410.
Helms, M.
1993 *Craft and the Kingly Ideal: Art, Trade, and Power*. University of Texas Press, Austin.
Hendon, J. A.
1987 *The Uses of Maya Structures: A Study of Architecture and Artifact Distribution at Sepulturas, Copan, Honduras*. Unpublished PhD dissertation, Department of Anthropology, Harvard University, Cambridge.
1991 Status and Power in Classic Maya Society: An Archaeological Study. *American Anthropologist* 93:894–918.
1992a Hilado y tejido en la epoca prehispanica: Tecnología y relaciones de la producción textil. In *La indumentaria y el tejido mayas a través del tiempo*, edited by L. A. D. Barrios and D. García, 7–16. Monographía 8. Museo Ixchel del Traje Indígena, Guatemala City.

1992b The Interpretation of Survey Data: Two Case Studies from the Maya Area. *Latin American Antiquity* 3(1): 22–42.

1997 Women's Work, Space, and Status. In *Women in Prehistory: North American and Mesoamerica*, edited by C. Claassen and R. A. Joyce, 33–46. University of Pennsylvania Press, Philadelphia.

2003 In the House: Maya Nobility and Their Figurine-Whistles. *Expedition* 45(3): 28–33.

2006 Textile Production as Craft in Mesoamerica. *Journal of Social Archaeology* 6(3): 354–78.

Hernández, C., R. H. Cobean, A. G. Mastache, and M. E. Suárez

1999 Un taller de alfareros en la antigua ciudad de Tula. *Arqueologia* 22:69–88.

Hester, T. R., J. D. Eaton, and H. J. Shafer (editors)

1980 *The Colha Project, Second Season, 1980, Interim Report*. University of Texas Center for Archaeological Research and Centro Studie Ricerche Ligabue, San Antonio.

Hester, T. R., and H. J. Shafer

1984 Exploitation of Chert Resources by the Ancient Maya of Northern Belize, Central America. *World Archaeology* 16:157–73.

Hicks, F.

1999 The Middle Class in Ancient Central Mexico. *Journal of Anthropological Research* 55:409–27.

Hirsch, Eric

1995 Landscape: Between Place and Space. In *The Anthropology of Landscape: Perspectives on Place and Space*, edited by E. Hirsch and M. O'Hanlon, 1–30. Clarendon Press, Oxford.

Hirth, K.

1998 The Distributional Approach: A New Way to Identify Market-Place Exchange in the Archaeological Record. *Current Anthropology* 39(4): 451–76.

Hodell, D. A., M. Brenner, and J. H. Curtis

2000 Climate Change in the Northern American Tropics and Subtropics since the Last Ice Age: Implications for Environment and Culture. In *Imperfect Balance Landscape Transformations in the Precolumbian Americas*, edited by D. Lentz, 13–38. Columbia University Press, New York.

Houston, S. D.

1986 *Problematic Emblem Glyphs: Examples from Altar de Sacrificios, El Chorro, Río Azul, and Xultun. Research Reports on Ancient Maya Writing 3*. Center for Maya Research, Washington, D.C.

1992 A Name Glyph for Classic Maya Dwarfs. In *The Maya Vase Book*, vol. 3, edited by J. Kerr, 526–31. Kerr Associates, New York.

1993 *Hieroglyphs and History at Dos Pilas: Dynastic Politics of the Classic Maya*. University of Texas Press, Austin.

1999 Classic Maya Depictions of the Built Environment. In *Function and Meaning in Classic Maya Architecture*, edited by S. Houston, 333–72. Dumbarton Oaks, Trustees for Harvard University, Washington, D.C.

2008 *The Epigraphy of El Zotz*. www.mesoweb.com/zotz/articles/ZotzEpigraphy.pdf.

Houston, S. D., and T. Inomata

2009 *The Classic Maya*. Cambridge University Press, New York.

Houston, S. D., Z. Nelson, C. Chiriboga, and E. Spensley
2003 The Acropolis of Kaminaljuyú, Guatemala: Recovering a "Lost Excavation." *Mayab* 16:49–64.
Houston, S. D., and D. Stuart
2001 Peopling the Classic Maya Court. In *Royal Courts of the Ancient Maya*, vol. 1, edited by T. Inomata and S. D. Houston, 54–83. Westview Press, Boulder, Colorado.
Houston, S. D., D. Stuart, and K. A. Taube
2006 *The Memory of Bones: Body, Being, and Experience among the Classic Maya.* University of Texas Press, Austin.
Hruby, Z. X.
2007 Ritualized Lithic Production at Piedras Negras, Guatemala. In *Rethinking Specialization in Complex Societies: Archaeological Analysis of the Social Meaning of Production*, edited by Z. X. Hruby and R. K. Flad, 68–87. Archaeological Papers of the American Anthropological Association, No. 17. Arlington, Virginia.
Hruby, Z. X., and R. K. Flad (editors)
2007 *Rethinking Craft Specialization in Complex Societies: Archaeological Analyses of the Social Meaning of Production.* Archaeological Papers of the American Anthropological Association, Number 17. Arlington, Virginia.
Huang, Y., F. A. Street-Perrott, S. E. Metcalfe, M. Brenner, M. Moreland, and K. H. Freeman
2001 Climate Change as the Dominant Control on Glacial-Interglacial Variations in C_3 and C_4 Plant Abundance. *Science* 293:1647–51.
Hutson, S. R., A. Magnoni, and T. W. Stanton
2004 House Rules? The Practice of Social Organization in Classic-Period Chunchucmil, Yucatan, Mexico. *Ancient Mesoamerica* 15(1): 75–92.
Hutson, S. R., T. W. Stanton, A. Magnoni, R. Terry, and J. Craner
2007 Beyond the Buildings: Formation Processes of Ancient Maya Houselots and Methods for the Study of Non-Architectural Space. *Journal of Anthropological Archaeology* 26:442–73.
Hutson, S. R., and R. E. Terry
2006 Recovering Social and Cultural Dynamics from Plaster Floors: Chemical Analyses at Ancient Chunchucmil, Yucatan, Mexico. *Journal of Archaeological Science* 33:391–404.
Hyman, D.
1970 *Precolumbian Cements: A Study of the Calcareous Cements in Prehispanic Mesoamerican Building Construction.* Unpublished PhD Dissertation, Johns Hopkins University.
Iannone, G.
2002 Annales History and the Ancient Maya State: Some Observations on the "Dynamic Model." *American Anthropologist* 104(1): 68–78.
2004 Problems in the Definition and Interpretation of "Minor Centers" in Maya Archaeology with Reference to the Upper Belize Valley. In *The Ancient Maya of the Belize Valley: Half a Century of Archaeological Research*, edited by James F. Garber, 273–86. University Press of Florida, Gainesville.
Iannone, G., and S. V. Connell (editors)
2003 *Perspectives on Ancient Maya Rural Complexity.* The Cotsen Institute of Archaeology, University of California, Los Angeles.

Ingold, T.

1993 The Temporality of the Landscape. *World Archaeology* 25(2): 152–74.

Inomata, T.

1995 *Archaeological Investigations at the Fortified Center of Aguateca, El Petén, Guatemala*. Unpublished PhD dissertation, Department of Anthropology, Vanderbilt University.

1997 The Last Day of a Fortified Classic Maya Center: Archaeological Investigations at Aguateca, Guatemala. *Ancient Mesoamerica* 8:337–51.

2001a King's People: Classic Maya Courtiers in a Comparative Perspective. In *Royal Courts of the Ancient Maya*, vol. 1, *Theory, Comparison, and Synthesis*, edited by T. Inomata and S. Houston, 27–53. Westview Press, Boulder, Colorado.

2001b The Power and Ideology of Artistic Creation: Elite Craft Specialists in Classic Maya Society. *Current Anthropology* 42(3): 321–49.

2006 Plazas, Performers, and Spectators: Political Theaters of the Classic Maya. *Current Anthropology* 47(5): 805–42.

2007 Knowledge and Belief in Artistic Producion by Classic Maya Elites. In *Rethinking Craft Specialization in Complex Societies: Archaeological Analyses of the Social Meaning of Production*, edited by Z. X. Hruby and R. K. Flad, 129–41. Archaeological Papers of the American Anthropological Association, Number 17. Arlington, Virginia.

Inomata, T., and S. Houston (editors)

2001 *Royal Courts of the Ancient Maya*, vol. 1, *Theory, Comparison, and Synthesis*. Westview Press, Boulder, Colorado.

Inomata, T., and L. R. Stiver

1998 Floor Assemblages from Burned Structures at Aguateca, Guatemala. *Journal of Field Archaeology* 25:431–52.

Inomata, T., and D. Triadan

2000 Craft Production by Classic Maya Elites in Domestic Settings: Data from Rapidly Abandoned Structures at Aguateca, Guatemala. *Mayab* 13:57–66.

Inomata, T., D. Triadan, E. Ponciano, E. Pinto, R. E. Terry, and M. Eberl

2002 Domestic and Political Lives of Classic Maya Elites: The Excavation of Rapidly Abandoned Structures at Aguateca, Guatemala. *Latin American Antiquity* 13:305–30.

Isbell, W. H.

1978 Environmental Perturbations and the Origin of the Andean State. In *Social Archaeology: Beyond Subsistence and Dating*, edited by C. L. Redman, M. J. Berman, E. V. Curtin, W. T. Langhorne Jr., N. M. Versaggi, and J. C. Wanser, 303–13. Academic Press, New York.

Ivic de Monterroso, M.

1999 Las Figurillas de Piedras Negras: Un Análisis Preliminar. In *Proyecto Arqueológico Piedras Negras: Informe Preliminar No. 3, Tercera Temporada, 1999*, edited by H. L. Escobedo and S. Houston, 359–73. Report submitted to the Institute of Anthropology and History, Guatemala City. Brigham Young University, Provo, Utah.

2002 Resultados de los Análisis de las Figurillas de Piedras Negras. In *XV Simposio de Investigaciones Arqueológicas en Guatemala, 2001*, edited by J. P. Laporte, H. Escobedo, and B. Arroyo, 555–68. Museo Nacional de Arqueología y Etnología, Guatemala City.

Jackson, S., and D. Stuart

2001 The *Aj K'uhun* Title: Deciphering a Classic Maya Term of Rank. *Ancient Mesoamerica* 12:217–28.

James, S. R.

1997 Methodological Issues Concerning Screen Size Recovery Rates and Their Effects on Archaeofaunal Interpretations. *Journal of Archaeological Science* 24:385–97.

Janusek, J. W.

1999 Craft and Local Power: Embedded Specialization in Tiwanaku Cities. *Latin American Antiquity* 10(2): 107–31.

Jarzen, D. M.

2006 *Guide to the Operations and Procedures Adopted in the Palynological Laboratory, Florida Museum of Natural History*. Florida Museum of Natural History, Gainesville.

Jarzen, D. M., and S. A. Jarzen

2006 Collecting Pollen and Spore Samples from Herbaria. *Palynology* 30:111–19.

Jensen, C., K. Johnson, and R. E. Terry

2001 Analisis Quimico de Suelos en Motul de San José. In *Proyecto Arqueológico Motul de San José Informe #4: Temporada de Campo 2001*, edited by A. Foias, 136–43. Report submitted to Institute of Anthropology and History, Guatemala. Williams College, Williamstown, Massachusetts.

Jensen, C., M. Moriarty, R. E. Terry, and K. F. Emery

2003 *Soil Typologies and Connections between Agriculture and Settlement at Motul de San José, Guatemala*. Paper presented at the SAA Annual Meetings of the Society for American Archaeology (session entitled "Testing Economic and Political Models of the Classic Maya"), Milwaukee, Wisconsin.

Jensen, C. T., M. D. Moriarty, K. D. Johnson, R. E. Terry, and K. F. Emery

2007 Soil Resources of the Motul de San José Maya: Correlating Soil Taxonomy and Modern Itzá Maya Soil Classification within a Classic Maya Archaeological Zone. *Geoarchaeology* 22(3): 337–57.

Johnson, A., and T. Earle

1987 *The Evolution of Human Societies*. Cambridge University Press, Cambridge.

Johnson, K. D., R. E. Terry, M. W. Jackson, and C. Golden

2007 Ancient Soil Resources of the Usumacinta River Region, Guatemala. *Journal of Archeological Science* 34:1117–29.

Johnson, K. D., D. R. Wright, and R. E. Terry

2007 Application of Carbon Isotope Analysis to Ancient Maize Agriculture in the Petén Region of Guatemala. *Geoarchaeology* 22:313–36.

Johnston, K. A.

2003 The Intensification of Pre-Industrial Cereal Agriculture in the Tropics: Boserup, Cultivation Lengthening and the Classic Maya. *Journal of Anthropological Archaeology* 22:126–61.

Jones, C.

1991 Cycles of Growth at Tikal. In *Classic Maya Political History: Hieroglyphic and Archaeological Evidence*, edited by T. P. Culbert, 102–26. Cambridge University Press, New York.

Jones, C., and L. Satterthwaite Jr.

1982 *The Monuments and Inscriptions of Tikal: The Carved Monuments*. Tikal Report No. 33, Part A. University Museum, University of Pennsylvania, Philadelphia.

Jones, G.

1989 *Maya Resistance to Spanish Rule: Time and History on a Colonial Frontier*. University of New Mexico Press, Albuquerque.

1998 *The Conquest of the Last Maya Kingdom*. Stanford University Press, Stanford, California.

Joyce, A.

2000 The Founding of Monte Alban: Sacred Propositions and Social Practices. In *Agency in Archaeology*, edited by M.-A. Dobres and J. E. Robb, 71–91. Routledge, London.

Joyce, A. A., L. A. Bustamente, and M. N. Levine

2001 Commoner Power: A Case Study from the Classic Period Collapse on the Oaxaca Coast. *Journal of Archaeological Method and Theory* 8(4): 343–85.

Joyce, R.

1986 *Classic to Postclassic: The Terminal Classic Transformation of Lowland Maya Political Ideology*. Paper presented in the session "Mesoamerican Political Ideology" at the 51st Annual Meeting of the SAA, New Orleans.

Junker, L. L.

1999 *Raiding, Trading, and Feasting: The Political Economy of Philippine Chiefdoms*. University of Hawai'i Press, Honolulu.

Kelly, E. F., C. Yonker, and B. Marino

1993 Stable Carbon Isotope Composition of Paleosols: An Application to Holocene. In *Climate Change in Continental Isotopic Records*, edited by P. K. Swart, K. C. Lohmann, J. McKenzie, and S. Savin, 233–39. Geophysical Monograph 78. American Geophysical Union, Washington, D.C.

Kemp, B.

1989 *Ancient Egypt: Anatomy of a Civilization*. Routledge, New York.

Kerr, B., and J. Kerr

1981 *The Painters of the Pink Glyphs*. Paper presented at the Fine Arts Museum of Long Island, New York.

Kerr, J.

1989–97 *Maya Vase Book: A Corpus of Rollout Photographs*, vols. 1–5. Kerr Associates, New York.

Kertzer, D. I.

1988 *Ritual, Politics and Power*. Yale University Press, New Haven, Connecticut.

Ketterings, Q. M., J. M. Bigham, and V. Laperche

2000 Changes in Soil Mineralogy and Texture Caused by Slash and Burn Fires in Sumatra, Indonesia. *Soil Science Society of America Journal* 64:1108–17.

King, E. M., and L. C. Shaw

2003 A Heterarchical Approach to Site Variability. In *Heterarchy, Political Economy, and the Ancient Maya: The Three Rivers Region of the East-Central Yucatán Peninsula*, edited by V. L. Scarborough, F. Valdez Jr., and N. Dunning, 64–76. University of Arizona Press, Tucson.

Kintz, E. R.

2004 Considering the Ties that Bind: Kinship, Marriage, Household, and Territory among the Maya. *Ancient Mesoamerica* 15(1): 149–58.

Kiser, E., and Y. Cai

2003 War and Bureaucratization in Qin China: Exploring an Anomalous Case. *American Sociological Review* 68(4): 511–39.

Klein, C., and C. S. Hurlbut Jr.
1993 *Manual of Mineralogy*. 21st ed. John Wiley and Sons, New York.
Kopytoff, I.
1986 The Cultural Biography of Things: Commoditization as Process. In *The Social Life of Things: Commodities in Cultural Perspective*, edited by A. Appadurai, 64–91. Cambridge University Press, Cambridge.
Kosakowsky, L.
1987 *Preclassic Maya Pottery at Cuello, Belize*. Anthropological Papers of the University of Arizona, no. 47. University of Arizona Press, Tucson.
2005 *The Problematical Terminal Late Preclassic: Ceramic Evidence from Northern Belize*. Paper presented at the 70th Annual Meeting of the Society for American Archaeology, Salt Lake City, Utah.
Kovacevich, B.
2007 Ritual, Crafting, and Agency at the Classic Maya Kingdom of Cancuen. In *Mesoamerican Ritual Economy: Archaeological and Ethnological Perspectives*, edited by E. C. Wells and K. L. Davis-Salazar, 67–114. University of Colorado Press, Boulder.
Kowalewski, S. A., G. M. Feinman, and L. Finsten
1992 "The Elite" and Assessment of Social Stratification in Mesoamerican Archaeology. In *Mesoamerican Elites: An Archaeological Assessment*, edited by D. Z. Chase and A. F. Chase, 259–77. University of Oklahoma Press, Norman.
Krosshavn, M., I. Kögel-Knaber, T. E. Southon, and E. Steinnes
1992 The Influence of Humus Fractionation on the Chemical Composition of Soil Organic Matter Studied by Solid-State ^{13}C NMR. *Journal of Soil Science* 43:473–83.
Kurtz, D. V.
2001 *Political Anthropology: Power and Paradigms*. Westview Press, Boulder, Colorado.
Lacadena, A. Garcia-Gallo
2008 El Título *Lakam*: Evidencia Epigráfica Sobre la Organización Tributaria y Military Interna de los Reinos Mayas del Clásico. *Mayab* 20:23–43.
Lacadena, A., J. Adanez, A. Ciudad, and M. J. Iglesias
In press El Proyecto "La Construccion social de la ciudad Maya: Identificacion de unidades administrativas en los centros urbanos del periodo Clasico (siglos II-X DC): Plateamientos y objetivos." In *XXII Simposio de Investigaciones Arqueologicas en Guatemala, 2008*, edited by J. P. Laporte, B. Arroyo. Ministerio de Cultura y Deportes, Direccion General del Patriminio Cultural y Natural, Instituto de Antropologia e Historia, Museo Nacional de Arqueologia y Etnologia, Asociacion Tikal, Guatemala City.
Lal, R.
2009 Soils and Food Sufficiency. A Review. *Agronomy for Sustainable Development* 29: 113–33.
Lane, C. S., C. I. Mora, S. P. Horn, and K. H. Orvis
2008 Sensitivity of Bulk Sedimentary Stable Carbon Isotopes to Prehistoric Forest Clearance and Maize Agriculture. *Journal of Archaeological Science* 35:2119–32.
Laporte, J. P.
2003 Thirty Years Later: Some Results of Recent Investigations in Tikal. In *Tikal: Dynasties, Foreigners & Affairs of State*, edited by J. A. Sabloff, 281–318. School of American Research Press, Santa Fe, New Mexico.

Laporte, J. P., and V. Fialko

1995 Un reencuentro con Mundo Perdido, Tikal, Guatemala. *Ancient Mesoamerica* 6: 41–94.

Laporte, J. P., M. A. Reyes, and J. E. Chocon

2004 Catálogo de figurillas y silbatos de baro del Atlas Arqueológico de Guatemala. In *Reconocimiento y Excavaciones Arqueológicas en los Municipios de La Libertad y Dolores y Poptun, Petén*, edited by J. P. Laporte and H. Mejía, 295–344. Atlas Arqueológico de Guatemala y Área de Arqueología, Guatemala City.

Lawton, C.

2007a Excavaciones residenciales en el grupo O: operaciones 1O1, 6A, 6B y 6D. In *Proyecto Arqueológico Motul de San José Informe #7: Temporada de Campo 2005–2006*, edited by M. D. Moriarty, E. Spensley, J. E. Castellanos, and A. E. Foias, 177–98. Report submitted to the Institute of Anthropology and History, Guatemala. Department of Anthropology, Tulane University, New Orleans.

2007b *Wheel within a Wheel: Local Commodity Trade in a Long-Distance Exchange Network.* Paper presented at the 72nd Annual Meetings of the Society for American Archaeology, Austin, Texas.

LeCount, L. J.

1996 *Pottery and Power: Feasting, Gifting, and Displaying Wealth among Late and Terminal Classic Lowland Maya.* PhD dissertation, Department of Anthropology, University of California, Los Angeles.

1999 Polychrome Pottery and Political Strategies in Late and Terminal Classic Lowland Maya Society. *Latin American Antiquity* 10:239–58.

2001 Like Water for Chocolate: Feasting and Political Ritual among the Late Classic Maya of Xunantunich, Belize. *American Anthropologist* 103(4): 935–53.

Lee, J. C.

2000 *A Field Guide to Amphibians and Reptiles of the Maya World.* Cornell University Press, Ithaca, New York.

Lee, T. A.

1969 *The Artifacts of Chiapa de Corzo, Chiapas, Mexico. Papers of the New World Archaeological Foundation No. 26.* Brigham Young University, Provo, Utah.

Lemenih, M., E. Karltun, and M. Olsson

2005 Soil Organic Matter Dynamics after Deforestation along a Farm Field Chronosequence in Southern Highlands of Ethiopia. *Agriculture, Ecosystems and Environment* 109:9–19.

Lemmonier, P.

1986 The Study of Material Culture Today: Toward an Anthropology of Technical Systems. *Journal of Anthropological Archaeology* 5:147–86.

Lentfer, C. J., and W. E. Boyd

1998 A Comparison of Three Methods for the Extraction of Phytoliths from Sediments. *Journal of Archaeological Science* 25:1159–83.

1999 An Assessment of Techniques for the Deflocculation and Removal of Clays from Sediments Used in Phytolith Analysis. *Journal of Archaeological Science* 26:31–44.

2000 Simultaneous Extraction of Phytoliths, Pollen, and Spores from Sediments. *Journal of Archaeological Science* 27:363–72.

Lentz, D. L.
1991 Maya Diets of the Rich and Poor: Paleoethnobotanical Evidence from Copán. *Latin American Antiquity* 2(3): 269–87.
1999 Plant Resources of the Ancient Maya: The Paleoethnobotanical Evidence. In *Reconstructing Ancient Maya Diet*, edited by C. D. White, 3–18. University of Utah Press, Salt Lake City.

Lentz, D. L., J. Yaeger, C. Robin, and W. Ashmore
2005 Pine, Prestige and Politics of the Late Classic Maya at Xunantunich, Belize. *Antiquity* 79(305): 573–85.

Lewis, B.
2003 Environmental Heterogeneity and Occupational Specialization: An Examination of Lithic Tool Production in the Three Rivers Region of the Northeastern Petén. In *Heterarchy, Political Economy, and the Ancient Maya: The Three Rivers Region of the East-Central Yucatán Peninsula*, edited by V. L. Scarborough, F. Valdez Jr., and N. P. Dunning, 122–35. University of Arizona, Tucson.

Leyden, B. W.
2002 Pollen Evidence for Climatic Variability and Cultural Disturbance in the Maya Lowlands. *Ancient Mesoamerica* 13:85–101.

Lichtfouse, E., S. Dou, S. Houot, and E. Barriuso
1995 Isotope Evidence for Soil Organic Carbon Pools with Distinct Turnover Rates—II. Humic Substances. *Organic Geochemistry* 23:845–47.

Lincoln, Charles E.
1985 Ceramics and Ceramic Chronology. In *A Consideration of the Early Classic Period in the Maya Lowlands*, edited by G. R. Willey and P. Mathews, 55–94. Institute for Mesoamerican Studies Publication 10. State University of New York, Institute for Mesoamerican Studies, Albany.

Lind, M.
2000 Mixtec City-States and Mixtec City-State Culture. In *A Comparative Study of Thirty City-State Cultures*, edited by M. H. Hansen, 567–80. The Royal Danish Academy of Sciences and Letters, Copenhagen.

Lindsay, W. L.
1979 *Chemical Equilibria in Soils*. John Wiley and Sons, New York.

Lindsay, W. L., and W. A. Norvell
1978 Development of a DTPA Test for Zinc, Iron, Manganese, and Copper. *Soil Science Society of America Journal* 42:421–28.

Littmann, E. R.
1957 Ancient Mesoamerican Mortars, Plasters, and Stuccos: Comalcalco, Part 1. *American Antiquity* 23:135–40.
1958 Ancient Mesoamerican Mortars, Plasters, and Stuccos: Comalcalco, Part 2. *American Antiquity* 23:292–96.
1959a Ancient Mesoamerican Mortars, Plasters, and Stuccos: Las Flores, Tampico. *American Antiquity* 25:117–19.
1959b Ancient Mesoamerican Mortars, Plasters, and Stuccos: Palenque, Chiapas. *American Antiquity* 25:264–66.

1960a Ancient Mesoamerican Mortars, Plasters, and Stuccos: The Puuc Area. *American Antiquity* 25:407–12.

1960b Ancient Mesoamerican Mortars, Plasters, and Stuccos: The Use of Bark Extracts in Lime Plasters. *American Antiquity* 25:593–97.

1962 Ancient Mesoamerican Mortars, Plasters, and Stuccos: Floor Construction at Uaxactun. *American Antiquity* 28:100–103.

1967 Patterns in Maya Floor Construction. *American Antiquity* 32:523–33.

Liu, R., C. E. Clapp, and H. H. Cheng

1997 Usefulness of the Carbon-13 Tracer Technique for Characterizing Terrestrial Carbon Pools. *Nutrient Cycling in Agroecosystems* 49:261–66.

Liverani, M. (editor)

1993 *Akkad, The First World Empire: Structure, Ideology, Traditions. History of the Ancient Near East Studies V.* Tipografia Poligrafica Moderna, Padua.

Lohse, J. C., and F. Valdez (editors)

2004 *Ancient Maya Commoners.* University of Texas Press, Austin.

Longyear III, J. M.

1952 *Copán Ceramics: A Study of Southeastern Maya Pottery.* Carnegie Institution of Washington, Publication 597, Washington, D.C.

Looper, M. G.

2009 *To Be Like Gods: Dance in Ancient Maya Civilization.* University of Texas Press, Austin.

Lopes, L.

n.d. *Maan Polity in Maya Inscriptions.* Manuscript in possession of the authors.

Lopes, L., and A. Davletshin

2004 The Glyph for Antler in the Mayan Script. Wayeb Note No. 11. www.wayeb.org/notes/wayeb_notes0011.pdf.

López Bravo, R.

2000 La veneración de los ancestros en Palenque. *Arqueología Mexicana* 8(45): 38–43.

López Varela, S., P. McAnany, and K. Berry

2001 Ceramics Technology at Late Classic K'axob, Belize. *Journal of Field Archaeology* 28(1/2): 177–91.

López Varela, S., A. van Gijn, and L. Jacobs

2002 De-Mystifying Pottery Production in the Maya Lowlands: Detection of Traces of Use-Wear on Pottery Sherds through Microscopic Analysis and Experimental Replication. *Journal of Archaeological Science* 29:1133–47.

Lopiparo, J. L.

2003 *Household Ceramic Production and the Crafting of Society in the Terminal Classic Ulúa Valley, Honduras.* Unpublished PhD dissertation, University of California, Berkeley.

Lucero, L. J.

1992 Problems in Identifying Ceramic Production in the Maya Lowlands: Evidence from the Belize River Area. *Memorias del Primer Congreso Internacional de Mayistas* 2: 143–54.

Lucero, Lisa J.

1999 Classic Lowland Maya Political Organization: A Review. *Journal of World Prehistory* 13(2): 211–63.

2002 The Collapse of the Classic Maya: A Case for the Role of Water Control. *American Anthropologist* 104(3): 814–26.

2006 *Water and Ritual: The Rise and Fall of Classic Maya Rulers*. University of Texas Press, Austin.

Lyman, R. L.

2008 *Quantitative Paleozoology*. Cambridge University Press, Cambridge.

MacKinnon, J. J., and E. M. May

1990 Small Scale Lime Making in Belize, Ancient and Modern. *Ancient Mesoamerica* 1:197–203.

MacLeod, B. and D. Reents-Budet

1994 The Art of Calligraphy: Image and Meaning. In *Painting the Maya Universe: Royal Ceramics of the Classic Period*, edited by D. Reents-Budet, 106–63. Duke University Press, Durham, North Carolina.

Macphail, R. I.

1999 Sediment Micromorphology. In *Boxgrove: A Middle Pleistocene Hominid Site at Eartham Quarry, Boxgrove, West Sussex*, edited by M. B. Roberts and S. A. Parfitt, 118–49. Institute of Archaeology, University College London, London.

n.d. *Advances in Interpreting Past Land Use and Cultural Activity Using Soil Micromorphology and Chemical Techniques*. Unpublished manuscript.

Macphail, R. I., and J. Cruise

2001 The Soil Micromorphologist as a Team Player. In *Earth Sciences and Archaeology*, edited by P. Goldberg, V. T. Holliday, and C. R. Ferring, 241–64. Kluwer Academic/ Plenum Publishers, Boston.

Macphail, R. I., and P. Goldberg

2003 Gough's Cave, Cheddar, Somerset: Microstratigraphy of the Late Pleistocene/Earliest Holocene Sediments. *Bulletin of the Natural History Museum of London* 58:51–58.

Madella, M., A. H. Powers-Jones and M. K. Jones

1998 A Simple Method of Extraction of Opal Phytoliths from Sediments Using a Non-Toxic Heavy Liquid. *Journal of Archaeological Science* 25:801–3.

Magaloni, D., T. Falcon, J. Cama, R. W. Siegel, R. Lee, R. Pancella, L. Baños, and V. Castaño

1992 Electron Microscopy Studies of the Chronological Sequences of Teotihuacan Plaster Technique. In *Materials Issues in Art and Archaeology III*, edited by P. B. Vandiver, J. R. Druzik, G. Segan Wheeler, and I. C. Freestone, 997–1005. Materials Research Society, Pittsburgh.

Mahaney, W. M., K. A. Smemo, and K. L. Gross

2008 Impacts of C_4 Grass Introductions on Soil Carbon and Nitrogen Cycling in C_3-Dominate Successional Systems. *Oecologia* 157:295–305.

Maler, T.

1908–10 *Explorations of the Upper Usumacinta and Adjacent Regions*, vol. 4, *Memoirs of the Peabody Museum*. Harvard University, Cambridge, Massachusetts.

Manahan, T. K.

2004 The Way Things Fall Apart: Social Organization and the Classic Maya Collapse at Copán. *Ancient Mesoamerica* 15(1): 107–25.

Manzanilla, L., and L. Barba

1990 The Study of Activities in Classic Households: Two Case Studies from Coba and Teotihuacan. *Ancient Mesoamerica* 1:41–49.

Marcus, G.

1983 "Elite" as a Concept, Theory and Research Tradition. In *Elites: Ethnographic Issues*, edited by G. Marcus, 7–27. University of New Mexico Press, Albuquerque.

1992 The Concern with Elites in Archaeological Reconstructions: Mesoamerican Materials. In *Mesoamerican Elites: An Archaeological Perspective*, edited by D. Chase and A. Chase, 292–302. University of Oklahoma Press, Norman.

Marcus, J.

1973 Territorial Organization of the Lowland Classic Maya. *Science, New Series* 180(4089): 911–16.

1976 *Emblem and State in the Classic Maya Lowlands: An Epigraphic Approach to Territorial Organization*. Dumbarton Oaks, Washington, D.C.

1983 Lowland Maya Archaeology at the Crossroads. *American Antiquity* 48(3): 454–88.

1992 Royal Families, Royal Texts: Examples from the Zapotec and Maya. In *Mesoamerican Elites: An Archaeological Perspective*, edited by D. Chase and A. Chase, 221–41. University of Oklahoma Press, Norman.

1993 Ancient Maya Political Organization. In *Lowland Maya Civilization in the Eighth Century A.D.: A Symposium at Dumbarton Oaks, 7th and 8th October 1989*, edited by J. A. Sabloff and J. S. Henderson, 111–83. Dumbarton Oaks, Washington, D.C.

1995 Where Is Lowland Maya Archaeology Headed? *Journal of Archaeological Research* 3:3–54.

1998 The Peaks and Valleys of Ancient States: An Extension of the Dynamic Model. In *Archaic States*, edited by G. M. Feinman and J. Marcus, 59–94. School of American Research, Santa Fe, New Mexico.

2008 The Archaeological Evidence for Social Evolution. *Annual Review of Anthropology* 37:251–66.

Martin, S.

2000 At the Periphery: The Movement, Modification and Re-use of Early Monuments in the Environs of Tikal. In *Sacred and the Profane: Architecture and Identity in the Maya Lowlands, Acta Mesoamericana*, vol. 10, edited by P. R. Colas, 51–61. Markt Schwaben, Berlin.

Martin, S., and N. Grube

1994 Evidence for Macro-Political Organization amongst Classic Maya Lowland States. *Mesoweb*. www.mesoweb.com/articles/martin/Macro-Politics.pdf.

1995 Maya Superstates: How a Few Powerful Kingdoms Vied for Control of the Maya Lowlands during the Classic Period (A.D. 300–900). *Archaeology* 48(6): 41–46.

2000 *Chronicles of the Maya Kings and Queens: Deciphering the Dynasties of the Ancient Maya*. Thames and Hudson, London.

2008 *Chronicle of the Maya Kings and Queens: Deciphering the Dynasties of the Ancient Maya*. 2nd ed. Thames and Hudson, New York.

Martin, S., and D. Reents-Budet

2010 A Hieroglyphic Block from the Region of Hiix Witz, Guatemala. *PARI Journal* 11(1): 1–6.

Marx, K.

1949 *Capital*. George Allen and Unwin, London.

1982 Selections from the Economic and Philosophical Manuscripts, the German Ideology, the Poverty of Philosophy, the Manifesto of the Communist Party, the Eighteenth Brumaire of Louis Bonaparte, Preface to a Contribution to the Critique of Political Economy, "Value, Price, and Profit," and Capital, Vols. 1 and 3. In *Classes, Power, and Conflict: Classical and Contemporary Debates* edited by A. Giddens and D. Held, 12–39. University of California Press, Berkeley.

Masson, M. A.

1999 Animal Resource Manipulation in Ritual and Domestic Contexts at Postclassic Maya Communities. *World Archaeology* 31(1): 93–120.

2000 *In the Realm of Nachan Kan: Postclassic Maya Archaeology at Laguna de On, Belize.* University Press of Colorado, Boulder.

2002 Community Economy and the Mercantile Transformation in Postclassic Northeastern Belize. In *Ancient Maya Political Economies*, edited by M. A. Masson and D. A. Freidel, 335–64. AltaMira Press, New York.

2004 Fauna Exploitation from the Preclassic to the Postclassic Periods in Four Maya Settlements in Northern Belize. In *Maya Zooarchaeology: New Directions in Method and Theory*, edited by K. F. Emery, 97–122. Institute of Archaeology, UCLA, Los Angeles.

2008 Animal Use at the Postclassic Maya Center of Mayapán. *Quaternary International* 191(1): 170–83.

Masson, M. A., and D. A. Freidel (editors)

2002 *Ancient Maya Political Economies.* AltaMira Press, Walnut Creek, California.

Mathews, P.

1985 Early Classic Monuments and Inscriptions. In *A Consideration of the Early Classic Period in the Maya Lowlands*, edited by G. R. Willey and P. Mathews, 5–55. Institute for Mesoamerican Studies Publication No. 10. SUNY, Albany.

1991 Classic Maya Emblem Glyphs. In *Classic Maya Political History: Hieroglyphic and Archaeological Evidence*, edited by T. P. Culbert, 19–29. Cambridge University Press, New York.

1997 *La escultura de Yaxchilan.* Instituto Nacional de Antropología e Historia, Mexico City.

Matthews, W.

1995 Micromorphological Characterisation and Interpretation of Occupation Deposits and Microstratigraphic Sequences at Abu Salabikh, Southern Iraq. In *Archaeological Sediments and Soils: Analysis, Interpretation and Management*, edited by Anthony J. Barham and Richard I. Macphail, 41–74. Institute of Archaeology, University College, London.

Matthews, W., C. A. I. French, T. Lawrence, D. F. Cutler, and M. K. Jones

1997 Microstratigraphic Traces of Site Formation Processes and Human Activities. *World Archaeology* 29:281–308.

Mayer, K. H.

1989 *Maya Monuments: Sculptures of Unknown Provenance; Supplement 2.* Verlag Von Flemming, Berlin.

1991 *Maya Monuments: Sculptures of Unknown Provenance; Supplement 3.* Verlag Von Flemming, Berlin.

1995 Stela 1 from Balamtun, Petén. *Mexicon* 17(4): 62.

2000a Stela 1 from Huacutal, Petén. *Mexicon* 22(6): 127–29.

2000b Stela 1 of Acte, Petén. *Mexicon* 22(4): 72–74.

McAnany, P. A.

1989 Economic Foundations of Prehistoric Maya Society: Paradigms and Concepts. In *Research in Economic Anthropology, Supplement 4: Prehistoric Maya Economies of Belize*, edited by P. A. McAnany and B. Isaac, 347–72. JAI Press, Greenwich, Connecticut.

1993a The Economics of Social Power and Wealth among Eighth-Century Maya Households. In *Lowland Maya Civilization in the Eighth Century A.D.*, edited by J. A. Sabloff and J. S. Henderson, 65–89. Dumbarton Oaks Research Library and Collection, Washington, D.C.

1993b Resources, Specialization and Exchange in the Maya Lowlands. In *The American Southwest and Mesoamerica*, edited by J. E. Ericson and T. G. Baugh, 213–45. Plenum Press, New York.

1995 *Living with the Ancestors: Kinship and Kingship in Ancient Maya Society*. University of Texas Press, Austin.

1998 Ancestors and the Classic Maya Built Environment. In *Function and Meaning in Classic Maya Architecture*, edited by S. D. Houston, 271–98. Dumbarton Oaks, Washington, D.C.

2004a Appropriative Economies: Labor Obligations and Luxury Goods in Ancient Maya Societies. In *Archaeological Perspectives on Political Economies*, edited by G. M. Feinman and L. M. Nichols, 145–65. University of Utah Press, Salt Lake City.

2004b (editor) *K'axob: Ritual, Work, and Family in an Ancient Maya Village. Monumenta Archaeologica 22*. The Cotsen Institute of Archaeology, University of California, Los Angeles.

2010 *Ancestral Maya Economies in Archaeological Perspective*. Cambridge University Press, New York.

McAnany, P. A., and S. Murata (editors)

2008 *Salt and Pottery Production at Wits Cah Ak'al and Further Excavations of Group A at Hershey: 2007 Field Season of the Xibun Archaeological Research Project*. Report submitted to the Institute of Archaeology, National Institute of Culture and History, Belmopan, Belize. Department of Archaeology, Boston University.

McAnany, P. A., and S. Plank

2001 Perspectives on Actors, Gender Roles, and Architecture at Classic Maya Courts and Households. In *Royal Courts of the Ancient Maya: Volume One: Theory, Comparisons, and Synthesis*, edited by T. Inomata and S. D. Houston, 84–129. Westview Press, Boulder, Colorado.

McCafferty, S. D., and G. G. McCafferty

2000 Textile Production in Ancient Cholula, Mexico. *Ancient Mesoamerica* 11:39–54.

McKillop, H.

1989 Coastal Maya Trade: Obsidian Densities at Wild Cane Cay. In Prehistoric *Maya Economies of Belize*, edited by Patricia A. McAnany and Barry L. Isaac, 17–56. Research in Economic Anthropology, Supplement 4. JAI Press, Greenwich, Connecticut.

1994 Ancient Maya Tree Cropping: A Viable Subsistence Adaptation for the Island Maya. *Ancient Mesoamerica* 5:129–40.

1996 Ancient Maya Trading Ports and the Integration of Long-Distance Trade and Regional Economies: Wild Cane Cay in South-Coastal Belize. *Ancient Mesoamerica* 7:49–62.

2002 *Salt: White Gold of the Ancient Maya*. University Press of Florida, Gainesville.

McKillop, H., and P. F. Healy (editors)

1989 *Coastal Maya Trade*. Trent University Occasional Papers in Anthropology, Peterborough, Ontario.

McKinnon, J. J.

1989 Coastal Maya Trade Routes in Southern Belize. In *Coastal Maya Trade*, edited by H. McKillop and P. F. Healy, 111–22. Trent University Occasional Papers in Anthropology, Peterborough, Ontario.

Means, P. A.

1917 History of the Spanish Conquest of Yucatan and of the Itzas. *Papers of the Peabody Museum of American Archaeology and Ethnology, Harvard University*, vol. 7. Peabody Museum of American Archaeology and Ethnology, Cambridge, Massachusetts.

Mejía, H. E., and J. M. García Campillo

2004 Dos nuevos monumentos de Itzimte, Petén. In *XVII Simposio de Investigaciones Arqueológicas de Guatemala*, edited by J. P. Laporte and B. Arroyo, 833–50. Museo Nacional de Arqueología y Etnología, Guatemala City.

Merwin, R. E., and G. C. Vaillant

1932 *The Ruins of Holmul, Guatemala*. Peabody Museum of American Archaeology and Ethnology Memoirs, vol. 3, no. 2. Harvard University, Cambridge, Massachusetts.

Michelsen, A., M. Andersson, M. Jensen, A. Kjøller, and M. Gashew

2004 Carbon Stocks, Soil Respiration and Microbial Biomass in Fire-Prone Tropical Grassland, Woodland and Forest Ecosystems. *Soil Biology and Biochemistry* 36:1707–17.

Miksicek C. H.

1991 The Natural and Cultural Landscape of Preclassic Cuello. In *Cuello: An Early Maya Community in Belize*, edited by N. Hammond, 70–84. Cambridge University Press, Cambridge.

Miksicek, C. H., E. S. Wing, and S. J. Scudder

1991 The Ecology and Economy of Cuello. In *Cuello: An Early Maya Community in Belize*, edited by N. Hammond, 70–84. Harvard University Press, Cambridge, Massachusetts.

Miller, D., and C. Tilley

1984 Ideology, Power and Prehistory: An Introduction. In *Ideology, Power and Prehistory*, edited by D. Miller and C. Tilley, 1–15. Cambridge University Press, Cambridge.

Miller, M. E.

1986 *The Murals of Bonampak*. Princeton University Press, Princeton.

1988 The Boys in the Bonampak Band. In *Maya Iconography*, edited by E. P. Benson and G. G. Griffin, 318–30. Princeton University Press, Princeton.

Miller, M. E., and S. Martin

2004 *Courtly Art of the Ancient Maya*. Thames and Hudson, New York.

Miller, M. E., and K. Taube

1993 *The Gods and Symbols of Ancient Mexico and the Maya: An Illustrated Dictionary of Mesoamerican Religion*. Thames and Hudson, London.

Mills, B. J.

2000 Gender, Craft Production, and Inequality. In *Women & Men in the Prehispanic Southwest: Labor, Power & Prestige*, edited by P. L. Crown, 301–43. School of American Research Press, Santa Fe, New Mexico.

2004 The Establishment and Defeat of Hierarchy: Inalienable Possessions and the History of Collective Prestige Structures in the Pueblo Southwest. *American Anthropologist* 106(2): 238–51.

Minasny, B., and A. B. McBratney

2002 *FuzME Version 3.0. Australian Centre for Precision Agriculture.* University of Sydney, Sydney.

Minc, L. D.

2005 Monitoring Regional Market Systems in Prehistory: Models, Methods and Metrics. *Journal of Anthropological Archaeology* 25:82–116.

Mock, S. B.

1997 Monkey Business at Northern River Lagoon: A Coastal-Inland Interaction Sphere in Northern Belize. *Ancient Mesoamerica* 8(2): 165–83.

Moholy-Nagy, H.

1985 The Social and Ceremonial Uses of Marine Molluscs at Tikal. In *Prehistoric Lowland Maya Environment*, edited by M D. Pohl, 147–58. Harvard University Press, Cambridge, Massachusetts.

1994 *Tikal Material Culture: Artifacts and Social Structure at a Classic Lowland Maya City.* PhD Dissertation, Department of Anthropology, University of Michigan.

1997 Middens, Construction Fill, and Offerings: Evidence for the Organization of Classic Period Craft Production at Tikal, Guatemala. *Journal of Field Archaeology* 24(3): 293–313.

2003 Beyond the Catalog: The Chronology and Contexts of Tikal Artifacts. In *Tikal: Dynasties, Foreigners, & Affairs of State*, edited by J. A. Sabloff, 83–110. School of American Research Advanced Seminar Series, Santa Fe, New Mexico.

2004 Vertebrates in Tikal burials and caches. In *Maya Zooarchaeology: New Directions in Method and Theory*, edited by K. F. Emery, 193–205. Institute of Archaeology, UCLA Press, Los Angeles.

Monaghan, J.

1990 Reciprocity, Redistribution, and the Transaction of Value in the Mesoamerican Fiesta. *American Ethnologist* 17:758–74.

Moore, J. D.

1996 *Architecture and Power in the Ancient Andes: The Archaeology of Public Buildings.* Cambridge University Press, Cambridge.

Morales, T., J. Drapkin, and M. D. Moriarty

2002 Las Operaciones de Cartografía en Akte, 2002. In *Proyecto Arqueologico Motul de San José Informe #5: Temporada de Campo 2002*, edited by M. D. Moriarty, 6–11. Department of Anthropology, Tulane University, New Orleans.

Morehart, C. T.

2002 *Ancient Maya Ritual Cave Utilization: A Paleoethnobotanical Perspective.* Unpublished MS thesis, Florida State University.

Morehart, C. T., D. L. Lentz, and K. Prufer

2005 Wood of the Gods: The Ritual Use of Pine (*Pinus* s) by the Ancient Lowland Maya. *Latin American Antiquity* 16:255–74.

Morgan, L. H.

1964 *Ancient Society.* Belknap Press of Harvard University Press, Cambridge, Massachusetts.

Moriarty, M. D.

2000 Investigaciones Preliminares en una Residencia Elitista en el Grupo G de la Periferia del Sition: Operacion 31. In *Proyecto Arqueológico Motul de San José Informe #3: Temporada de Campo 2000*, edited by A. Foias and J. Castellanos, 76–86. Report submitted to the Institute of Anthropology and History, Guatemala City. Williams College, Williamstown, Massachusetts.

2001 Notas Preliminares sobre la clasificación indígena de suelos en San José, Petén, Guatemala. In *Proyecto Arqueologico Motul de San José Informe #4: Temporada de Campo 2001*, edited by A. Foias, 131–35. Report submitted to the Institute of Anthropology and History, Guatemala City. Williams College, Williamstown, Massachusetts.

2002 (editor) *Proyecto Arqueológico Motul de San José Informe Preliminar #5: Temporada de Campo 2002*. Report presented to the Institute of Anthropology and History, Guatemala City. Department of Anthropology, Tulane University, New Orleans.

2004a Excavaciones en el Grupo C, Un Palacio Menor en La Trinidad de Nosotros: Operaciones 1C, 3C, 4A, y 7C. In *Proyecto Arqueológico Motul de San José Informe #6: Temporada de Campo 2003*, edited by M. D. Moriarty, J. E. Castellanos, and A. E. Foias, 75–104. Report submitted to Institute of Anthropology and History, Guatemala City. Department of Anthropology, Tulane University, New Orleans.

2004b Introducción a las investigaciones del Proyecto Arqueológico Motul de San José en el 2003. In *Proyecto Arqueológico Motul de San José Informe #6: Temporada de Campo 2003*, edited by M. D. Moriarty, J. E. Castellanos, and A. E. Foias, 1–14. Report submitted to Institute of Anthropology and History, Guatemala City. Department of Anthropology, Tulane University, New Orleans.

2004c *Investigating an Inland Maya Port: The 2003 Field Season at Trinidad de Nosotros, El Petén, Guatemala*. Report submitted to the Foundation for the Advancement of Mesoamerican Studies. http://www.famsi.org/reports/02061/index.html.

2004d Settlement Archaeology at Motul de San José, Petén, Guatemala: Preliminary Results from the 1998–2003 Seasons. *Mayab* 17:21–44.

2005 Entre el Centro y la Periferia en la Tierra de los Señores "Ik": Investigaciones Recientes en Sitios Satélites de Motul de San José, Petén. In *XVIII Simposio de Investigaciones Arqueológicas en Guatemala, 2004*, edited by J. P. Laporte, B. Arroyo, and H. Mejía, 440–54. Museo Nacional de Arqueología e Etnología, Guatemala City.

2009 *Behind the Ballcourt: Feasting, Ritual, and the Ancient Maya Ballgame at Trinidad de Nosotros, El Petén, Guatemala*. Paper presented at the Harvard University Archaeological Wing Lunch Series, Cambridge.

n.d. *Notes on Indigenous Soil Classification and Agricultural Potential in San José, Petén, Guatemala Region*. Unpublished manuscript.

Moriarty, M. D., J. Castellanos, and A. Foias (editors)

2003 *Proyecto Arqueológico Motul de San José Informe #6: Temporada de Campo 2003*. Report submitted to the Institute of Anthropology and History, Guatemala City. Department of Anthropology, Tulane University, New Orleans.

Moriarty, M. D., and A. E. Foias

2007 El Juego de Poder en el Centro de Petén: Evidencia Cerámica sobre Festejos Asociados al Juego de Pelota en La Trinidad de Nosotros. In *XX Simposio de Investigaciones Arqueológicas en Guatemala, 2006*, edited by J. P. Laporte, B. Arroyo, and H. Mejía,

1397–415. Ministerio de Cultura y Deportes, IDAEH, Asociacion Tikal, NWAF, Guatemala City. Moriarty, M. D., and C. Halperin

2003 Excavaciones alrededor de las estelas de Akte Petén, Guatemala 2003: Akte Operaciones 4A, 5A y 6A. In *Proyecto Arqueológico Motul de San José Informe #6: Temporada de Campo 2003*, edited by M. D. Moriarty, J. E. Castellanos and A. E. Foias, 149–62. Report submitted to Institute of Anthropology and History, Guatemala City. Department of Anthropology, Tulane University, New Orleans.

Moriarty, M. D., C. T. Halperin, A. E. Foias, and E. K. Thornton

2008 *Shifting Community Identity: A Perspective on Political Dynamics and Community Integration in the Motul de San Jose Area, AD 550–850*. Paper presented at the Society for American Archaeology Meetings, Vancouver, B.C.

Moriarty, M. D., P. Rivera, and F. Ramirez

2000 Reconocimiento y Mapeo de la Periferia de Motul de San José: Los Transectos Sur y Noreste. In *Proyecto Arqueológico Motul de San José Informe #3: Temporada de Campo 2000*, edited by A. Foias and J. Castellanos, 87–102. Report submitted to the Institute of Anthropology and History, Guatemala City. Williams College, Williamstown, Massachusetts.

Moriarty, M. D., F. Ramirez, E. Spensley, and J. Buechler

2001 Reconocimiento, Mapeo y Sondeos en la Periferia de Motul de San José: El Transecto Este. In *Proyecto Arqueologico Motul de San José Informe #4: Temporada de Campo 2001*, edited by A. E. Foias, 86–103. Report submitted to the Institute of Anthropology and History, Guatemala City. Williams College, Williamstown, Massachusetts.

Moriarty, M. D., and E. Spensley

2009 *Shifting Fortunes: Continuity and Change at the Ancient Maya Community of Trinidad de Nosotros, AD 550–850*. Paper presented at the Society for American Archaeology Meetings, Atlanta, Georgia.

Moriarty, M. D., E. Spensley, J. Castellanos, and A. Foias (editors)

2007 *Proyecto Arqueológico Motul de San José Informe #7: Temporada de Campo 2005–2006*. Report submitted to the Institute of Anthropology and History, Guatemala City. Williams College, Williamstown.

Moriarty, M. D., E. Spensley, C. Lawton, E. E. Kennedy-Thornton, and C. T. Halperin

2008 *Being "Portly": Assessing Economy and Community at the Ancient Maya Port of Trinidad de Nosotros*. Paper presented at the 107th Meeting of the American Anthropological Association, San Francisco, California.

Moriarty, M. D., and E. E. Thornton

2007 *Behind the Ballcourt: An Assessment of Classic Maya Ballgame Feasting at Trinidad de Nosotros, El Petén, Guatemala*. Paper presented at the 2007 Chacmool Conference: "Archaeology of Foodways," Calgary, Alberta.

Moriarty, M. D., and A. Wyatt

2001 Reconocimiento Preliminar de Algunos Sitios Menores en la Zona de Motul de San José. In *Proyecto Arqueológico Motul de San José Informe #4: Temporada de Campo 2001*, edited by A. E. Foias, 104–7. Report submitted to Institute of Anthropology and History, Guatemala City. Williams College, Williamstown, Massachusetts.

Moriarty, M. D., E. S. Kerns, C. T. Halperin, E. Spensley and B. Haldeman

2004 Operaciones de levantamiento en La Trinidad, 2003: con notas sobre asentamiento y organizacion. In *Proyecto Arqueológico Motul de San José Informe #6: Temporada de*

Campo 2003, edited by M. D. Moriarty, J. E. Castellanos, and A. E. Foias, 15–37. Report submitted to Institute of Anthropology and History, Guatemala City. Department of Anthropology, Tulane Unviersity, New Orleans.

Morley, S. G.

1938 *The Inscriptions of Petén*, 3 volumes. Carnegie Institution of Washington, Washington, D.C.

Morley, S. G., and G. Brainerd

1956 *The Ancient Maya*. 3rd ed. Stanford University Press, Stanford, California.

Morris, E.

1931 *The Temple of the Warriors*. Charles Scribner's Sons, New York.

Mueller, A. D., G. A. Islebe, M. B. Hillesheim, D. A. Grzesik, F. S. Anselmetti, D. Ariztegui, M. Brenner, J. H. Curtis, D. A. Hodell, and K. A. Venz

2009 Climate Drying and Associated Forest Decline in the Lowlands of Northern Guatemala during the Late Holocene. *Quaternary Research* 71:133–41.

Munera Bermundez, L. C.

1985 *Un taller de cerámica ritual en la Ciudadela Teotihuacan*. Tesis de Licenciado, Escuela Nacional de Antropología e Historia, Mexico City.

Murra, J. V.

1980 *The Economic Organization of the Inka State*. Research in Economic Anthropology, Research Annual, Supplement 1. JAI Press, Greenwich, Connecticut.

Murty, D., M. F. Kirschbaum, R. E. McMurtrie, and H. McGilvray

2002 Does Conversion of Forest to Agricultural Land Change Soil Carbon and Nitrogen? A Review of the Literature. *Global Change Biology* 8:105–23.

Nations, J. D., and R. B. Nigh

1980 The Evolutionary Potential of Lacandon Maya Sustained-yield Tropical Forest Agriculture. *Journal of Anthropological Research* 36(1): 1–30.

Nichols, D. L., M. J. McLaughlin, and M. Benton

2000 Production Intensification and Regional Specialization: Maguey Fibers and Textiles in the Aztec City-State of Otumba. *Ancient Mesoamerica* 11:267–91.

Nicklin, K.

1979 The Location of Pottery Manufacture. *Man* 14:436–86.

Nordt, L. C.

2001 Stable Carbon and Oxygen Isotopes in Soils. In *Earth Sciences and Archaeology*, edited by Paul Goldberg, Vance T. Holliday, and C. R. Ferring, 419–48. Plenum Publishers, New York.

Olson, G. W. (editor)

1977 *The Soi Survey of Tikal*. Department of Agronomy, Cornell University, Ithaca, New York.

Palka, J. W.

1997 Reconstructing Classic Maya Socioeconomic Differentiation and the Collapse at Dos Pilas, Petén, Guatemala. *Ancient Mesoamerica* 8:293–306.

Parmington, A.

2003 Classic Maya Status and the Subsidiary "Office" of Sajal: A Comparative Study of Status as Represented in Costume and Composition in the Iconography of Monuments. *Mexicon* 25(2): 46–53.

Parnell, J. J., R. E. Terry, and C. Golden
2001 The Use of In-Field Phosphate Testing for the Rapid Identification of Middens at Piedras Negras, Guatemala. *Geoarchaeology: An International Journal* 16:855–73.

Parnell, J. J., R. E. Terry, and Z. Nelson
2002a Soil Chemical Analysis Applied as an Interpretive Tool for Ancient Human Activities at Piedras Negras, Guatemala. *Journal of Archaeological Science* 29:379–404.

Parnell, J. J., R. E. Terry, and P. D. Sheets
2002b Soil Chemical Analysis of Ancient Activities in Cerén, El Salvador: A Case Study of a Rapidly Abandoned Site. *Latin American Antiquity* 13:331–42.

Pauketat, T. R.
2000 The Tragedy of the Commoners. In *Agency in Archaeology*, edited by M.-A. Dobres and J. E. Robb, 113–29. Routledge, London.
2003 Resettled Farmers and the Making of a Mississippian Polity. *American Antiquity* 68:39–66.
2007 *Chiefdoms and Other Archaeological Delusions*. AltaMira Press, Lanham, Maryland.

Paul, A.
1976 History on a Maya Vase? *Archaeology* 29(2): 118–26.

Peacock, D. P. S.
1981 Archaeology, Ethnology, and Ceramic Production. In *Production and Distribution: A Ceramic Viewpoint*, edited by H. Howard and E. Morris, 187–94. British Archaeological Reports International Series 120. Archaeopress, Oxford.
1982 *Pottery in the Roman World: An Ethnoarchaeological Approach*. Longman, London.

Pearsall, D. M.
2000 *Paleoethnobotany: A Handbook of Procedures*. Academic Press, San Diego, California.

Pearsall, D. M., and N. Duncan
2005 *University of Missouri Soil Processing Procedure*. University of Missouri Paleoethnobotany Laboratory, Columbia.

Pessenda, L. C. R., S. E. M. Gouveia, and R. Aravena
2001 Radiocarbon Dating of Total Soil Organic Matter and Humin Fraction and Its Comparison with ^{14}C ages of Fossil Charcoal. *Radiocarbon* 43:595–601.

Phillips, P., J. A. Ford, and J. B. Griffin
1951 *Archaeological Survey in the Lower Mississippi Alluvial Valley 1940–1947*, vol. 25, *Papers of the Peabody Museum of Archaeology and Ethnology*. Harvard University, Cambridge, Massachusetts.

Pierrebourg, F.
1999 *L'espace domestique Maya: Une approche ethnoarcheologique au Yucatan, Mexique*. In BAR International Series Monograph no. 764. Archaeopress, Oxford.

Piña Chán, R.
1996 Las figurillas de Jaina. *Arqueología Mexicana* 3(18): 52–59.

Piperno, D.
2006 *Phytoliths: A Comprehensive Guide for Archaeologists and Paleoecologists*. AltaMira Press, Lanham, Maryland.

Pohl, M. D.
1981 Ritual Continuity and Transformation in Mesoamerica: Reconstructing the Ancient Maya *cuch* Ritual. *American Antiquity* 46(3): 513–29.

1983 Maya Ritual Faunas: Vertebrate Remains from Burials, Caches, Caves and Cenotes in the Maya Lowlands. In *Civilization in the Ancient Americas: Essays in Honor of Gordon R. Willey*, edited by R. M. Leventhal and A. L. Kolata, 55–103. University of New Mexico Press and Peabody Museum of Archaeology and Ethnology, Harvard University, Cambridge, Massachusetts.

1985a Osteological Evidence for Subsistence and Status. In *Prehistoric Lowland Maya Environment and Subsistence Economy*, edited by M. Pohl, 107–13. Peabody Museum of Archaeology and Ethnology, Harvard University, Cambridge, Massachusetts.

1985b The Privileges of Maya Elites: Prehistoric Vertebrate Fauna from Seibal. In *Prehistoric Lowland Maya Environment*, edited by M. D. Pohl, 133–45. Harvard University Press, Cambridge, Massachusetts.

1990 The Ethnozoology of the Maya: Faunal Remains from Five Sites in the Petén, Guatemala. In *Excavations at Seibal, Guatemala*, vol. 18, number 3, edited by G. R. Willey, 144–74. Peabody Museum Monographs, Harvard University, Cambridge, Massachusetts.

1994 The Economics and Politics of Maya Meat Eating. In *The Economic Anthropology of the State*, edited by E. M. Brumfiel. Monographs in Economic Anthropology, No. 11. New University Press of America, New York.

Pohl, M. D., and P. Bloom

1996 Prehistoric Maya Farming in the Wetlands of Northern Belize: More Data from Albion Island and Beyond. In *The Managed Mosaic*, edited by S. Fedick, 145–64. University of Utah Press, Salt Lake City.

Pohl, M. D., and J. Pohl

1983 Ancient Maya Cave Rituals. *Archaeology* 36:28–32, 50–51.

Pohl, M. D., K. O. Pope, J. G. Jones, D. R. Jacob, D. R. Piperno, S. D. deFrance, D. L. Lentz, J. A. Gifford, M. E. Danforth, and J. K. Josserand

1996 Early Agriculture in the Maya Lowlands. *Latin American Antiquity* 7(4): 355–72.

Pohl, J.

1999 The Lintel Paintings of Mitla and the Function of the Mitla Palaces. In *Mesoamerican Architecture as a Cultural Symbol*, edited by J. Kowalski, 176–97. Oxford University Press, Oxford.

Polk, J. S., P. E. van Beynen, and P. P. Reeder

2007 Late Holocene Environmental Reconstruction Using Cave Sediments from Belize. *Quaternary Research* 68:53–63.

Pollock, H. E. D.

1919 Report of Harry E. D. Pollock on the Coba Expedition. *Carnegie Institution of Washington Yearbook* 2:328–29.

Pollock, S.

1999 *Ancient Mesopotamia: The Eden that Never Was*. Cambridge University Press, New York.

Pool, C. A.

1990 *Ceramic Production, Resource Procurement and Exchange at Matacapan, Veracruz, Mexico*. Unpublished PhD dissertation, Tulane University, New Orleans.

1997 Prehispanic Kilns at Matacapan, Veracruz, Mexico. In *The Prehistory and History of Ceramic Kilns*, edited by P. M. Rice, 149–72. The American Ceramic Society, Westerville, Ohio.

Potter, D. R.

1993 Analytical Approaches to Late Classic Maya Lithic Industries. In *Lowland Maya Civilization in the Eighth Century A.D.: A Symposium at Dumbarton Oaks, 7th and 8th October 1989*, edited by J. A. Sabloff and J. S. Henderson, 273–98. Dumbarton Oaks, Washington, D.C.

Potter, D. R., and E. M. King

1995 A Heterarchical Approach to Lowland Maya Socioeconomies. In *Heterarchy and the Analysis of Complex Societies*, edited by R. M. Ehrenreich, C. L. Crumley, and J. E. Levy, 17–32. Archaeological Papers of the American Anthropological Association No. 6. American Anthropological Association, Washington, D.C.

Powers, A. H., and D. D. Gilbertson

1987 A Simple Preparation Technique for the Study of Opal Phytoliths from Archaeological and Quaternary Sediments. *Journal of Archaeological Science* 14:529–35.

Pring, D. C.

2000 *The Protoclassic in the Maya Lowlands*. BAR International Series 908. Archaeopress, Oxford.

Proskouriakoff, T.

1950 *A Study of Classic Maya Sculpture*. Carnegie Institution of Washington, Publication 593, Washington, D.C.

1993 *Maya History*. University of Texas Press, Austin.

Pugh, T. W.

2003 The Exemplary Center of the Late Postclassic Kowoj Maya. *Latin American Antiquity* 14(4): 408–30.

2004 Activity Areas, Form, and Social Inequality in Residences at Late Postclassic ZacPetén, Petén, Guatemala. *Journal of Field Archaeology* 29(3/4): 351–67.

2005 Caves and Artificial Caves in Late Postclassic Maya Ceremonial Groups. In *Stone Houses and Earth Lords: Maya Religion in the Cave Context*, edited by K. M. Prufer and J. E. Brady, 47–69. University Press of Colorado, Boulder.

Quitmyer, I. R.

2004 What Kind of Data Are in the Backdirt? An Experiment on the Influence of Screen Size on Optimal Recovery. *Archaeofauna* 13:109–29.

Ramirez, F., A. Sanchez, and M. Alvarado

2000 Capitulo 3: Excavaciones de Sondeo. In *Proyecto Arqueologico Motul de San José Informe #3: Temporada de Campo 2000*, edited by A. Foias and J. Castellanos, 9–28. Report submitted to the Institute of Anthropology and History, Guatemala City. Williams College, Williamstown, Massachusetts.

Rands, R. L.

1965 Classic and Postclassic Pottery Figurines of the Guatemalan Highlands. In *Handbook of Middle American Indians*, edited by G. R. Willey, 156–62. University of Texas Press, Austin.

1967 Ceramic Technology and Trade in the Palenque Region, Mexico. In *American Historical Anthropology*, edited by C. L. Riley and W. W. Taylor, 137–51. Southern Illinois University Press, Carbondale.

Rands, R. L., and R. L. Bishop
1980 Resource Procurement Zones and Patterns of Ceramic Exchange in the Palenque Region, Mexico. In *Models and Methods in Regional Exchange*, edited by R. E. Fry, 19–46. SAA Papers No. 1, Washington, D.C.
Rands, R. L., R. L. Bishop, and G. Harbottle
1978 Thematic and Compositional Variation in Palenque-Region Incensarios. In *Tercera Mesa Redonda de Palenque, Vol. 4*, edited by M. G. Robertson and D. C. Jeffers, 19–30. Herald Peters, Monterey.
Rands, R.L, R. Bishop, and J. Sabloff
1982 Maya Fine Paste Ceramics: An Archaeological Perspective. In *Analyses of Fine Paste Ceramics, Memoirs of the Peabody Museum of Archaeology and Ethnology, vol. 15, no. 2*, edited by J. A. Sabloff, 315–38. Harvard University Press, Cambridge, Massachusetts.
Rands, R. L., and B. C. Rands
1959 The Incensario Complex of Palenque, Chiapas. *American Antiquity* 25(2): 225–36.
Rattray, E.
1988 Un taller de cerámica anaranjado San Martín en Teotihuacan. In *Ensayos de Alfarería Prehispanica e Histórica de Mesoamérica*, edited by M. C. Serra Puche and C. N. Cáceres, 249–66. Universidad Nacional Autonoma de México, Mexico City.
Reents, D.
1985 *The Holmul Style Classic Maya Pottery*. Doctoral dissertation, Department of Art and Art History, University of Texas at Austin.
Reents-Budet, D.
1987 The Discovery of a Ceramic Artist and Royal Patron among the Classic Maya. *MexIcon* 9(6).
1994 (editor) *Painting the Maya Universe: Royal Ceramics of the Classic Period*. Duke University Press, Durham, North Carolina.
1998 Elite Maya Pottery and Artisans as Social Indicators. In *Craft and Social Identity*, edited by C. L. Costin and R. P. Wright, 71–89. Archaeological Papers of the American Anthropological Association No. 8, Washington, D.C.
2000a Classic Maya Conceptualizations of the Royal Court: An Analysis of Palace Court Renderings on the Pictorial Ceramics. In *Royal Courts of the Ancient Maya*, edited by S. Houston and T. Inomata, 195–233. Westview Press, Boulder, Colorado.
2000b Feasting among the Classic Maya: Evidence from Pictorial Ceramics. In *The Maya Vase Book*, vol. 6, edited by J. Kerr, 1022–37. Kerr Associates, New York.
2003 "El Descubrimiento de la Historia Social en Artefactos: Teoría y Práctica de la Historia del Arte en la Arqueología Maya." In *XVI Simposio de Investigaciones Arqueológicas en Guatemala (2002)*, edited by J. P. LaPorte, B. Arroyo, H. Escobedo, and H. Mejía, 763–72. Museo Nacional de Arqueología y Etnología, Guatemala City.
Reents-Budet, D., E. Bell, L. P. Traxler, and R. L. Bishop
2004 Early Classic Ceramic Offerings at Copán: A Comparison of the Hunal, Margarita, and Sub-Jaguar Tombs. In *Understanding Early Classic Copán*, edited by E. Bell, M. Canuto, and R. J. Sharer, 159–90. The University Museum of Archaeology and Anthropology, University of Pennsylvania Press, Philadelphia.

Reents-Budet, D., and R. L. Bishop

1989 *The Ik' Emblem Glyph Pottery Corpus*. Manuscript and paper presented at the Seventh Mesa Redonda de Palenque, Palenque, Mexico.

In press *Classic Maya Painted Ceramics: Artisans, Workshops and Distribution*. Manuscript prepared for the Dumbarton Oaks catalog of its Maya art collection.

Reents-Budet, D., R. L. Bishop, J. Ball, and J. Taschek

2000 Out of the Palace Dumps: Ceramic Production and Use at Buenavista del Cayo. *Ancient Mesoamerica* 11:99–121.

Reents-Budet, D., R. L. Bishop, and B. MacLeod

1994 Painting Styles, Workshop Locations and Pottery Production. In *Painting the* Maya Universe: Royal Ceramics of the Classic Period, edited by D. Reents-Budet, 164–233. Duke University Press, Durham, North Carolina.

Reents-Budet, D., S. Boucher Le Landais, Y. Palomo Carrillo, R. L. Bishop, and M. J. Blackman

In press *Cerámica del Estilo Códice: nuevos datos de producción y patrones de distribución*. Paper presented at the XXII Simposio de Investigaciones Arqueológicas en Guatemala. Museo Nacional de Arqueologia y Etnologia, Ministerio de Cultura Y Deportes, IDAEH, Asociación Tikal, y Fundación Arqueológico del Nuevo Mundo, Guatemala City.

Reents-Budet, D., A. E. Foias, R. L. Bishop, M. J. Blackman, and S. Guenter

2007 Interacciones políticas y el Sitio Ik' (Motul de San José): Datos de la cerámica. In *XX Simposio de Investigaciones Arqueológicas en Guatemala, 2006*, edited by J. P. Laporte, B. Arroyo, and H. E. Mejía, 1416–36. Ministerio de Cultura y Deportes, IDAEH, Asociacion Tikal, NWAF, Guatemala City.

Reents-Budet, D., O. Gómez, R. L. Bishop, and M. J. Blackman

2008 *Un Análisis de Algunos Ejemplares Cerámicos de La Plaza de Los Siete Templos, Tikal, El Petén, Guatemala*. Paper presented at the XXI Simposio de Investigaciones Arqueológicas en Guatemala. Museo Nacional de Arqueologia y Etnologia, Ministerio de Cultura y Deportes, IDAEH, Asociación Tikal, and Fundación Arqueológico del Nuevo Mundo, Guatemala City.

Reents-Budet, D., S. Guenter, and R. L. Bishop

2001 *War and Feasts: Ceramic Styles of the Ik' Polity, Guatemala*. Manuscript and paper presented at the 2000 Chacmool Conference, University of Calgary, Calgary, Canada.

Reimer, P. J., M. G. L. Baillie, E. Bard, A. Bayliss, J. W. Beck, C. J. H. Bertrand, P. G. Blackwell, C. E. Buck, G. S. Burr, K. B. Cutler, P. E. Damon, R. L. Edwards, R. G. Fairbanks, M. Friedrich, T. P. Guilderson, A. G. Hogg, K. A. Hughen, B. Kromer, G. McCormac, S. Manning, C. B. Ramsey, R. W. Reimer, S. Remmele, J. R. Southon, M. Stuiver, S. Talamo, F. W. Taylor, J. van der Plicht, and C. E. Weyhenmeyer

2004 Intcal04 Terrestrial Radiocarbon Age Calibration, 0–26 Cal KYR BP. *Radiocarbon* 46(3): 1029–58.

Reina, R. E.

1967. Milpas and Milperos: Implications for Prehistoric Times. *American Anthropologist* 69:1–20.

Reina, R. E., and R. M. Hill

1978 *The Traditional Pottery of Guatemala*. University of Texas Press, Austin.

Reitz, E. J., and E. S. Wing
2008 *Zooarchaeology.* 2nd ed. Cambridge University Press, Cambridge.
Renfrew, C.
1975 Trade as Action at a Distance: Questions of Integration and Communication. In *Ancient Civilization and Trade*, edited by J. A. Sabloff and C. C. Lamberg-Karlovsky, 3–59. School for American Research Advanced Seminar Series, University of New Mexico Press, Albuquerque.
1977 Alternative Models for Exchange and Spatial Distribution. In *Exchange Systems in Prehistory*, edited by T. K. Earle and J. E. Ericson, p. 71–90. Academic Press, New York.
1982 Polity and Power: Interaction, Intensification and Exploitation. In *An Island Polity: The Archaeology of Exploitation in Melos*, edited by C. Renfrew and M. Wagstaff, 264–90. Cambridge University Press, Cambridge.
Renfrew, C., and J. F. Cherry (editors)
1986 *Peer Polity Interaction and Socio-Political Change.* Cambridge University Press, Cambridge.
Restall, M.
1997 *The Maya World: Yucatec Culture and Society, 1550–1850.* Stanford University Press, Stanford.
Rethemeyer, J., C. Kramer, G. Gleixner, B. John, T. Yamashita, H. Flessa, N. Andersen, M.-J. Nadeau, and P. M. Grootes
2005 Transformation of Organic Matter in Agricultural Soils: Radiocarbon Concentration versus Soil Depth. *Geoderma* 128:94–105.
Rice, D. S.
1986 The Petén Postclassic: A Settlement Perspective. In *Late Lowland Maya Civilization: Classic to Postclassic*, edited by J. A. Sabloff and E. W. Andrews, 301–44. University of New Mexico Press, Albuquerque.
1988 Classic to Postclassic Maya Household Transition in the Central Petén, Guatemala. In *Household and Community in the Mesoamerican Past*, edited by R. R. Wilk and W. Ashmore, 227–48. University of New Mexico Press, Albuquerque.
1996 Hydraulic Engineering in Central Petén, Guatemala: Ports and Inter-Lacustrine Canals. In *Arqueologia Mesoamericana: homenaje a William T. Sanders*, vol. II, edited by A. G. Pastache and J. R. Parsons, 109–22. Arqueologia Mexicana, Instituto Nacional de Antropologia e Historia, Mexico City.
Rice, D., and T. P. Culbert
1990 Historical Contexts for Population Reconstruction in the Maya Lowlands. In *Precolumbian Population History in the Maya Lowlands*, edited by T. Patrick Culbert and Don Rice, 1–36. University of New Mexico Press, Albuquerque.
Rice, D. S., and P. M. Rice
1980 La Utilizacion de las Sabanas del Petén Central por los Mayas Clásicos. *Antropologia e Historia* 2:69–80. IDAEH, Guatemala City.
1984 Topoxte, Macanché, and the Central Petén Postclassic. In *The Lowland Maya Postclassic*, ed. by A. Chase and P. Rice, 166–83. University of Texas Press, Austin.
1990 Population Size and Population Change in the Central Petén Lakes Region, Guatemala. In *Precolumbian Population History in the Maya Lowlands*, edited by T. P. Culbert and D. S. Rice, 123–48. University of New Mexico Press, Albuquerque.

Rice, D. S., P. M. Rice, and G. D. Jones
1993 Geografia Politica del Petén Central en el Siglo XVII: La Arqueologia de las Capitales Mayas. *Mesoamérica* 26:281–318.

Rice, D. S., P. M. Rice, and T. Pugh
1997 Settlement Continuity and Change in the Central Petén Lakes Region: The Case of ZacPetén. In *Anatomia de una Civilizacion: Aproximaciones Interdisciplinarias a la Cultura Maya*, edited by A. Ciudad Ruiz, Y. Fernandez Marquinez, J. M. Garcia Campillo, M. J. Iglesias Ponce de Leon, A. L. Garcia-Gallo, and L. T. Sanz Casstro, 207–52. Sociedad Espanola de Estudios Mayas, Madrid.

Rice, P. M.
1979a Ceramic and Nonceramic Artifacts of Lakes Yaxha-Sacnab, El Petén, Guatemala. Part I. The Ceramics. Section A. Introduction and the Middle Preclassic Ceramics of Yaxha-Sacnab, Guatemala. *Ceramica de Cultura Maya et al.* 10:1–36.

1979b Ceramic and Nonceramic Artifacts of Lakes Yaxha-Sacnab, El Petén, Guatemala. Part I. The Ceramics. Section B. Postclassic Pottery from Topoxte. *Ceramica de Cultura Maya et al.* 11:1–86.

1980 Petén Postclassic Pottery Production and Exchange: A View from Macanche. In *Models and Methods in Regional Exchange*, edited by R. Fry, 67–82. SAA Papers No. 1. Society for American Archaeology, Washington, D.C.

1981 Evolution of Specialized Pottery Production: A Trial Model. *Current Anthropology* 22(3): 219–40.

1985 Maya Pottery Techniques and Technology. In *Ancient Technology to Modern Science*, vol. 1, *Ceramics and Civilization*, edited by W. D. Kingery, 113–32. American Ceramic Society, Columbus.

1986 The Petén Postclassic: Perspectives from the Central Petén Lakes. In *Late Lowland Maya Civilization*, edited by J. A. Sabloff and E. W. Andrews V, 251–99. University of New Mexico Press, Albuquerque.

1987a Economic Change in the Lowland Maya Late Classic Period. In *Specialization, Exchange, and Complex Societies*, edited by E. M. Brumfiel and T. K. Earle, 76–85. Cambridge University Press, Cambridge.

1987b *Macanché Island, El Petén, Guatemala: Excavations, Pottery, and Artifacts*. University of Florida Press, Gainesville.

1987c *Pottery Analysis. A Sourcebook*. University of Chicago Press, Chicago.

1991a Specialization, Standardization, and Diversity: A Retrospective. In *The Ceramic Legacy of Anna O. Shepard*, edited by R. L. Bishop and F. W. Lange, 257–80. University Press of Colorado, Boulder.

1991b Women and Prehistoric Pottery Production. In *Proceedings of the 22nd Annual Chacmool Conference, the Archaeology of Gender*, edited by D. Walde and N D. Willows, 436–43. The Archaeological Association of the University of Calgary, Calgary.

1996 La Cerámica del Proyecto Maya-Colonial. In *Proyecto Maya-Colonial—Geografía Política del Siglo XVII en el Centro del Petén, Guatemala. Informe Preliminar al Instituto de Antropología e Historia de Guatemala sobre Investigaciones de Campo en los Años 1994 y 1995*, edited by D. Rice, P. Rice, R. Sánchez Polo, and G. D. Jones, 247–318. Report submitted to the Institute of Anthropology and History, Guatemala City. Southern Illinois University, Carbondale.

1999 Rethinking Classic Lowland Maya Pottery Censers. *Ancient Mesoamerica* 10:25–50.

2004 *Maya Political Science: Time, Astronomy, and the Cosmos.* University of Texas Press, Austin.

2009a Late Classic Maya Pottery Production: Review and Synthesis. *Journal of Archaeological Method and Theory* 16:117–56.

2009b On Classic Maya Political Economies. *Journal of Anthropological Archaeology* 28:70–84.

Rice, P. M., A. A. Demarest, and D. S. Rice

2004 The Terminal Classic and the "Classic Maya Collapse" in Perspective. In *The Terminal Classic in the Maya Lowlands: Collapse, Transition, and Transformation*, edited by A. A. Demarest, P. M. Rice, and D. S. Rice, 1–11. University Press of Colorado, Boulder.

Rice, P. M., and D. S. Rice

1979 Home on the Range: Aboriginal Maya Settlement in the Central Petén Savannas. *Archaeology* 32(6): 16–25.

1985 Topoxte, Macanche and the Central Peten Postclassic. In *The Lowland Maya Postclassic*, edited by A. Chase and P. Rice, 166–83. University of Texas Press, Austin.

2004 Late Classic to Postclassic Transformations in the Petén Lakes Region, Guatemala. In *The Terminal Classic in the Maya Lowlands: Collapse, Transition, and Transformation*, edited by A. A. Demarest, P. M. Rice, and D. S. Rice, 125–39. University of Colorado Press, Boulder.

2009 (editors) *The Kowoj: Identity, Migration, and Geopolitics in Late Postclassic, Petén, Guatemala.* University Press of Colorado, Boulder.

Rice, P. M., R. Sánchez Polo, and D. S. Rice (editors)

2007 *Proyecto Arqueológico Itza del Petén: El Sitio de Nixtun-Ch'ich.* Report submitted to the Instituto de Antropología e Historia de Guatemala (IDAEH), Guatemala City.

Rinck, B. A.

2007 *The Micromorphology of Archaic and Woodland Period Pits from the Sandy Hill Site, Connecticut.* Unpublished MA thesis, Boston University.

Ringle, W. M., and G. J. Bey III

2001 Post-Classic and Terminal Classic Courts of the Northern Maya Lowlands. In *Royal Courts of the Ancient Maya, vol. 2: Data and Case Studies*, edited by T. Inomata and S. Houston, 266–307. Westview Press, Boulder, Colorado.

Rivero Torres, S.

2002 *Figurillas Antropomorfas y Zoomorfas del Juego de Pelota de Lagartero, Chiapas.* Tuxtla Gutíerrez, Universidad de Ciencias y Artes de Chiapas.

Robin, C.

1999 *Towards an Archaeology of Everyday Life: Maya Farmers of Chan Nòohol and Dos Chombitos Cik'in, Belize.* Unpublished PhD dissertation, Department of Anthropology, University of Pennsylvania.

Roscoe, P. B.

1993 Practice and Political Centralisation: A New Approach to Political Evolution. *Current Anthropology* 34(2): 111–40.

Roscoe, R., P. Buurman, E. J. Velthorst, and J. A. A. Pereira

2000 Effects of Fire on Soil Organic Matter in a "Cerrado Sensu-Stricto" from Southeast Brazil as Revealed by Changes in $\delta^{13}C$. *Geoderma* 95:141–60.

Rosenswig, R. M.
2007 Beyond Identifying Elites: Feasting as a Means to Understand Early Middle Formative Society on the Pacific Coast of Mexico. *Journal of Anthropological Archaeology* 26:1–27.

Rovner, I.
1976 A Method for Determining Obsidian Trade Patterns in the Maya Lowlands. *Katunob* 9(1): 43–51.

Roys, R. L.
1934 The Engineering Knowledge of the Maya. *Contributions to American Archaeology* 2, 27–105. Carnegie Institution Publication No. 436. Washington, D.C.
1954 *The Maya Katun Prophecies of the Books of Chilam Balam, series I. Contributions to American Anthropology and History*, vol. 12, no. 57. Carnegie Institution of Washington, Washington, D.C.

Ruscheinsky, L. M.
2003 *The Social Reproduction of Gender Identity through the Production and Reception of Lowland Maya Figurines.* Unpublished PhD dissertation, Department of Art History, Visual Art and Theory, University of British Columbia.

Russell, B. W., and B. H. Dahlin
2007 Traditional Burnt-Lime Production at Mayapán, Mexico. *Journal of Field Archaeology* 32:407–23.

Rye, O. S.
1981 *Pottery Technology: Principles and Reconstruction.* Taraxacum Manuals on Archaeology, Washington, D.C.

Sabloff, J. A.
1975 *Excavations at Seibal, Department of Petén, Guatemala, Number 2: Ceramics.* Peabody Museum of Archaeology and Ethnology Memoirs, Vol. 13. Harvard University, Cambridge, Massachusetts.
1986 Interaction among Classic Maya Polities: A Preliminary Examination. In *Peer Polity Interaction and Socio-Political Change*, edited by C. Renfrew and J. F. Cherry, 109–16. Cambridge University Press, Cambridge.
2003 (editor) *Tikal Dynasties, Foreigners & Affairs of State: Advancing Maya Archaeology.* School of American Research Press, Santa Fe, New Mexico.

Sabloff, J. A., and D. A. Freidel
1975 A Model of a Pre-Columbian Trading Center. In *Ancient Civilization and Trade*, edited by J. A. Sabloff and C. C. Lamberg-Karlovsky, 369–408. University of New Mexico Press, Albuquerque.

Safronov, A.
2005 The Yaxchilan Wars in the Reign of 'Itsamnaaj B'alam (771–CA.800). In *Wars and Conflicts in Prehispanic Mesoamerica and the Andes. Selected Proceedings of the Conference Organized by the Société des Américanistes de Belgique with the Collaboration of Wayeb (European Association of Mayanists): Brussels, 16–17, November 2002*, edited by P. Eeckhout and G. Le Fort, 50–57. BAR International Series 1385. John and Erica Hedges, Oxford.

Sanchez Polo, R., D. S. Rice, P. M. Rice, A. McNair, T. Pugh, and G. D. Jones
1995 La Investigación de la Geographia Politica del Siglo XVII en Petén Central: La PrimeravTemporada. In *VIII Simposio de Investigaciones Arqueologicas en Guatemala, 1994,*

edited by J. P. Laporte and H. L. Escobedo, 707–20. Ministerio de Cultura y Deportes, IDAEH, Asociacion Tikal, Guatemala City.

Sanders, W. T.

1962 Cultural Ecology of the Maya Lowlands, Part I. *Estudios de Cultura Maya* 2:79–121.

1963 Cultural Ecology of the Maya Lowlands, Part II. *Estudios de Cultura Maya* 3: 203–41.

1992 Ranking and Stratification in Prehispanic Mesoamerica. In *Mesoamerican Elites: An Archaeological Assessment*, edited by D. Z. Chase and A. F. Chase, 278–91. University of Oklahoma Press, Norman.

Sanders, W. T., J. R. Parsons, and R. S. Santley

1979 *The Basin of Mexico: Ecological Processes in the Evolution of a Civilization*. Academic Press, New York.

Sanders, W. T., and Barbara J. Price

1968 *Mesoamerica: The Evolution of a Civilization*. Academic Press, New York.

Sanders, W. T., and D. Webster

1988 The Mesoamerican Urban Tradition. *American Anthropologist* 90:521–46.

Šantrucková, H., M. I. Bird, and J. Lloyd

2000 Microbial Processes and Carbon-Isotope Fractionation in Tropical and Temperate Grassland Soils. *Functional Ecology* 14:108–14.

Satterthwaite, L.

1958 *The Problem of Abnormal Stela Placements at Tikal and Elsewhere. Tikal Report No. 3, Museum Monographs*. University Museum, Philadelphia.

Savage, H. G.

1971 Faunal Material. In *Excavations at Eduardo Quiroz Cave, British Honduras*, edited by D. M. Pendergast, 523–29. Royal Ontario Museum of Art and Archaeology Occasional Paper No. 21, Toronto.

Scarborough, V. L.

1996 Ecology and Ritual: Water Management and the Maya. *Latin American Antiquity* 9:135–59.

2003 *Flow of Power: Ancient Water Systems and Landscapes*. SAR Press, Santa Fe, New Mexico.

Scarborough, V. L., M. E. Becher, J. L. Baker, G. Harris, and F. Valdez Jr.

1995 Water and Land at the Ancient Maya Community of La Milpa. *Latin American Antiquity* 6:98–119.

Scarborough, V. L., and F. Valdez Jr.

2009 An Alternative Order: The Dualistic Economies of the Ancient Maya. *Latin American Antiquity* 20(1): 207–28.

Scarborough, V. L., F. Valdez Jr., and N. Dunning (editors)

2003 *Heterarchy, Political Economy, and the Ancient Maya: The Three Rivers Region of the East-Central Yucatán Peninsula*. University of Arizona Press, Tucson.

Schele, L., and D. Freidel

1990 *A Forest of Kings: The Untold Story of the Ancient Maya*. William Morrow, New York.

Schele, L., and N. Grube

1994 Tlaloc-Venus Warfare: The Petén Wars 8.17.0.0.0–9.15.13.0.0. In *Notebook for the XVIII Maya Hieroglyphic Workshop at Texas*, edited by T. Albright, 79–167. University of Texas at Austin, Institute of Latin American Studies, Austin.

Schele, L., and P. Mathews
1979 *The Bodega of Palenque, Chiapas, Mexico*. Dumbarton Oaks, Washington, D.C.
1991 Royal Visits and Other Intersite Relationships among the Classic Maya. In *Classic Maya Political History: Hieroglyphic and Archaeological Evidence*, edited by T. P. Culbert, 226–52. Cambridge University Press, New York.
1998 *The Code of Kings: The Language of Seven Sacred Maya Temples and Tombs*. Scribner, New York.

Schele, L., and M. E. Miller
1986 *The Blood of Kings: Dynasty and Ritual in Maya Art*. 2nd ed. Kimbell Art Museum, New York.

Schiffer, M. B.
1976 *Behavioral Archaeology*. Academic Press, New York.
1983 Toward the Identification of Formation Processes. *American Antiquity* 48:675–706.
1985 Is There a "Pompeii Premise" in Archaeology? *Journal of Anthropological Research* 41:19–41.
1987 *Formation Processes of the Archaeological Record*. University of New Mexico Press, Albuquerque.

Schlosser, A. L.
1978 *Ceramic Maya Lowland Figurine Development with Special Reference to Piedras Negras, Guatemala*. PhD dissertation, Department of Anthropology, Southern Illinois University.

Schortman, E. M., and P. A. Urban
2004 Modeling the Roles of Craft Production in Ancient Political Economies. *Journal of Archaeological Research* 12(2): 185–226.

Schortman, E. M., P. A. Urban, and M. Ausec
2001 Politics with Style: Identity Formation in Prehispanic Southeastern Mesoamerica. *American Anthropologist* 103(2): 312–30.

Schwartz, G. M., and S. E. Falconer
1994a (editors) *Archaeological Views from the Countryside: Village Communities in Early Complex Societies*. Smithsonian Institution Press, Washington, D.C.
1994b Rural Approaches to Social Complexity. In *Archaeological Views from the Countryside: Village Communities in Early Complex Societies*, edited by G. M. Schwartz and S. E. Falconer, 1–9. Smithsonian Institution Press, Washington, D.C.

Sears, E. L., R. L. Bishop, and M. J. Blackman
2005 Las Figurillas de Cancuen: El Surgimiento de una Perspectiva Regional. In *XVIII Simposio de Investigaciones Arqueológicas en Guatemala, 2004*, edited by J. P. Laporte and B. Arroyo y H. Mejía, 745–52. Museo Nacional de Arqueología y Etnología, Guatemala City Guatemala City.

Service, E. R.
1962 *Primitive Social Organization: An Evolutionary Perspective*. Random House, New York.
1975 *Origins of the State and Civilization*. Norton, New York.

Shafer, H. J., and T. R. Hester
1983 Ancient Maya Chert Workshops in Northern Belize, Central America. *American Antiquity* 48:519–43.

1986 Maya Stone-Tool Craft Specialization and Production at Colha, Belize: Reply to Mallory. *American Antiquity* 51:158–66.

1991 Lithic Craft Specialization and Product Distribution at the Maya Site of Colha, Belize. *World Archaeology* 23(1): 79–97.

Shaffer, B. S.

1992 Quarter-Inch Screening: Understanding Biases in Recovery of Vertebrate Faunal Remains. *American Antiquity* 57:129–36.

Shaffer, B. S., and J. L. J. Sanchez

1994 Comparison of 1/8"- and 1/4"-Mesh Recovery of Controlled Samples of Small-to-Medium-Sized Mammals. *American Antiquity* 59:525–30.

Shah, A.

2010 Poverty around the World. *Global Issues*. http://www.globalissues.org/article/4/poverty-around-the-world.

Sharer, R.

1993 The Social Organization of the Late Classic Maya: Problems of Definitions and Approaches. In *Lowland Maya Civilization in the Eighth Century AD*, edited by J. A. Sabloff and J. S. Henderson, 91–110. Dumbarton Oaks Research Library and Collection, Washington, D.C.

1994 *The Ancient Maya*. 5th ed. Stanford University Press, Stanford, California.

Sharer, R. J., and C. W. Golden

2004 Kingship and Polity: Conceptualizing the Maya Body Politic. In *Continuities and Changes in Maya Archaeology: Perspectives at the Millennium*, edited by C. W. Golden and G. Borsgstede, 23–50. Routledge, New York.

Sharp, Z.

2007 *Principles of Stable Isotope Geochemistry*. Pearson Prentice Hall, New York.

Shaw, L. C.

1991 *The Articulation of Social Inequality and Faunal Resource Use in the Preclassic Community of Colha, Northern Belize*. PhD dissertation, University of Massachusetts.

Sheets, P.

1978 From Craftsman to Cog: Quantitative Views of Mesoamerican Lithic Technology. In *Papers on the Economy and Architecture of the Ancient Maya*, edited by R. V. Sidrys, 40–71. Institute of Archaeology, University of California, Los Angeles.

2000 Provisioning the Ceren Household: The Vertical Economy, Village Economy, and Household Economy in the Southeastern Maya Periphery. *Ancient Mesoamerica* 11(2): 217–30.

2002 (editor) *Before the Volcano Erupted: The Ancient Ceren Village in Central America*. University of Texas Press, Austin.

Sheets, P. D., and G. Muto

1972 Pressure Blades and Total Cutting Edge. *Science* 175:632–34.

Shepard, A. O.

1948 *Plumbate: A Mesoamerican Tradeware*. Publication 573. Carnegie Institution of Washington, Washington, D.C.

Sidrys, R. V.

1979 Supply and Demand among the Classic Maya. *Current Anthropology* 20:594–97.

Sinopoli, C. M.

1988 The Organization of Craft Production at Vijayanagara, South India. *American Anthropologist* 90(3): 580–97.

1994 The Archaeology of Empires. *Annual Review of Anthropology* 23:159–80.

Six, J., P. A. Schultz, J. D. Jastrow, and R. Merckx

1999 Recycling of Sodium Polytungstate used in Soil Organic Matter Studies. *Soil Biology and Biochemistry* 31:1193–96.

Smith, A. T.

2003 *The Political Landscape: Constellations of Authority in Early Complex Polities.* University of California Press, Berkeley.

Smith, B. N., and S. Epstein

1971 Two Categories of $^{13}C/^{12}C$ Ratios for Higher Plants. *Plant Physiology* 47:380–84.

Smith, C. A.

1976 (editor) *Economic Systems: Regional Analysis*, 2 vols. Academic Press, New York.

Smith, M. E.

1986 The Role of Social Stratification in the Aztec Empire: A View from the Provinces. *American Anthropologist* 88:70–91.

1987 Household Possessions and Wealth in Agrarian Societies: Implications for Archaeology. *Journal of Anthropological Archaeology* 6:297–335.

2008 *Aztec City-State Capitals.* University Press of Florida, Gainesville.

Smith, M. E., and K. J. Schreiber

2005 New World States and Empires: Economic and Social Organization. *Journal of Archaeological Research* 13(3): 189–229.

2006 New World States and Empires: Politics, Religion, and Urbanism. *Journal of Archaeological Research* 14(1): 1–52.

Smith, M. E., J. B. Whartoon, and J. M. Olson

2003 Aztec Feasts, Rituals, and Markets: Political Uses of Ceramic Vessels in a Commercial Economy. In *The Archaeology and Politics of Food and Feasting in Early States and Empires*, edited by T. L. Bray, 235–68. Kluwer Academic/Plenum, New York.

Smith, P. E.

2006 Children and Ceramic Innovation: A Study in the Archaeology of Children. In *Children in Action: Perspectives on the Archaeology of Children*, edited by J. E. Baxter, 65–76. Archaeological Papers of the American Anthropological Association, No. 15, Arlington, Virginia.

Smith, R. E.

1955 *Ceramic Sequence at Uaxactún, Guatemala.* Middle American Research Institute Publication 20, vols. 1 and 2. Tulane University, New Orleans.

1971 *The Pottery of Mayapan: Including Studies of Ceramic Material from Uxmal, Kabah, and Chichen Itza.* Papers of the Peabody Museum of Archaeology and Ethnology, vol. 66, 2 vols. Harvard University, Cambridge, Massachusetts.

Smith, R. E., and J. C. Gifford

1966 *Maya Ceramic Varieties, Types, and Wares at Uaxactún: Supplement to "Ceramic Sequence at Uaxactún, Guatemala."* Middle American Research Institute Publication 28. Tulane University, New Orleans.

Smith, R. E., G. R. Willey, and J. C. Gifford
1960 The Type-Variety Concept as a Basis for the Analysis of Maya Pottery. *American Antiquity* 25(3): 330–40.

Smyth, M. P., and C. D. Dore
1992 Large Site Archaeological Methods at Sayil, Yucatan, Mexico: Investigation Community Organization at a Prehispanic Maya Center. *Latin American Antiquity* 3:3–21.
1994 Maya Urbanism in Sayil, Yucatan. *Research and Exploration* 10:38–55.

Smyth, M., C. D. Dore, and N. P. Dunning
1995 Interpreting Prehistoric Settlement Patterns: Lessons from the Maya Center of Sayil, Yucatan. *Journal of Field Archaeology* 22:321–47.

Soil Survey Staff
2006 *Keys to Soil Taxonomy*. 10th ed. United States Department of Agriculture, Natural Resources Conservation Service, Washington, D.C.

Sorensen, K., J. B. Glover, and S. L. Fedick
2003 A Volumetric Assessment of Ancient Maya Architecture: A GIS Approach to Settlement Patterns. In *Enter the Past: The E-Way into the Four Dimensions of Cultural Heritage*, edited by R. M. d. S. Wien and S. R. K. Erbe, 308–38. British Archaeological Reports, Oxford.

Southall, A. W.
1988 The Segmentary State in Africa and Asia. *Comparative Studies in Society and History* 30:52–82.

Spaccini, R., A. Piccolo, G. Haberhauer, and M. H. Gerzabek
2000 Transformation of Organic Matter from Maize Residues into Labile and Humic Fractions of Three European Soils as Revealed by ^{13}C Distribution and CPMAS-NMR Spectra. *European Journal of Soil Science* 51:583–94.

Spensley, E.
2003 Excavaciones en el área de puerto en La Trinidad de Nosotros 2003: Operación 2. In *Motul de San José, Informe #6: Temporada de Campo 2003*, edited by M. D. Moriarty, J. E. Castellanos, and A. E. Foias, 105–32. Report submitted to the Institute of Anthropology and History, Guatemala City. Department of Anthropology, Tulane University, New Orleans.
2007a Investigaciones en el área del puerto de La Trinidad, 2005: operación 12. In *Proyecto Arqueológico Motul de San José Informe #7: Temporada de Campo 2005–2006*, edited by M. D. Moriarty, E. Spensley, J. E. Castellanos, and A. E. Foias, 167–75. Report submitted to the Institute of Anthropology and History, Guatemala City. Department of Anthropology, Tulane University, New Orleans.
2007b Investigaciones en la sabana Chächäklu'um, 2005: Operacion 1. In *Proyecto Arqueológico Motul De San José Informe # 7: Temporada de Campo 2005–2006*, edited by M. D. Moriarty, E. Spensley, J. E. Castellanos, and A. E. Foias, 219–26. Report submitted to the Institute of Anthropology and History, Guatemala City. Department of Anthropology, Tulane University, New Orleans.
2008 *Doctoral Dissertation Improvement Grant: Classic Maya Ceramic Technology and Power Dynamics in the Center Petén Lakes Region, Guatemala*. Boston University, Boston.

Spensley, E., and A. E. Foias
2001 *Elite Households at Motul de San José: Preliminary Results of Excavations in Six Epicenter Structures.* Paper presented in the session "Testing Economic and Political Models of the Classic Maya" at the 68th Annual Meeting of the SAA, Milwaukee, Wisconsin.
Spensley, E., and J. L. Garrido Lopez (editors)
2008 *Proyecto Arqueológico Periferia Motul de San José, Informe #1: Temporada de Campo 2008.* Report submitted to Institute of Anthropology and History, Guatemala City. Boston University, Boston.
Spensley, E., and M. D. Moriarty
2006 *An Ancient Maya Harbor at Trinidad de Nosotros, El Petén, Guatemala.* Paper presented at the 71st Annual Meeting of the Society for American Archaeology, San Juan, Puerto Rico.
Spielmann, K. A.
2002 Feasting, Craft Specialization, and the Ritual Mode of Production in Small-Scale Societies. *American Anthropologist* 104(1): 195–207.
Stark, B. L.
1985 Archaeological Identification of Pottery Production Locations: Ethnoarchaeological and Archaeological Data in Mesoamerica. In *Decoding Prehistoric Ceramics*, edited by B. A. Nelson, 157–94. Southern Illinois University Press, Carbondale.
2007 Pottery Production in the Gulf Lowlands. In *Pottery Economics in Mesoamerica*, edited by C. A. Pool and G. J. Bey III, 147–83. University of Arizona Press, Tucson.
Stein, G.
1994a Introduction Part II: The Organizational Dynamics of Complexity in Greater Mesopotamia. In *Chiefdoms and Early States in the Near East: The Organizational Dynamics of Complexity*, edited by G. Stein and M. S. Rothman, 11–22. Prehistoric Press, Madison, Wisconsin.
1994b Segmentary States and Organizational Variation in Early Complex Societies: A Rural Perspective. In *Archaeological Views from the Countryside: Village Communities in Early Complex Societies*, edited by G. M. Schwartz and S. E. Falconer, 10–18. Smithsonian Institution Press, Washington, D.C.
1998 Heterogeneity, Power, and Political Economy: Some Current Research Issues in the Archaeology of Old World Complex Societies. *Journal of Archaeological Research* 6(1): 1–44.
Steiner, W.
1987 Portrait: The Limitations of Likeness. *Art Journal* 46(3): 173–77.
Steinkeller, P.
1993 Early Political Development in Mesopotamia and the Origins of the Sargonic Empire. In *Akkad, The First World Empire: Structure, Ideology, Traditions*, edited by Mario Liverani, 107–29. History of the Ancient Near East/Studies V. Tipografia Poligrafica Moderna, Padua.
Stephens, J.
1979 *The Transition from Capitalism to Socialism.* Macmillan, London.
Stevenson, F. J.
1994 *Humus Chemistry: Genesis, Composition, Reactions, Second Edition.* Wiley, New York.

Stuart, D.

1985 The Yaxha Emblem Glyph as Yax-Ha. *Research Reports in Ancient Maya Writing* no. 1.

1987 Ten Phonetic Syllables. In *Research Reports in Ancient Maya Writing*, no. 14. Center for Ancient Maya Research, Washington, D.C.

1993 Historical Inscriptions and the Maya Collapse. In *Lowland Maya Civilization in the Eighth Century A.D.*, edited by J. A. Sabloff and J. S. Henderson, 321–49. Dumbarton Oaks, Washington, D.C.

2003 *La Identificación de Hixwitz*. Paper presented at the XV Simposio de Arqueología en Guatemala, Museo Nacional de Antropología e Historia, Guatemala City.

2007 *Inscriptions of the River Cities: Yaxchilan, Piedras Negras and Pomona*. Presentation at the XXXI Maya Meetings, University of Texas, Austin.

2008 A Stela from Pajaral, Guatemala. *Maya Decipherment*. http://decipherment. wordpress.com/2009/06/15/an-inscribedblock-from-pajaral-guatemala/.

Stuart, D., N. Grube, and L. Schele

1989 A Substitution Set for the "Macuch/Batab." *Copán Notes* 58.

Stuart, D., and S. D. Houston

1994 *Classic Maya Place Names*. Studies in Pre-Columbian Art & Archaeology, No. 33. Dumbarton Oaks Research Library and Collection, Washington, D.C.

Stuiver, M., and B. Becker

1986 High-Precision Decadal Calibration of the Radiocarbon Time Scale, AD 1950–2500 BC. *Radiocarbon* 28(2b): 863–910.

Stuiver, M., and P. J. Reimer

1993 Extended ^{14}C Data Base and Revised Calib 3.0 ^{14}C Age Calibration Program. *Radiocarbon* 35(1): 215–30.

Sullivan, L. A.

2005 *Reflections on the R. E. Smith's Influence: A Perspective from Northwestern Belize*. Paper presented at the 70th Annual Meeting of the Society for American Archaeology, Salt Lake City, Utah.

Sweetwood, R. V., R. E. Terry, T. Beach, B. H. Dahlin, and D. Hixson

2009 The Maya Footprint: Soil Resources of Chunchucmil, Yucatan, Mexico. *Soil Science Society of America Journal* 73(4): 1209–20.

Tambiah, S. J.

1976 *World Conqueror and World Renouncer: A Study of Buddhism and Polity in Thailand against a Historical Background*. Cambridge Studies in Social Anthropology 15, Cambridge.

1977 The Galactic Polity: The Structure of Traditional Kingdoms in Southeast Asia. In *Anthropology and the Climate of Opinion*, edited by S. A. Freed, 69–97. Annals of the New York Academy of Science 293, New York.

Tan, K. T.

2003 *Humic Matter in Soil and the Environment*. Marcel Dekker, New York.

Taschek, J. T.

1994 *The Artifacts of Dzibilchaltun, Yucatan, Mexico: Shell, Polished Stone, Bone, Wood, and Ceramics*. Middle American Research Institute, Tulane University, New Orleans.

Taschek, J. T., and J. W. Ball

1992 Lord Smoke-Squirrel's Cacao Cup: The Archaeological Context and Socio-Historical Significance of the Buenavista "Jauncy Vase." In *The Maya Vase Book, vol. 3: A Corpus of Rollout Photographs of Maya Vases*, edited by by J. Kerr, 490–97. Kerr Associates, New York.

2003 Nohoch Ek Revisited: The Minor Center as Manor. *Latin American Antiquity* 14(4): 371–88.

Tate, C. E.

1992 *Yaxchilan: The Design of a Maya Ceremonial City*. University of Texas Press, Austin.

Taube, K. A.

1985 The Classic Maya Maize God: A Reappraisal. In *Fifth Palenque Round Table, 1983*, edited by M. G. Robertson, 171–81. Pre-Columbian Art Research Institute, San Francisco.

1988a Prehispanic Maya Katun Wheel. *Journal of Anthropological Research* 44(2): 183–203.

1988b A Study of Classic Maya Scaffold Sacrifice. In *Maya Iconography*, edited by E. P. Benson and G. G. Griffin, 331–51. Princeton University Press, Princeton.

1989 The Maize Tamale in Classic Maya Diet, Epigraphy, and Art. *American Antiquity* 54(1): 31–51.

1992 Iconography of Mirrors at Teotihuacan. In *Art, Ideology, and the City of Teotihuacan*, edited by J. Berlo, 169–204. Dumbarton Oaks, Washington, D.C.

1998 The Jade Hearth: Centrality, Rulership, and the Classic Maya Temple. In *Function and Meaning in Classic Maya Architecture*, edited by S. Houston, 427–78. Dumbarton Oaks, Washington, D.C.

2000 The Breath of Life: The Symbolism of Wind in Mesoamerica and the American Southwest. In *The Road to Aztlan: Art from a Mythic Homeland*, edited by V. M. Fields and V. Zamudio-Taylor, 102–23. Los Angeles County Museum of Art, Los Angeles.

2005 The Symbolism of Jade in Classic Maya Religion. *Ancient Mesoamerica* 16:25–50.

Teeri, J. A., and L. G. Stowe

1976 Climatic Patterns and the Distribution of C_4 Grasses in North America. *Oecologia* 23:1–12.

Teeter, W. G.

2004 Animal Utilization in a Growing City: Vertebrate Exploitation at Caracol, Belize. In *Maya Zooarchaeology: New Directions in Method and Theory*, edited by K. F. Emery, 177–92. UCLA Institute of Archaeology, Los Angeles.

Teeter, W. G., and A. F. Chase

2004 Adding Flesh to Bones: Using Zooarchaeology Research to Answer Big-Picture Questions. *Archaeofauna* 13:155–72.

Terry, R. E., Hardin, P. J., Houston, S. D., Nelson, S. D., Jackson, M. W., Carr, J. and Parnell, J. J.

2000 Quantitative Phosphorus Measurement: A Field Test Procedure for Archaeological Site Analysis at Piedras Negras, Guatemala. *Geoarchaeology, an International Journal* 15:151–66.

Terry, R. E., F. G. Fernández, J. J. Parnell, and T. Inomata

2004 The Story in the Floors: Chemical Signatures of Ancient and Modern Maya Activities at Aguateca, Guatemala. *Journal of Archaeological Science* 31:1237–50.

Thompson, J. E. S.

1932 Monuments of the Cobá Region. In *Preliminary Study of the Ruins of Cobá, Quintana Roo, Mexico*, edited by J. E. S. Thompson, H. E. D. Pollock, and J. Charlot, 131–84. Carnegies Institution, Washington, D.C.

1942 *The Civilization of the Mayas*. Field Museum of Natural History, Anthropology Leaflet 25, Chicago.

1966 *The Rise and Fall of Maya Civilization*. 2nd ed. University of Oklahoma Press, Norman.

1970 *Maya History and Religion*. University of Oklahoma Press, Norman.

Thompson, R.

1958 *Modern Yucatecan Maya Pottery Making*. Memoirs of the Society for American Archaeology, no. 15. Millwood, New York.

Thornton, E. K.

2008 *Uso de los animales por los Mayas prehióricos de Cancuen: resultados preliminares del análisis zooarqueológico*. Report submitted to the Institute de Anthropology and History, Guatemala City. Florida Museum of Natural History, University of Florida, Gainesville.

Thornton, E. K., and K. F. Emery

2007 Uso e Intercambio Prehispanico de Recursos de Fauna en la Entidad Politica de Motul, Petén, Guatemala, edited by J. P. Laporte and B. Arroyo. In *XX Simposio de Investigaciones Arqueológicas en Guatemala*, edited by J. P. Laporte, B. Arroyo and H. E. Mejia, 1181–93. Ministerio de Cultura y Deportes, IDAEH, Asociacion Tikal, NWAF, Guatemala City.

2008 Patterns of Ancient Animal Use at El Mirador: Evidence for Subsistence, Ceremony and Exchange. Report submitted to R. T. Matheny, New World Archaeological Foundation, Salt Lake City. Manuscript on file with the authors.

Thornton, E. K., and M. D. Moriarty

2007 Analisis preliminar de los entierros humanos de Trinidad de Nosotros. In *Proyecto Arqueológico Motul de San José Informe #7: Temporada del Campo 2005–2006*, edited by M. D. Moriarty, E. Spensley, J. E. Castellanos, and A. E. Foias, 211–17. Report submitted to the Instituto de Antropología e História de Guatemala. Department of Anthropology, Tulane University, New Orleans.

Tokovinine, A.

2002 Divine Patrons of the Maya Ballgame. *Mesoweb*. www.mesoweb.com/features/tokovinine/Ballgame.pdf.

2003 A Classic Maya term for public performance. *Mesoweb*. www.mesoweb.com/features/tokovinine/Performance.pdf.

2008 *The Power of Place: Political Landscape and Identity in Classic Maya Inscriptions, Imagery, and Architecture*. PhD thesis, Harvard University.

Tourtellot, G., III

1988 *Excavations at Seibal, Department of Petén, Guatemala: Peripheral Survey and Excavation, Settlement and Community Patterns*. Memoirs of the Peabody Museum of Archaeology and Ethnology vol. 16. Harvard University, Cambridge, Massachusetts.

Tourtellot, G., III, F. Estrada-Belli, J. J. Rose, and N. Hammond
2003 Late Classic Maya Heterarchy, Hierarchy, and Landscape at La Milpa, Belize. In *Heterarchy, Political Economy, and the Ancient Maya: The Three Rivers Region of the East-Central Yucatán Peninsula*, edited by V. L. Scarborough, F. Valdez Jr., and N. P. Dunning, 37–51. University of Arizona Press, Tucson.

Tourtellot, G., III, and J. A. Sabloff
1972 Exchange Systems among the Ancient Maya. *American Antiquity* 37:126–35.

Tourtellot, G., III, J. A. Sabloff, and K. Carmean
1992 "Will the Real Elites Please Stand Up?": An Archaeological Assessment of Maya Elite Behavior in the Terminal Classic Period. In *Mesoamerican Elites: An Archaeological Assessment*, edited by D. Z. Chase and A. F. Chase, 80–98. University of Oklahoma Press, Norman.

Tourtellot, G., III, M. Wolf, F. Estrada Belli, and N. Hammond
2000 Discovery of Two Predicted Ancient Maya Sites in Belize. *Antiquity* 74:481–82.

Tourtellot, G., III, M. Wolf, S. Smith, K. Gardella, and N. Hammond
2002 Exploring Heaven on Earth: Testing the Cosmological Model at La Milpa, Belize. *Antiquity* 76:633–34.

Tozzer, A. M.
1911 *A Preliminary Study of the Prehistoric Ruins of Tikal, Guatemala: A Report of the Peabody Museum Expedition, 1909–1910*. Peabody Museum of Archaeology and Ethnology Memoirs, vol. 5(1). Harvard University, Cambridge, Massachusetts.
1941 Landa's Relaciones de las cosas de Yucatan. In *Papers of the Peabody Museum of Archaeology and Ethnology*, vol. 18. Harvard University, Cambridge, Massachusetts.

Tozzer, A. M., and G. M. Allen
1910 Animal Figures in the Maya Codices. *Papers of the Peabody Museum of American Archaeology and Ethnology* 4(3): 273–372.

Traverse, A.
2007 *Paleopalynology*. Springer, Dordrecht.

Triadan, D.
2007 Warriors, Nobles, Commoners and Beasts: Figurines from Elite Buildings at Aguateca, Guatemala. *Latin American Antiquity* 18(3): 269–93.

Trubitt, M. B.
2000 Mound Building and Prestige Goods Exchange: Changing Strategies in the Cahokia Chiefdom. *American Antiquity* 65(4): 669–90.

Tunesi, R.
2007 A New Monument Mentioning Wamaaw K'awiil of Calakmul. *PARI Journal* 8(2): 13–19.

Turchin, P.
2003 *Historical Dynamics: Why States Rise and Fall*. Princeton University Press, Princeton.

Turner, B. L. I.
1983 The Excavations of Raised and Channelized Fields at Pulltrouser Swamp. In *Pulltrouser Swamp: Ancient Maya Habitat, Agriculture, and Settlement in Northern Belize*, edited by B. L. Turner II and P. D. Harrison, 30–51. Texas Pan American Series. University of Texas Press, Austin.

1990 Population Reconstruction of the Central Maya Lowlands: 1000 B.C. to A.D. 1500. In *Precolumbian Population History in the Maya Lowlands*, edited by P. Culbert and D. S. Rice, 301–24. University of New Mexico Press, Albuquerque.

Turner II, B. L., and P. D. Harrison

1981 Pre-Historic Raised Field Agriculture in the Maya Lowlands. *Science* 213:339–405.

1983 (editors) *Pulltrouser Swamp: Ancient Maya Habitat, Agriculture, and Settlement in Northern Belize*. University of Texas Press, Austin.

Turner II, B. L., P. Klepeis, and L. C. Schneider

2003 Three Millennia in the Southern Yucatán Peninsula: Implications for Occupancy, Use, and Carrying Capacity. In *The Lowland Maya Area: Three Millennia at the Human-Wildland Interface*, edited by A. Gómez-Pompa, M. F. Allen, S. L. Fedick, and J. J. Jiménez-Osornio, 361–87. Food Products Press, New York.

Turner II, B. L., and C. H. Miksicek

1984 Economic Plant Species Associated with Prehistoric Agriculture in the Maya Lowlands. *Economic Botany* 38(2): 179–93.

Urban, P., and E. Schortman

2004 Opportunities for Advancement: Intra-Community Power Contests in the Midst of Political Decentralization in Terminal Classic Southeastern Mesoamerica. *Latin American Antiquity* 15(3): 251–72.

Urban, P. A., E. C. Wells, and M. T. Ausec

1997 The Fires without and the Fires within: Evidence for Ceramic Production Facilities at the Late Classic Site of La Sierra, Naco Valley, Northwestern Honduras, and in Its Environs. In *The Prehistory and History of Ceramic Kilns*, vol. 7, edited by P. M. Rice, 173–94. The American Ceramic Society, Westerville, Ohio.

Urquizú, M., E. C. Wells, I. Aguirre, N. Monterroso, E. Arredondo, and A. Roman

1999 Unidades residenciales en Piedras Negras: resultados de las investigaciones realizadas en las temporadas de campo de 1997 y 1998. In *XII simposio de investigaciones arqueol'ogicas en Guatemala*, edited by J. P. Laporte and H. L. Escobedo, 255–73. Museo Nacional de Arqueología y Etnología, Guatemala City.

Valadez, R., B. Paredes, and B. Rodríguez

1999 Entierros de perros descubiertos en la antigua ciudad de Tula. *Latin American Antiquity* 10(2): 180–200.

Valdés, J. A.

1997 Tamarindito: Archaeology and Regional Politics in the Petexbatún Region. *Ancient Mesoamerica* 8(2): 321–35.

2001 Palaces and Thrones Tied to the Destiny of the Royal Courts in the Maya Lowlands. In *Royal Courts of the Ancient Maya*, vol. 2, *Data and Case Studies*, edited by T. Inomata and S. Houston, 138–64. Westview, Boulder, Colorado.

Vaughn, H. H., and E. S. Deevey

1985 Pollen Stratigraphy of Two Cores from the Petén Lake District. In *Prehistoric Lowland Maya Environment and Subsistence Economy*, edited by M. D. Pohl, 73–89. Peabody Museum of Archaeology and Ethnology, Harvard University, Cambridge, Massachusetts.

Vázquez Negrete, J., and R. Velázquez

1996a Análisis químico de materiales encontrados en excavación, dos casos: porta-in-censarios tipo Palenque y cinabrio usado en practicas funerarias. In *Eighth Palenque Round Table, 1993*, edited by M. J. Macri and J. McHargue, 103–6. The Pre-Columbian Art Research Institute, San Francisco.

1996b Caracterización de materiales constitutivos de relieves en estucos, morteros, y pintura mural de la zona arqueológica de Palenque, Chiapas. In *Eighth Palenque Round Table, 1993*, edited by M. J. Macri and J. McHargue, 107–12. The Pre-Columbian Art Research Institute, San Francisco.

Velásquez García, E.

2009 La mascara de "rayos X": Historia de un artilugio iconográfico en el arte maya. *Anales del Instituto de Investigaciones Estéticas* 90:7–36.

2010 Los señores de la entidad política de 'Ik.' *Estudios de Cultura Maya* 21:45–87.

Villegas, M., X. Vázquez, D. Rios, L. Baños, and D. Magaloni

1995 Relative Dating of the Stucco Reliefs at Palenque, Chiapas, Based on Variation in Material Preparation. In *Materials Issues in Art and Archaeology IV*, edited by P. B. Vandiver, J. R. Druzik, J. L. Galvan Madrid, I. C. Freestone, and G. Segan Wheeler, 469–81. Materials Research Society, Pittsburgh.

Vogt, E.

1969 *Zinacantan*. Harvard University Press, Cambridge, Massachusetts.

1993 *Tortillas for the Gods: A Symbolic Analysis of Zinacanteco Rituals*. University of Oklahoma Press, Norman.

Wagner, E.

2006 Ranked Spaces, Ranked Identities: Local Hierarchies, Community Boundaries and an Emic Notion of the Maya Cultural Sphere at Late Classic Copán. In *Maya Ethnicity: The Construction of Ethnic Identity from Preclassic to Modern Times*, edited by F. Sachse, 143–64. Acta Americana 19. Verlag Anton Saurwein, Markt Schwaben.

Wailes, B. (editor)

1996 *Craft Specialization and Social Evolution: In Memory of V. Gordon Childe*. The University Museum of Archaeology and Anthropology, University of Pennsylvania, Philadelphia.

Wake, T. A.

2004 On the Paramount Importance of Adequate Comparative Collections and Recovery Techniques in the Identification and Interpretation of Vertebrate Archaeofaunas: A Reply to Vale and Gargett (2002). *Archaeofauna* 13:173–82.

Watanabe, J. M.

2004 Some Models in a Muddle: Lineage and House in Classic Maya Social Organization. *Ancient Mesoamerica* 15(1): 159–66.

Webb, E. A., H. P. Schwarcz, and P. F. Healy

2004 Detection of Ancient Maize in Lowland Maya Soils Using Stable Carbon Isotopes: Evidence from Caracol, Belize. *Journal of Archaeological Science* 31:1039–52.

Webb, E., H. P. Schwarcz, C. T. Jensen, R. E. Terry, M. D. Moriarty, and K. F. Emery

2007 Stable Carbon Isotope Signature of Ancient Maize Agriculture in the Soils of Motul de San José, Guatemala. *Geoarchaeology* 22(3): 291–312.

Webster, D. L.

1992 Maya Elites: The Perspective from Copan. In *Mesoamerican Elites: An Archaeological Assessment*, edited by D. Z. Chase and A. F. Chase, 135–56. University of Oklahoma Press, Norman.

1993 Study of Maya Warfare: What It Tells Us about the Maya and What It Tells Us about Maya Archaeology. In *Lowland Maya Civilization in the Eighth Century A. D.*, edited by J. A. Sabloff and J. S. Henderson, 415–44. Dumbarton Oaks, Washington, D.C.

Webster, D. L., B. W. Fash, R. Widmer, and S. Zeleznik

1998 The Skyband Group: Investigations of a Classic Maya Elite Residential Complex at Copán, Honduras. *Journal of Field Archaeology* 25:319–43.

Webster, D., and N. Gonlin

1988 Household Remains of the Humblest Maya. *Journal of Field Archaeology* 15:169–90.

Weiner, A. B.

1992 *Inalienable Possessions: The Paradox of Keeping-While-Giving*. University of California Press, Berkeley.

Wells, E. C.

2004 Investigating Activity Patterning in Prehispanic Plazas: Acid-Extraction ICP/AES Analysis of Anthrosols at Classic Period El Coyote, Northwest Honduras. *Archaeometry* 46:67–84.

2006 Recent Trends in Theorizing Prehispanic Mesoamerican Economies. *Journal of Archaeological Research* 14:265–312.

Wells, E. C., and P. A. McAnany (editors)

2008 *Dimensions of Ritual Economy: Research in Economic Anthropology*, vol. 27. Emerald Group Publishing, JAI Press, Bingley, UK.

Wells, E. C., and K. L. D. Salazar

2007 Mesoamerican Ritual Economy: Archaeological and Ethnological Perspectives. In *Mesoamerican Ritual Economy: Archaeological and Ethnological Perspectives*, edited by E. C. Wells and K. L. Davis-Salazar, 1–26. University Press of Colorado, Boulder.

Wells, E. C., R. E. Terry, J. J. Parnell, P. J. Hardin, M. W. Jackson, and S. D. Houston

2000 Chemical Analyses of Ancient Anthrosols in Residential Areas at Piedras Negras, Guatemala. *Journal of Archaeological Science* 27:449–62.

Welsh, W. B. M.

1988 *An Analysis of Classic Lowland Maya Burials*. BAR International Series 409, Oxford.

Wernecke, C. D.

2008 A Burning Question: Maya Lime Technology and the Maya Forest. *Journal of Ethnobiology* 28:200–210.

West, G.

2002 Ceramic Exchange in the Late Classic and Postclassic Maya Lowlands: A Diachronic Approach. In *Ancient Maya Political Economies*, edited by M. Masson and D. Freidel, 140–95. AltaMira Press, Walnut Creek, California.

Westenholz, A.

1993 The World View of Sargonic Officials: Differences in Mentality between Sumerians and Akkadians. In *Akkad, The First World Empire: Structure, Ideology, Traditions*, edited by Mario Liverani, 157–69. History of the Ancient Near East/ Studies V. Tipografia Poligrafica Moderna, Padua.

White, L.

1959 *The Evolution of Culture: The Development of Civilization to the Fall of Rome*. Mc-Graw-Hill, New York.

White, C. D., M. D. Pohl, H. P. Schwarcz, and F. J. Longstaffe

2004 Feast, Field and Forest: Deer and Dog Diets at Lagartero, Tikal, and Copán. In *Maya Zooarchaeology: New Directions in Method and Theory*, edited by K. F. Emery, 141–58. Institute of Archaeology, UCLA Press, Los Angeles.

White, C. D., and H. P. Schwarcz

1989 Ancient Maya Diet as Inferred from Isotopic and Chemical Analyses of Human Bone. *Journal of Archaeological Science* 16:451–74.

Whitmore, T. M., and B. L. Turner II

1992 Landscapes of Cultivation in Mesoamerica on the Eve of the Conquest. Special Issue: The Americas before and after 1492: Current Geographical Research. *Annals of the Association of American Geographers* 82(3): 402–24.

Wichmann, S.

2004 The Grammar of the Half-Period Glyph. In *The Linguistics of Maya Writing*, edited by S. Wichmann, 327–37. University of Utah Press, Salt Lake City.

Wilkinson, R., and K. Pickett

2010 *The Spirit Level: Why Equality Is Better for Everyone*. Penguin, London.

Willey, G. R.

1972 *The Artifacts of Altar de Sacrificios*. Papers of the Peabody Museum of Archaeology and Ethnology 64. Harvard University, Cambridge, Massachusetts.

1978 Artifacts. In *Excavations at Seibal, Department of Petén, Guatemala*, edited by G. R. Willey, 1–189. Peabody Museum of Archaeology and Ethnology, Harvard University, Cambridge, Massachusetts.

Willey, G. R., T. P. Culbert, and R. E. W. Adams

1967 Maya Lowland Ceramics: A Report from the 1965 Guatemala City Conference. *American Antiquity* 32(3): 289–315.

Willey, G. R., and R. M. Leventhal

1979 Prehistoric Settlement at Copán. In *Maya Archaeology and Ethnohistory*, edited by N. Hammond and G. R. Willey, 75–102. University of Texas Press, Austin.

Willey, G. R., and P. D. Mathews (editors)

1985 *A Consideration of the Early Classic Period in the Maya Lowlands*. Institute for Mesoamerican Studies, State University of New York, Albany.

Wilson, C., I. A. Simpson, and E. J. Currie

2002 Soil Management in Pre-Hispanic Raised Field Systems: Micromorphological Evidence from Hacienda Zuleta, Ecuador. *Geoarchaeology* 17:261–83.

Wing, E. S.

1975 Animal remains from Lubaantun. In *Lubaantun: A Classic Maya Realm*, edited by N. Hammond, 379–83. Monographs of the Peabody Museum of Archaeology and Ethnology, no. 2. Harvard University Press, Cambridge, Massachusetts.

1978 Use of Dogs for Food: An Adaptation to the Coastal Environment. In *Prehistoric Coastal Adaptations: The Ecology of Maritime Middle America*, edited by B. L. Stark and B. Voorhies, 29–41. Studies in Archaeology. Academic Press, New York.

Wing, E. S., and I. R. Quitmyer
1985 Screen Size for Optimal Data Recovery: A Case Study. In *Aboriginal Subsistence and Settlement Archaeology of the Kings Bay Locality*, vol. 2, *Zooarchaeology*, edited by W. H. Adams, 49–58. Reports of Investigations No. 2. Department of Anthropology, University of Florida, Gainesville.

Wing, E. S., and S. J. Scudder
1991 The Exploitation of Animals. In *Cuello: An Early Maya Community in Belize*, edited by N. Hammond, 84–97. Cambridge University Press, Cambridge.

Winter, M., and W. O. Payne
1976 Hornos para cerámica hallados en Monte Albán. *Boletín del Instituto Nacional de Antropología e Historia* 16:37–40.

Wiseman, F. M.
1985 Agricultural and Vegetation Dynamics of the Maya Collapse in Central Petén, Guatemala. In *Prehistoric Lowland Maya Environment and Subsistence Economy*, edited by M. D. Pohl, 63–71. Harvard University Press, Cambridge, Massachusetts.

Wolf, E. R.
1990 Facing Power, Old Insights, New Questions. *American Anthropologist* 92:586–96.
1999 *Envisioning Power: Ideologies of Dominance and Power*. University of California Press, Berkeley.

Wolff, E. N.
2004 Changes in Household Wealth in the 1980s and 1990s in the U.S. *Working Paper No. 407*. The Levy Economics Institute of Bard College, Annandale-on-Hudson, New York.
2010 *Recent Trends in Household Wealth in the United States: Rising Debt and the Middle-Class Squeeze—An Update to 2007*. Working Paper No. 589. The Levi Economics Institute of Bard College, Annandale-on-Hudson, New York.

Wright, D. R., R. E. Terry, and M. Eberl
2009 Soil Properties and Stable Carbon Isotope Analysis of Landscape Features in the Petexbatún Region of Guatemala. *Geoarchaeology: An International Journal* 24(4): 466–91.

Wright, L. E., and C. D. White
1996 Human Biology in the Classic Maya Collapse: Evidence from Paleopathology and Paleodiet. *Journal of World Prehistory* 10:147–98.

Wright, R. P.
1991 Women's Labor and Pottery Production. In *Engendering Archaeology: Women and Prehistory*, edited by J. M. Gero and M. W. Conkey, 194–223. Basil Blackwell, Oxford.

Wurtzburg, S. J.
1991 *Sayil: Investigations of Urbanism and Economic Organization at an Ancient Maya City*. PhD Dissertation, State University of New York, Albany.

Wyatt, A.
2008 Pine as an Element of Household Refuse in the Fertilization of Ancient Maya Agricultural Fields. *Journal of Ethnobiology* 28(2): 244–58.

Yaeger, J.
2000 *Changing Patterns of Social Organization: The Late and Terminal Classic Communities at San Lorenzo, Cayo District, Belize*. Unpublished PhD dissertation, Department of Anthropology, University of Pennsylvania.

2003 Untangling the Ties that Bind: The City, the Countryside, and the Nature of Maya Urbanism at Xunantunich, Belize. In *The Social Construction of Ancient Cities*, edited by Monica L. Smith, 121–55. Smithsonian Press, Washington, D.C.

Yoffee, N.

1988 The Collapse of Ancient Mesopotamian State and Civilization. In *The Collapse of Ancient States and Civilizations*, edited by N. Yoffee and G. L. Cowgill, 44–68. University of Arizona Press, Tucson.

Yorgey, S. C.

2005 *Rural Complexity in the Central Petén: A View from Akte, El Petén, Guatemala*. Unpublished MA thesis, Tulane University.

Yorgey, S., D. Glick, A. Sanchez, and F. Ramirez

1999 Programa de Excavaciones de Sondeo. In *Proyecto Arqueologico Motul de San José Informe Preliminar # 2: Temporada de Campo 1999*, edited by A. Foias, 22–34. Report presented to the Guatemalan Institute of Anthropology and History. Williams College, Williamstown, Massachusetts.

Yoshida, M., and K. Kumada

1978 Studies on the Properties of Organic Matter in Buried Humic Horizon Derived from Volcanic Ash. *Soil Science and Plant Nutrition* 24:481–89.

Zender, M.

2001 A Note on the Inscription of Iztutz Stela 4. *PARI Journal* 2(4): 17–22.

2002 The Toponyms of El Cayo, Piedras Negras, and La Mar. In *Heart of Creation: The Mesoamerican World and the Legacy of Linda Schele*, edited by A. Stone, 166–84. University of Alabama Press, Tuscaloosa.

2004a Sport, Spectacle and Political Theater: New Views of the Classic Maya Ballgame. *PARI Journal* 4(4): 10–12.

2004b *A Study of Classic Maya Priesthood*. PhD thesis, University of Calgary.

2005 The Raccoon Glyph in Classic Maya Writing. *PARI Journal* 5(4): 6–16.

Contributors

Daniel A. Bair is a Ph.D. candidate in the Land, Air, and Water Resources Department at the University of California–Davis. His research area is the application of stable carbon isotope ratios and elemental concentrations in the soil organic matter to identify ancient agricultural fields, feasting, workshop, and marketplace activities at ancient sites.

Ronald L. Bishop is curator for Mexican and Central American archaeology in the Smithsonian Institution's National Museum of Natural History. He has written extensively on the use of neutron activation and petrography in the study of cultural materials, integrating the analytical data obtained from the study of museum objects with analyses of artifacts from recent excavation and surveys. His mathematical modeling of compositional data incorporates both geological and social aspects of material production, use, and exchange.

M. James Blackman is senior research chemist in the Department of Anthropology of the Smithsonian Institution's National Museum of Natural History. He has published extensively on the chemical characterization and technological analysis of archaeological ceramics, clay objects, and obsidian (from the ancient Middle East, South Asia, and the Colonial Americas); trade and exchange; and craft specialization, especially as these topics relate to the flow of information in early state formation.

Jeanette Castellanos has worked in Guatemala over the last twenty years at many sites, including Kaminaljuyu, Piedras Negras, Motul de San José, and its satellite, Nuevo San José. She has received a FAMSI grant to support her research at the site of Nuevo San José that has uncovered the earliest occupation in the Motul de San José zone from the eighth century B.C. Her other research interests and publications have been in Maya pottery analysis.

Kitty F. Emery is associate curator at the Florida Museum of Natural History and associate professor in the Department of Anthropology at the University of Florida in Gainesville. Emery conducts environmental archaeology research at various Maya sites in Guatemala and Honduras and specializes in zooarchaeological reconstructions of Mesoamerican diet, environment, and economics. She is the author of *Dietary, Environmental, and Societal Implications of Ancient Maya Animal Use in the Petexbatun* and editor of *Maya Zooarchaeology.*

Antonia E. Foias is professor of anthropology in the Department of Anthropology and Sociology at Williams College. She is the coauthor of *Ceramics, Production and Exchange in the Petexbatun Region: The Economic Parameters of the Classic Maya Collapse* (with Ronald L. Bishop). She has published on the topics of ceramic analysis, economy and evolution of complex society, and most recently, *Geographies of Power: Understanding the*

Nature of Terminal Classic Pottery in the Maya Lowlands (with Sandra L. López Varela). Since 1998 she has directed the multifaceted archaeological research at the site of Motul de San José, located in the central Petén jungle of Guatemala.

Elizabeth Graham is senior lecturer at University College of London, Institute of Archaeology; associate fellow in the Institute for the Study of the Americas, University of London School of Advanced Studies; and adjunct professor in anthropology at the University of Western Ontario (London, Canada) and University of North Carolina–Wilmington. Her interests span Maya archaeology, urban environmental impact in the humid tropics, and religion and iconography in Colonial Mesoamerica. She has excavated at various sites in Belize since 1973, including Negroman-Tipu, whose results are currently being compiled in a monograph. Graham's most recent fieldwork has focused on the site of Lamanai with funding from Social Sciences and Humanities Research Council of Canada, National Geographic Society, British Academy, and Institute of Archaeology, UCL.

Stanley Guenter is affiliated with three archaeological projects in Guatemala, working at the sites of El Mirador, El Peru, and La Corona and has previously conducted excavations in southern Mexico and the Rocky Mountains of Canada. His primary research area is in Maya epigraphy and decipherment and has published broadly in topics related to epigraphy. His most recent interest is in Preclassic texts and iconography.

Christina T. Halperin is Cotsen Postdoctoral Fellow in the Society of Fellows at Princeton University. Her research focuses on political economy, textile and ceramic craft production systems, caves and sacred landscapes, materiality, ideology, and iconography. Her latest publication is as co-editor of the book, *Mesoamerican Figurines: Small-Scale Indices of Large-Scale Social Phenomena.*

David M. Jarzen is courtesy research scientist in paleobotany and palynology at the Cleveland Museum of Natural History in Ohio. His research interests in the nature of extant and fossil plant life have included extensive fieldwork in Canada and the United States, as well as Europe, Africa, Mexico and Central America, Colombia, the Caribbean, New Caledonia, New Zealand, Fiji, and Australia. His publications number over 230 papers, including professional papers, popular articles, and book chapters. In 2003, David was elected as Fellow National to the Explorers Club, and in 2005 he was elected Fellow of the Ohio Academy of Science.

Ellen Spensley Moriarty has recently finished her doctorate in Mesoamerican archaeology in the Department of Archaeology at Boston University. Her current research focuses on Late Classic Maya ceramics and political economy in the Central Maya Lowlands. She has worked at the site of Motul de San José and several of its peripheral settlements for several years, and she also has field experience in the western United States. She has published several co-authored articles on geomorphological studies of stucco and pottery in the Maya lowlands.

Matthew D. Moriarty is an archaeologist specializing in ancient Maya settlement patterns, ceramic development, and long-distance trade. He is currently completing his doctoral dissertation in Tulane University's Department of Anthropology. His research focuses on the dynamic interplay between trade and politics at the ancient Maya site of Trinidad de Nosotros, Motul's principal port on Lake Petén Itzá. Moriarty has participated in fieldwork in Guatemala, Belize, Mexico, Ireland, and the United States. As a member of the Motul de San José Archaeological Project, Moriarty directed settlement pattern investigations from 2000 to 2001 and all field investigations at the sites of Trinidad and Akte from 2002 to 2005. His recent publications include articles in the journals *Mayab*, *Mexicon*, and *Geoarchaeology*.

Dorie Reents-Budet is curator of the arts of the ancient Americas at the Museum of Fine Arts Boston and Visiting Curator at the Mint Museum, Charlotte, North Carolina. She is the art historian for the Maya Ceramics Project, Smithsonian Institution, which combines nuclear chemical and art historical analyses of ancient Maya pottery to address questions of socio-politics and economics. She has collaborated with archaeological field projects in Mexico, Belize, Guatemala, Honduras, and Perú, and has curated precolumbian art exhibitions in the United States, Canada, Guatemala, and Honduras. She is the author of many articles and several books, including *Painting the Maya Universe: Royal Ceramics of the Classic Period*.

Henry P. Schwarcz is University Professor Emeritus in the School of Geography and Earth Sciences at McMaster University and also adjunct professor in the Department of Anthropology. His main area of research is the study of stable isotope ratios in bones, teeth, and speleothems. He has carried out several studies on the paleodiet of the Maya in collaboration with other archaeologists, including Chris White, Lori Wright, and Kitty Emery. He is the author of about 300 papers and book chapters on diverse topics in geochemistry, archaeology, and paleoclimate. In 2004, together with Liz Webb and Paul Healy, he demonstrated the use of ^{13}C signals in soil to detect the former cultivation of maize.

Richard E. Terry is professor of soil science in the Plant and Wildlife Sciences Department at Brigham Young University in Provo, Utah. His research is in the area of carbon and nitrogen transformations in soils. For the past eleven years he has conducted research in soil chemical residues of ancient Maya activity areas, heavy carbon isotopes in Maya agricultural resources, and the geochemistry of the floors of ceremonial and marketplace plazas. He has worked at the sites of Piedras Negras, Aguateca, Seibal, Motul, and Tikal, Guatemala, and at Chunchucmil and Mayapan, Mexico. He has coauthored twenty-two articles on soils in Maya archaeology in professional journals.

Erin Kennedy Thornton is an environmental archaeologist specializing in the analysis of ancient animal bones (zooarchaeology). Her background in Maya archaeology and tropical ecology combines an interest in ancient environmental changes caused by human impacts and other factors such as climate change. She also specializes in stable isotope analysis, which she uses to address research questions related to ancient animal acquisition, management, and exchange. Since 2000, she has conducted zooarchaeological and isotopic research on materials from Mesoamerica, Peru, Florida, and the Caribbean. She earned her doctorate from the University of Florida in 2011 and is now an instructor and research associate at Trent University in Peterborough, Ontario.

Alexandre Tokovinine is research associate of the Corpus of Maya Hieroglyphic Inscriptions, Peabody Museum of Archaeology and Ethnology at Harvard University. His research interests span Maya epigraphy and archaeology. He participated in several projects in Guatemala including the Holmul Archaeological Project and Proyecto Arqueologico de Investigacion y Rescate Naranjo as well as in field research at Copan, Honduras.

Elizabeth A. Webb specializes in stable-isotope biogeochemistry focusing on the interactions among the soil-plant-atmosphere continuum. She develops paleoclimate models based on the isotopic analysis of ancient plant materials (organic molecules and biogenic minerals like phytoliths) preserved in soils in order to learn about climate change and biogeochemical cycles with implications for carbon sequestration, water resource availability, and ecosystem resilience in regions with high rates of natural or anthropogenic vegetation change. At McMaster University she developed a procedure to identify residues of ancient maize preserved in humin, the oldest fraction of soil organic matter. This technique has been successfully applied to soils of the Maya sites of Minanha, Caracol, and Motul de San José to distinguish soils that were used for ancient agriculture. She is associate professor at the University of Western Ontario where she has used stable isotopes to investigate carbon preservation in soils, iron biomineralization in plants, and climate signals preserved in the oxygen isotope composition of phytoliths.

Andrew R. Wyatt is assistant professor in anthropology at Middle Tennessee State University in Murfreesboro, Tennessee. His research interests include human-environment interactions, the archaeological study of anthropogenic landscapes, ancient agriculture and land use, and plant use in ancient societies. He is a specialist in the analysis of ancient plant remains to reconstruct ancient environments and subsistence practices. He has conducted archaeological research in Mexico, Guatemala, Belize, Belgium, and the midwestern United States and has analyzed plant remains from the sites of Motul de San José, Holmul, and Chiquiuitan in Guatemala; from Stela Cave, Actun Halal, Baking Pot, Pook's Hill, and Chan in Belize; and from the Eastep site in Kansas. His most recent publication in the *Journal of Ethnobiology* deals with the fertilization of ancient Maya agricultural fields with household refuse.

Suzanna C. Yorgey has worked with the Motul de San José Archaeological Project since 1997. She has conducted fieldwork both in North America and Europe and has specialized in Maya archaeology. She has conducted research in archaeology based on the analysis of the ceramic materials from Akte, one of the rural sites within the Motul de San José region.

Marc Zender is visiting assistant professor at Tulane University, where he teaches Mesoamerican indigenous languages and epigraphy. His research interests include anthropological and historical linguistics, comparative writing systems, and decipherment (particularly Aztec and Maya writing). He is project epigrapher for the Proyecto Arqueológico de Comalcalco, directed by Ricardo Armijo Torres, and has undertaken linguistic, epigraphic, and archaeological fieldwork in much of the Maya area. His recent publications include contributions to *Sacred Bundles: Ritual Acts of Wrapping and Binding in Mesoamerica* (edited by J. Guernsey and F. Kent Reilly) and *Reading Maya Art: A Hieroglyphic Guide to Ancient Maya Painting and Sculpture*.

Index

Italic page numbers indicate material in tables or figures.

MAYA STUDIES

Edited by Diane Z. Chase and Arlen F. Chase

The books in this series will focus on both the ancient and the contemporary Maya peoples of Belize, Mexico, Guatemala, Honduras, and El Salvador. The goal of the series is to provide an integrated outlet for scholarly works dealing with Maya archaeology, epigraphy, ethnography, and history. The series will particularly seek cutting-edge theoretical works, methodologically sound site-reports, and tightly organized edited volumes with broad appeal.

Salt: White Gold of the Ancient Maya, by Heather McKillop (2002)

Archaeology and Ethnohistory of Iximché, by C. Roger Nance, Stephen L. Whittington, and Barbara E. Borg (2003)

The Ancient Maya of the Belize Valley: Half a Century of Archaeological Research, edited by James F. Garber (2003; first paperback edition, 2011)

Unconquered Lacandon Maya: Ethnohistory and Archaeology of the Indigenous Culture Change, by Joel W. Palka (2005)

Chocolate in Mesoamerica: A Cultural History of Cacao, edited by Cameron L. McNeil (2006; first paperback printing, 2009)

Maya Christians and Their Churches in Sixteenth-Century Belize, by Elizabeth Graham (2011)

Chan: An Ancient Maya Farming Community, edited by Cynthia Robin (2012; first paperback edition, 2013)

Motul de San José: Politics, History, and Economy in a Maya Polity, edited by Antonia E. Foias and Kitty F. Emery (2012; first paperback edition, 2015)

Ancient Maya Pottery: Classification, Analysis, and Interpretation, edited by James John Aimers (2013; first paperback edition, 2014)

Ancient Maya Political Dynamics, by Antonia E. Foias (2013; first paperback edition, 2014)

www.ingramcontent.com/pod-product-compliance
Lightning Source LLC
Chambersburg PA
CBHW031807270326
41932CB00008B/334